THE BRITISH CANOE UNION

COACHING HANDBOOK

EDITED BY FRANCO FERRERO

With contributions by:

Bill Taylor, Nick Draper, Chris Hodgson, Phil Hadley, Franco Ferrero, Dino Heald, Bob Timms, Lara Tipper, Sue Hornby, Leo Hoare, Graham Campbell, Ian Coleman, Chris Forrest, Trys Morris, Nigel Robinson, Loel Collins, Alan Edge and Pete Catterall.

PESDA PRESS - WALES

WWW.PESDAPRESS.COM

Published in Great Britain 2006

by Pesda Press
Galeri 22
Doc Victoria
Caernarfon
Gwynedd
LL55 1SQ

info@pesdapress.com

ISBN-10   0-9547061-6-1
ISBN-13   9780954706166

FOREWORD

Congratulations must go to everyone involved in this fantastic project and indeed to all BCU Coaches, young and old, past and present. All have, in their own way, contributed to this great coaching resource.

Encompassed within this work are the coaching, technical and tactical experiences of BCU Coaches and the BCU Coaching service.

Integrating the 'How', the 'Why' and the 'What' of Coaching, the BCU Coaching Handbook will help the Paddlesports Coach at all levels appreciate the role of the Coach and build the Coaching Process and technical skills to assist and enhance Coaching performance in the Paddlesport environment.

This is a book that will aid existing Coaches and those coming into Paddlesport coaching for the first time. It will help place the theory of the Coaching Process in a practical context delivering theory through practice. The BCU Coaching Handbook shares the experiences of its contributing coaches focusing on the 'how' skills of coaching (the all important coaching process skills), alongside the 'what to coach' skills of Paddlesport. With sections covering all elements of coaching theory and delivery this comprehensive resource is a must on every coach's bookshelf and will be a major supporting element of the BCU's United Kingdom Coaching Certificate endorsed coach education programme when it goes live.

While presented here by the 'few' it would not have been possible without the enthusiasm, knowledge and skill of the 'many' coaches who have contributed to establishing BCU Coaching as the respected and progressive sport coaching body that it is today. That we have matured to this level of resource… thanks should go to every BCU Coach for their own individual commitment.

Enjoy the read

Mike Devlin
BCU Director of Coaching

ACKNOWLEDGEMENTS

Thanks are due to all the members of the BCU coaching scheme, past and present who have helped to develop our body of knowledge to what it is today. I would also like to thank those coach educators, coaches from other sports and Sports Coach UK who have influenced our development over the years.

A special thanks is due to those people who have contributed by supporting the writers by offering suggestions, support, proof reading, acting as models for photographs and in a hundred other ways. Apologies to those of you who were not brought to my attention, those who were are:

Richard Manchett, Lee Miles, Matt Cooke, Vicky Barlow, Richard Chrimes, Vicky Adkin, Peter Wood, Andy Spinks, Glyn Brackenbury, Howard Jeffs, Joan Ferrero, Rose Powell, Marianne Davies, Kelly Dyer, Stuart Bell, Andy Jackson, Samantha Turner, Clive Atkins, Barney Wainright, Richard Lee John Males, Bill Endicott, Hugh Mantle, Keith Lyons, Dave Crosbee, Reg Hatch, Shaun Pierce and Ian Raspin.

Organisations to be thanked include:

BCU Coaching Service, BCU World Class, BCU Young People's Programme, Leicester Outdoor Pursuits Centre, Holme Pierrepont Canoe Club, Plas y Brenin National Mountain Centre, Peak UK, Pyranha, Nigel Dennis Sea Kayaks and Palm International.

The Editor

PHOTOGRAPHS

Unless otherwise specified all photos in Chapters 1-11, 13, 18, 20, 21 by **Dave Leathborough** of Focused on Adventure, dave@focused-on-adventure.com, Tel: 0115-846-0575.
Also 12-1,2,12,14,15,16,17 ~ 19-9,10,11a,12 (19- is the chapter and 5,6,7 the photo numbers, T indicates a Title photo, P a portrait photo).

Unless otherwise specified all photos in Chapters 11,14 and 17 by **Lucinda Manouch**, www.freedomphotographs.co.uk. Also: 1-3 ~ 5-4c ~ 19-6,7,8.

Unless otherwise specified all photos in Chapter 12 by BCU World Class. Also 9-4 ~ 20-T.

Kevin Mansell 1-1 **Franco Ferrero** 1-7,8,10, ~ 2-1 ~ 3-7 ~ 5-T ~ 6-8,9,15,19,20,21,P ~ 12-3b ~ 13-1 **Peter Wood** 1-13, **Glyn Brackenbury** 2-3a,5a, ~ 16-T,12,14,15a,17 **Nicky Norris** 2-11,12,13,17,18,19,21 **Andy Biggs** 2-14 ~ 6-2 **Dino Heald** 6-10 ~ 5P ~ 7P **Nicky Mansell** 6-25 **Bob Timms** 8-1,2,5 ~ 15-7b,P **Alun Hughes** 9-2 ~ 15T **Andy Hall** 9-P **Gaele Atkinson** 11-1 **Richard Lee** 11-11 **Pete Catterall** 13-2 ~ 19-T,1,14 **Nigel Dennis** 15,1,3,20c,20f **Simon Burke** 15-2,17,18,19,25, **Trys Morris** 15-4,5,6,7c,8,9,11,12,13,14,20b,21,22,23,26 **Cackle TV** 15-7a **Jonathan Walpole** 15-10,16 **Adrian Trendall** 15-20a **Aled Williams** 15-20d **Les Wilson** 15-24 **Nigel Robinson** 16-1,3,5,8,9,18 **Andy Spinks** 16-2,4,6,7,10,11,13,15b,16 **Vicky Barlow** 19-2,3,4,5,13,P ~ **Paul O'Sullivan** 19-11b.

Coaching Service Contact Details

British Canoe Union, Adbolton Lane, West Bridgeford, Nottingham, NG2 5AS

info@bcu.org.uk   www.bcu.org.uk

Tel. 01159-821100

CONTENTS

INTRODUCTION

If you have picked up this book you probably have one main aim in reading it: to become a better paddlesport coach. Fortunately, the main aim of this book is to help you achieve just that. Although written by the coaching service of the British Canoe Union, this book is designed to be fundamental reading for anyone who coaches paddlesport, whether they be based in the UK or not.

GUIDING CONSIDERATIONS

In producing this book, the authors and editor have been guided by the following considerations:

1. This book is about how to coach. The assumption is made that the reader is familiar with how to paddle. So although, for example, key points may be given for a particular manoeuvre or stroke for the purposes of illustration, breakdowns of every stroke and manoeuvre are not included. The reader is referred to the BCU Canoe and Kayak Handbook for that kind of information and an excellent overview of paddlesport.

2. In recent years the BCU has made great advances in coach education, particularly in the area of making coaching theory more accessible. We are aware of the danger that the pendulum can swing too far the other way. Theory is only of use if it helps us to become better *practical* coaches. To this end there is a great emphasis on balancing the theory by providing practical tools to help the coach out there on the water.

3. The BCU Star Tests are invaluable as a means of measuring progress and providing proof of having achieved minimum technical competence before attending training for the various coaching awards. However, the downside is that some BCU coaches are putting far too much emphasis on measuring skill and not enough on developing it. The Star Tests are, and always were, designed as a means of measuring progress and *never* intended as a training syllabus. To this end they will only be mentioned in terms of being one of many ways of measuring progress or a possible aid to goal setting.

4. This book is intended for all paddlesport coaches, so plain English is used throughout. Jargon is only used where it aids rather than hinders understanding and is always explained.

5. A picture speaks a thousand words, so we have used many photos, drawings and diagrams.

COMPONENT PARTS AND TRANSFERABLE SKILLS

Even where a discipline is not specifically covered many of the coaching needs for that aspect of the sport can be met by combining different chapters. As an example, a wild water racing coach would benefit specifically from reading chapters 1 to 5, 8,9,11,12,17, 20 and 21.

Many of the concepts and techniques used in different disciplines are transferable. So do get around to reading those chapters that may not appear to apply to you. As an example, no matter what your background you would benefit from studying the ideas on teaching leadership outlined in Chapter 15 Sea Kayaking.

EFFECTIVE

We hope that you will find this book an informative and enjoyable read. However, the real proof of success will be if you find that some of the things you have read in this book help you improve the effectiveness of your coaching.

Read on!

Franco Ferrero

1 COACHING

Coaching paddlesport is both a rewarding and frustrating exercise, it seems simple one moment and extremely complex the next. It deals with numbers of individuals and groups of learners who come in all shapes, sizes, and ability levels, and with a variety of personal aspirations and motivations.

The environments that the coaching of paddlesport is mainly conducted in can change in the passing of a moment, providing fresh challenges to both coaches and learners. In fact, it is these very aspects: the unpredictability of the paddler, the rapid, the next wave, the opposition, and ultimately our own performance as coaches that draws us back time and time again to the water and our love of coaching.

INTRODUCTION

This chapter is about the art and science that is coaching. It has been written for coaches of all disciplines within paddlesport and aims to provide them with an overview of a number of concepts that would influence the nature and manner in which they coach. It will highlight examples of good practice and coaching behaviours that should make the process of coaching paddlers more enjoyable and effective for all concerned.

One thing that it will not, and never set out to do, is to provide a recipe-type format on how to coach.

The author fundamentally rejects the idea that such a chapter is desirable. Coaches will be more effective if they adapt these ideas so as to play to their strengths, and each person we coach is a unique individual.

What the chapter will aim to do is present an argument that suggests that although some of the goals, methods and delivery of recreational and competition coaching may differ, the true focus of any productive and effective coaching session must be the learners themselves.

▶ THE FOUNDATIONS

Coaching is a complex, thinking activity.

It shares certain characteristics with other activities, based around broad educational concepts, and is focussed on the psychomotor (physical and movement skills), affective (ideas and values) and cognitive (mental, thought processes) development of individuals and groups.

Coaching, like teaching, has a body of specialised knowledge borrowed from many of the sport sciences, such as physical education, sports physiology, psychology, biomechanics, as well as formal education, youth work, management training and other people-orientated activities and professions.

Slowly paddlesport coaching is developing a knowledge base of its own and beginning to share it among its fellow coaches.

In the last few years we have seen a limited number of excellent specialised books and texts, which have expanded and exposed some of the more successful coaching practices, that have been hidden from the wider coaching public by the diverse nature of our multi-disciplined sport.

The fact that paddlesport has looked to other areas and sports to add to its coaching knowledge I see not as a weakness but a strength. It has allowed us to select the best of what others have found out for themselves, and provides paddlesport with a rich and diverse base of coaches who all bring personal histories, sympathies and talents with them.

The connection is simple. The focus of good practice, in a great deal of these similar occupations, is that they put people at the centre of the process.

◯ KEY POINT

• Coaching paddlesport is a thinking activity. Its strength lays in the fact that we have gathered the best of what other sports and occupations have offered and used it to help paddlers get better at what they do.

COACHING COMPETENCIES AND SKILLS

Coaching is an intellectual activity; it often has at its core decision-making 'the best fit option' approach, meaning that there are often a number of differing ways that a coaching task or issues may best be tackled. The result of this decision-making may need to balance a number of conflicting elements, by the selective application and understanding of coaching tools and competencies.

Being able to identify the competencies that are required in the effective application of coaching is of benefit in a number of circumstances:

• It provides targets and goals for personal development. Without the ability to identify what you already do and which coaching behaviours you need to improve it is difficult to get better at what you do.

• Most coaches are involved in some form of formal or informal coach education. They might be willing to work alongside novice coaches, mentoring them and passing on their knowledge, or might see formal coach education as a part of their general coaching activity.

• The ability to be able to identify aspects of good practice and effective coaching competencies will make the observation of other coaches much more productive. It allows coaches to critically observe another individual's work and gather top tips and handy hints, which will in turn help them in their own development.

▶ So What Are These Competencies?

They can be separated into three groups:

 1. Knowledge

• About the subject matter – technical, tactical and physical.

• About the individuals you are working with – as individuals and within group interactions.

• About the venues and environments that you intend to work in.

◯ 2. Decision making

• That occurs before, during and after the session or programme.

• Decisions that are concerned with the selection of 'best fit' coaching methods and approaches.

• Decisions, which focus on aspect of safety and the personal well-being of the learners and group we work with.

• The management of the learning environment to provide a platform to achieve the identified learning outcomes.

 3. Action

• Overt behaviours by the coach in their efforts to meet the aims and objective of the session or programme.

• Action in the interactive nature of a coaching delivery. Those situations where the learning process will have to be managed and guided by the coach with the aim of producing more positive results.

One key feature of the coaching process is the interactive nature of what we do. By interactive we mean the manner in which we continuously change and modify our coaching behaviour in light of new information which is received by a constant stream of learner, task and environmental feedback.

When watching successful coaches this process seems almost routine and only partly conscious, to the point that they only seem to think consciously about circumstances which are more unexpected. This feature, the seemingly natural action of an effective coach, has led to the process of coaching being seen as and labelled as an art.

It would be easy to see an act of coaching as simply being the application and carrying out of hundreds of separate behaviours and sub-skills, which when thrown together produce effective and efficient end results.

If only it was as simple as that.

It is the mixing and blending of the ingredients that make up the artistry in coaching, and the realisation not only that the recipes have to continuously change as the learning processes develop, but each new situation will require a slightly differing mixture depending on the needs of the individual learner and the environmental, social and interpersonal context of their learning.

 KEY POINT

• Effective coaching can be likened to baking a cake. It's not just about the ingredients , but the subtle way a coach mixes those ingredients, in the right quantities to best suit the desired outcome of the session.

► DEVELOPING A COACHING PHILOSOPHY

All coaches, no matter who they coach, the paddling experience they have, and the level they work at, have some form of coaching philosophy.

Some of us may struggle to write it down in a five bullet point list, but you can be sure it's there.

This philosophy is like a set of guiding principles, a framework of scaffolding which colour the ideas we hold, influence the way we like to work and make us the coach we are. It is born from a number of influences, and will often reflect the kind of individual we are outside of our coaching and paddling life.

This helps shape the attitudes we bring to our coaching, the manner in which we deal with the performers and learners that we work with, and the priorities that we hold dear in the practice of coaching paddlesport. It helps give direction and clarity to our coaching, and allows others to assess what kind of coach we are, and the type of coaching they can expect to receive from us.

It may even mark us out and separate us from other individuals involved in coaching, and even bring employers who don't share our vision into conflict.

For some the result always justifies the process. For some coaches all learners must be taught under their rules or not at all.

Without some general agreement that the ideals of the learner and coach (and sometimes employer) are similar, it is unlikely that any coaching interaction will be productive. So don't hide your own coaching philosophy, be clear on why you coach and what beliefs guide you in that activity.

▶ The Influence Of Others

For some of us, that philosophy is shaped by our own experience of being coached and of observing other coaches working. We often come into contact with individual coaches and fellow paddlers who influence not just our skill development, but also the very nature of the way we learn and the way we think about our sport.

These individuals often provide both inspiration and a role model which consciously or not underpin a lot of what we do later in our paddling career. Although at the time of contact we may not have realised it, the point at which they came into our paddling career and unknowingly steered it in a new direction might have been just the right time.

It could be just what they said and why they said it. Most of us, in our coaching and paddling, are an amalgamation of individual experience and the influences and direction of other people.

This personalised history and bank of experiences that all paddlers have, help make coaches individualistic and sometimes, the coaching they provide, idiosyncratic.

Photo 1 An Individualistic Coach?

Is that a positive aspect for our sport? Yes, very much so.

The 'we should all coach the same way approach' is flawed, as the 'one size fits all camp' fails to take on board the diverse and individual nature of a sport such as ours. One of the strengths of having a number of differing coaches with differing approaches is that the learners should always find someone who best suits and fits their style of learning and individual ambition. It also forces us as coaches to challenge and re-assess what we do and why we do it. In fact the action of having other coaches and learners question what we do and why we do it, helps us achieve one of any coach's key goals, that of continuous improvement.

PUTTING THE PADDLER FIRST

Having argued that this diversity is a positive thing, a focus on the human nature of the interaction between coach and paddler allows us to both individualise the coaching process and to treat all learning opportunities as unique. This *humanistic* approach, as it is sometimes referred to, places the focus of the coaching process firmly on the needs and wishes of the learner.

When pressed to explain their own version of a paddler-centred paddlesport philosophy, coaches will usually come out with 'the individual should be at the centre of the process' or ' it is not about medals, it is about the medallist', all very individual learner based.

But what does this paddler-centred idea mean, and how does it relate to the manner in which we conduct and run our coaching sessions?

In a humanistic focus delivery the coach's role and the manner in which they carry out that role are centred on the personal goals and aspirations of the individual they are coaching. The delivery style is considered because of the needs of the individual learners, not just as a passing reference to them.

KEY POINTS

- *'Humanistic coaching'* is a coaching approach which puts the paddlers you are working with at the very centre of any coaching decision-making and delivery.

FUNDAMENTAL QUESTIONS

What is often missing from the process in the first place are the central questions, of why they are being taught that particular skill, what use is it going to be for them in the future, and who is really setting the agenda for the learning?

Is the structure of the training or coaching session based on the requirement of the individual learner, or the wishes of the coach?

Indeed do we have as starting premise, as coaches, the implicit permission from the learner to help set that particular agenda?

If a humanistic approach is to be followed we have to start thinking about the manner in which key decisions are made well before the start of that individual session or coaching relationship.

Lets be clear on this, I am not suggesting that all coaching, and coaching decisions, should be passed over to all learners whatever their age or experience. That would not work.

What I am suggesting is that many coaching sessions and relationships never even stop to think of the central questions, and in doing so the power always remains in the hands of the coach.

Critics of this approach suggest that some of the key principles (those being of fostering understanding, working towards independence and developing mature learning skills), are unachievable in most short term coaching situations, and that this giving of the responsibility over to the learner will not work when working with some young people.

Yes, in those situations that may be true, if the passing of responsibility over to a learner is really about abandonment, but it is not.

It is about, in the case of young people, the sharing of responsibilities so they can take charge of aspects which they have confidence and experience to deal with, at the same time allowing them to be aware of the aspects which the coach may have control of.

It is about being honest and gaining implicit permission. When paddlers sign up for an improvers course they should be told of the remit of the coaching and the expectations they should meet... by turning up for the first session they have, to a degree, allowed the coach to start making some decisions for them.

CHILDREN, AND A HUMANISTIC APPROACH

The coaching of children and the amount of responsibility you can pass over to them is an interesting and complex debate. Young people are often used to having adults make most of their decisions for them. They are also often at a stage in their mental development where collective action and the management of their own behaviours is sometimes problematic. A humanistic coach understands these physical maturation and emotional maturity issues, and conducts the session because of that appreciation, not just because they as a coach are an adult.

The overall safety of any learner you are working with is ultimately your responsibility, but too many

Photo 2 *Keeping them fully involved.*

coaches place learners in stressful positions, only to try, often unsuccessfully, to deal with its consequences later. Keeping learners fully informed and involved in any planning process concerning possible stressful situations is also your responsibility. It is about keeping the learner in the centre of the process rather than on the outside looking in, only being involved when the coach deems fit.

INDIVIDUALISATION AND THE TRANSFER OF POWER

Performers who seek out individual coaches, to add that something extra to their performance, are by the process giving a degree of responsibility over to the coach.

The key thing here is that the coach has been given it... they have not taken it.

The nature of the interpersonal relationship is key here. Sometimes the relationship between coach and learner has already been set, for example school children may find the situation awkward if they perceive a shift in power and decision-making they are not used to.

Paddlers may arrive with experiences of the coach providing all key input and structure within their own learning. Being involved from the start with setting their own goals and wishes may be something that they are not practised at. Taking responsibility for our own learning as a coach or paddler needs practice and patience from all involved.

As a result the learning moves away from being the subject of your coaching and into the possession of the individual you are working with.

Giving some of the responsibility to the learner helps free up coaches of some of the roles and responsibilities we have historically taken as our sole domain.

If we let go, much of the responsibility for providing motivation and direction shifts from coach to learner, and the roles you as a coach take on board are determined by the needs and wishes of the individual and not just by your own considerations.

Many argue that some learners don't want to be given ownership and responsibility. Well that is fine, because if it is clear to all parties that this is the case and you as a coach are prepared to take on that role, that is humanistic coaching.

The relationship is based on agreement and the wishes of the individual have been the driving force in that process.

ROLES

No matter whom you coach and for whatever reason, the act of coaching is a complex, dynamic and thought-provoking process. It can provide moments of sheer joy one moment and a few seconds later elements of deep despair. Each coaching session and each coaching relationship is unique; individuals will vary in the way they respond to your input, and the environmental conditions, often so critical in our sport, provide an ever-changing variable which the coach and learners must manage to the best of their abilities.

The role and responsibilities you take on board to meet these demands are numerous.

KEY POINTS

• Listing all the roles and responsibilities that a coach could take on is a lengthy and scary task. Which ones you need to enact at any given moment depends on the individual, the environment and the tasks that you are working on.

In fact if you listed all the jobs and tasks coaches could have responsibility for you would put off all but the bravest individuals from starting out on a coaching career.

Few coaches take all of these roles on.

It depends on your relationship with the paddlers you coach, the experience you have, the type of coaching you do, and the time and effort you can commit to the coaching of paddlesport.

It might be worth considering how these responsibilities and roles are balanced between these aspects. These aspects must be balanced along with many others such as the length and stability of the coaching relationship between coach and paddler.

Consider also the purpose of the coaching; is it performance driven, where the competitive performance is the major end goal, or a short-term participation based coaching relationship in which the goals are more open, and are likely to be driven by immediate personal aspirations and short-term satisfaction?

Needless to say the two given examples don't sit in totally opposite ends of a spectrum, but can be best seen as degrees of engagement.

Of course, these will change from one coaching relationship to another, and change as your interests in certain aspects of coaching and paddling come in to play.

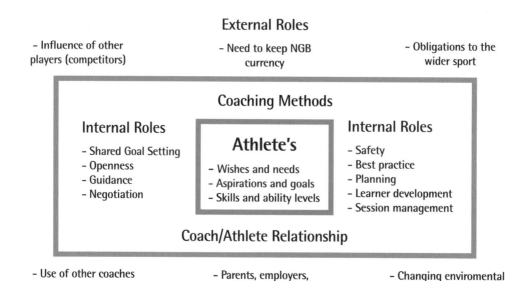

Fig. 1 An Athlete-Centred Model with internal and external roles of coaching

KEY ELEMENTS

These elements help set out the agenda. They map out the rules of engagement in which the role and responsibilities of all parties are made clear. They also provide a structure and focus for the coaching being undertaken.

▶ Planning And Invention

While every coaching event needs a certain degree of planning, some coaching activity only requires a single session or very short-term plans. On the other hand in a club competitive environment the planning and invention may take place over years of growth and paddler development. Developmental pathways may be mapped out to allow a logical and planned progression for paddlers from the junior to senior competition ranks.

▶ Nature And Purpose

The nature and purpose of the coaching will help determine the degree of concern a coach has to give to aspects such as short-term satisfaction and the individual's performance levels.

In some coaching relationships, such as a come and try session, the central aim may be to excite and enthuse the individuals with rapid skill gains and immediate satisfaction.

The competitive coach, however, may see the focus of their coaching as the establishment of sound and precise technical proficiency, where performance in a competitive domain is the driving focus. Each coach in the examples given will take on some of the same roles, but to a different degree of intensity, or not at all, as each situation determines.

▶ Specificity

All types of effective coaching will try to meet the needs of specificity in the way it deals with learners and their skill development. When working with highly skilled paddlers, specific coaching and a focussed approach is required if degrees of improvement are to be maintained. Here that focus is likely to be on fine motor skills such as the refinement of a particular aspect of a paddling technique, not the acquisition of base gross movement such as learning to steer the boat.

▶ Scale And Involvement

Many recreational paddlers, and the coaches they come into contact with, may have a loose and ad hoc involvement with each other on a coaching front.

Individuals may drift in and out of involvement with the sport and the scale of their activity will vary.

Performance-based coaching, on the other hand, usually requires a greater degree of intensity and involvement from all parties. The coaching is often committed to a longer-term cyclical process. Coaching sessions may be programmed to take place a number of times a week, or even on a daily basis at the elite performance level.

▶ Obligation

The degree of obligation is also important in identifying the manner in which the coaching process is conducted. In participation-based sessions the level of obligation on behalf of the learner may at times be marginal, they could be at the session for a whole number of differing reasons. In performance-based sessions there is usually a need for longevity in the process and a commitment to the longer-term planning nature of achieving technical, mental, tactical, and physical development.

▶ THE COACHING PROCESS

One of the difficulties when attempting to describe the activity of coaching is that it is relatively easy to compile a list of behaviours and roles, and give details about what the coach does, but difficult to provide an holistic picture of the interconnected nature of the real workings of all these behaviours.

Each piece of feedback offered to each student, task given to complete, individual session coached, all have a causational relationship with each other.

It is difficult to select and examine each independent act in isolation without stripping it of its real meaning and potencies.

One attempt to give the circular and interrelated nature of the relationship some clarity is to provide diagrammatic models of this process. These diagrams and models can both help and hinder any coach, it's is often connected to what kind of learner you are. Individuals who are strong visual learners find clarity and purpose from models, while those of us who are strong kinaesthetic learners need to see these concepts transferred into action before it all clicks into place. Some of these models describe what coaches do in the field and are best described as models *of* the coaching process; while others act as blueprints, and are models used to structure a coaching session. In other words models *for* the coaching process.

Fig. 2 *The simple Plan, Do, Review pathway with focus on the activity elements.*

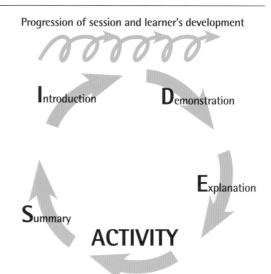

Fig. 3 *The IDEAS model of delivery indicating the progression and linkage.*

ASSUMPTIONS ABOUT THE NATURE OF COACHING

The following elements of the coaching process make up the skills, behaviours and applications of the coach's role. Not all coaches will use all of these, it will depend on the individuals you coach (competitive paddlers, or recreational), the intensity of the coaching relationship you have with the learners (how often you meet, and the importance of performance goals) and the level at which you are coaching.

The models that represent this interrelationship have at their centre the following criteria:

- The process can be seen as circular in nature.

- Each episode will bring immediate and short-term results but contribute to long-term improvement.

- Any model cannot do justice to the idiosyncratic nature of each coaching event.

- The path of the coaching process is rarely linear in direction and all the elements within it will alter their position and relationship with each other.

The coaching process is made up of a number of groups of behaviours, which can be subdivided under the following:

1. Direct intervention. The elements of delivery that are used in the construction and working of face-to-face coaching. They include:

- Verbal instruction.

- Observation and analysis.

- The use of questioning and command words.

- Giving feedback.

- Goal setting.

- Organisation of practice.

- The providing of models or demonstrations.

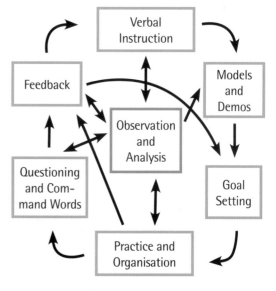

Fig. 4 *Aspects of Direct Intervention Model - indicating the relationship of elements and a possible order.*

2. Process management. The process of changing the immediate environment and influences that shape the process.

• The selection of venues.

• The use of equipment.

• The changing of tasks and short-term goals.

• Aspects of timing and length of session.

• The well-being and safety of the individuals.

• The reviewing of all plans and sessions.

3. Constraints management. The management of external influences that affect the nature and structure of the delivery.

• The planning of the coaching to fit in with both learner and coaching requirements.

• The meeting of a National Governing Bodies wider social and physical requirements.

• The influence of others: other water users, other competitors, other coaches.

• The management of support system: transport, facilities or coaches.

4. Strategic co-ordination.

• The setting of long-term goals and the allocation of resources to meet them.

• The long-term development of competitors and their competitive profile.

• The use of other partners in supporting the performer. Physiotherapist, exercise physiologists, performance psychologist and other sport science support.

• In the case of Elite performers the securing of funding, issues of selection and talent identification.

In Fig. 5 it can be seen that there is an interplay between the external factors which control and affect the process of delivery and the sub-process of the face-to-face delivery itself. While the coach may make every effort to manage these external constraints, dependent on the nature of the coaching, many may be beyond their sphere of influence. That is not to suggest that they are not of central importance to the coach, the paddler and the relative success of the coaching.

For example, in a competitive domain the action of other paddlers is a factor that a coach cannot directly control, but he will have to deal with the consequences of that competitor's action. This might result, in the case of a game of canoe polo, in a tactical switch, while in a marathon race it may lead to the reworking of a race plan.

There also are contextual factors that influence and colour the wider process such as NGB agendas, or an employing organisation's own goals.

While the performer's personal characteristics will affect the selection of methodologies and approach you may select within the delivery, there is limited influence a coach can exert in the short term to alter the view and attitude of the individual.

While the model may not be useful to guide the practice of coach it does indicate the nature of the wider setting that any coaching practice is delivered within.

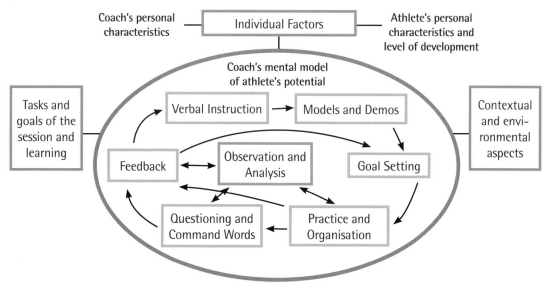

Fig. 5 The wider coaching process based on the Côte et al model.

It represents the coaching delivery process, and suggests that the process is not a haphazard, trial and error affair but one that involves a series of orderly and interrelated steps. It details the element of direct intervention which many coaches see as their bread and butter work.

It does however suggest that the process should be open to external influences, such as the interjection of other coaches, and that the process should be the subject of almost continuous internal revision and reassessment.

The delivery process model needs to be seen in the dynamic nature of the manner in which coaching both evolves and is progressive in its efforts to move the learning and learner forward.

▶ PLANNING, PREPARATION AND MANAGEMENT

Marcus Baillie once wrote that the coach should be… *the stage manager, not the star performer.* I don't think Marcus was underestimating the centrality of the coach's role or suggesting that just because successful coaches are often in the background their importance is any less. What he was suggesting however is that one of the key coaching roles is that of planner and manager.

Effective planning is critical in all aspects of paddlesport coaching. Coaches plan on short-term micro-issues, such as the next task they intend to set their learners, and on longer-term issues such as the physical training goals they might set their learner for the next two years towards a successful Olympics or world championship.

Whether it be short or long-term planning you are engaged in, plans help provide:

◎ Direction for the coach and the coaching session. They provide a framework by which success can be measured, as well as providing direction that can be broken down and used in goal setting exercises.

◎ The meeting of immediate personal needs such as reducing stress and anxiety by providing a handrail and a future to the process of coaching and learning.

◎ A means to an end. It provides a step-by-step structure for you to organise equipment, time, individuals and learning material.

◎ A way to direct learners in their learning by providing a road map of what has gone before and what is coming up. It also helps learners remember the flow of a session and the order in which aspects of a skill might be learnt and remembered.

◎ Evidence that may be useful in displaying the programming skills required through assessment procedures. They can also provide a reminder to learners of the longer-term process they have been through, and if recorded, an indication of the progress they have made.

FACTORS TO CONSIDER IN PLANNING

How much planning you do and the formality of that planning process is determined by a number of variants.

▶ The Learner's Experience

The nature of the group and the paddlers within it is one key element in starting to draw up your plan. Do they have certain expectations and desires about the possible outcome from the coaching? Have they a learning history that has been comforted by having a detailed tight and rigid structure?

We must remember that sometimes an individual's only real experience of learning has been via a highly organised school system. If you turn round and suggest that 'we will see where the coaching takes us', this lassez-faire approach may put the learner on the back foot before the coaching starts.

▶ Novices

Large novice groups provide a number of management problems, and without some degree of planning, a coaching session can quickly turn into something resembling a duck shoot.

One reassuring aspect of coaching novices is that they usually are at, or around the same experience level, and they will make progress quickly. The number of individuals you are working with will also make a difference. A smaller number of more mature learners with their own thoughts and desires can help steer plans and the direction of any session.

▶ The Environment

One aspect that is a key function of coaching is the management of the learning environment. While some disciplines conduct their coaching in a relatively stable and closed environment (canoe polo being the most obvious example), many others (and their coaches) need to be concerned with aspects of safety and environment change.

Planning can help manage the uncertainty that the environment may bring, by balancing the needs of the learner to experience those conditions, with the optimal conditions for acquiring skill and having a positive experience.

Not an easy task for the coach to get right all of the time.

▶ Experience

Your experience plays a major part here. Experienced coaches often rely on their memory of past coaching experiences to pull the right session out from their memory bank. They are confident that they have come across the situation in front of them before, and return to tried and tested patterns and schemes of work, which hopefully has produced positive results in the past.

Sometimes these experienced coaches have little written evidence of their immediate plan, but if you stopped them from coaching and asked them to explain where they are going with the next three hours, they could tell you.

One advantage with this approach which allows for flexibility and open-endedness, is that when unseen opportunities arrive they can be taken. Without the constraints of a plan the coaching session may find positive coaching moments that were unforeseen.

For the rest of us, and particularly for novice coaches with little experience to draw on, a written down structured plan may be the best option. Remember the focus, when drawing up any plan, should be improvement of the paddling, skill, enjoyment of the learners, not just to provide you with a security handrail.

3

Photo 3 Keeping all the balls in the air!

or a conductor, a ringmaster orchestrating a number of differing performances while keeping everybody in focus and in time. The act of coaching is like plate spinning; you have to keep a number of elements moving at the same time with enough momentum so they don't fall off (or in as the case may be).

You only get the full picture by standing back and watching all the individual elements in action, attending to each at the right time and with the right amount of contact to set it off onto the next phase of its movement.

You also have to be a resource manager; not only do you have to keep the session going but you need to get the right number of plates for the right number of poles.

Remember to include all the elements needed for a successful plan into your thinking. The simple things make such a difference when they are missing from the bigger picture.

MANAGING OTHERS

The action of coaching is seldom done in isolation. Just getting the paddlers to the session may involve parents, caretakers, club and competition officers, other coaches and the organisation of your own life to allow the coaching to happen.

I know of a polo coach of an under-18 team who spends most of her evenings leading up to a weekend competition organising car space so the youngsters can get to the pool just to compete.

She always said that the politics of dealing with parents was harder than any coaching she did. Much of this work of managing others is unseen and carried out before the actual water time begins, but is critical if things are to run smoothly during the session.

> ### ◯ KEY POINT
>
> - We need to separate the needs of learners from their wishes. Needs are those elements of performance that must be in place before effective learning can take place. Wishes are those skills which learners would like to work on, even if they don't have the necessary foundation skills. Coaches should try and convince the learner of the importance of addressing needs while giving the student some of what they want!

MANAGING THE PLAN

The art and science of coaching has been likened to a number of other performances. The coach is a juggler,

Some high level coaches find themselves taking on more of an administrative role, organising and facilitating junior coaches and sports science support working under their direction. Although in this situation the face-to-face coach paddler role is missing, their management role still comes under the responsibilities of a modern coach.

SETTING OBJECTIVES IN PLANNING

When planning, it helps if you structure the process by clearly setting out the objectives that the plan is designed to meet. They help provide an end point to the plan and allow you to understand when you achieve the purpose of the session or programme.

The manner in which these objectives are stated can differ. In a formal planning situation they may be written down as benchmarks, particular goals that you wish the learner and or yourself to meet. In a less formal setting the planning objectives may be less well defined. While this may help to steer the direction of the plan they can sometimes be difficult to measure. If the objective of the session is to have fun, (admirable but difficult to measure) then do we mean everyone has to laugh, what percentage of the group laughing at the same time meets the criteria?

You can see the problem. Providing objectives which are easily measurable, and identifiable will help you judge the relative success of any planning process you undertake.

TYPES OF PLAN

The following are various types of plans, each best applied to a particular situation, and having both negative and positive aspects.

They include:

• Recipe plans
• Short-term plans
• Episodic plans
• Periodisation
• Inclusive planning
• Long-term performer development

▶ Recipe Plans

These are plans that provide pre-worked out solutions to some of the problems and issues that coaches come across in their coaching. As we mentioned before some coaches draw upon experience to recog-

KEY POINT

• Plans *should be your slave, not your master*. It is important to see plans as helping you structure delivery. They should never get in the way of you grabbing those ideal teaching moments, or adjusting the programme because situations and opportunities change.

nize particular patterns in the coaching process and utilise their experience to come up with a programme to meet the requirements of the session.

In other situations organisations may impose these recipe systems on the coach, believing that if all learners are taught the same way, it provides clarity of processes and means that coaches could exchange students and understand what has gone before, and the stages they are at in their learning.

This rigid use of recipe planning takes the focus completely away from the learner and toward the perceived need of the organisation. While it may have some application in coaching team tactics such as in crew boats, polo teams, or other group activities, wholesale recipe planning usage restricts both the learners and coaches.

▶ Short-Term Plan

Short-term plans deal with periods of up to five sessions or so. They have at their focus a structure, which allows for meeting of the short-term needs of the programme and some elements of progress from one session, or week to the next. As with all planning the coach may have to balance the need for direction in a session with the ability to be flexible. For example, if after the second session, it becomes evident that the group are making faster progress than imagined, sessions 3, 4, and 5 can be redesigned with that in mind. Each session can provide a measurable sub-step while providing a logical progression to the next event (Fig. 6).

▶ Contingency Plans

Contingency plans are those which a coach may enact when aspects of the session they are running don't go to plan. Contingency plans provide a back-up when environmental conditions (weather, facility, access, equipment), learner condition (illness, injury, availability, performance levels), change without warning.

This decision-making process about when to change course and direction is a difficult one to advise on. Experience of the 'What if factor' usually provides an indication of when the second string plan should be employed.

Of course all this makes the assumption that you have made a contingency plan in the first place!

▶ Episodic Plans

Episodic plans are those that deal with the individual requirement of a session or weekly programme while maintaining the longer-term requirements of the season and paddlers. An example would be a coach working with performers towards an up coming slalom competition which may require a particular approach to that one-off event, while balancing this with the longer-term thoughts of where the paddlers are, in terms of their fitness training, peaking for major competitions and their seasonal goals.

The skill here is to place the immediate session in terms of the bigger picture, to blend the desire for quick fixes with long-term skill acquisition, and to motivate individuals both in the short and medium term while maintaining the long-term version of where a paddler may be in two or three years time.

▶ Periodisation

Periodisation is a version of long-term planning with a focus on the physical preparation of performers toward particular events or competitions. It is centred on the idea that certain types of physical conditioning and skill learning are most effective when planned in relation to each other and during differing phases thoughout the season or paddler's development.

Considerations such as physical, mental, tactical, and technical peaking are programmed to come together at certain key events to allow the performer greater chances of success.

It is difficult for elite athletes to peak for maximum performance more than a few times in each season, so competitive events will be given an order of importance. Some will be main competitions for that performer for that season, in others the experience of being at a competition will be of more importance than the result.

Increasingly this type of planning is being used in recreational disciplines and expedition training.

An understanding of these principles of physical conditioning and training can also help the rehabilitation of injured paddlers and individuals who might wish to return to paddlesport after a period away.

▶ An Integrated Approach To Planning

While modern recreational paddlers may get on the water two or three times a week and are beginning to see the benefits of cross training and physical conditioning to help ward off injury, full time training and commitment to paddling is usually found in competition-based performers. As standards rise and the time and effort needed to maintain these increases,

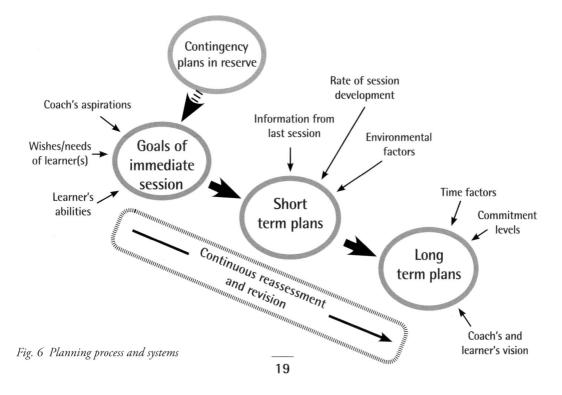

Fig. 6 Planning process and systems

19

the focus begins to fall not just on what the performer does while they are with the coach, but what they do outside of paddlesport.

Coaches need to take a holistic and integrated approach to planning if performers are going to be helped to manage their lifestyle and continue to paddle at the highest level. Aspects of preparation at competition level such as sleep patterns, nutritional intake, elements of social and personal stress can reduce the impact of successful coaching undertaken while the performer is under your wing. It is not unusual to find talented young athletes in paddlesport also in demand for the football and basketball teams as well!

Without the holistic picture being taken into account it is easy to see why many young talented performers either fail to make the progression to the senior ranks, suffer burn out and get lost to the sport, or end up with long-term overuse injuries.

▶ Long Term Paddler Development

Not only does long-term planning suggest that we should see where paddling fits into the jigsaw of an individual's life, but where it fits into the long-term planning of a paddler's long-term development.

▶ LONG TERM PADDLER DEVELOPMENT (LTPD)

Long Term Athlete Development (LTAD) Model has been, and continues to be, developed by Dr Istvan Balyi, a Hungarian/Canadian coach. Istvan has drawn together a wealth of experience and research, and developed LTAD as a model upon which sports can base their athlete development strategies. Through the autumn of 2004 the BCU worked to fine-tune the LTAD model to suit paddlesport and developed a Long Term Paddler Development (LTPD) Model. LTAD/LTPD has been established based on the principles behind human growth and development, and maximises the opportunities this offers to the paddler.

The model aims to provide a base of paddlesport and movement skills that will give an individual the opportunity to enjoy our sport to whatever level they choose, whether recreationally or high performance. It also aims to help deliverers provide the right opportunities at the right time, ensuring that paddlers are enjoying paddlesport and progressing at an optimal level.

The Long Term Paddler Development model supports paddlers from the day they first get into a boat

and over a span of many years, providing a logical progression of programme planning and skill development from the young paddler to the experienced performer.

THE THREE KEY AREAS

There are three key areas in the LTDP framework:

▶ 1. Foundation Paddlesport

This is applicable to anyone starting out in paddlesport and is split into three stages:

- ✓ FUNdamentals stage - learning to move
- ✓ Paddlesport start - learning to play sport
- ✓ Paddlesport development - learning to paddle

The Foundation Paddlesport stages are designed to develop a strong core of skills through enjoyable and appropriate activities. They aim to give paddlers a base to progress either into recreational or performance paddlesport or into other sports depending on their aspirations. This stage is based on having fun and developing quality movement skills. This foundation of skill development and enjoyment gives paddlers a base to progress either down the recreational or performance route depending upon their aspirations.

Optimal development requires an early start; ideally paddlers should be passing through these stages between the ages of about 5 and 13 years old. However the principles can be applied and be very beneficial for anyone in their first few years of paddling, whatever discipline, whatever age.

▶ 2. Recreational Paddlesport

This area aims to give paddlers opportunity and skills to maximise their enjoyment and satisfaction from the sport to whatever level they desire. This is applicable to

Photo 4 BCU LTPD Document

paddlers who wish to achieve personal goals, e.g. enjoy a surfing holiday, be able to paddle class 3, learn to cartwheel, be able to take the kids on a canoe camping trip, use paddling as a fitness session, or to enjoy regular trips on the local river. The Long Term Paddler Development model can be used as a goal setting and evaluation tool, helping individuals and coaches to identify specific areas that need development in order to reach those personal goals.

▶ 3. Performance Paddlesport

This area is applicable to anyone wishing to maximise their potential and equally applies to the competitive and non-competitive disciplines. It is split into three stages:

Train to train - develop skills and fitness

Train to perform - learn how to perform under pressure

Train to excel - producing the goods when it matters

Paddlers who come into this category would include, for example, those with high aspirations on the competitive strands of paddlesport, but equally those wishing to pursue a recreational discipline to the highest level, for example a solo sea kayaking expedition or a first descent.

At each stage specific principles and guidelines for physical, psychological, technical, tactical and ancillary development are identified. Once competencies have been achieved at one level, they form the foundation for the next level. The model takes the paddler from basic to complex skills, from general to specific, and from beginner to expert. It considers what the paddler should be doing and when, providing the best possible programme to ensure individuals come into the sport, stay in the sport and achieve performances that reflect their potential and aspirations.

As coaches we should be applying the principles of LTPD into all our delivery. More details of the specific stages can be found in the "BCU Long Term Paddler Development Pathway Document" available from the BCU. The underlying principle behind LTPD is that individual paddlers are given opportunities based on their personal needs.

Each of the following chapters discusses some of those needs in more detail:

- Physiology
- Psychology
- Safety
- First go
- Novices
- Coaching Young Paddlers

See also:

www.bcu.org.uk The BCU website has links to other reading material and useful websites.
www.worldclass-canoeing.org.uk

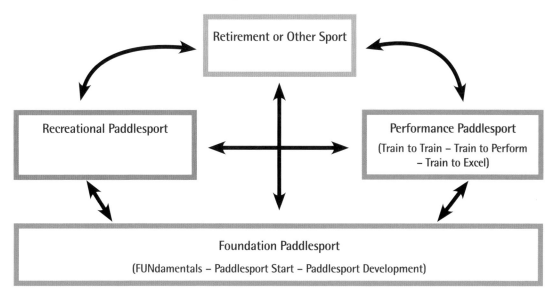

Fig. 7 BCU LTPD Pathway

▶ DELIVERING THE GOODS (COACHING BEHAVIOURS)

This section will consider the coaching behaviour and skills required to deliver the goods, to turn the plan you have developed into effective coaching practice.

Because of the numerous combinations and considerations that should be taken into account when making decision about delivery, it is misleading to suggest that there are ten easy steps to communication, or that practice should always be run along this or that line. What this section will do is to put forward suggestions of what constitutes good practice which should make the face-to-face coaching of learners more productive for all concerned.

COACH/LEARNER COMMUNICATION

It has been said that cut down to its fundamental parts the coaching process is no more than the act of effective communication, and it is to these elements that this section of the chapter turns:

- Verbal instruction/ information
- Demonstration
- Feedback

When used effectively these forms of communication are powerful and versatile tools, making links and connections in learners' minds that other forms of coaching delivery may fail to do. For example: the spoken word in the form of verbal instruction can help explain a paddling action in great depth and detail. It can also help, when timed correctly, to focus the learner's mind on an important aspect of their performance.

VERBAL INSTRUCTION

Verbal instruction usually relates to information that you want the learner to use in relation to tasks or practice that has been set. It is different in nature to giving learners background information which they will not necessarily turn into a physical response.

Because of the unique nature of the relationship we have with our learners it is difficult to recommend tight guidelines and structures for making verbal instruction more productive, but the following points should give coaches something to consider:

- Plan what you are going to say... before saying it.
- Remember the individual characteristics, and the stage of learning of the student. Make the

instruction understandable and related to those stages and characteristics.

- Give the instruction when the students are in the best physical and mental position to receive it. Wait until they have completely stopped any physical activity being undertaken. Only advanced learners can take on information while dealing with the physical nature of a task.

- If you want the information turned into a physical action, remember... less is more!

- For novices complex instructions may be best broken up by some practical activity. The next section of information can be relayed to the student after the student returns from practising the previous task.

- Check that the message has been understood. Getting students to repeat to themselves the instruction (self talk) helps them internalize the action.

- You must provide opportunities for the instruction to be carried out. Waiting a few seconds before letting them work on the new information may help some learners consolidate what has been said. While some individuals only really understand what has been said after they have turned it into an action.

◯ KEY POINTS

- Remember... less is more!

  Research indicates that there is a positive relationship between the brevity of instruction and the likelihood of the instruction being followed accurately.

▶ Hooks And Hangers

Verbal instruction is a powerful tool within coaching, however it is often overused in terms of the amount of information we give at any one stage. For our learners to turn the words spoken into a required action they must be able to understand, relate and remember what has been said. Using language you know the learner has experience of can help this process. Relating the description of a new activity to a past one will also help them associate the novel action with another learning experience. This action of relating novel action to their past experience is sometimes referred to as using hooks and hangers.

The use of descriptive phrases that evoke an action such as 'feel the squeeze' or 'plant the blade' conjure up pictures for the learner to work with, and seem to be most profitable when working with novices.

▶ Confirmation

Not all verbal communication is used to introduce new movements or concepts. Some verbal input is best used to reassure or keep the individuals on task.

Learners will often turn to the coach during a practice, looking for confirmation they are on task, a quick 'Yes' or 'Go on then' may be all that is needed.

> **TOP TIP**
>
> • Ask yourself: *Why am I saying this, and for who's benefit is this being said?*
>
> If you are not convincing in any of the answers you have given yourself, say nothing.
>
> Silence is a hard coaching skill to perfect but a powerful one.
>
> Remember… less is more!

VERBAL INFORMATION

Verbal information or input is what a coach says to students which helps give background information. So for example information on the merits of one boat design over another may be of interest to the individual, but the student will not turn that input in a particular action. The following pointers will help your verbal input:

Don't interrupt the learning to say something. Wait until the student has stopped performing the action they are engaged in, before speaking. Learners, particularly novices, require all their attention to be directed towards the new skill, not listening to new input while they are occupied.

Don't turn away students who come to you asking for additional input. Those are excellent and potent coaching moments. Take them.

Be clear and concise in what you say.

Try and link the input and new information to a past event, or indicate where it may be of use.

Think hard about the best time to give this input, too much information rarely helps.

> **TOP TIP**
>
> Any efforts you can make to individualize the verbal instruction/input given to the learners will help build positive relationships. Take time to learn individual names. Remember that events in past coaching sessions may provide linkage between the past and future learning.
>
> • *example one:* This is a development from the skill we looked at this morning.
>
> • *example two:* Helen, remember the action is similar to your snow boarding experience.

DEMONSTRATIONS

Another way of communicating with learners is by the use of demonstrations (sometimes referred to as modelling). Much of our early learning as children is achieved through this observational learning (watching others and then reproducing their action). Demonstrations help convey details of a movement that verbal instructions often cannot. They allow students to get a sense of the timing and flow of a movement, critical in, say, the action of breaking in and out. These visual pictures are internalized and then hopefully turned into a physical representation of what the learner has just seen.

Demonstrations (models) can also provide goals to aim for as students get to see what their effort should end up looking like. This can provide inspiration, and also spur the students to further their efforts. For some learners the visual elements of this type of communication can conjure up a very potent image.

Demonstration can be made more effective by:

Making sure that all of the students can see the demo and that additional environment markers are also in sight.

For example, it is of limited use to show a break out maneuvre if the observer (the student in this case) cannot see the relationship between the timing of the strokes and the eddy line, which is being crossed. Remember to give the demonstrations context.

Make sure that the demonstration can be copied by the observer.

Consider the appropriateness of the demonstration (if it is to be copied) at the particular stage of the learning. Target it so it is within the abilities of the students. Children and those who may feel insecure with their own learning may feel demotivated if they believe they cannot achieve what is asked of them. The finding of the research is mixed with regard to the appropriateness of who should demonstrate. Some research suggests that a peer model encourages individual novices to attempt the action, because they feel it is within their grasp. While other research suggests that novice learners attend to expert models more carefully.

Perform the action in silence.

Generally students are fully occupied when taking on this visual information and will only be distracted if you give a verbal commentary over the top of the demo.

Advanced learners may well be able to distinguish the verbal from the visual but as a rough rule separate them.

Perform the action in real time.

Early demonstrations that help fix in a learner's mind the overall shape and form of an action should be performed at the speed that the action would normally take place. Later, once that initial impression is fixed, slow motion could be used when 'spotlighting' particular aspects of an action.

Be wary when showing negative demonstrations.

If we are suggesting that demos are very useful and powerful tools, we need to be careful when showing what went wrong in a performance. It is asking a lot of learners to disregard the last set of visual information given, and then to return to the correct performance. Again this is not a hard and fast rule, showing poor form (via a negative model) can help some performers mentally compare their own model with the one which has been shown to them. A powerful tool to be used sparingly.

Help the learner in the observation.

Point out to the learner the key aspects of the movement that they should focus on. Just saying 'Watch this' can be very confusing for learners.

They may focus on aspects which contribute to the complete action, but are not key elements. So help the learner by giving a short list (no more than three, less if they have no knowledge of the action being shown) of clues for them to keep an eye out for. The research would support the idea that it is the effect and outcome of an action which we should be getting our learner to focus on when watching.

KEY POINT

A simple way to think of how people might prefer to receive information is to use the abbreviation VAK:

- **V**isual

- **A**udio

- **K**inaesthetic

Tell them when the demonstration is starting and finishing.

Imagine an intermediate paddler who is unsure of what an outside pivot turn looks like in an open boat. The coach paddles off, turns the boat around with a bow jam, then proceeds to demonstrate the outside pivot. Which action does the learner copy, the bow jam or the outside pivot?

Frame the demo, giving it a definite start and finish.

Use others to demonstrate to learners.

Sometimes novice students feel that their efforts to copy a coach's demonstration are doomed to failure. They have been paddling eighteen minutes, you eighteen years. How could they possibly think they could reproduce your actions? Using other members of the class may get over that problem of confidence. If Eric knows that Anna learnt the stroke only last week, then that may seem a more realistic task when you ask him to reproduce it himself.

Video of other paddlers also can produce excellent models.

Give the student opportunities to practise what they have seen.

The act of demonstrating may only take a matter of seconds but it can be the catalyst for the practical sessions that logically follow.

So, take time and consider the options that are open to you as a coach but move on to a student led practical opportunity as soon as possible.

Again, remember that some learners like watching pictures of what they are trying to achieve, and these individuals may benefit from a number of differing visual inputs.

KEY POINT

- Students must be given opportunities to practise any skill that has been demonstrated to them. Without the chance to conceptualize and customize the new skill the demonstration is rendered worthless.

Demonstrations help give learners a rough outline of the way a particular stroke or technical movement should be performed. So, for novices with little or no knowledge of the action this is both powerful and appropriate. For those who have the general movement and are picking up additional information the demonstration may be less potent. Expert paddlers will have their own style, and much of their own improvement is in the development of what they can already perform. The need for them to observe a demonstration of something new to them is limited.

What learners do (and we should encourage them to do this) is customise the information gained from these earlier demos. This customizing process enables individuals to adapt any techniques to best suit their body shape, size and physical characteristics. This moulding process should be overtly encouraged and allowed within the requirements of what is accepted safe and effective performance.

GIVING FEEDBACK

Feedback, so the sport scientists tell us, is a central and important factor in progressing any student and their learning. Feedback can be given by an outsider to the performer, such as the coach, the environment, a stopwatch, or even a watching crowd (external or extrinsic feedback).

The performers themselves can also receive their own feedback. The individual's own internal feedback is called intrinsic feedback, and can be in the form of the feelings and senses the paddler generates from within as the action is carried out.

Each of these types of feedback has its place and merits within coaching.

▶ What Is Feedback?

Feedback is about the quality and nature of the performance just seen, performed or experienced. It can also be general in nature, if being used to support and praise the learner. "Excellent effort Kerry. You really seemed to be focussing on the task this time".

If we wish to use it to change or reinforce an action or behaviour, then the feedback given to a student needs to be as specific as possible and related to an action that can be clearly identified.

▶ External Feedback From Coaches

The most common form of external feedback is that which is given to the performer by the coach. This itself can be in the form of verbal input, thumbs up sign, or an agreeable smile.

Any of these can have the desired effect of encouraging the individual in their efforts and giving reassurance that the performance they are displaying is the correct one.

The process of giving external coach-related feedback could be structured in this way:

After rehearsing what you want to say in your head, gain the learner's direct attention.

Wait a few seconds for the learner to finish the practice or activity undertaken.

When they are ready and only then, give the feedback.

Using this loose structure will help:

Example, effect, change or repeat.

EXAMPLES

- *example one:*

The Example: "Kerry. On that second to last gate, number thirteen, you took a wider path before turning downstream."

The Effect: "That is why your stern touched the inside pole, and we got a penalty."

The Change: "So, on the next two runs turn slightly before the gate, power through and go on to gate fourteen. Are you clear on that? OK, that's good, away you go."

- *example two:* As Derek comes paddling past, Clive the coach says "Well done Derek good effort. That last lap you really had the paddle extended way out in front of your body. It seems to be helping your forward stroke. Keep focussed on the forward position and watch how it helps you keep control."

Remember to give feedback on something which can be identified. General comments like 'well done' are good for showing support for your student but not if you need to change or reinforce their actions. This is because the term 'well done' is not about anything in particular. What aspect has been well done? Did it refer to the last pop out or the one before?

Saying, "It was well done because of 'X'" is of much more benefit to learners and their learning.

Always try to be honest with your feedback. Students often realize quickly when you are being insincere. Misuse of praise can also devalue the times when you are sincerely acknowledging an effective performance.

Make sure the student can perform the technical aspect, which the feedback is about, and give them an opportunity to practise again and work with your new advice.

▶ Video

A videotape of the performer is an additional form of external feedback. It is particularly useful for learners who may not take on the feedback given by a coach or outsider. As they say, the camera never lies! The use of video is beyond the scope of this chapter (see Chapter 11) but generally be careful with its usage. Video images of your own performance as a paddler or coach can be very disheartening. We are not always as we see ourselves. Ask the learner if they mind being videoed, explain what you are using it for and who might see it. When dealing with under-eighteen year olds remember you must have their parent's permission before you start filming.

Any video clips used should be previewed by the coach before being shown to the learner and be kept short and sweet. Video footage of learners does have advantages; young paddlers love to be filmed and it can allow them to get a permanent record of their performances and improvement.

There has been some research and evidence to show that teenage female athletes find it difficult to focus

on the technical aspects of their performance when watching video of themselves. When interviewed the athletes suggested that they were very aware of their own body image and this tended to consume much of their attention.

For technical aspects, the use of video as a performance/feedback tool allows the coach and learner to sit down and concentrate on those small details, which may only be observable with repeat viewing and the advantage of slow motion.

▶ The Environment

These forms of feedback tend to be about the end result of a paddler's action.

Photo 5 Feedback from the environment

Capsizing is feedback on your ability to balance! The fact that a learner makes it down their first rapid or caught a surf wave is feedback. Just as the clock is for downriver racers or the touch of a pole is for slalom paddlers.

As a coach, our job is to alert our students to be aware of the stream of information that is around them. Once they tune in and value environmental feedback, they are a step nearer to becoming independent learners.

▶ Key Pointers In Giving Feedback

These will help improve the quality of feedback:

✓ Make sure you are in a good position to provide feedback. This is often not the same place that is good for observation.

✓ Only give one or two points of feedback at a time. Mature learners may be able to deal with three points.

✓ Wait till the learner is ready to receive feedback. It takes 8-10 seconds for an individual to process their intrinsic feedback.

○ KEY POINT

- The use of advances in video has opened up a whole range of new and exciting possibilities within coaching. The key things for a coach to remember is: preview the footage, keep it short, and don't let the technology get in the way of the coaching. It's a tool not a toy!

TOP TIP

• Don't bother counting seconds to work out when a student is ready to give or receive feedback. Just wait for them to make eye contact!

Keep it brief. To make the most of external and intrinsic feedback the action involved should be practised again within 30 seconds to a minute.

Check with the learner that you are both talking about the same event.

Select aspects that will make the biggest differences first.

Focus on telling students what they are doing right, use feedback to rei nforce correct performance.

Separate the actions of the performance from that of the individual. They might be just having a poor session, that doesn't mean that they are a poor performer.

Foster internal feedback within learners.

▶ Internal Feedback

Internal feedback happens all the time. Our bodies pick up a whole range of sense and feeling about the paddling we undertake and the effect of the environment on our bodies.

Novices often in their early learning will concentrate on the external element to the exclusion of their own feeling. Only after the external input begins to quieten down can they begin to tune into their own internal feedback.

Internal feedback is like a radio that is on all the time. As a learner we may not be aware of the numerous messages it continues to send to us while we paddle.

The job of the coach is to get the students to tune into that radio, turn it up and listen to what is being played. The benefit of the radio is that it plays an individual's own tune. The feedback it gives is not somebody's impression of what happened but our own. The student just has to trust the messages coming from within. Getting to a position where a learner both listens to and values the internal feedback can take some time. Some people never seem to buy into the whole idea of letting their bodies respond to the information they receive, while others take to it with considerable ease. Like most aspects of learning it takes time. As a coach, introduce it slowly allowing the learner to sup-plement other forms of feedback with their own internal feedback. One of the major benefits of this avenue is that it allows the student to practise alone and still gain the benefit of additional guidance.

It may take time and some patience on behalf of coach and learner for this method to start working. But do persevere, as the benefits are considerable.

▶ Getting Feedback

Sometimes coaches are so concerned with providing or encouraging students to think about feedback, that they forget to ask for it themselves. Students are the central consumers and partners in the coaching process and we should value their views and perceptions of our input. We should make efforts to get their opinions. This can be via a feedback sheet to be filled out at the end of the session or day's coaching, or may be via a review session linked to goal setting. Whatever method you use the act of asking for feedback from other coaches and the learners you work with can only help you improve in the long term. Use feedback the right way and you can only get better.

ANALYZING PERFORMANCE

The performance or practice stage of the coaching process allows the coach to monitor the level of and progress of the learners. The main task of the coach in these practice or learning situations is to observe the performance and if needed, to use feedback to support and correct aspects of the movement being undertaken.

Some people refer to this as fault correction. For me this implies a negative approach to the process of feedback. A common fault of coaches is to concentrate on what the student is doing wrong, not supporting them in the reinforcement of the correct performance and what they are doing right. One thing that unites beginners in our sport is that they often don't understand or recognize when they are doing something right. If the coach sees feedback as fault correction they often fail to support the student who is getting it right but does not realize it, because they are looking for those in a group who need correction. Telling the student what is working and why it is will allow them to continue a practice routine with confidence and focus.

The skill in analyzing any paddler's performance is to understand both what the action should look like when performed correctly and if not, why that is the case. The coach also needs to understand the cause of the performance errors they observe.

In novices these errors in performance are often considerable and obvious and are known as gross motor errors. In more advanced performers they are referred to as fine motor errors. As the names suggest, these aspects of the performance need a keener eye to be identified acutely and a greater understanding of what is really happening in the execution of the movement.

There is no substitute for experience in this field, the greater the range of paddlers you observe, the more causes you will identify for something not working. It may be the case when you are trying to analyze some fine technical errors that you require the use of video or another analysis tools. The use of some form of notional analysis may be the most effective tool here. Notional analysis in its most simple form is a logging method of comparing and recording performances. Modern video technology has allowed both split screen facilities and the ability of some computer programmes to break down performance to its minutia components. These provide a degree of detail that is difficult for the human element in coaches to observe and identify.

One of the problems with the use of complicated systems is that they still have to have a coach/learner interface if they are to provide benefit.

Patterns will often emerge, which seem to come up time and time again. Be critical if this is the case within your own students and coaching, as these error patterns may only have one thing in common, the fact that you were the coach.

▶ Factors To Consider

When analyzing a performance consider the following:

🖊 Take time in observing and analyzing the performance - some errors are only temporary and the learner will self correct these after a number of attempts. Make sure that what you see is really consistent. Research again supports the notion that the effect of trial and error by the learners seems to produce a more secure and robust skill than if the end product is fed to them too quickly by the coach.

🖊 Make the effort to move to a position from which you can best observe the aspect of the performance you are concentrating on.

🖊 Some aspects of a paddler's performance may be very visible but not affecting the quality of the particular task which is being completed. Make sure you can identify and separate a symptom

Photo 6 Sometimes the problem is so obvious it 'leaps out'... you don't need video analysis for this one!

from a root cause. This understanding is born from a full understanding of both the mechanics of a particular stroke or performance, and the relationship the individual component parts have. Where do you get this knowledge? Well from having an open and enquiring mind, and by seeking out technical coaches who have worked out these relationships already.

🖊 Not all causes of error can be seen, what you see is only half the issue. Things such as movements below the spraydeck, the mental condition of the learner and their degree of arousal may not be easily noticed.

If you believe that there is more than meets the eye, you may have to question the performer to complete a fuller analysis of the action. In doing so you value the learner input, get them to conventionalize their own performance and will discover insights that only the originator of the action can truly give.

🖊 After analyzing an action, ask yourself the question, "Does this need me to pass comment on it"? Some learners develop their own particular style, it may not suit us, but it is effective for them. Also do you have the time to address the fault this session, as it might be best left for another day? Some issues are those which only a long-term approach may pay dividends. By dealing with only half the problem for a short period of time you may find that element of the performance you need to attend to fully is left in a worse state than if it was not tackled at all.

OBSERVATION APPROACHES

There are a number of ways to approach observation:

• *Holistic:* This is big picture observation where the answer simply leaps out at you. Holistic observation relies on the coach's experience. The process involves the direct comparison of what the coach actually sees against an image the coach holds of the skill being performed.

• *Deductive:* With experience a coach learns that a certain problem has a small number of probable causes. He can then focus his observation so as to isolate which of these is the *actual* cause, e.g:

Problem: Student performs draw stroke. Instead of moving sideways the boat turns.

Experience tells the coach there are 2 possible causes:

1. The paddle is being drawn too far forward instead of to the hip (Photo 7a).

2. The paddle is being drawn correctly but is not completely 'knifed' on the return (blade angle). In effect the stern is pushed around on the return stroke (Photo 7b).

• *Analytical:* Analytical observation relies on the use of specific flags and markers on the paddler (see over). One system is the 5 B's model which is a good place to start.

7a

7b

The picture is broken down so as to focus our observation. The B's stand for:

Body, **B**oat, **B**lade, **B**ackground, **B**rain.

Loel Collins

Body

• Head position
• Shoulder and trunk position
• Hand and wrist position
• Hip/knees/feet

Brain

• The effect of the environment
• Peer group pressure
• The type of learner
• The amount of learning

Whole Perfomance

Boat

• Direction
• Speed
• Edge
• Trim

Blade

• Angle of loom
• Blade angle
• Position of blade
• Penetration of blade
• Cadence/RPM

Background

• The actual background, position on the water, relative to the bank or shore
• The student background, experience, how they learn, etc.

Fig. 8 The 5 B's

OBSERVATION TOOLS

• *Flags:* Make yourself aware of indicators that flag up certain actions. Flags are something that will indicate that something is or isn't happening. An example of a flag indicating a problem is someone's face coming out of the water first when rolling. In this case the flag indicating a positive outcome would be the face coming out of the water last.

Photo 9a Water touching spraydeck used as a marker of amount of edge.

Photo 9b Tape placed by coach to indicate how far forward the paddle enters the water in the 'catch' phase.

Photos 8a-b Head flagging up incorrect and correct body action when learning to roll.

• *Markers:* Markers enable us to measure performance more accurately. Observers can either use existing markers or make their own (Photos 9a-b). See Chapter 11 Use of Video for more detail.

• *Noise:* Noise can tell the observer a great deal, e.g. Is the paddle entering the water quietly or making a big splash?

• *Rhythm:* Is the paddle stroke rhythmic? Are the bow waves even? Is there a pause in the set up for a stern-dip?

• *Shape:* Examples of using shape could be: when the paddler performs a bow rudder, what track does the boat make through the water? Is it like a 'J' or a 'C'?

Photo 10 The window formed when performing a bow rudder (in this case long and narrow, what does it tell you about his elbows if it was more of a square?)

Is the 'window' made by the gap between the paddler's arms, body and paddle loom long and narrow or almost a square?

• *Like with Like:* Use markers on the shore or in the water to make sure the paddler is performing the same manouevre and that you are comparing like with like.

Franco Ferrero

After making an analysis and before offering the student feedback, you might wish to question the students about their own paddling performance. Mature learners are quite often aware of their own technical faults and just need you to confirm that what you see is what they feel. If the right analysis and corrections can come from the student themselves we, as coaches, are on the road to producing independent learners. If we have achieved that, we have coached them to be competent learners, not just competent paddlers. Maybe we are then on the way.

EFFECTIVE PRACTICE

It used to be said that practice makes perfect, we now know it doesn't.

Practice makes permanent. Therefore poor practice will indeed make poor performance permanent. And how much practice do we need? Well it seems that if we are to produce high level performers we could be talking of up to 10,000 hours, that is about the equivalent of 3 hours a day for ten years, to hit our genetic ceiling and produce performers who excel at their chosen sport.

It is clear that paddlers who perform at the highest level have, and still practice a great deal. The Olympic 1,000m sprint champions still practise and are coached on their forward paddling. Top-flight slalom racers still practise flat water gates even if they have done it a million times before.

▶ Types Of Practice

There are also differing types of practice structures which are open to us as coaches which all have differing results and applications.

Blocked practice is where a particular motor action is performed time and time again. Paddlers practicing a particular skill over and over again have an opportunity to repeat that action. Coaches talk of practising a stroke so it becomes second nature to a learner. This does allow the paddler opportunities to gain a lot of experience in a short time, but it has the drawback of lacking variety and maybe interest, and may fail to represent the range of environmental applications the paddler will require when they need to produce it in a performance environment.

Random practice is where a number of different tasks are given to the paddler for them to perform. They are reproduced once or twice before going onto something new. Running a short section of white water may be an example of random practice in action.

The paddler would start off with a break-in on the right, ferry glide across the river, turn 180°, then reverse paddle passing the mid-stream eddy, pause, break out on their left, back into the flow surfing the standing wave, exit and paddle off downstream.

This type of practice has a number of advantages. It allows for a variety of tasks to be performed at the same time, and by a number of learners at different times. The main potency of this type of practice is it most closely mirrors what you might do normally on the river.

▶ Research

Research suggests that blocked practice (repeating the action again and again) may quickly improve the performance of the student, but that improvement may not last long and be turned into secure learning. However, it does seem to benefit novices who are trying a movement out for the first time, as it allows them to gain a strong picture of something new to them.

Random practice may well produce less immediate results, that is, the student seems to be taking longer to pick up the skill. But research suggests that the learning and later performances are more secure, allowing greater retention and transfer of the performance.

▶ Choices

The choice of which to use is down to a number of factors.

For students who need to see quick results, perhaps to keep their motivations high, or for novices learning an action for the first time, blocked practice is probably best, even if they forget it next week.

While efforts to produce long-term secure learning are best served by random practice routines.

It is a judgment call by the coach. Is the need to experience the motivation provided by rapid skill acquisitions more important for the learner, at that particular stage, than the longer-term goal of working a skill which is likely to be robust and environmentally secure?

There is little merit in the coach working solely on long-term skill development when because the student fails to realize their level of improvement, they drop out of the training programme altogether.

▶ Why Should This Random Mixture Work?

It is suggested that because the actions of the learner are broken up the paddler's brain can relate to the distinctiveness of the individual actions (remember the ferry, break out, surf etc.) This separation allows the mind to build a clear picture of what is required to reproduce the particular task. Having other tasks performed at the same time and practice may help the individual categorize these individual actions. This phenomenon is referred to as the contextual interference effect.

See Chapter 18 Slalom for more detail and specific examples of different practice types.

▶ Why Do We Practise?

So in an effort to make this crucial aspect of the coaching process as beneficial as possible we need to consider why we practise at all.

We set up and organize practice routines to allow our students to experience a number of things.

For cognitive learners:

It allows them to rehearse the model/demonstration they have just seen.

It begins to build a physical element to something, which before may have been only a mental picture.

It allows them to customize the action to suit their individual bodies and their intended outcomes.

It provides a memory of a physical action, which can be called upon in future to be reproduced when needed.

When successfully performed it provides motivation and reassurance to the learner.

It allows them to experience the effect of the practice environment on the execution of the skill.

For Associative and Autonomous learners:

It provides opportunities to adapt and mould the action to new environments.

It builds the experience base of the individual. They will increase the situations in which they can perform such an action.

It may allow the physical rehearsal of techniques, which if performed in the real environment would be stressful.

It allows the coach to observe the performance of the student.

▶ It All Depends On...

What we want the practice to achieve for the learner. Is it rapid performance improvement or long-term learning that we are after? Each method has drawbacks and merits. The problem with blocked practice is that it can become tedious if the student cannot see it applied. On the other hand, not all students may see the benefits of making the practice routines random. They believe they should keep at something until they get it polished.

You as a coach may only have a little time to produce results. If your goal is to make sure the class comes back next week, then practices should be organised with that in mind. Fatigue and apprehension are other aspects that should be taken into account. Random practice interwoven with breaks can help reduce these factors. Keep the learner informed and involved in the decision making with regard to the practice you are undertaking. With their agreement the session will produce better results.

KEY POINTS

There are three stages to learning a new skill, these are:

- Cognitive phase -Identification and development of the component parts of the skill.
- Associative phase - Linking the component parts into a smooth action.
- Autonomous phase - Developing the learned skill so that it becomes automatic.

KEY POINTS

- Effective coaches structure and provide practice environments that closely mirror the environment that the skill is to be used in.

▶ Practise Where You Would Paddle

As most paddling environments that we want students to perform in are ever changing, the practice situations we get should reflect this. The most effective environment to practise in is in the environment in which the skill is going to be used. This aspect of organizing practice cannot be overstated. Increasingly research is focussing on the relationships between the individual, the task to be completed, and the environmental demands placed on that skill. If you practise a skill in isolation it will remain in isolation, practise in a variety of situations and we equip our learners to perform in not just the differing situations of the next hour of practice, but in situations and environments as yet unknown to them.

TOOLS – VARIETY IS THE SPICE OF LIFE

We often have to work with quite limited resources, for example there may only be a simple jet of water to play on. Many of the benefits associated with random practice can be gained without having to change the task completely. The task only has to be different enough for the brain to have to process the action anew, rather than getting into a groove.

As an example, let us assume the main focus of our session is on improving the student's breaking-in skills.

• Using the simple jet we could start off with block practice by getting them to do 4 RH break-ins (Fig. 9a) and in order to get back into the eddy 4 RH breakouts.

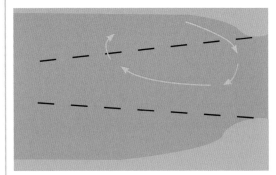

Fig. 9a 'C' shaped circuit

• We can then move to the other eddy and do 4 LH break-ins and outs.

• We can then get them to alternate by crossing the jet, RH break-in followed by LH breakout followed by LH break-in followed by RH breakout (Fig. 9b).

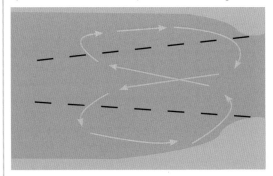

Fig. 9b 'X' shaped circuit

We can then vary some of the key elements of the break-in, i.e. attack angle, approach speed, amount of edge used and stroke combinations, e.g.

• Slow break-ins
• Medium paced break-ins
• Fast break-ins
• 45° attack angle
• Narrow attack angle
• Wide attack angle
• Average edge
• Lots of edge
• As little edge as possible
• Forward paddling throughout break-in
• Low brace
• Bow rudder

Having practised some or all the above they will have the tools with which to optimize each break-in by selecting the right combinations. We now need to get them to practise selection by using random practice. Ideally we would set them courses down a series of different rapids requiring different manoeuvres. Next best would be to paddle the same rapid several times in different ways, so that each time they descended they would have to use different combinations of manoeuvres. Assuming that we are stuck with our simple jet, we can still do our best to make the practice as random as possible, e.g.

• Approach from upstream of the jet, break out well down the eddy and without losing speed break back in.

• Starting at the bottom of the eddy, ferry glide across to the other eddy, break in, cross the jet and break out.

• Break in, reverse ferry glide and set in to the other eddy.

• Now do all those combinations again but in a different order and starting from the other eddy.

We are limited by our resources, but for many coaches the limiting factor is their imagination. With imagination we can dream up equally varied practices for any paddling skill!

Franco Ferrero

▶ The Importance Of Practising On Both Sides

One other element we should build into the practice routine is the use of both sides of the body (bi-lateral practice), try and select practice areas and routines, which use a two-sided element. The idea that we should gain competence on one side before moving on to the other is a false notion. Learners who have only practised on their good side use their new-found skills, to the exclusion of the weaker side.

One side gets better and the other relativity worse. How many of us have a roll, which is only dependable on one side? I am aware that if pressured I would prefer to sit in a hole on my left side.

Manage the practice session so that your learners have to interchange sides as they complete the tasks you have set them.

Some paddlers, particular beginners will tend to concentrate on actions which give them confidence and a feeling of success. So don't be surprised to see students given a choice practise only on one side, and working on something they are already good at.

Research would indicate that the time spent on an individual's weaker side has benefit for both the good and not so good sides. So be strict on this dualism. You owe it to the learner and any future coach that may inherit them not to disable them!

> ⦿ **KEY POINT**
>
> • Get students to practise all skills and strokes both sides, it is a falsehood that we should get good at one sided skills before turning to the other.

SETTING GOALS

Goal setting is a process that helps learners focus on targets for the present and targets for the future. If successful they are powerful tools, which can help bring about self-confidence, increased motivation and progressive learning.

Some paddlers are driven by their desire to learn an individual technique, to complete their first roll, to paddle and descend the local rapid, to make that gate, to start slalom racing, to win, to be selected, to have fun. Others may be focussed on the wilderness experience a gentle sea paddle may bring them. Whatever floats your individual boat, all of us have implicit or explicit goals, which our participation in this sport helps us achieve. Whatever it is, goal setting helps students and coaches achieve it.

Competition paddlers and coaches have long worked with goal setting as part of their normal routine. The act of slalom racing is a classic example of short-term goal setting - making that gate. Medium-term goal setting, get a top third place in this round of events, and long-term goal setting, in their desire to make the senior team by their twenty-first birthday.

Some of the benefits to all paddlers and their coaches of goal setting are that:

 Goals improve the quality of practice sessions. They give it tangibility.

✓ Goals help clarify expectations of both coach and student.

✓ Goals help relieve boredom by making training more challenging.

✓ Goals help coaches and students measure progress.

✓ Goals increase the intrinsic motivation to achieve.

✓ Goals can be short, medium and long term.

▶ The Coach's Use Of Goal Setting

Most coaches will use goal setting to some degree, even if they believe they don't. Very few of us start with no ideas on the direction a session will take, or what we would like the session to produce by the time it is finished. Taking time to focus your efforts toward a goal, or the setting of goals is rarely wasted.

Some sessions may start with a stated goal. "At the end of today I would like us to be able to..."

Others will be part of the questioning process the coach may undertake. "So Jake, what is your goal for this paddling season?"

Goal setting may be used in a particular practice routine, and be adjusted again and again to focus and refocus the paddler's efforts. For example, the paddler may be asked to make a ferry glide across a simple jet in under eight strokes. After the learner succeeds in that goal the target changes and a new goal is set, they have to do it in six, then four strokes. In these situations the coach and student need to agree on set goals which both parties believe are achievable and realistic for the paddler. Research suggests that without this agreement the student may be less inclined to make efforts to succeed, and in turn the quality of the learning will suffer.

Effective goal setting, which results in long-term learning, is nearly always a shared activity. The type of

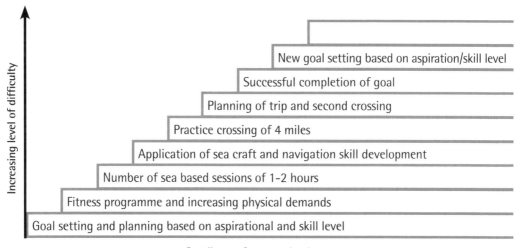

Fig. 10 Goal setting and support (staircase approach to goal setting). Example of goal setting to complete an open crossing of 12 miles.

goal set may also be subject to the degree of support that you can give the student, and their confidence.

Be careful in forcing goals onto your students without their permission, individuals may feel like they are being manipulated and end up being demotivated without any investment in the goal setting process themselves.

▶ Guiding Your Students

Having said that, some students, particularly novices have little idea of what is possible. They have limited experiences in learning the mechanics of paddlesport, while the coach on the other hand has seen dozens of beginners at their stage of development and learning. It could be that the coach may set a goal of completing the simple three-mile sea crossing because he or she understands that a fit adult beginner would be able to make such a journey. The beginner doesn't have that experience to call upon, and may not believe the crossing to be possible.

Here, the skill of the coach is to convince the paddler of the possibilities that lay before them, to encourage them to push themselves and not underachieve. Remember that if we are to aim for a truly humanistic coaching approach then we must consult and involve the learner with the process.

It is a difficult balancing game for the coach to get right, you want to involve the student in their learning, but wish them to get the most from the activity.

Remember, sometimes learners don't know what they don't know yet.

▶ Outcome Goals

Students who are motivated by goals and targets such as running a particular named fall, or reducing their time for the 1000m K1 by five seconds are said to be focussing on outcome goals. They just want to achieve that particular target.

These goals are easily measured and can be determined by a particular event. However, they can be problematic. The sprint racer who is striving to knock off five seconds from their personal best time may get injured a month before the end of their season. If that reduction of the time by five seconds is the sole goal of their season, then it could be argued that they have failed due to the goal set not being met.

The problem with outcome goals is that they fail to acknowledge the improvement process that has taken place in the effort to make the outcome goal, in this case to make that individual faster.

▶ Process Goals

Maybe a better focus is to set process goals which take note of the incremental improvement in technique.

For example, the journey is this case was more important than the arrival. In this case each element of the improvement, which when put together may help produce a faster 1000m, is given value because it was a goal in its own right. Gaining the sharper starts, smoother paddle action and increased physical strength left for a strong finish, had all been process goals, and helped towards losing those vital five seconds. Even with the end of season injury the improved elements of performance are still successful goals (process goals) due to successful goal setting.

▶ Long-Term Goals

Again differing individuals will be motivated by differing visions. It is unlikely that an eight-year-old novice can be driven by a ten-year master plan. But some people can be excited by the opportunities that long-term skills learning may give them. Those individuals can be motived by a long-term desire, each of us have different drives, so take time to value them.

▶ Our Job As Coaches

Our job as coaches is to make the goal setting process both challenging and achievable. We will often be in the best position to focus students on what is possible. Try and link the goals set at the beginning of the session or course with an assessment of what has been achieved at the end of it.

Photo 11 Goals have to be negotiated and agreed with your students.

Goals should be changed and developed as the learner and their skills develop. They are not obstacles to be overcome but bench marks of development. Used properly they can help coach and student achieve more than was first thought.

> ### ◯ KEY POINTS
>
> • Research suggests that when learners are involved in their own goal setting they are more likely to strive to attain those goals.
>
> • Read the chapter on psychology and what it has to say about motivation and goal setting.

▶ COACHING METHODS AND APPROACHES

The coaching methods and approaches you employ in your coaching are often referred to as your coach style. While it is true that it is difficult to separate an individual's method from their personality as an individual, I would suggest that to provide clarity these two aspects of the coaching process are treated separately.

Coaching strategies are the tools you use in your effort to progress the learners you come into contact with. As mentioned before the style you adopt in the delivery of these methods is more a function of you as a person and your overarching coaching philosophy.

One question that is never far from the lips of novice coaches is "What method should I employe in this or that situation?" Well that is not a simple question to answer, it depends on a number of factors and is related to issues such as:

◑ The time allocated to the session or skill learning.

◑ The type of learner(s) you are dealing with.

◑ Whether your aim is rapid skill acquisition, or the long-term learning and retention of that skill.

◑ The cognitive maturity of the learners.

◑ Whether you are coaching new skills, or developing existing ones.

◑ Whether the individuals you are working with are supportive of each other, and effective when working in groups.

◑ The facilities and equipment available.

◑ Where the session fits into any long-term development.

◑ The physical maturity of the individual or individuals.

There are of course numerous other independent aspects particular to each individual session and each coaching relationship.

▶ Being Positive In Your Coaching

Implicit in a number of coaching approaches is the idea that the coach should take on the role of fault finder, and that they should spend time observing, analysing, and correcting faults evident in a performer's skills and techniques. Now there is no doubt that learners, particular beginners, make errors and a number of these need to be picked up before they lead to poor practice or possible injury, but the encouragement of good practice can be met by focussing on what is effective and right about an individual's learning, not just what is wrong with it.

With this approach the whole atmosphere of the coaching changes. Language becomes more positive, individuals lose their fear of experimentation, and the whole focus of the session shifts from looking to do something right to building on personal success.

SOME METHODS AND APPROACHES

▶ Direct Instruction

Historically, direct instruction has been the main method of paddlesport coaching. It is attractive because it is the approach that most coaches are familiar with through their own experience and observation. It usually follows a set format and process, it is directed by the coach allowing them to monitor content and control time issues, and also provides a degree of security for both learners and coach. The process usually starts with a simple introduction of the task that is going to be taught, followed by some form of demonstration. The group or individual then attempts to reproduce the action, with the coach dealing with shared or individual development points as they occur. The most effective use of this stage of the process is where learners can put the skill into context, by allowing it to be reproduced in its correct environmental setting.

When used successfully direct instruction can produce quick and impressive results. This is the reason why it is often used to coach larger groups of complete novices who have little or no experience of the fundamental skills of canoeing and kayaking.

It is also the first methodology often adopted by novice coaches as it provides them with a structure and relies on less decision making, adaptation and blending demanded by other approaches.

When learners start off at a similar stage of development the group can be taught at a uniform pace and the opportunities for establishing sound technique can be managed by the coach via effective demonstration and monitoring.

As the learners begin to customise the fundamental skills into personal application the potencies of this approach may start to decline.

▶ Practice Methods

Alongside direct instruction the use of practices is a common theme in paddlesport coaching. After all the sport is practically based, and the physical nature and pleasure gained from paddling a boat is a reason given by many as to why they took up the sport in the first place.

Using practice as a coaching approach has many advantages:

1. It provides a core to the session allowing learners to apply skills in a contextual setting.

2. It provides continuous environmental feedback to the performer, even if the student is not aware of this.

3. It allows the individualisation of tasks and activities. With effective planning a number of differing practices can be conducted in the same location, and finally it can free up the coach to concentrate on the observation of progression, and provide support and feedback as required.

The amount of, and the difficulty of the tasks that are practised is a judgement call on behalf of the coach. Learning and developing new skills can be tiring and time consuming, so it is important that the coach continuously manages the learning by selecting the environments, number of repetitions and length of the practice involved.

It is worth restating some of the key elements a coach should have in mind:

Be clear in what the learners are practising and the purpose of any individual task set.

Manage the environment and the level of task difficulty, to allow for a degree of success.

Encourage learners to value errors in the practice environment. They allow the positioning of correct technical performance in relation to less successful applications. They also help deepen a cognitive understanding of the mechanics of performance.

Contextualise the skill within practice situations. That is organising practices that mirror those conditions of the performance environment as closely as possible.

Be aware of the law of diminishing returns. Practices should be stopped before the performance level drops to a point where errors are brought on by elements of fatigue.

Provide change, challenge and alternatives to both the task being practised and the environment in which the tasks are being carried out.

Coaching Approach and Strategies	Key Themes	Role of Coach	Advantages	Disadvantages	Applications
The Inner Game	Focus on dealing with the psychological barriers found in learning.	To encourage positivism within the learner.	Can provide eureka moments.	Needs skill application by coach- some learners just don't buy it.	Can be effective to get over certain mental blocks.
Coaching Principles And Concepts	Transferability of ideas across differing environments and tasks.	To focus on the principles of movement across water.	Encourages independent learners and transferability of knowledge.	May take longer for the learner to grasp the concepts.	All paddlers, all levels! Allows independent skill acquisition.
Guided Discovery	Values different processes of learning and the variety of outcome.	To set the loose goals but to value the range of applications and journeys.	Engages learner in judgements about what works best for them.	Can take longer for some to draw conclusions. In a group allows skills acquisition at differing rates.	All paddlers, all levels! Values unknown outcomes.
Coaching Via Learner Self Appraisal	Focus on learner(s) developing critical and reflective skills.	To judge if the students have enough knowledge to benefit from the application.	Students develop self coaching techniques. Frees coach up to manage the application, not just to provide all the input.	Some learners enjoy the outsider looking in, which is the coach. May not be so successful with less self motivated learners.	Where there is environment feedback present, paddling or training team situations can benefit from 'peer' appraisal.
Collaborative Learning	Puts learners into small groups and encourages peer learning.	To give the members of the group enough knowledge to be able to help each other.	Frees the coach to manage and direct.	Some groups will advance at differing rates and require pre planning.	Large groups, students at the associative stages of development.
Coaching Using Questioning	To encourage the learners to think and consider for themselves.	To build an open and questioning approach to learning.	Helps the individualisation of learning.	If overplayed can be very annoying.	All paddlers, all levels. Builds relationship and openness.
Shaping And Chaining	Provides logical and sequential patterns.	To shape and provide links for the learner to develop.	Learners often see quick developments, need to be kept moving.	The relationship of the parts must be focussed. Members of the group will advance at differing rates.	Can provide opportunities to link technical aspect into skill application within an environment.
Whole-Part-Whole	Breaks the action into parts, then rebuilds.	Make decisions about what parts to select and when to separate.	Helps complex skills seem achievable, provides sequences.	In separation parts often lose relationships of timing and application.	Skills that seem complex and confusing to learners, allows 'small wins strategy'.
Copy Me Method	Focus on observational learning.	To provide demos by self or others.	Suits visual learners, quick to structure. A lot of information included in demos.	Give basic pictures which will have to be adapted by learners. Requires framing and correct environment cues to be really valuable.	Helps provide a rough picture of skill very quickly. Children socially learn this way. Advanced learners can copy complex movement patterns.

Fig. 11 Comparison of Coaching Methods *continued...*

Coaching Approach and Strategies	Key Themes	Role of Coach	Advantages	Disadvantages	Applications
Direct Instruction	Coach drives the session.	To plan, carry out and structure the learning.	Allows coach to keep a time limit on activity. Lends itself to formal or potentially dangerous situations.	Learner often passive, little if any individualisation or cognitive development involved.	Introduction of closed skills, some aspects of safety training, more formalised coaching with direct outcomes.
Practice Methods	The application of a technique in a practical setting.	To provide focus of session and the right environment(s) to apply the skill(s) in.	Keeps learners very active and mobile. Helps contextualise techniques in applied situations.	There may be a fatigue element to consider. May be perceived as boring by some.	Lends itself to block and random practice approaches. Applicable where fitness training is the focus of the coaching.

Allow the practice to flow without interruption and the benefits of practice to take place. Too often coaches halt the flow of practice and provide input when it is not required.

The correct application and use of practice routines is a mainstay of paddlesport coaching. Because of this it is important that coaches consider the nature and purpose of what they are doing before setting up any practice routine. As they say practice does not make perfect, it makes permanent. Relearning and recoaching poor technique once it becomes second nature is both disheartening and time consuming.

▶ Copy Me

Here as the name suggests the focus is on the power of the demonstration, and the ability of learners to pick up the visual cues needed to observe, understand and then customize the action to their own individual needs. Young children with their experience of copying and watching often respond to this method. Simple verbal direction on what to look at, can help the internalisation of the demonstration. When working with children consider the options of using one of their peers to provide the demo.

Individual learners who have a history of observing others perform will often have the skills to help them pick up the salient points in a demonstration and transfer it to their own learning.

▶ Whole-Part-Whole

This is mainly used in situations where the coach is introducing a multi-task or complex skill. The whole part whole structure allows the skill to be demonstrated first in its fullness, then the individual elements that make up the skill are broken down, practised and hopefully learnt, followed by a return to the whole skill. This breaks down the movement into achievable chunks of learning, which once mastered are reassembled back into the complete movement.

Which aspect of the whole is tackled first is open to choice; it could be that with a new skill there is a logical sequence to its development and therefore the order in which it is taught. When working on a complex skill for which the learner has already learnt the constituent parts, it may be worth revisiting the learnt skill and using it as the building block on which to develop the more complex task.

An example of this might be a low brace turn. The learner may already know how to forward paddle, bow sweep, edge and low brace. All the coach has to do is show them how the parts fit together.

Because this method often relies on effective demonstration it seems to work well with visual learners.

▶ Shaping And Chaining

These similar approaches are just varieties on the practice theme. Shaping is the teaching of a simplified rough copy of a movement or techniques which are then moulded and shaped to the more polished article as the coaching and learning progresses.

The issue here is that the rudimentary stages must be moved through before the skill become too practised. Its advantage is that the basic model can allow quick progress and aid motivation providing the platform for future more detailed learning.

Chaining is the building of skill via a sequential and logical pattern. Like the whole-part-whole approach

Photo 12 Coaching By Questioning

the skill or movement is broken down into individual actions and linked as in a chain to build to the complete picture. It has at its advantage a logical structure, once the coach gets to understand the fundamentals of a stroke or technique. It also enables an opportunity for the use of small wins strategies (SWS) and incremental goal setting as the more complex movement is built into the full application.

One of the problems with using chaining is that the learners may not see the end result while working toward mastery, and may not be able to visualise the complete action for themselves.

 KEY POINT

• Which approach to adopt when and with whom is a central but difficult decision for the coach. There is no easy answer. You need to understand the merits and shortcomings of each method and to balance this against the needs and wishes of the learner and the goals of the session. If you are to do this you must practise each approach so when it is required you can pull it from your mental toolbox and let it run.

▶ Coaching By Questioning

Although the use of questions and questioning is commonplace in coaching, and often used as a tool in other methods of delivery, it is a skill not often considered in terms of the why and how we should use questioning.

At its simplest, questions can be used to check a base level of knowledge.

With more care and consideration they can be used to deepen and develop further levels of understanding. Such as:

⊙ 1. They can be of use in checking the knowledge and listening skills of the learner. These knowledge-based questions, as they are called, are often low in cognitive demand. They test mainly recall.

Example: "Remind me again Mike, was gate three an upstream or downstream gate?"

⊙ 2. Questions that ask for comprehension and application have an immediate cognitive demand as they might require the transfer of one skill into a differing domain and situation.

Example: "Have you paddled on a flooded river before Jo? What conditions would you expect to find behind that midstream boulder?"

3. High cognitive demand based questions ask for analysis, synthesis and evaluation.

Example: "Having competed against this pair before Dave, over a number of differing courses, what tactics are you going to employ in the race today?"

Questioning can also be considered to be narrow or broad, the former leading to specific answers and the latter providing the opportunity for alternative answers and solutions and is more open ended. Like most effective applications of a coaching skill we need to take time and plan our use of questions. This can be helped by doing the following:

Framing the question within the context of the session and the learning objectives.

Plan the level, timing and order of the questions. Inexperienced coaches often find questioning can lead to a loss of focus in the session, as it opens up differing areas of interest. Planning will help lessen the chance of that happening.

Remember to extend the question sequence. Think of additional questions that could bring out deeper levels of understanding.

Give time for an answer to be returned. Jumping in and providing the answer is a common error of coaches. Waiting gives value to the response and the person giving it, gets a better response, and is common courtesy.

Analyze the answers given to the question. Questioning should be seen as cyclical in nature. It is critical for the motivation of the learners that you listen and reflect on the answers given, before speaking again.

Don't overuse questioning, it can really irritate people.

It is unlikely that the random firing of questions here and there is going to produce productive results. If we want to ask questions, which get our learners to think, we've got to think ourselves about the question we are going to ask.

The use of questioning is not a complete single self-contained approach, but it is an important ingredient in other coaching methods that allows the development of deeper mental understanding.

Be cautious, overuse of this method can interrupt learning and is sometimes seen by learners as a reflection of a lack of knowledge on behalf of the coach.

▶ Collaborative Teaching

With collaborative teaching there can be considerable benefits in terms of the learner's own skill and social development. It is also an excellent method for dealing with large numbers of learners and encouraging group involvement. Sometimes called peer teaching, collaborative teaching focuses on the reciprocal nature of small group work and mutual support. Groups of two, three, or four are given a task to complete with the involvement of all members.

It could be as simple as using two others learners as marker buoys to turn around while practising the fundamentals of a pivot turn, or as demanding as the use of peer reviewing technique of a fellow slalom paddler's run, via the use of video.

The key element here is to use others within the coaching as a coaching aid. As well as practising the skill themselves they end up practising observation, analysis and feedback techniques, which in turn will help them in their own learning.

This method seems to produce the best results when the learners are well motivated and have clear directions on what is expected of them.

The other advantage of this method (if functioning well) is that it frees up the coach to act as monitor and trouble-shooter while the feedback and management is continued within the sub-groups.

▶ Coaching By Self-Appraisal

In this application, the learner is given more responsibility for his or her own learning. It relies on a degree of self-motivation and maturity on the part of the learners involved. Coaching by self-appraisal requires that the individual learner is clear on what constitutes success or the correct application of a skill. An example would be a sprint canoeist involved in a timed session using the fartlek principle.

As long as the distance is covered in the required time and the recovery needed before the next sprint is monitored then the performer can self-appraise.

With less independent learners the coach will need to take time to set up the system of self-checking. Providing laminated performance criteria cards, which highlight the conditions for a successful execution of a particular task, could help do this.

Self-appraisal like collaborative coaching can be tackled in small groups. It has particular application when working with doubles in crew boats.

▶ Divergent Problem Solving (Guided Discovery)

One aspect that unites paddlesport and all its disciplines is that there is usually more than one way of completing a task or solving a problem. One of the shortcomings with coach-directed methodologies is that they tend to restrict the inventiveness and alternative solutions provided by the learner.

Even with novices the use of the guided discovery approach may produce some weird and unworkable solutions, which after some trial and error and a little guidance from the coach are honed and refined into a workable solution.

The strength of this process is that the process of thinking and problem solving helps develop a reasoning and appreciation behind why something works or doesn't work.

The fact that a number of solutions are offered and owned by the learner helps both retention of the skill and the development of the capacity for future problem solving.

> ### ◯ KEY POINT
>
> • Much of the recent research on skills learning supports the central principles in guided discovery learning. The key themes for a coach to take away are that we should encourage individual customisation of strokes and skills, allow students to practice their techniques in a variety of environments, and foster decision-making in their application.

▶ Coaching Principles And Concepts

It is often said that if you coach a technique in isolation it will be repeated in isolation.

The merit of coaching using principles and concepts is that once they have been understood they provide considerable opportunities for transfer of knowledge to existing and future situations.

The caveat is that the coaching of concepts and issues is often difficult.

It is difficult because paddlesport has not had a history of putting these transferable notions in the forefront of learning. In addition many coaches fail to understand some of the core principles and concepts of moving a boat across water themselves, so cannot pass this understanding on to others.

Resistance is also there from the learners; learning a new technical skill has tangible aspects you can physically see, an improvement, a faster time, but the understanding of transferable concepts and principles may take some time to fully develop. This is because a fuller understanding of something doesn't always result in an immediate improvement, just a headache! This means that some learners find the approach frustrating and unproductive in the short term.

Photo 13 A relaxed uninhibited performance

Coaching principles and concepts, contrary to common belief, should not be just reserved for elite performers. The basic concepts of paddlesport have potencies whatever the level of learner. They help produce freethinking individual learners that find future problem solving easier to deal with.

▶ Using The Inner Game Approach

In his book 'Inner Game of Tennis', Tim Gallwey states: ' I know of no single factor that more greatly affects our ability to perform than the image we have of ourselves.'

For the inner game approach, this image of us and our performance potential is constructed by what Gallwey calls the self 1, and the self 2.

The self 1 is the ego-driven side of our mind which fills our head with a stream of self chatter and critical instructions. The self 2, our body, our natural fluid movement side, is distracted from achieving and reaching our potential because of listening to self 1, fills us with fear and self doubt, which in turn hinders and stifles our performance.

What the coach is trying to do when using the inner game approach is to quieten the self 1 side of the mind, unlocking the real possibilities of a confident and unrestricted performer. Gallway suggests that we often think too hard about completing physical tasks, and this manifests itself in a tenseness in the muscles that restricts our movement.

We can try to distract the chattering mind (self 1) by positive self-talk, repeating affirmation statements, and even singing while we paddle.

One of the problems with the inner game is that for many it lacks tangible and concrete examples. Converts would argue because of the individual nature of each situation there can only be principles. It is a method that works well for internal thinkers who are prepared to stick with it. The following example may help to give the approach some application.

 EXAMPLE

Anna employed a coach on a one-off session. They had talked over the phone about the focus of her learning and Anna's most recent experience of feeling there was a lack of polish in her paddling. A few years ago hitting every eddy on good grade three was not a problem, but recently the river seemed to take control of her and she often got swept out of the bottom of eddies and missed breakouts that she could previously have made with ease.

Anna, with encouragement from the coach, recounted events from a few years back, when micro eddies were not a problem, and the whole river would seem to slow to a pace that was determined by Anna. When they reached the top of the local rapid the coach asked Anna to remind herself of the way it used to feel when she was in charge of the boat. She leaned back in the boat, closed her eyes and smiled. As she did so the coach asked her to show him what it should look like when she had this control. Within a second she was off, the first three breakouts she made with ease, her body was turned to face the next eddy before she had left the last one. The final midstream boil and high cross were completed with a few smooth strokes. Anna arrived in the bottom pool still smiling and waited for the coach to join her. Anna had reminded herself what it was like to paddle like that.

This most recent success now becomes her most recent memory. It is now fresh and easily remembered.

▶ ASSESSING STUDENTS' PROGRESS

Coaches assess students' progress all the time. They make an almost continuous judgement on the progress that individuals are making, in order that they might best set new and appropriate targets for their development. One of the advantages of a coaching role is that it often provides an excellent opportunity to measure and quantify the progress that learners are making. As a result of their nearness to their own experience, paddlers often find it difficult to recognise the advances they have made.

Measuring progress can take many forms, returning the student to an old task to see if advancement in execution can be made is one method. Evaluating the performance against NGB set criteria is another way. These methods provide reassurance and motivation for most learners. They also help the coach establish the point the student is at in their progression, so further and more accurate planning can be applied.

▶ GETTING BETTER AT WHAT YOU DO

Coaching is a learnt skill, and like all processes involving cognitive decision-making, it needs practice and continued updating and development. It is easy for coaches to settle into comfortable and familiar patterns, producing similar session and delivery on a regular basis.

As they say 'How do you know where you are going, if you don't know where you started from'.

It could be suggested that if this situation is producing satisfactory results then what is the need for change?

Well, a number of factors indicate that if our coaching is to be as progressive and effective as possible we need to be active in adding and developing the range of tools, methods, and delivery skills we have at our finger tips. Hopefully making us better at what we do.

Knowledge and ideas about the process of coaching are developing at an impressive rate. Even if we reject a particular new approach we should do so out of an understanding and critical experience, not just because it is new, different and we don't understand it!

Undertaking new learning and training on aspects of coaching can help freshen up your coaching experiences and increase your own subject knowledge base. Using a new approach is exciting and stimulating. That freshness will be picked up by those you teach.

Returning to situations where you are once again a novice, with many aspects of a new skill still to acquire, is a benefit when it comes to dealing with your own learners. It helps you develop empathy and understanding about how hard the journey of learning can sometimes be.

There is a law of diminishing returns for a number of coaching and training methodologies. After years of similar type delivery some learners find that the method employed becomes stale. A change in your direction may just be the stimulus they need to take the next step.

Most organisations, national governing bodies, employers, and increasingly the paddlers you work with, expect coaches to be current and up to date. Without continuous professional development (CPD) you may fall behind the demands of the sport and limit the number and types of learner who are willing to be coached by you.

Learners will forgive you if you introduce something novel into the programme or delivery, but not if you are repetitive and boring.

KEY POINT

• When we talk of the 'currency' of teaching and coaching skills, we are referring to the need for all coaches to keep up to date with recent thinking and approaches. Only then can we give our students the best of what is on offer.

GETTING THE BEST OUT OF COACH EDUCATION COURSES

It both surprises and disappoints me to find a high number of coaches who fail to gain much from any coach education and training courses they attend. The reason for this situation is varied, occasionally it is the nature of the course itself, a clash between coach educator and coach but more often than not it is the manner in which the course was approached.

KEY POINT

• We all have a preferred learning style or blend of styles. Take time to discovery yours (search the web for on-line tests). It will help you understand about the way we take in information and give you additional empathy for your fellow learners.

▶ **Invest In Your Own Time**

Find out as much as you can about the staffing team delivering the course: are they current and up to date, how many courses do they run each year, what do past students say about the quality and standard of their delivery?

If the course is introducing new and challenging concepts, read up about the subject matter before hand, making your time on the course as profitable as possible.

It helps if you understand what kind of learner you are. Are you the type that needs to reflect on any new input for a week or so before drawing any conclusion, or the type that needs to see a new concept in action on the water before buying into its effectiveness?

A simple search on the web will provide you with a number of learning style questionnaires, which when completed will help you identify your own preferred learning style. Once you understand more about the ways you best learn, it will allow you to make any input more productive.

Progressive training courses and their coach educators should make efforts to find out about your learning history and preferences. If they don't explicitly ask you, make efforts to flag up your own preferences and learning styles.

Remember that for some of us, learning can be an uncomfortable and sometimes a painful process. We may have the very cornerstones of our own philosophy and delivery challenged and reassessed. One character of an effective coach with improvement potential is the ability to take these new ideas, value them, and to blend them into his or her own battery of coaching tools. The best approach to additional training opportunities is to go to the course with an open and inquisitive mind.

Give the new method a fair trial. Use it in a number of differing applications before considering rejecting it. Some new ideas will not work for everyone and in every situation, but like most aspects of learning, new

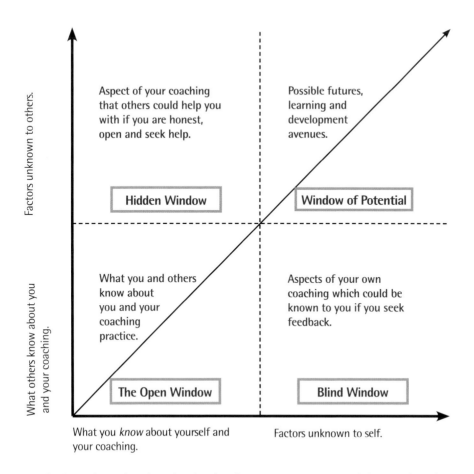

Fig. 12 Johari's window is based on the idea that the more open you are and the more knowledge you seek, the greater the size of the 'window' of potential.

material takes time and a number of errors in application before producing results. It might just be the tool you need to unlock the potential you saw in a particular performer.

▶ Transferable Skills

Attending other sports training programmes, and watching and talking to other sport coaches is a great way of broadening the range of knowledge and ideas you have access to.

If you take on board the general concept that we coach individuals to learn, and that the only real difference between say, coaching snowboarding and modern playboating is in the environmental application, it opens up a whole new range of opportunities to help you develop as a coach.

BEING HONEST ABOUT WHAT YOU DO

The worst type of feedback, they say, is the feedback you never get.

In the process of improving our coaching we need to recognise both what we do effectively and efficiently and what we don't. This process of being honest on our relative strengths and weaknesses can be a painful journey but it does provide excellent opportunities for improvement.

1. Actively search out feedback from fellow coaches, coach educators and your learners. Document it so patterns and trends can be identified.

2. Educate your paddlers in the skills of giving feedback.

3. Remember that critical feedback is about giving and supporting positive aspects, not just about correcting negative elements.

4. Learn to listen openly and objectively when getting feedback from others. For some the process of giving feedback to others may make them feel uncomfortable.

5. Remember that not all feedback you will get is well thought through or well delivered. Not everybody has those skills. You will have the best pictures of overall merits of the comments, and be able to identify if it represents an isolated instance or is part of a long-term pattern which you need to attend to.

6. Do something with the feedback, build it into your own coaching development plan. Use it as a springboard for future improvement.

7. Be honest with identifying your own areas that need development. Other coaches can only help you in a productive manner if you are open and honest in what you lack and value these areas as the way forward. This approach cannot only support you in aspects where you are aware of the need for development, but in areas in which you were not aware. Remember you do not need to be ill to get better.

POTENCIES OF REFLECTIVE PRACTICE

It is reported that a famous baseball coach on his retirement stated that his only regret in his long and successful career was that he hadn't made enough mistakes!

Now taking this at face value, you might think that the coach can't have been that successful if he made numerous mistakes.

But it is what he did with these errors that was potent. What mistakes can do is highlight areas that need improvement but this will only happen if you are open to recognising errors and using them in a productive manner.

One method that can aid this process is reflective practice. Reflective practice is the process of taking past experience and knowledge, and critically evaluating them in the light of new experiences and knowledge. Reflective practice can help us make sense of experiences which at first glance seem unstructured and unrelated. It is not about treating sections of learning in isolation, but blending them with other experiences, and using them to revisit existing ideas about effective and efficient practice.

The process of reflecting on what has happened allows you to build upon what you already know about coaching and utilise new ideas by adding value to past and present learnt skills. Taking time to analyse experience, to get behind the obvious, will provide greater benefit than taking what first appears at face value.

Because of the nature of the coaching process, it being a process of decision-making and selection of best-fit options, reflective practice encourages a multi-answer type approach to problem solving. It encourages deeper learning in both coaches and performer by giving values to individualised solutions to a variety of problems that affect what we do in our coaching and learning. The result is, not just a broadening of the pool of skills and solutions that a coach can call on, but a deeper understanding of the reasons behind why some things work and some things don't.

Reflective practice works at all levels of coaching and coach education.

When used by paddlers it helps develop free thinking individuals who can make independent decisions on the water.

Reflective practice is aided by:

Providing time and space in any training situation for both you and your paddlers to reflect on the learning undertaken. It is tempting, when time is limited, to cut the time out for this in a programme, but if you are to give the process value you must give it time.

Programme it into all coaching or training schemes. Reflective practice processes can be used to link one session to the next. In a coach education programme it can play a central part of an individual's short and long-term development.

The use of training diaries, session planners and coaching logbooks all provide opportunities for written reflective practice. Some coaches keep an individual coaching journal in which they reflect on the experience they have, and their feelings about those experiences. The key thing here is to keep these documented so they provide a history of development and can in turn support longer-term goal setting and motivation.

Facilitation of reflection in a group setting is a skilled and often difficult process, but the advantages of group learning and the experience of sharing others' thoughts on their learning, may outweigh the negative aspects.

Photo 14 The relationship of mentoring

It is not the experience that you gain that helps you get better but what you do with that experience.

BENEFITING FROM MENTORING

In the last twenty years or so the act of mentoring has been widely used in all forms of skill and personal development. The relationship of mentoring can be as formal or informal as the situation allows and demands. It's like getting a coach to help you improve your coaching.

The key starting place for developing this supportive relationship is finding someone with whom there is an element of trust. They do not have to be a more experienced or senior coach than yourself, they could be at the same level. Peer mentoring can also be beneficial because of the shared experiences of someone at a similar stage of coaching development.

Crucial to the mentoring role is the idea that you are not trying to copy the attitudes and approaches of the mentor, (nor should mentors focus their own approaches on anyone) but using the relationship to develop your own individual skill and talents as a coach.

How Mentoring Works

Mentoring works at differing levels by giving you someone to bounce ideas off, go to for advice and generally use as a sounding board. Mentors can help when things don't quite go to plan by helping you see things through a different set of eyes.

They can be used to directly observe your performance as a coach. They may bring forward elements for discussion, which because of your closeness to the action, may be difficult for you to identify.

The use of video here is excellent as a recording tool. Sometimes our behaviours are not as we perceive them, and aspects of our coaching that we mean to be interpreted by learners and others may not be as we had intended them. The use of video can be a frank reminder of these elements.

Mentoring can be beneficial to all involved parties. Working with other coaches can help you revisit aspects of your own delivery with a critical eye. The role of mentor can expose you to alternative views and approaches that you have not been aware of and help you on the road to getting better at what you do.

But remember… adapt it, don't adopt it.

FURTHER READING AND ACKNOWLEDGEMENTS

The following texts have the Sport Sciences as their knowledge base, and therefore they will have varying degrees of accessibility to those without a basic sport science background. Texts that lend themselves to an easy introduction to the subject area are indicated in blue.

Much of the information and ideas covered in pages 13 to 15 draws heavily on the work of John Lyle (2002) his excellent book is referenced below.

Coaches Guide to Teaching Sports Skills, Christina R & Corcos D, 1988, Human Kinetics, 1-800-747-4457

The Coaching Process: Principles and Practice for Sport, Cross N & Lyle J, 1999, Butterworth-Heinemann, 0-7506-4131-2

Inner Skiing - Revised Edition, Gallwey T & Kriegel B, 1977, Random House, 0-679-77827-6

A Guide to Mentoring Sports Coaches, Galvin, B, 1998, NCF, 1-902523-03-2

Developing Decision Makers: An Empowerment Approach to Coaching, Kidman L, 2001, Innovation Print 0-473-07587-3

The Coaching Process: A Practical Guide to Improving Your Effectiveness, Kidman L & Hanrahan S, 1997, Dunmore Press, 0-86469-285-4

Sport Coaching Concepts, Lyle J. 2002, Routledge 0-415-26158-9

Coaches Guide to Sports Psychology, Martens R, 1987, Human Kinetics, 0-87622-022-6

Successful Coaching, Martens R, 2004, Human Kinetics, 0-7360-4012-9

The Effective Teaching of Physical Education, Mawer M, 1995, Longman 0-582-095220

The Centered Skier, McCluggage D, 1986, A Bantam New Age book, 0-553-24508-2

Better Coaching: Advanced Coach's Manual, Pyke F, 2001, Human Kinetics 0-7360-4113-3

Motor Learning and Performance, Schmidt R & Wrisberg C, 2000, Human Kinetics 08801155009

Sporting Body Sporting Mind - An Athlete's Guide to Mental Training, Syer J & Connolly C, 1984, Cambridge University Press, 0-521-26935-0

Coaching Kids for Dummies, Wolff R, 2000, IDG Books world wide, 0-7645-5197-3

BILL TAYLOR

Bill is a Londoner by birth and spent most of his early paddling career racing up and down the River Thames in sprint boats. It was only in his early twenties that he widened his interests to include the rest of what paddlesport has to offer. Bill made first descents in Africa, Mexico, Pakistan and the former Soviet Union, completed a six month solo sea paddle in the South Pacific, and a three month solo canoe paddle along the length of the River Danube. He even managed to represent Britain at white water rafting.

His career path has taken him from working as an outdoor pursuits instructor in Scotland, to being a co-director of Mobile Adventure Ltd. Bill is presently employed in the Department of Exercise and Sports Science, Manchester Metropolitan University where he is subject leader in Coaching.

2 PHYSIOLOGICAL PRINCIPLES

Whether you are coaching elite athletes for world class competition, preparing your paddlers for a multi-day sea expedition or simply need to ensure that your students get the best out of themselves and come to no harm... this chapter is for you. A good understanding of how our bodies work is an essential part of any coach's 'toolbox', whatever the level they are coaching.

INTRODUCTION

Physiology is the study of how our bodies function, how we produce the energy we need for paddling. Knowledge of the physiological or physical principles that apply to each canoesport discipline will further improve the paddler or coach's ability to interpret paddling performance. Our paddling performance is related to the interaction of the technical, tactical, psychological and physiological elements involved in our chosen discipline, as shown in Figure 1.

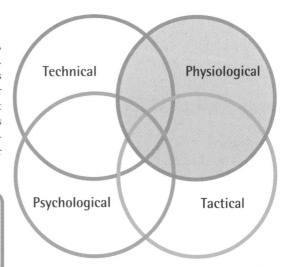

Fig. 1 *The Relationship between the Components of Paddling Performance.*

> ### ○ KEY POINT SUMMARY
>
> • Paddlesport performance is determined by the interaction of technical, tactical, physiological and psychological factors. As paddlers we need to identify which factor is the rate-limiter at any stage in our development.

PADDLING PERFORMANCE

The relationship between the technical, tactical, physiological and psychological elements for any one of us must be viewed as dynamic. At any one time an individual paddler can be limited by physiological, psychological or skill-based (technical or tactical) constraints. The relative size of the four components will change over time, between disciplines and individuals. For example, the importance of the mental, physical and skill components may differ for playboaters, slalom canoeists and marathon paddlers.

The trick for us as paddlers, seeking to improve our performance, is to identify which of the components is our rate-limiter at any particular stage in our development. For example a kayaker or canoeist could have difficulties crossing a strong eddy fence. This could be due to skill errors (technical), such as not having all the blade pulling in the water, not being physically powerful enough to punch through the eddy line (physiological), a lack of understanding of the attack angle required (tactical), or anxiety created by the thought of capsize (psychological). A coach will need to be able to analyse performance and decide the underlying problem for a paddler. This chapter concerns the physiological aspects of paddlesport. Table 1 provides some examples of problems that might appear to be technical, tactical or psychological but in fact have a physiological root cause. Coaches and paddlers will need to be able to identify when a paddling rate-limiter has a physiological cause. Once identified this chapter can be used to help create physiological solutions for improving paddling performance.

As a highly skilful activity sport many chapters within this book will focus on the technical aspects of the sport. In the next chapter Chris Hodgson will provide details of psychological factors that can help to improve canoe and kayak performance. The main function of this chapter is to begin to examine the physiological principles that can usefully assist us as paddlers (these will be developed further in the Performance Coaching chapter in Part 2). Figure 2 identifies the major elements that can influence our physiological performance. There are, however, a number of factors in Figure 2 that have an interaction with the other two performance components, skill development and psychological principles. These factors, gender differences, growth and development and injury prevention and recovery, will be discussed in this chapter from a physiological perspective, but will

Symptom of Problem	Misleading Causal Component	Root Cause of Problem (Physiological Component)	Possible Solution
Poor forward paddling action during a sea paddling expedition.	Technical	Lack of local muscular endurance, aerobic fitness or poor nutrition during paddling could undermine physical ability during a day of paddling.	Aerobic Training – in-boat, Circuit Training, review of food and fluid intake during expeditions to highlight any useful changes.
Paddler appears anxious during the paddle out when taking part in surf sessions.	Psychological	Lack of power to build up speed quickly and punch through waves.	Mixture of strength training and in-boat drills to develop power for use during paddle out in surfing.
Paddler capsizes on eddy turns due to incorrect application of edge.	Tactical	Lack of core strength development to hold high degree of edge required in faster eddy turns.	Work on general strength and specific core stability – possible alternatives: in-boat exercises, weight training, circuit training, pilates, cross-training - cycling.

Table 1 Examples of misleading problem identification where the actual root cause is physiological.

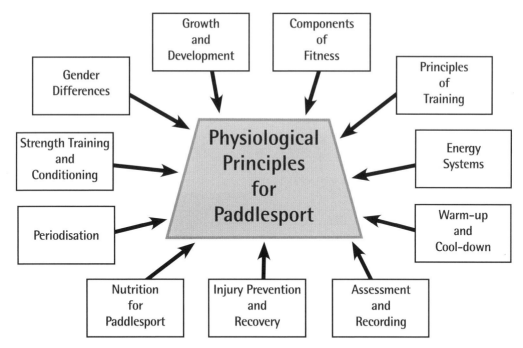

Fig. 2 *The Physiological Principles for Paddlesport.*

be discussed further in subsequent chapters in a discipline/skill or psychological context.

▶ Improving Paddling Performance

To improve paddling performance it is beneficial to adopt a long-term approach to development. This chapter is based on such an approach, for the physical, mental and skill (technical and tactical) development of a paddler should be viewed with the future in mind.

▶ COMPONENTS OF FITNESS

The physiological aspects of paddling are concerned with fitness. To develop any sort of training programme for canoe or kayak sport we must ask some fundamental questions about the nature of the activity. One of the key questions has to do with fitness and how it can help improve paddling ability. If we are fitter it will help us to improve our performance, whether this is seen through quicker times or improved decision making due to lower overall stress on the body.

We will first consider the mature adult system as this differs quite significantly from a child or adolescent. The young paddlers physiological system is discussed in Chapter10.

At its most basic level, to be fit is to be healthy or in good athletic condition. Fitness for paddling, however, is specific – fitness for sea paddling journeys means something very different than for slalom. As a paddler or coach you must be able to identify the components of fitness that are the most important to your discipline. This section identifies the major components of fitness that may impact to a greater or lesser extent on a paddler depending on their discipline. In developing a training programme for your discipline you will need to identify which of these components is fundamental to improving your performance.

🔘 KEY POINT SUMMARY

- Fitness is specific, so paddlers or their coaches need to be able to identify the key components of fitness for their discipline.

The components of fitness for paddlesport can be divided into those that are physically trainable, and will be discussed in this chapter, and those that are skill-related and are discussed within other chapters of this book. The components are identified in Table 2. The terminology used by sports scientists can differ, but within the context of this book the definitions of each of these components will be maintained by all authors.

Physiologically Trainable Components of Fitness	Skill Related Fitness Components	
Muscular Endurance	Agility	
Aerobic Capacity	Co-ordination	} Dynamic Balance
Anaerobic Power & Capacity	Balance	
- Speed	Reaction Time	
- Strength		
Body Composition		
Mobility		

Table 2 The Components of Fitness

MUSCULAR ENDURANCE

Muscular endurance relates to the ability of a certain muscle or muscle group to maintain repeated muscular contractions against a given resistance. This resistance could represent a small percentage of your maximal contraction (see strength below) or a higher percentage. The closer a load is to your maximum the shorter the time that the movements can be maintained. For paddlesport an example of muscular endurance would be the ability to paddle for a day's white water paddling or on a sea journey. The load for each individual paddle stroke would be small, relative to the maximum thus enabling you to maintain the action for long periods of time. If you fatigue before the end of a day's paddling, one aspect you might need to develop would be your muscular endurance.

AEROBIC CAPACITY

While muscular endurance relates to the ability of a muscle or group of muscles to maintain work without fatiguing, aerobic power or capacity refers to the ability of the body to produce energy for exercise involving the whole body over a relatively long period of time. Canoesport disciplines that last for longer than one and a half minutes will produce the energy for paddling largely through aerobic mechanisms. The term 'aerobic' means in the presence of oxygen . The body has a variety of systems or 'gears' that can be used to provide the energy we need for paddling, and the '3rd gear' or 'overdrive', (the aerobic system), uses oxygen to assist in the conversion of the food we eat into fuel for our paddling. A marathon paddler will require oxygen to produce energy for the several hours duration of the event. Aerobic capacity is often measured using maximal oxygen uptake. This represents the maximum amount of oxygen the body can use each minute to provide paddling energy. There are a variety of ways this can be measured or estimated such as through the multi-stage fitness test (Bleep test) or in a laboratory on

Photo 1 A day's sea journey requires muscular endurance.

a treadmill; it is also possible to measure this for kayak and canoesport. In a physiology laboratory a gas analyser can be used to examine how much oxygen a paddler uses per minute. This can give the paddler, their coach and the physiologist information about their aerobic fitness. You do not, however, need expensive equipment to estimate aerobic fitness and the section below on assessment tools provides details of a number of aerobic fitness tests that could easily be used or developed for use by any paddler. In addition, training for aerobic fitness will be addressed further below.

Photo 2 Marathon paddler

ANAEROBIC POWER & CAPACITY

As 'aerobic' refers to being in the presence of oxygen, 'anaerobic' relates to energy produced without the need for oxygen. Energy production utilising oxygen takes longer than anaerobic methods to become a main fuel source and is produced at a lower rate than can be achieved via anaerobic sources. Thus for events that last less than 1½ to 2 minutes, such as sprint events, a sprint finish or intermittent events (with sprints and recovery periods such as canoe polo or a surf kayak heat), anaerobic methods provide a major fuel source. Anaerobic mechanisms, ones that do not require oxygen to operate, provide the 1st and 2nd gears for our paddling energy production.

BODY COMPOSITION

Body composition refers to the chemical make-up of the body. For sports physiologists this basically refers to two components, fat mass and fat-free mass. Research into canoesport and body composition has concentrated on the body fat percentages for Olympic canoeists. This found that gold medallists were heavier than the average competitor for each event. This difference has been shown to be related to an increased muscle mass for the most successful canoeists. Body composition has health implications for all paddlers, however, as a non-weight bearing and non-weight categorised sport, percentage fat mass has fewer implications for performance than in other sports. In addition, if diet remains unchanged increased training volumes will normally lead to a positive shift in body composition (i.e. a decrease in fat percentage in relation to lean mass).

MOBILITY

The terms flexibility and mobility are often used interchangeably to refer to the range of motion about the joints of the body. Often linked in with warm-up and cool-down mobility and flexibility have a significant role to play for paddlers. Research indicates that most often mobilising exercises should be utilised during the warm-up to get joints and soft tissue ready for the movements they will encounter during the exercise and static flexibility – stretching – should be carried out during the cool-down when the muscles and soft tissues are thoroughly warm. A good range of motion in the wrists, shoulders, trunk and hips are important for the canoeist. Trunk rotation for a variety of kayak strokes and cross-deck paddling for open boaters, flexion and extension onto front and back decks for rolling rely on good levels of mobility

Photo 3a Surf kayaker taking off
Photo 3b Sprint start

and are improved by flexibility work carried as part of a training programme. Mobility is an excellent illustration of the close relationship between the physical and the skill-based elements of paddlesport. A lack of trunk rotation flexibility can easily become a rate-limiter for improvements with, for example, cartwheeling for playboaters. Hyper-mobility is also a concern for canoeists where too much shoulder flexibility can create problems with shoulder dislocations so there is a balance to be maintained. A balance between strength training to protect joints along with flexibility training to maintain and/or improve range of motion is a useful concern for us as paddlers. **See Appendix A.**

Photo 4 Freestyle paddler cartwheeling

DYNAMIC BALANCE

Physiologists describe three different balance-related components that are more meaningfully combined for canoesport and can be termed 'dynamic balance'. Balance is the ability to hold a static position such as a handstand for a length of time under control. Agility relates to a moving form of balance such that an agile athlete is able to make a series of movements with changes of direction but remain in balance. Co-ordination is the ability to effect efficient movements to achieve a goal. As individual components they have some relation to canoesport but, as a sport based on water rather than land, are more meaningful when combined to comprise 'dynamic balance'. In a paddlesport context this refers to the ability to use skilful co-ordinated movement to maintain position or make progress on the water. Balance and agility as part of this movement are fundamental to the body, boat and blade aspects of any particular stroke. Ian Coleman, in the Canoe and Kayak Handbook (page 149) describes the 'Dynamic Seating Position' as being the central foundation to the development of many boating skills. This 'locking' of the paddler into the boat is a first step in employing skilful dynamic balance for closed cockpit craft. For those using open boats, waveskis and open cockpit kayaks, whilst not always being locked into position, the need to adopt a position in the boat that allows for maximised body, boat and blade control is central to dynamic balance. Dynamic balance is very closely related to the skill aspects of all paddling disciplines.

REACTION TIME

Reaction time is the interval between the introduction of a stimulus and the beginning of a response. For example, on paddling a new river how quickly does a kayaker react to an event horizon and if necessary take evasive action – catching a 'must-make' eddy before a waterfall. It is a key aspect of sports performance and as such is defined by physiologists as one of the components of fitness. However, reaction time is much less trainable in a physiological context than components such as strength or aerobic endurance and is best developed as part of skills training.

▶ A Skilful Activity

Paddlesport is clearly a skilful activity, within all disciplines, and as such any fitness training needs to be balanced with skill development. Improvements in fitness can help skill development and lead to improved performance. With the highly varied nature

Photo 5a Carving a bottom turn
Photo 5b Open boater shifting weight

of paddlesport and the confines of this chapter it would be impossible to examine the components of fitness important to every canoe discipline. With your knowledge of the sport, however, you should be able to identify the main components. The key texts listed at the end of this chapter can give you further useful information to assist you with this process.

▶ PRINCIPLES OF TRAINING

To improve our paddling we must focus on the performance model and decide which of the components (technical, tactical, psychological, physiological or a combination of all four) needs to be addressed to make further progress. If we decide to develop our physical fitness there are a number of key principles that should guide us as paddlers when designing training programmes.

OVERLOAD PRINCIPLE

The Overload Principle is based on research that has shown the body will respond to training loads above those that it normally meets. If a sedentary person takes up a training programme all exercises would be new and would therefore be overloading their body. This will bring about physiological adaptations for

2 Physiological Principles

that individual, or in other words, improvements in their fitness. A paddler must apply this same principle when designing a training programme. To improve fitness we must train with loads that are above those that we would normally meet. To do this we can adjust the frequency, intensity or time (FIT) for which we train. Frequency is the number of times per week we train, intensity is the level at which we work (for example, at what percentage of our heart rate maximum we work) and time being the duration of each training session. Each of these parameters can be manipulated in programme design to create a training overload through which to achieve an improvement in fitness.

KEY POINT SUMMARY

- The principles of fitness should be used as guidelines for the development of any training programme.

PROGRESSION PRINCIPLE

The principle of progression is very closely linked with that of overload. As physiological adaptation takes place (as we become fitter) a training load that was an overload will decrease in its difficulty. To continue to progress in our training the FIT of training need to be adjusted to cater for improvements in fitness. We must progressively increase the training overload. An example of this can be made with weight training. You decide that a resistance (weight) training programme would improve your paddling and design a programme that you carry out 3 times per week at a local gym. The load for each exercise in the initial weeks will represent an overload, however, as you get fitter you will need to increase the weight lifted to maintain progress. A simple way to do this is to use the 2 for 2 rule. If you can complete two repetitions more than the assigned repetition goal in the last set of an exercise over two consecutive sessions, you should increase the weight lifted. For example, if for biceps curl you are performing three sets of 10 repetitions but in the last set, for two sessions in a row, you can complete 12 reps it is time to increase the load. By adjusting the FIT you can manipulate any aspect of your training to maintain a progressive overload.

SPECIFICITY PRINCIPLE

Research into physiological adaptations has provided us with a number of guidelines regarding specificity of training. The specificity of training principle

Photo 6 Weight training being used to develop strength

refers to the need for training to be particular to the desired goals.

▶ Resistance Training Specificity

Resistance training is commonly employed by athletes from many sports including paddlesport to help improve performance. Research tells us that resistance training can help improve strength, power, speed and muscular endurance, all of which can be beneficial, to a greater or lesser extent (depending on our discipline) to our paddling performance. The goals of resistance training can be different by design, and as such, should be made specific to the discipline. Firstly, the exercises selected should be specific to the activity chosen. For example upper body exercises for a kayaker should take priority over lower body exercises and movements made with weights should match as closely as possible movements made in the activity. Secondly, strength gains have been found to match the speed at which training was carried out. For example if training was carried out at slow speed to develop strength the maximal expression of strength would be found moving at that slow speed. If you are training for an explosive event that requires power then training speeds should reflect this to maximise possible gains.

▶ Conditioning Training Specificity

A number of studies have been carried out regarding specificity and conditioning that can be of benefit to us as paddlers designing training programmes. Training results are specific to the muscles trained and there is often little transfer to other muscles even between events like running and swimming. One good illustration of this is a study that involved 15 healthy but sedentary subjects swim training for one hour per day, 3 days per week, for 10 weeks. All subjects carried out swimming and running tests at the start and end of the study. Not surprisingly, the results found a 1.5% improvement in the running test scores for the group, but an 11% change in the swim test scores. When training for a specific activity such as kayaking or canoeing the training overload should engage the specific muscles and energy systems used for the discipline. In other words, if you wish to get fit for paddling you need to train in your boat as a regular part of your programme.

In a similar fashion to the speed aspect of resistance training, discussed above, the conditioning aspects of training should match the activity for which you are training. Sprint training for anaerobic sprint events, endurance training for aerobic events and a mixed protocol for intermittent events such as canoe polo.

▶ Programme Specificity

There are a number of aspects with regard to programme design where specificity needs to be addressed. In developing a training schedule the focus of training should move from generalised to more specific training as time comes closer to competition. This will be addressed further in the section below on periodisation. The time at which training is carried out should match competition or performance times as closely as possible. Research has shown that adaptations to training are specific to the time of day during which the training took place. If you are training for a slalom event which will take place in the morning it is better if you can do some of your training at this same time of day. Paddlers training for the DW race also need to consider training their bodies to work during the night. In a similar way research has found that modelling competition in training can help make adaptations specific to the event. It is important for you, as a paddler or coach, to know about the aerobic and anaerobic contributions to energy production for your discipline. Training should mimic or 'model' these relative contributions.

REGRESSION PRINCIPLE

When an athlete stops training they will lose any gains they have made relatively rapidly. The effects of detraining can be seen very clearly in anyone who has broken a leg or arm and had it kept in plaster for six weeks. When the plaster is removed the resulting atrophy (loss in muscle size) is due to detraining or regression. The regression principle states that ceasing training, dependent upon the period and degree of detraining (ranging from normal active life but no training to complete bed-rest), will result in a loss of fitness gains made through previous training. This has clear implications for breaks in training or off-season phases and the need to maintain some level of fitness.

Photo 7 Canoe Polo

It is for this reason that many top athletes have recovery phase training programmes to maintain a reasonable level of fitness before commencing pre-season training. The same principle can guide planning the training programme for any level of paddler.

INDIVIDUALISATION PRINCIPLE

If you set two very similar wild water racing paddlers on a training programme the response of each to training would vary for each aspect of training. Individualisation, whilst making sound physiological sense, is a fundamental coaching principle. Just as skill development sessions should be devised on an individual basis, training programmes should be developed in response to each paddler's fitness assessment results (see below) and their training goals. Research tells us that optimal training benefits are obtained through individually developed programmes. This does not, however, mean that all training should be carried out individually.

VARIATION PRINCIPLE

Adding variety such as by changing the venue, number of paddlers training or by having changes in training programme can help with motivation and enable a paddler to avoid any boredom with training.

Photo 8 Training in groups is good for motivation

Dependent upon the level of performance the training volume for a canoeist can be up to and over 1,000 hours per year, as such the paddler or their coach needs to add variety to the programme to maintain enthusiasm. Variation in training loads can help not only with motivation but also assist in avoiding overtraining illnesses. Training close to your maximum in every session can overstress the body. By adding variety to sessions, for instance by having hard and easy training days, a paddler can avoid such illnesses or injuries. This can be achieved by manipulating the FIT in a training programme, a central aspect of the next section which deals with long-term training programme development – Periodisation.

▶ PERIODISATION

Periodisation is based upon the General Adaptation Syndrome (GAS) - the body responds to a situation of stress (in the case of training the stress is the different forms of exercise that can be undertaken) by first showing alarm - shock to body and muscle soreness, then adaptation which leads to improvement of performance and finally exhaustion when a body is able to make no further improvement as a result of the training. If training is not reduced at this stage an overtrained state may occur. Periodisation is a system of training programme design through which a paddler can best develop their training overtime, to peak for a major event or for a competition season, without going into the exhaustion phase.

Since the original model of periodisation was proposed by Matveyev in 1965, a number of variations in programme have been developed to suit athletes from different sports. Boaters from every discipline and level of performance now have a wide range of periodisation options from which they can develop an appropriate training programme. As well as avoiding overtraining, having a periodised programme can help a canoeist avoid boredom with training through having a phased programme and knowledge of what is coming next in preparation for an event. The athlete can see clearly why they are training and how they are progressing to their goal. This aspect of physiology can be closely linked with the psychological tool of goal-setting that Chris Hodgson will discuss in the next chapter. Before designing a programme for a paddler it would be useful to have read both sections from this book.

See also Chapters 18, 20 and Appendix B.

KEY POINT SUMMARY

- Periodisation, dividing the training year into manageable and progressive sections, is an excellent way to set realistic goals for the paddler and to enable him or her to identify exactly where they are in the progress towards a main competition or event.

▶ Phases

The concept behind periodisation is to divide the training year into distinct phases. These phases build upon one another to prepare a paddler for a specific event or season of performance. Programmes can be designed over a short or long period of time and be designed individually for each paddler. The possible units within a periodised programme are detailed in Table 3. The most common lengths of time for a periodised programme would be between several weeks and one year depending on the level of performance and age of the paddler. Within periodisation these phases of training have specific names. A macrocycle is the largest unit of a programme such as a training year; this is divided into a number of mesocycles which last for one to several months. Mesocycles are divided into microcycles which are typically one week long. By dividing the programme in this way it is possible for a paddler to see what they are doing for the next training session, how this fits with their week's training and how this builds up to the next mesocycle and how that leads to the event for which they are training.

PROGRAMME DESIGN

The basis behind the success of periodised training is the variation for the volume (quantity) and intensity (quality) of training. Figure 3 provides a model of how the relationship between volume and intensity of training is managed through a periodised programme. The paddler or their coach needs to manage the volume and intensity through the programme so as to avoid overtraining. During the early part of training the volume of training is kept high with a much lower intensity. As time comes closer to the main event the intensity is designed to rise to performance level and as a result the volume of training decreases dramatically. As can be seen, the model training period (macrocycle) is divided into four mesocycles. Each one of these would then be divided into a series of microcycles. The hypertrophy phase is a preparatory phase and is designed to 'get the body ready to train', con-

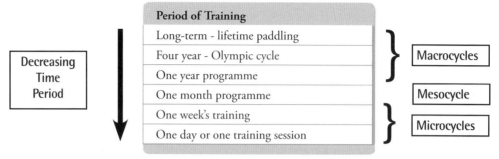

Table 3 *Possible Training Units Within a Periodised Programme*

centrating on increasing muscle mass and endurance. The strength phase sees the cross-over between intensity and volume of training with quantity decreasing to allow a greater focus on the quality of the sessions. The strength and the strength/power phases represent the key phases of training when the hard work is completed by the paddler, ready for the final peaking phases that taper training in order to be rested and in peak condition for the competition.

▶ When To Carry Out Fitness Assessments

The next section looks at the variety of tests that can be used to assess a paddler's fitness. They are based upon the components of fitness and should be devised into a battery or group of tests according to the phase of training. A fitness assessment would be carried out with a canoeist to evaluate how a training programme was working. For instance, has strength improved at the end of the strength phase? If strength has not improved the programme might not have included the correct exercises, reps and sets to bring about an improvement and may need alteration for future events. Completing a battery of testing is normally hard work for a paddler as they will want to do their best and as such the schedule needs to be well thought out. If following a periodised programme the tests undertaken should reflect the phase of training. At the start of a macrocycle, like that for instance at the start of a training year, a complete battery of testing might be carried out to assess baseline fitness levels. From this the training programme could be designed and re-testing phases be linked with the completion of each specific mesocycle, i.e. hypertrophy or strength.

KEY POINT SUMMARY

• The phases in a training programme are designed to build one upon the next. The hypertrophy phase is a foundation stage to get the body ready for the hard training to come. The strength phase is a physically hard stage for any athlete and should provide the strength base for the speed and power development in the strength/power phase. In the peaking phase the quantity or training is reduced but the quality is maintained as the paddler nears the event for which they are training.

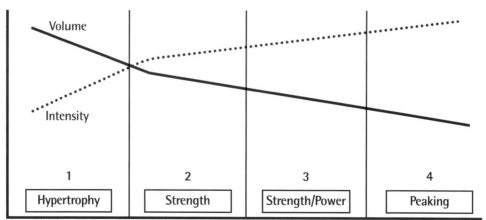

Fig. 3 *General Periodisation Model shown over 4 Mesocycles*

▶ PROGRAMME ASSESSMENT

There are a wide variety of assessment tools available that can be used in paddlesport. A key question though, is why we should use them?

There are three main reasons why assessing fitness is important to the paddler or their coach:

◎ 1. If you do not test you cannot know the level at which to set the training programme a paddler should follow. Similarly, if you do not carry out testing at the end of a phase of training you will be unable to decide if the programme is working.

◎ 2. If you do carry out a testing programme it can help to give you or your paddler some positive feedback that the hard work in training is working and can provide excellent information for setting realistic training goals for the next phase of training (as mentioned above, goal setting with paddlers will be covered in more detail in the next chapter).

◎ 3. If you do not carry out testing for a programme a paddler is following you will have an incomplete profile of the paddler. The paddler and coach need a more complete picture in their search for the developmental rate-limiter at any particular stage.

This is made possible by:

- Using video to analyse technique and tactical development.
- Good communication with an athlete about their psychological preparation.
- Physiological assessments of fitness improvement.

It is possible for the paddler or their coach to have a more complete picture in the search for the developmental rate-limiter at any particular stage.

Photo 9 Paddlers being tested

▶ Choosing The Tests

The battery of tests you decide upon for a programme will be based on the components of fitness for your discipline. The exact components of fitness will be different for each area of canoe and kayak sport and the exact schedule of tests you decide to use should reflect this.

This section will be split into three main parts:

◎ 1. Aspects of assessment that can be common across disciplines.

◎ 2. Discipline-specific assessment tools.

◎ 3. A short section with guidelines for the organisation of a testing schedule.

◯ KEY POINT SUMMARY

- Keeping race results, video clips and height and weight measures for a paddler can form the basis of monitoring long-term paddler development.

GENERIC PADDLING ASSESSMENT TOOLS

For all paddlers, especially growing ones, it is useful to keep a record of height and weight. Keeping previous race, performance and test records is a really useful way of monitoring development for a paddler. Although most often used as a coaching tool, a video clip diary kept over time can additionally provide an excellent record of performance development in skill based tests.

Photo 10 Using video to record progress

DISCIPLINE-SPECIFIC ASSESSMENT TOOLS

The development of a battery of tests should be specific to the components of fitness relevant to each discipline. When designing a battery of tests it is really useful to be inventive. It would be impossible in a chapter such as this to decide on a battery of tests for each paddlesport discipline. The tests described are therefore examples that you should modify and adapt as you feel is most appropriate for your discipline.

KEY POINT SUMMARY

• In order to evaluate whether a training programme is working – checking whether the paddler is getting fitter- you need to assess its impact. Tests should be specific to the discipline, the components of fitness and carried out before and after the phase of training.

▶ Muscular Endurance

A variety of 'body weight resistance' circuit training style exercises or in-boat paddling drills can be used to assess muscular endurance. The key with these exercises is to maintain the quality of the movements throughout the test time. Exercises can be carried out on a singular basis, such as how many sit-ups can be completed in a minute, or in a mini-circuit, for example with press-ups, sit-ups, tricep dips, star jumps for 30 seconds on each activity. The type of exercises would be determined by the paddlesport discipline and could include appropriate in-boat drills.

▶ Aerobic Capacity

The traditional gold standard (seen as the most accurate measure) for assessment of aerobic capacity is the maximal oxygen uptake or $\dot{V}O_{2max}$ test (the V of $\dot{V}O_{2max}$ stands for volume, the dot above the V shows it is measured per minute, the O2 means oxygen and the max being short for maximum). In a laboratory setting the test is carried out using a treadmill, cycle ergometer (literally a work measuring device), rowing machine or kayak ergometer. The testing device to be used is based on the athlete's sport due to the specificity of fitness. After a warm-up the athlete being tested will then complete an 8 to 12 minute protocol designed to take them to their maximum work rate with increases in the workload at regular increments throughout the test. The test time is designed to allow the aerobic or oxygen transport system to get to its maximum. During the test the amount of oxygen consumed for each stage, up to the athlete's maximum, is recorded. The aerobically fitter the athlete the longer they will be able to carry on the test and the higher the amount of oxygen they will be able to use to produce energy.

One of the useful benefits of this test is that heart rate (HR) and oxygen consumption have a very close

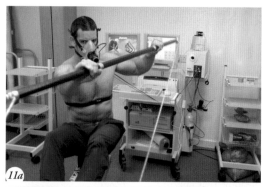

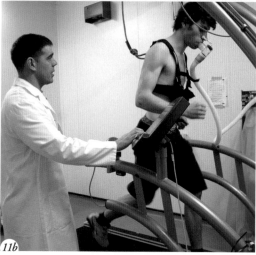

Photo 11a $\dot{V}O_{2max}$ *test using paddle ergometer*
Photo 11b $\dot{V}O_{2max}$ *test using treadmill (if no paddle ergometer available)*

AEROBIC CAPACITY TESTS

The $\dot{V}O_{2max}$ test requires laboratory facilities that are expensive and difficult to come by. Fortunately, due to the relationship between HR and oxygen consumption, many sub-maximal* aerobic tests and maximal tests based on HR have been developed for assessing aerobic fitness.

These include:

• *1.5 mile run.*
• *Coopers 12 minute run.*
• *Queen's College Step Test.*
• *Multi-Stage Fitness Test (Bleep Test).*
• *Rockport Walk.*
• *Astrand-Rhyming Nomogram.*

* Sub-maximal tests do not take an athlete to maximum but use a level below maximum to estimate maximum.

KEY POINT SUMMARY

- In order to evaluate whether a training programme is working – checking whether the paddler is getting fitter – you need to assess its impact. Tests should be specific to the discipline, the components of fitness and be carried out before and after the phase of training.

linear relationship. This is not really surprising as it is the heart that pumps the oxygen we need for paddling round to the working muscles. The harder you work at each stage in the test, the more oxygen you need to use and the harder the heart needs to work to supply the required oxygen.

In addition, a number of performance-related tests, where time to complete a test is the parameter measured, have been developed for work with rowers and paddlers. These include 1000m, 2000m, or further timed distance tests. The key concept with all these tests is to match as closely as possible the requirements of the paddling discipline to the test to be used. Research has shown that kayakers, being tested for aerobic fitness, score higher on a kayak ergometer than they do on a treadmill (running) or a cycle ergometer and higher still when they are tested in their own boats. Specificity as a principle of training is as important for testing as it is for training. The use of HR monitors as a training tool will be discussed further in the section on strength training and conditioning below.

▶ Anaerobic Power And Capacity

Exercises for the assessment of anaerobic power are covered in discussion of the next two components of fitness: strength and power/speed. Anaerobic capacity assessment would need to be based around the anaerobic demands of the activity. As mentioned in the components of fitness section above, anaerobic energy production related to capacity relates to the '2nd gear' of energy production for events such as 200m – 500m sprints, sprint finishes in distance races or for intermittent events such as canoe polo. Again activities would be best carried out in-boat but could also be carried out on Concept II rowers or arm ergometers. The duration or nature of the test should reflect the discipline for which the assessment is being devised. There is a wide variety of tests that can be used to assess anaerobic capacity, some of which were not developed for canoe and kayak but could be easily adapted and adopted by an inventive coach. The demands of the discipline should dictate the test to be employed with a paddler.

Photo 12 Basketball Sprint Test

ANAEROBIC CAPACITY TESTS

There are a variety of anaerobic tests that can be used to assess a training programme. Choose or develop ones that are most specific to your discipline and the type of training being undertaken. Where possible they should be carried out in-boat.

- *The basketball sprint test* - could be adapted to use in a boat on a marked course. This test involves four out and back increasing distance sprints. The distances would need to be adapted to the activity, i.e. canoe polo etc. The time taken should be recorded.

- *6 x 150m rowing anaerobic test* on Concept II with 30 seconds recovery between each sprint, time being recorded for each sprint.

- *Varying distance repeat sprints* - straight course or out and back course - then five minutes recovery with a repeat immediately after. The time taken for each sprint being recorded.

- *'T'-Test* - Marked 'T'-shaped course where you paddle out to top of the 'T', scull sideways to the edge of the top of the 'T', back to other top edge of the 'T', and back to the middle where you paddle backwards to the finish line. The time to complete the course is recorded.

▶ Strength

Assessment of strength development would need to be based around the most appropriate exercises for the paddlesport discipline. The methods for assessing could include one repetition maximum lifts, for instance the maximum amount that can be lifted for one repetition for bench press, or a 5-10 repetition maximum could be utilised. The number of repetitions should be based upon the discipline or the age of the athletes (see the section on growth and development below). Exercises, depending on the experience of the paddlers, could be carried out as free weight Olympic lifts or on multi-gym machines. The advantage with free weights is that they tend to require groups of muscles to work together, to lift the bar and control sideways movement, and so more closely match paddling whereby canoeists use muscles working in groups, i.e. forward paddling requires co-ordinated leg, back, abdominals and arm movement.

▶ Power/Speed

The most appropriate method for assessing power in paddlesport would be to do this in-boat where possible. Short courses could be set to assess take-off power or sprint speed. For flat water paddlers this would be very close to boat-based skill work. Power assessment for surf kayakers would most logically be based around the four or five power strokes needed to pick up a wave and could be measured on flat or moving water and be assessed by the distance travelled after the power strokes. Out of boat power tests could be carried out on a Concept II rower or with an arm crank ergometer, both of which can usually be found in the gyms at fitness centres.

▶ Body Composition

The most accurate and easily available method for body composition assessment would be using skinfold callipers. The reading list at the end of the chapter provides details of books that cover the necessary techniques. The key concerns with this aspect of fitness assessment are the reliability of measurements (see below) and the way in which results are used. As a society we have become obsessed with body size and shape. When assessing body composition we need to be sensitive in handling results; who really needs to know, and do we really need to know about a particular paddler's result?

▶ Mobility

In-boat mobility assessments would again be the most appropriate for assessing flexibility of paddlers.

Photo 13 Sit and Reach Test

These should be based around functional discipline-specific movements, i.e. trunk rotation and flexion/extension of the lower back, with the aim being to develop appropriate levels of mobility for all aspects of your paddling. In addition, the 'sit and reach' flexibility test could be used to provide a general out of boat assessment of mobility. Photo 13 (sit and reach test) provides a picture of the test apparatus, which should be carried out after a warm-up, with straight legs, at a slow speed and with three trials. The best of the three trials - how far the paddler can reach (in centimetres) is recorded. *(This uses facilities available in any gym, for more paddler-specific tests see Chapter 18).*

▶ Advanced Assessment Tools

There are a number of advanced assessment tools that can be employed for testing paddler fitness. As mentioned above the VO_{2max} test has traditionally been the gold standard measure or predictor of aerobic fitness. More recently, however, research has shown that lactate threshold is a more accurate predictor of success in aerobic events. The measurement of lactate levels is based on studies showing that, as an athlete increases their effort towards maximum, they increase the amount of lactate they produce. With regard to assessment of fitness levels, the testing of lactate levels relies on the fact that in shorter duration events that do not allow the aerobic system to come to full power when operating near to or at maximal levels, the anaerobic (lactic acid system) has to contribute some of the energy produced. A result of this is the release of the metabolic by-product lactic acid into the blood. The harder an athlete is working the more lactate is produced. Knowledge of this allows coaches and sports scientists to assess time and lactate production after a set distance run, paddle or swim. If fitness is improving over time then lower lactate levels should be recorded for successive tests.

KEY POINT SUMMARY

- Lactic acid is produced in glycolysis when there is insufficient oxygen to enable the aerobic system to continue the breakdown of carbohydrates. Once lactic acid is produced it quickly dissociates to form lactate and a free hydrogen ion which is what causes the rise in acidity in the muscle and blood. The terms lactic acid and lactate are often used interchangeably.

Lactate produced by working muscles can be transported to the heart (where it can be used as a direct fuel source), non-working muscles or to the liver where it can be converted into fuel sources for energy production. The lactate threshold represents a level of work after which an athlete's removal of lactate from the blood cannot keep pace with production. After this threshold, lactate begins to accumulate in the blood and will lead to an athlete having to stop exercising due to the lactate in the working muscles and blood. Research has found that for aerobic events, the higher percentage of an athlete's $\dot{V}0_{2max}$ at which this occurs the better for performance in races. In other words, if two marathon paddlers had the same $\dot{V}0_{2max}$ but one could operate at 90% of this and the other could operate at 85% before passing their lactate threshold the first paddler would be able to operate at a higher workrate/speed and would complete the race first. Researchers have shown that knowledge of the level at which lactate threshold occurs is a better predictor of performance than $\dot{V}0_{2max}$ alone. As a result many sports scientists are now using a test of lactate threshold as a measure of aerobic ability/performance for elite athletes.

GUIDELINES FOR TESTING

There are a number of useful principles that can be followed to assist with designing and administering the tests to be used and the order in which they are used.

▶ Validity Of The Test

Does the test measure what it really should measure? For example, does the distance paddled assess the aerobic system, the anaerobic system or a combination of both? How does the test match the requirements of your discipline? There are many tests that can be employed for each component of fitness and you need to select the most valid. Are they specific to your discipline?

▶ Reliability Of The Test

There are two aspects of reliability that you need to consider, test-retest reliability and inter-tester reliability. If you test someone one day and then retest again the next day, before any changes in their fitness have taken place you should get very close to the same score if the test is reliable. If scores are different this may be due to a lack of test-retest reliability with the test. In a similar way, there may be situations where two people carry out the testing for a paddle. In a reliable test a paddler would achieve their score regardless of who was testing; if so, the test can be said to have inter-tester reliability. It should not matter who is carrying out the test – an effective test needs to provide consistent results.

KEY POINT SUMMARY

- Tests need to be valid and reliable measures of performance. An analogy for this can be drawn from archery. The validity of a test refers to the ability of the arrow to hit the target and the reliability refers to the consistency with which the target is hit with each arrow.

▶ Ordering Of Tests

An element that is highly specific for paddlesport fitness assessment is that of environmental factors. Due to the nature of our sport, changes in weather, the river, the boat, etc. can have a significant influence on test results. That is not to say testing should be abandoned if there is a change in environmental factors, but they should certainly be recorded and taken into account when evaluating results. The period before testing can also have an influence on results, for instance a really heavy training session the night before testing can influence testing results. When administering a test battery you should try to mimic as closely as possible the lead-in to the previous tests and where possible allow paddlers to take tests in a rested state. Each time a battery of tests is carried out they should ideally be carried out in the same order to enable you to evaluate like with like. The order in which a paddler performs a series of tests will also influence the levels they achieve. For example, scores for strength tests will be negatively influenced by any maximal aerobic test carried out before the strength test, whereas aerobic results, after an appropriate rest, are not detrimentally affected by strength assessment.

The following assessment schedule is therefore proposed:

- Non-exercising tests – Height, weight, body composition
- Maximal strength tests
- Flexibility and agility tests
- Sprint tests
- Muscular endurance tests
- Maximal aerobic or anaerobic tests

If you are worried that having one test before another might influence the score achieved on the latter, consider completing testing on different days rather than one.

▶ NUTRITION

Our diet provides the fuel for our paddling. This section will examine our nutritional requirements, guidelines for a balanced diet, modifications for power and endurance athletes and suggestions for pre-competition, during exercise and recovery meals. How our bodies use the food we have eaten, to provide the energy we need for paddling, will then be covered in the next section on energy systems.

THE SIX NUTRIENTS FOR HEALTH

The food we eat is vital for our health and providing the energy we need for our paddling and daily lives. Carbohydrates, fats and protein make up the main nutrients in our food and provide energy for our bodies. Vitamins, minerals and water, while not providing energy directly, assist the body with energy production, transport of nutrients, removal of waste products, health and immunity from illness.

▶ Carbohydrates

These form a major source of energy for the muscles and brain in the form of sugars and starches. There are several ways of classifying carbohydrates according to the structure. Carbohydrates that are of one simple sugar are monosaccharides (glucose or fructose), and disaccharides such as sucrose or lactose are formed of two monosaccharides. Sucrose, (household sugar) is made from a glucose and a fructose.

◯ KEY POINT SUMMARY

- A balanced diet is a healthy diet and will form the foundation for successful performance and, except at elite level or due to illness, very little in the way of supplements are required.

The largest carbohydrate units are polysaccharides which include starch and glycogen. Both are composed entirely of glucose units, with glycogen being the form in which glucose is stored in the body to provide energy. Very often nutritionists talk in terms of simple (monosaccharides and disaccharides) and complex carbohydrates (polysaccharides). Simple and complex carbohydrates have also been known to athletes as quick and slow 'carbs', with simple sugars being thought of as less useful than complex carbohydrates that enter the bloodstream more slowly. This is not entirely true as the food's glycemic index (see recovery meals below and reading list), amount eaten, and food preparation also affect the speed of entry to the blood.

▶ Fats

Fats, also known as lipids, provide highly concentrated stores of energy. Fats are broken down in the body to form smaller units such as triglycerides, free fatty acids and cholesterol. Fats form an important part of our diet and serve several functions within the body, such as providing energy (70% when we are at rest), support of organs in the body and storing fat soluble vitamins. The most basic unit of fats are free fatty acids which occur as saturated or unsaturated fats. Saturated fats tend to be solid at room temperature and derived from animal fats whereas unsaturated fats (monosaturated or polyunsaturated) tend to be liquid at room temperature. Saturated fats have been linked with a higher risk of cardiovascular disease than unsaturated fats.

▶ Proteins

These are nitrogen-containing food stuffs that provide the basis for building and repairing muscles, other tissues, red blood cells and hormones. Proteins are broken down in the body into amino acids. Twenty amino acids have been identified as necessary for our growth and metabolism. Importantly, nine of these are essential within our diet as they cannot be produced within the body. Complete proteins, such as meats, fish, eggs and milk, contain all of the essential proteins. Protein derived from plants and grains cannot individually provide all the essential proteins and so vegetarians need to gain their protein from a variety of sources.

▶ Vitamins

Although required in relatively small quantities, vitamins form an essential part of our diet, assisting the body with chemical reactions for energy production, promoting growth and maintaining health.

▶ Minerals

Are found throughout the body, for example as iron in red blood cells or as calcium in bones and are essential for allowing cells to function normally.

▶ Water

We are made up of approximately 60% water and it is second only to oxygen in its importance to our bodies. Within our bodies water assists with maintaining body temperature, carrying nutrients and waste products, along with assisting cell function.

GUIDELINES FOR A HEALTHY DIET

A healthy diet is the basis for sound nutrition and the need for supplements and dietary manipulation is seldom necessary if a paddler has a sound diet.

Figure 4, below, provides a guide to the food groups that form the basis of a healthy diet, which can in a natural way provide all the nutrients necessary for a healthy athletic life. In percentage terms for the 'big 3' that make up the bulk of our diet, it is recommended by researchers that we consume 55-60% of our calories through carbohydrates, up to 30%, but ideally less than this, through fats (with under 10% saturated fats) and 10-15% from proteins.

Figure 4 provides the recommended daily servings for the food groups within the pyramid. For the bread group, an example serving size for bread would be 1 slice, or half cup (cooked) of pasta or rice. For the fruits and vegetables groups examples of serving would be an apple, a small banana, a medium tomato, or a small stalk of broccoli. For the milk and meat groups, example serving sizes would be 1 egg, 1/3 of a can (small) of tuna or 3oz chicken breast (about the size of a pack of cards).

In addition to the basic diet there are some useful considerations you can make in your diet to improve upon these basic guidelines. Variety, moderation and naturalness will add to a healthy diet. There is no one food that can provide all the nutrients we need, having variety with meals helps us to gain all the nutrients

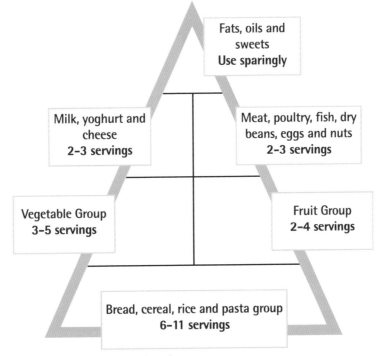

Fig. 4 The Food Guide Pyramid with Suggested Daily Servings

we need. There is nothing wrong with having 'treats' occasionally; these add variety to the diet and increase enjoyment of your food - the secret to this is moderation and cutting back in other areas. The more natural your food is, that is the less it has been processed by manufacturers before you consume it, the better. Processed food tends to have fewer nutrients than natural foods. Choosing wholemeal bread over white bread or cooking foods yourself rather than buying processed meals can help to retain the nutrients in the food you eat. In Britain people are encouraged to eat 5 portions of fruit and vegetables a day. The food pyramid includes fruit and vegetables - both can contribute to the five a day, selecting both in your diet helps in the variety you get in your diet. It is better to eat a mixture of fruits and vegetables rather than eating 5 apples a day. Including fibre in your diet will aid digestion and can be found in whole wheat grains, some cereals, beans and peas.

KEY POINT SUMMARY

- As well as the basic healthy diet, adding variety, moderation and naturalness to the food we eat will help our paddling performance. What we eat does count in our paddling.

▶ Modifications For Paddlers In Power And Endurance Disciplines

The main manipulation of diet for us as paddlers concerns the overall energy expenditure we have in our daily lives. The more exercise and training a canoeist takes part in the greater the energy expenditure. The daily energy requirements for sedentary people are 2000-2500kcal for women and 2500-3000kcal for men whereas those involved in kayaking may need 30% and more above these levels. Paddlers involved in the Devizes to Westminster or similar marathon races may expend in the region of 5000 - 6000kcal per day and would need to replace as much as possible of this during the race. So to a large extent modifications in diet for paddlers involve increasing total calorific (food) intake rather than changing the percentages of our daily intake.

Paddlers involved in power events can benefit from some additional protein intake, but the requirements for athletic performance are far less than people often imagine. There is not normally a need for a paddler in a power-based discipline to take protein supplement or drinks. It is recommended that power athletes do

not exceed 1.4 - 1.8g of protein per kg of body weight. Thus a 75kg paddler each day would need between 105-135g of protein. By way of example, an 8oz chicken breast would provide about 70g of protein.

▶ Pre-Competition, During Exercise And Recovery Meals

Research tells us that canoeists do benefit from a pre-training or pre-competition meal. Ideally this meal should be eaten 3 – 4 hours before the event, be low in fat, protein and fibre, high in carbohydrate and include fluid to help maintain hydration. This meal should also comprise foods with which you are familiar. It is better to eat foods that you know suit you than to try some new suggestion just before you go into a competition.

Maintaining blood glucose levels during exercise through ingesting carbohydrates has been shown to improve exercise performance. For intermittent disciplines such as canoe polo this would be best achieved through a sports drink. For paddling events of longer duration, such as a day white water or sea paddling, the maintenance of blood glucose levels can be maintained through sports drinks, and or, a mixture of carbohydrate snacks such as wine gums, jelly babies, dried fruits, cereal bars or sandwiches. Sports drinks can also help with maintaining hydration as they are absorbed more readily than water and can assist with replacement of minerals lost through sweating.

Photo 14 Sea paddler snacking

KEY POINT SUMMARY

- After a paddling session a meal including protein and carbohydrate helps with tissue repair and restoring glycogen stores.

After a paddling session, as a recovery meal, both carbohydrates and proteins are beneficial. The meal should be eaten as soon as possible after completing canoeing. The glycemic index of the food is also important for the post-exercise meal. Carbohydrates that have a high glycemic index and more quickly enter the bloodstream are more beneficial in the process of replacing glycogen stores in the muscles. These include baked potatoes, cereals and bread. Eating protein as part of the post-exercise meal will help with muscle repair and building. Research indicates that eating a combined carbohydrate and protein meal can help with the building process. If it is not possible to eat a meal after finishing paddling, a sports drink can help with energy replacement and will also help with replacing fluid loss which needs to be addressed after training or competition.

▶ ENERGY SYSTEMS

This important section within the chapter contains information about how the food we take into our bodies is used to provide the energy we need for different paddling disciplines. It is also intended to make clear the differences between aerobic and anaerobic energy production that is essential knowledge for a paddler in making decisions about the components of fitness relevant to their discipline. The basis for understanding energy production is to understand where this takes place – within the cells of our bodies. This section will begin with a review of what we are made up from – cells, then look at anaerobic and aerobic energy systems along with information about muscle fibre types and the adaptations to the body brought about by training.

THE CELLULAR BASIS FOR LIFE

The foundation of all living things is the cell – the smallest unit capable of carrying out all the processes associated with life. Humans are made up of many different cells that work in co-ordinated groups to accomplish functions within the body. The body's systems - skeletal, muscular, respiratory and nervous etc. - are made up from cells working in co-operative units. All cells have specialised functions that contribute to the functioning of the body and are dependent on the other groups of cells carrying out their functions to maintain life. For example muscle cells use energy to bring about movement, but are dependent on the circulatory system (blood and blood vessels)

Photo 15 Paddler drinking sports drink

for supplying oxygen, the food necessary to produce energy and for removing the waste products that result from energy production. Cells within the body have to work co-operatively in this integrated fashion for us to sustain life. The various cells within our bodies, while serving different functions, all require energy for the roles they play and have the same basic structure. As can be seen from Figure 5, a simplified diagram of cell structure under an electron microscope, all cells have a similar structure. Most cells have three main parts, the cell membrane (outer skin), the nucleus and the contents of the cell, the cytoplasm. It is this structure that enables cells to produce the energy required for us to go paddling.

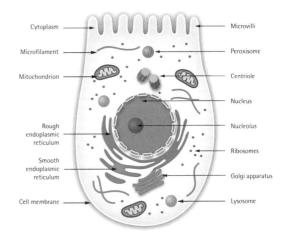

Fig. 5 The structure of a 'typical' cell

The cell membrane is a very thin structure that encloses every cell and keeps it separate from its surrounding environment. The nucleus, normally the largest single unit in the cell, contains the deoxyribonucleic acid (DNA), the blueprint for controlling the operations of the cell. The cytoplasm comprises the inside of the cell except for the nucleus. It is made up of a gel-like substance, cytosol, which houses and protects six main sorts of small structures called organelles. These organelles (meaning small organs or structures) serve a variety of roles for the cell. In Figure 5 one of these organelles, a mitochondria, is shown as it is vital in the process of energy production. Mitochondria are the power plants of the cell and they are responsible for producing about 90% of our energy.

KEY POINT SUMMARY

- All cells in the body need energy to carry out the work they do. Cells comprise a cell membrane that separates the cell from other parts of the body, a nucleus that controls the cell's functions, and the rest of the cell which is known as the cytoplasm. Within the cytoplasm are mitochondria - tiny organs that are the power plant for energy production.

The key concept to take from this section is that energy production does not take place within some 'factory' or a particular organ within the body. The body is made up of cells, every one of which needs energy to carry out its work. When we go paddling the muscles that we use, which are made up of cells, each with a nucleus, cell membrane and cytoplasm (containing mitochondria) produce the energy they need to allow us to paddle. The energy produced comes from the food we eat - carbohydrates broken down

to glucose in the body, fats broken down to free fatty acids (FFA) and proteins broken down to amino acids that are mainly responsible for growth and repair, but can be used for energy production.

ENERGY PRODUCTION

Energy production for use by the body begins with digestion or breakdown of our food after we have eaten. The process of digestion can be thought of as the mining or drilling for crude oil or the fuel that we need for energy production. The crude forms of fuel produced after digestion are glucose, FFA and amino acids. These crude fuels are shipped (via the blood) to cells throughout the body where they are converted into the refined fuel of Adenosine Triphosphate (ATP). Adenosine triphosphate, shown in Figure 6, is the 'petrol' for our bodies – the fuel every cell uses to do work.

▶ Adenosine Triphosphate (ATP)

Adenosine triphosphate is named as such because it has one adenosine molecule bonded (joined) to three phosphate molecules. It is these bonds that make ATP the 'petrol' for our bodies, for each one is created using energy, but when created, stores energy for work. ATP stores large amounts of energy in each of these bonds so that when a bond is broken it will release the stored energy to allow a cell to do its work, for instance when the energy muscles need to contract and bring about movement. The most common breakdown of ATP is for one phosphate to be broken from the chain to release energy and leave behind the free phosphate and ADP (Adenosine diphosphate). This energy release reaction is shown in Figure 7.

ATP

Adenosine Triphosphate with high energy bond (‿‿)where energy is stored for use by the cell.

Fig. 6 Adenosine Triphosphate

Stored ATP

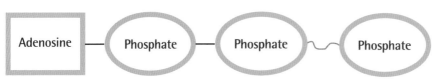

Adenosine Triphosphate with high energy bond (〜〜) where energy is stored for use by the cell.

ADP created from breakdown of ATP

Adenosine Diphosphate where the last phosphate has been broken from the chain to release energy for work.

Fig. 7 Adenosine Triphosphate converted to Adenosine Diphosphate, so releasing energy.

◯ KEY POINT SUMMARY

- Adenosine Triphosphate (ATP) is the petrol for our paddling performance. Carbohydrates, fats and proteins are broken down in the cells of the body to produce the ATP every cell needs. Cells have three systems (two anaerobic and one aerobic) with which to produce ATP. Each of these systems act as 'gears' for energy production. First and second gear, the ATP-PC system and glycolysis (see below), become the dominant fuels relatively quickly, but have a limited duration, whereas the overdrive third gear (aerobic system) is slower to become the main fuel source but can enable activity for long periods of time. Each paddlesport discipline will place different demands on the energy systems.

Cells within the body keep some stores of ATP, for if they did not, every time we wanted to make a movement we would have to delay before the ATP was created. However, this stored ATP (fuel) is limited in its supply, enough for a few seconds work, so very quickly we have to create new supplies of ATP. We have three energy systems that can be used to create ATP from the food we eat to produce the energy we need for paddling. There are two anaerobic energy systems and one aerobic system.

▶ Changing Gear

Anaerobic and aerobic energy production is concerned with creating ATP for the working muscles to allow us to paddle. The simple question is why do we have more than one system, surely if any one of these systems can produce the ATP we need for work then that should be enough? This is not, however, the case. Just as a car has gears so the body needs a variety of systems to produce ATP. Two low gears (1st and 2nd) for power and acceleration along with a high gear (3rd)- overdrive – for efficiency and long journeys. The human 'car' has three gears, 1st and 2nd gear are the anaerobic systems while 3rd gear is the aerobic system. The purpose for all three systems is to create ATP to replace the stores in cells as they are used up when the cell is working.

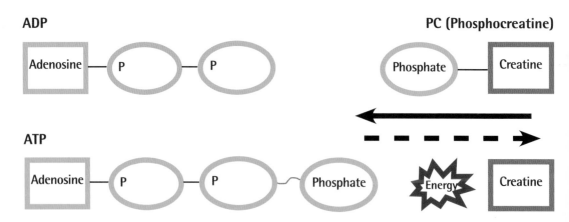

The bond between the creatine and phosphate (PC) is broken to release the energy required to join the phosphate to the ADP to recreate ATP.

Fig. 8 The Phosphocreatine System

THE ANAEROBIC ENERGY SYSTEMS

The two anaerobic sources of energy production are the phosphocreatine system and glycolysis.

▶ Phosphocreatine System

The most rapid source for creating ATP is the phosphocreatine (PC) system. Each cell stores within the cytoplasm PC which can be used, as shown in Figure 8 above, to recreate ATP for use as a rapidly available short term energy system. Through this reaction phosphocreatine is broken down to release the phosphate to create a third high-energy bond with ADP, forming ATP and leaving creatine. The arrows in Figure 8 show that the reaction is reversible and at times of rest PC will be recreated to be stored in the cytosol of the cytoplasm. Events of up to 10 seconds duration will use this source of energy as the main fuel source.

▶ Glycolysis

The second source of anaerobic energy production is glycolysis. For events lasting longer than 10 seconds and less than one and a half minutes of maximal effort or for a sprint finish this will increasingly become the dominant source for ATP production. As can be seen from Figure 9, glycolysis involves a ten step breakdown of glucose (carbohydrate) to produce Pyruvate and ATP. The breakdown of glucose glycogen (the storage form of glucose. Glucose is stored in the liver and muscles as glycogen – chains of glucose molecules linked together) takes place in the cytoplasm of each cell. It is not important for you as a practising coach

to know each of the 10 reactions and so they are not included in Figure 10. The important concept to gather from the figure is that there are many more reactions to produce ATP through glycolysis than through the PC system and it is for this reason that it becomes the second system for energy production. It is, however, faster in producing ATP than the aerobic system.

The end product of glycolysis is pyruvate. If sufficient oxygen is present, i.e. we are paddling below maximum rate and for a period of time over 1½ minutes, the aerobic system can utilise the pyruvate to help produce more ATP (this will be discussed in the next section). However, if a paddlesport discipline requires maximal effort for a short period of time or a sprint at the end of a race there will not be sufficient oxygen to metabolise (use) all the pyruvate. In this anaerobic situation lactic acid, or lactate as it is sometimes called, is formed.

The formation of lactic acid, creating acidity in the working muscles and pain in your muscles when you exercise, for instance in an all-out 1 minute sprint, will limit the duration for which you can continue to exercise at a high intensity. The lactic acid, produced through exercising maximally and using glycolysis to form ATP, causes a rise in acidity in the cells. The enzymes (catalysts) that assist the reactions of glycolysis can only work within a narrow pH range. As lactic acid levels rise and change the pH within the cell, the enzymes are inhibited in their work, impairing our ability to continue to produce ATP through glycolysis and leading to fatigue.

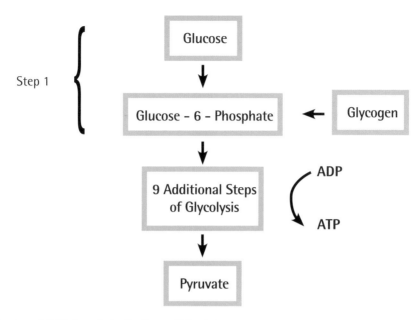

Fig. 9 The Creation of ATP through the Ten Steps of Glycolysis

THE AEROBIC ENERGY SYSTEM

Whereas glycolysis can utilise only carbohydrates, in the form of glucose or glycogen to produce ATP through aerobic metabolism cells can use fats and proteins as well as carbohydrates to produce ATP. The production of ATP within each cell for anaerobic purposes takes place within the cytoplasm of the cell. Aerobic metabolism takes place within the mitochondria (powerhouse) of each cell. Depending on their function each cell can have from a few hundred to several thousand mitochondria. The mechanisms through which fats, proteins and carbohydrates can be, in the presence of oxygen (supplied to each cell from the lungs via the bloodstream), used by cells to create ATP is shown in Figure 10.

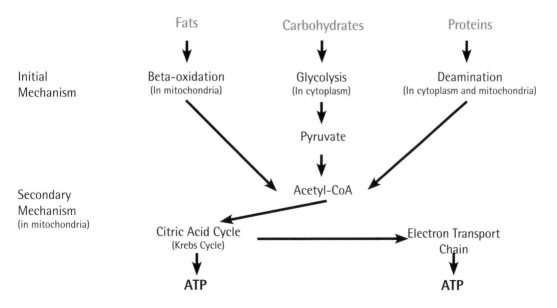

Fig. 10 Breakdown Mechanisms for Aerobic ATP Production

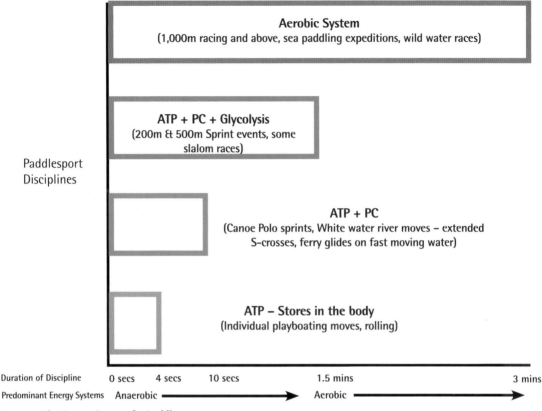

Fig. 11 The Energy Systems for Paddlesport

Even from looking at the steps in the process it is clear why producing ATP from aerobic methods is a slower method for producing energy than using anaerobic mechanisms. Although all three nutrients can be used for energy production it is thought that proteins are responsible for supplying only 10% of our energy needs so the main aerobic fuel sources are fats and carbohydrates. Carbohydrates (glucose or glycogen) are broken down in the cytoplasm through glycolysis, proteins in the cytoplasm and mitochondria through deamination and fats in the mitochondria through oxidation. After this initial breakdown the fate of all three food substances is Acetyl Co-Enzyme A (Figure 10). From Acetyl CoEnzyme A the three nutrients are broken down further through the citric acid cycle (also known as the Krebs Cycle) and the electron transport chain to produce ATP. The largest supply of ATP is available through aerobic metabolism and can provide relatively inexhaustible supplies such as the majority of the energy required to complete marathon paddling races or a day sea paddling.

Figure 11 shows the relationship between the sources of energy production for paddlesport.

MUSCLE FIBRE TYPES

The body is made up of cardiac (heart), smooth (around blood vessels) and skeletal muscle fibres. For energy production in paddlesport, clearly the heart is vital for supplying the oxygen we need, however, we are most concerned with the ability of skeletal muscles to bring about movement. The strength, power and endurance we need for canoeing and kayaking is provided by our skeletal muscles. Just as we have different ways to produce the energy we need for canoesport, there are a variety of muscle cell or fibre types that can be used by our bodies to move our boats around.

Two main distinctions have been made, Type I (slow twitch) and Type II (fast twitch) fibres.

▶ Type 1

Type I fibres have greater aerobic capabilities than Type II fibres. Type I fibres have a higher density of blood vessels supplying oxygen to the fibres, a larger number of mitochondria and increased aerobic enzyme activity (catalysts that enable reactions to take place).

▶ Type 2

Type II fibres have greater anaerobic qualities and are able to generate greater forces than Type I fibres but fatigue more quickly.

▶ Percentages

Each one of us has a slightly different make-up of Type I and Type II fibres and this is what makes us physiologically more suited to some disciplines than others. A paddler with a higher percentage of Type I fibres would be more suited to endurance events, a paddler with a predominance of Type II fibres being more suited to power disciplines. Through training, however, we can affect our fitness and our bodies can make adaptations according to the type of training we undertake. This forms the final part of this discussion of energy systems.

◯ KEY POINT SUMMARY

• We have two main muscle fibre types, Type I and II. Type I are more suited to aerobic activity and Type II are more suited to anaerobic activity. Each of us as paddlers are made up of different proportions of fibre types. If we are made up from more Type I fibres we may be more suited to aerobic disciplines or if Type II fibres predominate we may be more suited to sprint and power type activities.

ADAPTATIONS TO TRAINING

After making decisions about the predominant energy systems for your discipline, the training programme should be based around the specific demands of the activity because the adaptations to training will be highly specific as well.

▶ Adaptations To Aerobic (Endurance) Training

Endurance training such as longer distance paddling sessions or interval work will bring about a number of changes to the body that will enhance aerobic performance including:

◯ Increase in size and number of mitochondria.

◯ Increased blood flow round the body (the heart, also a muscle, will increase in size through training thus improving the ability of the heart to pump blood to the muscles that need it).

◯ Increased ability to use fats as a fuel source (we have relatively unlimited stores in our bodies) thus sparing glycogen stores which are limited.

◯ Increased lactate removal from the blood to enable a canoeist to paddle at higher intensity of exercise with the same level of lactate.

▶ Adaptations To Anaerobic (Strength And Power) Training

If a paddler follows an anaerobic programme this will have a number of positive effects on their anaerobic capabilities including:

Photo 16 Endurance training

◯ Increased anaerobic stores such as ATP, PC, glycogen stores and strength of muscles.

◯ Increased ability to produce lactate and sustain high levels of lactate before ceasing exercise.

◯ Increased activity and stores of enzymes involved in anaerobic energy production.

▶ In Summary

In summary, the energy systems are concerned with producing ATP, the fuel for paddling and exercise. To start any movement or activity we have stores of ATP

Photo 17 Strength and power training

that are quickly used up so we have 3 gears or systems for creating ATP and continuing movement. The first two anaerobic systems (ATP-PC and glycolysis) are relatively fast in being able to supply energy, but have a limited duration as a main fuel source. The third aerobic system is slower to initiate due to the number and nature of reactions required for the system to get 'up to speed' but is a long-term fuel source for producing the ATP we need to paddle. As paddlers we need to analyse our discipline to identify the predominant energy system(s), and then our training can be based around maximising the efficiency of the systems through the adaptations identified above. Without the knowledge in this section it is very difficult to accurately develop training for any canoesport discipline.

▶ STRENGTH TRAINING AND CONDITIONING

So far we have discussed the components of fitness that might apply to any particular canoesport discipline, general principles for designing a training programme, how to divide up a training year to peak for an event and how to evaluate the success of the programme. Having done this, and with knowledge of the energy systems, the next step is to examine the range of strength (also called resistance or weight) training and conditioning exercises that can form the basis of a training programme for a paddler. This section will provide the specific training suggestions that can help you to address physiological improvements in performance.

STRENGTH TRAINING

There are a great number of gyms and sports centres in Britain now where you can undertake a resistance training programme. If you lack power or muscular endurance in your paddling, resistance training can help to address this. Strength or resistance training can be carried out using free weights or machine weights or a combination of both. With this range of equipment there are numerous exercises that can be performed for each muscle group working in isolation or in functional groups. Carrying out a preacher curl would be an example of working a muscle in isolation – the biceps muscle – whereas a power clean, a very popular exercise for athletes, works large groups of muscle in co-ordinated movement pattern and is, as mentioned above, much more specific to sporting performance. For canoe and kayak sport we work our muscles to a large extent in functional groups - several muscle groups working together - to bring about propulsion in our boats. Therefore, following the specificity principle we should try to match this in the weight training programmes we follow to improve our strength, power or muscular endurance.

Resistance training can be used to bring about a variety of results through manipulating the weight, repetitions and sets carried out for each particular exercise. Table 4 provides details of the variation in reps and sets that would be required for each particular outcome. The weight for each exercise should be decided by experimenting with the weights until you find a load at which in the last set you can just complete the repetitions required. Start with lower weights and build up; after you have been to the gym for a short period you will be able to find the appropriate weight quite quickly – do not sacrifice technique for extra weight. The 2 for 2 rule could then be used to make decisions about increasing training loads as your body makes adaptations to training. An instructor at a local gym should know all of these exercises and would be able to provide you with further advice on choice of exercises and technique.

KEY POINT SUMMARY

- Strength training programmes can be designed to develop a wide range of muscular goals including pure muscular strength, power, muscle size and endurance. The repetitions, sets and weight can be manipulated to bring about desired results.

Outcome	Strength/Power	Strength	Hypertrophy	Muscular Endurance
Repetition Range	1 - 3	5 - 8	8 - 12	15+
Sets	3 - 5	2 - 4	2 - 4	3
Rest Between Sets	3 - 5 mins	1 - 3 mins	1 - 3 mins	1 min

Table 4 Possible Training Units Within a Periodised Programme

Body Part	Exercise	Equipment
Shoulders	Lateral Raise	Dumbells or Machine
	Shoulder Press	Barbell, Dumbells or Machine
	Deltoid Raise	Dumbells
	Upright Row	Barbell
	Lower Arm Abduction/Adduction	Cable Pulley
Legs	Back Squat	Olympic Bar
	Front Squat	Olympic Bar
Upper Back	Seated Row	Cable Pulley or Machine
	Lat Pulldown	Machine
	Bent Arm Pullover	Barbell or Machine
	Dumbell Row	Dumbells
Lower Back	Back Extension	Machine or Floor Exercise
Chest	Fly Curls	Dumbells
	Pec Deck	Machine
	Bench Press	Barbell or Machine
	Incline Press	Barbell or Machine
Tricep Press	Tricep Press	Machine
	Tricep Extension	Machine
	Bicep Curl	Barbell, Dumbells or Machine
	Wrist Curls/Raises	Barbell
Abdominals	Abdominal Curls	Machine, Floor or Physio Ball
	V-ups	Floor
	Chinnies	Floor
	Hanging or Dip Machine Leg Raise	Hanging from pull-up bar or dip
	Hip Crunch	Floor with Medicine Ball
	Hip Rotator	Floor with Medicine Ball
Combination Exercises	Power Cleans	Olympic Bar
	Deadlift	Olympic Bar
	Bent-over Row	Olympic Bar

Table 5 Suggested Resistance Training Exercises for Paddlesport

▶ A Range Of Exercises

There are a wide range of exercises that can be usefully undertaken in a general fitness programme for kayak and canoesport and these are listed in Table 5. The number of exercises in a session would be between 8-12 and those selected should be those that you believe are the most specific to your discipline. In terms of specificity it is clear that the major element of paddlesport is upper body dominant, however the low back, abdominals and legs are important as assistor muscles, and weaknesses in these aspects of your development can impact negatively on your performance.

▶ Ordering The Exercises

Having selected the exercises for a programme, there are a number of ways that exercises can be ordered depending upon the outcomes desired. For maximal strength and power gain, exercises can be carried out from largest to smallest muscle groups (for example bench press before tricep extension), or changing from upper body to lower body exercises (for example Lat Pulldown to Squat to Pec Deck) where maximising rest is important. For hypertrophy and muscular endurance training you could consider moving from small to large muscles groups (tricep extension before bench press) or completing all exercises for one body part before moving on to the next. Weight training exercises can also be linked in with matched plyometric exercises (see below) in 'complex' training that can also impact upon the power or endurance capacity of muscles. An example of this would be bench press being matched with clap press-ups - a strength exercise to pre-load the system followed by a plyometric power exercise.

By altering the order of exercises or splitting routines into separate body parts it is possible for us to train in the gym up to six days per week. However, this degree of weight training specialisation would be more appropriate to sports where the physical domain is larger than the skill component. This is not the case for paddlesport and, as such, a maximum of three weight training sessions per week would allow a more appropriate focus on skill development.

▶ Alternatives

As well as weight training there are a number of alternative forms of resistance training that might prove beneficial to paddlesport. One of the most important of these is, as mentioned above, plyometrics which can be used in conjunction with the above. In the reading list below the book by Chu (Power & Strength) has a very good focus on plyometric exercises and how they can be linked in with strength exercises to form complex training programmes. Plyometric exercises use pre-tensioning of muscles to increase force generation and research has shown that they can help with power development, especially when linked in with weight training exercises. Yoga and pilates both offer forms of training that can help with core strength and mobility for paddling and could be considered as part of your resistance training programme. Finally, circuit training, a form of training that combines strength and conditioning can provide an efficient form of training for canoesport. The key with all aspects of resistance and conditioning training is not to lose your focus on the most important aspects of your paddling. It would be very easy to have yoga, pilates, weight training and conditioning sessions dominating your training. Paddlesport is skill dominant and as such, for most times in our development, paddling should be at the centre of our training.

CONDITIONING TRAINING

Conditioning training involves anaerobic and aerobic training sessions that are specific to the demands of your canoe or kayak discipline. Table 6 provides details of the various forms of conditioning that can be undertaken as part of your training programme.

▶ Measuring Effort

For sprint training and short duration interval training the method for measuring each of the efforts is how close you are to your maximum. For longer duration intervals and all other forms of training in Table 6 it is possible to use heart rate as an indicator of effort. The development of heart rate monitors has made it relatively easy and inexpensive to monitor your training effort. The more exact you can be with monitoring your training the more accurately you can evaluate the success of your training programme. In working out heart rate training zones a simple way to do this is to take your age away from 220 beats per minute, (your approximate heart rate maximum at birth which decreases by about one beat per year), so if you were 20 your heart rate maximum would be 200 beats per minute. From this basis you can then work out your training zone for each type of training.

▶ Specificity

The majority of the conditioning training for paddlesport can and should be carried out in-boat, however, it is worth thinking about rowing machines and cycling as two possible additional forms of training that could add variety to your programme. Rowing machines, such as the Concept II rower, are available in many gyms and have a more similar muscle pattern usage than any other gym equipment for developing aerobic and anaerobic fitness. Cycling, as an almost perfect opposite to paddlesport has a crossover in that it will provide general cardiovascular improvements but also contributes well to the development of core stability, an important aspect for paddlesport and a feature of pilates sessions. Cycling power comes from the legs, with the upper body and abdominals working as fixators, whereas in paddlesport the power comes from the upper body with the legs and abdominals as fixators.

◯ KEY POINT SUMMARY

- Conditioning training programmes can be designed with a great deal of variety. One of the most versatile forms of conditioning training is interval work where the repetitions, sets and intervals can be varied to meet many training goals.

Type of Training	System Trained	Intensity	Repetition	Sets	Duration of Repetitions
Sprint Training	Anaerobic	90 - 100% of maximum effort	5 - 10	1 - 5	5 - 30 secs
Interval Training	Anaerobic/Aerobic	85 - 100% of maximum effort/heart rate	3 - 10	1 - 3	30 secs - 2 mins
Medium Paced Continuous Training	Aerobic	70 - 80% of maximum heart rate	1 - 3	1	3 - 10 mins
Fast Paced Continuous Training	Aerobic	80 - 90% of maximum heart rate	1 - 3	1	1 - 5 mins
Fartlek* or Speedplay	Aerobic	70 - 85% of heart rate maximum	1	1	40 - 60 mins
Long Slow Distance Training	Aerobic	50 - 70% of heart rate maximum	1	1	40 - 60 mins or more

Table 6 Anaerobic and Aerobic Training Programmes

INJURY PREVENTION AND REHABILITATION

A carefully planned and balanced resistance training programme can be a central part of injury prevention and rehabilitation for a canoeist. A key part of injury prevention is about keeping a balance between muscle groups around the main joints. Canoeing and kayaking, as 'pulling from the shoulder activities', place a heavy load on the muscles around the shoulder. To avoid muscle imbalances, do weight training and conditioning exercises that develop the 'pushing' muscles around the shoulder. Having suitable rest and recovery periods between training and a good basic diet can also help with avoiding both overtraining illnesses and injuries. Finally, the use of warm-ups and cool-downs have, through research, been shown to help with injury prevention.

See also 'Functional Stability' Chapters 18 and 20, and 'Achieving Correct Posture for Paddling Kayak' in Chapter 18.

▶ Professional Help

For rehabilitation purposes the use of a physiotherapist or similar medical professional can help with specific recovery strategies. In addition, they can provide specific resistance training exercises that can be used during the later stages of injury recovery to assist with strengthening the muscles around joints. An example of this is the lower arm abduction and adduction exercises from Table 5 that can be incorporated into a resistance training programme and can assist in both rehabilitation from, and prevention of, shoulder impingement injuries.

Photo 18 A heart monitor used for conditioning training.

Photo 19 Strengthening the 'pushing' muscles to avoid muscle imbalance.

WARM-UP AND COOL-DOWN

Aspects that should be considered as part of skill, strength training, and conditioning sessions are the start and end of the training. Research tells us that both warm-up and cool-down can improve performance, help avoid injury and promote recovery. The following points should be considered with regard to warm-up and cool-down:

◎ Warm-ups should consist of a pulse/heart rate raiser and mobilising exercises.

◎ Cool-downs should consist of gradual pulse lowering activities and stretching or flexibility exercises.

◎ Improved flexibility, within healthy limits, has been shown to be beneficial to performance and a lack of mobility can limit skill development. In other words, hypermobility (too much flexibility) and hypomobility (too little flexibility) of a joint can lead to injury and have a detrimental effect on performance.

◎ Specifically, research has shown us that warm-ups can improve:

• Blood flow to muscles and muscle temperature. Sudden bouts of strenuous exercise without warm-up have been shown to lead to abnormal heart performance through inadequate oxygen supply to the heart muscle.

• Oxygen utilisation and the functioning of the energy systems including reducing lactic acid build up.

• Nerve transmission.

• Psychological readiness for the activity by focusing the mind and body on the session ahead.

• Performance during the first minutes of strenuous exercise.

◎ Warm-ups should be specific to the activity to be undertaken, so where possible should include in-boat activities and paddling related pulse raisers and mobilising exercises.

◎ Pulse-raising activities can move from general to discipline-specific activities and can be completed entirely within your boat.

◎ Mobility exercises involve developing intensities of range of movement activities around the key joints to be used for the discipline, such as trunk rotation and shoulder rotation.

◎ Cool-downs have been shown to have an impact on:

◎ KEY POINT SUMMARY

• An appropriate sequence for a paddlesport warm-up would begin with a *pulse raiser* and then light *mobilising* exercises *before* the lifting of any boats. Once on the water a secondary boat-specific *pulse raiser* and *mobilising* exercises can be carried out. All *flexibility* exercises should be carried out at the end of the session.

• Reducing delayed onset of muscle soreness (DOMS) that is often felt 1-2 days after strenuous training sessions.

• Stretching to improve flexibility has been shown to be most effective for warm muscles. Stretching carried out during the cool-down is the most beneficial for reducing DOMS and improving flexibility.

◎ A gradual lowering of heart rate and activity levels at the end of a session can assist with removal of waste products from working muscles.

◎ There are a number of forms of stretching that can be undertaken during a cool-down. Two that could be usefully undertaken for paddlesport flexibility are static stretches, held in a comfortable position for 3 x 30 seconds, and proprioceptive neuromuscular facilitation (PNF) which is discussed further in the texts within the reading list. Proprioceptive neuromuscular facilitation involves stretching with a partner whereby a partner assists you to hold a stretch then, as you relax, take your body a little further into the stretch. This is a very useful stretching technique but it requires skill and care in execution to avoid over-stretching and injury.

◎ Flexibility exercises for paddlesport should focus on the shoulder, trunk rotation, flexion and extension, lateral flexion and extension, and hip flexion.

◎ KEY POINT SUMMARY

• Warm-ups are now frequently used as part of a training session for paddlers. The most appropriate are those that closely match the demands of the discipline and can be carried out in-boat. Cool-downs are less frequently carried out at the end of a paddling session, but can have a very positive impact upon recovery from training. The end of the session can also usefully include flexibility exercises. **See also Appendix A.**

► GROWTH AND DEVELOPMENT

The purpose of this chapter is to discuss paddler development from a long-term context rather than to think of it as session-by-session planning process. With such a starting point it is important to briefly look at the implications of growth and development on our paddling. If we start paddling at a young age or coach younger canoeists, what are the differences between these athletes and adults - are there some fundamental differences that we need to take into account? The short answer to this, not surprisingly, is yes. The individualisation principle of training is a key concept for all paddlers including younger canoeists. Children are not simply mini-adults and we must take notice of differences between them and adults, and between males and females.

Growth refers to increases in size both of the body as a whole and of individual components, such as the heart which increases by between 10-20 times in size between birth and adulthood. Development refers to the gaining of skills and behaviours for life such as social, emotional and sporting learning and progress. Maturation, a term often associated with growth and development, refers to progress towards the mature biological functioning of the body. This section examines these differences before the implications of these differences are brought together in Chapter 10 Coaching Young People.

MEASUREMENT OF AGE IN GROWTH AND DEVELOPMENT

There are many different ways in which age can be assessed. Traditionally for teaching and coaching we group by chronological age (years, months, days), however, the biological age (developmental stage) of the group may show a wide variation. Through the pubertal years adolescents can differ biologically by as much as 8 years, i.e. a 13 year old could developmentally be more like a 9 year old, and his friend more like a 16 year old. Research tells us that while we follow a similar pattern of development from birth to adulthood, the timing and extent of changes is highly individual, in addition, girls tend to mature physically about 2-2½ years before boys. As coaches we must attempt to take these differences into account when working with groups.

Photo 20 *They may be the same biological age but are at very different stages of growth and development.*

HEIGHT AND WEIGHT

Two of the most widely studied and easily recorded measures of progress to maturity are height and weight. There are a variety of points at which height and weight measures in childhood can be used as predictors of adult values, for instance on average 50% of adult height is reached at the age of two years old. From birth to puberty weight gain is constant and similar for males and females. During puberty there is a significant rise in weight for boys and girls. For males this rise is mainly in muscle mass, for females it results from an increase in bone mass, fat mass and muscle mass.

► PHV And PWV

A measure of great interest for physiologists and coaches working with young athletes, found by keeping longitudinal (long-term) records of height and weight, is the individual's peak height and weight velocities (PHV and PWV respectively). That is the periods in growth where height and weight gain are at their maximum rates. For each of us there are two peaks in height and weight velocities, the first between birth and two years of age, the second during puberty. The start of the second increase in height gain starts before puberty with PHV occurring at about 12 years for girls and 14 years old for boys. For girls PWV is reached on average at the same time as PHV (12 years old) while for boys it is reached after PHV (14½ years old). Research indicates that knowledge of the timing of PHV in particular, for an individual is an important indicator for long-term paddlesport development. PHV gives us a reference point for the design of optimal training programmes, as the body grows critical periods of trainability occur that can be maximised. Children usually grow at about 5-6 cm/year before puberty, this increases to about 9-10 cm/year during the growth spurt, which lasts anything from 1.5-5 years. (Menarche occurs in girls approximately 6 to 18 months after PHV. Girls rarely grow more than 5 cm after the menarche has occurred.)

KEY POINT SUMMARY

- Peak height and peak weight velocities are critical stages in development for each paddler. Monitoring height/weight changes on a regular basis for younger paddlers can enable a coach to time when to introduce new aspects of training.

▶ Measuring PHV

The best way to identify the growth spurt is to take accurate height measurements:

- ✔ Use a reliable tape measure.

- ✔ Take measurements at the same time everyday.

- ✔ Measure height without shoes and socks.

- ✔ Stand with heels flat and together and legs straight.

- ✔ Stand with heels, buttocks and scapulae against a flat wall.

- ✔ Keep eyes looking straight ahead.

- ✔ The arms should be hanging loosely at the sides with the palms facing the thighs with the shoulders relaxed.

- ✔ The paddler is asked to breathe in and stand tall.

- ✔ Height is measured, with a level rule, from the top of the head, to the nearest mm.

Photo 21 Measuring PHV 21

In order to ensure the growth spurt is recorded these measurements should be taken monthly from age 9-10 for girls and 11-12 for boys. This is perhaps earlier than necessary, but avoids the danger of missing the initial growth acceleration.

KEY POINTS

- Before the growth spurt children should focus their sporting activity on learning sport skills in varied environments.

- During the growth spurt accelerated adaptation of the aerobic system occurs, and flexibility is important to help the growing body remain flexible and injury free.

- For girls, the optimal time for strength development comes at the onset of menarche.

- For boys, the optimal time for strength development comes 12-18 months after PHV.

It is also important to realise that during this time hormonal and emotional changes are taking place as well as physical development. These are discussed in an article titled "Characteristics of Physical, Mental/Cognitive and Emotional Development" by Istvan Balyi. This is available on www.bcu.org.uk by following the LTPD link. This discusses the basic characteristics, general consequences and implications for coaching of Physical, Mental/Cognitive and Emotional Development from childhood to early adulthood.

MOTOR DEVELOPMENT

A major part of childhood is spent learning basic movement patterns and skills such as walking, running, jumping, hopping, skipping, throwing, kicking, catching and striking. These movement patterns are the foundations for developed sport-specific skills learned in later life. Research has shown that a rounded and fulfilled motor development in childhood is vital to future sporting performance. Skills that are not developed during this vital stage are not compensated for later in life and will leave deficits in global motor performance that can impact on sports performance. Researchers are indicating that for successful long-term development a paddler and his/her coach should address these core motor movement patterns at the appropriate stages in development. Gender differences in these basic motor abilities are most clearly evident for throwing and striking and may reflect societal differences in programmes for boys and girls. This is certainly a concern for the paddler, as there are much smaller differences between common movement patterns such as running, hopping, skipping and jumping.

THE IMPLICATIONS OF GROWTH AND LTPD

As the body develops from childhood, through adolescence, into adulthood the physiological systems undergo a number of changes.

To summarise:

• The pre-adolescents (approximately under 12s, ± 2 years) should focus on quality skill development and do not need to 'train' the physiological systems other than through general sporting activity. Development of flexibility, agility, balance and co-ordination should be at the heart of all sessions. Children in this age group are good aerobic machines and find the low intensity environment preferable with equipment and activities that are sized appropriately to the strength and size of the child. The LTPD Skill and Speed Development Windows of Opportunity apply during this age range.

• Adolescents (approximately 12-14 year olds) become able to withstand a higher intensity of exercise, their aerobic system is continuing to develop and their ability to tolerate lactic acid accumulation is improving. Adolescents should avoid working in the 20-120 second range as this puts excessive stress on their underdeveloped anaerobic system. They are particularly responsive to aerobic and short speed work during this age. Strength training can be started using light weights and focusing on high quality movements. The LTPD Speed and Aerobic Development Windows of Opportunity apply during this age range.

• As adolescents' physical development slows down they become able to withstand higher levels of intensity especially in the 20-120 second range, and can cope with higher strength demands both in the gym and on the water. The LTPD Strength Development Window of Opportunity applies during this age range.

See Chapter 10 'Coaching Young People' and for more details.

See Chapter 1 'Coaching' for an introduction to LTPD.

AEROBIC DEVELOPMENT

As our heart and lungs - our respiratory and circulatory systems - improve with development so does our aerobic capacity. With smaller hearts and lungs children can transport lower levels of oxygen to their working muscles when paddling, however, as they grow this ability continues to develop. The maximal oxygen uptake of children in absolute terms is lower than adults, but when expressed in terms of body weight is similar to adult levels. The differences in aerobic performance between adults and children are related to economy of effort - adults are more efficient than children. This difference in economy for paddling ability is related to limb length and co-ordination. With longer limbs and more efficient movement patterns adults use less oxygen at all sub-maximal levels when compared with children. The greatest improvements on aerobic development coincide with the PHV for boys and girls. The absolute $\dot{V}O_{2max}$ is higher on average for boys than girls before and after PHV.

ANAEROBIC DEVELOPMENT

Children have a lesser ability to generate energy from glycolysis – they are essentially aerobic machines with lower abilities to work maximally anaerobically. That is not to say that they do not work anaerobically; lots of activities that children take part in - games and pastimes - involve short burst anaerobic activity. Each child's ability to produce energy anaerobically increases linearly with age. Before puberty boys and girls tend to have similar anaerobic abilities. Children have a lesser ability to produce a key enzyme for glycolysis, phosphofructokinase, which is thought to be a significant reason for their lower anaerobic abilities as shown through a lower ability to produce lactate. In addition children have a smaller muscle mass than adults and lower stores of ATP in their muscles and these will contribute to lower anaerobic abilities.

STRENGTH DEVELOPMENT

Strength improves, not surprisingly, with increases in muscle mass, maximising in females by about 20 and for males by 20-30 years of age. The hormonal changes we experience through puberty will bring about significant increases in strength for males but have a lesser effect for females who continue with linear increases in strength that are related to muscle mass increases. Prior to puberty strength differences between boys and girls are small, but males become stronger than females from puberty onwards. The greatest gains in strength occur after the PHV and are linked with increases in muscle mass and hormonal changes.

IN CONCLUSION

Whatever the age you enter paddlesport, or the level at which you wish to take part, adopting a long-term approach to planning your development will help your progress. Using this chapter to unlock the physical aspects of your planning can help you to improve your overall paddling performance.

For discipline specific examples and further exploration of many of the issues in this chapter read Chapters 18 and 20.

Photo 22 Enjoying paddlesport

FURTHER READING

Essentials of Strength Training and Conditioning, Baechle, T.R. and Earle, R.W. (2000). Human Kinetics: Champaign, IL. ISBN 0-7360-0089-5.

Theory and Methodology of Training, Bompa, T.O. (1994). Kendall/Hunt: Dubuque, Iowa. ISBN 0-7872-3371-4.

Explosive Power and Strength, Chu, D.A. (1996). Human Kinetics: Champaign, IL. ISBN 0-87322-643-7.

Training in Sport, Elliott, B., (Ed.) (1998). John Wiley & Sons: Chichester. ISBN 0-471-97870-1

Advanced Fitness Assessment and Exercise Prescription, Heyward, V.H. (1998). Human Kinetics: Champaign, IL. ISBN 0-7360-4016-1.

Physiological Aspects of Sport Training and Performance, Hoffman, J. (2002). Human Kinetics: Champaign, IL. ISBN 0-7360-3424-2.

Physiological Assessment of Human Fitness, Maud, P.J. & Foster, C. (1995). Human Kinetics:Champaign, IL. ISBN 0-87322-776-X.

Exercise Physiology: Energy, Nutrition and Human Performance, McArdle, W.D. Katch, F.I. & Katch, V.L. (2001). Lea & Febiger. ISBN 0-7817-2544-5.

Physiology of Sport and Exercise, Wilmore, J.H. & Costill, D.L. (1999). Human Kinetics: Champaign, IL. ISBN 0-7360-4489-2.

The Food Guide Pyramid, Leaflet No. 572. U.S. Department of Agriculture. (1992). U.S. Government Printing Office

NICK DRAPER

Nick is a keen kayaker and canoeist having taken part in trips on rivers and lakes all over Britain. In addition, he has paddled rivers in Europe, New Zealand and South Africa. His favourite aspect of paddling is running new rivers in kayak or canoe. Nick is a Senior Lecturer at the Centre for Adventure Science Research within the School of Physical Education at the University of Chichester where he teaches physiology. Before joining the University of Chichester he was Performance Planner for the Great Britain Judo Team and was Team Manager for Judo at the Sydney 2000 Olympic Games. His research interests include the effects of environmental and exercise demands on performance in paddlesport and mountaineering.

3 PSYCHOLOGICAL PRINCIPLES

*H*ave you ever... *Coached a performer who did well in practice but struggled under pressure? Struggled with a learner who never seemed to believe that they could succeed? Known a really talented paddler who just gave up after training intensively for years? Worked with a learner whose expectations were so high that they could never fulfil them?*

If you were frustrated by the underachievement of any of these learners then this chapter is for you...

INTRODUCTION

In Chapter 2 we were introduced to the 'components of paddling performance model' and the concept that overall performance is dependent on the relationship and interaction between technical skill, tactical accuracy, physiological and psychological components. We were also introduced to the idea that paddling performance, in any particular paddler, could be limited by deficiencies within any one of the four performance components. In order to develop paddlers effectively one of our key roles is to identify areas for improvement that will result in the greatest gains in terms of overall performance. This skill is one of the key elements in effective paddlesport coaching.

Often a paddler will suffer from a problem where the solution can clearly be found within the same component of the paddling performance model. For instance a white water paddler may be prone to capsizing in rapids as a result of not developing effective

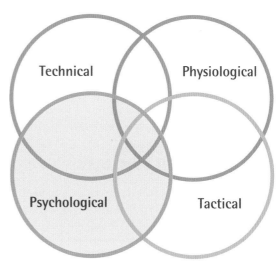

Fig. 1   The Relationship between the Components of Paddling Performance.

83

Photo 1 Capsize... tension or technique?

bracing strokes. The (technical) problem of capsizing would be best tackled by improving the paddler's skill in bracing and recovery strokes (technical). More challenging and possibly more intriguing for the coach are those problems that present themselves in one component when the root cause lies within another. Another white water paddler may not be capsizing due to a lack of technical skill but because they 'tense-up' (psychological) and become stiff on rapids. In this scenario it would not make sense to work on bracing strokes; instead equipping our paddler with relaxation skills may be more effective. In fact a problem in any one of the performance components can be caused by deficiencies in any other. Within the psychological component of performance this will often be the case.

Psychological factors can impact on performance in three different ways during the acquisition and performance of paddlesport:

• Psychological factors play a part in a paddler's attitude to training and skill acquisition and therefore impact on technical, physiological and tactical preparation.

• Psychological factors can facilitate or retard skill acquisition during practice.

• Psychological factors can enable or hinder the efficient, appropriate execution of learned skills during performance.

KEY POINT SUMMARY

• Psychological factors will impact on paddling performance through preparation, skill acquisition and ability to cope during performance.

This means that as coaches we are already working with the psychological component of paddling performance. Every time we give praise or reinforcement, every time we offer feedback and every time we plan a coaching session we are having a psychological impact on our paddlers and considering psychological factors in our decision making. Some coaches feel slightly uncomfortable with the idea that they might become involved with a specialist body of knowledge complete with its own language but this is really not the case. Psychology can be involving enough for a lifetime's study but at its most basic it is just making the most of 'good old fashioned' coaching.

Sports psychology and mental skills training is often viewed as being the last piece in the jigsaw of top level performance to be 'bolted on' when technical, tactical and physical training are close to their natural limits. If there were to be a single message of this chapter it would be that this view is a mistake. Arousal control, attentional style, maintaining motivation and the other topics in this chapter can enhance the paddlesport experience at any level of learning or performance. Therefore coaches at all levels of participation should find a basic understanding of these topics useful.

The other problem with the 'adding psychological skills last' approach is that, like any other learned skill, strong psychological skills require practice. If we try and add a new technical component just before a performance we would not be surprised to see our paddlers fail to get it right, this is also true with mental skills. Developing psychological skills should go hand in hand with all other sporting development if we want paddlers to have robust psychological skills when they need them most.

Physical conditioning can be thought of in terms of two objectives:

• Staying healthy
• Increasing fitness for our activity

As paddlesport coaches, increasing our knowledge of the way mental processes can affect learning and practice in canoesport can enable us to get the best out of our paddlers. It can also allow us to help our paddlers get the most out of their sport in terms of enjoyment and satisfaction. Sport psychology is often viewed simply as a way to increase performance for high level athletes but this view is both narrow and restrictive. Sport psychology is also about enhancing enjoyment, learning and remaining mentally fresh and healthy as paddlers and coaches involved in any level of activity.

Symptom of problem	Component	Root cause of problem (Psychological Component)	Possible Solution
Paddler shows poor levels of control in basic paddling.	Technical	Paddler believes that paddling skill is down to 'natural ability' that he or she doesn't possess, and therefore doesn't practise basic skills.	Work on allowing paddler to see technical element of performance as controllable.
Paddler is too tired to paddle effectively towards the end of a day.	Physiological	Anxiety causes the paddler to 'try too hard' during early part of day, consequently depleting energy reserves.	Coach paddler in methods of coping with anxiety.
Paddler consistently fails to follow the correct line on rapids.	Tactical	Attention of paddler fixed on hazards rather than the route through the rapids.	Train paddler to view a rapid's most important feature as the route to be paddled.

Table 1 The Psychological Root of Deficiencies Displayed in other Paddling Performance Components.

A deeper understanding of the link between our coaching behaviours and our own mental functioning can also enable us to structure our coaching activities in such a way as to enhance our own enjoyment of the coaching experience.

This chapter will look at issues that we, as coaches, need to be aware of in order to maintain our learners' full involvement in paddlesport and help push performance forward. It aims to provide coaches with a greater knowledge of how our behaviour and the sessions we plan can impact on learners' development, learning and performance. This information is intended to help coaches plan sessions and programmes that will maintain and build on motivation, improve self-confidence and result in performance improvements for their paddlers.

The chapter also provides an overview of some common psychological sporting problems and issues, and provides solutions that coaches can use in a practical setting. Whilst not exhaustive the intention is to give the coach a flavour of the kind of approaches and solutions that can be used to target specific problems.

Finally it contains information on using psychological skills to boost performance in a paddlesport setting. This provides an insight for the coach or paddler who wants an edge in competitive or pressurised situations. Techniques like arousal control and imagery are basic psychological skills that, once learned, any paddler can use to enhance their learning and performance over a lifetime of paddling.

► GOAL SETTING

Goal setting is probably the most common psychological tool in sport. In fact goal setting is so common that often we can forget that goal setting is really a psychological component of performance and development. Even those coaches among us who would claim to have little knowledge of psychological skills training will accept the value of clear appropriate goals. Engaging in sporting development without goals is a bit like getting into a car with no steering wheel. You might cover a lot of ground but you can't be sure you will have moved in an appropriate direction.

Despite the widespread use of goal setting among coaches not all approaches have been shown to be equally effective. Goals can be thought of as objectives that a paddler will work towards, the nature of these objectives can be quite different and these will result in us setting different kinds of goals. One of our jobs as coaches is to help our paddlers set the right kind of goals.

SHORT-TERM VS LONG-TERM GOALS

Goals can differ in terms of the time period that they refer to. Some goals can be targets years in the future, others can be short-term or even immediate in nature.

Fig. 2 Staircase model - Goals are there to assist our progress.

▶ Long-Term Goals

Long-term goals are like a mission statement; they will often refer to events or outcomes quite far into the future. Long-term goals are good for painting a picture of where a paddler would like to be but the large number of factors that will need to be achieved to reach that goal means that we will need more detailed directions on how to get there. This is where medium and short-term goals come in. These goals outline highly specific phases of development and act as "stepping-stones" on the way to achieving the long-term goal. Within a single coaching session we might set immediate goals related to a particular skill, exercise or drill. Long-term, medium-term and some short-term goals may be formally recorded and others, including some immediate goals, may never even be spoken aloud.

▶ Short-Term Goals

Short-term goals should be structured in a way to lead the paddler to eventual success in their long-term goal. A long-term goal can be too daunting or remote to elicit an appropriate response in the paddler and valuable time can slowly leak away until it is too late. Day to day, session by session, the focus should generally be on the short-term goals that underpin the long-term plan.

 KEY POINT SUMMARY

• Goals can be related to physical preparation, skill development, mental training or any other aspect of preparation that might lead to the final performance.

OBJECTIVES

Goals can differ in terms of the kind of objectives they display. These objectives can be outcome focused, performance focused or process focused. This results in three different kinds of goals.

▶ Outcome Goals

An outcome goal is directed towards the end result of an event or competition – completing a first descent or circumnavigation, winning a polo competition or coming first in a race. The problem with outcome goals is that there can be many factors impacting on the realisation of that goal. Since many of these factors may be outside the control of the paddler, a large element of luck comes into play. The performance of opponents is an obvious uncontrollable factor in competition but there are many uncontrollable factors in expedition paddling – genuinely unforeseen events, bad weather, illness or injury for instance. A young white water paddler may be paddling better than they ever have before and yet the group may be unable to paddle the complete section of river they had hoped to. If their only goal was to paddle the section then they will fail to achieve it.

▶ Performance Goals

Performance goals are focused on achieving a set standard of performance independent from others in the group or fluctuating environmental challenges. These will often be set by referring to previous performances and long-term goals. Working to improve your high brace from two star to three star standard would be an example of a performance goal, so would aiming to set a new personal best time in a downriver race. Rolling successfully 60% of the time during a pool session would be a performance goal. Performance goals should relate to factors within the control of the paddler. This makes performance goals a far more reasonable measure of a paddler's personal achievement and progress.

▶ Process Goals

Process goals focus on controllable factors within a paddler's performance that will result in improvement. Maintaining bent elbows during high bracing practice would be a process goal. Optimising the trim of an open canoe before each change of technique on an open canoe journey would be another. Process goals emphasise particular factors or coaching points that a paddler specifically needs to work on to improve their performance.

Athletes who focus mainly on performance and process goals have been shown to be more confident, less anxious and better able to concentrate. This is not to say that paddlers should not set outcome goals, simply that most goals for paddlers in any discipline and level of skill development should be of the performance or process variety. As coaches we need to make sure that our paddlers understand that only performance and process goals are related directly to their efforts and that these are the important goals to measure their successes and achievements.

MOTIVATION AND DIRECTION

Goals can provide motivation and direction for paddlers. They also provide a framework for reviewing and appraising development, performance or a training session.

▶ Specific

For goals to be useful to us as paddlers and coaches they need to be specific. "Improve my rolling" is not

specific "learn to reverse screw roll on both sides" is more specific, adding a context; pool, open water or moving water will improve this goal further.

▶ Deadlines

Goals with deadlines are more likely to motivate positive behaviour. "Attend six training sessions by the end of October" or "complete 3 star by the start of August" gives the paddler a time frame to work to. Goals like this can allow a paddler to review their commitment and assess whether they are really prepared to stick to the programme that will lead to their long-term goal.

▶ Challenging But Achievable

The best goals are challenging but achievable. Little will be gained from a series of goals that are too easily achieved. Likewise unachievable goals will only serve to demotivate our paddlers. A paddler who gives up or one who is not really trying will not end up fulfilling their potential. As coaches we need to ensure that the goals our paddlers set give them the biggest possible chance of success. This means setting goals that are realistic in terms of commitment and difficulty, identify strategies to achieve success and provide the opportunity to evaluate progress.

 KEY POINT SUMMARY

As a quick guide we can do well if we remember to set SMART goals:

- Specific – goals should state exactly what is going to be accomplished.

- Measurable – we need to know precisely when we have achieved a goal and when we haven't.

- Action Orientated – they should indicate actions necessary for their achievement.

- Realistic – goals should be sensible and able to be carried out.

- Timely – goals should be tied to a reasonable time frame for accomplishment.

▶ MOTIVATION

Understanding what people gain from paddlesport is very useful to the coach interested in working with paddlers over any period of time but especially those involved in longer-term development. Motivation can be thought of as the psychological and social factors that impel a paddler to act in a certain way and engage in particular activities.

Photo 2 Motivated paddler!

As coaches we often discuss motivation as if it was a single measurable variable within a paddler; we might describe a paddler as being highly motivated or poorly motivated. In fact motivation is not as simple as this. Human beings, even canoeists, are actually motivationally complex creatures and our overall motivation is actually a result of interactions between different kinds of specific motivations. We may take part in activities because we enjoy them, because we receive some other kind of reward or even to avoid some other less agreeable activity. The exact composition of the specific motivational factors is different for all of us and, as coaches, we need to remember this whenever we work with paddlers.

◯ KEY POINT SUMMARY

• A paddler's motivation can come from many different factors and even paddlers displaying the same behaviours may hold different motivations.

Some coaches view increased motivation as the answer to many problems – lack of fitness, absence from sessions or a lack of concentration or effort during practice or performance. Efforts by these coaches to increase motivation using 'pep talks' or demands for 'positive thinking' can often lead to frustration rather than success. Equally the commonly held assumption that motivation is innate and unalterable can be unhelpful as this is simply not true. It is quite possible to increase or decrease motivation or even change the type of motivation responsible for a paddler's participation.

INTRINSIC / EXTRINSIC

Motivation in paddlesport can be divided into two types:

• **Intrinsic Motivation** - Intrinsic motivation springs from direct participation in the activity. Natural curiosity, feelings of pleasure or satisfaction related directly to the experienced activity and the enjoyment of movement fall into this category. Intrinsic motivation increases when we feel that we have competence in an activity and control over our participation.

• **Extrinsic Motivation** - Extrinsic motivation can relate to financial or material reward, peer pressure or social contact, approval of others or competitive success. Extrinsic motives can be very powerful and rewarding for both paddlers and coaches and can even be very important in allowing paddlers to continue their participation in paddlesport.

▶ Demotivating

So, imagine a coach who runs a pool session once a week. They decide to increase motivation by keeping score over the number of sessions youngsters attend during the winter. They announce that there will be prizes for those who attend three out of four sessions each month.

By adding an extrinsic motivator (payment for attendance) to an activity that youngsters attend for fun (intrinsic motivator) the coach will have increased overall motivation, right? - Maybe not.

Perhaps surprisingly it has been found that increasing levels of extrinsic motivation can actually reduce intrinsic motivation for a sports performer. Unfortunately some forms of extrinsic motivator can be interpreted as disempowering or even coercive by the paddler. Parents of young performers have been known to link 'pocket money' or other rewards to sporting participation. Whilst this may be viewed as 'motivating', the paddler can start to view material rewards as the primary reason for participation and can feel compelled to take part. Eventually the paddler can feel they have no say in their continued participation. In this case the extrinsic motivator has undermined

Fig. 3 Extrinsic motivation!

the original intrinsic motivation for participation. This undermining of intrinsic motivation by extrinsic motivators can also occur to coaches who become dependant on financial or material rewards and begin to feel they have no choice but to continue coaching.

▶ The Role Of The Coach

Whilst extrinsically motivated activity is not necessarily bad the possible reduction of intrinsic motivation should be a concern to coaches. Extrinsic rewards are often more fickle and less reliable than intrinsic rewards and focus the paddler on outcomes rather than the performance. This can undermine positive work done in goal setting. As paddlesport coaches we need to be careful not to over-emphasize extrinsic rewards when working with paddlers. Ultimately we need to build a culture that values factors responsible for intrinsic motivation.

A paddler's motivation will result from the interaction between their own personality and situational factors. As coaches we contribute significantly to the situational factors and have a very real impact on the motivation of our paddlers. Coaches can often unknowingly give off subtle but powerful messages that influence their performers. Clubs and squads can also develop cultures that display a particular set of values and expectations, which add to the mix of situational factors affecting motivation in individual paddlers. Sometimes these team cultures can be helpful but sometimes they are not; the astute coach will need

to be aware of this and may need to monitor developing or existing team or club culture. As coaches we should always be looking to build and maintain intrinsic motivation regardless of the level of performer we are working with.

Intrinsic motivation can be enhanced if we adhere to some principles when coaching:

- Paddlesport coaches should structure activities so that learners experience a certain amount of success. Paddlers should not be successful in everything every time they do it, as this is not realistic in sport or any other worthwhile activity.

- Paddlers should be allowed a significant role in their own goal setting and decision making. This will result in a greater sense of control and the assumption of responsibility.

- Coaches should ensure that all their performers receive realistic praise (positive reinforcement) for their successes.

- Paddlers should have realistic goals that can feed their feelings of competence. This will mean goals that involve building on past skill levels or positive behaviours, not just competitive results.

- Coaches need to avoid boredom by varying the content and sequence of practice sessions. Participation should be fun at any level in sport and practices do not need to be overly repetitive.

▶ SELF-CONFIDENCE

As paddlesport coaches we are often engaged in activities that we hope can result in increased self-esteem and self-confidence. Self-confidence is a measure of our beliefs about our abilities. Self-confidence is 'contextual' which means that it can be different in different areas of a person's life. We can be self-confident in relation to communication but lack confidence in examinations. Likewise we may be high in self-confidence as open canoeists but low in self-confidence as polo players (or vice-versa).

There is a clear relationship between self-confidence and success. Generally, successful performers are also self-confident, and self-confident performers are successful (Fig. 4).

This means that as coaches we are going to be concerned with self-confidence, whether our primary aim is sporting development or personal and social education.

Confident performers tend to:

- Show perseverance, even when things aren't going well.

- Attempt challenging tasks and set realistic goals.

- Display a positive approach.

- Share responsibility for their performance.

- Show enthusiasm.

A confident paddler is far more likely to be able to remain calm and collected under pressure. High self-confidence has been shown to act as a 'buffer' against the negative effects of anxiety.

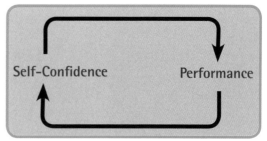

Fig. 4 Reciprocal Relationship between Self-confidence and Performance

▶ The Continuum

It is important to realise that self-confidence has different levels running along a continuum, at one end is self confidence about a very specific paddling skill in a particular situation (sometimes referred to as self-efficacy). At the other end is a kind of self-confidence that a paddler takes with them throughout all aspects of their lives, a personality wide level. Somewhere between these two extremes is self-confidence in a particular paddlesport discipline.

Photo 3 A confident performance!

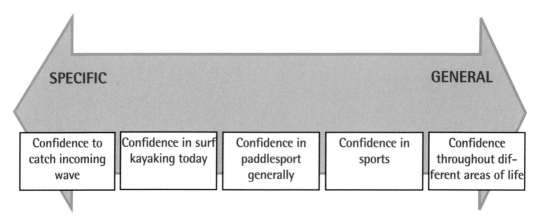

Fig. 5 Spectrum of levels of self-confidence for a paddler.

Increases in a paddler's self-confidence at any level can move along the spectrum. Repeated success in one skill will eventually result in increased confidence in that skill. As confidence in that particular skill improves then this will begin to be reflected in confidence in that area of paddlesport; eventually increasing self-confidence can reach the general sporting levels and personality level. Likewise increased self-confidence from other life experiences can filter down into the paddlesport levels. As coaches we also need to understand that this will be a slow process.

▶ The Coach's Role

Our everyday behaviour as coaches is likely to have a strong effect on the self-confidence of our paddlers. We should be sure that the message we give out is that all our paddlers can improve and succeed. We also need to show that we value all of our students no matter where they are in terms of skill development.

> **Specific sports psychology techniques can be used to increase self-confidence in paddlesport performers:**
>
> • Goal setting can help a paddler develop self-confidence. The coach should ensure that a paddler's goal setting allows them to achieve success on a regular basis. Goals should still remain challenging, as paddlers will be quick to pick up on goals that are designed to make success too easy and will take no credit for achieving them.
>
> • Imagery (mental rehearsal) can allow paddlers to develop self-confidence by enabling a paddler to repeatedly 'experience' a successful past performance.
>
> • Self-talk can be used to increase self-confidence by replacing negative or neutral self-talk with positive self-talk.

These topics are discussed elsewhere in the chapter.

Photo 4 Coach showing that he values the performance

▶ ATTRIBUTIONS

> Think back to a recent paddling performance: -
>
> • Was it successful or unsuccessful?
>
> • Did you achieve your goal or did your performance fall short of your expectations?
>
> • What caused you to be successful or unsuccessful, to succeed or fail?

Perhaps a new piece of equipment, your level of physical fitness, or the amount of practice you managed to fit in prior to the performance influenced the outcome. Whenever we perform as paddlers we tend to find ourselves searching for explanations for our success or failure. Psychologists refer to these explanations as attributions; we attribute success or failure to certain causes.

Long-term paddler development is essentially about us as coaches facilitating a process of change in our paddlers. We want our paddlers to make changes or improvements in order to arrive at a new state of physical, mental and technical preparation. One of the biggest barriers for learners can be their own belief about their ability to make these changes.

Attributions are the explanations a paddler will use to account for outcomes in their sport. Coaches need to realise that attributions are not always the actual cause of the outcome but are the things that our paddlers believe explain their performances. Attributions are linked to the paddler's beliefs about paddlesport and can either be helpful or unhelpful in the process of change and long-term development.

> **Imagine a slalom paddler who does poorly in an event. The paddler could believe that their poor performance is a result of several different factors and their response will vary accordingly:**
>
> • The paddler attributes this to poor fitness and starts a physical training programme to improve their performance.
>
> • The paddler attributes the poor performance to poor accuracy of line and they may engage in a skill-based programme.
>
> • The paddler attributes this result to lack of natural ability in paddlesport and decides to give up slalom altogether.
>
> • The paddler attributes the outcome to bad luck and decides to do nothing at all.

	Stable	Unstable
Internal	Example - Natural Ability	Example - Effort
External	Example - Task Difficulty	Example - Luck

Table 2 Model of Attributions (Weiner, 1972)

Clearly two of these attributions might result in positive behaviour – though they may not necessarily be the correct response. Two of the attributions result in either no response or a negative response.

▶ Attributional Types

Attributions can be categorised into four types using a two-dimensional model (Table 2). Attributions can either be stable or unstable. If a performance is given an attribution that is stable then the performance will be viewed as relatively unchangeable, alternatively an unstable attribution will mean the paddler views the performance as being very changeable. A paddler may also view the cause of a particular outcome as being external or internal. In an internal attribution the paddler views the cause of a particular outcome as lying within him or herself. If the paddler views the outcome as resulting from the performance of fellow paddlers, the coach, the environment or the opposition then the attribution is said to be external.

▶ Attributional Style

Paddlers often have a tendency to attribute performances in particular ways despite the actual cause of the outcome. This is referred to as attribution style. For instance one paddler may tend to attribute success to external /unstable factors such as good luck, poor performances by opponents or a favourable judgement by an official or judge. Understanding how a learner tends to attribute success or failure can allow a coach to understand why a paddler might experience a learning plateau or period of very slow development. It can also help to explain poor motivation in some performers.

A paddler who attributes most of their successes to external /unstable factors (luck) cannot expect to maintain or improve their performance through training since no matter what they do luck will remain the deciding factor next time. Also a learner who attributes failure to low natural ability will not expect to improve or succeed irrespective of the task difficulty since this is an internal/stable factor and therefore unchangeable. From a coaching perspective both these attributions are dysfunctional in that they effectively demotivate the learner.

Perhaps a simpler way of looking at attribution is to consider the controllability of the attribution as the important factor. A paddler who perceives that the outcome of their performance is within their control will be more likely to be motivated to engage in positive behaviours. This should result in changes that improve performance. Attributions with a high degree of learner controllability are therefore functional for the coaching and development of paddlers.

As we have heard, many paddlers will have a tendency to explain the outcome of performances in relatively consistent ways. This style or disposition can have a large impact on (intrinsic) motivation. As paddlers if we believe that the outcome is related to factors controllable by us (i.e. effort) we will be more likely to continue in paddlesport and train than a paddler who feels that success and failure is outside of their control. In order to feel pride or satisfaction in a performance we need to feel that the result was due to our own actions.

KEY POINT SUMMARY

- Learners must believe that they can control the outcome of a performance in order to be motivated to make changes to techniques or strategies or even practice.

▶ Attributional Retraining

It is important for us to understand as coaches that attributional style is not rigidly fixed and can be affected by coach behaviours, peers, parents or psychologists. Studies have shown that the way instructions are delivered to performers can influence the attributions they are likely to make. As coaches we should be sure to emphasize the controllable nature of factors contributing to our paddler's outcomes when giving instructions and reviewing a performance. We should emphasize that improvements and success are a result of application, dedication and practice and avoid implying that natural ability or lack of ability is a strong factor in success or failure.

Attributional retraining is the process of actively redirecting an individual's awareness so that they begin to make attributions that we would see as helpful or functional. For instance the coach may make a concerted effort to get a paddler to see that they were responsible for their own success and that future success is therefore a controllable factor. Changing the attributional style of a paddler can be a long process that may well need to be implemented alongside goal setting. The good news is that improvements in attributions have been measured after very short interventions, where athletes were given feedback promoting the belief in a high degree of control over the outcome of sporting tasks.

Coaches hoping to encourage learners to view their performances as controllable should:

- Emphasise that the main difference in performance will come from effort and practice.
- Avoid suggesting that some learners will naturally do better than others.
- Concentrate on the areas that a paddler can change when examining outcomes.
- Be realistic about what a paddler can't change.
- Avoid consoling learners by suggesting their abilities lie elsewhere.

▶ BURN-OUT

Burn-out occurs when either a paddler or coach withdraws from an activity due to excessive stress or dissatisfaction over a longer period of time. The desire to improve or maintain performance can be a tremendous source of pressure on those involved in paddlesport. Often a burned-out athlete or coach does not physically drop out of sport since social or financial pressure may ensure that they remain involved. Psychological withdrawal can occur accompanied by emotional and psychological exhaustion, negative responses to others, low self-confidence and depression.

The view that more and more training is necessary for success can lead a highly committed paddler to overdo it. Eventually this can lead to overtraining or burn-out. Overtraining is mainly a physiological problem that occurs when an athlete is exposed to an excessive training load for a relatively short period of time resulting in decreased performance. Burn-out occurs as a result of a longer process of psychological stress.

Coaches are unlikely to suffer from overtraining but can certainly suffer from burn-out. Generally this

occurs due to accumulated stresses in and outside of sport coupled with an apparent lack of success or recognition for our effort and hard work.

KEY POINT SUMMARY

- Coaches or paddlers can become burned out if they feel that they are not equipped to cope with the demands on them or are not recognised for their efforts.

▶ Avoiding Burn-Out

How can we, as coaches, avoid burn-out in our paddlers or ourselves?

We need to accept that we all have limits on the levels of physical and psychological stress that we can endure. All of us have different individual limits. Conditions that one paddler can cope with will result in burn-out in another.

We need to be aware that stresses that we can cope with for short periods of time may be unsustainable for long-term development or involvement in paddlesport.

Photo 5 Keep a sense of humour!

Coaches and paddlers can best avoid burn-out if they ensure that they remember to retain a balanced lifestyle:

- Always remain aware that no one is immune to burn-out. Males and females, performers and coaches at all levels, 'winners' and 'losers' are all potential victims if stress gets out of control.

- Adopting a lifestyle that maintains physical health at an optimal level can provide some inoculation effect. Coaches and paddlers who are healthy are more likely to feel good and radiate enthusiasm to others.

- Maintain social support systems by having associations with others who understand the importance of your sporting situation. Coaches and paddlers can release tension by venting frustrations in the presence of others who understand.

- Keep a sense of humour.

▶ AROUSAL

Arousal is best thought of as our physical state of activation, or excitation. This can range from deep sleep to extreme excitement. Arousal is characterised by increased heart rate and respiration, sweating and butterflies in the stomach. Arousal is emotionally neutral and is the mind and body's natural preparation for action.

Several models of arousal attempt to explain the relationship between the intensity, or amount, of arousal and performance. Essentially these models all share the concept of an ideal, or optimal intensity of arousal for performance. An under or over-aroused paddler would fail to do well. An over-aroused paddler may be too jumpy and an under-aroused paddler might not be able to display their full physical potential. As coaches we should realise that optimal levels of arousal will be different in different sports and different tasks within sport and for different individuals. A paddler in a situation that requires high levels of physical work but low levels of motor control and decision making can be more aroused than one who needs delicate control or to choose between different possible responses. The different requirements of different activities would be illustrated by the difference between snooker and power-lifting. The snooker player would want a low level of arousal but a power-lifter may want a very high level. Different paddlers can also need different

levels of arousal to perform at their best so a coach needs to know the individual nuances of their own performers or learners.

⭕ KEY POINT SUMMARY

- We all have different responses to arousal and coaches need to be aware of how their own individual paddlers tend to perform best in order to help them reach or maintain that state.

▶ The Catastrophe Model

The catastrophe model (Hardy, 1990) shows that the relationship between arousal and performance is generally a smooth curve with a peak or optimal zone (Figure 6). However, beyond a critical point the performance of an over-aroused paddler will not slowly decline but instead will crash. Recovery from such a crash is difficult and the paddler may need to be removed from the stressful situation, only re-engaging in the activity after returning to almost resting levels of arousal if there is to be any hope of a reasonable performance. Whilst the actual point of catastrophe cannot be measured by a coach in the field, the real lesson here is that coaches need to be vigilant and prepared to respond to the signs of over-arousal and decreasing performance in their paddlers before the catastrophe threshold is reached. Once a paddler has 'gone over the top' the session is effectively over and the coach will spend the rest of their time picking up the pieces. Knowing the individual differences and responses of your paddlers is your best chance of avoiding catastrophic levels of arousal.

Photo 6 Anxious or excited?

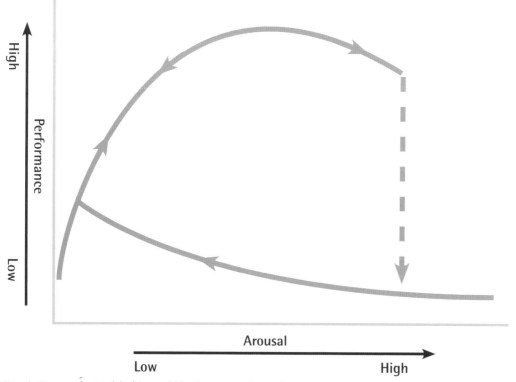

Fig. 6 Catastrophe Model of Arousal / Performance Relationship

▶ ANXIETY

Anxiety is often blamed for poor performances when an athlete or player fails to display the level of skill that coaches or observes know they are capable of. With the extra environmental factors that can add stress to canoesport it is hardly surprising that many coaches have an interest in anxiety. As coaches many of us are aware that a relationship between anxiety and performance exists. Unfortunately, whilst in our everyday lives we would all claim to know what we mean by anxiety, our everyday understanding can be limiting when trying to unlock the components of sporting performance.

Anxiety is an emotional state characterised by negative thoughts, nervousness and worry. Anxiety can be broken down into two sub-components; cognitive (mental) anxiety and somatic (physical) anxiety. Somatic or physical anxiety is simply the paddler's awareness of their own arousal. As the paddler becomes more aware of their shallow breathing and racing heart their somatic anxiety increases. Cognitive or mental anxiety is the presence of negative self-talk and feelings of dread or apprehension. The paddler may become preoccupied with the consequences of failure instead of concentrating on the task at hand.

▶ Reversal Theory

If arousal is seen as being the body's natural preparation for action then anxiety can be viewed as one possible emotional impact of high arousal. Reversal theory (Kerr) suggests that high arousal can be experienced as either positive or negative, depending on the motivational state of the paddler. At any time we will be in either an arousal-seeking state or an arousal-avoiding state. In an arousal-avoiding (telic) state then we will interpret high arousal as anxiety. Alternatively if we are in an arousal-seeking (paratelic) state then we will interpret the same high arousal as excitement.

Reversal theory suggests performers can move from non-facilitative (unpleasant) to facilitative (pleasant) states by reinterpreting their own experience as desired or undesired. Studies of slalom paddlers have shown that switching from arousal avoiding to arousal seeking states can take place during canoesport.

Imagine a white water paddler who feels their heart rate increase and starts to get butterflies in the stomach while inspecting a rapid that is actually within the

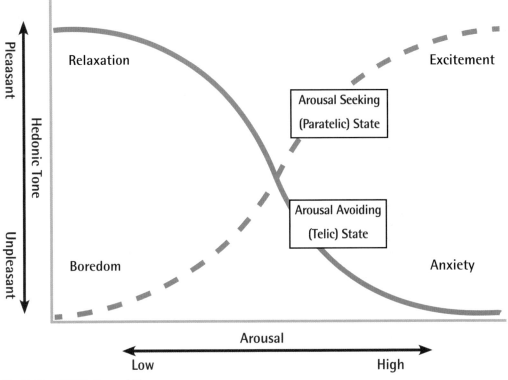

Fig. 7 Kerr (1987) Reversal Theory

limits of their ability. If they interpret this as negative (unpleasant) they will become anxious and may find themselves either paddling poorly or even deciding to walk the rapid. However, if they can become convinced that their arousal symptoms are positive and desired they will interpret their condition as excitement.

Successful performers often view the symptoms of high arousal (elevated heart rate, sweating, increased respiration and butterflies in the stomach) as positive indicators of their readiness. Many describe the sensation as 'a buzz' and look forward to it. We as coaches can help by encouraging paddlers to view high arousal as positive rather than negative, use the term 'excited' rather than 'nervous'. We know that hearing accounts from successful, experienced athletes of their experiences of viewing arousal symptoms as positive can actually facilitate younger, less experienced performers in their attempts to reappraise their symptoms as both positive and desired. As coaches we can encourage this process of reappraisal of arousal symptoms either by intervening ourselves or by encouraging other paddlers to help less experienced and younger performers. It is quite possible to learn to associate paddling and high arousal with excitement so that this becomes the normal response.

▶ Other Strategies

Other strategies for dealing with high levels of anxiety tend to concentrate on lowering arousal. Instead of switching to an arousal-seeking state we move back along the curved line of Figure 7 to reach relaxation. Techniques for this can include relaxation training or stress inoculation. Both are longer-term solutions and will need a paddler to participate in a progressive training programme.

Relaxation techniques rely on the link between the body and the mind. If a paddler's body is relaxed it is very difficult for them to remain anxious. Progressive relaxation is a technique that paddlers can learn in order to induce a state of relaxation. A paddler will practise deliberately tensing a muscle group and then relaxing it. These exercises raise awareness of the feelings of contrast between the tense state and the relaxed state. Often for paddlers, tension will be held in the shoulders and gripping muscles and so it would make a lot of sense to practise tensing and relaxing these areas. A paddler could even practise whilst holding a paddle deliberately over-gripping and tensing the shoulders, holding the tension and then releasing it, paying attention to the contrast in sensation. Like any

Photo 7 Using breathing exercises to lower arousal levels.

learning this will require practice before it can be used with any effect in a stressful situation but eventually it is possible for the technique to become an automatic response to anxiety.

Breathing exercises are another popular relaxation technique for lowering arousal and dealing with high anxiety. By concentrating on deep, diaphragmatic breathing it is possible to lower physical tension and trigger a relaxation response. Conversely when we are anxious we often either hold our breath or take shallow, rapid breaths from the upper chest. If a paddler can deliberately control their breathing they can avoid becoming over-anxious or effectively lower anxiety. Yoga classes are a good way to learn and practise the correct breathing technique.

As coaches involved in a group of sports with high potential for stressful situations we are very likely to find ourselves from time to time dealing with over-anxious paddlers.

We can help our performers to enjoy their paddling, learn effectively and perform at their best if we can:

- Identify the signs of increased arousal and anxiety in our paddlers.

- Monitor our paddlers over time and learn to identify the optimal level of arousal and emotional state for optimal performance.

- Recognise that anxiety is a result of situational and personal factors.

- Tailor our practice to our individual paddlers.

- Develop confidence in our performers so that they can cope with stress and anxiety.

- Increase our knowledge of effective techniques for coping with anxiety.

▶ CONCENTRATION

Concentration, or lack of concentration, is a term that is often used to explain differences in sporting performance. Concentration is often a poorly understood phenomenon. Many coaches will assume that a paddler is concentrating if they are succeeding and not concentrating if they are performing below par. We might even instruct a performer to concentrate harder, pay attention or 'focus'. It might be easier if we think of concentration as being the same as attention. As coaches it is not enough to ask a performer to concentrate, we need to let our paddlers know what we want their attention on.

Some paddlers may seem to be very easily distracted; their attention flitting to irrelevant events or elements in the environment. As a coach we may know that optimal performance is about not attending to unhelpful elements in the environment as much as attending to the helpful ones. However, asking a paddler not to concentrate on something is a bit like asking someone not to think of a blue bear with large ears. Are you not thinking of it? Instead we need to think about what we do want our paddlers to attend to and direct them to concentrate on those things instead.

◯ KEY POINT SUMMARY

- We are always concentrating on something, the question really is... are we concentrating on the right things in the right way?

As coaches we should also realise that our style of concentration or attention is not always the same. The width, or amount of things we can attend to can change and so can the type of thing we attend to (Figure 8). Some situations require us to attend to a lot of information from different sources. For example a canoe polo player engaged in play will need to monitor their own position in the pool, that of the ball, their team-mates, their opponents and spaces that allow for movement to take place. This requires a broad focus of attention. A sprint paddler waiting for the start may be attending to nothing but the sound of the starter. They might not even be aware of their opponents at all. This would be a very narrow focus of attention, however, in this situation it may be totally appropriate.

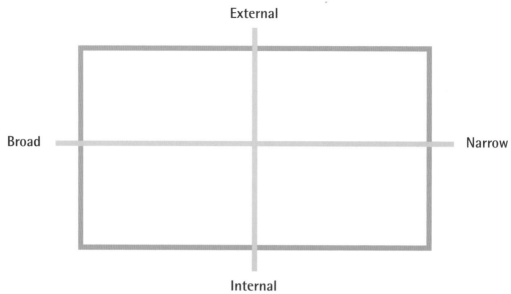

External

Broad   **Narrow**

Internal

Fig. 8 Dimensions of Attention

▶ Direction

Concentration or attention can also have direction and be said to be either internal or external. If we have an internal focus then we are concentrating on some aspect of our own performance, our thoughts, feelings or movements. If we are concentrating on the environment, other paddlers or even our equipment, then we have an external focus.

We are likely to already have an attentional style, which means that we will often drop into one attentional width and direction, for example narrow / internal. This is also true of our paddlers although their natural style may be different from ours. What is important is that the type of attention or concentration we find ourselves using is matched to the needs of the activity. If it is not matched then we need to change our focus of attention.

▶ Attention Control Training

Attention control training is about learning to switch between different types of concentration, moving between an internal focus and an external focus or moving from broad to narrow width of attention. Paddlers should practise activities that empathise one particular style of attention and practise moving from one style to another. For instance scouting a rapid will generally require a broad/external focus of atten-

tion. Assessing a particular hazard might then require a narrow/external focus. Controlling the pitch of the paddle blade during a sculling draw might require a narrow/internal focus, then controlling the direction of the boat's movement might require a narrow/external focus. Avoiding other paddlers during a game of tag would then require a broad/external focus.

Many paddlers believe that concentration is only really important in competition or for top level performance. The problem with this thinking is that they have actually missed the opportunity to practise the very skills they find themselves needing. Concentration or attentional skills need to be practised alongside technical skills and physical training.

One of the difficulties concerning concentration during stress or competition is that increased arousal tends to narrow attentional focus. To a point this can be good for certain activities making it easier for a paddler to ignore distractions. Unfortunately, if this process continues the focus can become too narrow for the activity and relevant, useful information can be ignored. This is one explanation for the decline in performance with over-high levels of arousal shown in catastrophe theory (Figure 6).

Photos 8a-c Differing paddling activities requiring different levels of focus.

As coaches and paddlers it is a good idea to remember a few basic principles related to concentration:

- Concentration needs to be focused on relevant factors in a paddling performance; these need to be identified if the term concentration is to be meaningful.

- Different paddling tasks need different attentional styles; we may need to work out what these are.

- Different paddlers will be stronger in different attentional styles.

- Paddlers can learn to adopt more appropriate attentional styles but this will require practice.

- Under stress our attention may become narrow if we allow ourselves to become too highly aroused; relaxation techniques may help to counter this.

▶ IMAGERY

Imagery, also referred to as visualisation or mental practice, is one of the most well known and commonly used mental skills. Reports of successful athletes and sports people using mental practice are common across all avenues of sport including golf, athletics, tennis and rugby. The popularity of imagery as a performance enhancement tool is a result of two factors. Firstly imagery has a vast array of possible uses once the basic technique has been developed and secondly it builds on mental processes that we already use daily.

KEY POINT SUMMARY

- Imagery is a skill we use every day; mental skills training simply aims to make us better and more effective at it.

Imagery has been used successfully to increase and maintain motivation, build confidence, regulate arousal, practise physical skills, learn new skills and rehearse strategies. This versatility and adaptability means that if you are interested in adopting mental skills training that could provide both an edge now and be used throughout a sporting career, imagery would come second only to goal setting.

Imagery has been described as "going to the movies". It has also been described as having your own virtual reality system. Think of a recent sporting performance of your own, picking a successful one will make this more fun. Now close your eyes and try to recreate the event in your imagination. Try to see the performance as it actually happened. Can you imagine the event in colour? What about the things you could hear? If this was easy to do try adding information from your other senses, try and feel the paddle in your hands and the footrest pushing against your feet. This is imagery, all of us can do it but some people are better than others. However, we can all train to be better at it and those well practised in imagery have often learned to be exceptional at it. There are Olympic level sportsmen and women who can 'image' a whole future event. They can see the path they will take through the course, feel the resistance against the paddle and the boat sliding over the water, hear the splash of the boat and paddle and the noise of the crowd. The length of time taken to complete the imagery run is within fractions of a second of the actual time they will get.

▶ Uses Of Imagery

Whilst this level of skill in imaging is uncommon, imagery is not only an obtainable skill for all paddlers but also a highly useful one. Imagery can be incorporated into the inspection of rapids, warm up for a polo match or race. It can be used to practise freestyle manoeuvres on days when getting to the water is impossible or for fault finding in a three star skill. Imagery can be used to enhance the learning and performance of any level of paddler in any paddling situation. It can be used to improve reviewing or to prepare for a future performance. Imagery can involve recreating a past event or experiencing an event that has not yet taken place.

▶ Training To Use Imagery

Having accepted that we are already able to use imagery without any training or practice it is important to realise that there are far more effective ways to go about imagery if we are prepared to put some time and thought into how we go about it. Holmes and Collins (2001) have developed the PETTLEP model based on the assumption that what we do in imagery should fit as accurately as possible to what we do in the real world:

Physical - Try and mimic the physical condition you would be in during the performance, this is likely to be alert and active rather than relaxed or lying down. Imagine being out of breath, perhaps even hold your paddle during imagery.

◎ Environment - Imagine as much of the environment you will perform in as you can, sounds, smell, and colour. Use photographs or videos to recreate environmental features if necessary.

◎ Task - Imagine very specific tasks and concentrate on the things that you would want to concentrate on during physical performances.

◎ Timing - Try and imagine the performance in 'real time', no slow motion. Leave that for videos!

◎ Learning - As you improve your physical performance you need to make sure you review your imagery and are not imaging 'old' techniques.

◎ Emotion - Include appropriate emotional content to your imagery. If you feel exhilaration or worry during a real performance then you should include these in your imagery.

◎ Perspective - Imagery can be internal where you imagine the view you get during the performance or external where you observe your performance from outside. Internal perspectives are normally better for warm-ups and preparation, external perspectives may be better for building confidence or for an aesthetic assessment such as an analysis of a freestyle move.

▶ SELF-TALK

As human beings we spend huge amounts of time talking to ourselves. Any time we actively think about something we are in effect talking to ourselves. We may be evaluating what we have done, "I think that went pretty well", what we are doing or our chances of succeeding in what we are doing. We often talk to ourselves about the consequences of failure, "If I don't make this last eddy I'm going to end up swimming the next rapid". Sometimes we talk to ourselves about other people's performance, either team-mates or opponents, "That was a nice move" or "I thought they were supposed to be good!".

In fact no matter what we do and how we perform as paddlers we will continue to talk to ourselves sometimes during a performance but certainly before and after performances, perhaps when maintaining or selecting equipment, in the car afterwards or talking to friends before getting on the water. Remember that when we are talking to others we are actually also talking to ourselves (since we are listening). Not

Photo 9 Slalom paddler imaging her run

only do we listen to ourselves when we are talking to others and ourselves but there is a lot of evidence to say that we actually take notice of what we say. The bad news is that often what we say isn't helping either our performance or our enjoyment.

▶ Negative Self-Talk

Negative self-talk includes labelling ourselves as "loser", or "poor under pressure" or "just not good in these situations". The problem with negative self-talk is twofold. Firstly negative self-talk is immensely powerful and has been shown to result in poorer performances. It can be highly disruptive during a performance but can also erode confidence and self-esteem between performances. Secondly negative self-talk can become habit forming. We probably all know people who have a habit of making negative remarks about their own abilities. Over time paddlers who continually label themselves as losers or not good under pressure expect to fail in those situations and when we expect to fail we normally manage to meet our expectations.

▶ Positive Self-Talk

Positive self-talk on the other hand has been shown to positively boost performance. A paddler who makes positive statements during self-talk, or in general discussion, can actually build up their expectations of success. Comments like, "I can do this", "I have the ability to learn this skill" or " I know I can succeed if I put the work in" are all positive outlooks for self-talk. Some psychologists will help athletes put together a series of positive self-talk statements that are often referred to as affirmations. Affirmations are a simple way of trying to control self-talk by ensuring that a paddler becomes used to self-talk of a positive and helpful nature. Since it is only possible to be engaged in one form of self-talk at a time they can be used to prevent negative self-talk from creeping in by default.

KEY POINT SUMMARY

• Affirmations are a form of positive self-talk that can be used to boost confidence over a period of time or in stressful situations.

Anyone who might want to improve their performance through control of self-talk should think about creating key phrases using the following six rules (Mikes, 1987):

• Keep your phrases short and specific.

• Use the first person and present tense.

• Construct positive phrases.

• Say your phrases with meaning and attention.

• Speak kindly to yourself.

• Repeat phrases often.

Self-talk can also be targeted at improving concentration or attention control. It is easy to get caught up in the past during performances. If you are the sort of paddler who finds yourself reviewing your performance during your activity then you might want to try using self-talk to draw your attention back to the areas that will enable you to do well.

▶ MOVING ON FROM HERE...

The main aim of this chapter has been to encourage coaches to view sports psychology as a body of knowledge that can enable us to be more successful in our work with paddlers. Also to view psychological skills training as a natural part of sporting progression and development that should go hand in hand with technical, tactical and physiological training.

See also Chapter 18 Slalom for useful examples of discipline-specific mental skills training.

FURTHER READING

Weinburg, R.S. and Gould, D. (2003). *Foundations of Sport and Exercise Psychology.* IL: Human Kinetics.

CHRIS HODGSON

Chris is a Senior Lecturer at the University of Chichester where he teaches psychology to adventure education and physical education students. Originally from the north-east of England he started his paddlesport career in a rock pool on the Northumberland coast aged twelve. Since then paddling has taken him all over the world from the Canadian Arctic to the Himalayas.

Chris is fascinated by the areas of learning and performing in complex and challenging environments and how we can improve performance during environmentally induced stress. He has been involved in the coaching of paddlesport at every level of experience from total novices through to international competition. Chris is a BCU Level 5 Coach holding coaching qualifications in inland, sea, open canoe and surf and also a postgraduate degree in sport psychology.

4 DUTY OF CARE

The reasons why people become coaches are many and varied. Some people coach at their club and regard coaching as a rewarding hobby, others are coaching their paddlers to become elite athletes, some are making a living from coaching paddlesports. As coaches we must accept that we have a duty of care and responsibility for all those who put themselves under our care and guidance.

INTRODUCTION

There is a growing concern that some coaches are giving up because they are concerned about the 'duty of care' issue! Their concern being that they might become involved in litigation.

Most of these worries and concerns are largely unfounded and as long as you are aware of the issues and your coaching follows 'current best practice' then the perceived risk of having a claim made against you should never arise.

Over the past few years many voluntary organisations have struggled to find volunteers to lead activities; this is especially true of organisations that take children and young people into challenging environments, such as scouts, guides and canoe clubs. Thankfully this situation is presently being turned around.

The government have realised that young people need to be exposed to a certain amount of risk in a controlled yet challenging environment, in order to be able to manage risk and solve problems in their own lives. Although we, as coaches should not be afraid to take people paddling we do need to be very aware of the issues involved. The bottom line is, as long as you are not negligent and follow current best practices, you have little to fear. So how do we know what these current best practices are?

All the information is on the BCU website. Coaching forums are a great way to get expert advice as well as network with other coaches. Sports Coach UK offer various workshops. Once you make the initial step, keeping up to date isn't such a daunting task – if in doubt, ask!

▶ DUTY OF CARE

The BCU wishes to ensure that all those taking part in canoeing are able to do so, protected and kept safe from harm while they are with staff, coaches and/or volunteers. This is particularly true in respect of children and vulnerable adults.

With this in mind, the BCU recognises that they have a duty towards all those taking part in paddle-sport activity and to any club providing paddling opportunities. That is to ensure that support is provided to enable all to do so with the highest possible standards of care.

All coaches and clubs should have a clear understanding of operating within an appropriate code of ethics, aware of what their 'duty of care' is and how this relates to their position in providing activities and being responsible for others.

As an organiser of activity, there is a possibility of someone in your care being harmed. In a small percentage of cases action may be taken against you if the person decides to make a claim. This action may result in financial losses but can also harm your reputation or the reputation of your club and the BCU itself.

A good definition of 'duty of care' is:

"The duty which rests upon an individual or organisation to ensure that all reasonable steps are taken to ensure the safety of any person involved in any activity for which that individual or organisation is responsible"

In an activity such as canoeing, safety and keeping people safe is all about risk assessment and minimising the risks involved at all levels of participation. While all taking part in activity have a duty to their neigh-

bours, in organised activity we all have a heightened duty of care and as such we should be aware that the principal risks extend to the quality of control exercised by those in charge. Trainers, coaches, referees, umpires or administrators should all take 'reasonable' steps to safeguard those directly taking part in activities and at any time they may be deemed responsible for those in their charge - in vehicles, during journeys to and from the activity, during events, team training events and camps etc.

THE COACHES' CHARTER

1. Coaches must respect the rights, dignity and worth of every person and treat everyone equally within the context of their sport.

2. Coaches must place the well-being and safety of the performer above the development of performance. They should follow all guidelines laid down by the British Canoe Union and hold appropriate insurance cover.

3. Coaches must develop an appropriate working relationship with performers, especially children, based on mutual trust and respect. Coaches must not exert undue influence to obtain personal benefit or reward.

4. Coaches must encourage and guide performers to accept responsibility for their own behaviour.

5. Coaches should hold up-to-date nationally recognised governing body coaching qualifications.

6. Coaches must ensure the activities they direct or advocate are appropriate for the age, maturity, experience and ability of the individual.

7. Coaches should at the outset clarify with performers, and where appropriate their parents, exactly what is expected of them and what performers are entitled to expect from their coach.

8. Coaches should co-operate fully with other specialists (e.g. other coaches, officials, sport scientists, doctors, physiotherapists) in the best interest of the performer.

9. Coaches should always promote the positive aspects of their sport (e.g. fair play) and never condone rule violations or the use of prohibited substances.

10. Coaches must consistently display high standards of behaviour and appearance.

Photo 1 Working with children is very rewarding and involves an enhanced duty of care.

Photo 2 Involving parents and carers

This Charter is reproduced by courtesy of Sports Coach UK. For more information on guides for sports coaches visit www.sportscoachuk.org.

BCU CHILD PROTECTION AND VULNERABLE ADULTS POLICY

It is recommended that all coaches make themselves familiar with the BCU Child Protection Policy, available to download from www.bcu.org.uk.

GOOD PRACTICE GUIDELINES

By following these guidelines you will help to protect both the children in our sport and our coaches/helpers from wrongful allegations.

Avoid situations where you are alone with one child. The BCU acknowledges that occasionally there may be no alternative, for example, where a child falls ill and has to be taken home. We would stress, however, that one-to-one contact must never be allowed to occur on a regular basis. Further guidance on this is contained in the BCU Code of Ethics/Sports Coach UK Code of Conduct.

If any form of physical support is required ask the paddler's permission, explain what you are doing and why to both the child and their parents/carers.

Where possible ask parents/carers to be responsible for children in changing rooms. Always ensure that whoever supervises young people work in pairs.

Where there are mixed teams/groups away from home, they should always be accompanied by an adult male and female coach/helper.

Don't allow physically rough or sexually provocative games, or inappropriate talking or touching.

If it's necessary to do things of a personal nature for children who are young or disabled, make sure you have another adult accompanying you. Get the consent of the parent/carer and if possible the child. Let them know what you are doing and why.

Ensure that any claims of abuse by a child are taken seriously and that it is dealt with by people who know what to do.

Ensure that the nature and intensity of training does not exceed the capacity of a child's immature and growing body.

Follow the BCU guidelines for photography and video use (see reference sheet 'Guidelines for use of Photographic and Filming Equipment' from BCU website).

CLUBS

Ensure your club adheres to the BCU best practice guidelines with particular reference to:

🛶 The BCU Code of Ethics/Sports Coach UK Code of Conduct.

🛶 The BCU guidance on child protection and the Paddlesafe Guidelines provided.

🛶 The requirements for coaches and helpers to have undergone disclosure.

🛶 Publicise the NSPCC Child Protection Helpline.

0808 800 5000

Regular Child Protection workshops are held at coaching forums, and Sports Coach UK offer a Child Protection workshop which is well worth attending, details from www.sportscoachuk.org.

FURTHER INFORMATION

BCU Coaching Directory
BCU Coaching Code
Sports Coach UK Code of Conduct
BCU Duty of Care Policy
BCU Harassment Policy
BCU Articles of Association and Disciplinary Procedure

Child Protection in Sport Unit
NSPCC National Training Centre
3 Gilmour Close
Beaumont Leys
Leicester LE4 1EZ

Telephone 0116 234 7278/7280
Facsimile 0116 234 0464
Email: cpsu@nspcc.org.uk

PHIL HADLEY

Phil started paddling at about ten years old with the scouts and later at school. He started paddling seriously whilst completing a BSc Hons Degree in Sports Studies at the University of Wolverhampton, and has been associated with the University ever since as a visiting lecturer. Phil has been involved in the management of outdoor centres for the past ten years or so, and uses the experience gained to advise other centres and LEAs of the best ways to manage risk and unlock the potential of the outdoors learning environment. He now works part-time as a Paddlesport Development Officer for the BCU, as an Outdoor Education Consultant for the local LEA, as well as coaching paddlesports as often as time (and a young family) permit. Phil holds coaching awards in four BCU disciplines, as well as yachting, dinghy sailing, windsurfing, climbing and powerboating.

5 GENERIC SAFETY ISSUES

A coach has both a moral and a legal duty of care to those being coached. In addition to the duty of care, safety considerations can affect the effectiveness of one's coaching.

▶ THE COACHING ENVIRONMENT

Effective learning can only take place in a suitable learning environment. In its broadest sense, 'the coaching environment' refers to any physical or psychological factors that affect students' ability to learn. These could include whether they trust their coach, whether an atmosphere where mistakes are seen as learning opportunity rather than a source of embarrassment has been cultivated, or whether they perceive themselves to be in real physical danger.

If learners perceive the environment to be too threatening, they will only be concerned with survival and coping strategies. No thought will be given to examining performance, there will be no room for experimentation, and no notice will be taken of any feedback offered by the coach.

It is equally the case that the more that coaches have to concentrate on safety and leadership issues, the less effort they can put into their coaching!

DIFFERENT DISCIPLINES

Different aspects of canoeing and kayaking are affected by the environment in different ways. Marathon paddling, for example, takes place on canals and gently flowing rivers. If the student is being coached in forward paddling technique, both the coach and the student can be quite relaxed about safety as it is only a short swim to the bank in calm water. In fact, in this aspect of the sport it is the norm for paddlers not to wear buoyancy aids and the coaches to work from the bank. However, if it is a very cold day and the winds are blustery, the wise coach may well decide that, on this occasion, buoyancy aids will be worn.

On the other hand, a coach and student sea kayaking in rough seas and an offshore wind may decide that this is not the time to work on the finer aspects of forward paddling technique. However, there is nothing to stop the coach from waiting for better conditions or moving to a more sheltered location.

Photo 1 Coaching beginners, coach in boat providing safety cover.

Photo 2 Coaching improvers on white water. In this location the coach chooses to work from the bank, but is in paddling kit with a kayak nearby.

Photo 3 Coaching elite paddlers. In this particular situation the coach has decided that it is reasonable to rely on the paddlers to take care of each other.

SAFETY COVER

When working with competent or elite paddlers it is often appropriate for the coach to work on the premise that the students will take care of their own and each other's safety and the coach will concentrate on coaching. At the other extreme, coaches working with complete beginners will be actively providing safety cover as well as coaching input, unless they are fortunate

enough to have the assistance of a competent paddler who can take over the safety cover role. When working with improvers one can compromise. Coaches will sometimes work from their boats and sometimes from the bank, though when doing so they will probably be in paddling kit and have their boat handy.

▶ Positioning

The best position for the coach is dictated by one or all of three factors:

Observation - The best position from which to observe the performance (Photo 4a).

Feedback – The best position from which to provide feedback (Photo 4b).

Safety – The best position from which to provide safety cover! (Photo 4c).

If the performance of the students requires that safety cover be provided, then safety cover must be the priority. However, it is possible to compromise so that all three factors are addressed satisfactorily.

▶ ASSESSING THE RISKS

The more demanding and prone to change the environment, the more observant and flexible a coach will have to be. In advanced situations, any guidance that a meaningful risk assessment could give would have to be very general in nature, allowing the coach to be flexible in order to adapt to rapidly changing conditions.

Sometimes a coach will be required to supervise less experienced coaches. In situations where there are definite boundaries and the local environment is not subject to significant changes or these changes can be easily observed and quantified, it may be appropriate for an experienced coach to undertake a formal written risk assessment that provides firm safety guidelines.

FORMAL RISK ASSESSMENTS

The purpose of a written risk assessment is to draw attention to any hazards, assess the level of risk they pose and highlight measures that can be taken to control those risks, (which may of course include deciding not to use the location in question).

The dangers inherent in any form of written risk assessment are:

- It becomes an exercise in management absolving themselves from responsibility rather than a useful tool.

- People expect these assessments to be written by experts and may take their content as 'gospel'. However… if the system has failed and it is written by someone who lacks the knowledge and experience required, the assessment is worse than useless in that it is misleading.

- It gets filed away and the people who should benefit from its advice are unaware of its existence.

- Users become over-reliant on it and stop using their own observation skills and judgement.

If done well, written risk assessments are a valuable tool, drawing attention to dangers and solutions that the reader may not have been aware of.

DYNAMIC RISK ASSESSMENTS

Dynamic risk assessment is just a posh phrase describing what any paddler who is still alive and doesn't rely on luck does all the time. We keep our eyes and ears open, we anticipate problems, and when in any doubt we ask ourselves "What if… ?" We then adapt our behaviour to avoid or deal with the changes in the environment causing us concern.

Dynamic risk assessment relies on alertness, observation skills and good judgement, and is the most important form of risk assessment. You have probably heard someone remark about a good coach, "He's got eyes in the back of his head!"

▶ Factors To Consider

Useful guidance on what factors should be considered when making a formal risk assessment can be found in the AALA (Adventure Activity Licensing Authority) website www.aala.co.uk.

▶ Control Measures

Different students will have differing skill levels and experience. A location with water/weather conditions that are perfect for one group may be too threatening or even downright dangerous for another group. If a coach decides that a given location is too threatening for effective coaching, or too risky from a safety point of view, he or she will need to put in place one or more control measures.

Possible options are to:

Move to a location better suited to the student's ability.

Change the way in which the site is used so as to avoid the hazards that cause concern.

Increase the level of personal protective equipment (PPE) worn by students and coaches (e.g. wear helmets).

Put in place additional rescue tools (e.g. have someone ready with a throw line).

Increase the staffing levels. This could be in terms of quantity and/or quality, (i.e. it may be more appropriate to have one more experienced coach than to double the number of less experienced coaches).

▶ Cut-Offs

If a location is prone to changes in conditions it may be appropriate to provide less experienced coaches with clear indicators of at what point the site becomes unsuitable for the activities they wish to undertake.

For example it may be that a site or stretch of river is perfect for novices at low water levels, but becomes dangerous due to trees becoming strainers and the novices' inability to avoid them at higher water levels. The risk assessment and resulting safety guidelines may indicate that if a certain boulder is covered by water the site is not to be used with novice groups.

On the sea it may be that a sheltered bay is deemed suitable for use with groups by Level 2 coaches providing the wind is onshore, or if offshore no more than a Force 2.

▶ THE STANDARDS BY WHICH WE ARE MEASURED

Accidents happen… but so do preventable accidents. If something happens that was a genuine accident that could have happened to anyone we will, first and foremost, be able to live with ourselves, and secondly, be able to justify our actions to a court should that prove necessary.

The questions a court will ask (as will your fellow coaches) are:

Did the coach owe his students a duty of care? The less experienced and skilled the student, the greater the duty of care, but a coach will always have some duty of care. (Duty of care is a factor

Photo 5 Finishing on a high! (With appropriate equipment).

that affects coaches, leaders and individual paddlers so I refer you to the chapter Safety and Leadership in the BCU Canoe and Kayak Handbook where it is well covered).

Were the coach's actions reasonable in the circumstances? If coaches ask themselves, "What if?", stay alert and work within their own limitations they should be able to cope with the second question.

How a coach's actions compare with the 'norms of the industry.' It is certainly worth bearing in mind that a court (and your peers) will not judge your actions and precautions by your standards. Your actions will be judged by the standards that are deemed to be the norm. That is to say a consensus view of what most coaches operating at that level would regard as best practice.

So, for example, if a student was paddling on placid water, fell out of his boat and banged her head on a car that had been dumped in the canal and was a hazard no one could have foreseen, there would be no problem. This is because it is the norm in placid water situations to paddle without helmets. If on the other hand you were paddling on a placid water section of

river without helmets and then decided to allow your students to run a broken weir, you would be in an entirely different situation. If someone capsized and received head injuries you would be hard put to justify your decision. The norm in such a situation would be to wear helmets.

STUDENT PRESSURE

• It is easy to imagine how pressure from students could lead a coach astray. A boisterous group who have had a good time, made rapid progress and feel insufficiently challenged, might well place a coach or leader under a lot of psychological pressure to finish on a high by running the weir. The coach may feel so pressured to do this that he or she chooses to ignore the lack of helmets. "It'll be all right just this once".

I know of a number of accidents that have occurred because the coaches felt under pressure to give the students a more exciting time… and went against their better judgement. You must resist!

▶ COACHING YOUNG PEOPLE

There are a number of extra factors that must be taken into account to ensure best practice when working with young people. This is for their protection and for yours. Read the relevant section in the Safety and Leadership chapter of the BCU Handbook. In fact it is important that you are familiar with the whole of that chapter.

IN CONCLUSION

As an individual coach there are certain attitudes and approaches that we can adopt to help us to keep on top of the situation:

✓ Stay alert!

✓ Communicate effectively (avoid misunderstandings).

✓ Develop your observational skills (this will also help your coaching).

✓ Develop a 'healthy' sense of paranoia (i.e. yes it can happen to you)!

✓ Be in the right place at the right time.

✓ Practise safety and rescue skills.

✓ Make yourself aware of and read any safety policy documents or risk assessments that apply in your place of work.

FURTHER READING

BCU Canoe and Kayak Handbook, Pesda Press - Read the chapter on Safety and Leadership and the safety and rescue information in chapters that cover your specialist areas.

WEBSITES:

Adventure Activities Licensing Authority - www.aala.co.uk

FRANCO FERRERO

Franco is a Level 5 Coach (Inland and Sea). Most of his work time is taken up running Pesda Press, though he still does some free-lance and voluntary coaching. He was formerly the head of the canoeing department at Plas y Brenin, and was honoured with the Geoff Good Coach of the Year Award (coaching adults category) in 2000.

His main paddling interests are white water and sea touring, though he occasionally 'dabbles' in other aspects of paddlesport and is also a keen mountaineer and skier. He has paddled throughout Britain and the European Alps, as well as in Norway, Nepal, Peru and British Columbia in Canada.

6 FIRST EXPERIENCES

Can you remember your first introduction to paddlesport... the anticipation and excitement you felt as you were about to go paddling for the first time? What was it that attracted you? Was it while at school, going on an outdoor pursuits holiday, or maybe your parents were keen paddlers, introducing you to paddlesport at an early age?

My own first experience was while on a residential course with school in the Lake District. It was wonderful being outdoors on the lake and in the mountains. I remember the magic of being on the water, the wind in my face, the waves rocking the boat and making it dance. We paddled out to a little island, where we found a secret pool. There we sat eating our lunch, drinking in the breathtaking scenery and feeling on top of the world.

How little I knew then that it would consume me and entice me back time and time again. I suppose it's the feeling you have when you are totally at peace and doing a sport that you love. Just being on the water was more than enough to bring a smile to my face.

INTRODUCTION

This chapter looks at introducing people to paddlesport. There are many ways in which we can do this. Looking at the points in a logical progression, from the first steps through to them returning time and again, seems the most appropriate and beneficial when applying them practically.

When introducing people to paddlesport we tend to guide them into a particular area, which may be our main area of interest, be this kayak, canoe, slalom, sea or white water racing. Whilst this may work well initially, being able to offer a wide and varied introduction in a variety of crafts will allow the beginner to see which area they enjoy and which direction they then choose to follow. This means that the broader your knowledge of the different areas of canoesport, the greater the opportunity for those participating to be guided into the areas that interest them. Remember that there is a great crossover between the different disciplines and this can be applied at all levels.

Throughout the chapter the emphasis is on paddleability; all this means is focusing in on the individual's ability and on what they can do rather than what they can't do. There is a great chapter in the BCU Canoe and Kayak Handbook on inclusive canoeing and kayaking.

▶ FIRST CONSIDERATIONS

The most important aspect of introducing people to paddlesport is that they are safe, are having fun and that learning is taking place. The technical side of their paddling will come later. As a coach you are at the forefront when introducing the complete beginner. This is where you can ensure that they have really enjoyed themselves, wish to return and do it again. Even better, they tell all their friends and bring them along too! Remember, these could be the stars of the future and their first insight into the sport could be through you.

For many people, being in a water environment is very natural and poses no problems but for others the fear of going into water can be nerve-racking. The experiences they have had will have a large impact on how they view water. For some people this will be something that they relish and will require little encouragement, whilst others will need careful nurturing, encouragement and guidance.

The way in which you present yourself and the sport will have a lasting impression. All too often you hear that for some their experiences within paddlesport have not been positive. Others feel that they have tried the sport and that it is not for them. That's fine, not everybody that has a go will want to continue. What is important is that they have a positive experience. This means that you as a coach will make an impression on the people that you come into contact with and must act in a professional manner at all times.

MEDICAL

It is important to ascertain at the beginning of the session whether any of the students have a medical condition or are taking any medication that could affect them during the session. For instance asthma is common in children and it may be that you will need to look after their inhaler in your buoyancy aid during the session in case they need it. When asking medical details be aware that it can be very embarrassing for people to discuss their personal details in front of the whole group. Always allow people to approach you alone to discuss any medication that they may be taking. It will not usually exclude people from taking part in the activity, but should an incident occur and you have some background knowledge you will be able to deal with it quickly and effectively.

CONSENT FORMS

When coaching anyone under the age of eighteen who is not accompanied by parent or guardian, consent for the child to take part in the activity must be obtained. This can be done by way of a form, which is completed in advance of the planned activity. A copy of a consent form can be downloaded from the BCU webpage www.bcu.org.uk/aboutus/childprotection-policy.html.

Photo 1 Working together to lift an open canoe.

MANUAL HANDLING

There is a need to be aware of manual handling when working with complete beginners. Whilst most will have had some experience of lifting, they will probably not be aware of the type of loads when lifting closed cockpit kayaks and open cockpit kayaks and canoes.

Manual handling is well documented in Chapter 6 of the Canoe and Kayak Handbook and there is also a BCU course that covers all the issues.

Below are some tips to help:

- When lifting open canoes with young adults, gather all of them around the canoe and lift it together.

- With kayaks and white water racers, double people up so that there are two people to one boat.

- When seeing small children or young adults dragging a boat, *think!* They have done a good risk assessment, decided that they can't possibly lift the boat and have dragged it along the ground instead.

 TOP TIP

- Ask yourself if the briefing and instructions were clear; you may know what you meant but did the students?

▶ PLANNING A SESSION

There are many ways in which a session can be planned. If you are new to coaching, using a pre-prepared session plan as outlined in the following page may well give you a starting point until you gain more experience in the planning process. For an experienced coach writing headings down on the back of an envelope that outlines the session could be more than adequate. Certainly everybody will plan their session thinking about the various points outlined below.

The six successful steps to practical session planning are:

- ◎ Setting session goals
- ◎ Setting session content
- ◎ Warm up
- ◎ Practice development
- ◎ Cool down
- ◎ Evaluate the session

Remember that the session plan is not set in stone. If during the session things are not working, change the activity.

When planning a session it is important to identify the following areas:

- ◎ **Who** are you going to coach?

Age and sex, numbers, experience/ability, and how the groups are mixed. For example: are they all adults, all children, mixed adults and children, male, female or mixed?

- ◎ **What** are you going to coach?

Things that affect the process are: is it a one-off session? Is it a series of sessions, one session a week for four weeks? Aims and objectives.

- ◎ **How** are you going to coach?

These can be affected by: water conditions, weather conditions, coaching style, location, what are their expectations and are they realistic?

Being able to identify the type of students that you will be coaching will help to steer the session from the outset. If for instance the students are children and this is a one-off session then giving too much formal coaching input could make the session stale and boring. Playing lots of games and having fun is much more appropriate and reflects the group dynamics, giving a much better balance to the session.

AIMS AND OBJECTIVES

When planning a session it is important to have aims and objectives. These specify what is to be attempted and what the students are likely to achieve.

▶ Aims

Aims state what your students hope to achieve during the session and give a general outline of the session. For example: Have fun - by the end of the session feel they have achieved a degree of control of the boat.

▶ Objectives

Objectives are more specific – what the students will know and be able to do as a result of the planned learning event. For example, an objective may be that by the end of the session the student will be able to:

1. Paddle a boat in a reasonable straight line.
2. Stop at will.
3. Turn the boat on the spot.

At the end you can review the session, checking your objectives to see if they have been met.

GOAL SETTING

Goal setting helps set a target that can be achieved both on the day and in the future, which needs to be agreed by both the coach and the student. This is individual to a person and those in the group may have very different goals for the session. Certainly when introducing beginners to canoesport and when mixing adults and children together their expectations from the session will be very different.

Beginners may not have much of an idea as to what their goals will be from the session since they will have no starting point. The first session may well be observing where they are at, and using your experience as a coach as to what is likely to be achievable for the session. Some will need support and encouragement so that they don't underachieve.

SESSION CONTENT

Having set the aims and objectives, the session content should have more detail with an introduction, the main content and the summary. Break the session down into the different areas then make short notes so that you can use and understand them at a quick glance.

EVALUATING THE SESSION

It is important that once the session has finished you evaluate it. This can be done directly after the session or once you are changed. It only takes five minutes and will help identify areas of improvement for future sessions.

If this is done soon after the event then it is simply asking yourself the following questions:

- What went well?
- What could have been improved?
- Changes to be made?

Making a note of these on the session plan allows you to refer back to these at a later date. Over a period of time you will have a comprehensive set of plans that can be used or modified accordingly. Remember, just because something that you tried didn't work with a particular group doesn't mean that it won't work with another group on a different day.

► LOCATIONS

The locations that you choose for your group will dictate whether the session will be successful or not and whether the group enjoy themselves or feel very frustrated.

There are many factors that will influence a decision as to the location that you use, these being:

- The type of group
- The number in the group
- Weather
- Access and egress
- Hazards
- Water levels
- Other users

All these factors need to be taken into consideration when choosing a suitable venue. If you are not familiar with a site a visit beforehand would be recommended. This will allow you to plan what your group is likely to do. When choosing a location think about *what if* circumstances change. Maybe on the day you visited the site the weather was calm, yet when you return there is an offshore wind blowing.

Even as an experienced coach, you should always perform a dynamic risk assessment to see if any factors have changed since your last visit or indeed as the day progresses. It is very easy to become complacent when using a site regularly.

Photo 2 This holiday beach looks placid enough but there is a strong breeze blowing offshore!

► MEETING THE GROUP

When introducing the complete beginner to canoesport they may be apprehensive so always introduce yourself, the location, what they can expect from the session and a very rough outline of what is planned. Smile! It costs nothing, makes people feel welcome, and puts them at ease.

People much prefer it if you use their name, so take the time when you first meet them to do this. Names can be difficult to remember but with practice this becomes easier. Those in the group may not have met each other either so getting them to know the group is important. You can use the following activities:

- With adults you can get them to introduce themselves to each member of the group, maybe telling the other person about something that they enjoy doing.

- Using a game such as getting everybody to stand in a circle then, using a throw bag or a ball, get the person who throws the object to call out his or her name. Once everybody has become familiar with peoples' names, they can then call out the name of the person who they are throwing the object to.

Photo 3 Getting to know people's names

▶ EFFECTIVE USE OF EQUIPMENT

When introducing people to canoesport we tend to think about getting straight onto the water with little thought about the equipment that they may use. For beginners, having a paddle that is the correct diameter and length, a boat that has a footplate or a ladder footrest, a backrest, thigh braces that are fitted correctly and properly secured are all very important points which need careful consideration.

PADDLES

This means having a variety of different length paddles that are suitable for all the individuals within the group, and a variety of different sizes of craft.

Think of everybody within the group as individuals and kit them out accordingly.

Photo 4 A rough guide to measuring white water or general-purpose kayak paddles

Photo 5 A rough guide to measuring open canoe paddles.

BOATS

When introducing kayaking there are advantages to putting beginners in a general-purpose or a touring kayak and not a shorter, white water kayak or playboat. This is because the longer designs are easier to paddle in a straight line and encourage an early development of good forward paddling technique. However, the more modern boats are generally wider, making them more stable than the longer, thinner boats and many of the newer boats are scaled for different size paddlers. This is certainly an advantage when faced with the issues of fitting people in boats.

Some people have a fear of being in a boat; they are concerned that the boat is unstable and that should the boat capsize they would be unable to exit properly. For a variety of reasons some people would be physically unable to power or to control the boat by themselves. This does not necessarily exclude them from taking part in paddlesport. A big advantage of using open canoes is that two can be joined together to make a very steady platform, which allows people to participate in the session. When joining canoes together care must be taken to ensure that they are properly secured. Leaving a gap of about two feet will allow the water to pass between the open canoes without building up resistance and create a solid platform, similar to a catamaran.

▶ INTRODUCING THE BEGINNER TO EQUIPMENT

Where possible, introduce equipment well away from the water. Here the kit is the link to the planned activity. At the water's edge they will be focused on the water instead of the kit.

BOATS

When introducing a boat, gather the group around so that everyone is in a position to see and hear you.

Introduce the varying parts of the boat, highlighting the following areas:

- The type of boat, where and when used, e.g. "This is an open canoe…"
- Highlight the bow and stern (front and back)
- Painter lines
- Thwart
- The seat
- Gunwales
- Yoke
- Air bags, explaining that they displace water and help the kayak float high in the water,(if fitted).

Photo 6 Different boats being used in beginners' session.

Photo 7 Introducing beginners to an open boat.

For general-purpose kayaks the process is the same as outlined above except that the points highlighted will change to those specific to kayaks.

PADDLES

There are a number of different paddles that can be used to introduce beginners. Usually these can have a flat blade on either end and therefore can be used left or right-handed. For the paddle to be used in this way there must be no feather, or set at 90° for kayaks. The only advantage of these paddles is that they are cheap. Starting beginners with curved paddles from the outset is much more productive from a coaching rather than an accounting perspective.

▶ Kayak Paddle

When using a very sheltered location where the group is well contained, group control is not a problem. In these circumstances simply letting the group get on the water and experiment with the paddle and then correcting those who need help individually is very effective.

Introducing the kayak paddle before getting on the water has the advantage that you can allow people to get the feel of the movement before getting on the water. This will certainly be an advantage where the students need to be able to demonstrate a reasonable amount of control due to the conditions.

An example of coaching methods that can be used for introducing the paddle are 'copy me' and experiential. This is outlined as:

1. Hold the paddle out in front of you with the right-hand blade facing down, as if you were riding a motorbike.

2. Make a right angle with the elbows with the paddle in front of the chest.

3. Return the arms to the outstretched position.

4. Check that the hands are held evenly on the paddle.

5. Get the group to rev the bike up (roll their wrist on the control hand to line the other blade up for entry). Making the noises here helps.

6. The non-control hand is slippy and slips through whilst the control hand moves.

7. Demonstrate the whole action.

Photos 8a-c One method of introducing the kayak paddle.

 TOP TIPS

• Face the same way as the group so that they can imitate the correct actions.
• Don't forget that those doing it right also need feedback!

Photo 9 *Face the same way as the group.*

Then go round the group giving individual feedback to those who have not quite mastered the movement. Actually standing in front and moving the paddle for them will help them develop the feel for what the actual movement is. In this way you are not highlighting the weaknesses in front of the whole group, but are able to identity those that require additional help quickly. You should always be aware of people's personal space and consider how you deal with this. Always stand in front of the person when helping with this exercise, informing them how you intend to help them.

▶ Canoe Paddle

Again, coaching methods that can be used for introducing the paddle are 'copy me' and 'experiential'.

1. Hold the paddle using the 'T' grip. Hook the 'T' bar over the thumb then curl the hand over the top, see diagram (Photo 10a).

2. Grip around the shaft with the lower hand (Photo 10b).

3. Demonstrate the whole action.

Once again this allows you to go round the group giving individual feedback, particularly to those who have not quite mastered the movement. Standing in front and moving the paddle for them will help them develop the feel for what the actual movement is.

▶ Spraydecks

The main purpose of the spraydeck is to keep the water from entering the kayak. It also helps to keep out the cold. If the conditions were such that the group would need spraydecks for an introductory session perhaps a change of venue or activity would be in order.

If spraydecks are used it is a good idea to use loose fitting nylon ones that come off easily and to ensure that everyone practises removing them.

TOP TIPS

• Getting people to do this exercise first will highlight whether they are right or left-handed. If they are struggling with the above movement, ask them to hold the paddle as for a left-handed person. (Make sure that you have a left-handed paddle available if using curved paddles). Just because they are left-handed normally does not mean that they cannot paddle right-handed. Letting them experiment first as to how they find holding the paddle will work much better. If they appear to find the motion confusing only then get them to change to a different paddle.

• Careful observation of what your students do and listening to what they tell you will prove invaluable.

▶ Personal Kit

The personal kit that people need will depend on the time of year and the length of the session. As an absolute minimum, each individual within your group will always need a buoyancy aid and footwear.

During a very warm summer, it may be sufficient for the group to wear loose comfortable clothing such as tracksuit bottoms and sweatshirt. The wind can make

Photos 10a-b *One method of introducing the canoe paddle.*

what could feel like a warm day very cold once on the water, so they would normally also require waterproof top and bottoms as an absolute minimum. These would keep the wind off but not necessarily keep the group warm if they were to capsize. If you were to go on a journey you would have to make sure that the group had sufficient clothing to allow for weather changes.

Wetsuits can be used throughout the year, are warm once the person is wet and also give protection to the wearer. They are usually combined with a cagoule, which will not necessarily stop them from getting wet but will keep the wind off.

It is essential that all those participating should be wearing some type of footwear. This is due to the risk of infection and also the possibility of glass and other foreign objects which may be in the water and could cause a serious injury. The types of footwear the group have with them can vary although usually it tends to be trainers. Always make sure that they are correctly fastened or they may fall off should they capsize. Note that chunky trainers can make it harder to enter and exit the kayak safely. Good planning beforehand here is the key. You as the coach have a responsibility to the

TOP TIP

Having spare clothing handy for those who may not have brought sufficient clothing with them will prevent problems later on in the session.

group to ensure that they have the right clothing for the session.

Photo 11 *Kitting people out.*

KITTING PEOPLE OUT

When kitting the group out it is really important to go through the equipment, how it works, how to put it on and the order in which it should be worn, starting from what to wear underneath through to the buoyancy aid and helmet. This can be shown as:

• *One:* A brief explanation about the equipment with a set of kit laid out in front of you for demonstration purposes.

• *Two:* Go through what they will need to wear underneath their wetsuits, i.e. swimming trunks, costume and, when colder, a fleece, jumper or thermal top.

• *Three:* Explanation of the wetsuit, how it works and how to wear it.

• *Four:* Then the cagoule, explaining that it is designed to keep the wind off and not necessarily keep them dry if they were to go in the water.

• *Five:* Next the buoyancy aid, explaining how it works, how to wear it and that it helps the person in the water to float and swim.

• *Six:* Lastly the helmet, if the coach decides that helmets are to be worn. Paddlers do not usually wear helmets on placid water, however with beginners it may be advisable as the risk of minor head injuries from capsizing in shallow water or hitting each other with a paddle is high.

If you were based near the water's edge where access to changing facilities was close at hand then you could go through points 1- 4, allow them to change then go through points 5 and 6. This would save time, as taking everything into the changing rooms can prove chaotic especially with children.

If you have to travel a short distance then getting them changed, going through points 1 - 6 beforehand, then travelling to the venue might be appropriate.

The other situation is where you have to travel some distance, with the group getting changed at the venue. If this is the case then it is very important to make sure that everybody has the kit checked before travelling and that you carry spares to be able to deal with any eventually.

▶ INTRODUCING THE WATER ENVIRONMENT

In the 'bad old days' it was thought that a capsize drill must be performed at the beginning of the first session. Why? Having said that the emphasis should be on fun and enjoyment, making people get wet and cold at the very beginning of the session manages to have the opposite effect, with very little purpose. This would be reinforced by going through a whole session with the group already cold, wet and becoming more so as the session progresses, with the consequent risk of hypothermia.

CAPSIZE DRILLS

A capsize drill can seem daunting and shape the way the sport is viewed as a whole. With closed cockpit boats there is a need to show them the capsize drill, but it is not necessary to get everybody wet at the start of the session. In addition, modern boats with 'keyhole cockpits' are much easier to get out of.

12

Photo 12 Water fight!

 TOP TIPS

• When doing a capsize drill, allowing the student to either get their head wet, or totally submerge in the water before the capsize drill, will help to build their confidence since they are already wet and therefore have one less thing to worry about.

• In closed cockpit kayaks a dry land drill is sufficient before getting the group on the water. However, if they are to progress they will have to master capsize drills sooner or later. If the weather is nice and the group are 'up for it', why not do one at the end of the session after getting them thoroughly wet playing games?

Sudden immersion in cold water can disorientate the student and stops them from thinking clearly. Hyperventilating can also occur, where the person keeps trying to breathe in and is unable to breathe out. This usually doesn't last very long but can be distressing to the student. If this happens it is important to remain calm and reassure the student, telling him or her to remain still until they breathe normally; only when they are calm and have regained their breathing should you attempt to place them back in their craft.

▶ Closed Cockpit Kayak

Actually going through the dry drill on the bank before getting on the water is quite sufficient. Begin with giving a full and clear explanation followed by a good demonstration near the water's edge. Start with how to enter the craft, how to sit properly and how to exit the craft. Then ask them to do the same. This makes sure that they have understood what to do, but also allows them to experience what it's like in the craft without having to get onto the water. Whilst they are all sitting in the kayaks you have the opportunity to go round checking that they are in the correct sitting position and that their legs are actually touching the footrests. This helps alleviate some of the fears that they may have.

The first steps to the dry drill are:

1. Enter the kayak, sitting in the correct position.

2. Lean forwards.

3. Then place your hands on the side of the kayak, level with your hips.

4. Explain at this stage that you would normally allow the craft to capsize, and wait until the boat is totally upturned before moving.

5. Put your knees together.

6. Then push the boat away from your legs with your hands (this is not a forward roll).

7. On exiting the kayak in deep water, brief the students to leave the boat upturned, move to the end of the kayak, hold onto the end grab, and if possible to retain their paddle.

8. If close in to the bank, to make their way to the shore.

This can be done several times on the bank beforehand if you feel that it is necessary for your group.

Before going on the water it is important to stress that they remain calm throughout if they capsize, and to wait until the kayak is totally upside down before attempting to exit.

Photos 13a-d Dry land capsize drill sequence

▶ Open Canoes And Open Cockpit Kayaks

For the open canoe, give a full explanation followed by a clear demonstration, highlighting the specific points about how to enter, sit or kneel correctly and how to exit the canoe. If an open boat does capsize, *count heads and right the upturned craft **before** dealing with any swimmers, so as to be absolutely certain that no one is trapped underneath.*

*Photo 14 Righting a capsized open boat **before** dealing with any swimmers.*

The sequence for the drill is far simpler than with the closed cockpit kayak as the canoe is easier to exit:

1. How to enter the canoe.

2. The correct sitting or kneeling position .

3. How to exit the canoe.

4. What to do if the canoe were to capsize.

Keep explanations simple and concise, and demonstrate several times.

If using open cockpit kayaks or sit-on-tops (surf skis) the sequence is the same as for the open canoe. With sit-on-tops care is needed if there are waist or foot straps fitted as there is a real risk of entrapment. For beginners, removing the straps would deal with this very effectively. Be especially careful if the conditions change as sit-on-tops tend to be very light and, when caught by the wind, can be blown away or into another member of the group.

▶ Capsize Drill Using The Swimming Pool

The pool can be a great tool for introducing paddlesport in a safe, warm environment, which can be used throughout the year. The majority of people have been in a pool before so are a lot more relaxed and comfortable. Being able to perform capsize drills here will then lead to more confidence once this progression is taken outside.

When you demonstrate the capsize drill, go through it on the side of the pool. Run through the features of the boat and the correct method of exiting. When demonstrating the capsize in the water, bear in mind that it can be difficult for the group to see what is happening. All they see is the upturned boat and then a head popping up. Going through the dry drill as outlined above works much better.

For those with special needs, the pool is a particularly valuable resource allowing easy access and warm water; this allows more time to be spent in the water. The BCU Canoe and Kayak Handbook covers the full safe use of the pool and capsize drills.

WARMING UP AND COOLING DOWN

It is generally accepted that warming up helps to prepare the body and mind for exercise. The risk of injury is greatly increased by not doing any at all. Chapter 2 explains the process and the BCU Handbook fully covers the appropriate ways in which this can be achieved.

The type of warm-ups that you choose will depend solely on the group. If for instance you have a group of young children, then incorporating the use of games to do this will work well, but with adults make the warm-up applicable, which simply means don't make fools of them.

Being able to incorporate a theme throughout the session will keep the session flowing whilst at the same time give continuity. An example of this is role-play for the warm-up, using a pizza as the theme.

For this you must have a clear understanding of warming and mobilising exercises and the sequences in which to deliver these.

SETTING BOUNDARIES

Boundaries are principally there so that students have a defined area to stay within. This is so that you as a coach can keep control of the group and avoid any hazards.

The students may have little or no experience of being in that medium so could potentially put themselves in danger if they stray too far.

The factors that you will need to take into account when defining the boundaries are:

- What are you coaching?
- Are the boundaries that you have chosen suitable?
- What are the hazards?
- Will you need to change them when using games?
- Can the group see and identify them clearly?

When choosing boundaries remember to keep to two or three markers, any more will become confusing. When there are insufficient markers to use, it is sometimes feasible to use yourself as one of the markers. This works particularly well when supervising games. If the site has very few markers then you can bring your own. You can make these by using empty 2 litre plastic drinks bottles with caps on, painted a bright colour and tied to some string, with a weight on the end. Care must be taken when putting these out as

 MAKING A PIZZA

- Find a safe working area, identifying any hazards.

- Have the group line up. Tell them that they are going to have a pizza for dinner, but that they must make it themselves first. Identify and walk to the cupboard, which is situated a little distance away, to check which ingredients are on the shelves, going several times, with each turn increasing the pace. (This is to increase their heart rate).

- Once warmed up, start introducing the ingredients needed to make the pizza base, using flour, yeast, and water. Then mix them together and knead the dough into a ball, rolling out the shape into a circle, raising it above their heads and spinning it, changing hands several times. Then reach on the shelves for the different toppings before popping it in the oven. (This is to mobilise the whole body).

- It is worth mentioning that once a warm-up has been completed then you should move straight onto the activity with little pause between.

Photo 15 *The shoreline is a natural boundary on the right and an imaginary line between the wrecked boat and the point forms the boundary on the left.*

you could become entangled in the line. If changing the activity simply pull them in and reposition them.

GETTING AFLOAT

For those people who have never been in a boat before it can be very difficult.

The following are typical access points:

On a slight incline and/or bank.

From a step or jetty, where the craft is afloat but level with the bank.

From a step, jetty or canal bank where there is a small distance to the craft.

▶ Open And Closed Cockpit Kayak

By far the easiest is from a slight incline. This allows you to line the kayaks up by the water's edge and using your hands to launch into the water. The down side of this method is erosion of the environment, so every effort should be made to avoid all unnecessary damage. Care must also be taken with the boats as the constant sliding can damage the boats.

The students observe you entering the water and copy you. This is a very simple and quick way of getting on the water. Sometimes you will be able to have the entire group lined up together by the water's edge, but this will depend on the venue chosen. If you have an assist-

ant then you can launch first whilst the assistant helps to organise the students as they get onto the water.

Access from a step where it is at or near the water-

> ## KEY POINT SUMMARY
>
> - The 'norm' is for the coach to get on the water first, partly to provide a demonstration and partly so as to provide safety cover. If you have an assistant who is a competent paddler who can tow and perform deep water rescues there is no reason why he or she can't do the demo and get on the water first.

line takes a little more time, as the students will have to place their craft in the water. The simplest way to get in is if one holds the craft and the other student gets in; they can steady each other's craft until there is only one person left. This is great for teamwork and gets everybody involved in the activity.

A good demonstration is sufficient to put this across. Gather the group round so they can all see then demonstrate the procedure.

The key points are:

Place boat in the water, making sure that your paddle is within reach.

Sit next to the kayak with your feet pointing to the bow (front) of the kayak (Photo 16a).

Lean back on one hand while your other hand holds onto the middle of the kayak at the back of the cockpit rim (Photo 16b).

Place your feet into the middle of the kayak (Photo 16b).

Transfer your weight towards the centre of the craft and slowly enter the kayak (Photo 16c).

If the students enter the boat where there is a small distance down to the boat such as a canal bank the student will step into the boat keeping their weight central, sit on the back of the cockpit and then shuffle their way into the kayak (Photos 17a-c).

Photos 16a-c Demonstrating a method of getting afloat from a step that is more or less level with the kayak.

Photos 17a-c Demonstrating a method of getting afloat from a step that is higher than the kayak.

▶ Open Canoe

Entering the open canoe is very much about keeping the weight to the middle of the canoe and then sitting/ kneeling down. This can be shown as:

Place the canoe so it is afloat in the water.

Step into the centre of the canoe and sit/kneel down.

If in a double, one person steadies the canoe while the second person steps in.

It is important to make sure that the canoe is afloat as it is difficult to launch once the canoe becomes weighted.

When getting off the water the actions are reversed for the above methods.

Photos 18a-c Demonstrating a method of getting afloat in an open canoe.

▶ GROUP CONTROL

Group control is all about being in the right place at the right time. Your students should be concentrating on the fun element of the session whilst you are providing the safety. Ensure that your group are close together so that if anybody capsizes or an incident occurs, you can deal with it quickly and effectively. Group control is just as important on the bank as it is on the water; the factors highlighted below apply to both situations.

When coaching beginners, you as the coach will need to provide the safety for the whole group as well as the coaching input. Having an assistant to provide safety cover helps enormously and allows you to con-

TOP TIP

• Before starting your demonstration, think about where to position your beginners so that they can see what you really want them to see.

centrate more on the coaching than on the safety. You have full responsibility for the session and need to keep this in mind at all times. Therefore there may be occasions when you will need to take control.

This can be broken down into the following areas:

• Your positioning

• Students' positioning

• Distractions

• Other water users

• A capsize occurs

POSITIONING

Your positioning throughout the whole session is one of the keys to a successful session.

▶ Briefings

When talking or briefing the students make sure that you have everybody's attention, so they can all hear you, and are in a position to see any demonstrations that you choose to give. Another factor that affects your positioning is the sun, so place yourself so the sun is in your eyes and not in the students'.

▶ First On Last Off

When getting on the water, the coach or another competent paddler should always be afloat before any of the students. When getting off the water the coach

Photo 19 Coach briefing group. The sun is behind them and there are no distractions behind the coach.

or a competent helper should be last. This is so that if any incidents do occur they can be dealt with quickly and effectively, as well as allowing you to control the students at all times.

▶ On The Water

When on the water, position yourself so that you can see the whole group at all times and ensure that the group are between you and the bank. This will stop anyone drifting off or putting him or herself in any immediate danger. *Remember that this will be their first time on the water* and the students will only have a limited amount of control.

Photos 20a-c Methods of positioning the group so as to retain their attention. a Sterns on beach. b Rafted up (only if the wind is light or going your way). c Paddling gently into wind so as to hold position.

DISTRACTIONS

Any distractions that are close by will draw the attention of the group. Wait for it to pass (for example an aeroplane or another water user) then continue on with the session. Avoid trying to talk over it as all the information will be lost and you will have to repeat yourself. If the distraction is static then either reposition the group so their backs are to it or move to a different working area.

OTHER WATER USERS

Being aware of water users is another factor that you will need to consider. There might be other groups using the area you intended to use. If there is insufficient room to use the same site safely then you may need to use an alternative venue. Try approaching other coaches working in the same location. It might be possible to coordinate so you can take turns to use different parts of the site. Whilst on the water, other users may enter the area you are using. Make sure that your group stay together and that you are still able to see the entire group and position yourself in the appropriate place.

CAPSIZES

If a student does capsize it is important to get them back in the craft quickly but safely. Position yourself so that you can see the whole group. Ask them to paddle so they are close together but *not rafted up;* rafts tend to catch the wind and can be blown away from you very quickly, separating the group. If it is windy get them to paddle gently into the wind to hold their position. Alternatively if the shore is close, get them to ground the bows of their boats on the shore and wait there until you have finished the rescue.

Photo 21 Those not involved in rescue made safe!

 TOP TIP

• Read the chapter on Safety and Leadership in the BCU Canoe and Kayak Handbook for a lot more detail on group control.

▶ COACHING METHODS AND STYLES

There are numerous methods and styles that you can adopt in your coaching. These are very well documented in Chapter 1. Using a variety of the different methods means that all students will understand what you are trying to put across.

ON THE WATER

You do not necessarily need to use paddles at the beginning of the session, but this will very much depend on the venue that you are using (see locations within the chapter). Everybody has at some time or other messed around at the beach, in the pool on a lilo or the large foam floats which most pools have, where they have used their hands to paddle around. Once on the water give the students time to experiment; this may be with or without paddles, allowing them time to discover how things work. They will try manoeuvring the boat so that they can talk to others within the group and also look to you for help and encouragement; choice of location really is the key here. Sitting back and observing the students whilst on the water will allow you to gather a lot of information about them.

The decision is now whether to stay in the same area or to go on a small journey. There are plus points for both of these; the advantage of going on a small journey straight away is that the group start to explore the surrounding area and practise paddling in a straight line. This method is very much about discovering how to move the boat forward and the students are active very quickly. The plus points for staying in a more confined area are that the group can gain confidence by being close to the bank.

Photos 22a-b Swapping boats

Photo 23 Chariots

 SIMPLY MESSING ABOUT IN BOATS

There is a lot to be said for "simply messing about in boats". Fun and games can be used to get people used to the way boats behave and how to stay in balance… or not!

• *Swapping boats:* If the kayaks being used have simple 'ladder' style footrests get people to raft up in pairs and swap boats. The same game can be played in canoes.

• *Chariots:* One person uses a paddle to hold the two kayaks together and sits on it, the other stands with one foot in each cockpit and paddles with the other paddle. This can also become a chariot race.

• *Stand up and paddle:* Both the crew of a tandem canoe stand up and paddle. This can also be turned into a race.

• *Raft walk:* Can be done in canoe and kayak. The boats are rafted up and, one at a time, the paddlers have to walk across the back of the raft and stand on each of the outermost boats before returning to their own boat.

▶ Setting A Theme

Setting a theme for the session can help get the information across and make the learning enjoyable. This also allows the group to link together the knowledge that they already possess.

One theme that can be used throughout a session is 'a pizza', since everybody will at some time have had a pizza and be able to associate with the shape and the various toppings. Remember that this is only one theme and there are many more that you can use. You are only limited by your imagination. (An example of this is shown for sweep strokes).

▶ Position In The Boat

From the outset of their introduction to paddlesport people should be encouraged to sit and/or kneel correctly. The correct position is sitting upright and leaning slightly forwards. To be able to do this the boat needs to be fitted out correctly for each student. Taking time to do this when introducing the boat will make all the difference.

Photo 24 Stand up and paddle

Photo 25 Over-ambitious raft walk? One at a time is more usual!

SWEEP STROKE (TURNING THE BOAT)

This stroke turns the boat and is also used to initiate turns whilst on the move.

▶ IDEAS

An example of a coaching method that can be used to introduce the sweep stroke is IDEAS :

✓ Introduction - Which is " how to turn the boat". That's all you need to say.

✓ Demonstration - Do this at normal speed, repeating it on both sides and in such a way that the students view it from different angles. Demonstrations give a 'rough coding' which gives the students an overall shape and timing. First impressions are hard to change so the first demo is the most important. It should be done without explanations.

✓ Explanation - The explanation highlights the key points. The paddle is placed at the front near the feet, the blade is just under water, the paddle is swept round drawing a letter 'C' with the arm slightly bent, the blade is removed as it meets the back of the boat. The head is looking in the direction they are going.

✓ Activity - This is where the students imitate the movement, which should be the largest part of the whole process. During the activity go round and give the student individual coaching to improve the stroke.

✓ Summary - This review of the activity is done by the coach and students.

The process can be repeated again in a loop, but this time highlighting a key point of the demonstration, becoming much more specific as to what you want the student to focus in on.

◯ KEY POINT

• 'Spotlighting' can be used as part of the explanation process. Once an initial demonstration has been fixed in a student`s mind as a rough code of the action, it can be further refined by verbal explanation and spotlighting. This involves focusing the student`s attention on a particular aspect of a 'demo' before it is performed, e.g."As I perform this sweep stroke watch my elbow". This refined version of a demonstration is sometimes referred to as modelling.

▶ Pizza Theme

Another example is introducing the sweep stroke by using a theme:

🛶 Set the scene by getting the students to imagine that they are sat in the middle of a pizza with the ends of the kayak being the edge of the pizza.

🛶 Explain that the pizza has just come out of the oven but that the edge of the pizza has been burnt, having been left in the oven too long.

🛶 Tell them they will need to scrape the outside of the pizza to get rid of all the burnt bits, starting at the front of the boat and working towards the back on both sides of the pizza.

🛶 Demonstrate to the group several times how they could do this.

🛶 Now get them to scrape the burnt bits off while you go round the group.

🛶 Go around the students giving individual feedback on how they can improve.

🛶 They can then scrape the pizza from the back of the boat to the front, again on both sides.

Your explanation of the game must be clear and concise or people will become confused, which could have safety implications.

▶ Command Style

The full sweep stroke is only really used to spin the boat on the spot, so getting the students to go round and round in circles is not very relevant. Now that they can demonstrate how to turn the boat a progression from this is to be much more controlled as to where they want the boat to point. The following 'command style' of coaching could be used here:

🛶 Set the scene for a clock face.

🛶 Pick a prominent point on the bank.

🛶 Call this 12 o'clock.

🛶 Get the students to point the front of their boats towards 12 o'clock.

🛶 Explain that when you call out a time they must then point the boat in that direction, e.g.: 3 o'clock, 6 o'clock, 10 o'clock.

🛶 When you call out the time the students must turn their boats to face that time.

🛶 Vary the practice.

KEY POINTS

• **Verbal Instructions:** Keep verbal explanations brief. Think about the key points. Rehearse in your mind what you are going to say to make sure that it makes sense.

• Make sure that what you say = what you mean = what they understand?

▶ Using Games

With beginners, giving them too much input can overload them, so having games that reinforce the coaching input are invaluable. An example of a game which reinforces this is:

Photo 26 Start position

🛶 Set three people as in Photo 26.

🛶 Explain that the person in the middle is an island and stays still. The other two's task is to touch the back of each other's boat with their paddle whilst going round, but avoiding contact with the island.

🛶 The person in the middle judges as to who touched first.

🛶 Set them off. Once they have gone one way round, play the game again but this time going the other way round.

🛶 Change round the group so everybody has a go.

With this game the activity provides its own boundaries as the students are focused round the person in the middle. The game also emphasises turning whilst on the move, as the students will need forward motion.

All the above methods are generic, i.e. can be used with any boat. All you would need to do is make the points specific to the boat.

PADDLING IN A STRAIGHT LINE

When introducing beginners, looking at paddling the boat in a straight line and correcting some common faults will be the main focus. It will certainly take more than one or two sessions to be able to coach forward paddling effectively.

▶ Open And Closed Cockpit Kayaks

There is no doubt that if you introduce people to kayaking in straight-running craft such as sea kayaks and the more stable marathon boats it will be easier for them to develop a good forward paddling action. This will stand them in good stead as they progress, whatever the discipline.

When paddling in a straight line in a general-purpose kayak, every stroke that is placed will have a slight turning effect on the boat. This means that the boat will tend to zigzag, with the stern of the boat skidding out. When beginners first start to paddle forwards they tend to start off by doing a series of sweep strokes, keeping the paddle low. Then as the boat starts to veer off they try correcting it by using a sweep stroke at the bow of the boat. As the problem is caused by the stern skidding, this just makes things worse.

The way to stop the boat skidding out is to use a stern sweep that brings the boat back in line. Some will do this naturally at the end of the forward stroke to correct the skid. Others will need to use a sweep at the stern of the boat to do this.

An example of a coaching method that can be used for paddling in a straight line is "experiential/discovery". Allow the students to become familiar with the paddle action then embark on a small journey straight away. As they are travelling along you will be able to aid them if they find it difficult by using your boat to nudge the stern of the student's boat, which will then correct the skid, allowing the boat to run straight. You may have to stay close as this could happen several times.

Another way in which you can help the kayak go in a straight line is by having a skeg fitted to the stern of the boat so it skids a lot less and runs straighter. An alternative method, if the kayaks do not have a skeg fitted, is by attaching a length of tape or cord to the stern of the boat. What this does is extend the length of the keel line, though this can have the effect of causing drag, slowing the boat down.

Another approach is to start people in touring kayaks that are designed to run in a straight line.

TOP TIP

• Beginners will find it easier to paddle a short boat in a straight line if they are paddling into wind as the boat tends to 'weather cock' into the wind. The other advantage of paddling into wind is that you can raft up and drift back to your start point if they become tired.

An example of a game that highlights forward paddling is Bulldogs:

Use a suitable site, define the boundaries and warn of any hazards.

Explain that the purpose of the game is to get from one side to the other without being caught by those who are 'on'. The way they are caught is by their boat being tagged with the paddle. Once tagged they are also 'on'; this continues till everyone has been caught.

Decide who will start by being 'on'.

Allow the group to line up then, on your signal, set them off.

Continue until everybody has been caught.

If during the session a student is still finding that the kayak will not run straight and is unable to correct the kayak, try the command coaching method using the pizza theme.

Set the scene for a pizza.

Ask the student to choose two toppings for the pizza.

Divide the boat into six sections as in the diagram, allocating two toppings to the last third of the stern on either side, say ham for one side and pepperoni for the other.

Practise this by asking the student to scrape the topping off the pizza when you call the topping name out.

Now get the boat moving and as the boat is starting to turn, call the topping.

They will now find that the stern is swept into line and they have corrected the boat.

Now when paddling in a straight line, if the student starts to veer off and is finding it difficult to recover, using the command word agreed beforehand will help correct the turn.

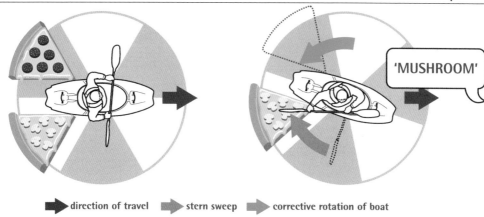

direction of travel ➡ stern sweep ➡ corrective rotation of boat

Fig. 1a Allocate your ham and pepperoni toppings.

Fig. 1b Call topping to initiate correction stroke.

▶ Open Canoes

Once the students have had the opportunity to get a feel for the canoe then you can think about how to paddle in a straight line. This will depend on the number of students in the craft, which could be from one to three. Normally if there were three they would be children. With canoes things tend to happen slower; this means that when the boat has started to turn, correcting the boat will be slower due to the length.

With beginners it is the person in the front who sets the stroke rate and initiates a turn. The person in the rear steers the canoe using a stern rudder and follows the stroke rate set by the person in the front. With beginners solo canoeing, they will usually kneel in the centre of the canoe and use a stern pry or a 'J' stroke to keep the canoe running in a straight line. There are two parts to the stroke, the power and the steering. Allowing the students to experiment will give them time to see and feel how the canoe responds.

 ## THE IMPLICATIONS OF LTPD

The LTPD pathway promotes the concept that initial sessions need to be FUN and focus on learning basic paddling and movement skills.

Someone's first paddling experience needs to be fun, it needs to get them hooked and wanting to come back for more. It must be remembered that paddlers who come into the sport will enjoy a range of its different aspects and that a 'fun' session will need to be planned based on individual preferences.

Before someone can learn complex paddling skills they need to have a basic level of movement skills. Skills such as balance, co-ordination and agility are fundamental. When working with children these movement skills are still being developed and we can use paddlesport to help them improve. Whilst working with adolescents and adults we are often trying to patch up gaps in these basics. Games and clever task setting can help the individual develop these core movement skills.

It is vital that during the first few paddling sessions good technique is developed; what is learnt at this stage will become ingrained. Practice doesn't make perfect... it makes permanent! Perfect practice makes perfect!

Paddlers need to develop quality skills with:

- Active posture.
- Balanced and co-ordinated movement.
- A feel for the movement of the boat over/through the water.
- An effective transfer of power from the body into the movement of the boat.

These qualities are fundamental to skilful paddling and need to be taught alongside any technical skill development. The concepts are not just the domain of the experts, but should be introduced gradually from the first time a person sits in a boat!

See Chapter 10 'Coaching Young Paddlers' for more details about how these principles should be applied specifically when working with young people.

See Chapter 1 'Coaching' for a basic introduction to Long Term Paddler Development.

An example that can be used for paddling in a straight line is "discovery". Allow them the opportunity to propel the canoe forwards using the method that they find works. They soon realise they will need to work together to achieve this. After a while they will find that they are able to go in a reasonably straight line.

With beginners they can sometimes find that they are not paddling together but working against each other. An exercise that can help them gain a greater understanding of working together is:

 Set the students so that they are kneeling in the centre of the canoe facing each other.

 Ask one of the students to hold the paddle normally with the 'T' grip, the other to hold the same paddle just below that of the other.

 The person who has their hand on the 'T' grip then starts to paddle forwards. The other person who is holding onto the paddle is also active in the stroke.

 They can then paddle backwards, and also swap sides.

 The students then reverse roles, with student number two holding the paddle with the 'T' grip.

This helps the students understand that they both need to synchronise their paddling so as to work as a team.

A game that gets the group paddling forwards and turning is:

> ### KEY POINT
>
> • **Command Words:** These are used to aid timing. A command word is used to trigger an action or a sequence of actions. The word or words to be used must be agreed beforehand with the student, e.g. "Left" or "Ham" means: "Use a powerful stern sweep on the left as a correction stroke".

 Use a suitable site, define the boundaries and warn of any hazards.

 You have a ball that floats.

 The aim of the game is to get the ball into the canoe that is positioned in the middle. The person in the middle is the keeper and their job is to stop the ball from landing in their canoe using their paddle to do this. They will work in two teams and the first team to reach 5 points wins. Everybody can then swap round so they are either in the middle or on a different team.

 Decide who will be in the middle and divide the rest into two teams.

 Start the game by throwing the ball away from the keeper.

Always remember that there are many different ways in which things can be done; the examples are only a selection. Be imaginative! As a coach have fun, enjoy what you do, and pass that on to the people you coach.

FURTHER READING

BCU Canoe and Kayak Handbook, British Canoe Union, Pesda Press, 0-9531956-5-1
Canoe and Kayak Games, Editor: Loel Collins, Rivers Publishing, 0-9550614-0-7

DINO HEALD

Dino is a Level 5 Coach and currently works at Plas Y Brenin.

His main interests lie in white water, freestyle and sea touring, and is also a keen mountaineer. His has paddled throughout Britain and the European Alps as well as Norway and America.

7 COACHING NOVICES

When I first began coaching paddlesport, I was thrilled to have the opportunity to introduce others to an activity which had brought so much into my life and had fundamentally changed it forever.

INTRODUCTION

I know that I am not alone in having experienced this feeling of privilege. My early teachings were to non-canoeists, mostly people on multi-activity taster holidays. My enthusiasm endured for first one and then a second summer of this type of teaching, but slowly the novelty began to wear off as I became jaded and less motivated. I hungered to teach canoeing at a higher standard; I sought out friends and colleagues who had the basics but wanted to get better and I made opportunities to teach beyond 'taster' sessions. I found my enthusiasm returned, there were new challenges to cut my teeth on and once again I was an excited coach.

Sadly I was young, impatient and misguided. Eventually I felt I had discovered all there was to learn about coaching beginners and I wanted to move on once more. I foolishly bought into the idea that the more advanced your students and the environments that you coach in, the more exciting your work and the better a coach you were. I embarked upon a journey to reach the top of the coaching ladder to teach at the most advanced level, and I remember thinking arrogantly that a day would come when I would never have to coach beginners again!

How little I knew about both coaching and life. The journey was long, but I got there only to discover that the most exciting coaching is that of beginners!

A problem with 'advanced' coaching can be that the more canoeing or kayaking experience a person has, the more deeply ingrained any bad habits are likely to be and the less a person is likely to accept they have them. They may also have been influenced by a number of different coaches, all of whom have their own strong opinions about how things should be, each leaving behind a legacy for the next coach to work with or overcome.

By complete contrast however, the beginner is a totally blank sheet of paper, "they don't know what they don't know yet" so they are a joy to coach. They trust you implicitly, not questioning where a series of exercises may be going, not comparing your approach to that of another coach. They just let you get on with moulding them into the best possible expression of a canoeist that they can be.

I've been fortunate to coach in a number of different disciplines up to advanced levels. I have seen, experienced and coached all manner of paddlers and thus witnessed the results, both good and bad, of my own and others' coaching. I've seen the pitfalls created by teaching particular techniques in certain ways, training skills in others and introducing things either too late or too early.

When a paddler has a weakness in their paddling it can be traced back to a root cause. This root cause is invariably something they either started or didn't start doing early in their paddling career. Either way the problem started when they were a beginner. The longer we leave these unchecked the bigger the problems in the future:

It is a lot harder to undo bad habits or replace them with better practice than it is to teach the correct thing in the first place. The analogy of a wall is the best way to explain it:

'A wall can only be built as high as the strength of its foundations will allow.

Eventually you get so high and realise that to go any higher the foundations need strengthening and improving. But as the wall is now quite high, it's going to be a bigger and harder job to take the wall down to get to the foundations than it would have been to put better ones in place to start with'.

So if we can give beginners a good foundation in basic techniques in the first place there will be little to put right later on and they can just keep on adding and improving. To understand what are good foundations and how best to coach them, we need to examine some of the common bad legacies that more advanced paddlers carry with them.

OVERHEARD ON THE WATER

Coach: "Ah but there's no 'right' way to do anything". (Referring to the fact that skilful application of technique involves adapting it to the individual's physiology, the context of the environment it is being used in and the use it is being put to).

Experienced Coach: "Quite right... but there are some definite 'wrong' ways of doing things". (Referring to movements that could cause injury or are demonstrably less efficient or effective).

▶ THE COMMON LEGACIES

These can be grouped into 3 areas:

1. Flawed or weak basic techniques and skills.

2. Inability to adapt.

3. Lack of self-awareness.

BAD LEGACY 1. – FLAWED OR WEAK BASIC TECHNIQUE AND SKILLS

As techniques are the basic building blocks, which become adapted and applied skilfully to become 'Skills' then it makes sense that our basic technique should be as perfect as possible. Common errors or weakness in basic techniques often stem from paddlers learning 'cheating' tactics or coping strategies. This is where a technique is learned that enables a paddler to achieve an outcome quickly or with less effort. They get results and are happy, but they haven't learned the best way or process of doing it. Left unchecked the paddler can become highly proficient at the 'coping strategy' and practises it so frequently that eventually it becomes their reaction. The paddler will still get the results they want, particularly where the environment is flat and not too testing. However when put under more pressure, coping strategies are seldom a sufficient substitute for good technique, and ultimately the technique and consequently any future skills based on it are likely to fail.

▶ Example – Edge Control In A Kayak

A beginner learns a basic version of edging and recovering an off-balance boat using their trunk, hips and legs. In an attempt to hold the boat further and further off balance, they discover that leaning backwards and laying on their rear deck seems to makes it easier. This is their 'coping strategy'. This apparent increase in performance is because the paddler's centre of gravity has been lowered by leaning backward therefore allowing them to take the boat further over before reaching the point of no return! Unfortunately, leaning back causes the trunk muscles to be far less effective at hip flicking and thus less effective at righting the boat. This is because when leaning back, the trunk muscle groups are stretched out and are not able to create the necessary hip flicking movement. However the paddler doesn't realise this because on flat water they are able to compensate for the ineffective hip flick by using their shoulder and arm muscles to pull the boat back upright with a strong support stroke or brace. The paddler continues to consolidate this 'coping strategy' through further practice and their natural reaction to being off balance becomes leaning back.

As edge control is fundamental to all support strokes, the paddler imports and adapts this technique into all support strokes, rolling and anything involving hip flicking and edge control. Whilst still on flat water they are likely to maintain a high degree of success due to support from their support strokes. They continue to be successful, unaware that brute strength is making up for the poor technique.

However if they progress on to paddling in white water and/or on the sea they will encounter problems. In these environments the water no longer has as much support as it has a broken surface and is seldom flat. They find themselves failing to support or roll in waves and rapids and consequently they swim a lot. Their coping strategy has reached the limit of its effectiveness, their upper body strength is no match for the sea or river. The only way they will upright their boat is using the powerful trunk and hip muscles, but because they are leaning back these are not able to work properly.

To progress they must go back and relearn the basic fundamentals of hip flicking, edge control and support strokes. They need to remove the instinct to lean back and instead sit upright or forward.

COPING STRATEGIES

It makes sense for the coach to identify the common coping strategies found in paddlers and, based on these, form strategies to prevent them occurring in beginners.

Here are some examples of good technique, common coping strategies, what problems they may cause and how we might proactively prevent them.

▶ Posture In Edge Control

Photo 1 Upright or forward using edge control.

🌀 *Desirable outcome:* Sitting upright or forward whilst edging/hip flicking allows trunk and core muscles to move unhindered and provide powerful, uprighting movements and effective balance control.

Photo 2 Leaning back using edge control/hip flick.

❌ *Problems:* Restricts movement - causes trunk muscles to be ineffective, puts reliance on upper body strength; weakens all forms of edging, hip flicking, stability and rolling.

◎ *Prevention:* Encourage good form and technique in early trunk and edging use, sitting upright or forward. Discourage leaning back in all stability situations.

▶ Head Position

Photo 3 Head low, towards water when rolling or recovering.

🌀 *Desirable outcome:* Keeping head low, towards the water when rolling or recovering causes good spinal 'C to C' movement, keeps centre of gravity low and allows effortless finish.

Photo 4 Head high reaching away from water when rolling or recovering.

❌ *Problems:* Head high discourages good spinal hip flicking movement and raises centre of gravity, making recovery harder.

◎ *Prevention:* Encourage head to be last thing to come out of water/upright when rolling/recovering.

▶ Positive Correction

Photo 5 *Using forward strokes to correct when paddling forward.*

✓ *Desirable outcomes:* Using only forward strokes to correct encourages the paddler toward good, fluid, forward paddling where subtle corrections occur instinctively within the cyclical pattern of movement. This helps to retain forward speed whilst correcting.

Photo 6 *Using reverse strokes to correct when paddling forward.*

❌ *Problems:* Reduces speed, discourages corrective forward paddling, can encourage stalling later on, i.e. in white water break-ins/outs or paddling out through surf.

◎ *Prevention:* Teach forward paddling corrective strokes and stern rudders at the earliest opportunity. Teach sweep strokes in forward only version and in two halves, front half (change direction) and rear half (correct direction), see BCU Canoe and Kayak Handbook. No reverse strokes early on.

▶ Forward Paddling

Photo 7 *Good forward paddling technique showing rotation, upright posture and push/pull action.*

✓ *Desirable outcomes:* Underpins everthing, early good posture and rotation here breathes the same into all other movements.

Photo 8 *Weak forward paddling technique.*

❌ *Problems:* Underpins everything! Bad posture and no rotation will undermine all their other paddling.

◎ *Prevention:* Teach and encourage good forward paddling; go for flat water journeys early in paddlers' learning, and work on forward paddling whilst on these.

▶ Trunk Rotation

Photo 9 *Good trunk rotation throughout all manoeuvres.*

Desirable outcomes: Maximises reach and keeps shoulder joints within a safe range of movement. Encourages paddlers to turn toward the new direction and look where they are heading. Encourages use of powerful trunk and core muscles, as well as dynamic rotation to help the boat turn.

Photo 10 Poor trunk rotation throughout all manoeuvres.

Problems: Limits reach and leverage of strokes. Power comes from weaker arms and shoulders, rather than from stronger trunk and torso movements; encourages dangerous strain on shoulder joints; discourages paddlers from looking where they are heading; discourages dynamic rotation and stability in turning movements.

Prevention: From the outset, teach turning the torso and presenting the chest and shoulders before using the paddle when learning strokes. Encourage rotating the body into the turn when teaching turning manoeuvres.

▶ Future Water

Photo 11 Paddler looking to the future water whilst turning.

Desirable outcomes: Getting paddlers to look where they are going encourages kinaesthetic paddling (feeling what the boat is doing) and allows the brain to collect more information and anticipate the next manoeuvres, thus smoother paddling.

Photo 12 Paddler staring at their bow whilst turning.

Problems: Discourages awareness and anticipation of water features and environment ahead of boat. Discourages kinaesthetic awareness and feel of lower body movements.

Prevention: Encourage paddlers to 'look where they are going' from the outset.

Remember that paddling is developing very fast, so we will continue to discover that what we are teaching today may be creating bad habits for tomorrow. Therefore this is an area that, as coaches, we should be continually evaluating and updating.

See if you can think of some more common coping strategies!

BAD LEGACY 2. – INABILITY TO ADAPT

Time and time again you come across paddlers who are only able to perform when they are in their boat, gear and often at a familiar venue, paddlers who don't like change, or having to do things in a different way. If you delve deep you will usually find that these paddlers were not exposed to a wide variety of changes in their early paddling experiences. They probably used the same boat, paddle and gear and associated their performance with this.

> ### KEY POINTS
>
> • Canoesport is an open skill. Open skill development benefits from exposure to a variety of experiences. This includes equipment and venues, not just what you do.

An early learner who is encouraged to try different boats and visit different places will create a broad skill base to build on and will be open to a great many experiences. They will also overcome one of the greatest bad habits, that of developing a paddling style which only reflects one type of paddling; this is very limiting.

▶ Example

A beginner joins a club that has a white water bias. They learn to paddle in a 2.5m river kayak on flat water. Consequently they develop a forward paddling style appropriate to a short boat, i.e. very limited trunk rotation and never paddling for more than a few moments before stopping. They find certain strokes difficult to learn, such as sideways strokes on the move. As these strokes seem to have no useful application in such a short boat they don't persevere.

Much later in their paddling career they develop a passion for sea kayaking, but find that it exhausts them. This is due to having a paddling style that is less effective and efficient in a sea kayak. Unfortunately due to the lack of variety in their early paddling experiences and having strongly reinforced a particular paddling style, they will have more difficulty in developing and adapting than someone who had a broader range of experiences in their early learning stages.

▶ Varied

Ultimately the broader, richer and more varied the experiences a paddler receives early on, the more adaptive and versatile they will be later. This is exactly what we do with children's education – general early on, specialising only later when sufficient breadth has been attained and a specialism has been chosen.

BAD LEGACY 3. – LACK OF SELF-AWARENESS

Skills within paddlesport fall into two main areas. There are those which are tactics and strategies based on knowledge of the activity and the environment in which it takes place, i.e. tidal planning or choosing a line down a rapid. These we call cognitive skills. Then there are the other skills, which are about physical movements and controlling your boat. These are motor or the physical skills of boat handling.

It is generally the motor skills we are most concerned with when coaching beginners, because without the ability to move around within the environment we can't take them into it to learn more about it!

If, when learning and improving motor skills, a student relies too heavily on feedback from the coach to gauge their performance, their progress can be slow and often confused - *Why?*

Answer - The coach can only say what they have seen and they may of course have missed things. They also have to communicate their observations to the learner; the learner receives this, processes it and incorporates it into the preparation for their next practice. Each of these stages has the potential for the clarity of information and relevant detail to be lost because of an individual's different interpretation. A bit like a game of 'Chinese whispers'- the end message may not be the same as the intended message.

To avoid these interpretation/translation difficulties, it is far better to encourage the learner to 'listen' to their own kinaesthetic feedback. That way they will know for themselves what the practice felt like. This route has little room for misinterpretation and encourages self-learning.

This doesn't make the coach redundant in terms of feedback. There is still a very important role for the coach. Sometimes the student's perception of what they are doing may be different to what they actually are doing. In this situation the coach can help point this out to the student.

▶ Example

A coach is trying to encourage a paddler to sit more upright when they are paddling. Based on their own internal feedback the student feels they are sitting upright. The coach however sees that the student is still slouching, though not as much as before. The coach suggests that the student tries leaning forward. When they do this, they are in fact sitting upright. The coach then explains that when the student feels upright they are actually leaning back a little and when they think they are leaning forward, they are in fact upright. The coach helps the student to 'recalibrate' their awareness of their movements.

TOP TIP

• Video playback can be a powerful tool to helping these situations, letting the student see exactly what they are doing and compare it with what their movements tell them they are doing.

▶ Self Recalibration

The earlier the student learns to do this the better a learner they will become and the more open to constant learning and improvement they will be. They will be able to adapt and modify their practice even without the coach being present because they are able to be self-aware and analyse their own movements against what they have seen others do, what they have learned recently and what they have experienced feeling before. Most people do this naturally, but the more conscious of this process we become, the better we are able to use it, and the less likely we are to practise bad habits without realising it.

Having briefly looked at the common bad habits a beginner can pick up, we should now incorporate these into the broad principles of how to coach beginners in a positive way.

▶ GETTING THEM HOOKED AND CONTEXTUALISING

It doesn't matter how good your coaching may be, if your students don't come back for more they aren't going to get any better and turn into a paddler. As we know, paddlesport can be a very frustrating activity to learn as a beginner and certainly not the most exciting if it takes place at the same flat water venue every time. People will soon tire of practice, exercises and playing games unless they see a purpose to boating that justifies all the effort involved in getting better at it.

One of the most exciting and attractive aspects of kayaking and canoeing is journeying, exploring places and seeing views that are unique to being in a very small manoeuvrable craft. It's possible to give beginners, even with very limited abilities, regular tastes of this. This will keep them motivated, give them an idea of what it's all about and hopefully help them to catch the paddling bug!

The double bonus is that journeys and exploring allow newly acquired techniques and skills to be adapted and applied in a variety of different ways and environments, leading to a broader skill base.

The triple bonus is that if recently acquired techniques are used and applied appropriately in the correct environmental context, understanding and retention of these is far higher. It makes total sense that if you learn something new but don't apply it in its intended way, you won't understand it as well. If you just practise it because that's what your coach says you need to do, then its application, context and use in the intended environment has to be imagined. This is far more likely to lead to the technique being practised in an abstract and often misunderstood or incorrect way, one that doesn't help its future use in the correct environment.

In contrast, applying new techniques and skills in the appropriate environment and context instantly cements their place and use in the paddler's mind. The retention is far greater because their brain has understood and personally experienced an application for it. They understand the whys and hows of it and they are using it in response to the real environment... the environment is doing the teaching for the coach, as long as the coach has chosen the correct environment to start with.

▶ Example

The Stern Rudder. This can be learned relatively quickly and then practised repeatedly with games etc., but it is not contextualised or applied in a varied way.

If you went for a journey on a canal, or narrow river you would use this again and again to go through narrow gaps. Alternatively, on an open lake trip if you had to paddle downwind (the wind on students' backs) they would have to use the stern rudder to keep the boat running straight against the wind and any possible swell. They would also learn how to use the rudder as a continuation of a forward power or sweep stroke, thus breaking down the barriers between stroke boundaries!

TOP TIP

• If you have paddled into the wind to make it easier for a group of novices to paddle in a straight line and practise their forward paddling, what better way to get back to your start point than to introduce the stern rudder and then ask them to practise it in context, i.e. running downwind?

KEY POINTS

• If you have introduced the stern rudder using the IDEAS model, remember that the A for activity should be the largest component. As well as practising by using games that involve using the stern rudder, try and include as many activities that use the stroke in context, such as steering the boat through narrow gaps and steering the boat whilst travelling downwind.

This kind of practice is more natural and occurs with less conscious effort than in a formal coaching session, where it is often practice for practice's sake. You can't get better at a physical activity without doing it, so what better way of doing it than go on a journey?

That said, games also have an important part to play:

1. They are fun.

2. If all you have is a small pond, a journey may not be an option, in which case make your games many and varied.

So incorporate journeys into your sessions and where possible take your students to places that are new to them so the fascination of exploration and discovery distracts their attention from the process of paddling, meanwhile contextualising learning and improving without even being aware of it.

▶ FAMILIES OF STROKES

If you read the Star Test syllabi or one of the many technique books on canoesport, you would be led to believe that there are a vast number of different strokes to be learned. Each of these appears to be an isolated 'paddle waggle' that does a specific thing, a stand-alone stroke of its own rather than a variation of another. Reality is that most strokes have far more similarities between them than differences. When we paddle without thinking, our strokes tend to blur and blend together making it very hard to isolate and identify individual named strokes.

The point of isolating and defining strokes is meant to be an aid to learning and coaching to present a logical structure and progression and to allow coaches to explain specific techniques in isolation. However this tends to present a bewildering number of strokes, which is often an obstacle to most students.

The danger is that, rather than see the similarities between strokes, learners see the differences and in doing so miss the fundamentals of boat manoeuvring. Coaches may likewise see and teach them as different, almost unrelated strokes and techniques, which adds to the difficulty and complexity of learning. The learner also perceives strokes as having one definitive version to aspire to, rather than a number of subtly different versions, all of which are acceptable in the right circumstances. This is best illustrated through the so commonly heard question: " Is my 'so and so' stroke correct?"

All of this leads the paddler away from fluid paddling, and toward a more robotic, mechanical style where paddling appears to be a series of pre-organised sequences put one after the other, rather than a fluid movement.

It's important to remember that paddlesport takes place in an extremely open environment, so it is inappropriate to encourage pre-organised sequences or versions of strokes. Instead they should be adaptable and have a myriad of applied interpretations.

It is better to nurture good quality basic movements that move the boat in all directions and keep it upright. We can then progressively apply and adapt these to an infinite number of situations. We will end up with a far greater range and variety of effective 'strokes' in this way... they just won't all have specific isolated versions with accompanying names.

▶ How Can We Do This?

We can take all of the traditionally isolated 'strokes' (both canoe and kayak) and, based on the way in which they work, trace them back to a basic version from which a beginner can develop them. By starting with a basic movement or stroke and developing it into other versions, confusion is reduced, progression is more gradual through adaptation and we remove the perception that there are so many different new strokes to master. Probably of most importance is that we encourage the students to understand the dynamics of how and why a boat reacts the way it does through experimentation and personal discovery, thus having much greater ownership, understanding and belief of what they have learned.

The other plus side is that this requires little in the way of complicated explanations from the coach as each version is a small step or adaptation from another previous one, consequently making coaching far easier and less problematic.

THE FAMILIES

A natural, logical learning progression can be found within each stroke family... but what are the families?

Each one of us may take a slightly different approach to these families. It is important for the coach to understand the interrelationship between the strokes, and based on that, establish their own families and progressions.

As an example here is the way I view them:

• Propulsion - is paddling forward and backwards.

• Steering/Turning - is sweep strokes and stern rudder.

• Sideways - all sideways movement and bow rudders, cuts and jams.

• Balance - edging, leaning, supporting and bracing.

STEERING/TURNING

Steering/Turning includes what people would commonly call sweep strokes, but broken into two versions, the bow sweep, which is a 'new direction' stroke (first half) and the stern sweep which is a 'correction' stroke (last half) as described in the Basic Strokes section of the BCU Canoe and Kayak Handbook. In addition 'stern rudders' fit in here as they are little more than a correction 'sweep' stroke that has reached the back of the boat. I teach them as exactly this and refine them later. All other strokes which have an effect on directional control fall in the sideways family.

▶ Coaching Forward Paddling Through Steerage

The steerage strokes are usually the first ones people learn and they underpin most other strokes, techniques and manoeuvres. They are also an inherent part of forward paddling because of the correction element. A beginner trying to paddle in a straight line will be spending more time correcting than actually driving the boat forward. We all know this, so why not concentrate on coaching corrective steering strokes before getting people to work on forward paddling!

Remember the point about applying strokes correctly and contextualising them? Well, sweep strokes are a classic example of how people don't do this!

Typically sweeps are introduced as one long stroke from one end of the boat to the other. This will turn the boat round on the spot, something we all need to do from time to time, but not the most frequently used application of the sweep. What we far more regularly do is use it as two very separate halves: correction, back half, or new direction, front half.

When a sweep is introduced and taught as a going round in circles stroke, it has exactly that effect… people perfect going round and round, but they don't learn to stop the spin and point in a particular direction. Pointing in a particular direction is the application of virtually all sweep strokes usage whether that be correcting back to where you were heading, or steering away to point in a new direction. Spinning round in a circular pattern is a process of using a sweep, it is not outcome or goal, therefore we should concentrate our coaching and exercises on the applied use of the strokes and their intended outcomes.

In practice this is very simple. People are introduced to the corrective and new directive versions of sweeps and are given the opportunity to practise a basic working version of this. Earlier on I highlighted the pitfalls of encouraging reverse strokes as correction, so at this stage all the directional control is applied through forward strokes. You then coach its application through various games. Here are some examples:

Photo 13 The Clock Game

EXERCISES

• *exercise one:* Using physical markers, or the analogy of a clock face, students use the new strokes to turn the boat to point in specific directions. The directions are called out by the coach. When they have turned the boat they must hold it still, pointing in the new direction.

A by-product of this game is that the stern rudder position is 'accidentally' discovered when corrective strokes finish at the stern, thus beginning to establish the blending of rudders with corrective sweep strokes. You will find that if you spend ten minutes playing this game the positive effects on forward paddling are immense - students will correct naturally with little prompting. They will be using appropriate corrective sweeps and stern rudders to maintain a direction.

• *exercise two:* Later on you can get students to use the new direction sweep as well as the correction by paddling around buoys or markers or in the shape of a box or triangle, etc.

SIDEWAYS

Sideways is by far the biggest family of strokes. It is all strokes that displace the boat sideways. It includes all forms of drawing, but also hanging draws and turning strokes that use a drawing effect like the bow rudder. For the canoeist this family is twice as large because of the 'pry' and the 'jam'. I will explain the sideways family from the kayak perspective first of all. The canoe strokes follow the same logical pattern but twice, once for draw and once for their pry/jam cousins.

TOP TIP

• A coach I know thinks of the family of strokes I call 'sideways strokes' as 'Vertical Paddle Strokes'. Whatever works for you!

▶ Draws

The basic stroke from which all the kayak sideways family stems is the 'draw', the basic version being performed without an underwater recovery. All the other strokes develop from this because they are a draw

KAYAK SIDEWAYS FAMILY

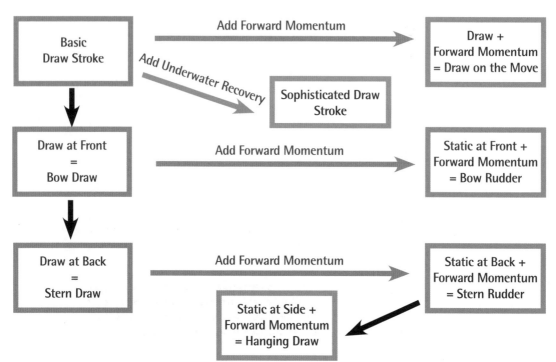

Fig. 1 The kayak version of the Sideways family

placed either further forward or back to get a different effect, or they are held statically whilst the boat's forward momentum creates the draw effect on the boat like air does on an aeroplane wing.

The flow charts shows one way of viewing the similiarities and how the strokes develop out of the basic version.

For the ease of communication I have used the conventional names for these strokes, however when coaching beginners, I avoid the use of traditional names and also the approach of presenting each of the above 'pigeon holed' strokes as a defined isolated version. They don't need to know the name of the stroke to be good at it, they just need to know what it can do for them and then to begin practising it with context and application.

Names can be introduced later as a reviewing tool as they progress and precise terminology becomes a help rather than a hinderance.

CANOE SIDEWAYS FAMILY

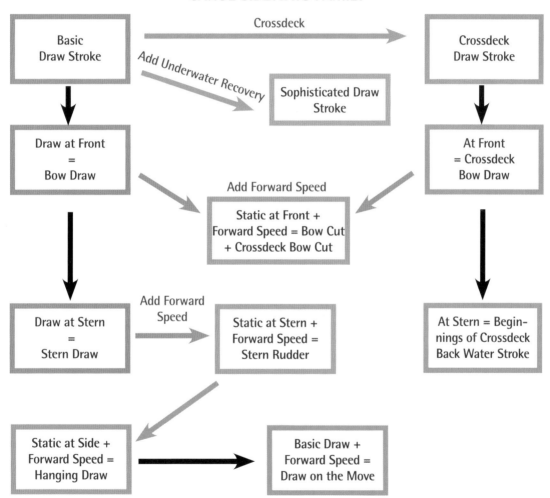

Fig. 2 The canoe version of the Sideways family

▶ The Pry Cousins

Draws are all strokes that move the boat toward the paddle. Pries and their static version, 'jams', move the boat away from the paddle. A jam is really a running pry positioned away from the centre of the boat to encourage a dramatic turning effect.

THE PRY COUSINS

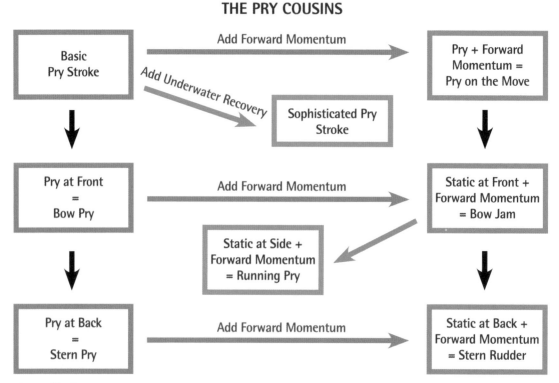

Fig. 3 The Pry cousins

▶ Coaching Tactics For Sideways Family

All these strokes either move the boat, or part of the boat toward the paddle or away from it. If we adopt this approach of 'growing' each stroke from a version before it, as in the previous diagrams, the students understand that there is no definitive position for the paddle, but that by subtly changing its position and feathering we can get different results. It is important to encourage this by getting students to experiment with positioning throughout their practice and to be able to say what the effects of the different positions are.

There are some strokes that fall into the Sideways family that people often find the most difficult to both coach and learn, for example the hanging draw or bow rudder.

There are three probable reasons for this:

1. Many of these strokes require the boat to have a certain degree of forward momentum to work. Student practice is undermined by the inability to move consistently forward with enough speed to engage with the stroke.

2. When the boat has forward momentum and the paddle is entered into the water to initiate a stroke, the shock or resistance of the water is often too much for the learner to control and this undermines success.

3. The kinaesthetic feel of a bow rudder, hanging draw, bow jam, etc. done well cannot be explained – it has to be experienced. Once a student has felt this, it is easier for them to replicate it. However getting that first time experience is difficult.

All three of these problems can be reduced greatly by adopting a common principle when coaching Sideways displacement strokes:

Get the student to concentrate on the sideways stroke and you create the forward momentum – for them!

The principle for this relies on the student positioning themselves, or being positioned by the coach through direct physical guidance. Momentum is then applied by either pushing or pulling the boat. This requires either being out of your boat, or getting the students to work paired up, one in a boat, one doing the positioning, pushing and pulling.

BOW RUDDER

• *one:* Get the student to present the paddle as if they were going to draw the boat sideways.

• *two:* Adjust their position to be appropriate for a bow rudder turn.

• *three:* Give their boat a big shove forward. *Voila! You have a bow rudder being experienced.*

• *four:* The student now knows what it feels like. Next time they can be shoved out and *slice*, not stab, the paddle into position, thus increasing fluidity and reducing stalling and loss of control.

 HANGING DRAW

• *one:* Attach a throw line to the bow of the boat.

• *two:* Get the student to present the paddle as if they were going to draw the boat sideways.

• *three:* Push the student away until they reach the full stretch of the line.

• *four:* Pull them slowly in toward you. They can adjust and experiment with the position of the blade as much as they want because the boat is not slowing down.
Voila! You have a hanging draw being experienced.

• *five:* The student now knows what it feels like. The next time the student is pulled in they can *slice* the paddle, not stab it, into position, thus increasing fluidity and reducing stalling and loss of control.

N.B.: Because of the sideways movement the line puller should ideally move sideways along the bank, staying in front of the boat, otherwise the line will affect the sideways movement too much.

All manner of sideways strokes (and the stern rudder) that require forward momentum to work can be introduced this way. It has the advantage that students learn to feel pressure build up on the blade and adjust to it, because they are not distracted with getting the boat moving forward. They can concentrate on the new element of the stroke and add the momentum themselves later when they are ready.

Another advantage is pairing students up to work in collaboration with one another (see coaching methods).

Photos 14a-b Bow Rudder exercise

Photos 15a-b Hanging Draw exercise

Very little positioning problems occur because direct physical guidance removes complicated and misunderstood explanations and demonstrations. However, if you have a very visual learner, a demo will be a good idea and later on, when it comes to refining the movement, explanation will come into its own (see next chapter). By using this holistic approach to strokes we can significantly speed up the learning curve with an increase in performance and more skilful, fluid and adaptive paddling in the long term.

 KEY POINT

- When coaching this way it is important to select the appropriate method of propulsion - there is no point in pulling a boat on a throw line if you want a student to experience a turning stroke, as their bow will be pulled back on line away from the intended direction!

BALANCE

Balance is a family not based so much on strokes, but on the technique of balancing the boat using the trunk and hip muscles - *essentially edging and leaning*.

We have previously discussed why it is important to introduce correct balance control early in a paddler's career. What I will do now is talk about how.

▶ Coaching Tactics For The Balance Family

The biggest obstacle to learning with this family is the fear of getting wet or being upside down. Most people are not relaxed enough and are too stiff to improve, because they don't want to get wet. This makes sense because the very reason we are learning these strokes is to avoid getting wet in the first place!

To reduce the impact of this we should reduce the environment to be less intimidating. This could mean using a pool to introduce balance strokes, or use shallow areas of an outdoor environment.

I typically use the latter, choosing an area shallow enough that should someone go too far and begin to capsize, they can put their paddle on the bottom before they go all the way over. An alternative in good weather is to get people to work in pairs with one partner stood in the water to right a capsized student (see BCU Canoe and Kayak Handbook).

All of these approaches increase effectiveness of a coaching session because students are less intimidated.

Another interference connected with not getting wet is the body's natural reaction to keep the head above water at all costs. This results in many people rearing their head away from the water when being near, or off balance.

As previously discussed, this can create a really bad habit in the long term.

Photo 16 Rearing their head away from the water when being near, or off balance.

To prevent this from establishing itself as a bad habit, we must encourage students from the outset to use a 'C' shape with the trunk and neck when edging and balancing.

When done correctly this gives maximum control and power from the trunk, and looks like this:

This equates to head away from the water whilst still in balance and head toward the water as you upright the boat.

Photos 17a-b 'C to C' - Head away from the water whilst in balance and head toward the water as you upright the boat.

Below is one method I use to introduce edging:

INTRODUCING EDGING

• *one:* Begin teaching edging by getting students to do this 'C to C' action slowly on the land, sat down out of their boats. This way it is slow and controlled, the 'below the deck' action is visible and, most of all it's definitely dry!
During this, focus on the use of the outer buttock as a point of contact.

• *two:* They can then transfer it to their boats on the land, or go directly to the water. Persistently reinforce the head movement. Focus on the outer buttock and also upward lift on the knees.

• *three:* Once people have this basic edging action get them to find the maximum amount of edge they can hold without falling in; this is their edge score of 3.

• *four:* If a flat boat is scored zero, then they should be able to find edge score 1 and 2.

• *five:* Now we can play a game where the coach calls out left or right followed by number 1,2,or 3 and the students have to hold that edge until a new number is called out.

In a similar way to the sweep stroke exercise, this gives a controlled application to edge control, rather than alternate edge to edge wobbling which does not encourage holding an edge.

All this is done without a paddle. Without the complications of paddle movements it makes it easier for the beginner to understand the basics of boat balance. It is then a simple progression to add the paddle as a point of contact on the water, which allows the trunk to flick away from it, first in a down-pushing position (low brace) and then for more dramatic loss of balance by hanging the body from under the paddle (high brace).

Introducing balance and hip flicking without the paddle allows the emphasis to be on posture, co-ordination of body parts and development of a powerful side bend in the trunk. It also discourages reliance on upper body strength when paddles are introduced.

It is the co-ordination of the head and the hips coupled with a powerful side bend that are the essential foundations of good supporting and rolling technique.

So often when coaching rolling it is these two ingredients which are missing or weak that are the obstacle to success. The stability family starts with edging, evolves through supporting, to finish with rolling as the extreme version of a high brace. Also included is the relationship between edging and leaning.

Photo 18a Edging on land.
Photo 18b Edging in the boat without a paddle.
Photo 18c Edging with paddle.

▶ Dynamic Balance

As the boat speed increases with forward or backward momentum, it is possible to substitute edging (with an upright body) for leaning the boat and body together. Many coaches refer to this as static and dynamic balance.

We can begin coaching dynamic balance very soon after students have successfully completed the balance exercise. The following exercises could be used:

DYNAMIC BALANCE

• *exercise one:* Students to paddle a straight line holding edge, different edge scores on both sides.

• *exercise two:* Students paddle large diameter circles holding their boat on an edge score throughout. Paddle circles with different scores on both sides.

• *exercise three:* Paddle a 'figure of eight' course holding the boat on edge and changing it for the different turns. Try different scores.

• *exercise four:* Get the boat up to maximum speed and then, using a new direction sweep, carve a turn using edge. Use different scores.

• *exercise five:* Do the last exercise again, this time edge the boat as much as possible.

Photo 20 Dynamic balance Exercise 2

Photo 21 Dynamic balance Exercise 5

During this last exercise students should discover that they have exceeded their static score of 3. This is because speed gives you more stability and therefore allows you to go further over before the point of no return - dynamic balance!

Balancing then needs applying and contextualising, perhaps within journeys, or polo. Polo is a great activity as it usually involves more unpredictable off-balance opportunities than most other things, making people react and stay upright.

Just make sure that coping strategies don't begin to creep in. This may happen as the focus will move from process (good technique) to outcome (winning and not capsizing).

If a student is able to achieve this level of performance using good trunk control then they will have an excellent foundation for their future paddling.

Photo 19a Static balance
Photo 19b Dynamic balance

THE IMPLICATIONS OF LTPD

The LTPD pathway promotes the concept that novices need to focus on developing quality skills and that this is best done by experiencing a wide variety of craft, venues and situations that are individually suitable.

The art of successful paddling lies in the paddler being able to create a union between themselves, the boat, paddle and the water around them, to such a degree that to an onlooker these components look as if they are working together as one. In order to achieve this, a strong connection between the paddler and their boat, paddles and the water is vital. Imagine a pony carrying a heavy load; the pony will move far more freely if the weight of the load is well balanced and attached firmly to the pony in the right place, rather than being loose and shifting. Now replace the pony with the boat, and you, the paddler for the load! The goal is to balance your weight in your boat, in a manner that allows you to follow the motion of the boat, and become part of it. If your weight is not centralised (either forward/back or side/side) the motion of the boat, its balance and flow are severely compromised.

The connected paddler has not simply outfitted their boat correctly, but:

• Has active posture, allowing the body to move freely, with the muscles being sensitive to movement and being quick to act.

• Is balanced, giving the body the freedom to generate powerful and efficient movements, allowing the paddler to react to the movements of the boat/paddles around them, and has co-ordinated efficient movements.

This allows the paddler to feel and anticipate the movement of the boat through the water and efficiently transfer power from the body to create movement of the boat. The paddler can perform strokes that generate power, turning and stability, control the speed, angle, edge and trim of their boat, and move efficiently and economically, resulting in the controlled and efficient movement of the boat to achieve a desired outcome.

These qualities are fundamental to skilful paddling and need to be taught alongside any stroke or technical development. The concepts are not just the domain of the experts, but should be introduced gradually from the first time a person sits in a boat. The more varied a paddler's experiences the better these concepts will be developed and the easier it will be for them to develop complex specialist skills as they progress.

See Chapter 10 'Coaching Young Paddlers' for more details about how these principles should be applied specifically when working with young people.

See Chapter 1 'Coaching' for a basic introduction to LTPD.

► BRINGING IT ALL TOGETHER

Ultimately you can take all the best coaching methodology there is and apply it to your students, but there are certain things that are essential for your students to be able to learn.

BOATS AND GEAR

At this level where students are trying to become paddlers, their boats and paddles need to be sized and fitted appropriately for them. It is very hard to learn about balancing a boat if you cannot reach the footrests! Take the time and effort to help students gain the most from their efforts and your coaching – make sure they have a good fit in their boat and their paddle is appropriately sized for them and tell them why this is so.

TEMPO AND ANIMATION

By tempo and animation, I mean the changes in pace and flow of the session. This includes the variety of different approaches used, e.g. some paired up work, some individual, some group. Try changing location within a session even if there are no environmental benefits, it will still be a change for your students. Within a whole session try contrasting static sessions with short journeys to a different location for another static session. Some of the paired work involving pushing and pulling boats gets people out of their boats and again adds variety. All these changes keep the students' minds alert and interested, it also makes the session more interesting for you. It is incredibly important that beginners are having fun and learning experiences are enjoyable. This may sometimes mean compromising on coaching ideals to maintain student excitement and your session's tempo and animation.

FEEDBACK AND REINFORCEMENT

Throughout all your coaching remember to reinforce good practice with praise and explanations of why it is good. At a beginner's level this is more important than corrective feedback in many ways.

▶ SUMMARY

Now after many years of coaching, my personal mission is to strive to find the perfect progression and structure from novice through to early improver, helping the paddler to create a sound foundation so they are able to pursue any avenue within paddlesport without hinderance, bad habits or coping strategies that will have to be undone later. This is a noble misson to have, but my parting thoughts are these:

Left to their own devices, most people will work out for themselves how to manoevure a boat forwards, backwards, stay upright and generally go where they want. A coach can speed up this process, and make it more efficient. Students can only progress at their own pace. Sometimes they under or over-estimate how fast that pace is and the coach can help them gain a more realistic view, but the pace must be dictated by the students' needs rather than the coach's desires.

The most effective thing a coach can do is to help each student find their own personal way of boating, whilst being mindful of not letting them acquire bad habits!

A coach does not give a student knowledge and skills, the student ultimately learns the skills themselves through direct personal experience. Your job as the coach is to provide the student with useful feedback and create the right environment in which this process can happen.

In essence this environment should be:

- Stimulating/challenging
- Fun
- Contextual/applied
- Varied

BOB TIMMS

Bob began kayaking in north-east London through school and, spurred on by the guidance of Clive Atkins, a local Level 5 Coach, he has never looked back.

Bob is a Level 5 Inland Kayak Coach and is also qualified in sea, canoe and as a raft guide. He has kayaked in South America, Asia, Europe and Australasia with some of his more bizarre achievements including a Bronze at the first (and probably last!) World Sea Kayak Championships and kayaking from Folkestone to Athens!

He's worked full time in the outdoors since leaving school, including managing Canolfan Tryweryn and instructing at Plas y Brenin.

Bob now lives permanently in Briancon, in the southern French Alps, working as a coach and International Mountain Leader for amongst others PGL, Plas y Brenin and himself as 'Bob Timms Boating and Trekking'.

8 COACHING IMPROVERS

I joined the school canoe club in late autumn. Being London and winter we went to swimming pools mostly, 3 nights a week at times. I learned to go backwards and forwards (but not very far) and to roll. I learned to go sideways and to roll a different way. I learned to do fast turns and another kind of roll. I learned hanging draws and support strokes. By February I could do heaps in a kayak, I was mustard, I could get to every part of that 15m pool in milliseconds and had a different type of roll for each square metre of its surface, but I was bored. I had all these skills, but nothing exciting to do with them.

On cue, our coach took us to a different pool, then another, each time with different boats to use. Then a pool so big it had a slalom course set up on it. Next came a rolling competition, followed swiftly by a trip on a lake (spring had sprung). Then during the next few months we were all over the place. Weekends away, weeks away, summer evenings paddling down the Lea Navigation Canal chasing rats along chains, first night paddle camping on an island, and the highlight... my very first time on the sea, the classic trip around The Stacks on Anglesey!

Looking back, my coach did an awesome job. Just at the point when my friends and I had mastered the basics and were about to lose interest, he picked us up and guided us through an amazing journey of development and progress. He improved our paddling no end, the proof being what we achieved, and all so effortlessly as far as we were concerned. My fading memory only holds onto the exciting highlights, but I know for a fact that there were endless training ses-sions in between, developing, learning and improving and I hope - no, I am sure - the experience for Clive was as rewarding as it was for us.

That's what comes with the territory of coaching improvers. You take a bunch of people who are perched on the cusp and, handled the wrong way they could be leaving the boating, but led the right way hooked for life!

▶ WHAT'S THE DIFFERENCE?

So what is so different about coaching a novice paddler to coaching an improver? That's someone who has moved on from the beginnings of paddling, but is not yet a Jedi. Not such a big difference in terms of coaching surely? Just a case of being a few steps further on, so why should we need a different approach?

Well those few steps further on are a critical few steps. There are a number of reasons why we should approach the improver differently. Let's take a closer look why.

REASONS TO BE DIFFERENT PART 1 – NO LONGER A BLANK CANVAS!

The novice paddler is a blank canvas. They have no preconceived ideas about how to paddle or how to learn to paddle. They are a joy to teach because we can start from scratch, coaching, developing and shaping them into our personal ideal of a paddler. Never having to deal with the legacies of other coaches' teaching. We are free to put in place all those perfect foundations for their future paddling career, avoiding short-cut coping strategies and all the while giving them a fun time! The novice is fresh clay on the potter's wheel, a blank sheet of canvas on the easel.

The improver on the other hand comes to us with a history that needs researching. They may be self-taught, taught by friends, family, a centre, a club, one coach, or twenty different coaches. They may have never performed a capsize drill, but be used to wearing a spraydeck, or have never paddled outside of a swimming pool, though they can hold their own in a polo match! They are most definitely not a blank canvas. Someone has already set to work shaping and outlining. But do they have good technique? Are the right foundations in place for you to build on? What teaching approaches have they come to expect?

This means there are far more unknowns for us to deal with than with novices, and for us to do the best job we can in coaching our improvers we need to understand who we are coaching, what we need to coach and their history, right down to the nitty-gritty bad habits they might bring with them.

So before we can coach them we need to both know our paddlers' abilities and get to know them as people - *Observation*.

Then depending on what we find out it may be that before we can go forward we may have to go back and

repair a few foundation stones that have been put in back to front or left out all together - *Revisiting foundations and weeding your garden*.

REASONS TO BE DIFFERENT PART 2 – MOTIVATION AND INTEREST

Novices do not know what they do not know yet. They are keen to learn to paddle though they do not know where it will lead, or have any idea of how difficult it may be. We all know that the first few hours are frustrating but get through those and the apparent advances seem huge. Suddenly the novice is motivated by their quantum leaps in performance .

"Yesterday I couldn't stay upright or go in a straight line. Today I managed to go for two hours up the lake and visited an island, I'm great!"

Throughout the novice stage the results come thick and fast, learning the basic crude working models to go in any direction, stay upright and maybe even get themselves back upright! Games are fun, it seems that the bar is never too high for them and if they do occasionally fail at something, well they are so new to the sport, one can't expect them to get everything right!

A little further down the line though and things begin to look and feel different.

They've been going at this a while now, and to be honest they don't feel that they are able to do a great deal more than they could weeks ago. The steep performance curve has flattened out and with that the rewards of new successes on a daily basis have disappeared. Consequently their interest and motivation is on the wane and so will their participation in paddling if we as coaches don't make the right decisions.

This is by no means unique to paddling. At this stage in most sports you'll find the greatest drop-out rate; check out the amount of second-hand sports gear on E-bay described as 'little used'. However what tends to increase this effect in paddlesports is that up until now it is more likely that the learning has taken place in the same or a similar environment and probably involves doing similar things. For example:

The club, group or centre only has access to one or two flat water venues and due to transport/safety/time/qualification/other constraints or sometimes lack of imagination and awareness, the same paddling sessions keep on happening at the same venues. The improvers get bored and under stimulated. At this stage in other sports there are often natural progressions which distract from this performance plateau - informal competition, sparring in martial arts, matches in racquet sports. The environment may be more easily changed to create a new stimulus and challenges, such as in skiing choosing steeper slopes. However in paddling we often don't have those natural opportunities and it all falls to the coach to make up for this.

So the coach faces a big challenge in keeping the improver interested and motivated. This will require a greater level of sophistication in *goal setting* than was necessary with novices and a greater awareness of medium to longer term *planning and strategies* to be mindful of where you are heading with your coaching.

REASONS TO BE DIFFERENT PART 3 – FOSTERING SELF-DISCIPLINE, SELF-COACHING AND INDEPENDENCE

At some stage the beginner has enough basic technique and foundation skills to start to become independent of the coach and a good coach will encourage this, realising the pitfalls of creating a coach-dependent student. However it is now that all the hard work of the early coach's influence is most at risk! Why? Because it is now that the paddler is competent enough to go away and find others to paddle with.

Up until now all their paddling experiences happened with a coach around to keep them safe. All the while the coach was ever-present, reminding, teaching, shaping and demonstrating good practice, technique and form. But now the paddler is more frequently without this support and all too easily performance can begin to slip especially if the other paddlers around them don't model the best techniques themselves.

It is also now that the paddler has enough skill and basic mastery of the craft to start really enjoying canoesport through exploration, journeys, races, matches, socials, trips and all manner of great opportunities afforded by our small and versatile craft. And throughout all these great exciting times the paddler is less interested in how they are paddling and much, much more interested in what they are taking part in! Thus the acquisition of new skills and the maintenance of foundation skills risk being neglected. Bad habits can easily appear, undermining future performance.

So a good coach would do well to encourage their paddlers to be aware of this and to foster a degree of self-discipline and self-awareness so that when they paddle independently of the coach, the coach's teaching continues even though they are not there. If this happens the paddler will continue to progress unhindered by bad habits and lazy technique.

Achieving this is easier said than done. Some students love to explore their own understanding of paddling and their own performance, really buying into the whole concept of making the coach ultimately redundant. Others however look to the 'teacher-student relationship' as being one way only, the teacher providing all the answers and the student only learning when the teacher is there!

The coach has yet another challenge - raising awareness of *internal feedback* and encouraging *independent self-discipline.*

REASONS TO BE DIFFERENT PART 4 – MANAGING THE STUDENT-COACH RELATIONSHIP

Coaching improvers is further complicated by a psychological transition which often takes place between novice and improver. Novices have little experience with which to evaluate or question the teachings they receive, so they will hang on every word and demonstration, eagerly trying to emulate the coach, who is of course to them, the font of all knowledge!

Soon the student paddler learns more and more and changes from being out of control to in control. With that their self-image as a paddler changes too. Exit stage left the keen learner… enter stage right the over-confident paddler who thinks they have no need of a coach any more. Here lies the problem of the student having enough understanding to achieve current outcomes, but not enough understanding to accept or realise that it is still worth improving the way they are doing it, and that they still have a lot to learn.

Another complication is that the gap between ability levels in groups of improvers can vary massively. Novices' ability gaps are often small, and are frequently changing as people learn, and so the gaps go relatively unnoticed amongst a group. By the time they have become an improver there is much more scope for the differences in ability to show up, and students themselves are much more aware of the differences. This can lead to frustration on the student's part, either from being the worst in the group and feeling bad, or from being the best and being held back by others.

Add to this the unrealistic wants that students sometimes have and you find yourself staring into a volatile cocktail of egos and expectations!

So as a coach you will find yourself dealing with this regularly - *managing student expectations* is an important coaching competence.

REASONS TO BE DIFFERENT PART 5 – LESS FROM SCRATCH, MORE BY ADAPT

This is the obvious one, which at the same time is very subtle! By using the word 'improver' we are suggesting that the person is not learning from scratch, but is improving what they already have… building, adapting and developing, but not really starting from zero. Most of us would accept that in principle, but how about in practice!

By this I mean that we should never have to present anything from a complete new beginning. Every skill and technique that they have yet to experience, learn or discover in a boat should be able to be coached from an existing skill or technique! They should already have all the foundation skills!

In some circumstances this may be as simple as taking an existing skill and using it in a new environment where it will naturally adapt and evolve into a more sophisticated and skilfully applied version of itself. For example:

Some paddlers can keep their boat running straight on a flat windless environment. They have also learned to use a stern rudder. If we now take them out onto a windy lake with a long fetch they will slowly adapt their paddling to become skilful in windy conditions and eventually to use a rudder within their forward paddling, particularly when running downwind. This may even evolve into what some people call a 'keyhole' stroke where the forward power stroke sweeps out into the latter half of a sweep and finishes as a stern rudder.

In other circumstances it could be as complicated as taking a collection of techniques or skills that the student would think of as separate and unconnected, and recombining them in a new sequence to gain a totally new outcome. For example:

Coaching paddlers to turn a boat with a long waterline (river racer, marathon, sprint, sea kayak) on the spot. They will combine forward and reverse sweeps with plenty of trunk rotation, with low braces used in a sculling action and edge changes. A student should possess each of these components, but this new task will adapt and recombine them to give a new skill.

So if we accept that improvers will always be adapting and evolving from what they already have, then our approach to how we directly introduce and coach a 'new' technique or skill will be very different to that of a novice. It may involve more complicated or multi-stage ways of breaking down a skill or technique to present it as a bite-sized chunk. More of this later.

▶ STAGES OF LEARNING

So having justified the reasons for taking different approaches with the coaching of improvers it is now time to look at the detail, but first it is worth just pointing out one more issue.

▶ Stages Of Learning And How It Affects Our Decisions As A Coach

Many of the approaches and coaching strategies within this chapter are not exclusive to improvers. You will find they are appropriate to coaching students of most levels beyond the novice or early learner stage. Why is this? Well everyone is an improver. The person who says they have learned everything is either deluded or at the brink of transcendence to a higher plane!

Anybody who chooses to be challenged by learning and taking part in an activity is a potential improver and as such will benefit from being coached. If we look at one of the more commonly accepted models for 'Stages of Learning' (BCU Canoe Handbook p123) we can see that a student would develop through these stages. What is not immediately obvious is that a person does not go through this process once in a sport like paddling, but in fact goes through it an unaccountable number of times. Each time an unfamiliar or 'new' challenge is encountered the learner is likely to return to the cognitive stage and has to think about what they are doing to get the desired performance. With practice they move up to the associative and eventually to the autonomous stage.

Advanced students differ from improvers in that they have been through this process many more times and have a greater breadth of skills on which to draw as their starting point for a new action. Therefore they will probably spend less time in the cognitive and associative stages than the improvers.

It is also true that improvers have more performance and learning experience than novices and thus will spend less time in the cognitive stage than them. That might suggest to you that the novice spends their whole learning time in the cognitive stage. Not so! Though they clearly spend more time there than more advanced learners, they do have some skills that have moved into the associative stage and some even into autonomous. Two good examples are balance and forward paddling:

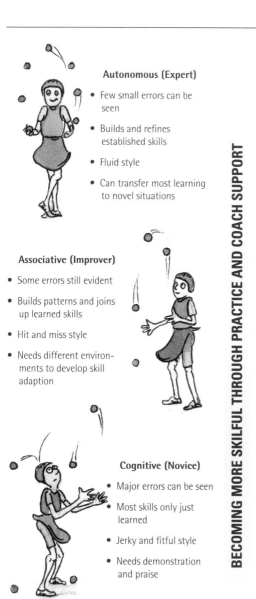

Autonomous (Expert)

- Few small errors can be seen
- Builds and refines established skills
- Fluid style
- Can transfer most learning to novel situations

Associative (Improver)

- Some errors still evident
- Builds patterns and joins up learned skills
- Hit and miss style
- Needs different environments to develop skill adaption

Cognitive (Novice)

- Major errors can be seen
- Most skills only just learned
- Jerky and fitful style
- Needs demonstration and praise

BECOMING MORE SKILFUL THROUGH PRACTICE AND COACH SUPPORT

Fig. 1 Stages of Learning (Fitts and Posner 1967)

Most novices will at some stage stop thinking continuously about trying to paddle forward in a straight line and just do it, then every now and again they will go off course and consciously have to correct. In time the correction will become automatic. Neither do novices spend their whole time concentrating on not falling in. So on flat water these skills are in the late associative or possibly even autonomous phase. Let us now imagine that we took the same paddlers onto choppy or moving water. Balance, which was operating beyond the cognitive stage, is very quickly back

there – the students have to think hard and work hard at staying upright again!

The key point here is that it is not where the paddler is in the overall scheme of things that should dictate whether you coach them as a novice, improver or advanced, but it is their level of familiarity with the task at hand. A good illustration of this is that I have coached some very advanced performance paddlers to correctly throw a throw bag. So unfamiliar were they with this motor-physical task that I employed teaching strategies and approaches that would have equally been suitable to introduce a novice to move their kayak sideways. They were clearly in the cognitive stage of learning when it came to throwing a bag.

So although we can generalise about beginners, improvers and advanced, it is pertinent to be mindful of where the task in hand sits in the stages of learning for that individual and how much background and experience they have to develop it further. All these things clearly affect your planning and direction of a session.

▶ PREPARATORY WORK

Let us now go into some detailed aspects of preparing the way for improving improvers.

WHAT ARE THE STUDENT'S GOALS?

Coaching is all about making decisions and enacting them. With novices most of the decisions about what you are going to teach your students are made for you. They are beginners and don't have the full repertoire of foundation skills yet. Therefore, these foundations are likely to be what you coach. By contrast, with improvers you can't instantly assume you know what you are going to be coaching. They know enough about paddling that they may have views about what to work on next, even if it is simply "I want to get better at doing X, Y and Z". If you don't give your students the opportunity to tell you this you are damaging your relationship with them. You can't expect your students to buy into your coaching if you have 'inflicted' it on them without first asking what they want to do!

So it is important to spend time with your student before starting any session or course, establishing what your student's goals are, but also clearly defining what is realistic in the time available. Be careful what you suggest at this early stage. You may not have seen their paddling ability, or have any idea about how quickly or slowly they learn - don't make promises you may not be able to honour!

All successful coaching relationships are built on trust and mutual respect. This begins with the coach listening to the students' wants and being mindful and respectful of them throughout the coaching relationship. Taking time to chat early on is invaluable to ascertain the students' goals, but also to learn other things about them.

OBSERVATION AND ANALYSIS

If you go to Chapter 1 Coaching, there is an excellent section on analyzing performance. All the nuts and bolts are laid out to choose from. What I would like to discuss is how to apply that within the context of meeting students who can already paddle but about whom you know nothing.

It would be better to call this 'evaluating current reality'. What are these paddlers actually capable of? How different are their abilities across the group? Without the answers to these questions and more, a coach cannot begin to do their job. We need to know what we are working with before we can make any decisions about where we are going to next.

Below is a list of all the things that, in an ideal world, would be useful for a coach to know about, to be able to begin making decisions:

- Current performance levels
- Comfort zones and arousal
- Preferred ways of receiving information
- Preferred learning styles
- Levels of independence
- Levels of self-discipline
- Levels of self/kinaesthetic awareness
- Levels of motivation
- Understanding of boating and learning
- Fast vs slow learner
- Fitness
- Confidence
- Desire to be coached
- Goals for the session and for the future

Those in blue can be observed relatively easily depending on the tasks you set or don't set, but those in black require the coach to interact with the students beyond simply observing and setting tasks.

▶ Structured Or Unstructured Observation?

Structured observation is where the coach sets the students specific tasks, sequences, or routines to do, which the coach can then observe. The benefit to the coach is that this takes less time to gauge student performance levels than unstructured observation and allows the coach to dictate exactly what is to be observed.

For example: a student had expressed a desire to improve their canoe poling in a half day session. The coach sets the following structured observation:

- Gunnel bobbing and moving from end to end in canoe - Evaluates balance
- Forward and reverse ferrying (current or wind) - Evaluates understanding of trim
- Poling up in shallow flat water - Evaluates current ability at poling

Photo 1 Evaluating balance

By structuring the observation to include the three different tasks, the coach has created the opportunity to observe the whole performance in question, but also some of the prerequisite key elements in isolation. By choosing to test balance and understanding of trim separately from the whole performance it helps the coach to spot weaknesses that may have been missed by only watching the whole performance.

Unstructured observation is where the coach does not set the students any specific tasks but instead gives the students a free reign to do what they want within an area. The benefit of this is that, as well as seeing the students' level of performance as they 'mess around', it also allows the coach to make some other observations of the students' personality and approach to paddling through their behaviours – whether they push themselves, or do very little, whether they do everything on one side. Do they struggle to do anything without an imposed task from a coach, do they interact with other students or stay in isolation? All of the things you might observe through unstructured observation can help to build a picture of the student, which in turn will help the coach be more effective by individualising their coaching.

The disadvantage of unstructured observation is that it can take more time and you still may not end up seeing everything you need to be able to decide on the direction of the session. In this case the coach would be wise to add on a period of structured observation to gain the essential bits of performance information.

Many coaches will typically start a session with some unstructured observation (which they 'sell' to the students as continuing the warm-up on the water) and then move into a more prescribed period of structured tasks to fill any gaps. This allows you to benefit in all the ways mentioned above, but of course takes more time, which may be precious!

Eventually you should come to a stage where you have a clear idea of the current reality for each student, which should in turn lead you to decisions about what you are going to coach. Can you move on to the next stage in their development, or do you need to go back and correct a few existing problems?

▶ Wants VS Needs

The problem at this stage can be that what you feel the student 'needs to learn' can be very different from what the student "wants to learn".

This is the classic dilemma of the student's 'wants versus needs'. It is common for students to desire to move on to new and different skills before they have either refined, or even learned correctly, the ones they have recently acquired.

Reconciling this difference and making the student aware that they need to take a few steps back before they can move forward is the duty and job of the coach. It would be wrong to knowingly leave a student with bad habits or poor/incorrect technique. We know that the effects of this weakness would only grow in size and proportion affecting more of the paddler's skills and taking more effort and hard work to put right the longer it is left. If the coach is concerned about upsetting the student they should remind themselves of how upset the student will be when they do inevitably realise the truth and wonder why no one mentioned it before!

So having mutually decided on what you are going to work on, there are still some highly important issues to consider that fall within observation before you get stuck in…

FINDING OUT MORE THAN JUST WHAT YOU CAN SEE

What you are going to coach is only half the picture of what we need to know. We also need information about the student to help us decide how we are going to coach. Below are two areas we might like to explore:

▶ Preferred Way Of Receiving Information

By this I refer to whether an individual prefers to understand how to do things by watching, by listening to explanations, or by trying to understand how it will feel. This preference is often represented in the simple model of VAK (Visual, Audio, Kinaesthetic).

How can we find this out? Simple - ask them! They may know. If not, talk to them openly about their past learning experiences. Most people will have an idea (though they are not always right) of how they prefer to 'pick things up', whether they are a watcher (V), a listener (A), whether they need to know how it will feel (K), or a combination of these.

An alternative to asking them directly, (or to test the validity of what they have told you) is to restrict the information you give them about a task to just one of these channels and then see how they cope. Try to present a new task by either mostly explaining, mostly demonstrating, or mostly physically guiding, then see how your students cope.

If after being given only a demo, a student comes back to you and says, "Could you give me a bit of an explanation?" then it is likely that this person prefers verbal information. If another student, given the same demo, rushes straight off seeming to have a clear idea about what to do, then they are likely to be more visually oriented. On the other hand, if another student sits in their boat and physically goes through the motions, trying to mimic your demonstration as a 'dry run' then there is a good bet that they are quite kinaesthetic in their approach.

Later you could then set a new task, but this time present it just by explanation. See what kind of reactions you get from your students now! Depending on the task you want to present, it may be possible to give the information just by physically guiding the students.

Eventually, by cross-referencing results you will pick up an indication of what their preferences are. Remember that this is not a proven clinical method of analysing students' preferred ways of receiving information. These are simple, crude, diagnostic tools which will give you a hint, but not a definitive answer. There is no substitute for spending lots of time with people and being observant of their behaviour and reactions to your coaching over a period of time.

It is also possible to help determine people's preferences through the words they use and the way in which they structure their language. This is a huge area and anyone wanting to know more should seek out books, information or courses on the subject of 'Neuro-Linguistic Programming'.

▶ Backgound

This covers a vast area including many items on our list of things a coach should ideally know:

- ◎ Comfort zones and arousal
- ◎ Preferred learning styles
- ◎ Levels of independence
- ◎ Levels of self-discipline
- ◎ Levels of self/kinaesthetic awareness
- ◎ Levels of motivation
- ◎ Understanding of boating and learning
- ◎ Fast vs slow learner
- ◎ Fitness
- ◎ Confidence
- ◎ Desire to be coached

Many of these subjects can be delved into through straightforward conversation. When discussing student goals before a coaching session you can take the opportunity to chat to your students and find out more. Alternatively wait until later on and chat to them during the session as a way of providing a rest or breaking up a period of practice.

Whenever you do it, it is important that you try to make it easy for your students to tell you truthfully about their paddling and learning backgrounds. Don't talk as a group, as people will feel under pressure to play down or up what they say. Instead try to do it informally on a one-to-one basis and avoid it becoming an inquisition. Sometimes there is no substitute for a direct question like: "Are you familiar with thinking about how things feel within the boat? Pressure on your feet, knees, hips, etc?"

The picture you build of your paddlers will be based on a combination of what they tell you and what you see. Sometimes these two things don't quite match and it is the gaps between them that may lead you to probe deeper and find out more.

Photo 2 Getting into a conversation

For example if someone tells you they have been paddling once a week for a year with regular instruction, but their performance on the water is weaker than you would expect for this, you may want to know more. Get into a conversation, slipping in some carefully directed questions that might lead them into telling you whether:

- 🗨 They have really been going that regularly?
- 🗨 They have received coaching from lots of different people?
- 🗨 The sessions are formal or not?
- 🗨 They progress slower than their peers who started at the same time?
- 🗨 They have a physical condition that makes it harder for them?

The list of questions we could ask goes on and on. The only defining factor should be: "Will this information help to build a fuller picture and help me coach this person as an individual?"

This is important! Remember, it is people we coach not strokes or manoeuvres! The skill in gathering this kind of information is in your ability to relax people and ask the right questions. Like anything it takes practice, the more you do the better you will be at it.

Eventually, through our observation phase we should have gathered lots of information which contributes to making our coaching decisions, such as:

- 🗨 What is right with the person's paddling
- 🗨 What is wrong with their paddling
- 🗨 Whether we need to go back and fix some older skills or embark upon learning some new ones
- 🗨 The beginnings of how the students might like to receive information and be taught.

So now we are armed to go forward and start having an effect.

REVISITING FOUNDATIONS AND WEEDING YOUR GARDEN

If our improver's foundation skills have flaws, they may be significant enough to have to go back and relearn or adapt and correct. As a coach we are then faced with the challenge of either teaching someone from scratch or developing them from a good base. This is different because we have to 'undo' something and then learn to do it in a different, but better way. I have written undo in apostrophes because it is misleading to think of undoing a learnt skill; we can't actually unlearn something. Once learnt it is always there, but what we can do is to learn a new version of the skill and then train the brain and body to choose the new version in preference to the older one. For example:

A paddler (canoe or kayak) forward paddles with no trunk rotation, all their power comes from their arms and from throwing their body forward and back. The coach has recognised that their technique will undermine their paddling and that in the near future, when on white water or covering distance on open water, they will not have enough power or stamina to cope. So the coach bites the bullet and renegotiates with the student the focus of the coaching over the forthcoming sessions.

Through a series of exercises the coach trains the student's forward paddling to be more efficient and incorporate more rotation. The student can still paddle in their original style as well as in their newer rotating style, so they have not unlearned the original skill, but learned a new additional one. At this stage, without the coach to remind and nurture the student, the student falls back into their familiar habit of no rotation. This happens even though they are consciously aware and understand that rotating is more efficient. Why? Because this is the one they have done far more times and therefore is what the brain chooses as its 'default' when it goes into autopilot for forward paddling.

KEY POINT

- At this stage you could describe the change as a change in *performance,* but it is a change which has not yet been fully learned, i.e. it is not permanent or autonomous. It is still in the associative stage of learning. When it is permanent and autonomous we could describe it as having been *learned*.

Having created the new skill, the task for the coach and the student is to make it a learned skill – for the brain to choose the rotating version, over the non-rotating version, when on autopilot. This is done by making it the new habit, by filling our brain's memory with many *recent* records of doing it. So many recent records that when it goes on autopilot and selects its 'preferred forward paddling style' the *recent* memory bank is dominated by the new version and is therefore what it chooses!

I have highlighted the word recent, because it is not necessary to have more total practices of one skill than another before the brain switches its first choice. What you need is to dominate the brain's recent memory with the new skill, or more accurately the selection of the new skill (the more times you select a skill to use the more you reinforce it). One of the fastest ways of doing this is to use lots of distributed and variable practice, so that the skill is retrieved from the memory many more times and is applied variably to reinforce its need to be used in all forward paddling situations rather than only when one is practising forward paddling. This last point about practice is exceedingly important when trying to reinforce a newer and better version of an old skill. If it is only selected in contrived or artificial practice sessions it will not transfer into all of your paddling!

▶ DELIVERING THE GOODS

There are several key areas within the delivery of coaching information to our students that should be given a different approach in comparison to delivering to novices:

- Individualising input and feedback
- Use of models vs demonstrations
- Encouraging understanding

INDIVIDUAL INPUT AND FEEDBACK

This is essentially tailoring your delivery to suit each student. If we have limited contact time we should maximise the effectiveness of our coaching to get the most results in the short time frame. If we are working with the students over an extended period of time we have no excuses about not knowing the students well enough to individualise the coaching to them.

Let us briefly look at why individual input and feedback is so effective:

Remember the IDEAS model? (See Chapter 1 Coaching). This model is designed to help with delivery to a group of students who we are less familiar with. It uses:

Demonstration to cater for Visual input

Explanation to cater for Audio input

Activity to cater for Kinaesthetic input (see below)

IDEAS covers all bases because we want to make sure that everyone in the group gets enough information to set off and start having a go.

TOP TIP - IDEFAS

• Note about activity catering for Kinaesthetic input – Demo and Explanation are about getting the intended message over, but Activity is not. It is the practice element of the session and although this does involve Kinaesthetic learning by physically doing, it does not necessarily get the intended message over through a Kinaesthetic route.

Direct physical guidance, analogies or movements that convey the 'feel' of the intended message would cater for the kinaesthetic learner. Therefore to be all things to all people IDEAS needs enlargement:

IDEFAS - IDEAS with a silent 'f' for 'FEEL'

A good analogy for IDEAS is that the coach is in front of the group with the delivery equivalent of a blunderbuss, spraying them with information in the hope that some will hit the target! A lot of information is given, much of it misses the target and in the chaos some students may get confused in the information crossfire!

However if the coach knew their group better they could put down the crude and wasteful blunderbuss, use the equivalent of a target rifle and fire one well-aimed message at a time. A quick one line explanation for that student (Audio), a demo for those two (Visual) and a quick rearranging of those two into the correct position and add an analogy that will convey the correct feeling of movement to them! (Kinaesthetic).

Of course you could argue that even though a demo was not that person's cup of tea it would not harm them to see it as well as hear the explanation? In some cases that's true and virtually all of us benefit from a combination of VAK. Very few individuals are exclusively one channelled but most of us are biased towards one. So we are usually biasing our input to a preferred but not exclusive channel. However, we may receive a message through our preferred channel

and be happy with what it means, then get some extra info through another, which then makes us confused and question our original understanding. Most of us will have experienced this at some time in our lives.

"I was alright till he added that other bit, now I'm completely lost!"

So if you can, keep the amount of info to a minimum and deliver it via the student's preferred channel, you will have more potent and effective coaching that leaves you more time to observe and plan where you are going next with your session!

Example:

A coach has a group of 4 improvers who are working on developing their hanging draws in canoe. Three of the four each have a different bias in their preferred way of receiving information. The fourth does not have a strong bias being comfortable with all three ways.

Having observed and come to some coaching decisions, the coach is aware that all four are failing to locate the correct position and feather combination for the paddle and as a consequence are turning. Leaving two students to carry on practising for a few moments, the coach calls in the Kinaesthetic and Visual learner to the bank. The coach then physically manipulates the Kinaesthetic learner into the correct general position for the stroke, moves the blade up and down the side of the boat and then adjusts the feather by steering her top hand. Adding the simple instruction:

"Experiment with these variations until you feel the sweet spot - off you go".

Then turning to the Visual learner, the coach says:

"See that? Copy her. When you've got it, show me."

Having given the Kinaesthetic learner a guided feel of what to do, with the visual learner getting the same info by watching, the coach then calls the other two in.

The coach first tells the all-channel learner to watch the others, focussing particularly on the position of the blade along the boat and the amount of feather.

Then, turning to the Audio learner, the coach says:

"I'd like you to experiment with the position of the blade alongside the boat. Move it back and forth till you find the perfect spot for moving sideways. You can also try changing the feather to make fine adjustments as well. Come back and explain what differences it makes."

The multi-channel learner has now seen and heard what the task is. If they need further input then the coach can physically guide them into position as per the kinaesthetic learner.

Remember that most people need a little bit of input from most channels in addition to a big chunk from their preferred one. Don't starve people of info, it's as bad as overloading them.

MODELLING VS DEMONSTRATION

Early learners who have little idea what canoeing and kayaking strokes and manoeuvres look like require lots of demos to convey the overall form and shape of the techniques and skills. These early demos form the basic skeleton in the paddler's memory on which all later knowledge is hung. Improvers by contrast have most of the foundation movements etched in their heads. For them only new unknown movements are worth seeing as full-blown, normal speed demos.

This has implications for the way in which we should use demonstrations with our improvers:

When teaching a new skill or technique that students have not seen before, following all the normal guidelines for demonstrations is appropriate.

When developing an existing skill or technique further, the use of modelling and highlighting is far more appropriate.

So for the development and improvement of skills from existing techniques, the improver requires modelling and highlighting of the pertinent issues. Modelling is simply the use of demonstrations after a skill is already understood at a basic level. It is the use of demos to convey fine detail, subtle aspects of timing, etc. It could even be to demonstrate a series of slightly different adaptations of the same stemming from the same base skill.

Modelling should focus in on detail that the student needs to refine or begin to understand. Thus exaggerating, or presenting in slow motion are ideal ways of drawing focus onto a specific area, as are narrating over a model and the use of abstracts (explained below). What is common in modelling is that some of the basic rules of giving demos are broken. This is okay as long as the student already has a blueprint of the movement in question etched in their head. Then all the subsequent modelling will aid fine analysis by the learner and thus absorption and understanding onto their original blueprint.

Photo 3 Coach demos a draw stroke 'highlighting' the knifing action by deliberately keeping the paddle blade half out of the water.

Before I give an example to illustrate this, we should briefly look at what an 'abstract' is. An abstract is like a model but is not of the actual kayaking movement in the boat, but rather is something you can do to illustrate a specific point better by removing the boat, or paddle, etc. A good example is from surf, using the steep face of a sand dune to walk slow motion through surf manoeuvres to model things like height on the wave face, etc.

Example:

At a beginner stage when demonstrating the basic (above water recovery) draw stroke, you would demonstrate the whole thing, following all the typical demo rules. You might slightly later show the more complex version with knifed recovery, but not train this yet. Later, when you want to start to develop away from the basic version it could be necessary to model what the blade is doing under the water by showing the stroke out of the water, holding the paddle almost at the blade neck and doing it in slow motion so that the students can follow the action. These models break many demonstration rules, but we know they will convey important information and that the student already understands the stroke well enough not to be mislead by the 'false images' given by them.

ENCOURAGING UNDERSTANDING

An important element of coaching improvers is that they have reached a stage where understanding is an essential part of the learning process. Let us once more contrast this against the beginner.

The beginner is an empty container waiting to be filled up. In the early stages of learning to paddle, what they need most are direct instructions in robust techniques that will form the foundations of all their future skills in canoes and kayaks. These techniques need to be presented in a clear and understandable way and the student needs to understand what these techniques do. But beyond this basic understanding little more is needed. In fact it is more likely that confusion and doubt will be sown if the coach tries to teach the mechanics, physics and all the possibilities of variation and adaptation at this stage.

Why? Well the student in this early learning stage is more than likely close to overload anyway. With the sensory and learning experiences of getting to grips with boating there is little or no mental space left to attempt understanding things beyond the basics.

As the student gains more and more control of their boat and moves away from the cognitive stage of learning and further into the associative stage, they have more mental or cognitive space available whilst paddling. If they have persevered to reach this stage they are also likely to be more interested in paddling beyond that initial 'wow this is different' phase. This interest in paddling usually leads to a natural curiosity about the 'whys' behind 'how a boat moves'.

The timing of this interest isn't coincidence, it's a natural consequence of a person's learning having reached a level where understanding is an important factor in their next steps. It is this innate curiosity that is probably responsible for man's incredible development to who we are today. It is the need to know 'why', not just 'how' that drives us to be so versatile and successful.

The other very important reason why the improver would benefit from greater understanding is that paddlesports are activities which take place in highly open environments and thus require well-developed open skills. Understanding how things work helps the individual to develop open skills quicker and explore more possibilities of adaptation via structured experimentation. This process of understanding, adaptation and experimentation is supported through the use of teaching styles that encourage reflective learning like guided discovery, collaborative and self-appraisal (see Chapter 1).

As the beginner consolidates their foundation skills and becomes an improver it is the perfect time to add in a greater degree of understanding, both from a motor skill development point of view and from the point of view of satisfying the student's interest, curiosity and consequently their motivation.

For example, in the novices chapter we looked at teaching sweep strokes in a way that would help quickly develop forward paddling, but there was little focus on understanding being passed on to the students. The focus was on 'how' to do the stroke. Later, when students have progressed onto improvers level, one can revisit this most basic of foundation strokes and add in a whole lot more, the understanding of 'why' the stroke and your body movements do what they do. The following exercise assumes the use of short kayaks:

In pairs you could start off by getting the students to paddle forward and then let their boat go off course, leaving it to spin without trying to correct. Do this in both directions. Ask them to watch one another and to describe the movement of the boat and what is happening.

Ideally I am looking for them to recognise that the boat is 'skidding', the back is trying to overtake the front. Also that in most circumstances, once the boat has turned through 180° it ceases to spin and simply travels backwards. Most importantly, it travels backwards in exactly the same direction that the boat was originally travelling! If the students do not arrive at this conclusion, then careful questioning and further experiments should steer them to this conclusion.

Still in pairs and taking turns to watch, do the same but this time ask the students to correct the 'skid' with only the front half of a sweep, a 'new direction' stroke – starting at the bow, coming out of the water just before the hips. Ask them to try this on both sides and come back to you when they can answer how effective this is for straightening up/correcting.

Typically it will take many strokes of this type before the boat corrects, sometimes it will not correct at all! The occasional flaw here is that the student's stroke will be too long and go past their hips, affecting the result of the experiment. We don't want them to do that yet, as it will spoil the exercise.

Still in pairs get them to do the same again on both sides, but this time the correction comes from the latter half of a sweep, a 'correction' stroke – entering at the hips, sweeping back to the stern. Ask them how effective that is.

What they should discover is that one stroke of this type corrects the boat with no effort at all. In fact it may require that the sweep is trailed as a stern rudder to prevent over-turning. (This could be trained, by using further questioning to steer student's thoughts in the direction of over-correcting and then asking them how this could be solved.)

Now ask them to decide what is the better way to correct when losing directional control –the front half sweep or the back half? When they have an answer to this (which will hopefully be the back half) then finally you could throw in the clincher - "Why is this stroke better?" Send them away to analyse why this works.

This exercise is a classic example of "Guided discovery" but also incorporates collaborative learning style teaching to encourage dialogue between students and increased observation. They have used contrasting techniques to solve a problem, been given the chance to experiment with them and evaluate their effectiveness and finally to decide why they work.

Photos 4a and 4b Students working in pairs, one observing...and then providing feedback

All of this should mean they understand the underpinning mechanics of the techniques which will in turn improve their performance both now and in the future. This will help the stroke become more skilfully applied and in turn become one of the foundations for other skills.

Another example would be trim in a canoe when turning. Trimming the boat bow heavy or bow light or central, what are the effects? This approach is essential for a canoeist to be able to embrace the concept of trim and then apply it fully to all future manoeuvres and situations rather than be told what is the 'correct amount' of trim in each case.

BREAKING IT DOWN

When teaching beginners, most techniques are fairly simple and don't involve too many stages, apart from perhaps forwards paddling, which certainly can be introduced at a very crude but working level. Later the paddler develops and starts to learn more complicated techniques and manoeuvres, or refines earlier crude working versions into more sophisticated and varied adaptations. At this stage it will become increasingly necessary to break these larger and more involved skills down into smaller parts to aid learning and development.

A good example is rolling - even when coaching this in the most modern and effective way, there are still several component parts and a specific sequence which needs to be followed to get a successful outcome. It can't all be presented at once and so it must be separated out.

A good analogy is that you can't fit a whole chocolate bar in your mouth at once. Even though you might want to, you have to take it a bite at a time!

There are several different ways of breaking down skills and techniques to make them presentable in more manageable bite-sized chunks. These are:

- Whole-part-whole
- Shaping
- Chaining
- Reverse chaining

As I have stated, these ways tend to lend themselves to improvers more than beginners so let's run through some classic examples to illustrate their application...

Whole-Part-Whole

The classic for this has to be forward paddling. The student already has the whole action, but what we want to do is improve it. Let's say that they have limited trunk rotation and we feel that they could be more efficient if they gained more.

What we do is look at the whole skill and take out the trunk element. This we then train through a series of exercises to encourage rotation.

Some of these exercises don't necessarily make the paddler feel they are making any progress at the time as the outcome of forward paddling is temporarily worse, i.e. holding the paddle shaft at the neck of the blades and paddling forward without bending your arms. Doing this exercise, the student clearly isn't going to feel they are getting better, as it is an exercise to increase awareness of rotation. However it will have an effect when their paddling is allowed to return to something closer to 'normal' forward paddling – when this 'part' is put back into the 'whole'.

Shaping

This we have already illustrated a number of times. It is where a crude working model is established early on and, before it is over-practised, it is developed/shaped into a better version of its former self. A good example would be making a bow rudder develop out of a draw stroke.

Chaining

A good example would be rolling, where each stage is a link in the chain and when all the links are strong and in place, the roll should work. Another example is introducing people to surfing:

First you teach understanding wave selection and then 'take off'. Having got that, you add a bottom turn. Next a diagonal run, then changing direction on the wave. So eventually you have a complete basic ride.

Reverse Chaining

I added a second example under chaining because I use reverse chaining when I teach rolling, and so this is my example for that.

Having established that the student has enough side flexibility and a very good high brace I begin to reverse chain. Standing in the water next to the student I roll them over toward me and support them just above the water. From here I get them to high brace and right themselves. Repeat left and right.

Next support them in the water the same way, but this time position the blade in the roll set-up position. Sweep the blade round to the high brace position and then hip flick upright again. Repeat left and right until ready to progress.

Continue with the same task as above but each time slowly lower the student a little further into the water before they begin the sweep. Stage by stage they will be working toward a fully submerged roll in tiny increments. This way they will fully comprehend the orientation and pattern of movement once they are fully upside down.

Once they are successfully doing this, add on self-capsizing and you have a roll from reverse chaining.

VARIETY AND SKILFUL DEVELOPMENT

By now you should be well aware that successful paddlers are highly adaptable and able to cope with constantly changing open environments. To reach this 'successful paddler' position it is essential that a student's skills are developed through the best-designed practice possible. By practice we mean all the activities which a paddler undertakes. This does not just include practice sessions where the coach organises exercises, routines, games, circuits and training, but also trips, journeys, competitions, events, etc. as all these activities require the student to 'do' and through 'doing' we are practising for the future. Any physical action we produce relies on the physical actions that have gone before for their quality, consistency and adaptability.

Cast your mind back to my opening story about my early paddling experiences. Within the constraints of our London environment and the resources available, my coach set out to consolidate my early learning with as diverse and varied activities as possible. This is exactly what the improver needs.

Once we have developed out of being a beginner and we are starting to expand and improve our skills we need the right circumstance to maximise our potential development. Take a look back at the section on practice within the coaching chapter. Reading this you will quickly come to realise that simply practising for practice sake and learning a few new tricks every now and again is not enough.

From both an understanding point of view and from a skill development point of view the improver needs the opportunities to apply their skills in the correct context and in a variety of different places. Using newly developed skills to journey, play and explore are

Photo 5 Action... Variety... Practice!

exactly the kind of things to do. Getting away from the familiar environments that the learning has so far taken place in will lead to much more variety in practice which will in turn lead to greater adaptability for the paddler in the future.

On a practical level, what this means is going on simple trips where the journey takes over focus from direct practice, but that practising of skills, like forward paddling, manoeuvring, and so on are happening constantly without conscious thought.

So we need to organise journeys on lakes, canals, slow-moving rivers, maybe the sea, surfing trips, or an introduction to some of the competitive disciplines such as slalom, polo or marathon.

Even if you don't have the resources, time or circumstances to do this, at least trying different things on the water you do use will help. Try organising polo games, flat water slaloms, or just trying out different boats and paddles to introduce at least some variables into their learning. Basically, introduce them to as many different possible avenues of canoesport as you can manage!

And finally, all practice should of course be bilateral from a very early stage.

GOAL SETTING AND MOTIVATION

As I stated in my opening gambit, it is very easy to lose people from sports at the improver stage. It is therefore of paramount importance that students are kept interested and motivated in what they are doing and learning. Easily said, harder to do! Or is it?

If you follow some basic principles you should be okay:

🛶 Keep it fun – the fastest way to lose people is to make it boring. Inject some humour, keep it light.

🛶 Don't force your expectations on your students - you may want your students to develop quickly and they may be able to, but you might find you are scaring them off by mapping out a serious training plan for them. Let them develop at their own natural speed. This will also allow appropriate consolidation.

🛶 Remind them how far they have come – as their progress slows down you will need to remind your students of just how much they have achieved already; contrast their current performance with their earlier ones.

Do something different – when the monotony begins to set in, do something different to shake everyone up.

Get out there and adventure - you keep people interested and motivated to keep learning by regularly giving them a real experience of what it is all about. This excites them, makes them realise what a great wealth of experiences are waiting for them and motivates them to learn more skills so they can have more adventure next time. Canoes and kayaks were made for journeys and exploring.

As I sit here writing, my thoughts are brought instantly back to today - a perfect example of this:

I was out helping some coaches who are working on a winter training scheme. The scheme's aim is to get a number of paddlers through the star tests and ultimately onto their Level 2 coach training. For the past 4 days the students have been working hard on the same lake, focusing on their personal skills and receiving an introduction to coaching others. For a change and an opportunity to put certain techniques into a moving water context the coaches had decided to take the students on a gentle river trip with a couple of harder grade 3 drops along the way.

When we got to the river it was lower than the ideal level for the group, but after a chat the coaches decided that the group would probably still enjoy it.

By the end of the trip the other coaches and myself were thoroughly beating ourselves up about what a waste of time the day had been, the jets weren't powerful enough and the eddies not well-enough defined, it hadn't stretched the students enough. Then I stopped and listened to the conversation amongst the students as they were changing – they were buzzing, totally elated with their river experience, exclaiming how 'the river rocks like the lake sucks!' It had worked and I'm sure they will return to the lake tomorrow with refreshed new interest in *improving* their paddling skills.

IN CONCLUSION

As I have written this last piece another coach poked his head round the door. He has just come back from a day off that he chose to spend with his own group of trainee Level 3 kayak coaches that he is mentoring. For the last week he has been developing their leadership, coaching and personal skills on white water.

"How was your day off on the surf?" I asked.

"I have some tired, but very excited people" replied Jim.

" And you?" I smiled.

"I'm very tired and excited too, but they're worth it!."

For the coach 'energy in = results out'. This is never truer than when coaching improvers. Take a deep breath and enjoy!

FURTHER READING

BCU Canoe and Kayak Handbook, British Canoe Union, 2002, Pesda Press, 0-9531956-5-1

BOB TIMMS

Bob Timms is a Level 5 Kayak Coach, MIC and IML who has worked full-time in the outdoor industry since 1988. Having lived and worked in England, Scotland, Wales, France and Austria he has finally settled down in the Southern French Alps with his young family. Professionally Bob shares his time between educating coaches and coaching and guiding clients.

"I am fascinated by people, the way that we learn and develop; I get excited about encouraging them to reach their true potential. Four words steer me - journeys, adventure, fun and development."

Bob runs 'Bob Timms Boating and Trekking' - www.bobtimms.co.uk

9 COACHING ADVANCED PADDLERS

By definition, advanced paddlers are already competent. Novices need techniques and skills introducing from scratch, improvers already have some understanding and ability but need those skills developing. With advanced paddlers we are talking about making small but significant improvements… the difference between making a micro-eddy above the waterfall or not, between being in the medals and being fourth.

INTRODUCTION

Whether they be a competitor wanting to make the team or win the worlds, or an adventure paddler wanting to be fit and efficient enough to complete that 60 mile crossing, coaching advanced/elite paddlers is both very demanding and rewarding.

That said it requires tenacity. You don't get the obvious improvements that you see with novices and to a lesser extent with improvers. The improvements are small but the satisfaction gained in the knowledge of the amount of skill and effort required on the part of both paddler and coach is great.

'The difference that makes the difference'

▶ WHAT MAKES AN ADVANCED COACH?

'The difference that makes the difference'

Refined understanding of the coaching process, coaching delivery, critical analysis, individualised practice, cutting edge solutions and decision making – all contribute to making the difference that makes the difference!

Coaching advanced paddlers and making the significant improvements that make a difference, requires that the coach has the ability to use integrated approaches within the coaching process and develops a learning environment that maximises performance. An in-depth understanding of skill development, problem solving, decision-making and the ability and desire to empower performance and independence are essential.

At this level a coach should be continually refining their approach to the coaching process and coaching delivery. They should be able to critically analyse performance and provide 'individualised' approaches in relation to 'individualised' performance. They should be able to design and apply specialised coaching, with outcomes that meet student needs via a range of activities appropriate to the technical, tactical, mental and physical skills and knowledge of the student.

For example:

The coach of an elite performer who is overtrained must be able to assess the physical, mental, and technical components of the coaching environment and use specialist support to solve problems.

The coach of teenagers working in a socially deprived area must be able to assess the peer pressures, understand youth culture and work out a practice environment and regime that is acceptable to the youngster paddling in that culture.

Coaches at this level would also exhibit the ability to use an effective combination of personal attributes and skills in order to manage change within the advanced paddlers.

Here the coach would be able to analyze and interpret the requirements of the specialist coaching environment, selecting and using supporting concepts in order to manage change and affect performance. The coach should also have a broad range of communication strategies and the ability to analyse and positively harness the personalities of others when working with participants, teams and support staff.

For example:

Working with the very talented, there may be very little technical that the coach wishes to, or needs to, work on, and physical training may be becoming routine. It is essential therefore to observe and listen in order to pick up the slight nuances and mood changes that will guide your coaching input.

Working with the very young requires communication to suit the age and the individual. Understanding how the youngster perceives words such as 'ability' 'effort', etc. is vital.

It is of equal importance that the coach at this level also has the ability to:

Be creative when problem solving and decision making within selected areas of coaching planning

and practice; perhaps bringing a range of ideas and solutions from a variety of sources both within and external to the recognised field of coaching.

Have the ability to review and analyze your own self-reflection skills so as to enable personal development and further develop your own coaching delivery.

► KNOWING YOUR PADDLER/ATHLETE

A coach may work with advanced paddlers over a long period or they may have someone come along who requires a 'quickfix'. Either way a coaching relationship is always a two-way process.

The more advanced the paddler, the more of an equal partnership it needs to become. Coaching is always ultimately about the student's needs. However, a novice accepts that the coach knows what he needs in terms of paddling experience better than he does. An advanced paddler will have strongly held views and will need to buy in to your solutions. Goals and *methods used to achieve them* will have to be truly agreed and understood.

Some coaches find it useful to write down a formal 'coaching contract' where the coach and athlete/paddler agree what their roles and responsibilities are and what level of commitment they expect from each other. Even without a formal contract these areas will need to be explored and understood.

SHORT-TERM

If a paddler comes to you with a particular problem, he has approached you because your reputation has led him to believe that you can help. It should not be too difficult to have the paddler buy in to your way of doing things, at least until you get to know them and can adapt your approach to their preferred learning style and ways of receiving information and feedback. Right from the start it is important to listen and show that you value their input and feedback.

A coach can observe what is going on but only the paddler can know how it feels. A lot of good coaching can be done by the coach simply acting as a 'sounding board'; the coach acts as a facilitator while the paddler verbalises his intrinsic feedback and works out the solution for himself.

LISTENING SKILLS

An attentive listener:

• Appears attentive.

• Avoids interrupting.

• Bridges – this means doing things that let the speaker know that you are still with him such as:

▸ Maintaining eye contact.

▸ Nodding your head in agreement.

▸ Making agreement sounds such as "mm-hmm'.

• Paraphrases - e.g. "so what you're saying is…"

• Listens 'between the lines' - e.g. notices that the words are saying one thing but the body language something quite different.

COACH'S TIP

• When a paddler has completed a circuit or exercise, give him a few seconds to internalize his own intrinsic feedback. When he makes eye contact, try saying nothing and simply raising an eyebrow quizzically. Odds are that he will tell you how it felt and what he thinks he should do to correct the problem.

• Don't do this all the time! Sometimes you will want to reinforce a good performance with praise, sometimes they will need you to give corrective feedback.

LONG–TERM

With long-term relationships the most important thing is to develop the paddler's trust and confidence in the coach.

This is done by:

⦿ Having your paddler's best interest at heart

⦿ Demonstrating by your actions that the above is true.

⦿ Being consistent.

⦿ Being honest. (But not necessarily brutally honest!)

As your relationship develops you will learn what makes them tick and how to motivate them. The fact that Erica learns better if she is guided towards working out the solution for herself, whereas John learns best if you give him a solution and then allow him to experience the solution kinaesthetically. The fact that Gerry can't take anything on board for an hour before lunch and Erica works best if sessions are interspersed with 'playtime'.

▸ Record Keeping

Keeping records when coaching people over a long period of time is crucial. They enable you to:

• Assess the paddlers' progress.

• Evaluate the effectiveness of particular coaching techniques and methods used.

• Record and review goals (See Chapter 3).

• Record and compare the results of fitness tests (see Chapter 2).

• Motivate paddlers by comparing performance results.

• Motivate paddlers by comparing technical improvements.

With performance testing it is best if you can reduce the variables as much as possible so that the only difference being measured is the improvement in the paddler, e.g. time taken to paddle 1,000m on flat water on a windless day or the same course on a rapid at the same water level.

Technique comparison records are best made using video review, (see Chapter 11 Use of Video). Once again, try and reduce variables to the minimum and use flags and markers so that you compare like with like.

Paddlers should be encouraged to keep their own training diary. It will:

• Help them to 'learn to learn'.

• Reduce 'coach dependency' by getting them to review the effectiveness of their training.

• Make it easier for them to share their thoughts… how tired they were at a particular stage, whether they found a particular session helpful or demotivating, etc.

▶ WHAT TO WORK ON

With long-term paddlers you will have your coaching records of previous sessions, goals set and progress made to help you decide what to work on. Nonetheless if your student has been working on a skill since you last saw them, a period of reviewing the work done, questioning and observation will pay dividends.

In a 'quick fix' situation the coach will need to rely on questioning and on 'diagnostic circuits'. For example through questioning you find out that Helen is concerned that on tight bow rudder breakouts she is always successful on the right but occasionally 'blows it' on the left. Set up a circuit that will allow you to observe/video left and right-handed breakouts. This will allow you to compare her 'strong and 'weak sides'. By a process of observation, analysis and comparison you will be able to spot 'the differences that make a difference'.

In the case of someone who doesn't have a 'strong' side you will have to make comparisons with an 'expert model'. This can be an image that you carry in your head from your long experience as a performer and/or coach, or literally an expert model in the form of another paddler who is more skilful in that area than the person you are coaching, or even a video of the World Champion performing the manoeuvre/technique in question.

WEAK LINK THEORY

A skilful performer needs to have all four aspects of the components of skill developed. As the coach you will need to be able to help your athlete improve in all four areas:

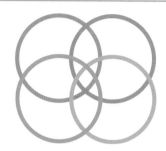

- **Technical** – technique, (Boat, Body and Blade).
- **Tactical** – understanding what is required (Brain, Background)
- **Physiological** – Fitness (Body)
- **Psychological** – Mental Preparation (Brain)

The best way to make a significant improvement is to work on that aspect of skill that is the weakest.

⊙ OBSERVE IN CONTEXT

• Always try and observe the technique or manoeuvre in the context it is going to be used, e.g. with a slalom paddler observe the technique in the context of a timed run. With a sea kayaker preparing for a long expedition observe the technique in the context of a heavily laden boat at the end of a long day.

1

▶ Example 1

A sea kayaker preparing for a committing expedition is concerned about her abilities to cope with big following seas. The coach observes her surfing on an overfall in a light boat and notes that there is no problem with her understanding of how waves behave and how to surf them (Tactical) or her ability to handle the boat on the wave (Technical) or her confidence (Psychological). She then observes the paddler on a day out with a heavily laden boat in a following sea. To start with the paddler is completely at ease (Psychological) and strong enough (Physiological) to handle the boat with ease. However as the day goes on her strength flags and performance drops markedly. The coach concludes that the weak link is the paddler's stamina and helps her design a training schedule to address this.

Photo 1 Varying your observation position will give you different perspectives and insights.

▶ **Example 2**

A slalom paddler achieves consistently good times against the clock but fails to deliver on race days. Observation and discussion with the athlete leads the coach to the conclusion that the athlete is getting stressed out while waiting for his run. They agree to concentrate their efforts on mental preparation and developing a pre-race routine (Psychological).

Photo 2 The paddler is observed to be at ease surfing overfalls, not a psychological problem.

Many coaches concentrate far too much on technique and neglect Tactical and Psychological issues. I have worked with people who paddled up to grade 4 white water and still didn't really understand what was happening when they made a breakout… and I've lost count of how many paddlers I've helped with their self-confidence after they had been pushed too hard too soon.

Many recreational coaches are loathe to address Physiological issues. Although fitness is less of an issue than in the competition world, where a difference of hundredths of seconds can mean you are out of the running, recreational paddlers who set themselves hard enough challenges still need to be fit enough for the challenge set.

SYMPTOM OR ROOT CAUSE?

At this level the 'differences that make a difference' are going to be subtle and even disguised. Inexperienced observers often latch onto a difference that is actually a symptom of the problem rather than the root cause. As a result attempts to correct the issue are

doomed to failure and the whole process can be very demotivating for the paddler concerned.

This is why the coach working at this level has to have a thorough and in-depth understanding of technical and tactical aspects of the discipline they coach.

▶ DELIVERING THE GOODS

The whole point of coaching advanced paddlers is that their needs are so unique that there is no simple answer. When working with advanced performers we need to individualize our coaching to meet that individual's needs. We all have our favourite exercises that work for most people, but even when using them we will need to know when to use them and how to tweek them.

The subjects in this section have been well covered in Chapter 1 and elsewhere so I will restrict myself to offering some comments aimed specifically at their pitfalls and advantages when working with advanced paddlers.

COACHING STYLES AND METHODS

Every coach, whatever the level of paddler they are working with, has a range of coaching styles and methods that they are happiest working in. The experienced coach is able to work in a wide range of styles and methods and will slide in and out of different methods depending on the requirements of the students and the situation. Certain methods are seen as being more coach-centred and others as being more student-centred. In general coach or task-centred methods work best where you need a quick fix, and student or process-centred methods lead to a more thorough understanding and are retained in memory better.

However, a coaching method has no intrinsic value of its own. There is only one justification for using a coaching method and that is that it is what the student needs at that moment in time. I have seen a paddler seething with frustration because he couldn't understand where the coach's patient questioning was leading. I later asked the coach why he didn't just show (demo/model) what he was trying to put across. He looked at me in absolute horror and said: "But I'm a student-centred coach". Talk about a little knowledge being a dangerous thing!

USE OF QUESTIONING

Questioning is particularly useful when exploring Tactical issues. It is often used as part of a guided experimentation approach enabling the paddler to take ownership of the answer. This means that they will more fully understand and remember the answer. The big danger when working with advanced paddlers is that the coach may be tempted to overuse it. It can get very irritating and the paddler may feel that they are unable to get a straight answer. Use it sparingly and well.

FEEDBACK

Feedback is a powerful tool, to be used carefully.

Well delivered positive feedback can be used to:

- Motivate people.
- Reinforce desirable behaviour/technique.
- Correct behaviour/technique.

Poorly delivered/negative feedback can:

- Demotivate people.
- Reinforce poor behaviour/technique.
- Change behaviour/technique for the worse.

The following points are generally valid whatever the level of paddler you are working with but are particularly applicable to those coaching advanced paddlers:

• Don't feel you have to provide feedback or praise every time your paddler completes a task/circuit. Your feedback will be devalued and your voice just another background distraction. Try asking them to do 3 reps before they come back to you.

• Do not praise them if they are doing something undesirable or you will reinforce the problem. If you feel you need to motivate them praise the effort but not the technique, e.g. (in a neutral voice) "OK we're still having a problem with the timing there"… (then in an upbeat voice), "But credit where it's due, you're working away at it."

• Give the performer time to internalise their intrinsic feedback. (In theory this takes about 8 seconds, don't bother counting, when they are ready for it they will make eye contact).

• If you are going to give corrective feedback be brief. For it to be at its most potent they need to repeat the exercise within 30 seconds.

• Beware paddlers becoming over-reliant on video feedback. Develop their use of intrinsic feedback.

• Be careful with your body language. Make sure you are giving the message intended and that it doesn't contradict what you are saying!

PRACTICE

Practice has been covered in Chapter 1 and there are some excellent practical illustrations of different types of practice in Chapter 18 Slalom. Some of the terminology used in describing practice types are used interchangeably and cause confusion, so read the practice section of the slalom chapter for a clear definition.

However there are a number of pitfalls that you may come across when working with advanced paddlers:

• Advanced paddlers may be highly motivated so that variety is less important for motivational reasons. However, variable and random practice is essential for skilful performance in that it includes the element of selection. So although block/constant practice has its place… don't overuse it.

• When practising a 'grooved in' skill, the brain sets a margin of error that it is prepared to accept as adequate. Therefore once your athlete/paddler reaches a certain standard the brain may not notice small errors and make adjustments to eliminate them. This is where contextual interference can be useful. By changing the context the skill is being performed in (e.g. performing the skill with eyes shut), it forces the brain to treat the practice as a new and challenging experience. (See Chapter 18 for more examples).

• When setting a circuit/exercise in a challenging adventure environment, do a quick dynamic risk assessment. Once you are happy with the safety issues it makes sense for you and your paddlers to have a play in the area. This enables:

▶ You to assess the potential of the site.

▶ Your paddlers to familiarize themselves with the site so that they are comfortable with the environment and able to concentrate on the practice and learning.

OBSERVATION AND ANALYSIS

Although we have already touched on this subject under 'What to Work On' it is worth examining some issues that particularly affect coaches working with advanced paddlers. Observation and analysis is the key to your coaching at this level. You can't make improvements if you can't see what needs improving and work out what needs to be changed to effect that improvement.

Photo 3 The power of body language and facial expression.

Observation and analysis points to consider:

• Observation is a skill and like any skill it can be honed. Work with other coaches and ask them what they see and more importantly *how* they see it.

• Take the trouble to move around. Observe from different angles and work on the assumption that the best place to give feedback from is probably *not* the best place to observe from.

• The better the paddler, the smaller the differences you are trying to spot. Set practices up carefully with precise start and finish points. Create your own flags and markers.

• Fifty percent of what goes on happens where you can't see it. Encourage feedback from your paddlers about what is happening below deck.

• Never rely on one observation… the error might be a one-off.

• Use video… as a precision tool. It is a great servant but a poor master, don't let it take over your session.

• Analysis at this level requires a deep understanding of the skill. If you can perform the skill spend time analysing your own intrinsic feedback and understanding.

• Use video review and questioning to develop *your* understanding by analysing expert models.

• Equipment, tactics, techniques, conditions and people change and develop. *Question your assumptions!* What was true yesterday might not be true today.

▶ I KNOW A MAN WHO CAN

No one person can be an expert at everything. Quite often the very best thing you can do for your paddler is to help them access a person or a service who can provide what they need. A coach working at an advanced level may need to be able to access all sorts of specialists.

Depending on his strengths and weaknesses a coach may wish to access:

- Fitness Trainers
- Sports Physios
- Sports Psychologists
- Motivational Trainers
- Technique Specialists
- Knowledge Specialists
- Sports Equipment Specialists
- Disability Equipment Specialists
- Disability Awareness Trainers

Photo 4 Bringing in expert help

CONCLUSION

It is vital that you stay abreast of new developments. This applies to both new developments in the discipline you are coaching and new coaching developments. Coaching advanced paddlers is immensely rewarding, but it requires a great deal of effort and commitment on your part to stay current and deliver the goods.

FRANCO FERRERO

Franco is a Level 5 Coach (Inland and Sea). Most of his work time is taken up running Pesda Press, though he still does some freelance and voluntary coaching. He was formerly the head of the canoeing department at Plas y Brenin, and was honoured with the Geoff Good Coach of the Year Award (coaching adults category) in 2000.

His main paddling interests are white water and sea touring, though he occasionally 'dabbles' in other aspects of paddlesport and is also a keen mountaineer and skier. He has paddled throughout Britain and the European Alps, as well as in Norway, Nepal, Peru and British Columbia in Canada.

A special thanks is due to Mike Devlin and Pete Catterall for their input to this chapter.

10 COACHING YOUNG PEOPLE

The information contained in this chapter is a culmination of the combined efforts of the BCU Young People's Programme, Phil Hadley, Sue Hornby, Lara Tipper and the coaches, volunteers and helpers who not only contribute to keeping our sport alive by nurturing and encouraging young paddlers but also, by sharing their experience and knowledge, are constantly improving the way we all teach and coach paddlesport. This chapter is based on a resource developed to support the BCU Coaching Young Paddler workshop, it is an introduction and is by no means exhaustive; it is up to you as a coach to constantly review and improve your coaching skills, to ensure you are an inspiration to the next generation of paddlers.

INTRODUCTION

Most coaches will probably spend a large proportion of their coaching career working with children and young people. It is therefore important that coaches understand that a different approach is required when coaching young people compared to coaching adults. In the past children were almost seen as 'mini-adults' and coached as such.

Children undergo massive changes in their physiological, psychological and cognitive development. The modern coach needs to understand how to utilise these changes in order to develop the talents of young potential athletes and to maximise their own coaching

skills to enable them to provide stimulating, inspirational and fun sessions for young people which will whet their appetites for a future within paddlesport.

Paddlesport is a hugely diverse sport which can cater for many tastes and abilities, from paddling on a pond to tackling raging torrents, to adventure and leadership challenges, individual achievement and teamwork, to competition and Olympic success – a fairly impressive range! In order to give young people the best chance in our sport we need to give our young paddlers a broad-based introduction and encourage them to be the best they want to be, in whichever discipline they choose.

▶ LONG TERM PADDLER DEVELOPMENT

Over the years researchers have identified key factors that encourage children to become long-term participants in sport and to achieve their full potential. In recent years the work of Istvan Balyi has strongly influenced many sports both in the UK and abroad with his Long Term Athlete Development Models. In paddlesport we are working to a framework of paddler pathways that encompasses these ideas for both competitive and recreational/lifestyle paddlers. Our aim is to give children the opportunity to achieve their potential in any aspect of the sport, should they so wish.

Balyi's LTAD model promotes sport as a valuable activity which is enjoyable and contributes to a healthy lifestyle. It forms a pathway of development, coaching and training opportunities that helps participants improve skill, and achieve their potential. The BCU have adapted the work of Dr Istvan Balyi to create a paddlesport-specific model that caters for paddlers from all disciplines and with varying levels of personal goals.

At each stage within the model, specific principles and guidelines for physical, psychological, technical, tactical and ancillary development are identified. Once competencies have been achieved at one level, they form the foundation for the next level. The model takes the paddler from basic to complex skills, from general to specific, and from beginner to expert. It considers what the paddler should be doing and when, providing the best possible programme to ensure individuals come into the sport, stay in the sport and achieve performances that reflect their potential/aspirations.

A basic summary of the model is included within Chapter 1 on page 20.

One of the underlying principles behind the BCU LTPD model is that the Foundation Stages focus on developing co-ordinated control and competence (physical literacy), quality skills, and help to prepare the individual for lifelong participation in sport. This aims to set the paddler up for a successful paddlesport career, whether recreational or high performance, competitive or non-competitive.

Ideally young people should pass through the Foundation Stages before they reach puberty. Any pre-pubertal child should follow these guidelines as the first stages are all about skill development rather than physical training.

THE FUNDAMENTAL STAGE

Paddlers would follow the guidelines of the FUNdamental Stage, for about 3 years, between the ages of:

- ⦿ Girls: 4 to 9 years
- ⦿ Boys: 5 to 10 years

The FUNdamental Stage should be structured and fun! The emphasis is on developing basic movement literacy and fundamental movement skills in a positive and fun environment, with a focus on the ABC's:

✔ Balance: Control of the centre of gravity and supporting base to create stable postures and steady movements.

✔ Co-ordination: Spatial awareness and co-ordinated movement.

✔ Agility: Balanced and co-ordinated movement at speed.

Photos 1a-b Quality movement patterns

As paddlesport coaches, we encounter many paddlers who fall outside of these age bands and have not had the opportunity to develop such skills. We need to be able to recognise if an individual has these skills and how we can use our sessions to further develop them. This can be achieved on the water using games that develop the feelings of sliding, gliding, floating, spinning, spatial awareness, starting, stopping and stability skills. For example, games that involve getting in and out of the boat develop balance and the ability to transfer weight from a solid medium (i.e. the bank) to a moving object (i.e. the floating boat). Warm-up games, land-based exercises, or sessions in the gym are a really good opportunity to develop the other fundamental movement skills.

The BCU LTPD Pathway document states key outcomes for each stage. If most of these have been fulfilled, the paddler can move onto the next stage with appropriate goals set to cover any gaps.

PADDLESPORT START STAGE

Age at start of phase:

- Girls: 7 to 9 years
- Boys: 8 to 10 years

Age at end of stage:

- Girls: 8 to 10 years
- Boys: 9 to 11 years

The key focus during paddlesport sessions at this stage is to provide an enjoyable introduction to the sport that enthuses people to want more!

Photo 2 Paddlesport Start Stage

During the Paddlesport Start Stage, young people should begin to develop a range of sport specific skills. Young paddlers should be encouraged to be involved in at least three sports in order to develop diverse and transferable skills across a broad range. During this stage of development young people are particularly good at learning skills, and coaches should ensure ses-

sions are focused on high quality skill development; this can be delivered in a structured manner and through fun and games.

The key paddlesport skills that should be developed include:

- A feel for how the boat moves.

- A feel for how the paddle and the body are used to create power, turning, balance and momentum.

- The ability to choose effective and efficient skills to manoeuvre the boat around the water.

- Correct posture.

PADDLESPORT DEVELOPMENT STAGE

Age at start of phase:

- Girls: 8 to 10 years
- Boys: 9 to 11 years

Age at end of stage:

- Girls: 11 to 13 years
- Boys: 12 to 14 years

The key focus during this stage is still high quality skill development, and FUN, but taken in more diverse environments. It is recognised that varied paddling experiences will aid sound skill development. For example, paddlers should be encouraged to participate in a wide range of paddlesport, canoe and kayak, in different environments. This needs to be taken in context of local opportunities; it is obviously restricted by availability of venues, boats and coaches. Paddlers should be encouraged to specialise in areas where they show particular talent and interest.

Photo 3 Paddlesport Development Stage

Key paddlesport skills that should be developed in varied environments include:

- ✓ Sound forward paddling technique.

- ✓ Posing - looking good!

- ✓ A feel for how the boat moves and balances.

- ✓ A feel for how the body (upper body, lower body, trunk & core) are used to assist turning, power and balance.

- ✓ A feel for how the paddle is used for power, turning and support.

- ✓ The ability to choose effective and efficient skills to manoeuvre the boat around the water.

- ✓ Correct posture.

Paddlers should move on from this stage when they start puberty. This can be monitored through measuring their growth spurt (see Chapter 2).

RECREATIONAL PADDLESPORT

This phase of the LTPD pathway aims to provide guidance to those involved in 'recreational' paddlesport. It outlines how the principles of LTPD can be practically applied to help any paddler, no matter

Photos 4a-b Recreational Stage

what their age, ability, aspirations, or specific interest. It outlines the LTPD approach to helping paddlers build on the generic Foundation Stages to maximise enjoyment and satisfaction in the time they have available for paddlesport.

This is applicable for any paddler (adolescents and adults) wishing to achieve personal goals. Activities for children should always be focused around the Foundation Stages. Reference should be made to the Performance Phase, using the guidelines as a template for goal setting, toning the guiding principles to suit individual needs and cherry picking the relevant information. For example, a paddler identifies a need to improve their strength; they can refer to the Performance Phase to establish the most effective method of doing this based on their development.

The recreational stage is designed to help:

- ✓ Non-competitive recreational paddlers, e.g.
  - • Enjoy a surfing holiday
  - • Paddle class 3
  - • Enjoy a family canoe camping trip
- ✓ Competitive recreational paddlers, e.g.
  - • Gain promotion to Slalom Division 2
  - • Enter a Peak Challenge
  - • Complete the DW race

PERFORMANCE PADDLESPORT

The Performance Paddlesport Stages are applicable to anyone wishing to maximise their potential. They apply equally to the competitive and non-competitive disciplines and are split into three stages:

- ✓ Train to Train - develop skills and fitness
- ✓ Train to Perform - learn how to perform under pressure
- ✓ Train to Excel - produce the goods when it matters

We are only going to look at the Train-to-Train stage here, as the next two stages (Train to Perform, Train to Excel) are applicable to adults. The details of these stages are discipline specific and the age ranges can vary considerably from one discipline to another.

▶ Train To Train

Age at start of phase:

- ◎ Girls: 10 to 13 years
- ◎ Boys: 11 to 14 years

Age at end of stage:

- Girls: 12 to 15 years
- Boys :   14 to 17 years

Paddlers should follow the guidelines through this stage when they are passing through puberty. It is vital that height is monitored regularly to ensure peak height velocity can be pinpointed and training set appropriately (see Chapter 2).

Paddlers in this stage would be expected to specialise and use other sports and other paddlesport disciplines to help them develop as good all-round athletes. The focus during this stage is physical development of aerobic, strength and speed based on windows of opportunity. (See Appendix 1 of the BCU Long Term Paddler Development Pathway Document). Skill development is continued along with learning the finer details of the discipline involved.

Photo 5 Train to Train

For further information regarding the BCU Long Term Paddler Development Pathway, please refer to the Pathway Document.

SEE ALSO

- www.bcu.org.uk

for Tables of the Stages of Athlete Development

- www.worldclass-canoeing.org.uk

for Physical, Mental/Cognitive and Emotional Development

The BCU website has links to other reading material and useful websites.

▶ SOCIAL AND PSYCHO-LOGICAL DEVELOPMENT

There has been a lot of research carried out regarding participation in sport and why young people drop out of a particular sport or activity. Research conducted by Southampton University in 1996 concluded that less than 1% of all young people who are introduced to canoeing actually take up the sport. Considering how many children take part in taster sessions through adventure holiday organisations, BCU Approved Centres, school activity days, youth clubs, scouts, guides, etc, the number of people taking up the sport is probably way below 1%.

Over the past few years there have been numerous references to the 'tick box' mentality of today's young people, trying an activity, 'ticking it off' then moving on to the next. Another important recent change is the way technology has influenced youngsters' lives; computer games, internet and mobile phones can all contribute to less interest in physical recreation.

At the Institute for Outdoor Learning National Conference in April 2003, Rod Carr opened the Conference with a rousing keynote speech of "Converting a One-off Experience into a Lifelong Passion". He outlined that Outdoor Education was competing with the 'electronic bedroom' and the 'pick & mix' culture which we had to match by giving young people excitement, lively fun, young friendly instructors and also a realisation that some do not like to be scared or out of control.

Photo 6 Social paddling scene

There are other factors which may detract from a young person's dedication to paddling, a newfound interest in members of the opposite sex, other sports and hobbies, peer group pressure, part-time jobs, school commitments or simply becoming bored with canoeing. With girls, a lack of female coaches or other female paddlers can often contribute to 'drop out'. As a child gets older, their perceptions of leisure and their interests change. As a coach it is important that you can adapt your coaching practice to ensure your sessions are fun, challenging and stimulating enough to inspire young paddlers to keep turning up to your sessions.

You may, at times, need to adapt sessions to meet specific needs such as:

Pleasure and enjoyment, friendship and acceptance, sense of achievement, demonstrate competence and independence, improving health and fitness, changing attitudes at different stages of development.

How athletes feel about themselves (self-image) is important. If they don't feel good about themselves in a particular setting they avoid that environment – they don't come paddling again, or do not perform to their potential. You play a large role in the development of an athlete's self-image.

Photo 7 Friendly coach

SEE ALSO

Further details can be found in Sports Science texts such as:

• Physical Education and the Study of Sport, Bob Davis, Mosby, 2000.

• Science for Exercise and Sport, Craig Williams, David James. Routledge, 2000.

Or coaching websites such as:

• www.brianmac.demon.co.uk

GOOD PRACTICE

• Know their names and use them (first names) when addressing them.
• Establish eye contact.
• Smile - often and readily.
• Give approving nods, winks, thumbs up.
• Develop a 100 ways to say "well done" (and remember to add their name)!
• Applaud effort, not just results.
• Be enthusiastic, energetic.
• Involve them in decisions.
• Let paddlers assume leadership in an appropriate situation.
• Spend time with everyone.
• Give them responsibilities.
• Remind them of their achievements.
• Treat them as you'd like to be treated when you are learning or being evaluated on some new task or skill.

▶ PHYSICAL FACTORS AND SKILL DEVELOPMENT

Refer also to the section on Growth in Chapter 1.

Physical growth is a process that is associated with steady increases in height, weight and muscle mass, whilst development refers to the functional changes that occur with growth. As we are looking to coach paddlers sometimes from a very early age, it is important that we have an understanding of paediatric exercise physiology.

GROWTH SPURTS

As children develop, they experience growth spurts where parts of the body grow at differing rates, the legs tend to grow faster before puberty and the trunk grows faster in the later stages of puberty. Adolescents can have disproportionately long limbs, and can appear clumsy and have difficulty in controlling their movements. These effects can often be minimised by co-ordination and agility exercises and supportive coaching. An example of this was when young tennis hopeful, Anna Kornacova could no longer hit the ball when her arms had grown so much. She could easily have been lost to the sport if a coach had not understood the reason and worked with her to resolve the problem.

A major growth spurt occurs at the time of puberty. Around age 8 to 13 in girls and 10 to 15 in boys, children enter puberty, which lasts from about 2 to 5 years. This growth spurt is associated with sexual development, which includes the appearance of pubic and underarm hair, the growth and development of sex organs, and in girls, the onset of menstruation.

By the time girls reach age 15 and boys reach age 16 or 17, the growth associated with puberty will have ended for most teens and they will have reached physical maturity. Physical changes to the shape of the child also take place, boys develop wider shoulders as girls develop wider hips, boys gain muscle as girls develop more fat. These changes alter biomechanics of movement, change the centre of gravity of a child, and alter strength to weight ratios. This can lead to a post-pubescent loss of performance, especially in girls, which can be very frustrating and upsetting to the young athlete. Girls who found they could beat all the boys in, for example Lightening sprints at ten years old, could well be very disappointed to find that, as the same boys mature and become stronger, she can no longer keep up. It is important for coaches to be aware and sympathetic to these changes.

Another important consideration for coaches is that not all children develop at the same rate, there can be as much as four years difference in developmental age between children of the same chronological age. This is further compounded by the way we take a specific reference point for age qualification. For example, when the BCU Young People's Programme run an event, the age is sometimes taken at 1st September to ensure school classmates are together. Children in the same event may have almost a year age gap, therefore a potential five year developmental age gap. Coaches can quantify growth spurts by measuring young athletes at regular intervals. (See Appendix 2 of the Long Term Paddler Development Pathway Document).

BONE DEVELOPMENT

Bones develop from cartilage growth plates, called epiphyseal plates, at each end of the bone shaft. These growth plates divide the calcified head of the bone (epiphysis) and the calcified shaft (diaphysis). The bone lengthens as cartilage is calcified into bone on the diaphyseal border, thus lengthening the shaft. At the same time, cartilage continues to grow on the epiphyseal border, so the epiphyseal plates retain a constant

Photo 8 *They are on the same session but their biological ages vary enormously.*

width of cartilage throughout. Growth ends when the plate eventually calcifies.

Growing bones are sensitive to stress so repetitive loading should be avoided. The epiphyseal plate is susceptible to injury and therefore a fracture to the epiphyseal plate prior to full growth could be a serious injury as it could disrupt bone growth.

A more common kind of epiphyseal plate injury, and the one coaches must take care not to cause, is called epiphysitis. This is a repetitive-strain injury that occurs when excess loads are placed on the tendons that attach to the epiphysis, causing an inflammatory response. The way coaches can avoid these kinds of injuries is to make sure that the young paddlers are using the right equipment. Long heavy paddles with looms so wide the child's fingers hardly meet are very likely to cause injury over long-term paddling as well as being very uncomfortable and unwieldy.

STRENGTH AND FLEXIBILITY

Strength is dependant on muscle type and size, hence as a child grows, their muscles enlarge and they become stronger. Smaller children are generally not only weaker but disproportionately so, therefore as a coach you cannot expect them to perform strength activities in the same way as adults or more mature children. This is especially relevant when children are helping to transport heavy boats; better to have a little army working as a team moving boats one at a time than risk injury.

As far as training goes, it is a myth that children should not participate in resistance training until they have stopped growing due to the danger of damaging the epiphyseal plates of the growing bones. The risk is only an issue if the young person is lifting exceptionally heavy weights, i.e. maximal lifts, or if they don't have enough rest between resistance sessions. (Children should undertake a maximum of three resistance sessions per week; remember some paddling sessions will be classed as resistance work).

There are far more arguments to promote the concept of young people undertaking resistance training:

To strengthen muscles / tendons / ligaments and bones to prepare the body for the demands of paddling and to reduce the risk of injury.

To learn correct techniques involved in lifting weights.

To learn how to train safely with weights and develop a training concept.

To reduce muscular imbalances developed as a result of paddling.

We need strong sitting muscles for paddling, without which a poor posture and ineffective paddling technique can lead to back problems.

The shoulder joint needs a strong set of balanced muscles to keep it stable.

Resistance training can be used to develop the muscles neglected by paddling and help create a balanced muscular system. Wherever there is muscular imbalance there is a risk of injury.

Strength training as a youngster makes the bones stronger by increasing bone density and reducing the risk of injury. This is especially good news for the girls, as high bone density can decrease the risk of osteoporosis in later life.

Paddling puts a heavy demand on the muscular system, a suitably designed strength-training programme can help develop these muscles, forming a strong base... safely. The demands on strength are far greater on the water than they will be during appropriately designed resistance-training sessions on the land.

Photo 9 Youngster strength training with coach.

Pre-pubertal children will become stronger from resistance training, by making improvements in movement efficiency, learning movement patterns and through improved muscle activation. The muscles do not increase in size because of training, but become better at doing their job.

Think low weight or no weight before puberty, with an increase in weight and decrease in reps after the growth spurt. Be aware some children may experience a strength 'lag' during the growth spurt and so may not be as strong as their physical size might suggest.

Photo 10 Youngster flexibility training (poor hamstrings).

Flexibility and stretching are very important to improve range of movement and reduce risk of injury, however because the epiphyseal areas of immature bones are prone to damage through over-stretching, it is important that the coach adapts sessions to avoid ballistic or bouncing stretches. It must also be appreciated that when the growth spurt begins, a sudden lengthening of the bones, tendons, ligaments and muscles occurs; this can cause the body to become tight, stiff and prone to injury. It is therefore important to include flexibility training into the young person's training.

(See Appendix 1 of the Long Term Paddler Development Pathway Document for details of the Strength Window of Opportunity).

THERMO-REGULATION

The body needs to maintain an optimum operating temperature to function properly; as we exercise we burn calories, producing excessive heat that is then dissipated through increased blood flow to the surface and evaporation of sweat. Children have a large surface area when compared to adults and so are not so efficient at maintaining their optimum body temperature. They overheat very quickly, sweating more and so becoming prone to dehydration and heat exhaustion. In cold conditions they lose heat quicker than an adult. These points are very relevant to us as a capsize on a hot day can take a young paddler to potentially dangerous extremes very quickly. All canoeists are aware of how much heat is lost through the head, so a child whose head is proportionately larger than an adult's is especially vulnerable and on cold days should wear some sort of insulating hat.

Photo 11 Appropriate headgear for the conditions.

AEROBIC/ANAEROBIC CAPABILITIES

Aerobic exercise in simple terms is low intensity, prolonged activity such as marathon paddling. This is sub-maximal and if repeated often with rest periods will result in increased endurance fitness in both adults and children. Adolescents' aerobic systems are particularly trainable; aerobic work should be specifically trained from the start of the growth spurt for approximately 4 years. (See Appendix 1 of the Long Term Paddler Development Pathway Document for details of the Aerobic Window of Opportunity).

Anaerobic exercise is high intensity, short duration, bursts of activity, this utilises carbohydrates stored in the muscles without the use of oxygen. This has the side effect of producing waste products such as lactic acid, which result in fatigue. Children often do not cope well with this sort of training and a coach should use it sparingly until a child's capacity for anaerobic work has gradually increased. It is generally better

Photo 12 Youngsters doing short sprints.

to increase a child's fitness aerobically. Pre-pubertal children should work hard in the 5-15 second range, and over 2 minutes, but avoid 15 second – 2 minute length sprints / hard work until after puberty.

INFORMATION PROCESSING

There are three stages to learning a new skill, these are:

- Cognitive phase -Identification and development of the component parts of the skill.

- Associative phase - Linking the component parts into a smooth action.

- Autonomous phase - Developing the learned skill so that it becomes automatic.

The learning of physical skills requires the relevant movements to be assembled, component by component, using feedback to shape and polish them into a smooth action. Rehearsal of the skill must be done regularly and correctly. In the first phase of learning children are concentrating very hard on the movement, hence it appears 'jerky' or unco-ordinated, and parts of the movement are missing or incorrect, such as not twisting the paddle shaft between alternate strokes resulting in one blade constantly skimming the surface and the boat spinning. Young paddlers rely heavily on coach feedback at this stage. Simple commands such as 'right', 'wide', 'low', 'twist' may be repeated until the child starts to advance into the next phase. In the associative phase, feedback can be delayed a little to allow the performer to experiment and experience the way the skill is working, however incorrect technique does need to be corrected during this phase.

PRACTICE MAKES PERMANENT NOT NECESSARILY PERFECT

In the final phase the skill can be produced time and again without much thought, allowing the performer

| Rudimentary Skill Development 0-5 years | → | Fundamental Skill Development 5-8/9 years | → | Specialist Movement Development 9+ years |

Fig. 1 Skill Development

to concentrate on tactics, strategies, reading the water etc. The performer should not need so much feedback now as they should be in a position to recognise their own mistakes and correct them accordingly.

SKILL DEVELOPMENT

The stages of skill development are outlined in Fig. 1.

▶ Rudimentary Skill Development

During the first two years of life children gradually develop voluntary movement control. For example, they develop the skills to crawl, walk, stand, sit, reach and grasp. By 12 months most children are walking independently and achieve a mature walking gait by 5 years of age.

▶ Fundamental Skill Development

Once a child has learnt to walk, a door is opened to a completely new world. Improvements in balance and co-ordination mean the hands are no longer required for support and can be used for a whole range of new skills.

The movement patterns for these skills are usually at a proficient level by the age of 6-8, but often take longer to reach a fully mature state; this is especially true of the skills that require higher levels of co-ordination, i.e. catching or hitting.

Photo 13 Fundamental skill stage

▶ Specialised Movement Development

The fundamental movement skills form the foundation upon which more complex movements and combinations are subsequently formed. Through practice and instruction the fundamental movement skills are refined and developed, the basic movement patterns are integrated into more complex skills that are fundamental to many games and sports.

Within paddlesport we can categorise the generic foundation skills as in Fig. 2.

It is vital that high quality skills are developed during the childhood years, these will stay with the paddler for the rest of their life.

Photo 14 Specialist skill development

REACTION TIME AND CO-ORDINATION

Children have slower reaction times than adults and so cannot react to situations as we would. Their co-ordination is sometimes lacking, especially during growth spurts therefore they often struggle to perform smooth and accurate motor tasks. When setting tasks the coach needs to be aware of these limitations, making the tasks fairly simple initially, with few decisions to be made by the young person, e.g. simplifying polo rules, making the pitch smaller, gradually making slalom courses more complex, and explaining the importance of lining up for the next gate.

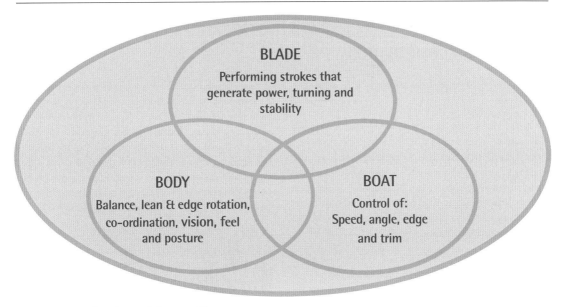

BLADE

Performing strokes that generate power, turning and stability

BODY

Balance, lean & edge rotation, co-ordination, vision, feel and posture

BOAT

Control of: Speed, angle, edge and trim

Fig. 2 Generic foundation skills in paddlesport

ADAPTING SESSIONS FOR YOUNG PADDLERS

As coaches we need to be aware of the limitations of young paddlers; with reference to the previous sections try to think about considerations you would make when coaching young paddlers. For example, one issue that has been raised on a number of occasions is high kneeling C1 and C2 paddling; the general consensus of opinion is that the young paddler should alternate paddling sides often during training. Ergos are often used to develop technique with close feedback from the coach; this allows the paddler to concentrate purely on one element of paddling without being distracted by the boat wobbling or going off line etc.

In specific disciplines with their unique potential problems it is vital that you keep abreast of the latest research and best practices.

> ### ◯ SEE ALSO
>
> Further details can be found in Sports Science texts such as:
>
> • Physical Education and the Study of Sport, Bob Davis, Mosby, 2000.
>
> • Science for Exercise and Sport, Craig Williams, David James. Routledge, 2000.
>
> • Motor Learning and Performance, Richard A. Schmidt, Craig A. Wrisberg, Human Kinetics Europe Ltd, 1999.
>
> • An Introduction to Sports Physiology, Martin Farrally, Coachwise Ltd, 1995.
>
> • Or coaching websites such as www.brianmac.demon.co.uk.

15

Photo 15 Correctly sized equipment

EXTRA CONSIDERATION

Some groups of youngsters require a little more consideration:

• *Girls:* As previously mentioned, girls develop differently to boys and as a result sometimes lose proportionate strength. This, coupled with hormonal changes, can make them self-conscious around boys and so sessions may need to be adapted to take these needs into consideration. Girls often respond better to female coaches. The BCU is currently piloting a scheme called Girl Power.

• *Gifted and Talented:* As a coach you have a moral obligation to place a young athlete where they are most likely to excel. Sometimes this is difficult for a coach, to 'lose' a promising athlete to another club or coach.

Photo 16 Talented youngster

• *Low Performers:* Some children are not quite so quick to learn as others. Slow things down, break the skills into manageable chunks, make the sessions fun and reward effort as well as results.

• *Disability Groups:* This is a complex area, but one that should not be overlooked, the BCU is keen to encourage anyone to paddle, and so runs disability awareness courses. The key issue is to see past the disability and concentrate on the paddler. Young people with learning difficulties especially gain personal self-esteem and experiences from paddling sessions. As a coach you should be able to find ways to enable anyone to paddle. See BCU Canoe and Kayak Handbook.

Photo 17 Ethnic groups

• *Ethnic Groups:* Some religions and cultures make participation in sports difficult for some youngsters, parents sometimes discourage their children from playing certain sports. A lack of swimming ability or inbred fear of water, sometimes makes paddling seem an impossible pastime for some children. It is important to reassure both the parents and the children that the sport is safe, and discuss any misgivings either may have. Special consideration may need to be given to religious practices.

KEY POINTS

• Your sessions should be youth focussed and paddler centred, each paddler should be treated as an individual and sessions will need to be differentiated to allow everyone to benefit from coach input.

• Children are not mini-adults.

• Every child is different, some develop quicker than others, each one is an individual case.

▶ COACHING YOUNG PEOPLE

Coaching children can be highly rewarding. You should be having fun and the children should be having fun! This doesn't only mean splashing and falling in the water. Having fun is achieving a goal set by the coach, managing to keep the boat in a straight line, getting around a slalom course cleanly, winning a medal for the club, etc. There is tremendous satisfaction for a coach when young paddlers do well, but you must remember to keep your sessions enjoyable.

COACHING CHILDREN

You may have many years experience of coaching children or you may be a novice. Below are listed some guidelines that may be useful.

Photo 18 Working with a group

▶ Response And Adaptation To Exercise

Give a correct warm-up. Young children do not need to realise it is a warm-up, it could be in the form of a game. The warm-up should be activity specific; that means that some of the warm-up should be done on the water. The best warm-ups start with some cardiovascular activity to raise body temperature and so warm up muscles and prepare not just physically but mentally. Dynamic flexibility and mobility must play a large part in the warm-up.

Finish the session with a cool-down, including gentle paddling and static stretches - this may reduce muscle and joint tightness throughout the week.

Children become warmer earlier than adults when exercising, this affects hydration. It is therefore very important that you stop your group for a short water break every 20 minutes.

Whist the children may not be under your direct control at meal times continually stress the importance of good eating habits, you are what you eat, exercise needs fuel. The most important meal is breakfast. Don't forget it is very important to eat after exercise, preferably within twenty minutes, and consisting predominantly of carbohydrates.

Photo 19 Water bottles lined up on the bank

Sleep is of paramount importance also, please stress this to young paddlers.

▶ Learning Techniques And Developing Skills

Do:

- Work within the children's limitations.
- Explain what they are trying to do clearly and simply.
- Demonstrate - suggest how they might do it.
- Instruct through visual information as well as verbal information.
- Give enough time for practice.
- Be patient and correct errors one at a time.
- Communicate slowly in simple terms, with one key factor or sub-skill/component at a time.
- Keep corrective feedback simple - no paralysis by analysis.
- Point out the important things to attend to.
- Help children evaluate their own performance through effective questioning.
- Keep practices shorter with younger children.

Photo 20 Smiley coach

Don't:

❌ Expect too much too soon.

❌ Give them too much to think about.

❌ Talk in technical jargon: who are you trying to impress?

❌ Be critical when giving feedback: be positive.

Psycho-Social Development

Do:

✔ Try to achieve maximum involvement for everyone.

✔ Be sensitive to the adolescent who seeks independence and identity.

✔ Give confidence by encouraging children to try new things.

✔ Give everyone some success during a session.

✔ Pay attention to everyone, not just the 'stars'.

✔ Change the rules to suit.

Don't:

❌ Expect children to understand the activity completely.

❌ Put them down for trying.

❌ Make children specialise too early.

WHAT DO CHILDREN LIKE IN THEIR COACHES?

Young athletes have preferences about how they are treated and the sort of things they like in their coaches. In principle, it is important to treat them with respect and not as if they were objects. They like you to listen and take notice of their feelings and opinions.

A recent series of interviews with 140 young athletes in different sports gives an idea of those aspects of coaching which young athletes think are important. The opinions that were given may change according to sex, age, and sport. These are just the general comments:

✔ **Knowledge** - Coaches should know their sport well and most children prefer coaches who have participated in the sport. It provides them with credibility.

✔ **Personality** - Children like coaches who are friendly, happy, patient, understanding and have a sense of humour.

✔ **Authority** - Children like coaches to be firm but fair, and while boys particularly, like to be worked hard, they don't like to be shouted at.

✔ **Taking personal interest** - As they get older and more able, many young athletes like coaches to take an interest in the things they do besides sport.

✔ **Reaction to performance** - When they do well, children like the coach to say "Well done" but they don't like them to "go over the top." (OTT) When they do poorly, they like to be given some encouragement and told what went wrong. They want to be told how to correct mistakes and not to be shouted at or ignored.

✔ **Encouragement** - Most children, particularly in team sports, like to have the coach shout encouragement to them when they are competing.

✔ **Decision making** - Few young children express a wish to have a say in the decisions which affect them; they expect coaches to coach and trust them to make the right decisions. As they get older and more experienced, they are more likely to want to be consulted. This may be the case with 13+ children.

✔ **Organisation** - Children like coaches to be organised and present structured coaching sessions. They also like them to take responsibility for seeing that they are in the right place at the right time.

✔ **Instruction and feedback** - Children do like to be shown what to do, how to do it and to have mistakes corrected. In short: teach them!

⭕ SEE ALSO

- Coaching Children in Sport: Principles and Practice, M.J. Lee, Spon Press, 1993.

- Working with Children (Introductory Study Pack) Coachwise Ltd, 1996.

BCU Coaching Young Paddler Workshop - details from BCU, e mail: youth@bcu.org.uk

▶ BCU YOUNG PEOPLE'S PROGRAMME

The BCU Young People's Programme aims to tackle the challenges and develop strategies to provide a comprehensive paddlesport programme that meets the needs of young people in the 21st century.

The key aims of the programme are:

◉ Translating taster activity into regular paddling.

◉ Supporting clubs and centres to develop safe, effective, child-friendly programmes and encourage better links with each other.

◉ Helping clubs, centres and other organisations to develop quality programmes that offer a range of paddlesport experience.

◉ Recruiting and training more volunteers to provide quality experiences and coaching to young people.

◉ Providing more opportunities for young talent to improve and progress.

◉ Provision of appropriate equipment for youth, locally and regionally.

The BCU Young People's Programme has developed a number of initiatives to support the above – such as the Paddlepower Scheme, Cadet Leader Award, Top Club, Diamond Slalom Award, and the Curriculum at Key Stage 2 & 3. To assist with implementation there are a number of part-time Paddlesport Development Officers (PDO) working at a local level and who can help providers who wish to develop more opportunities for youth.

Details of all BCU YPP initiatives can be found on the youth pages of www.bcu.org.uk.

PADDLEPOWER

Paddlepower is an exciting scheme which has been designed to meet the needs of young people. Its colourful and youth-centred approach is aimed at the under-16 age group. It comprises of progressive levels to take the paddler to just beyond 2 Star standard.

For more information see BCU website.

CADET LEADER AWARD

The Cadet Leader Award aims to encourage and introduce young people into leadership roles within paddlesport, through a training programme based at their own club, centre or the organisation where they paddle. Many young people have much to offer their club, bringing a variety of skills, willingness, enthusiasm, and provide a valuable role model for younger paddlers. This scheme hopes to encourage their involvement, development of skills and recognise those already helping out.

See Cadet Leader Award Syllabus on the BCU website.

CLUB DEVELOPMENT AND ACCREDITATION

Clubs play an important role for young people in paddlesport. To support clubs to develop safe, effective child friendly practices there are currently two main schemes which lead to accreditation. These are the BCU Top Club Award and Sport England Clubmark Award. Together these schemes provide a kite mark to recognize clubs across sports, agencies working in sport, local authorities, schools and for parents.

Clubmark is the new club accreditation scheme across sports which has been linked to the BCU Top Club scheme to meet the needs of our clubs and paddlesport. This means that a club can gain accreditation for both schemes at the same time.

Both schemes are based on the principle that clubs demonstrate:

🗷 A commitment to young people.

🗷 Provision of safe, quality activity and coaching programmes.

For clubs that have achieved the standards it gives public recognition. For clubs that wish to improve what they do it is like a blueprint/model to help and guide which areas to work on. The Top Club award is not just for clubs - BCU approved centres can work towards the award.

To enter the Top Club programme you should contact your PDO or the Young People's Programme at BCU Head Office. For further details of the Top Club Criteria see BCU website.

DIAMOND SLALOM CHALLENGE

Based on the Diamond figure formed by 4 slalom gates, it is the ideal way to test boat handling skills and to practise those strokes needed on moving water, whether taking part in a slalom or just paddling down a river. It has been designed to fit into a one-hour pool session and can be used as a goal setting and motivation tool for young paddlers and, whilst aimed at 8-12 age group, it has proved to be very popular with all age groups.

Photo 21 Diamond slalom

XSTREAM CHALLENGE

This is a great new challenge to help young people develop better moves in their boat – and have FUN! There are lots of different formats which include freestyle, slalom and polo – including spins, limbos and ball work.

XStream (pronounced cross stream) can be done individually or as a team – and can be set up in a swimming pool or at your club. Each challenge is marked out by slalom poles or buoys and there is a set course to follow.

THE PERCEPTION WAVEHOPPER CHALLENGE SERIES

A fun series of events are held around the country, which are run by the BCU Youth Programme to introduce young people to Wild Water racing. The races are either over two short runs or one slightly longer run. The age categories are U12 (under 12), U14, U16 (on 1st January). It's great for learning more about rivers and developing skills… even better, it's challenging, fun and exciting!

Photo 22 Wavehopper

Wavehopper Kayaks can be provided through the community boat scheme; contact your Regional Paddlesport Development Officer for details. To find out more about the Wavehopper Kayaks, please visit the Perception website at www.perception.co.uk.

PYRANHA LIGHTNING CUP SERIES

The Lightning Cup is a series of Sprint and Marathon events, timed to run alongside some of our main National Sprint and Marathon competitions. The regattas are designed to cater for youngsters (boys & girls) under the age of 12 and who are not competing in the main event. The aim of these events is to encourage the participants to train, improve and to compete together.

To find out more about the Lightning K1, please visit the Pyranha website at: www.pyranha.com.

Photo 23 Lightning

THE BELL BOAT

The Bell Boat is a team boat for all, which has been used by every section of the community. It is 9m long and the catamaran design makes it very stable. This enables safe transportation of up to 8 adults or up to 14 children plus a helm/coach. It can be used by all ages and abilities. It truly is a boat for ALL!

The Bell Boat is ideally used as a school on water and gives those taking part a greater understanding of teamwork, individual strengths and co-operation. Above all, it's fun!

▶ Bell Boat Events

The BCU Young People's Programme run a series of Bell Boat events throughout the year around the country. These are fun events in which all ability levels are welcome. There is also an annual Bell Boat National Championships each year with prizes for age classes and scout/guide groups. For more details see Events, on the youth pages of www.bcu.org.uk.

Photo 24 Bell Boats

THE BELL BOAT HELM AWARD

This award is specifically aimed at teachers and youth leaders to enable them to take children and young people on the water. A person with no previous paddling skills can qualify as a helm after a 2 day course (this includes 4 hours first aid). Courses are available through the Coaching for Teachers scheme. For more details of the Bell Boat Helm Awards, and Coaching for Teachers see the youth pages of www. bcu.org.uk.

ACCESSING BELL BOATS

There are a number of "community" Bell Boats around the country which can be accessed on agreement with the organization where they are based. For details of location and see Community Bell Boats on the youth pages of www.bcu.org.uk.

Bell Boats can be purchased new direct from the manufacturers - for full details and prices contact Main Sport on 01386 861034, Fax 01386 861008.

PADDLESPORT AND THE CURRICULUM

▶ Paddlesport At Key Stage 2

Paddlesport can meet many aspects of the Key Stage 2 Curriculum and not just outdoor and adventurous activity. Aspects such as games, history, geography, science, technology and, importantly, environmental aspects can be enjoyed more through taking the classroom onto the water.

There is a BCU booklet which is full of ideas and guidance entitled The Curriculum at Key Stage 2 and Watersports which includes 10 resource lesson plans.

▶ Paddlesport At Key Stage 3

Paddlesport can meet the requirements of the National Curriculum at Key Stage 3 in Outdoor & Adventurous Activities, Athletic Activities, Games.

▶ Paddlesport At Key Stage 4

Canoeing can be an integral part of your curriculum. The various disciplines within the sport cater for all demands made by the National Curriculum at Key Stage 4. All you need is access to canoes and the water, appropriately qualified coaches and the willingness to offer your pupils the excitement and diversity of the sport.

As with KS3, various aspects of the National Curriculum can be easily and comprehensively met. Outdoor and Adventurous Activities comes quickly and easily to mind, but other aspects, sometimes overlooked, can also be included:

Games are played in canoes up to international level - canoe polo.

Photo 25 Youngsters playing a non-contact variant of canoe polo.

Running with your arms in linear, competitive and recreational events, the same as other linear athletic activities - marathon and sprint canoeing.

Inclusion of the activity as part of Duke of Edinburgh Awards is also popular.

GCSE Examinations are also included in the possibilities for your pupils. All examination boards have specifications including canoeing, and if contacted can advise on content and assessment procedures.

Clubs are only too happy to help with candidates wishing to use canoeing as part of their GCSE, and Paddlesport Development Officers can offer further advice and help.

PADDLESPORT DEVELOPMENT OFFICERS (PDO)

These are professional staff (mostly part-time) whose role is to initiate and facilitate activities to promote and support the development of youth opportunities and progressions in paddlesport. They work with clubs, centres and youth organizations and run a range of workshops and events for coaches and youth.

Contact details for PDO's can be found on the BCU website.

FURTHER READING

How to Help Children Find the Champion Within Themselves, David Hemery 2005
Physical Education and the Study of Sport, Bob Davis, Mosby, 2000.
Science for Exercise and Sport, Craig Williams, David James. Routledge, 2000.
Motor Learning and Performance, Richard A. Schmidt, Craig A. Wrisberg, Human Kinetics Europe Ltd, 1999.
An Introduction to Sports Physiology, Martin Farrally, Coachwise Ltd, 1995.
Coaching Children in Sport: Principles and Practice, M.J. Lee, Spon Press, 1993.
Working with Children, (Introductory Study Pack), Coachwise Ltd, 1996.

WEBSITES:

www.bcu.org.uk
www.brianmac.demon.co.uk
www.worldclass-canoeing.org.uk

BCU YOUNG PEOPLE'S PROGRAMME

Phil Hadley, Sue Hornby and Lara Tipper

Sue Hornby enjoys paddling now just as much as when she started 35 years ago, whether it's competition or recreation, on flat water, white water or the sea! This has taken her around the world and includes winning medals at World WWR Championships, competing in 9 World Championships, taking the first GB Ladies Team to compete in the Molokai Hoe Outrigger Canoe Race and being a member of the River Fraser Kayak Expedition on the first descent in 1981. Sue has worked in personnel, coached the RYA Olympic Windsurfing Squad, manufactured throw bags and currently works for the British Canoe Union as Head of Young People's Programme.

Sue Hornby

Lara Tipper started kayaking when she was 10 years old and has been driven by the sport ever since! Under her belt she has achieved successful international slalom and freestyle results, Level 5 Coach, and has had the experience of paddling some of the best white water around the world. She now works for the BCU on the Long Term Paddler Development project and coaches white water paddling and coach education on a freelance basis.

Phil Hadley is described in Chapter 4.

Lara Tipper

11 USE OF VIDEO

Video is the ultimate tool for providing feedback; it beats having to run next to your student with a full size mirror! Feedback can be instant through the viewfinder or it can be reviewed after the session on a larger screen. As a tool it can be used to measure progression in performance and comparisons can be made with other paddlers, which in turn can be used for motivation. This chapter will show you how powerful a video camera can be within your coaching, and give you some helpful tips on what to buy and how to use it.

SAFETY

Safety must underpin our coaching.

The coach must always consider safety before getting the camera out. A quick risk assessment of your students' abilities is essential. Do they have the ability to rescue each other, or to roll… and where are they going to end up if they don't? Your reaction time to a rescue situation is a lot slower whilst using a camera.

There are two options: to film from your boat, (inevitably with your spraydeck off if you're in a kayak) or to film from the bank. A canoe is a great 'halfway house' because you don't have to 'faff' with a deck.

Filming from your boat also creates some practical issues such as camera shake and your movement on the water you are filming from. To avoid all these problems:

- Wedge yourself on a rock.
- Avoid using the zoom from a distance.
- Use a site that has a run-out, allowing you time to get your spraydeck back on.

When filming from the bank, always have a throw bag to hand, and set up a system where your students look after each other. On the sea you won't have the problem of having your spraydeck off because you will want to carry the camera in a deck bag and tether it because they don't float. However, make sure your system does not hinder your ability to perform rescues in any way. Surf coaches have the potential problem of getting their camera stolen when they are rescuing. Working a buddy system will give rescue cover to solve this problem, freeing you up to film.

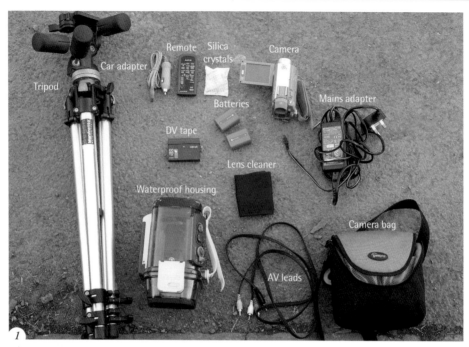

Photo 1 Camera and accessories

► TECHNICAL

... but not scarily technical! Just some information that will help you make informed choices and avoid some of the pitfalls.

CAMERAS AND TAPES

There are now cameras available that put the footage staright onto a hard drive. However for now mini-DV format is still the best option because of storage costs and ease of cataloguing. Nowadays a mini-DV camera is very affordable. Clubs, universities or even groups of paddling friends could share the costs. The tapes are also relatively inexpensive and are usually of one hour's duration. They can be used numerous times, taping over existing footage without a loss in quality, and are a format which PC's or Mac software can work with when importing for editing purposes.

When you compare the specifications of cameras between manufacturers, Sony are at present the only company who sell hard-shell housing which allows you to fully immerse your camera, a consideration for boat-based coaches. If you buy another make you would have to rely on the soft type of waterproof case which, with cold hands, prove very fiddly and make reviewing through the LCD virtually impossible. A cheaper option is a pelicase, which is a hard, water-tight box. Pelicases offer great protection, however

you cannot use your camera when it is inside it, so I advise you to also invest in a brolly and a towel for when it rains.

Photo 2a Camera in housing

Photo 2b Camera in 'Pelicase'

BATTERIES

You can never have enough battery power. It is typical that when you have put lots of time into setting up a video session, or promised your group that they were going to see themselves on telly you'll run out of power! When you buy a camera it usually comes with a standard-sized battery, which is inadequate, so buy 2 or 3 additional batteries when you purchase your camera, ideally long-life heavy duty ones which are bigger, remembering to check they still fit in your waterproof housing.

Always be sure to have them charged. The batteries do not have a memory, which means you can top them up whenever you like without the need of running them out first. However they will still be greatly affected by the cold and their life will be much less on colder days. You should also be aware that the LCD viewfinder also zaps the batteries so, to save power, use the eyepiece viewfinder for when you are filming. When using the camera for instant review you will need to use the LCD screen rewinding; slow motion and freeze-frame functions all eat your battery. A useful gadget is a charger, which works off a car cigarette lighter. Another feature to look for in a camera is for it to show how many minutes you have left of battery time, not just a picture of a battery and its demise in its viewfinder.

CONDENSATION

Condensation always has the potential to spoil our plans. A modern camera just refuses to even switch itself on in the presence of moisture. So always have small bags of silica crystals inside the housing or peli-case and regularly dry them out on a radiator or replace them. Carry a piece of silk or chammy leather to wipe away any steam from the lens and viewfinder, but most importantly of all, avoid touching the camera with wet hands or getting it out when its raining – easier said than done I know! Place the camera into its housing before you go out, and take a towel and some form of shelter for when you change the battery or tape. If you're a sea coach use the camera sparingly! A top tip for pool sessions is to take the camera into the pool about half an hour before your session to allow it to grow accustomed to the environment. Linked closely to the moisture issue is that of oxidation on the playing heads in the camera; you'll need a cleaning tape and want to use it regularly.

ZOOM/FOCUS

A video camera has a zoom lens, which will have 2 types of zoom. They are digital and optical. The optical zoom is just like a conventional zoom lens, which allows you to zoom in on your picture without any loss of picture quality. The higher the magnification number the more you can zoom in, i.e. optical x25. Digital zoom takes it a stage further, but in doing so it reduces the resolution of the image, in turn losing quality and making it useless to film moving subjects. Cameras can be as much as 800x digital; this makes it hopeless even with a tripod. Avoid using any digital zoom at all costs. Your camera should let you know when you are venturing out of optical zoom or will even allow you to turn off the digital function. Using the optical zoom is useful to frame a shot whenever your subject is a distance away. You can also use it, carefully, to follow them as they paddle towards, or away from you. Avoid doing this fast or in a stop-start fashion. It's worth practising getting it slow and smooth. Some cameras are better than others for achieving this. Be aware! Overuse of the zoom is very off-putting when you are analysing performance… our eyes don't have a zoom!

Key points when using zoom/focus:

◎ It is best to keep your camera on auto-focus as opposed to manual because our subjects are moving, however you must be careful when you are working on a river bank with overhanging trees, slalom gates or even other paddlers in the foreground or the camera will cleverly/annoyingly focus in on that rather than your student!

◎ When filming white water/overfalls or play-boating it's best to keep the camera aimed at the paddler as opposed to aiming it at the piece of water/wave they are about to paddle into. This is because it takes the camera time to refocus from the wave you are pointing at to the paddler when they join it, thus missing any initiation/angles/speed due to being out of focus for a split second.

◎ When you move the camera to keep the subject in the frame it's called panning. By panning you will keep your paddler accurately focused.

◎ Panning is best done with a tripod to avoid camera shake.

◎ A tripod is very useful in avoiding camera shake, especially if you are working from a distance and having to use the zoom. They are a must for surf coaches. They are also good for keeping the camera away from sand! A tripod makes a frame and background consistent, with no movement; it allows you to compare performances which have the same objectives with accuracy.

Photo 3 A tripod in use

FREEZE–FRAME

Freeze-frame, frame by frame and slow motion allows you to take analysis to a much higher level than you could ever dream of. This is where the video camera is worth its weight in gold. Just make sure the camera you buy has these functions and includes a remote control, which makes these functions easier to perform without the need of holding the camera. Whilst using freeze-frame a modern day digital video camera will not blur the picture.

KNOW YOUR CAMERA

In my view the top 5 boo boos include:

⊗ Pressing record and forgetting to turn the camera on.

⊗ Turning the camera on and pressing the wrong button thinking it was record.

⊗ The old lens cap trick.

⊗ Recording over some great footage.

⊗ (My favourite) in front of a group reviewing the footage, not being able to find the freeze-frame, or frame by frame functions, and spending quarter of an hour analysing the students going at a rate of knots forwards and backwards numerous times.

 TOP TIP

• Have a good play with your camera before using it in a work capacity.

▶ FILMING

Before filming you should gain permission from your students and if you work with minors it is paramount to get their parent or guardian's permission (see Chapter 4 Duty of Care and Chapter 10 Young People and BCU Child Protection Policy, available from www.bcu.org.uk).

It is really easy for both coach and student to overload and be overloaded because you get to see everything, so it is important to both film and review objectively. To ask yourself 'What do you want to show? will be a good start and will direct you to how it should be filmed.

I will now go through some examples of what you may want to show. In each example the footage would be captured in different ways, considering Framing, Angles, Markers and the best way to 'feedback' your findings.

See yourself as a film director creating a storyboard.

FRAMING

Framing can be craftily used if you focus in on one area, i.e. just have head and shoulders in the frame or the back of the boat. This will allow you to concentrate on that element and nothing else.

Photo 4a A tight, focussed frame.

Photo 4b A wider angle used to include entry and exit.

But if your objective is angles of entry/exits, take-off speed or to feedback shapes and background you will need to make sure the frame includes them.

▶ Angles

The angle from which you film is important. Photos 6a-d are shot from different angles - they are of the same boater performing the same skill.

Which is the best angle to show the following?

- Rotation
- Stroke length/blade depth
- Plant and exit point of blade
- Head movement
- Entry angle/speed
- Trim and body position
- Amount of edge

▶ Markers

Remembering the most important point 'What do you want to show?' the use of markers within a video session is very useful to emphasize, measure or compare (see photos 6a-d and 7).

Photo 5 shows how you can compare differences in strokes or cadence. You can film paddlers next to each other so that there is a direct comparison.

Photo 5 3 paddlers lined up

▶ Comparing Like With Like

You could set the camera on a tripod and keep the frame identical, then give your paddlers start and finish points. Get your footage, and then count the number of strokes in between the two points in your review. You can also time how long it takes them. This comparison is useful for coaching competitive disciplines and if you keep the footage and repeat the session another day it allows you to monitor progressions.

Photo 6a From directly in front
Photo 6b From behind
Photo 6c From left bank
Photo 6d From right bank

Height of logo relative to water and amount of inside of hull showing make great markers for assessing amount of edge used.

Photo 7 Possible markers - a) top hand relative to gunnel, b) amount of rotation, c)and d) amount of edge.

▶ **Distractions**

Background distractions can give unexpected problems, which can be overlooked at the time of filming.

If the sun is out don't have it as a backdrop. Film with the sun behind, or the footage will be overexposed and unusable.

Avoid commentary/talking or turn the volume down when showing your student. It can be confusing and also has the potential of being very embarrassing. Another distraction is having other paddlers in the background. It is easy not to notice them in the frame when it is taking all your effort to keep your student in focus but it is a disaster when it comes to reviewing footage.

▶ **REVIEWING**

When people watch themselves on film for the first time there is a great novelty factor.

'Look Mum I'm on Telly!' It is best to get this out of one's system; play it with a bit of music and give them the opportunity to watch it a couple of times. You could even vary the angles and edit to make it fun. Once the novelty has gone you can start being productive.

When reviewing footage *everybody tends to be too critical*. This can be soul destroying and have a negative effect on performance. Don't forget that video can bring out positives in a performance and can be used as a confidence builder or motivational tool. Remember a positive frame of mind is directly related to performance.

There are essentially 2 different ways we can analyse the footage. These are through the LCD screen, (for quick and instant feedback). This can be used during journeys or sessions and is brought out by the coach to give quick-fix visual feedback that directly related to the performance just completed by the student. The other method takes the form of a review done via the camera through TV, projector or computer. The review method inevitably entails delay between performance and feedback, but does have the benefit of a larger screen and more scope/tools to enable us to be even more analytical.

Watch it yourself first holistically. This will make sure you have captured what you wanted but also find the point with which to start and end the feedback or to freeze-frame. You may also find there are more pressing issues to address, which you may not have found initially. If you have captured footage with no coaching objectives, it will hopefully give you some.

When you watch it with your students do it at real speed first, it is similar to a demo and the first image is important. If you go straight to slow motion or freeze-frame they will have trouble putting it in the context of their whole performance.

SLOW MOTION AND FREEZE-FRAME

An advanced performer will complete movements within a sequence quicker than the naked eye will be able to pick them up, some so subtle that the only way to analyse them is to slow them down. *All hail the camera!*

Watching a performance in slow motion also makes it easier for people to visualize doing it themselves. With the camera you can also see the movements over and over again. In the review the coach can physically move their student through the sequence, making it kinaesthetic. This is a perfect way to introduce mental

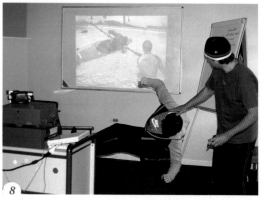

Photo 8 Kinaesthetic feedback during review

Feedback through	Pros	Cons
CAMERA LCD Feedback (instant) 	• Feedback is instant and on the spot. • No need to leave coaching site allowing the full coaching process to be immediate. • Does not require power or other hardware. • You can be selective on what you film and what you show. • Incorporates a rest in between sessions. • It's fresh and relates directly to a performance. • Forces individual coaching when working with a group.	• Screen is small. • Eats the batteries. • Can be cold for your student and fiddly for the coach with cold hands. • Hard to watch both footage and the safety/performances of others in the group.
DIGITAL PROJECTOR (£800+) onto a WHITEBOARD Review 	• Big screen. • Warm and dry so more time can be spent on feedback. • Time lag between review and next session forces more reflection time. • Projected onto a whiteboard allows you to draw. • Can be used like a mirror.	• Takes time and organisation. • Requires a classroom. • Feedback time loop. • Expensive. • More technical stuff to get to grips with. • Relating a performance seen to the same one done on the water.
COMPUTER/LAPTOP Review 	• Allows you to edit. • Comparison through split screen software. • Can be used at the venue with care. • Bigger screen compared with lcd.	• Cost. • More technical stuff to go wrong.
TV Review 	• A cheap big screen that's not too hard to work out.	• Portable but awkward. • Needs a power source.

Table 1 Pros and Cons

Photo 9 Projecting onto a whiteboard enables you to mark points for emphasis or comparison.

rehearsal (which is a useful but hard skill for anyone to master.)

A frozen frame allows you to analyse a position or shape. These can be reciprocated in the classroom/review. It can be of them, in order to copy their own position and used for confirmation of something positive, or alternatively it could be to copy another paddler, used as in modelling.

Once the position has been achieved, ask them to shut their eyes, come from and then return to the position a few times. This will help it sink into short-term memory.

Watching footage at the normal speed will have brought out a coaching point. By then, using it frame by frame, you will confirm and highlight its extent. Going from one frame to the next will do this with clarity and accuracy for you to make observations like: exactly how wide or how low, timing, and consistency.

USE OF A PROJECTOR AND WHITE BOARD

If you have access to a digital projector you can have the pleasure of seeing the footage projected large on a wall, but even better than that a white board. A whiteboard will let you draw in paddle angles, where a stroke is planted, angle of trim, boat positions, exit angles etc. By leaving your scribe on the board you

can compare the next performances or other paddlers. (This works best if the footage is consistent, i.e. on a tripod, with the same frame and same amount of zoom with each performance).

Another clever trick can be used to coach forward paddling or individual strokes. This is achieved by having the camera on in the 'camera mode', pointing at your student who is positioned in the frame and in view of the whiteboard, on a bench with their paddle in hand. Their movements will be projected directly up on the board without the need to record. The coach can manipulate the paddler into the positions and the paddler is able to feel and see for him/herself the position/movement they are making. With relation to forward paddling, with the paddler side-on to the camera, they can see their plant, reach and exit marks on the board. It will give the paddler something visual to aim for and make consistent.

Whilst having them face-on to the camera it will show rotation, head movement and punch; again marks on the board can be used in the same way (see Photo 10).

SPLIT SCREEN

There is software which allows you to have two performances shown simultaneously side by side on

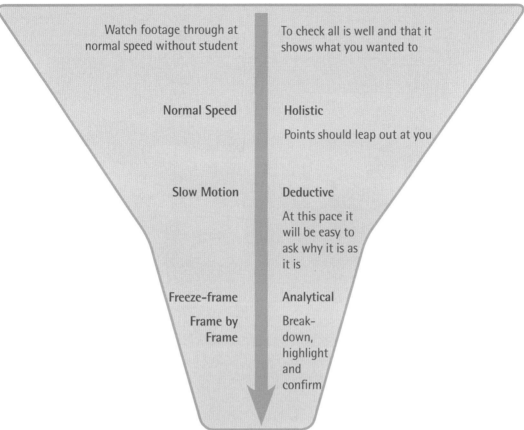

Watch footage through at normal speed without student — To check all is well and that it shows what you wanted to

Normal Speed — **Holistic**

Points should leap out at you

Slow Motion — **Deductive**

At this pace it will be easy to ask why it is as it is

Freeze-frame — **Analytical**

Frame by Frame — Break-down, highlight and confirm

Fig. 1 Video Review / Observation Funnel

10

Photo 10 With this set up the paddler can see herself paddling in actual time.

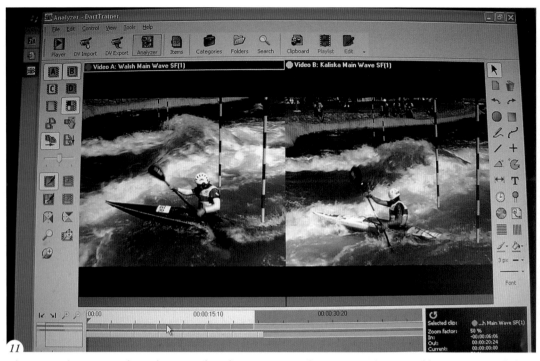

Photo 11 Split screen can be used in a number of ways. For example to compare the same athletes progress on different runs or the same course, or to compare one performer's run against another.

a split screen. This is expensive but valued by the British and Welsh Slalom Teams where comparison between performances is essential to gain extra points of a second.

Competitive discipline coaches can also take stop-watch splits from the footage, again very useful in comparing the speed of techniques.

Finally, if your video session has gone well and you have worked through the observation funnel with definite objectives, your student will have fine-tuned their own observation skills and learn't to analyse and reflect on a performance. They will have learn't to be objective and analytical when watching others, and as long as they had someone to hold the camera, they could give themselves feedback. Remember, once our paddler is an independent learner we have done our job.

LEO HOARE

The video camera has gone full circle in Leo's career, from being coached by the British Slalom Team, analysing his own paddling, to analysing his students' performances while working has a Level 5 Coach and now to make paddling education films.

For more details see www.rockandseaproductions.com and www.lookinggoodproductions.com.

12 FORWARD PADDLING

*O*ur sport's commitment in signing up to our Long Term Paddler Development model is to be
athlete centred, and coach led. It is to give quality coaching so that a paddler is equipped to get
the most out of the sport wherever he/she wishes to go, be it to cross the Atlantic, be Olympic Champion
in sprint racing over 1000m or paddle recreationally along the local river, in kayak or canoe.

*How to paddle efficiently in a forward direction is an essential part of every paddler's development
and is therefore the core area for the teaching of paddling.*

INTRODUCTION

Paddlers may have varied goals in approaching our sport, but be they purely recreational, competition based in any discipline, or seeking challenges in the adventure world, forward paddling will be the core of their success and enjoyment.

The paddler wishing to travel from point to point on a canal will want to do so as efficiently as possible. The sea canoeist on a long trip and the marathon paddler will want to conserve energy while producing good cruising speed. The slalom paddler will want fast movement from gate to gate in fast moving water. The sprint paddler will want absolute maximum speed over a set distance; the polo player will need short bursts of fast movement to gain positions.

Built onto this efficient forward paddling will be a multitude of other paddling skills to enable the paddler to effectively deal with steering, stopping, changing direction, sideways movement, boat agility, in very varied water conditions and under varied stresses created by conditions, competition etc.

The biomechanics of the specialist manoeuvring strokes and skills will use the same essential biomechanical elements as the forward paddling stroke.

As coaches we need to recognise the central nature of forward paddling and gear our paddling curriculum accordingly, giving sufficient time to this central area of paddling, so that our learners become confident in this skill before moving onwards to a whole range of new skills.

This will mean that it will not be viable to introduce and practise many varied paddling strokes in the same session as basic work on forward paddling. There will be contradictions that will confuse the paddlers.

They need time to develop and groove each skill before going on to the next one.

Elsewhere in this coaching handbook there is discussion of the process of coaching and the philosophy of a coach or athlete-centred style of approaching this.

In teaching good forward paddling, it is the athlete who is central to the process.

There is no exact coach-created template that a paddler/athlete can fit into, as only the athlete can find the best fit for them as individuals. The paddler will be a unique physical individual with a unique combination of body and limb size, strength, endurance, coordination, functional stability, skill acquisition attributes, balance, etc. etc.

What they will need from us as coaches is support to find this best fit for themselves, and much of coaching skill is centred around helping the paddler become sensitive to their own body and the boat and its movements.

However, in searching for this most efficient paddling technique for the individual, the paddler will never get near their optimum if he/she is working contrary to simple biomechanical principles.

The coach has a vital role here in leading the paddler.

In this section of the handbook there is:

◎ An outline of the biomechanical structure of efficient forward paddling.

◎ A breakdown of the forward paddling stroke.

◎ An examination of the process of teaching this in an athlete-centred style.

◎ Material to develop forward paddling onto a higher level of excellence.

▶ PREREQUISITES

There are certain prerequisites for teaching efficient forward paddling.

Teaching any skill is made easier by use of good quality and appropriate equipment.

1. STRAIGHT-RUNNING BOATS

If forward paddling is to be seen as the core of paddling, then the ideal is that it will be introduced and developed in a boat that has inherent straight-running characteristics.

Similarly when more sophisticated manoeuvring skills are introduced, there will be the need for boats specialised for that purpose if the skill is to be learnt well.

Straight-running boats will enable the paddler to focus on the skill of forward paddling without the frustrations of a boat tending to spin, or the boat failing to glide through the water.

This may initially create a challenge for coaches in terms of equipment, but with forward planning this challenge can be overcome.

As a temporary measure skegs and other devices can be fitted to short boats to improve forward stability. In the long term coaches will need to endeavour to have suitable boats available for all aspects of skill development.

2. SEAT AND FOOTREST

If the paddler is to have good contact with the platform they are paddling on, i.e. the water, then a seat will be needed, and an adequate footrest that can be firmly pressed on for support and good connections, ideally centrally in a kayak so the knees and feet can be kept together. That connection point could later develop to be the knees in specialist moving-water boats, and in kneeling canoes.

Photo 1 Lightning junior K1 showing footrest and seat.

3. STABILITY

Although a little instability in the boat will increase its forward running capability, it is initially of little value to the paddler to be in a very unstable boat. Whereas a Lightning junior K1 will be easy to keep running forward, in a racing K1 the beginner paddler will almost certainly be dominated by staying upright, not developing a good forward paddling technique.

4. BOAT AND PADDLE SIZE

In an athlete-centred world, in all sports, good coaching demands that the equipment suits the paddler. It is vital that the paddler has a boat that is scaled to his/her size, both in breadth and in weight.

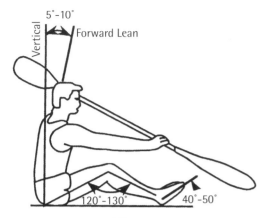

Fig. 1 Appropriate paddling position

Coaches should expect the boat to allow the paddler to take up an appropriate position to paddle (see Fig. 1).

▶ Paddles

Coaches should expect to provide a suitable range of paddle lengths with blade area appropriate to the paddler being taught.

Appropriate length can be measured using the paddler's reach - see Photos 2a and 2b.

Paddles for use largely in paddling forward will usually be set at 65-70°, where the angle is most comfortable for the catch.

Blade size is very important, with children and young adults as well as many adults needing small blade areas to suit their strength and coordination capability.

Remember that too long paddles or too large blades will prevent the acquisition of a sound forward paddling technique.

Passing down old adult paddles to juniors, or having one set of full-sized club paddles for all age paddlers is therefore something to be avoided.

Paddles usually need to be smaller than coaches and parents think!

Specific advice is available from the BCU Young Peoples' Programme.

▶ PADDLING – A HIGHLY SKILLED TECHNICAL SPORT

Coaches are introducing their paddlers to a sport where, to be effective, there is a demand for high levels of coordination, skill and body awareness. This skill is certainly up there with the most challenging of sports such as gymnastics and dance.

Unlike most landsports the paddler functions on an unstable platform, i.e. the water, but this water platform also provides support for the paddler.

Every movement that the paddler makes produces a contrary response from the water, even the most placid. On moving water this response can be more powerful and less predictable.

The water will also bring its own independent forces that will affect the paddler and the boat.

The paddler in their boat and paddling is inextricably linked to the water.

The paddler does not just sit in a boat and paddle.

The whole system is therefore the paddler, the boat and the water.

Photos 2a-b Appropriate paddle length

Photo 3 *Two elite paddlers working in harmony with their boat and the water.*

Efficient paddling requires the paddler to use this relationship in a positive way.

No matter what age, type of sport background, or branch of kayaking/canoe, it is useful for an athlete to develop a feeling for how the boat and paddle are reacting to the water. After some practice, athletes realize how important it is to feel the boat-paddle reaction to the water, and to feel the water through the boat. This ability develops after much practice.

Photo 4a *Paddle catch is just behind buoy. NELO sticker is behind buoy.*
Photo 4b *Paddle leaves water a little forward of where it went in. Boat has moved forward - see NELO sticker.*

The paddler and the boat have a structure that must remain intact if the system is to be moved efficiently in the direction chosen.

The integrity of this structure can be seen as an architectural model.

If a part of the body/boat/water relationship is compromised then the whole structure loses its integrity and effectiveness.

At its most extreme this will cause an unexpected loss of perhaps balance, or speed. At the least, it will result in ineffective paddling.

In its simplest form, efficient forward paddling is the process of moving the boat forward, while minimising all forces and movements that are not positively producing forward movement.

If therefore the boat moves contrary to the intended direction, if it snakes, rocks from side to side, lifts up and down at the bow, then a proportion of the forces are being used negatively and the forward motion will not be efficient.

▶ FORWARD PADDLING – WHAT HAPPENS

The paddle stroke is based on some very simple principles.

The paddle blade is driven into the water, well in front of the boat cockpit, using the power of the whole body.

The stability to do this is given by the legs pressing on the footrest and a strong upright posture in the body.

The blade is fixed in the water – the "Catch".

The blade remains stationary in the water while the whole body slides the boat past the fixed paddle.

The body and boat move past the blade. The blade does not move back, (in fact it will tend to move slightly forward especially with wing paddles).

▶ Objective:

🔹 Paddlers use a whole body rotational movement to transmit power from their body into forward movement of the boat.

🔹 The paddle is locked in the water at the front of the stroke and the whole trunk unwinds to transmit forward movement to the boat through the seat and footrest.

🔹 The boat moves past the fixed blade.

🔹 Boat and paddler are supported by the water.

5a

5b

Photos 5a-b The use of legs and lower body, the trunk, the shoulders and arms are all being used to create a powerful forward paddling stroke by this multi-World Champion paddler.

In efficient forward paddling the whole stroke takes place in front of the body, i.e. in front of the hip.

When the blade reaches the level of the hip it will be already out of the water.

It is desirable for the paddler to drive the blade into the water as far forward as they can reach, using the rotation of the body to extend their reach but without compromising a good posture – see earlier photos.

6

Photo 6 The blade has left the water by the time it reaches the paddler's hip. The whole stroke is in front of the hip and body.

If the paddle stays in the water after the hip, this slows the boat down but also delays the movement to the stroke on the other side of the boat, compromising that stroke in turn.

▶ THE STRUCTURE OF PADDLING

Bearing in mind the above fundamental points, we can look at the structure of forward paddling.

Although there is never only one way to look at skill acquisition, Imre Kemecsey's analysis of forward paddling as a movement is a sound basis for understanding what efficient forward paddling is.

Imre is a Hungarian master-coach who has coached paddlers from Hungary, Canada and Great Britain. He has Olympic medals as a performer himself, but has coached numerous World Champions and Olympic medallists.

He is accepted as the leading specialist in kayak technique, though all his analysis is equally applicable to canoe.

His approach to paddling technique is very useful for most coaches.

The analysis suggests that coaches and paddlers look at the whole stroke from different perspectives. His approach is to teach concepts and structures and encourage the paddler to find the best way to achieve that movement skill for them as individuals.

THE BASEMENT OF THE STROKE

Legs and buttocks.

This can be called **Power Circle 3.**

◉ The forward paddling stroke is built on the support of the water.

The body is connected to the water by the feet/footrest and the bottom on the seat.

◉ Each foot compresses the footrest to gain support for the stroke on that side.

◉ There should be a good connection with the hip as the foot presses on the footrest. If that is in place then there is a firm base for the paddling stroke.

The illustrations overleaf show the connections between foot and hips.

Power Circle 3

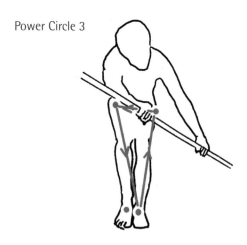

Fig. 2 Power Circle 3

Photo 7 The powerful compression of the footrest and the connection to the hip is the basis of forward paddling.

Key Teaching Points:

- Compress the footrest.

- A strong leg movement with both legs alternating.

- Good connections between the footrest(boat/water) and bottom (seat/water).

- Press on the footrest and the movement of buttock on the seat is going backwards and round.

Images for Coaches to Use:

- Squashing a peach under the foot and squeezing out juice.

- Bicycling.

Practices to Make Clearer:

- Set yourself to pull open a very stiff door - front foot presses hard onto floor to give support. This is the role of the foot on the footrest.

In Tug of War - the front foot is placed forward and presses hard to give support for maximum pulling power.

BODY ROTATION

The trunk rotates.

This can be called **Power Circle 2**

The whole upper body, the trunk, rotates on the firm base provided by the legs and pelvis.

This whole structure moves as one, keeping an upright posture.

The arms connect the trunk to the paddles but do not work independently.

The diagrams show the trunk structure rotating from the hip upwards.

There are good connections between shoulders and the paddle blades, and from shoulder blade to shoulder blade.

Power Circle 2

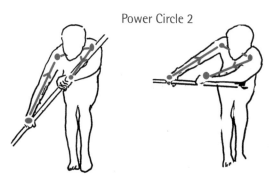

Fig. 3 Power Circle 2 - The upper body remains connected and functions as a strong structure.

Photo 8 The trunk rotates vigorously ready for the next stroke, then transmits power to that stroke.

Key Teaching Points:

🌀 Trunk rotation is round a central axis.

🌀 There is a good connection between shaft and shoulders – a strong structure.

🌀 The paddle shaft and chest/shoulders remain parallel – the body rotates.

🌀 The body follows the shaft round.

🌀 The two arms work as one.

🌀 The stroke is kept in front of hips – the blades come out before hip – so hand will finish the stroke just past the knee.

Images for Coaches to Use:

🌀 Think of a stretched membrane between the paddle shaft and shoulders. Keep it stretched, with no wrinkles. Wrinkles = a lost connection.

🌀 Think of two arms working as one – see canoe paddling.

🌀 Think of the structure as an eggshell (Bako) - as long as it is complete it is strong. Bend the arms at the front of the stroke or during the stroke, or lose the whole rotating trunk, and you lose the strong structure. It becomes weak like a dented eggshell.

Practices to Use:

🌀 In the warm-up - horizontal arm swings at shoulder level keep whole structure rotating as one.

🌀 The coach holds the paddle shaft. The paddler tensions and feels the tension/compression in both shoulders.

🌀 Horizontal rotation with a shaft in the boat or on an 'ergo'.

THE CATCH

The lower arm is straightened and the paddle is driven down into the water in front of the cockpit using the power of the whole connected trunk.

This can be called **Power Circle 1.**

The paddle blade becomes a fixed point in the water to move the boat past.

Power Circle 1

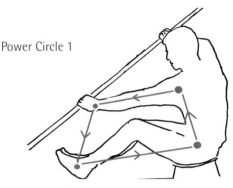

Fig. 4 Power Circle 1

Photo 9 The footrest, hip and trunk are all connected to the paddle blade to drive it into the water and then hold onto the blade in the water throughout the stroke.

Key Teaching Points:

🌀 Drive the paddle downwards in front of the cockpit.

🌀 Ensure there is a good connection between shoulder and blade, hip and foot on each side.

🌀 The foot/water on the stroke side provides a good support for the catch.

🌀 Fix the blade in the water. Lock the blade.

🌀 Hang on the fixed catch.

🌀 Put the body weight onto the paddle blade.

Images for the Coach to Use:

🌀 Spearing fish – beware slapping the water, so think of spearing a fish 30cm below the surface.

🌀 Think of the blade being stuck in a concrete block just under the water. (This is close to the facts - a full-size wing blade can grip a block of up to 35kg of water at the catch).

🌀 Holding onto a fixed post in the water.

Practices to Use:

🖐 The coach holds the shaft so the paddler can tension and feel a good connection with the shoulder, hip and foot.

🖐 The paddler hangs from chin bars – feeling the tension as they pull themselves up.

🖐 The paddler holds an upright pole and tensions against it.

MOVE THE BOAT PAST THE PADDLE

The blade is locked at the catch and the opposite hip drives the boat forward as the trunk unwinds powerfully against this fixed point.

This can be called **Power Circle 4.**

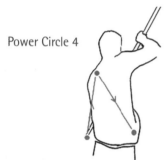

Fig. 5 Power Circle 4

Photo 10 *The crucial connection between blade and opposite hip (boat) allows the powerful sliding forward of the boat.*

Key Teaching Points:

🖐 Slide the boat past the fixed paddle.

🖐 Make a good connection between the blade and the opposite hip, and back to the blade.

🖐 The opposite hip moves the boat forward against the fixed catch.

🖐 Keep the connection between the hip and the blade all through the stroke.

○ **KEY POINT**

• The often used word "Pull" can be very confusing. It is suggested that coaches try to avoid its use, especially with beginners, as it encourages the incorrect image of pulling the blade back through the water. In fact the idea of pulling against a fixed point is fine, but the beginner may not grasp this to start with, causing confusion, and may forget the overriding principle that the blade stays still in the water and the boat moves forward.

Images the Coach Can Use:

🖐 Walk like a penguin and see how the hip swings forward.

🖐 Squeezing and gliding the boat forward.

🖐 In a tennis backhand - using the hip movement for power.

Practices to Use:

🖐 Sit on a trolley on wheels or a skateboard - grab a fixed point and slide boat past arm.

🖐 Walk like a penguin - walk using the hip to move leg and body forward.

🖐 Warm up on land, practise a visualised catch + move past it with eyes closed.

🖐 Sit on floor and move forward by moving hip and buttock forward - bumwalking - a good circuit training game.

TOP ARM CONNECTION

The top arm is pushed forward as the trunk rotates but remains connected to the movement of the trunk structure.

This can be called **Power Circle 5.**

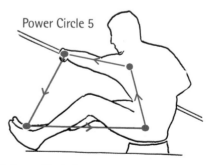

Fig. 6 Power Circle 5

Photo 11 Power Circle 5

Key Teaching Points:

Make a good connection between the stroke-side foot and opposite (top) hand, compressing the shaft.

Keep the top arm as part of trunk structure.

Make both arms and trunk work together.

Images the Coach Can Use:

Keep the strong eggshell structure.

Practices to Use:

Paddler puts the stroke-side foot on the coach's foot and presses down. With the opposite(top) hand push against the coach's hand and feel the connection.

SUPPORT IN THE WATER

The paddler in the boat is on a liquid base, the water, which must provide the support for all the paddler's movement.

Key Teaching Points:

The support when paddling is from the water.

There are several connections with water – four in boat, two feet and two buttocks, and the paddle blade outside the boat.

The body needs a stable support in order to paddle vigorously.

The harder you paddle the more support you need.

Images the Coach Can Use:

The Eiffel Tower is supported by four legs on a rock base. What would happen if any of the legs were in quicksand. Would it be stable? Four legs = paddler's buttocks and feet. Can you paddle well without being well supported?

Leaning on the water.

Practices to Use:

Figure of 8's in warm-up, leaning the boat away from the turn, using water to support.

Paddle in circles leaning the boat away from the turn.

Paddle for 50m in a straight line – alternately leaning the boat to left and right for 10m at a time, leaning on the water.

Hold onto the landing stage. Move the boat with body and feel the water support.

Hold onto an overhanging pole or branch and move the boat with the trunk against the water resistance.

BOAT MOVEMENTS

As the paddler gains better control of the kayak, the paddler develops an awareness of how the movements of the body affect the movement of the kayak and vice versa.

Key Teaching Points:

Help the paddler understand that they should work to keep the boat level and straight running, without bouncing, snaking or rocking.

Help the paddler recognise how their movements interact with the kayak.

Help the the paddler begin to support themselves well and control the boat movement while they paddle at increasing speeds.

Recognise the connection between the movement around the centre of gravity of the boat and boat instability and rocking. It will develop into counteracting one movement with another.

See Page 216 for tips on correction of negative boat movements).

► EARLY STAGES

It is essential that coaches develop a successful approach to coaching the initial stages of forward paddling.

Coaches are advised to carefully consider using aspects of these proactive approaches to ensure that good basic technique is quickly acquired, so that ingrained bad habits do not need to be corrected later.

Remember:

◎ Bad technique habits will quickly become difficult to change.

◎ Teach technique well from the start.

◎ It may only take 6 sessions to acquire bad technique but a year or longer to correct that.

A new environment on the water can be a distraction to a new paddler learning paddling skills. Coaches need to gear their approach to allow for this.

All serious athletic sports with a high skill element give much attention to the high quality of the initial introduction to the technique of the sport. Paddling can be no exception.

There are a number of approaches to introducing forward paddling skill to the best effect.

🍃 **1. Introduce the basic technique elements on land** using a paddle shaft, before going onto the water. This may involve sitting on a dummy seat, or on a step, or resting the feet on a curb (Photo 12).

The basic necessities of coordination and balance can be introduced and practised at this stage. The paddler would only go on the water when there is a sense of fluency in these movements and they have passed this land test.

Photo 12 Introduce the basic technique elements on land.

🍃 **2. Introduce the basic elements on land on a paddle ergo** with minimum resistance - achieved by using a fully covered fan and a small shaft, or a small fan, (Photo 13).

This removes much of the balance problem and enables the paddler to concentrate on mastering the basic movements - feathering, rotation, keeping the stroke in front of you, pressing on the footrest and feeling the need to stay on a central axis in the boat to avoid losing balance. The resistance of the paddling machine is not always necessary and

with a small junior may be a hindrance. Sometimes just the shaft is enough. Once again the paddler would need to become fluent in these movements before going onto the water.

Photo 13 Paddle ergo in use.

🍃 **3. Begin on the water but in a very stable series of boats.** Most of the basic skills of kayak can be introduced using a single-bladed paddle used in a canoe or Bell Boat. Fears of overbalancing are removed while the skills of steering, stopping, draw-stroking, forward and reverse paddling are introduced. Good use of both arms and pressure on the blade at the catch is easily emphasised. The stroke is always in front of the paddler and ends at the hip.

Alternatively in a plastic, but straight-running stable kayak, the paddler will feel safe enough to think clearly about the basic technique elements.

(A reminder here, as mentioned earlier, that stable plastic boats should be matched to the size of the paddler, should encourage a good paddling position, and should have a suitable central footrest and seat. Side footrests are not ideal here.)

Following the chosen introductory method for putting paddlers on the water, coaches will need to teach paddle feathering and the basic steering, forward and reversing, and braking strokes as tools for controlling the boat and safety procedures.

However at this stage it is purely giving the paddler the basics of stopping and turning the boat for practical reasons.

At this stage the prime focus is on forward paddling.

Coaches should begin to emphasise good basic technique at as early a stage as possible.

▶ COACHING STYLES

The above is a series of concepts of forward paddling for the paddler to learn to feel and understand. The process of introducing these concepts is dependent on the coach adopting an athlete-centred approach.

OUR OBJECTIVES AS COACHES

◎ Introduce forward paddling in such a way that junior paddlers have a clear understanding of this aspect of paddling.

◎ Help paddlers have a sound basic understanding of the biomechanics of paddling and the holistic paddling process.

◎ Help paddlers recognise and feel what is good paddling and be able to verbalise their feelings, and have the skills to self-correct to that good model.

▶ Empower The Athlete

Coaches are advised to adopt a style of teaching technique that encourages feedback and understanding from the paddler.

This will militate against a 'Critical Analysis' approach to coaching, where the coach tends towards listing the negatives, giving numerous detailed coach dominated instructions, and in favour of one that empowers the athlete.

The effective skills coach will offer the paddlers visual and kinaesthetic images to help them understand their movement. These images will address areas the coach recognises as needing work.

The skill of the coach lies in the choice of tools that is given to the paddler to help them improve their skill.

▶ Expectations

Paddlers' skill and knowledge will rise to the level of your expectations. If your expectation is that your paddlers will be sophisticated and advanced in their understanding of their forward paddling it is likely that they will be, and vice versa.

A SUGGESTED TEACHING PROCESS

 1. Demonstration

Carry out a quality silent demonstration – by the coach, another paddler or on video. Quality is the key word here. Use a paddling machine or boat on water according to skill area being coached. This could be on land before a session or on the water. It could be at the start of the week followed by several follow-up sessions.

 2. Talk through the demonstration

 3. Practice

Ask the paddlers to work on the practice.

 4. Feedback

Ask for their individual feedback on how well they accomplished the task.

a. Use open-ended questions to encourage the paddler to think and verbalise his/her feelings.

b. Use questions that cannot be answered by yes or no.

c. Develop the questions to direct the paddler to think about the area you want to work on.

d. When the paddler has gained some understanding of the coaching point, move onto the next area to work on.

e. Use a variety of linguistic formats - words associated with hearing, seeing, feeling, thinking about - to engage the paddler and kick-start the communication. Remember, verbal explanations from the coach will almost always be the most inefficient way of getting a point over.

 5. Plan your feedback

a. Plan opportunities to receive and give individual feedback during the session.

b. Work with paddlers passing your coaching point in rotation, e.g. staggered paddling in loops passing you at different times.

c. Pull out a paddler next to your boat or near to the side by the bank where you cycle, so you can give them individual feedback and hear theirs.

d. Make opportunities to follow up problems and improvements after the session.

e. Take advantage of paddling ergos for individual coaching.

f. Use a video camera on the water, playing back through a TV or computer to enable paddlers to see themselves paddling on the water, or on an ergo from different angles.

 6. Keep it simple

Remember, work on one simple aspect of forward paddling at a time.

Avoid working on the whole stroke at once and swamping the paddler with advice they may well not understand.

 7. Cues

Develop a series of simple cues that mean areas of technique to the paddler. You will have taught these specifically before, and will continue to work on them in detail, but out on the water cues are very important, and simple for the paddler to latch onto in difficult conditions. Always use the same cues and develop new ones that prompt your individual paddlers. A cue will be more effective on the water than a long explanation. Imre Kemecsey's Power Circles are excellent cues.

8. Cue Cards

Use laminated cue cards that the paddlers can attach to their boat where they can read it to help them be systematic in work on technique.

9. Plan your input to your coaching

Think about the format of your communication with the paddler:

Paddler's Name - recognition/praise - simple task/ coaching tip.

Examples:

- "John… Well done… Now - Powerful leg drive".

- "Sue… Going well… Work on more Power Circle 2. Trunk rotation".

- "Jack… That's a good try… Think about spearing fish on your catch".

- "Mark… Your catch is much better… Now try Power Circle 4, moving your boat past the locked blade".

- "Mark… OK… More PC 4".

10. Types of questions to ask, to encourage paddler feedback and understanding. (Don't forget that the coach will need to use a variety of language according to the paddler's linguistic preferences).

a. What could you feel when you were paddling then?

b. How did that go?

c. What do you see when you… ?

d. What can you feel in your… when you… ?

e. What is happening in your… when you do that?

f. Does working on … make it seem different/feel different?

g. Where does it make a difference?

h. Can you see how it makes a difference?

i. How stable do you feel when you… ?

j. Does working on… make you feel more or less stable?

k. Sounds as if you have got an idea how to do this better?

l. Where did you get your support in the water to do that?

Develop your questions to make the paddler have to work to develop their understanding.

Remember… your expectations will drive the success of their understanding.

▶ CANOE RACING - TECHNIQUE

Having looked at kayak forward paddling. It is time we looked in detail at the technique elements of forward paddling in canoe.

THE CATCH PHASE

The aim of the catch is to lock the blade in the water, to enable the paddler to draw the boat past the paddle. The secret to a good catch is to transfer the paddler's body weight onto the paddle. This lifts the boat higher in the water, thus reducing the wetted surface area, which in turn increases boat speed.

Photo 14 The Catch Phase

▶ Key Elements Of The Catch

1. Long Reach: Rotate as far as possible using the hips and shoulders (paddle-side hip and shoulder forward, top shoulder back).

2. Firm Entry: Hit the water by falling on the blade. Bend from the waist, drop paddle-side shoulder and keep arms straight. During this action drop and rotate around centre line of boat and keep side lean to a minimum.

3. Blade Angle: around 60° and running parallel with boat.

4. Weight on Paddle: Transfer body weight onto paddle, keeping all connections fixed.

5. Bury the Blade: Lock the blade before draw/pull and press down.

▶ Catch Development Exercises

1. On land and using a short paddle

• Kneel on 2 knees with paddle at exit/recovery position.

• Let body fall forward, keeping knees, hips and shoulders in line.

• Bring paddle forward into catch position.

• Let the paddle hit the ground in front of you as if catching the water (do this on grass to avoid damage to paddle).

• Repeat the above while rotating paddle-side hip/shoulder into stroke and top shoulder backwards.

2. In a TC2 or stable C1

• Repeat exercise 1 (above).

• Move to high kneel position, with a very short step (front foot close to knee block). Hold bottom hand higher on paddle shaft and repeat exercise 1.

3. In stable racing boat

• Bring front foot back to side of knee block. Paddle dropping weight onto blade.

4. In stable racing boat

• Stand up and hold paddle with bottom hand higher on paddle shaft. Paddle dropping weight onto blade.

5. In racing boat

• Repeat exercises 2-4.

• Move hands to normal paddling position and repeat.

THE DRIVE/POWER PHASE

The aim of the drive/power phase is to propel the canoe forward as quickly as possible while minimising any boat movement other than in a forward direction.

Photo 15 *The Drive/Power Phase*

▶ Key Elements Of The Drive/Power Phase

First 2/3rds of stroke

1. Pull with Hip: Uncoil paddle-side hip by pulling it back.

2. Pull with Shoulder: Uncoil paddle-side shoulder by pulling it back.

3. Pull Up: Use back muscles to pull trunk into upright position. Feeling of growing/vaulting over paddle. This keeps paddle vertical as long as possible. Keep arms straight and fixed.

4. Weight on Paddle: Keep weight on paddle by pushing down with straight top arm.

Last 1/3rd of stroke

1. Hip and Shoulder: Paddle-side hip and shoulder start to move forward, top arm moves across boat to aid steering.

2. Front Foot: Push off front foot and feel the boat slide underneath you.

▶ Drive/Power Phase Development Exercises

1. On land using a short paddle

• With body rotated, arms straight and fixed get paddler to move from high kneeling to standing by vaulting/growing over paddle.

• On a paddling machine or paddling from landing stage repeat vault/growing effect.

2. In a TC2 or stable C1

• Paddle with arms straight and fixed trying to repeat feeling in exercise 1.

• Repeat above while moving paddle-side hip and shoulder forward into the stroke and moving top shoulder backwards to give full rotation.

- Repeat above concentrating on uncoiling rotation during the first 2/3rds of the stroke.

- Repeat above and concentrate on paddle-side hip and shoulder moving forward during last 1/3rd of stroke.

- Repeat above and add push from front foot during last 1/3rd of stroke to slide the boat forwards.

3. In racing boat

- Repeat exercise 1 & 2.

THE RECOVERY/SET-UP PHASE

The aim of the recovery/set-up phase is to achieve a clean exit of the paddle from the water and to move quickly and efficiently into the next stroke.

Photo 16 The Recovery/Set-up Phase

▶ Key Elements Of The Recovery/Set-Up Phase

1. Exit at Hip: Pull the blade out quickly when lower hand is just in front of hip. The motion is similar to throwing a frisbee.

2. Relax: Breathe in and relax whole body. Start to rotate and move forward.

3. Set-up for catch: Firm muscles, rotate paddle-side shoulder and hip forwards, opposite shoulder rotates backwards. Keep paddle blade close to the water (5-10cm) during recovery.

4. Long reach: Rotate as far as possible using the hips and shoulders.

▶ Recovery Phase Development Exercises

1. On land with short paddle

- In high kneeling position practise frisbee throwing action.

- Repeat above but move paddle-side hip/shoulder forwards at same time.

- Repeat on paddling machine or paddling from landing stage.

2. In a TC2 or stable C1

- Repeat all of the above.

- Try to clip water as paddle comes forward to prevent lifting too high.

3. In racing boat

- Repeat exercise 1 & 2.

▶ MOVING THE BOAT - NEGATIVE FORCES

Coaches and paddlers can sometimes concentrate on body movements, and ignore the movement of the boat as a symptom of structural faults in paddling technique.

Paddlers are trying to concentrate their muscle recruitment into those muscles that are propelling the boat in a forward direction, and though there are some forces that inevitably cause the boat to move out of that line, there are forces that the paddler can create that are not necessary.

Wherever the waterline or 'water moustache' changes from one side to the other side of the boat there is the potential for negative forces and a deterioration in boat running.

Remember! All movements of the boat are created by the paddler, be they positive or negative.

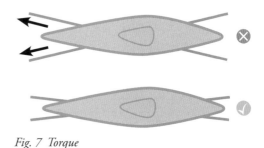

Fig. 7 Torque

SNAKING

Each stroke produces torque that pulls the front of the boat from one side to the other.

To correct this movement the paddler has to squeeze the boat straight with the body through the hips, compressing the water wall at each side of the boat. The effect of this will be to reduce the amount of snaking movement by the boat.

This is closely linked to the effect of Power Circle 4 with the hip moving forward and across as it drives the shell forward.

▶ What Can Cause It?

🌊 Tipping the boat on the pushing side.

🌊 'Soft' power transmission.

🌊 Too much emphasis on power on blade at the catch.

🌊 'Pulling' the blade too far from the boat after catch.

▶ What Can Eliminate It? Exercises

🌊 Powerful leg movement.

🌊 Rotation of opposite hip forwards and sideways - squeeze boat straight.

🌊 Squeeze the stern of boat sideways with help of the paddle.

🌊 Keep power lines straight.

🌊 Swing your trunk above the shell of boat.

🌊 Rotate your lower body towards the blade.

BOUNCING

Rather than running flat in the water the kayak will rise up at the front and simultaneously drop down at the back.

This is often caused by instability in the trunk, with movement transfer from the central point in the boat forwards and backwards, as the body searches to recruit more muscles to cope with the demands of the power generated elsewhere. This can be corrected by general technique work and by functional stability training.

It may be caused by misuse of 'pull bars'. The name itself implies misuse as pulling on the bar is not correct practice. The bar is to help stabilise the paddler and prevent the foot sliding off the footrest to the side or lifting up excessively.

If the paddler pulls hard on the footbar the front of the boat will rise up, bouncing.

TOP TIP

• Have paddlers take the 'pullbar' out of the boat for a week now and then.

Fig. 8 Boat rocks up and down at front and back

▶ What Can Eliminate It? - Exercises

🌊 Only rotation with the trunk.

🌊 Powerful support in the water before recovery.

🌊 Practise without "pull bar".

🌊 Lift up bow of boat with feet.

🌊 Focus on the stern of the boat.

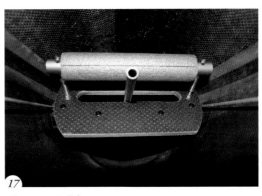

Photo 17 Pull bar

ROCKING

The boat moves from side to side in an exaggerated way, with the deck dropping to one side and then the next. This is more difficult to correct but severely prevents the boat gliding, with the water resistance increasing as it happens.

▶ The Paddler Has To Work On

🌊 Keeping body weight on the paddle throughout the stroke.

🌊 Keeping the connection with the catch throughout the stroke.

🌊 Connecting the opposite hip back to the catch-side blade.

🌊 Finding support in the water with the opposite hip to achieve the above three improvements, by leaning with the hip on the water through the boat, so that the body weight can remain on the other side of the boat, the stroke side.

What Can Eliminate This? - Exercises

- Tip/lean the boat at catch on the pulling side.

- Tip/lean the side of the boat all through the stroke on the pulling side.

- Tip/lean the boat at recovery on the pulling side.

- Figure of 8 exercises leaning boat.

- Turning exercises leaning boat.

- Slalom.

- Push the footboard with opposite foot.

Control of all these boat movements will increase the gliding and efficiency of the boat movement by decreasing resistance.

SUMMARY OF KAYAK STROKE

The Basic Start Position (Photo 18)

This position is an artificially frozen point in the whole cycle, but is often used by coaches in drills as a position to pause in... ready for the next stroke.

The trunk is rotated so there is a maximum reach forward with one arm, while the other is contracted. The top arm elbow is level or a little higher than the shoulder and the hand about level with the top of the head.

The paddle shaft is pointing forwards and downwards towards the water.

The paddle blade is feathered.

Entry and Catch (Photo 19)

The paddle enters the water and becomes a fixed and locked point.

With correct posture (see Fig. 1) and the top hand around forehead height, and the trunk rotated at approximately 70°, the blade is driven down and forward into the water using body and both arms together as one. Muscles are firm and there is a good connection between blade and body.

The blade should be moving towards vertical as it enters the water.

The blade should enter the water fairly close to the side of the boat to prevent the torque forces causing snaking.

The leg push should be synchronised with the catch. The foot is compressing the footrest slightly before the catch, looking for support for the catch, with the knee flattening as the trunk unwinds its rotation.

The Power Phase (Photo 20)

Against the fixed point of the locked blade at the catch, the body transfers energy into forward boat movement through legs and hips, accelerating the trunk and boat movement past the blade.

The pressure on the blade is always down, and from catch to exit there is a good connection and power transmission throughout, as the trunk rotates.

The paddle blade is locked in the water. Simultaneous trunk and arm rotation move the boat forward against this locked point. The opposite hip and legs transfer the forward thrust into the boat.

The two arms, trunk and legs work together. The arms alone do not pull the paddle.

For the phase to be powerful, there must be a locked blade at the catch. Especially at high stroke rates and therefore in crew boats, the catch and power phase are a continuous movement.

From the catch close to the boat, the wing blade will follow a path ending at about 70° to the boat.

21

22

Exit, Recovery And Airwork (Photos 21–22)

The paddle travels from exit on one side to the next catch on the other.

With the blade approaching the level of the hip, the lower wrist snaps sideways and upwards with little drag, with a quick clean action, and feathers the blade for the next stroke. This will happen in reality when the hand is level with a point just behind the knee.

THE KAYAK STROKE CYCLE FROM THE SIDE

Tim Brabants Olympic 1000m bronze medallist 2000

Note the maintenance of good connections through the whole body as outlined in the earlier Power Circles section.

THE KAYAK STROKE CYCLE FROM THE FRONT

Holman (Norway) Olympic and World Champion K1

Holman demonstrates the strong upper body Power Circle 2 and its rotation. Note how his swing takes his hands way over the centre line of the boat. He is also leaning his boat slightly towards the paddle-stroke side on every stroke, while compensating for this by pressing against the water with his opposite hip to keep balance.

GRAHAM CAMPBELL

Graham is a L4 coach, specialising in the placid water and racing side. He worked as a volunteer coach for nearly 20 years and for 4 years as National Development Coach for flat water. While coaching international juniors and seniors, he developed his interest in teaching technique and worked with top international coaches to search for the most effective way of introducing these high level skills.

He has recently retired to France, but is still involved in coach development.

13 ROLLING

The intention of this chapter is to deal with the 'how' of coaching rolling rather than the 'what'. There are many texts covering the mechanical and technical knowledge a coach would need to understand in order to be an effective coach of rolling, some of which are contained in the references. It is not the role of this chapter to repeat the technical manuals. If you are interested in further reading around the act of rolling and its coaching why not begin with the Inuit whale hunters in skin boats and icy waters in an era when your grandfather or father was the only coach you had.

The main issues dealt with will be:-

○ Equipment and Dynamic Seating Position.

○ The need to deliberately coach the action of rolling in appropriate environments, after acquiring the basic movement vocabulary.

○ The effects of attribution and goal setting on the psychological well-being of the learner.

○ The effect on performance as 'cold shock' and 'diving reflex' compete for control over the submerged paddler.

○ Variability and its pivotal position in a roll for all occasions.

Rolling is one of the most difficult of all coaching challenges. This chapter will help equip all coaches interested in developing their input into rolling skills with a set of principles and guiding concepts around which they can construct their coaching. As we pro-ceed through the chapter there will be examples of 'tools' a coach could use or adjust as necessary. It is important to remember that one of the most rewarding aspects of coaching is the creation of original coaching tools. This ability to create your own tools and exercises in changing environments is a skill all coaches should nurture. It could be argued that the point at which you step beyond the training or education received at any level in coaching is the start of the coach's development. The analogy that we could apply to both this coaching context and an underpinning philosophy behind the development of a paddler's roll would be the often heard 'you learn to drive after you pass your test'. In both rolling and coaching the most significant learning takes place after a person has realised a minimum level of competence.

The order the material is presented here should not indicate a priority, moreover it is important that the individualised coaching is a diet, based on the learner's needs and desires. It is worth mentioning at this point that the indoor swimming pool should not be cast in the role of novice-only territory, and should be used with integrity and ambition for developing rolling at every level of proficiency. The mere fact that your learner can capsize many times without real discomfort is important, particularly when the alternative is where one capsize is extremely uncomfortable for the learner.

► EQUIPMENT AND THE DYNAMIC SEATING POSITION

There is a great deal of merit in achieving the best fit for your learner in a craft, as rolling puts enormous strain on the interface between boat and body. The locking of the feet, knees and bottom against the control surfaces of the boat is the dynamic seating position (DSP). In younger or smaller paddlers this is extremely difficult to achieve accurately, hence learning to roll is often left until the youngster is able to solve this physical problem. This is a pity since the principles of Long Term Paddler Development (LTPD) state that from around the age of 12 body awareness and general co-ordination are the key areas, both addressed in the action of rolling.

There are a number of satisfactory solutions to this problem. Easy to fit re-usable kits are now available providing extra foam sections supporting 1,2 or 3 of the contact points. Alternatively, much can be done with closed cell foam and glue or 'Gaffer' tape. Combining this with improved backrest systems helps many young paddlers achieve a functional fit in the cockpit.

Although the footrest is often the easiest of the contact points to adjust, it is in some respects the least important. Keeping the relationship between the knee pressure and the bottom position is critical; to this end solutions that allow smaller people's legs and thighs to reach the front of the cockpit rim are better. In some boats it is possible to move the seat forward and/up so the knees can reach the front of the cockpit, allowing contact to be established. Provided the solution does not trap the paddler in any way, imagination and some basic DIY skills usually provide the answer.

There is a direct link between the speed and accuracy of learning and the quality of the equipment used, including fit. Easy to manage hull shapes, appropriate paddle lengths, blade shape and a spraydeck which does not pop the moment water pressure or torso/knee pressure is applied all need to be considered.

Equipment or props can take on many roles, the common pool equipment is one level, another use is to distract the learner from a specific outcome by using props to change their point of focus. An example from trampolining is where a coach might put tennis balls in the hands of the performer to heighten the awareness of the arm position during flight.

Performance rolling is usually 'blind' (dark or aerated water/eyes closed in polluted water). It is possible to practise the feel and timing of limited visual feedback by the use of dark goggles. We can use the coach as a prop gripping the hull of an upturned boat to provide friction against the righting action; this might be for several constructive reasons. It could be to simulate a loaded boat in sea paddling or to check for fit in a paddler who is prone to let the lower body release when concentrating on upper body or arm movements.

One final point is that of 'surfer's ear', a condition that can occur if people constantly flush cold water into the ear. Try to use either a specialist ear plug, a skull cap or even Blue-tac to lessen the chances of damage to the ear.

► DEDICATED ROLLING COACHING

It is stating the obvious to say the act of rolling a craft is extremely skilful; successful completion of the action is a synthesis of many sub-skills which need to be selected and blended to a time scale which can be demanding (sometimes too demanding). As coaches we therefore have an equally skilful challenge. This is one of the key points and probably the most important message of this chapter. If the learner is in need of a roll both as a useful skill in terms of their physical comfort, i.e. not swimming on a rocky river at 11.00am in March, or because of the psychological comfort of being able to tackle tougher challenges secure in the knowledge that the odds of swimming are less, then *we* as coaches have a responsibility to structure rolling coaching in many more contexts and environmentally varied situations than we do currently.

Simply put we need to *coach* rolling in a similar context to that of any other paddlesport skill, in a structured, organised and technically informed manner.

The coaching action I refer to is not the off-the-cuff advice for the 'next time'. It is easy as a coach to jump in and assist a learner who has fallen in and pulled an ugly recovery or work in the pool with a novice. The effective coach should design programmes that use exercises and organise varied practice in types and

Photo 1 Coaching rolling in context

temperatures of water which will allow learning to take place both in performance and at the cognitive decision-making level.

These deliberately chosen opportunities might include:

   A summer beach with small or no waves, where tasks include using firstly the sand as an introduction followed by progressively deeper water.

   Warm water lake (summer or abroad!) with a stiff breeze blowing on-shore, where a task involving the beginnings of flat water cartwheels blended with informed coaching on the effect of starting position on recovery.

   The local jet at low water levels in the autumn using the direction of flow to give variance to the roll.

   Slow-flowing deep water rivers in autumn, looking at timing issues in the righting of the hull.

   A dedicated canoe course in low season or midweek, using the safe hole/wave, free from the pressure of eddy queues and river runners.

   Canals and outdoor pools, taking the initial steps to stress proof the foundation skills, leading to the concept of learning 'how to fall in', maximising the learner's chance of rolling from a series of practised pre-positions.

   In a swimming pool focusing on the transfer to the outdoor next autumn by rolling in buoyancy aids, cags and helmets.

All of the above, if used imaginatively will create environments where coaches can help the learners build variability into their movements and decisions. A further layer of coaching effectiveness is to move the emphasis away from the technical coaching context; this is achieved by using the 'tactical' approach.

In paddlesport coaching generally there is a simple model to explain the options available to the coach in terms of session construction. The aspects we can change are: the *task*, the *environment* or the *equipment*, what you are doing, where and with what. In rolling coaching we can use this to change the emphasis to give the learner new enthusiasm. This innovation and creation of inventive exercises particularly applies in contexts the learner might perceive to be lacking challenge because of familiarity; some ideas might be:

   By changing site we are now in a faster moving piece of water.

   Swapping boats means that boxy rail is less of a problem.

   Trying to roll faster or in slow motion gives the learner better feel for the timing aspects of the action.

   Complete immediate rolls, up and downstream.

   Introduce paddle mitts in a low threat environment.

   Use a set of splits in a scenario-based task.

   Roll in the eddy, on the eddy line and in the current.

▶ PSYCHOLOGICAL AND PHYSIOLOGICAL ASPECTS

Let us now look at two psychological and one physiological principle important to all coaches but extremely significant for the coaching of rolling activities. These are variability, self-esteem and cold shock (competitive reflex reaction).

VARIABILITY

This is a term used in conjunction with the organisation of 'practice', more specifically 'random practice'. It is the concept of equipping learners with the ability to solve increasingly varied questions generated by the environment. The most effective method of equipping the paddler with this variation of solution is to practise in a manner that will demand increasingly varied solutions.

If you imagine the initial set of solutions as a 'narrow' track, only wide enough to cycle down, as the metaphor for the paddler's limited solutions at the beginning of the process. The coach's role is to 'broaden' the track giving the learner a wider range of solutions, turning the track into dual carriageway in terms of the choices of route for the cyclist. As a performer if the choice of skill is from a 'narrow' band of solutions or worse still a single solution, then it may prove to be inadequate or mismatched. In reality it is this narrow movement solution learner paddlers are all too regularly relying on.

In the skill of rolling, if you possess a 'wide' band of options or a variety of solutions it will result in a more reliable roll in a greater range of environments, underwater positions and craft.

Example exercises:

 Even at the early stages keep a good balance of left and right (allowing for success necessary to maintain the motivation of the learner).

Capsize in different starting positions by putting a skill before it, i.e. reverse sweep.

On a jet, variations in position relative to the flow but also the speed and direction of the paddler, i.e. reverse paddling strongly across the flow, capsizing upstream.

In small waves face left and right and encourage the learner to feel for the wave and use the pressure on the blade to initiate a roll (the results should be varied i.e. back/front of the blade and different sides).

In a safe hole using 'real' situations encourage the paddler to verbalise the pressure build-up they feel on the blade. This can be done upright at first, developing into an inverted exercise.

An alternative type of variability is to remain within a solution but vary the demands made upon it. These

demands are constructed by the coach to allow the learner to develop specific aspects of the skill.

The example used here is a screw roll, which is well established in a stable environment with a deliberate capsize. Although not initiated from a set-up position the preparation phase of the skill needs to develop considerable width to cope with a moving water environment. The 'noise' generated cognitively when a situation new to the learner is experienced can be enormous, requiring a great deal of practice to overcome and allow the paddler to achieve the position from which to begin the righting action. Developing progressive achievable tasks for the learner to succeed in the roll but develop aspects of its make-up is the coaching skill.

These might include:

Exercises on broken waves in surf where a partner or coach rights the paddler to a pre-arranged timescale, the capsized paddler completing a cognitive task whilst underwater.

Moving through different body and paddle positions before righting themselves.

Capsizing without a paddle, the coach then presenting it in different positions and orientations, i.e. vertical, blade first or behind them. As a progression it can be agreed before capsizing where the paddle will appear. If the water is clear enough to use vision to solve the problem then limiting the visual feedback would build better kinaesthetic awareness.

Photo 2 Rolling exercise in a safe hole

3a

3b

3c

Photo 3a-c Capsize whilst performing another skill and then roll, in this case a 'stern squirt'.

⚓ Complete another skill immediately prior to the capsize, i.e a draw stroke. This can be combined with variations in the water speed and direction; with a rope it can also be simulated in a pool.

PADDLER WELL-BEING

As stated in the chapter on Psychology, the coach needs to find clarity and a sympathy between the 'what' of the physical requirement of tasks and a developed understanding of the 'how' to construct an effective coaching framework.

In an activity so obviously success (product) related, failure to achieve the product has a heightened mental cost to the learner. The coach therefore has extra responsibility to the learner to buffer the negative effects this failure might generate. To maintain the learner's self-confidence when the outcomes are apparently so polarised is a significant coaching skill, underpinned by a greater understanding of three areas of coaching knowledge: goal setting, motivation and attribution.

The initial aim of the coach in a rolling context is to equip the learner with an understanding of the process, pitched at an appropriate level, allowing suitably small and technically achievable process goals to be set. If these goals are sympathetic to the technical level of the learner and understood cognitively, the odd failure, although unfortunate, will not detract from the learner making sense of the situation and keeping their confidence high.

Expectations prior to the activity can be guided away from the yes or no of the final product. This technique, usually termed 'frontloading', helps the learner adjust their expectations to be more aware of the process involved, seeing success in different parts of the skill and happy that they are learning. There is an especially strong case in rolling to support a far more incremental approach to the tasks chosen by the coach. The ability to break down the whole movement skills into much smaller achievable goals will allow the satisfaction of regular success in progressively more demanding tasks. This blend of accurate technical input with regular success will develop the foundations of key skills in the learner so as to allow the next steps to be taken accurately. The integrity of the increments used by the coach will help reinforce a difficult concept for some learners, that the development of rolling skill may not always be the roll itself.

If the context of the learner shifts to 'a person who may well be able to right themselves with some consistency', then as coaches we also shift the goals to begin developing focal points within the process. This top-end goal setting, beyond the simple product of success is the important link into rolling effectively in progressively more demanding situations and not stalling the learning curve at a particular part of the process.

An example would be a paddler who has a consistent roll in green water, but in aerated water struggles with the recovery phase, particularly the head. The coach would use the timing and positioning of the head recovery in a coaching session to give an improved understanding and efficiency in this aspect, possibly taking some of the leverage away by varying the paddles or slowing the movement down to understand the subtlety of the head's influence on the accuracy of the action.

To summarise the goal setting subtlety necessary in coaching rolling, the coach should:

⚫ Understand the full range of increments available with which to break the process down.

⚫ Be skilful in allowing the learner access to the key information at the appropriate times and through the appropriate medium.

⚫ Provide internalised feedback points so the learner is capable of self-checking the process (not just the product), scoring themselves on pressure points in the DSP.

⚫ Set small enough challenges to allow confidence to remain high but keep the learner in a tangible progression.

⚫ Once 'product' success is achieved begin the methodical improvement on key components in an individual, based on accurate technical analysis of their needs.

⚫ As before, construct learning opportunities matched to the learner's needs… *coach rolling*… not the recovery of other paddling errors.

⚫ Front-loading sessions so as to keep the learners' expectations accurate and achievable.

Using a technically accurate and audience-friendly vocabulary at this stage is key. Much of what we are coaching is 'feel' and 'timing', extremely difficult concepts to verbalise, so avoiding left/right, up/down, push/pull and in/out or such words will help enormously in keeping the process clear. Rely on kinaesthetic input or questions to elicit cognitive registry when analysing the actions.

Helping the learner understand through their actions technically accurate concepts such as leverage and pressure is a crucial element in the battle against loss of self confidence and thus the motivation to learn.

Developing the awareness of the function of accurate goal setting also gives a positive spin on the other main principles likely to interfere with the learning efficiency, that of motivation and attribution. What will the learner gain from this learning, AND who, why or what might your learner be attributing their perceived lack of progress on or to. The main skill needed here is to be aware of your learner's emotional strength and pre-empt the situations, adjusting the goals and feedback accordingly.

A last point on the maintenance of a psychologically robust learner is to avoid if at all possible the learner

swimming out of a task. Wherever possible, either as the coach or by using other paddlers, provide a safety net to allow some degree of attempt and failure without the potentially demoralising outcome of swimming. In practical terms this often means being in the water close to the action, in more situations than the swimming pool. Be clear about the sequencing of the practice to ensure the learner knows when the system, which is agreed and understood, takes over to recover the situation. This will allow the learner to experiment, practise and occasionally fail without always ending up swimming. Examples of tasks to ensure this would be:

⚫ Working in water shallow enough to use the bottom for recovery on a beach or on the edge of a lake.

⚫ Extremely accurate positioning and proactive shepherding in boat-based recoveries in jets to allow for immediate rescues (not motionless observation followed by a sprint after an increasingly urgent tapping on the bottom of a kayak).

⚫ The donning of appropriate clothing (dry suit etc.) to allow you to be in the water and effect a rescue.

On a point of personal experience, the sympathy between the fit of the craft (DSP), the spraydeck (neoprene) and the type of the paddle used (feather, length, blade shape, shaft profile) is of critical importance, particularly in moving water with learners working beyond the basic mechanics.

COLD SHOCK VS DIVE REFLEX

This topic is not as simple as the reflex action of sucking in breath or ice-cream head. The terms 'cold shock' and 'dive reflex' are in fact far more subtle physiological phenomenon which affect the human organism when its safety or survival is threatened by water or cold water. It is therefore important for a coach to understand their impact in situations where the paddler might have to roll unexpectedly.

When a person is put into threatening situations such as being underwater, the brain has been programmed over thousands of years to respond to survive. In the case of cold shock the brain triggers a number of responses. Heart rate increases, peripheral blood flow is reduced which, combined with the squeezing effect on the body from the pressure of the water, raises blood pressure dramatically, usually within only a few seconds. In extreme cases particularly where heart disease is a factor death has

Photo 4 Cross-deck splashing games!

occurred within five minutes. Even though a person may be upside-down in a kayak the physiological responses are the same. The second condition, that of the dive reflex, is a contradiction and is character-ised by a reduction in heart rate and motor activity (movement). The brain tries to limit unnecessary use of oxygen by limiting blood-flow to peripheral areas of the body thus maintaining a supply to the brain. Although this all seems strange there have been inci-dents where people (often babies) have survived long periods underwater with no ill effects.

Due to the conflict between these two innate responses the brain takes time to make a decision. Think of it as the processor on your computer chutter-ing along, red light flickering happily, when suddenly ten programmes are switched on simultaneously. The red light stays on as the processor tries to make sense of the inputs and takes decisions to action the demand. During this process it follows a programmed logic, very similar to the human body. In the case of cold shock versus dive reflex, research indicates that around 15% of people show evidence of the dive reflex, how-ever the predominant response is that of cold shock.

Although this is termed cold shock it can still occur indoors or in relatively warm water, as a reac-tion to overload, simply asking the learner to take too big a step or misjudging the difficulty or pressure a task requires.

In a practical coaching context this means that the coach should 'prepare' the learner for the situation before it arises; a good phrase to use in this respect is 'roll to roll'. If you play in a hole where the roll-ing to recover the situation is likely to be near your skilful limit, give yourself the best chances of success by reducing the impact of the cold shock/dive reflex battle. This can be achieved by engaging your learner in small progressively more wet and inverted contexts, thus when a capsize occurs you are ready to over-ride a survival instinct.

An effective coach will imaginatively use games and challenging tasks to lead the learner to this point. Below are some thoughts:

- Dampen or wet your helmet and put it back on.

- Cross-deck splashing games.

- Head dips in the side surf position in small surf (reform).

- Recoveries off the bow or stern of boats placed in different eddies.

Using rocks, shallow water on a beach or the bank to pick floating or submerged objects up with your hand or teeth.

Supported support strokes (coach, bank, or boat).

Edging games using buddies, rafted in moving water.

I have watched literally hundreds of coaches working and can count on one hand the few who have actively pursued coaching rolling on behalf of their learner as the focus in the session. It is clear that the appeal of the journey or the full experience of the activity seems to put rolling coaching in the shadows as an objective. Yet learners frequently state that they have insecurity because of the lack of confidence in their ability to successfully roll when randomly challenged by their circumstances.

It is this shock tactic of the circumstance that we as coaches have to supply solutions to; coaching the varied responses to the action of a capsize provide us with our challenge.

IN CONCLUSION

This chapter sets out to help coaches work more accurately with learners of all types and abilities in a varied coaching environment. It is an accepted starting point that the founding principles of good coaching, held true in other paddlesport activity and outlined in the first chapter of this book, apply to the coaching of rolling.

An appropriate starting point might be the most significant misconception, that of 'one size fits all'. The name of the roll is not the priority, good coaching should be applied to the individual and can be applied to any rolling technique.

FURTHER READING

Essentials of Sea Survival, Golden, F & Tipton, 2002, Human Kinetics
Life at the Extremes, Ashcroft F, 2001, Flamingo
Motor Learning and Performance, Schmidt R, 1991, Human Kinetics
Acquisition and Performance of Sports Skills, McMorris T, 2004, Wiley, 0-470-84995-9
BCU Canoe and Kayak Handbook, British Canoe Union, 2002, Pesda Press, 0-9531956-5-1
Kayak Rolling, Collins L, 2004, Pesda Press, 0-9531956-8-6

IAN COLEMAN

Ian is a senior lecturer at the University of Chichester and has been actively involved in sports coaching since becoming a basketball coach in 1981. The transfer of knowledge from areas in sport where significant developments have already been made has guided his input into the coaching scheme, mainly centred in the 'acquisition of skill'. As a recipient of 'old school' rolling coaching it is a personal priority to help coaches improve their understanding of the pivotal principles coaches must embrace to develop the coaching of rolling. Having swum in the sea and on a river recently, continuing to improve rolling coaching techniques is a vested interest.

14 OPEN CANOE

The open canoe is an infinitely diverse craft, being used today for anything from day trips to full on expeditions over weeks in remote wilderness areas. Recreational canoeing has evolved and adapted from a variety of practical uses and consequently there is a whole suite of skills for open water, moving water and journeying.

The Canoe Coach, perhaps more than any other discipline, has an incredibly broad scope, and for newly-fledged coaches the number of skills that need to be honed can be quite intimidating. But take heart, because like any coach in any discipline or sport your knowledge base grows and grows with experience. Always keep in mind the important role you as a coach play in developing canoesport.

WHERE TO START

First you need to know your group. Their technical ability, depth of knowledge, understanding and prior experiences determine your starting point. Discovering where their motivation lies guides the scope, content and environment. Homing in on their main learning style(s) will guide you into the most effective coaching approaches. Your informal chats with students (remember to listen) will give a lot of information, and using a combination of unstructured and structured observation in introductory sessions will provide the rest.

Choice of venue is key to running successful sessions. It is easier to plan sessions for sites you know well, as the site provides an outline plan of where to coach

what. For unfamiliar venues you have to react more to what the site or voyage offers, using more demonstrations so you can assess suitability of sections for any given exercise, and leading from the front more.

Above all our job is to motivate and inspire our students. Coaches should focus on a holistic approach to developing students. Ask yourself why a student needs to acquire a skill and where will they use it in the future? Focus on helping students understand why they do things (i.e. process) and where and when, not just what and how. Vary exercises as much as possible to maintain interest and help ingrain learning.

I firmly believe that skilled coaching is about a set of ideas and themes for delivering sessions, rather than how to do strokes per se. This holistic approach is primarily paddler-centred and the truly skilled coach takes their students from point A to point B in a seamless transition where the student is not even aware of the process.

Key Themes

When coaching canoe I return again and again to several key themes, which are fundamentally important for the learning process. Symbols are used throughout this chapter to highlight where they come into play:

 Students should practise strokes on *both sides.* This is called bilateral transfer. See Chapter 1 Coaching.

 Bow and stern paddlers should *swap over* in tandem. This develops a full stroke repertoire and a deeper understanding of how paddlers' actions affect canoe movement. It also provides a smoother transition for those who wish to progress to solo paddling.

 Communication and teamwork are essential skills for tandem pairs. As paddlers learn and consolidate new stroke combinations and practise in new and more challenging environments, the coach may need to reinforce these key skills.

 Having learnt the basics of a new skill it is important to apply and develop further on a *journey.* The onus is on the coach to find venues to challenge students, allowing them to experiment and fine-tune Boat, Body, Blade elements, power, etc. In other words it's all about mileage!

▶ BOAT, BODY, BLADE

BOAT (Trim)

The canoe's sheer size means that Boat, or correct trim, becomes far more significant in an efficient and skilled performance. Hence, the order of priority for canoeing is 'Boat, Body, Blade'.

As coaches we focus on how total body weight and weight distribution in the canoe affect trim, because these are the factors we can easily influence. We should also be aware of the impact manufacturers have on trim, particularly through design and position of seats. For example, take the GP canoe typically found in outdoor centres and clubs.

Seats are often:

• Fixed high above the floor, which raises paddlers' centre of gravity and reduces stability.

• Fixed too close to the stern and bow, which creates a very confined space for the bow paddler, and throws the stern paddler's weight back, affecting trim.

• Shaped moulded plastic, which encourages students to face forwards, which conflicts with learning and maintaining correct body position.

Encourage your students to experiment with seat position, height and angle to find the best set up. Boat settings are personal and you and your students will benefit if you dedicate time to kitting your canoes out properly.

Trim is generally adjusted through a choice, or combination, of:

• Paddler(s) leaning/moving forwards or backwards.

• Paddler(s) actually moving, using kit bags to sit on if necessary (major adjustments).

• Moving kit bags forwards or backwards (minor adjustments).

 COACH'S TIP

• Moving back from students gives a visual on their canoe and you can move paddlers and/or kit bags around until the trim looks right.

Photo 1 Canoe well trimmed - stern slightly heavier than bow.

Photo 2 Canoe badly trimmed - bow heavy and digging into water.

BODY

The beginner most often orientates their body to face the bow. This needs to be corrected from the outset as the body blocks the full path of the paddle and severely hampers the development of effective and efficient strokes.

Encourage them to rotate knees and upper body towards the gunwale on paddling side. This allows maximum upper body rotation during stroke sequence and importantly uses the skeletal system and strongest muscles to provide power. Strokes can now be performed with maximum efficiency, which is crucial for preventing muscle fatigue on long journeys.

Photo 3 Tandem paddler rotated towards gunwale on their paddle side. Photo 4 Orientated facing the bow.

Beginners often sit centrally in the canoe as this makes them feel stable. They should be encouraged to sit slightly off-centre and low in the canoe.

Encourage them to shift bottom (and body weight) towards paddling side. For tandem paddlers this allows a more upright, and therefore more efficient, paddle stroke. For solo paddlers this allows them to edge the canoe, presenting a slimmer keel-line to the water, which reduces drag, and is invaluable for journeys on flat water and easy flows.

Photo 5 Good - tandem paddlers sitting close to gunwale on their paddle side.
Photo 6 Bad - tandem paddlers sitting on centre line.

BLADE

The vast variety of strokes and stroke combinations makes open canoeing a never-ending voyage of discovery. For the coach this variety presents a challenge in its own right, which is why I adopt a holistic approach, focusing on sets of skills needed by students to go on a journey, rather than on the individual strokes.

▶ COACHING TANDEM

COMMUNICATION & TEAMWORK

The most experienced coach in the world is doomed to fail if they can't get tandem pairs working together effectively. I cannot stress the importance enough, except to say that I return again and again to communication and teamwork throughout my own sessions.

Coaching Progressions:

 Tandem pairs face each other in the canoe. Paddlers can introduce themselves. Get one to paddle forwards and the other backwards (don't worry at this stage about the canoe going in circles).

Benefits ▶ Develops timing; provides reinforcement for visual learners; and introduces peer coaching.

 With paddlers in normal seating position, get them to initiate strokes by tapping their paddle shaft on the gunwale:

- Forward and reverse strokes
- Forward and reverse sweep strokes
- Draw strokes – first on same side and then on opposite sides

Benefits ▶ *Develops timing; provides input for audio learners; and can be repeated as necessary - timing often falls apart when new strokes and stroke combinations or sequences are introduced.*

Have students sit facing each other in the centre. One student holds the top-hand position of both paddles, whilst the other holds the lower-hand position of both paddles. Have them 'row' forwards and backwards.

 Have students move around in the canoe changing positions.

 Have students sit on gunwales in centre of canoe with hands linked, and both lean out over the water, counter-balancing each other (trust game).

 Have one student gunwale bobbing, standing either on the floor or on the gunwales.

Benefits ▶ *Develops a high level of trust between teams, since the consequence of getting it wrong is likely to be a wet one!*

ROLES IN THE OPEN CANOE

Bow and stern paddlers each have distinct roles.

The *bow* paddler is responsible for:

- Route choice.
- Timing and pacing of strokes.
- Decision making for, and initiating of, major changes in direction.

The *stern* paddler is responsible for:

- Providing power (momentum) to assist the bow paddler's strokes.
- Minor corrections to direction to maintain a straight running course.

Without wanting to over-generalise, the coach often witnesses the scenario of male/female tandem partnerships, where the man takes the stern seat and assumes the status of decision-maker. Whilst often providing the ideal trim (with the heavier paddler to rear and lighter paddler to front), it does not permit effective development of teamwork and skills development.

COACH'S TIP

- Set a square or triangular course and have tandem pairs follow it first with the stern paddler carrying out steerage, whilst the bow paddler provides power only; then swap roles.

▶ OPEN WATER SKILLS

STRAIGHT RUNNING

Every time the coach moves onto new skills, elements of Boat, Body, Blade will need adjusting. In the case of forward paddling, good body position and an evenly balanced canoe are essential (see above). Beginners will benefit from visualising the paths of the bow and stern paddle. Drawing a diagram in the sand or using a waterproof notepad can be very effective. Correction should be introduced from the outset as appropriate, applying a short stern pry (similar to stern rudder).

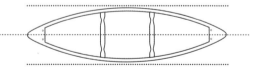

COACH'S TIP

- When swapping bow and stern roles, rather than physically moving up and down the boat, paddlers can turn on their seats to face the opposite direction, adjusting trim accordingly.

TURNING THE CANOE
Coaching Progressions:

🛶 Have teams perform sweeps, with bow paddler using a forward sweep and stern paddler using a Reverse Sweep (and vice versa).

🛶 Have teams experiment with edging to assist turning.

🛶 Introduce sweeps on the move, combining with other strokes.

> ### COACH'S TIP
>
> • Make sure students look in the direction of travel. (There is a particular tendency with sweep strokes for paddlers to focus on the passage of the blade through the water and if this is a forward sweep this will edge the canoe the wrong way.)

🛶 The coach stands in the canoe or on the bank and holds his/her paddle pointing skyward. As students paddle towards you, let your paddle swing down to left or right and they have to respond with the appropriate sweep strokes to turn in that direction.

🛶 Have teams paddle in a square clockwise and then anticlockwise.

🛶 Play 'follow my leader' or 'mother duck', with coach or assistant initiating a series of zigzags, which become progressively tighter and tighter as students become more proficient.

MOVING SIDEWAYS

This section focuses on specific skills for bow paddlers. Coaches often introduce cross-deck strokes much later. Personally, I find it is a natural progression to develop cross-deck draws in tandem with draw strokes, as it is easy to adapt the draw/cross-deck draw into a bow-cut/cross-bow cut.

Coaching Progressions:
▶ Bow Draws

🛶 Paddlers practise draws on the same side as each other.

🛶 Paddlers practise draws on opposing sides.

🛶 Once proficient in a stationary setting, students should practise on the move, with bow paddlers changing direction using draws and stern paddlers assisting with forward sweeps.

▶ Cross-Deck Draws

🛶 Repeat draw stroke exercises, but in the third exercise the stern paddler now assists the bow paddler's cross-bow draw with a reverse sweep.

> ### COACH'S TIP
>
> • In the Cross-Deck Draw, the body tends to block recovery of the paddle, so get paddlers to slice the blade forward (and out) at the end of the stroke.

▶ Bow Cuts/Cross-Bow-Cuts

🛶 Repeat the draw stroke exercises getting the bow paddler to place the blade further towards the bow, with full shoulder rotation and elbow tight (lower hand) to hip on a bow-cut and elbow close to chest to produce a cross-bow cut.

🛶 Have students paddle in a square (clockwise and anticlockwise), focussing on maintaining speed and reducing stalling throughout the turns.

🛶 Use the 'follow my leader' and 'zigzag' exercises to develop the stroke further.

EDGING

This is a good time to look at edging, because effective edging leads to greater efficiency in turns and helps maintain hull speed.

Coaching Progressions:

🛶 Students can explore edging through knee wobbling, i.e. shifting body weight over each knee in turn, gently at first and then with increasing commitment.

🛶 Introduce a 1-3 grading for degrees of edging and call out a number which students have to initiate and hold.

> ### COACH'S TIP
>
> • Throw balls into the bottom of the canoe, giving students instant visual feedback on trim and edge.

Photo 7 *Balls loose in the bottom of the canoe*

🪶 Have students stretch hands out in front (no paddle) and sweep them from left to right over the gunwales, with head and shoulders following line of hands. Emphasise the feel of a gentle rolling of the canoe, i.e. a smooth transition, rather than rocking from edge to edge.

Photo 8 *Head and shoulders leading the edging*

Advanced Coaching Progressions:

🪶 Get students to shift centre knee towards the paddle-side gunwale. This uses body weight to aid edging, and is especially useful for lighter students.

🪶 Have students paddle forwards whilst maintaining an inside edge. The canoe performs a wide-radius turn as a result of edging rather than steering.

Once students can hold an edge, they can use edging effectively to assist turning on the move (this is awkward for paddlers on their off-side).

STEERING THE CANOE

Here we are focusing on specific skills for stern paddlers, primarily stern prys (goon strokes) and 'J'-strokes.

▶ Stern Prys (Goon Strokes)

The stern pry is a crucial stroke for stern paddlers, but as with all strokes it has its time and place. It is a natural progression for the stern paddler as it has less of a stalling effect on the canoe when turning on the move and so provides a more efficient tandem combination with a bow-cut. It is also favoured in moving water because it provides maximum leverage making it extremely effective on technical water.

Beginners tend to pick this stroke up quickly as it feels less awkward than the 'J'-stroke and they get positive kinaesthetic feedback from the pressure on the blade. Students with experience in other disciplines find they transfer their knowledge of the stern rudder, achieving a relatively effective pry in a short space of time.

Coaching Progressions:

🪶 Have students perform gentle stern prys focusing on the pressure on the non-drive face of the paddle during the push-away phase.

 COACH'S TIP

• If students struggle try a kinaesthetic approach, with the coach standing in the water and applying pressure to the blade (some students benefit from closing their eyes during this exercise).

continued..

• Now hold the stern end of the canoe and once the stern paddler has the correct paddle position (push-away phase), push the canoe away. This provides a feel for the pressure on the blade whilst performing on the move.

Practise on the move with bow paddlers using bow-draws/cuts and stern paddlers assisting turning with stern prys (rather than the reverse sweeps used earlier).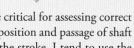

▶ 'J'-Strokes

'J'-strokes come in many forms. At one extreme there is the short-'J', a 'snappy' stroke with strong correction. This allows a high stroke rate and its effect is immediate and powerful so it is often favoured by river runners and by tourers (to reach cruising speed from a stationary start). At the other end of the spectrum there is the classic long-'J', a slow almost luxurious stroke where both hands work beyond the gunwale and the paddle trails for longer at the end of the stroke.

Coaching Progressions:

Adapt the stern pry coaching progressions.

REVERSE PADDLING

The principles of effective reverse paddling are the same as for forward paddling, in reverse, i.e. trimmed stern light and paddle strokes parallel to bow-stern centre line, not following the gunwale line.

The bow paddler now needs to apply the steering stroke, either trailing the paddle at end of the stroke (rudder) or performing a reverse-'J' (remember top

thumb turns down into 'breast' pocket allowing lower hand to extend forward).

Coaching Progressions:

Have students exaggerate trim to bow and then stern.

Benefits ▶ *trimming to extremes provides instant kinaesthetic feedback, helping students develop an instinctive awareness of the forces at play on the canoe.*

Have students experiment with adjusting trim so that the bow paddler applies less and less correction.

Benefits ▶ *this exercise develops awareness of minor alterations to trim, but be mindful that steerage is almost always required and so bow paddlers still need an effective correction stroke.*

Put paddlers back to normal paddling positions to practise.

Set a 'slalom' course around buoys or other obstacles.

Photo 9 Coach applying pressure to student paddle in reverse 'J'-stroke position.

MOVING SIDEWAYS CONTINUED... PRYS

This is a good time return to skills to move the canoe sideways, looking at the pry. The pry is often introduced relatively early, but I have found that it is better to let students consolidate a basic stroke repertoire first. Meanwhile, a cross-deck draw can be substituted for a pry. Once confidently performing draws on the move students are ready to look at the pry.

Coaching Progressions:

 Adapt the draw stroke coaching progressions, with students focusing on a deep blade and using the gunwale for leverage.

 Have students practise on opposing sides, with one using prys and the other draw strokes.

 Practise pry/draw combinations on the move.

COACH'S TIP

• Timing for the pry/draw combination is critical. If students struggle with this initially, have the bow paddler count into the combination from a forward paddling start.

▶ MOVING WATER SKILLS

If your students' end goal is to paddle rivers they will be thirsty for their first taste of moving water.

Coaches need to adapt sessions according to students' prior experiences:

• Novice canoeists need to consolidate some basic open water skills, and at least be able to paddle in a straight line. Moving water skills can then be developed using gentle currents with big eddies and forgiving eddy lines!

• Experienced flat-water paddlers can transfer knowledge of strokes and trim, but need to focus on manoeuvring skills, controlling speed and reading the water.

• White water kayakers will transfer their knowledge of moving water and paddle strokes, but now need to understand how the canoe behaves in a moving water environment, and learn how to adjust trim.

Introductory Coaching Progressions:

 Review open water skills in easy flows.

 Paddle into/out of the current, experimenting with degrees of edging.

 Execute wide turning circles in/out of the current, focusing on a point downstream (this encourages correct body position).

COACH'S TIP

• Use trim to assist your students develop new skills, moving them back to normal paddling positions once they have grasped the basics of what you are trying to coach:

  ▶ Bow light if coaching straight running or forward ferries.

  ▶ students closer together for developing skills for breaking in/out, setting, etc.

  ▶ stern light for developing any reverse ferries/setting.

• Edging also has a major impact on efficient tracking of the canoe:

  ▶ Ensure correct body position and get students to look in direction of travel. (The shoulders tend to follow the head and shift weight to one knee).

  ▶ Return to exercises to maintain an edge, if necessary.

FORWARD FERRIES
Coaching Progressions:

 Choose a venue with a gentle and consistent flow at the bottom and faster flow at the top. Start students at the bottom and move them upstream to work in faster flows as skill levels improve.

 Choose a rapid with a wide sweeping bend and have students focus on adjusting angle in different flow speeds.

 Choose a rapid with a series of waves and have students use these to move back and forth across the river (high crosses).

 Find a narrow fast flow with eddies either side and have students power across eddy line with a shallow canoe angle, using a running pry/running draw combination to shoot across. If the canoe loses momentum paddlers can provide forward power.

FAST OR SLOW?

There have been two main schools of thought on the best techniques for running rivers - one favouring setting and the other breaking in/out. Over the years I have found that the situation dictates the best approach and so I place equal emphasis on coaching both skills.

BREAKING IN & BREAKING OUT

Start with a venue offering a gentle current and eddies either side.

Coaching Progressions:

▶ Draw/Forward Sweep Combination

🌀 Break in and out at various entry speeds and angles, focusing on edging and looking in direction of travel.

🌀 As paddlers cross the eddy line have the bow paddler draw on the inside of the turn whilst the stern paddler uses a forward sweep, leaning away from the stroke (this feels quite awkward at first).

▶ Cross-Deck Draw/Heavy-'J' Combination

🌀 Once comfortable with the draw/forward sweep combination, introduce the cross-deck draw/ heavy-'J' combination and follow the same coaching progressions as above.

COACH'S TIP

• It is common for students to spin too early on the eddy line, so get them to focus on waiting until the bow starts to turn before placing a bow-cut. If the venue is suitable, use a kinaesthetic approach and get students to close their eyes as they power towards the eddy line and wait to feel the change in pressure.

• Encourage your students to work together matching time and rhythm. C+T

▶ Using Both Combinations

Once competent with both combinations, students can return to their normal paddling sides. Set exercises which encourage both combinations to be used naturally, eg:

🌀 Break in and out of an eddy, i.e. Making circles, (create a circuit involving the whole group).

🌀 Break in and out using eddies on both sides and return, i.e. Making a figure of 8.

🌀 Break in and out using eddies on either side and forward ferry back. S B

Advanced Coaching Progressions:

🌀 From the bow-draw/cross-bow draw position shift the top hand slightly forward creating a more vertical paddle, similar to a bow rudder and draw this towards the bow, linking into a powerful forward stroke, which regains hull speed.

🌀 The students have absorbed several combinations in a short period of time, so give them freedom to explore what they have learnt through student-led exercises, providing them with a suitable venue and give key areas to focus on:

- Experiment with different angles on exit and entry.
- Experiment with different speeds of approach.
- Maintain knee pressure to aid edging.
- Stroke timing as a team when crossing eddy lines.

A student-led approach gives space and time to consolidate the skills learnt and gets them reading the water speed and adjusting approach angles accordingly.

REVERSE FERRIES & SETTING

When students make the transition from open to moving water a key skill is the ability to avoid obstacles without going broadside. Paddlers are often seen frantically sweeping above obstacles, which increases speed, reduces reaction time/space and is more likely to take them broadside.

Reverse ferrying has two major advantages:

• It reduces and controls speed, which reduces water intake and increases reaction time. It takes a lot of power to completely kill the momentum of a canoe moving at the speed of the current, and all but the most powerful students will struggle, with the result that they mentally tick reverse ferries off their toolbox list. So remember that the goal is speed reduction.

• It keeps the canoe straighter, so avoiding pinning, and puts the canoe into position for side-slipping (setting) into eddies. This is an invaluable skill in tight spaces or when running rapids on sight.

GENTLE FLOWS
Coaching Progressions:

 Adapt the reverse paddling from the open water coaching progressions.

 COACH'S TIP

• Bow paddlers should use a competent reverse-'J'. They will find this easier on their downstream side at first (return to kinaesthetic input if need be).

• Use a consistent flow and avoid crossing eddy lines initially or you risk overloading your students with too many variables and they will tend to spin out on eddy lines.

 Use different venues, introducing variable and faster flows.

 Have students break in, switch to a reverse ferry and paddle across the flow to set into another eddy.

 Windscreen-wiper ferries - have students ferry across flow part way, change direction (bow paddler initiates with draws/prys) and return.

Benefits ▶ *develops defensive tactics for running faster water and rapids on sight.*

FASTER FLOWS

As students become more proficient on using reverse ferries on faster flows, they will realise the advantage for paddling white water. This defensive approach to paddling white water is essential in open canoe along with the ability to anticipate and read the water.

Coaching Progressions:

 Set angles according to the clock (12 o'clock is downstream), experimenting with angling the canoe between 10.30 and 1.30.

Benefits ▶ *increases students' awareness of how to use the force of the current on the canoe to cross currents. The aim is to find the optimal angle, which maximises speed and efficiency, and involves surprisingly little effort from the paddlers, aside from a few final power strokes to cross the eddy line. If the angle is too little it will take a long time and many paddle strokes to cross the current. If the angle is too great the force of the current on the canoe will overpower the paddlers and spin the canoe round.*

 Return to edge-holding exercises, using balls on the canoe floor if necessary, and emphasise the gliding or slide-slipping motion.

Benefits ▶ *edging aids tracking, so it is important to stop students rocking from edge to edge.*

 Space Invaders – paddle downstream and then coach/students call out about an imaginary obstacles (or real ones as students progress) to left, right or ahead and students take evasive action.

Having mastered the basics of reverse ferries/setting, students can resume normal paddling positions. Choose a venue where they can practise and experiment 'in anger', with the stern paddler shifting forward to adjust trim, if necessary, and bow paddler adjusting canoe angle with prys/draws.

▶ DEVELOPING SKILLED PERFORMERS

So far the student experience has been largely task-orientated focusing on strokes and stroke combinations in isolation. This approach provides students with a reasonable toolbox allowing them to become fairly proficient.

In order to become skilled performers paddlers need to consolidate what they have learnt so far and develop the ability to select and adapt these skills in different situations. The coach does this by exposing students to as many venues, exercises and challenges as possible. You will be limited only by your imagination.

Try and resist the temptation to be too prescriptive, but set broad goals and circuits such as:

• Break out and return by forward ferry.

• Break in and reverse ferry across to other bank.

• Set a slalom course down a rapid using eddies.

• Run rapids only using reverse paddling/setting.

• Run rapids under forward power.

If you get this right you will have mastered the skill of moving your students onto the next plateau, from task-orientated and conscious application of strokes, to skilled performers who read the river and unconsciously apply and adjust strokes as appropriate.

▶ SOLO PADDLING

Your students should have a reasonable foundation of skills and understanding of how the canoe responds from being coached tandem. 'Boat, Body, Blade' principles need to be revisited when making the transition to solo work:

- Boat - trim has an even greater significance for the soloist, as does matching the paddler's size (height/weight) to the canoe.

- Correct 'Body' position is essential for effective stroke work and to maintain an edge to assist with turning manoeuvres and forward paddling.

- All strokes now incorporate a steering phase, usually by adjusting 'Blade' position on entry or exit. The most important addition to a soloist's stroke repertoire is a competent 'J'-stroke.

This section assumes that students are building on and transferring skills already learnt in tandem. However, this may not be the case and so the coach may find it appropriate to draw on coaching progressions from the tandem section.

▶ OPEN WATER SKILLS

STRAIGHT RUNNING

Students must be able to maintain an edge now. Many students, however, are initially reluctant to commit to sitting off-centre and the level of edging required, as they feel unstable, so coaches may need to devote time to developing confidence in this skill. Have students run through a range of forward strokes - practising various 'J'-strokes, Indian, Canadian strokes and so on.

COACH'S TIP

- To aid your observation and analysis of Body and Blade positions place markers on the paddler and canoe using coloured tape.

The coach needs to also note the way the boat reacts once at hull speed:

- Rolling – if the canoe rocks from side to side, this generally indicates that the paddler is shifting their weight from edge to edge. Get paddler to shift more weight to their paddle-side gunwale.

- Pitching – the paddler applies too much power on the blade and/or enters the blade too far forward and exits too far back, having the effect of lifting the bow and killing the canoe's forward momentum. Encourage paddler to adopt a shorter and more vertical stroke.

- Yawing – the bow continually swings from left to right. This can be caused by a number of factors:

  ▶ Canoe tilt

  ▶ Canoe not on paddle-side edge

  ▶ Paddler not focusing on a clear marker ahead

  ▶ Too much power and correction on each stroke

Encourage paddler to aim for a target; start slowly with just enough correction to allow the canoe to maintain a straight line. ◀Ⓑ▶

TURNING THE CANOE

The classic textbook turning stroke combinations for the soloist is the inside and outside pivot turns. In reality, soloists tend to use the first phase of the outside pivot combination (cross-bow cut) and the second phase of the inside pivot (bow cut).

Coaching Progressions:

First let students experiment with using just forward power and edging to paddle in wide arcs to left and right. Emphasize weighting the paddle-side knee for both turns. When turning on-side (paddling side), more correction is needed.

Get students to practise using forward power, using different combinations to initiate turning and focusing on the effect on speed and turn, eg:

- Forward sweeps, which create long carving turns.

- Reverse sweeps, which kill hull speed.

- Short forward sweep followed by cross-deck draw, which minimises loss of hull speed and produces a relatively tight turn.

- Forward power with a heavy-'J' and bow draw, which minimises speed loss and produces tight turns.

⚙ Set circuits, eg:

- Squares - clockwise and anticlockwise
- Triangles - clockwise and anticlockwise
- Zigzags

Advanced Coaching Progressions:

⚙ Once students are skilled in turning the canoe using various combinations, they can perform the same exercises keeping the blade in the water throughout. Try:

- Indian strokes
- Inside pivot turns
- 'C'-Strokes

⚙ Now allow paddlers to explore stroke combinations and edging themselves. There are infinite combinations, each provoking slightly different responses from the canoe. Guided experimentation allows competent paddlers to develop a deeper and more instinctive understanding of 'Boat, Body, Blade' interaction. Paddlers may find this awkward at first but with perseverance they learn to maintain pressure on the blade (apart from during the recovery phase) with minimal loss of hull speed.

⚙ If some guidance is required try:

- On-side turning, which is relatively easier – moving from power stroke to 'J'-stroke, slicing forward and completing with a bow cut.

- Off-side turning requires forward speed, followed by a forward sweep from the hip back, slicing the blade to a bow jam and following through with forward power before momentum is lost.

COACH'S TIP

- Have students focus on quiet paddle strokes - no ripple and no splashing.

MOVING SIDEWAYS

Correct body position is essential to allow effective blade work in draws and cross-deck draws. Sitting off-centre with knee and upper body rotated lets both hands work over the gunwale and allows a high paddle angle.

Coaching Progressions:

⚙ Have students focus on a deep blade, pushing water under the canoe rather than onto the gunwale.

⚙ Have students experiment with the blade slightly forward or backward to pull the bow or stern more. ◀ B ▶

⚙ Repeat exercises for cross-deck draws.

SIDE–SLIPPING

These strokes come into their own on moving water for avoiding obstacles, allowing the canoe to side-slip and maintaining a straight running canoe. The foundations of the strokes, however, are best learnt on open water.

Coaching Progressions:

All strokes need to be practised under forward power:

▶ Running Draws

⚙ Have students experiment with opening the leading edge of the blade. Blade angle determines whether the canoe moves sideways or turns.

⚙ Have students experiment with blade position, which again influences whether the result is a sideways movement or turn.

⚙ To initiate get students to try the following:

- Forward stroke, exit blade and re-enter in running draw position; or
- Forward stroke slicing blade forwards into running draw position.

⚙ Having established correct angle and position, students can be introduced to sculling draws to maintain sideways movement once the hull loses speed.

▶ Running Cross-Deck Draws

⚙ Follow the same progressions as for running draws.

▶ Running Prys

⚙ Follow the progressions for running draws, except the leading edge of the blade is angled toward the gunwale. Pressure on the blade pushes the shaft onto the gunwale.

🔹 The blade can be placed directly or sliced into position from the stern.

🔹 As momentum is lost, the blade can be pushed forwards along the gunwale maintaining pry position, and repeat entering the blade slightly further back, and increasing the stroke rate. This is the basic reverse pitch, which is an excellent stroke incorporating power and steerage in one action, and mostly used for reverse setting.

▶ MOVING WATER SKILLS

Moving water is the ultimate test of the soloist's understanding of the interaction between Boat/Body/Blade.

Coaches can help the transition to moving water by:

• Venue choice. Students need consistent flows with large eddies and forgiving eddy lines to allow them to start transferring the basic skills into a moving water environment.

• Giving students basic skills for running moving water from day one, focusing on:

▸ Forward power and correction

▸ Reverse cross-deck paddling

▸ Sweeps with edging to assist turning

▸ Line choice to avoid tight manoeuvres and sharp eddies

The sooner coaches give their students sufficient skills and get them running short sections of moving water the better. Rather than drilling in lots of strokes, give them the satisfaction of running easy rivers. Their thirst for more will provide all the motivation needed to aid your coaching.

FORWARD FERRIES

As a rule of thumb, I keep students in their normal paddling position for river running. A well-balanced boat allows a range of movements to be performed and sliding forwards or leaning backwards allows for minor trim adjustment. Heavier canoeists obviously have greater impact on trim than lighter people. Broadly speaking, trimming by changing position or moving bags is only practical on open water and very easy rivers. Having said that, lighter paddlers may need to be prepared to throw a heavy kit bag around

to adjust trim and it is still useful to exaggerate trim when learning specific skills. Hence, for coaching forward ferries, you may need to move your students back or get them to throw a bag behind them.

Whether paddling on upstream or downstream side, paddlers should maintain good body position so that they weight the knee on their paddling side. They should also look where they are going, not where they've come from.

Coaching Progressions:

🔹 Start students on their downstream side (minimal correction is required), and have them experiment with varying boat speed and angle. ◀Ⓑ▶

🔹 Now progress to upstream side. A slight upstream edge should be maintained (easier for the body to sustain). There will be a trade off between the amount of correction required and loss of speed (and therefore loss of ground). Have students start with entering the current at a shallow angle, experimenting with the amount of correction needed. ◀Ⓑ▶

🔹 Windscreen-wiper ferries - have students ferry across flow part way and change direction:

• When paddling on downstream side initiate change of direction using a stern pry and a forward power stroke.

• When paddling on upstream side initiate change using a bow draw and forward power stroke (with a heavy-'J' if necessary).

🔹 Change venues and find variable currents.

BREAKING IN & BREAKING OUT

The secret to effective breaking in/out is to let the water do the work. Forward momentum drives the bow into the current/eddy and water pressure turns the canoe assisted by edging and turning strokes. So students need to focus on timing and developing ultra-slick and intuitive stroke combinations. Just like stepping onto a moving elevator, commitment (to edging) and timing (of strokes and edging) is needed or you will turn on the eddy line or capsize.

Breaking in when paddling on the upstream side is simpler to start with because the paddler can assist the turn and maintain momentum as the canoe enters the current. It does, however, require a change of edge and so timing is crucial.

Coaching Progressions:

 Paddling on upstream side have students gain forward speed towards the current, forward sweep, and simultaneously look downstream, change edge, placing a cross-deck bow-cut in the current.

 Paddling on downstream side, have students gain momentum towards the current, increasing edge as the bow starts to turn and place a bow-cut in the current. The canoe performs a large arc and quickly loses momentum on entering the current.

 Following on from the last exercise students use forward power strokes with a heavy-'J' on entering the current, then change to a bow-cut, which is drawn towards and continues under the hull (deep 'C'-stroke) finishing in a 'J'-stroke. This combination will maintain hull speed.

COACH'S TIP

• Have students close their eyes and sweep only when they feel the pressure of water start to turn the bow. For this you need to choose the site and manage your site safety carefully, but the exercise offers excellent kinaesthetic reinforcement.

Dip into the coaching progressions used for the tandem pairs to further develop breaking in/out skills.

REVERSE FERRIES & SETTING

Reverse ferries are one of the more difficult strokes to learn as solo paddlers, but are essential for running white water.

Coaches can adapt most of the exercises and techniques used for tandem crews. Choice of venue is critical, a steady consistent flow with no strong eddy lines is ideal; or coach in gentle flows whilst travelling downstream. Remember to trim boats stern light, exaggerating when first introducing the skill and then encourage students to develop from normal river-running position (slightly stern light).

Solo paddlers have two main stroke choices for reverse ferries:

• Reverse paddling combined with reverse cross-deck strokes are often taught to beginners. However this combination has several disadvantages:

▸ Students need to be relatively flexible and not suffering any back problems.

▸ It involves constant changing from edge to edge which means the canoe does not track well.

▸ The pause between strokes results in a greater loss of ground.

• Reverse paddling with a reverse 'J'-stroke allows the canoe to track consistently and less ground is lost. It is better to start students on their downstream side, focusing on adjusting amount of steerage according to flow speed and canoe angle. Ground tends to be lost during the steering phase.

COACH'S TIP

• Either on the bank or with coach in the water apply pressure to student's blade when in correct position for reverse 'J'-stroke (kinaesthetic input). Again some students will benefit if they do this with their eyes closed.

REVERSE PITCH

This is the 'Rolls Royce' of the solo paddler's stroke repertoire and, although rarely mentioned in canoe books, experienced paddlers seem to naturally discover and develop this stroke. The reverse pitch is both efficient and effective, because it eliminates the pause created by the reverse-'J', producing a faster stroke rate and moving the canoe swiftly across the current.

Unlike reverse ferries it is easier to learn the reverse pitch stroke on the upstream side. In both downstream and upstream applications, note that additional steerage strokes may be needed. I often use the occasional powerful reverse-'J'/reverse cross-deck draw to push the stern across eddy lines.

Coaching Progressions:

 Start students on their upstream side. Focus on placing the blade behind the paddler, keeping the shaft almost upright, and at a 45° angle to the gunwale and leading edge forward. Hold this position throughout the stroke.

 Now progress to downstream side modifying the stroke by starting the stroke at the hips and pushing the blade further forwards.

Photo 10 Reverse pitch, blade angle and position

Windscreen-wiper ferries - have students ferry across flow part way and change direction by adjusting paddle position forwards or backwards.

Change venues and find variable currents.

Raft slide - as with driving a car at high speed, anticipation of what's ahead is critical. Canoeists must plan ahead, identifying eddies in plenty of time and setting the canoe at an angle so the water pushes the canoe across the river assisted by a gentle paddle rate and edging. The raft slide technique is not concerned about losing ground, and a long oblique angle is taken towards eddies with an increasing paddle rate to assist the last push into the eddy.

▶ DEVELOPING RIVER RUNNING SKILLS

Coaches have endlessly discussed the merits of paddling rivers using predominantly forward or reverse power strokes. Personally I believe both methods are equally valid and should be coached along with an understanding of the pros and cons of each.

• Forward power combined with breaking in/out as necessary is effective where space and time allow, and for regrouping, briefings, portaging, etc.

• Reverse paddling is a more defensive approach and very effective for running rivers on sight. Speed is controlled allowing more time to react and read the river. The canoe is kept straighter - ideal for setting into eddies, or slide-slipping to avoid obstacles. Most importantly the risk of going broadside is minimised. This approach comes into its own on narrow, technical rivers.

The skilled performer, regardless of approach, must learn to react quickly and change canoe angle with minimal ground loss. For this, the soloist must be able to apply various stroke combinations, linking strokes and keeping the blade in the water as much as possible and above all not switch paddling sides!

Practices:

• Bow draws, sliced back to the stern and into a stern pry, if necessary.

• Bow pry and forward sweep finishing with a stern draw, if necessary, moving the canoe the other way.

The result is a square-shaped passage of the blade in the water, hence box strokes, of which there are infinite variations and forms.

Advanced Coaching Progressions:

Look at different box strokes emphasising quick changes of direction and focusing on maintaining pressure on the blade in the water throughout rather than the individual strokes that the blade forms.

Run rapids down the main flow using only reverse strokes.

Space Invaders - using side-slipping on rapids to avoid obstacles.

Run rapids using power strokes and breaking in/out.

Practise breaking in, forward ferrying and breaking out into the opposite eddy using the minimum number of strokes. If there is a wave to assist the crossing, a high-cross can be performed, but the principle is fine-tuning the angle so the power of the current pushes the canoe across.

Figure-of-8 - return to original eddy creating a continuous circuit.

'S' manoeuvres - choose an eddy half the length of the canoe in mid-stream. Break out and break in on the other focusing on maintaining hull speed/ momentum and minimising the number of strokes (effectively slalom in a big boat!).

Use your imagination and enthusiasm to come up with other ideas and combinations. Also remember to allow students to take control of their own learning at this level, using more student-led exercises. This will develop a deeper understanding of the Boat, Body, Blade dynamics, allowing them to apply skills more instinctively, so they can enjoy river running independently without their coach being on hand to guide them.

▶ TRADITIONAL SKILLS

In my experience, I found that the traditional skills opened up a whole new world of possibilities for journeying. These skills evolved for practical reasons - to make travelling by canoe fast, efficient and functional. Generally speaking, I have also found that the traditional skills are hugely undervalued and under-coached.

In my coaching I often find a section where I can look at a range of traditional skills, teaching not only the skills, but also letting students experiment so they can assess what will be efficient in different environments. For example, a portage may be described on a trip, but on inspection it may be quicker and easier to pull the canoe over a small lip, grab the painters and line a short section and then jump in and use a half-pole to stub down the final rocky section, jumping out and wading if it gets too shallow. By being able to apply all these skills and judge when and what to use, the paddler may have saved themselves a difficult and slow portage down the bank. Plus the satisfaction is tremendous!

▶ POLING & STUBBING

Poles come into their own on long shallow river and lake sections or shallow boulder rapids, where there is insufficient paddle depth. Venue choice is crucial for these sessions as it is important to practise these skills in context, i.e. where they would be effective.

HALF-POLING

I start poling sessions with half-poling, which is executed from a normal paddling position using the pole just as you would a paddle. Paddlers can make very effective use of half-poles on journeys by quickly transferring between paddle and half-pole as water depth changes.

- Tandem – get teams to pole on their paddle-side, avoiding cross-deck strokes, which increases the chance of hitting their partner. C+T

- Solo – half-poling is used to effectively perform a range of on-side and cross-deck strokes.

Remember to present the end with aluminium tip to the river (you may wish to tape the open end to prevent it becoming a lethal weapon!).

FULL-POLING

Full-poling allows the paddler to stand. Stability is a big issue when learning the art of poling, but once mastered it provides a welcome change, relieving tired paddling muscles and knees on long journeys.

Boat, Body, Blade factors:

- Boat - needs to be trimmed bow light, to aid forward movement and turning.

- Body - some adopt a feet-together stance and applying maximum edging; whilst others find that a wider stance, with trunk and hips rotated to poling side, provides a more stable platform.

- Pole (Blade) the key markers are:

    ▶ Both thumbs upright.

    ▶ Pole planted at angle to paddler and water.

    ▶ Knees bent, transferring pressure through feet.

    ▶ Mentally focus on moving canoe around the pole.

    ▶ Recovery of the pole for forward power achieved either through walking hands up and down the shaft, or by adopting the windmill technique.

Two extremes of body position for full poling and good blade/pole position (see key points above).

Photo 11 - feet together

Photo 12 (across the page) - wide stance

Coaching Progressions:

📌 Once students have grasped the basics they need lots of exercises to improve balance, eg standing up and shifting back and forth in the canoe.

👆 COACH'S TIP

• Lowering the centre of gravity reduces the wobble-factor! Have students lean forwards holding the pole across the gunwales and sliding their hands up and down the gunwales.

📌 Get students to focus on transferring power from hips, down through knees and feet to move canoe towards and away from pole, and then turning with pole on inside (like going around a maypole) and outside of the turn (pushing away from the pole).

📌 Have students do different circuits - circles, squares, etc. - using the pole as a point of leverage.

📌 To practise using the pole for steerage, find a shallow area and have students adopt a low stance and position the pole behind them. Keep the pole steady and apply pressure through the hips and feet to push/pull the canoe from side to side and swing to right and left.

👆 COACH'S TIP

• For tandem crews have one paddler practise, whilst the other sits on the floor facing their partner. This improves stability and allows them to give peer feedback.

Some coaches use bow rope to aid direction to start with, but I find that if you have to use a rope, you have probably chosen the wrong location.

Advanced Coaching Progressions:

📌 As students grow in confidence get them to push harder on the pole, transferring power using a hip thrust. The canoe accelerates and proficient polers find they can travel significantly faster than by any other method.

📌 To negotiate shorter, faster sections, lighten the bow (shift weight back) and increase poling rate by not using the full length of the pole length (reduces recovery time and produces short quick stroke sequences).

STUBBING

Watch a skilled performer and stubbing will look like a rapid series of short little stabbing actions. This prevents the build up of speed and allows directional control using the feet as in poling.

The ideal coaching venue has a shallow gravely bottom with consistent and minimal flow.

Boat, Body, Blade factors:

• Boat – needs to be trimmed light upstream. To achieve this either move paddlers forward *or* make them face the other way and spin the canoe around 180° (thus avoiding stepping over the central yoke, kit bags, kids, dogs, etc!).

• Body – the same as for poling but even lower so the knees are flexed to take the impact.

• Pole (Blade) – as with poling both thumbs are upright, but the pole is now held at a lower angle, placed further forward in water and downstream end over shoulder.

Photo 13 Boat, Body, Pole (Blade) - correct position

Coaching Progressions:

▶ Half-Pole

 From normal sitting position, have students slow their descent, by planting the pole downstream, and practise pushing the canoe sideways. Work on both sides of the gunwale (except for stern paddlers in tandem).

 Find a rocky section with variable depth, where students can practise transferring quickly between half-pole and paddle.

▶ Full-Pole

 Have students slow their descent, working on both sides of the gunwale.

 Have students hold position in moving water.

 Have students push canoe sideways developing into a reverse ferry.

 Have students pole downriver in gentle flow and then transfer to stubbing where flow speeds increase.

> ### COACH'S TIP
>
> • Stand holding the stern in position to coach control, position and steerage.

▶ LINING

The Canoe and Kayak Handbook contains an excellent section on lining. I would just like to emphasise that the first priority is the safety of the canoe and its contents, so always consider portaging, and remember the golden rule that ropes and water don't mix, and caution is required at all times:

• Minimise the number of knots.

• Keep knots close to the hull.

• Always have a clean end.

Lining Workshops

A good demonstration is essential. I often line my canoe part way first, showing the students how to manage a solo canoe and how to deal with the problems commonly encountered.

Find a venue with trees that have to be negotiated – to pass the tree, the student should let the canoe pass, go to the other side themselves, and reach through for a bite of rope, using the 'T'-grip to retrieve the rope.

I then pass the canoe to the students. The other canoes can be lined using a mix of team or solo methods.

Photo 14 Lining past a tree

▶ TRACKING

Tracking techniques are covered in the Canoe and Kayak Handbook. I have found that the traditional long-line approach often causes problems for students with ropes snagging on trees, boulders, etc. Instead, I favour the short-line method of tracking, which still uses bridle, but half the normal length of tracking line. The student has greater control and a firm tug on the ropes usually allows the canoe to ride over any obstacles.

> ### COACH'S TIP
>
> • Carry a large water bag for sessions, as standard kit bags are often insufficient to adjust trim.

▶ Quick Short-Line Method

A colleague taught me this gem and I use it all the time, usually ending up at the top before the other paddlers have set up their bridles. With no bridle, this technique is incredibly quick and easy to set up. Just be aware that if the bow swings towards you too far, the painter will slip out from under the gunwale, so the angle must be maintained.

 Take bow painter (minimum length is 1 canoe length); pass it down through bow seat (shore side); take across the back of the seat and up on the far side; pass rope over the gunwale and under the hull.

 Stern painter should be approximately 1 canoe length.

Photo 15 Tracking set-up

Tracking Workshops:

Key points:

• Clear demonstrations are essential.

• Venue choice is important, starting with no obstacles.

• Group control is essential because of the number of ropes in use.

• Set up one long and one short-line system to reduce the number of canoes and ropes on the water. Get students to take turns, practising both systems.

COACH'S TIP

• Place a student in the downstream end to help trim, and using paddle to steer.

▶ SAILING

For many years, I failed to recognise what sailing has to offer canoeing for journeying, firmly believing that sailing was best left to sailors. But after various long distance trips around the world I am a convert - harnessing the power of the wind offers the potential, on extended expeditions, to cover many miles in a short time allowing more time to explore other areas.

The many different options for sailing rigs – all with pros and cons for different situations – are well documented in other texts. However, I have included some practical ideas for running sailing sessions.

Sailing Workshops:

▶ Rafted Sailing

Simple rafted pairs using paddles to support the sail are quick to set up and keep more members involved working as a team.

Larger rafts bring entire groups together. Set up can take 20 minutes plus and is very coach led, unless there are two rigs to organise, so I only use it when sailing long distances. However, large rafts can use bigger sails (and so sail faster and in lighter winds) and can sail across the wind. They are also very sociable for groups who mainly spend their time in ones or twos in a canoe.

Trim (Boat) is sorted once afloat – stern heavy for sailing downwind, and more central for sailing across the wind.

Paddles (Blade) are used as rudders for sailing downwind and held centrally, like a leeboard for sailing across the wind.

Whole rafts have been known to flip, so if you have 'all your eggs in one basket' take the weather/water conditions out on the open water into account. You need bailing out systems and a plan for an all-in (including re-righting the raft).

'Man overboard' is a distinct possibility. Some suggest using a trailing line, which can be grabbed by a swimmer, but the most important thing is having a quick release system on the sail.

▶ Solo & Tandem Sailing

Before venturing out onto open water with a team of solo sailors, make sure you give clear briefings on safety cover and group control. If a canoe gains ground faster it should drop the sail and allow the others to catch up. If there is a capsize all canoes should drop sails, turn into the wind and hold position. Appoint a front canoe (your assistant, if you have one) and buddy systems. I find it best to take the rear, so I can see the whole group and sail over to any capsizes.

Generally the canoe needs to be trimmed stern heavy. In tandem canoes make sure there is something for the bow paddler to sit on further back.

For soloists, controlling the sheet (rope to adjust the sail) and steering are hard work over long distances, so cleats and leeboard tie-in (releasable) systems can be used.

WIND

Wind can be a nightmare for everyone, coaches included. Factors affecting canoes in wind include design, amount of freeboard, and paddlers' positions. The coach needs an awareness of these, plus the range of ability in the group.

▶ Heading Into Wind

There are two schools of thought on paddling into wind:

• Paddlers move forward to weight the bow, allowing the canoe to act like a flag. The disadvantage with this is that more correction is required and so it takes more effort over any distance and ground can be lost.

• Paddlers move back to lighten bow, paddle on downwind side and head slightly off-course until no steerage is required (the wind on the canoe cancels out the turning power in the stroke). After a while, change direction and paddling side. I prefer this method because, although a greater distance is covered, the method is far more efficient and less tiring.

Coaches must position themselves to cover safety and look for sheltered havens for the teams to regroup and rest. When faced with headlands the coach must keep students in line of sight either from the bank or water. If wind is too strong for soloists, they can team up as tandem pairs and tow one canoe, or track round if possible.

▶ Travelling Across The Wind

I use the same methods described above, but the coach can help the group by setting a ferry angle to follow. In the safety briefing I tell groups that if I blow the whistle and point downwind the group should run with the wind in a close pack.

▶ Running With The Wind

Fetch can dramatically increase wave size, so be cautious in assessing likely conditions further out. Keep trim bow light (soloists be careful as moving back puts you in the narrowest part, reducing stability). The coach is usually best positioned at the rear so they can paddle quickly to a swimmer. The safety brief should include a point for the group to aim at.

CHRIS FORREST

Chris has been paddling since the late 70's. In kayak, he ran many of the first descents of steep creeks and burns in Scotland throughout the 80's and 90's. In canoe he has linked just about every coast and loch in Scotland to put together new wilderness trips. Canoesport has also offered an excuse to explore other parts of the world - Europe, Scandinavia, Canada, New Zealand and Nepal.

Chris has worked for Glenmore Lodge and Plas y Brenin, playing a part in developing open canoeing at both national centres. He is a Level 5 Coach (Canoe and Inland Kayak) and an International Mountain Guide and now runs his own business, Inspirational Coaching (www.inspirational-coaching.co.uk) focusing on skills improvement, higher level governing body courses and guided trips.

Acknowledgements - I would like to thank: Stuart Bell for passing on his enthusiasm and passion for the open canoe and encouraging me to explore and develop my understanding of this craft; Andy Jackson for the many adventures and near-epics running and playing on Scotland's finest rivers; Samantha, my partner, for her support.

15 SEA KAYAKING

The wonderful thing about coaching sea kayaking is the rich diversity of both physical and cognitive skills we have to teach our clients in order to enable them to paddle safely and efficiently... and all this in an ever-changing environment.

They need to have the paddling skills to cope with a vast array of sea conditions as well as planning skills, navigation skills and an awareness of what is going on around them.

INTRODUCTION

This chapter identifies the physical and cognitive skills you need to teach to your clients and provides you with session ideas, exercises and progressions that will help you in your coaching of sea kayaking.

▶ What Do You Need To Coach On The Sea?

Have a look at the flow chart overleaf, it summarises all the conditions and environments our sea kayakers have to be trained for. Before you delve into the rest of the chapter, consider which physical skills, i.e. strokes, combination of strokes, adaptation of strokes and which cognitive skills you use yourself, in these environments?

Photo 1 Penrhyn Mawr in tranquil conditions

Title Photo Penrhyn Mawr on a moderately rough day

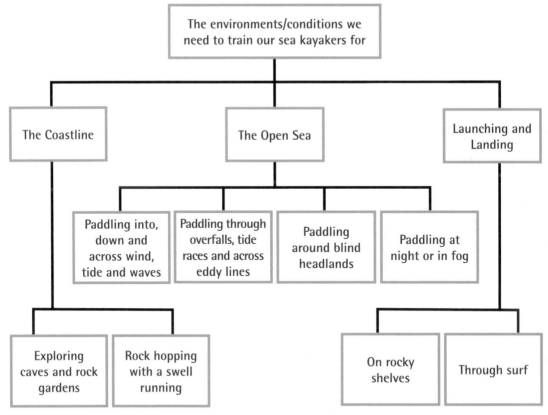

Fig. 1 The environments/conditions we need to train our sea kayakers for.

Physical skills required by sea kayakers:

- Good boat awareness
- Effective forward paddling in various conditions
- Close quarter manoeuvring skills
- Rough water handling skills
- Skills for launching and landing
- Skills to rescue others
- Rolling and self-rescue skills

Cognitive skills required by sea kayakers

- Group awareness
- Wind and water awareness
- Planning skills
- Deck top navigation skills
- Leadership skills
- Risk assessing and incident management skills
- Environmental awareness

The session ideas outlined are not in any strict coaching order, they are grouped together in the categories listed above. You may therefore need to pull out sessions described in later chapters before using those in earlier ones. For example, before trying out the forward paddling progressions in all the various conditions, ensure they have mastered (or at least tried) turning and manoeuvring in a calm bay.

Before we can start any coaching sessions we do need to consider our coaching strategy for the day. As mentioned in earlier chapters, a plan, whether it be in our heads, written down, a few scanty notes or a detailed scheme of work, is invaluable if we are to create a successful coaching session. Our plans, however, do need to be flexible and open-minded allowing for those unanticipated coaching opportunities, to be taken as they arise throughout the day. Nevertheless, we don't want any nasty surprises, so anticipating the effect of the predicted tides, weather and swell for the day is absolutely essential.

▶ PLANNING OUR STRATEGY

Having some sort of teaching strategy based around the client's needs and wishes, as well as the sea conditions for the day, is essential in order to give your clients a productive day. Of course you can just do things on the hoof, but if time is short and there are very specific needs to be addressed, more precise planning is required.

Below is an example of one of my coaching strategies, scribbled onto the back of an envelope. Not your typical well-presented lesson plan, but, nonetheless, it has all the necessary information on it, takes less than 10 minutes to prepare (with practice) and most important of all, ensures that I am prepared for whatever the day brings. Popping the envelope into a clear

TOP TIP

• Discussions with new clients prior to their day will help you identify what they wish to learn and will give you an idea of their ability. This will enable you to choose an appropriate location for them. 10 minutes of quiet observation of their actual ability once on the water will then tell you exactly what they need to learn, thus helping you decide on how best to use the location and tailor your initial coaching strategy to them.

plastic sleeve allows me to leave it on my deck and refer to it all day. Any such plan should include the following information:

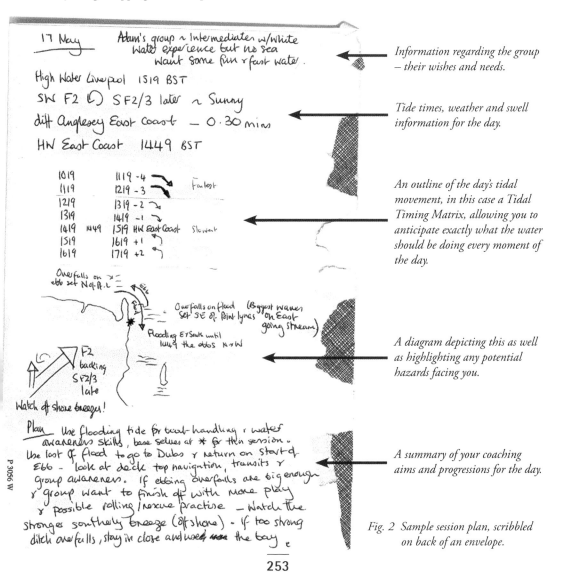

Information regarding the group – their wishes and needs.

Tide times, weather and swell information for the day.

An outline of the day's tidal movement, in this case a Tidal Timing Matrix, allowing you to anticipate exactly what the water should be doing every moment of the day.

A diagram depicting this as well as highlighting any potential hazards facing you.

A summary of your coaching aims and progressions for the day.

Fig. 2 Sample session plan, scribbled on back of an envelope.

A NOTE ABOUT TIDAL TIMING MATRICES

I can't stress enough that this matrix is only one way of laying out tidal movement. There are lots of ways of laying out such tidal information for you to see at a glance and there are many excellent kayaking and yachting publications that give good step-by-step guidelines, so find one that works well for you. If you wish to try out the above matrix it's easy to construct.

• **one:** Look up the time for high water (or low water if appropriate) for the standard port nearest your chosen venue.

• **two:** Look up the difference in tide for the area you will be paddling in. This information can be found in an almanac, tide tables, pilot or worked from the tidal diamonds off a chart.

• **three:** Take 30 minutes either side of this time and write down the hours you envisage being on the water.

• **four:** Arrows will help you visualise the tidal flow for each of those hours at a glance, this may prove useful later if your plans need to change.

• **five:** Add in any other detail you feel is important to your lesson. For example, note when the race around the headland begins, so that you have the opportunity to teach some initial water awareness skills before embarking on the overfall.

You will notice that the Timing Matrix does not refer to a specific time, but rather an hour of time. The reason for this is that the tide rarely turns at the exact time calculated. For example, a high-pressure system can exert so much pressure on the water's surface that it can make movement physically harder, thus the tide will turn later than predicted, or the wind can either make the tide turn earlier or later depending on its direction and strength in relation to the direction of the tide.

It's a good habit to always write BST or GMT after a time in order to remind yourself and others that you have taken into account the extra hour for British Summer Time – not taking it into account is a very common mistake likely to foil your day's coaching.

Finally, with your strategy prepared, ensure it's waterproofed and place it under the deck lines of your sea kayak, allowing you to anticipate and effectively use every teaching opportunity the sea has to offer you.

Prepared with this knowledge, you can really work a venue, gaining the optimum learning conditions for each of your students.

TOP TIP

• Encourage your intermediate students, in later sessions, to make a similar plan, regarding their journey and what they should expect, thus increasing their weather and water awareness (see Planning session later). Such planning abilities are invaluable to have and will begin the process of their independence from you.

Before moving on, it is important to consider introducing complete novice paddlers, especially young novices to the sea. Should we put complete beginners, especially children, on the sea without any prior paddling experience? Yes of course we should, but in appropriate conditions and with a constant eye on changes in the weather and the sea state.

▶ What Constitutes Suitable Conditions?

The initial area needs to be contained, a natural or man-made harbour is good and any breezes should be onshore. The physical skills required by the novice paddlers when first on the sea are no different to those described in earlier chapters. Remember to anticipate sea breezes in the afternoon if the day has been hot. They may have a dramatic effect on your group as the day goes on. A beautiful windless day can within minutes turn into an environment your group is unable to cope with.

▶ Venturing From The Safe Bay Out Along The Coast

Once you have established the ability of your students and what they are potentially capable of, then it's time to leave the bay and venture out. Teach-

Photo 2 Sheltered bay with an onshore breeze

ing opportunities are plentiful along the coastline, especially rocky ones. See Close Quarter Manoeuvring Skills below for some games and exercise ideas amongst the rocks.

Photo 3 Student turning in an indent

Some days when the wind is too strong, it may be more appropriate to go surfing with your novice group rather than go for a journey. The chapter on Surfing describes how one can introduce beginners.

Photo 4 Group surfing

▶ COACHING PHYSICAL SKILLS

Armed with our plan and thus all the information we need to know about the tide, weather, sea conditions and our client's wishes and needs, we are ready to begin coaching. The very first session should be one of familiarising the students with their sea kayak.

GOOD BOAT AWARENESS

Some clients may find sea kayaks strange, especially if they've only ever paddled kayaks of a more general purpose nature. Your first session therefore needs to involve transferring your client's skills from one craft to the other and building on what they already know. For clients who have only ever paddled sea kayaks this session will form an excellent revision of their basic skills.

Ideal Teaching Location

Calm bay or quiet area of a harbour with a beach or slipway available and no effect from the wind or tide.

Skills To Coach And Practise

Edging, leaning, edging to assist a turn and trim.

Session Progressions

When coaching boat awareness you are really trying to make your client aware of their kinaesphere (see earlier coaching theory chapters). You need to set exercises that encourage them to feel feedback coming from the water, through the kayak, through their joints and muscles and ultimately into their cognitive awareness.

▶ Edging And Leaning

The first element of this session involves exercises to learn edge control and the difference between edging and leaning.

Begin on the beach or slipway:

　Ask your students to sit in a paddling position.

　Next ask them to move all their weight onto their right buttock and hold that position for a short while. Explain that this is a right edge.

　Do the same on the left, but this time after a short while ask them to move their head in line with their spine and then wait to see (rather, kinaesthetically feel) what happens next. (A demo of this will help.) They should go off balance and fall over. This, tell them, is leaning.

5

Photo 5 Leaning/edging exercise

Have them practise edging and leaning on both sides again.

For students who learn visually or audibly, do the exercise once more but give them markers to look out for (visual), e.g. "In the edging position, if you look down you will see your spraydeck, in the leaning position if you look down you will see the water or in this case the beach." Explain what is actually happening and why (audio) i.e., "The weight of your head has made you go off balance."

Next have them work out 4 different amounts of edge for each side and label them numbers 1, 2, and 3, 3 being the hardest to maintain and 4 being off balance. Try to focus their attention on their muscles and joints, specifically differences in upper body shape, position of head, amount of foot and knee pressure exerted, as they perform each degree of edge. Ask them to remember these feelings which constitute intrinsic feedback from their bodies (their kinaesphere), which will prove useful to them later on.

Now have the group get into their sea kayaks and try exactly the same exercise on the water. Pairing the students up during this exercise and having each take it in turns to practise edging will further increase their knowledge. For example, they will be able to observe each other and the kayaks for differences they can see as each amount of edge is applied. Using buddies in this way is allowing you to teach the person edging kinaesthetically and the person watching visually. Both are learning audibly and vicariously through what's called collaborative coaching.

▶ **Turning Using Edge**

The next logical step is to explore edging as a means of assisting the sea kayak to turn. Firstly, edging towards the paddle will give your client extra reach and thus leverage when turning their kayak, especially when turning on the spot or when making very tight turns. Secondly, using an outside edge (i.e. a right edge to go left) will greatly assist the paddler turning their sea kayak through a longer turn on the move. The effect of edging to the outside of a turn is similar to other sports, e.g. skiers put pressure on the outside (downhill) ski to perform a parallel turn; sailors weight the side of their dinghy, i.e. the right side to go left, when practising rudderless sailing drills.

Note that some sea kayaks with more rounded hulls can be turned as effectively using either inside or outside edge. Be aware of this especially if your teaching method for the session is experimentation or guided discovery, it can throw you awfully. An exercise to illustrate the effect of outside edge would be helpful here. Line the paddlers up, explain that as you gently push them they are to apply a right edge – their kayaks will turn left. Try the exercise on both sides.

Harbours and bays with moorings make the perfect classroom for teaching turning and edging to assist turning. In this environment your choice of exercises are endless: forward paddling using different edges, backwards paddling using edges, turning using a combination of edging and sweeps, turning using a combination of edging, leaning and support strokes or ruddering (bow and stern) strokes, etc.

Guided discovery and coaching by self or peer appraisal in buddy pairs is ideal for this very dynamic and active session. Set individual tasks, circuits, have them set tasks for one another. Provided all have clear directions as to what is expected, your students flourish. This method of coaching is so useful, it frees you up to act as monitor and trouble-shooter, whilst feedback and management is continued by being in the buddy pairs. Just be aware of other water users and keep a vigilant eye on the comings and goings of any other bay or harbour traffic.

Photo 6 Sheltered harbour with buoys

▶ Trim

When considering trim, unlike river kayaks, moving our weight forwards and aft will have less effect in a sea kayak because they are so long. Nonetheless, trim is still important especially for control in big water, or in heavy winds or just for comfort over long distances. Many sea kayaks come with a skeg or rudder to address this problem. (Rudders are used to turn the sea kayak, skegs to trim it.) Some sea kayaks don't have rudders or skegs, and invariably any mechanical device may break at some point. It's important therefore to increase your client's awareness of the effects of trim, not only by using a skeg or rudder but by load distribution and packing.

Ideal Teaching Location

Sheltered bay and open sea area affected by the wind.

Skills To Coach And Practise

Alerting trim using both a skeg and then load distribution.

Session Progression

Firstly practise with a skeg (if applicable). Get the student to experiment with their skeg up, down and part way down. Have them experiment again in windier conditions.

Set a square course in the teaching area (with or without markers), one leg paddling into the wind, the next paddling across the wind, then paddling downwind and the last back across the wind again.

🌀 On their first circuit have the group do nothing but paddle skeg up. You want them to consider, through their kinaesphere, how the skeg alters their directional progress through the water. Do so by asking them to consider which leg required the least amount of correction strokes - this helps them to quantify the task.

🌀 Repeat the same exercise, this time skeg down.

🌀 Discuss their findings and reinforce effective use of the skeg by one final circuit, having their skeg up when paddling into wind, halfway down across the wind, and fully down with the wind on their backs. If necessary explain the theory of why this helps their paddling.

Afterwards, change the course from square to triangular, facilitating the use of a skeg in a quartering sea. Any course set out will need to be reasonably long, and in quite windy conditions to have any real opportunity to feel the different effects. Effects that are too subtle may get missed.

Your next session should address paddling without a skeg and the effect of load distribution. Armed with some full water bladders to weight your clients' sea kayaks appropriately, have your students repeat the above drills. Exaggerated distribution of equipment within the sea kayak will mimic the effect of a skeg reasonably well. Unfortunately, your students will have to land after each circuit to redistribute the load, unlike open canoes the load cannot be moved easily from one end of the kayak to the other whilst on the water.

Herein lies the danger of over-trimming the sea kayak for forecast wind conditions. Invariably conditions will change whilst you are miles out to sea! So encourage your clients to load their kayaks with the weight as near to them as possible and evenly distributed. Encourage them to really use their edges and foot pressure to make small corrections to their course. If a client has no skeg or rudder and is finding it hard to steer and keeps turning up into wind whilst you are journeying, attaching a short line to the back of their kayak will work wonders. If they keep turning downwind, place a full water bag as far forward in their cockpit as possible to ease the situation.

FORWARD PADDLING SKILLS

Different conditions require different adaptations of the forward paddling stroke. When paddling through big choppy water or through surf a powerful upright stroke is required providing that surge of speed at the crucial moment. A relaxed, less dynamic but more flowing stroke is required for cruising long distances.

Ideal Teaching Location

The best way to coach your students any such adaptations and more importantly, the timing of those adaptations, is in as wide a variety of conditions as possible. Golden opportunities could present themselves to you at any time; a change in the weather or sea state could warrant a change in paddling style not yet tried by your students. Your client might be using a less effective forward paddling style for the present conditions and some polishing of their skills is called for.

Skills To Coach And Practise

Basic forward paddling in a variety of conditions.

Session Progression

Forward paddling is not something that can be taught in just one session. It will need to be revisited time and time again. The progression of this session and individual elements of it can be rerun in the various conditions outlined on the flow chart at the start of the chapter.

Photo 7a Upright sprint style, top hand at eye height.
Photo 7b Long distance, top hand at shoulder height.
Photo 7c High winds, low paddle action.

Ideas for your first session should include observations of their current style on simple water. If their forward propulsion involves a lot of correction strokes, encourage them to alter their direction through the use of their edges and foot pressure or rudder rather than sweep strokes – this will instantly improve their paddling effectiveness.

Move out of the bay (preferably into onshore conditions) and look at paddling into wind, downwind and across gentle wind and wavelets.

 KEY POINT

- A common theme you'll see throughout this chapter is to find:

  Testing conditions with low consequences.

  When working on the sea the above cannot be stressed enough. Your students will be relatively new to sea kayaking and the potential for capsize still high. If it all does start to go wrong you want to end up somewhere safe!

Gradually, over the next day(s), begin to introduce your students to windier and wavier conditions (Force 2, onshore is ample). Before heading out into the windier water revisit turning and introducing turning on waves, this skill will be very necessary for the remainder of this session. Once able to turn, buddy up more able paddlers with less able/less confident paddlers and have them paddle directly into the wind. Your clients will find this the easiest of the forward paddling skills to master. Follow close by and ask them to turn back; turning one at a time is safest (especially if paddlers are not confident). For a client new to windy, wavy water, turning completely downwind is something they will try to avoid at all costs and will often keep paddling further out to sea.

▶ Turning Downwind

For many students, turning downwind in a following sea is the scariest part of any paddling in windy conditions. More scary for you however, will be seeing most of the group able to turn downwind and one or two unable to, creating a sudden star-bursting effect within of the group. In this instance, bring those who have managed the turn back into wind with those who still have not turned. Now, go to the upwind side of the client(s) who can't turn and be slightly ahead of them. Coax the scared person around, forcing them to turn by practically blocking their way. Positioning yourself slightly ahead of them means their head and

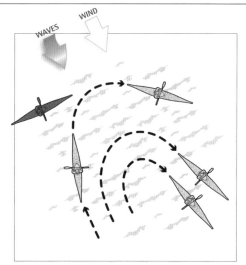

Fig. 3 Coach/buddy coaxing their partner around ready to paddle downwind.

body position will be in the most stable position as they go through the turn. Once round and paddling again they will relax a little.

It's important to encourage students to keep their momentum when turning or paddling down and especially across bigger waves. People tend to low brace, rather than paddle forwards, effectively killing the kayak's speed and leaving them marooned and at the mercy of the wind and waves. Encourage nervous clients, or better still ask their buddy to encourage them, to keep forward paddling. It is important for them to understand that stability comes from momentum; without that speed, they will stall and capsizing becomes more likely.

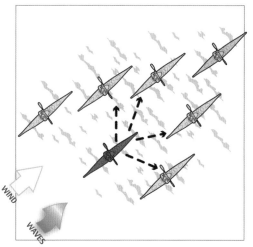

Fig. 4 Paddling downwind in a following sea - the group spread out in a 'V' shape to prevent collisions.

Downwind and downwave work essentially turns into an awesome surf session for some and a tense ride for others. Ensure your group is spread out either in a line or in a V-shape, so no kayaks will run into one another. Get your clients to feel the waves pass under them, help them to identify that moment when they need to put in a couple of vertical and strong power strokes and when to stern rudder down the wave. Again be ever watchful. Some people will love this, 'whooping' and 'yahooing' for hundreds of metres, whilst others will feel totally unstable, and will low brace or reverse paddle, stalling the flow each time a wave passes under them, thus spreading your group. Choice of venue (onshore wind into a gently shelving sandy bay), good group management, positioning and communication are paramount.

▶ Paddling Across The Wind

When paddling across the wind some of your clients will find their kayak doing something very different compared to their buddy's. Some little tips that will help you remedy these minor problems include:

For students paddling across the wind, finding their kayaks constantly turn up into the wind:

1. Ask them to edge towards the wind (i.e. almost leaning on it as they paddle forwards).

2. At the same time they should push firmly with their upwind foot, the effect of these two actions will be to cause the kayak to turn downwind.

3. If using their body and boat to counteract the effect of the wind is not enough, they can also use their paddle, either by extending the upwind side and paddling normally, or by using a keyhole stroke (half sweep from bow to centre, finished with a forward power stroke on the windward side) or maybe a sweep stroke on the windward side followed by a regular forwards stroke on the downwind side.

All 3 actions have the effect of counteracting the kayak's desire to turn upwind. Combining the body, boat and blade actions will have the greatest effect.

For those whose kayaks track downwind, life will not be so easy and to be honest without a skeg can be positively painful, with constant sweeps or keyhole strokes applied to the downwind side. In this instance, it might be prudent to follow a course whereby the affected kayak's trim is neutral allowing all to hold a single course en route for the shore. You will invariably land downwind of your intended target but with far less pain and greater ease. A quick paddle back up the coast will soon bring you to your original target.

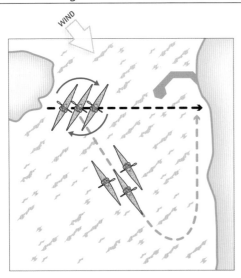

Fig. 5 Going with rather than fighting the wind.

As previously mentioned, the forward paddling skills need to be revisited with every new environment your students come into contact with. Most will adapt naturally, others may need a little coaching, even coaxing, as fear of the conditions prevents their bodies from paddling effectively.

CLOSE QUARTER HANDLING SKILLS

Close quarter handling amongst the rocks or during rescues requires a combination of manoeuvring skills and techniques, such as:

- Edging
- Power strokes
- Vertical turning strokes - such as the bow rudder and hanging draw.
- Horizontal turning strokes - such as low brace turns or stern rudders.

A close quarter handling session will involve being close to the rocks, and as students' skill level increases, close to the rocks in larger swell. Positioning yourself effectively with regards to coaching and rescuing students during the session is crucial for the success and safety of it (see effective leadership below). It is advised that helmets are used throughout the session and that the wind is gentle and offshore.

Ideal Teaching Location

Rock gardens, caves, arches and general rock hopping exploration of the coastline. You will need some sheer vertical sections of coast as well as some sloping ones. Conditions need to be calm to start with, but a little swell further along on a more exposed section of coastline will facilitate really good progressions and skill development, as well as increase the student's boat handling confidence.

Skills You Need To Coach And Practise:

Revisit some of the vertical and horizontal turning and correction strokes, bow rudders, low brace turns, stern rudders, etc. Adapt them, to create such strokes as bow draws, stern draws, bow and stern pries, sculling draws, sculling pries, etc and put all into practice within the rock gardens.

Session Progression

The following exercises do follow a progression, getting harder as you work through them with the increasing demands of the environments used. Please note that these exercises are the foundation exercises for Rough Water Handling Skills and Incident Management sessions later.

▶ Tight Turning Exercises

You may have already revisited low brace turns, using a combination of edging, leaning and sweep strokes on the move in the earlier sessions where you used edging to assist turning. If so... great, if not take the time to look at them now. Due to the combination of strokes the low brace turn lends itself well to the whole-part-whole method of coaching.

Once mastered in the bay, vary the practice and move to a more restricted location, increasing the challenge of the stroke efficiency by using ever-harder environments - narrowing coves or indentations in the coastline are ideal. Repeat the same low brace turns in here. Remember keep the practice bilateral and consider when and how you are giving your feedback (see earlier chapters).

Again we need to vary the practice, this time remaining in the same environment but experimenting with other types of turn, stroke combination or adaptations. Try switching your coach-led style of session to one that is more student-led in nature. As an example, ask them to create 3 different types of turn using all the strokes in their collective repertoire. Really encourage ideas from other paddling disciplines. It's a terrific opportunity to give the group the chance to create a whole new range of strokes, adapting all their old favourites and naming new strokes they have concocted.

Once again step back and observe, feed in if asked, cut in if necessary, but let them have the space and time

Photo 8 *Turning in a tight cove*

to come up with their ideas. Once everyone has finished, have a member of each team demonstrate a turn, encourage the other team to identify the combination of strokes used and facilitate any discussions that ensue. Take care to highlight elements of the demo or discussion you consider important coaching points.

Journeying along the coastline, dodging in and out of small spaces, playing follow my leader and giving the students the opportunity to lead various sections is terrific fun and very engaging. The desire to explore takes over their minds allowing their bodies to get on and perform the necessary strokes (see Inner Game theory).

Photo 9 *Rock hopping*

Try progressing now from boat awareness to water awareness. Take your students to an indent that is subject to a little swell (beware of onshore breezes) and allow them plenty of time to practise timing their turns to coincide with the rise of the swell for optimum manoeuvrability.

As you paddle along the coastline look out for any other potential teaching opportunities. Such opportunities constantly occur. For example, consider the following: your students are just ahead of you exploring the coastline's nooks and crannies. As they do, it becomes apparent to you that a weakness in their manoeuvring skills or possibly a lack of awareness of

the risks associated with a particular feature they're exploring needs desperately to be addressed. Let's use the example of them paddling forwards into a cave.

You may wish to stop them and say it's better to go in backwards, but try to wait (unless they are in danger of course). Once they're outside again, build on the experience they have just had. Suggest they paddle in again, this time backwards. Afterwards, see if they consider that paddling in backwards has any advantages over paddling in forwards. If the answer you want doesn't come immediately, you could just tell them or better still take them to an appropriate venue such as a cave with surging swell running into it. (Remember testing conditions/low consequences. Do choose an appropriate amount of surging swell.) Here they can experience the advantages both kinaesthetically and visually for themselves.

Photo 10 *Paddling backwards into a cave means you can come out forwards... Useful if a wave is coming!*

Undoubtedly, whilst at the same venue, other necessary skills will become apparent, for example, holding position in swell, cognitive skills such as group management and communication. Address the cognitive skills by scenario role playing, demonstrating the need for a person sat outside watching for rogue waves, ready to rescue as one or two others explore inside. "Ah, management of rescues! Maybe now would be a good time to practise some of those incident management drills we learned earlier in the week?" Teaching opportunities will just keep throwing themselves at you. After a while, the hardest thing about your session will be deciding on what not to teach!

Anticipation of the 'What if' factor, especially when managing exploration through rock gardens makes up a large part of the cognitive skills needed by our trainee sea kayakers. All of these close quarter manoeuvring ideas and exercises help you to coach anticipation of the 'what if' and 'what to expect'.

▶ Paddle Dexterity Exercises

Being able to move your paddle around with ease and dexterity is invaluable when handling a sea kayak in close quarter conditions.

Firstly, warm and wake up your clients' wrists. Have them sit static in their sea kayaks and place their paddle in a bow rudder position, then do it on the other side. Reach around and place the bow rudder towards the right stern of the kayak, followed by crossing to the left bow of the kayak… and so on. This will help limber up their bodies and minds and begin to speed up the reflexes with respect to general paddle dexterity.

Next ask the students to draw a rectangle in the water by the side of their kayak with their paddle. To begin with let them experiment with the combination of strokes required (kinaesthetic learning). If any student doesn't understand, switch to a different style and either show them (addressing any visual learners) or talk them through the paddle sequence (addressing any auditory learners). Remember to work bilaterally, doing the exercise on both sides. Increase the challenge by asking the students to maintain the paddle under the surface of the water at all times.

Vary the practice by changing from a rectangle to an oval, to a figure of eight and for any very able students, finding it really easy, have them try to etch out their names. Differentiation between abilities in the group is easily achieved with this exercise, as group members get to grips with one or other of the shapes.

Now give their wrists a well-earned break, by paddling to another venue that will allow you to do the next part of the exercise. Ideally you need to paddle a short distance to a vertical cliff or harbour wall. The aim of the next part of the exercise is to paddle

Photo 11 The exercise requires concentration.

along the cliff or wall using a combination of any strokes on one side only – the really hard bit is that their paddle must stay in the water.

Have them come back the other way thus using the other side and completing the bilateral work.

Finish the exercise by switching off the mind again, and continuing the journeying, allowing your students to experiment with all sorts of weird and wonderful combinations of strokes as they continue through the rock gardens more skilfully.

▶ Swell Positioning Exercises (Riding The Bronco)

Swell moving up and down the face of a steep cliff is necessary for this exercise. Definitely steer clear of breaking swell on a sloping cliff. Point out to your students the hallmarks of breaking swell, white foam (due to the sideways moving water) compared to brown foam (dead plankton brought to the surface after a storm).

Photo 12 Riding the Bronco.

Buddy up your clients and have them number themselves.

Clients number 1 should position themselves between a wide cleft in the rocks. Ask them to identify a mark on the walls either side of them and explain that the surging water will try to move them back and forth, but that they are to remain central between these two markers, using a combination of forwards and reverse strokes. Leave them in there for a short while with their buddy, client number 2 encouraging them to 'ride the bucking bronco'.

After a time swap over; second time around suggest they go as deep as they dare into the cleft. Don't allow them to go so deep that any surge in the swell will break on them and push them to the back of the cleft - it won't make for the easiest of rescues and all their hard-earned confidence will be dashed.

Photo 13 Riding a wave through a gap in the rocks.

You may consider, after a quick risk assessment of the venue and water, that helmets are necessary for this exercise.

▶ Timing Exercises Through The Rocks

Small amounts of swell will help focus people's attention on timing their ride through any gaps in the rocks. Too much swell and anxiety will override any learning opportunities so choose your rock hops carefully. Avoid areas where any surge in the swell will push your client onto other rocks rather than into an open space and only allow one student through at a time. Ensure all are wearing helmets. To begin with signal the correct time for a student to come through the gap.

Afterwards have your students determine when to go through the gap themselves and finally have them determine when their buddy goes through. To further develop your client's water awareness and build their confidence, move to narrower gaps, or areas of increased swell or complexity.

Exercises of a similar ilk are easy to come up with. Any rock garden or area creating vertical or horizontal movement of water will provide you with ideal teaching opportunities and one really cannot do enough of such water awareness and boat handling exercises. These simple exercises form the foundations of your students' boat handling skills in the big water found with overfalls and tidal races and are the initial warm-up exercises to an introduction to overfall surfing.

The exercise also develops self-awareness on the moving water, encouraging them to look around and stay observant whilst they are being moved and tossed around by the water. Additionally, awareness of themselves responding to the water, awareness of what the water is doing around them and to them, anticipation of what it might do in a few moments, as well as developing patience to sit and wait for the right moment to make their move, and anticipation of what it will do around similar features elsewhere are all learned during these sessions.

Rock gardens are great for exploring and whether you purposely go into rock gardens to facilitate any of the above learning opportunities or just go in to explore, be assured some student-led learning will be taking place all the time with every stroke. So when there is an opportunity to explore some rocks, caves or arches, take it.

SKILLS FOR LAUNCHING AND LANDINGS

Below is a list of typical launching and landing sites that our sea kayakers will have to deal with at one time or another in their paddling careers. Each requires a variety of skills ranging from surfing and swimming skills right through to skills better suited to a gymnast. The best way to teach these skills is to go out and experience all sorts of launchings and landings in a safe and constructive manner. Remember, testing conditions, low consequences. Here are some launching and landing sites used by sea kayakers:

- ⊙ Floating pontoons
- ⊙ Slipway
- ⊙ Shallow sheltered beach
- ⊙ Shallow exposed beach
- ⊙ Steep beach
- ⊙ Rocky beach
- ⊙ Sloping rock shelves
- ⊙ Steep rock ledge (or quay at low tide)

There are many good sea kayaking texts outlining suggestions on the physical techniques you could employ for each of the above launches and landings. Have a good look through them, try them out and work hard at identifying the key elements you need to teach your students.

When first coaching anything but the easiest of these landing or launches on the water, choose windless days. A small amount of ground swell is OK, even useful, but ensure there is an area of calmer water available close by to shelter from the full force of the wind and waves and facilitate your discussions before and after each launch or landing. This is a good habit for your students to get in to, as they will need to discuss similar landing strategies before any serious landing with their own peers.

🌀 Firstly, demonstrate the landing (or launch) with you managing it, run through the whole thing with no interruption or discussion. Like the concept of the first demo being silent to show the flow of the whole thing from start to finish in real time, this is in effect your 'silent demo', with any talking being that which is only necessary to the management of the landing.

🌀 Once landed, use questioning to draw from the group any key points, with specific reference to which physical skills were involved, what risk assessments they felt you made (see SAFE later) and lastly what group management/leadership strategies they felt you employed (see CLAP later).

Ensure they understand there is no single solution to any one landing or launch and that the variables of weather, sea state, group and individual ability and condition, all make it impossible to allow for a single solution. Insight into your thinking in such conditions is really helpful to your students' learning. Even little things like why you choose a specific venue to discuss your landing, prior to the landing,

Photo 14 *Talking through a landing before doing it.*

will help your trainee sea kayakers make their own assessments later.

Now that you have landed, you will soon need to demo a launch and repeat the above before you can work through a group-led landing.

Variety of practice will occur with every new landing or launch you try. Be aware that if wet, especially their heads, the students will get cold fast and their window for learning will drop quickly. Any really wet landing or launches should be left to last and any that require a person in the water would best be done by someone with a dry-suit. Helmets are essential during these exercises. Finally, with every new landing or launch, more and more of the decision making should be theirs, moving away from your earlier coach-led session and into a far greater student-led scenario. Always bear in mind testing conditions/low consequence when choosing a site.

Due to the numerous variables caused by the sea environment, rarely will there be one correct way to approach a specific landing or launching. The key principle to put across is to approach all landings and launches with safety in mind and ultimately, if it's not safe don't land. Stay out and find a better spot.

Photo 15 *Group undertake landing while coach observes.*

ROUGH WATER HANDLING SKILLS

Once again whole-part-whole teaching lends itself well to rough water training. Its important that the student experiences the whole first, e.g. being led through an overfall as part of a journey with no intention to go back and play, not yet anyway! If you have students who have the skills from other disciplines to play then sure, their first experience of an overfall can be one of playing almost immediately. However for those with little or no big volume moving water experience a more progressive approach is needed. An opportunity to see a race running from the top of a cliff and pointing out all of the water features visible below is very useful, especially if the weather that day prevents you getting anywhere near it.

Arriving at an overfall or tidal race when it's at its biggest gives a student insight into what the feature actually is but is not conducive to learning. Ideally you want to be there as it builds. So our first rough water handling session may involve a water awareness revision session using more challenging conditions/environments for the general manoeuvring skill exercises listed earlier, followed by a run or two through the race. It could be that you are fortunate enough to teach in an area where races occur on the flood and ebb, in

Photo 16 Dealing with rough seas.

which case you can stop for lunch after this first session and then after lunch as the race builds in the other direction, start your second rough water handling session. The tidal plans you made for the day are crucial if this level of learning opportunity is to be gained. Some days the tide will not allow for this and the second session may need to be run at another time.

The second session requires you being there as the overfall develops. At what point during the development of the race you time your arrival depends on the confidence and ability levels of your clients. For less able or confident clients arrive early, more able or confident arrive later.

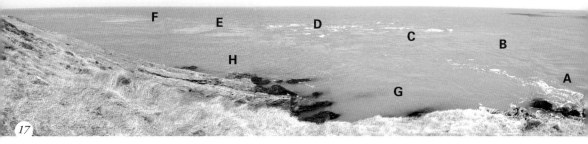

Photo 17 Anatomy of a tide race/overfall - please feel free to photocopy and use this for your students.

A Start of the overfall, more of a tidal race at A, as the water is squeezed vertically sideways around the headland.

B The smooth run in to the main section of overfall.

C The front wave of the overfall. As the flow of water is forced up over the shallower ground it breaks on the surface.

D The wave train.

E,F Dissipating wave train, that in this instance runs parallel to the coast, making it a safe overfall to train intermediate paddlers. Many other overfalls can run up to 2kms or more offshore. When using such an overfall it is important to work with small groups who are able to at least attempt to roll and are able to rescue one another quickly and confidently, whilst being towed perpendicular to the flow, back towards the coast.

G Strong eddy, nearest the headland.

H Weaker eddies further away from the headland.

▶First Overfall Session

Begin your session with some ferry glides, breaking in and out of the race, exercises paddling up to the front of the race and even into the area of calm water beyond, whilst the race is still weak, building confidence, boat handling skills and water awareness.

Next, buddy the students up and create circuits for the students to follow. Initially, give each student a target or goal, afterwards let them choose their own targets within the circuit and later encourage buddies to set suitable goals for one another. This will allow the student to begin to identify suitable circuits and thus water features for others, beginning to encourage them as leaders in their own right, responsible for their friend.

This sort of strategy again encourages awareness, this time group awareness, in determining the levels of flow their buddy is comfortable in, and what individual needs their buddy has, for instance feeling they ought to follow their buddy around the circuit to provide psychological support. Don't force these things to happen, just facilitate the opportunity for them to happen. As a coach it is so wonderful to step further and further back, seeing your sea kayakers grow in independence and begin to look out for one another. At this stage the less talking you do the more learning they experience and the better a coach you are.

Do keep your eye on the speed of the race, remember it's building all the time and you want your students confident with their use of edge, their ability to look around for eddies/calmer water, each other, before it builds too much. There will come a point when the teaching stops and management of the playing (and rescues) begins – the learning won't stop though, it will continue whatever, you just need to make sure it's positive learning they are experiencing and not negative.

Finally, once it has built to a level where the waves are surfable, have them paddle to the front of the overfall again. By this stage only those with arms of Popeye, or those who have mastered surfing will be able to move up the overfall.

Wait a while and then call everyone back into the eddy. They should ferry glide back to you.

Regroup the buddies according to how well they are doing; put more able with less able. Set them off again with the goal of remaining together at all times.

This has 3 effects:

• Firstly, for you - the buddy pairs stick together making management of the session easier for you.

• Secondly, for the more able buddy – he or she will have to move up and down the overfall to stay with their buddy. They will have to look over their shoulder for them, staying aware of them at all times, they will encourage and 'coach' the less able student thus increasing their own knowledge of the physical skills they are using to surf.

• Finally, for the less able buddy – he or she does not feel alone out there and thus their anxiety is reduced (self 1) allowing their muscles to relax and the body (self 2) to concentrate on surfing rather than being scared (Inner Game).

With all this collaborative coaching going on you can continue monitoring people's progress, feeding in where necessary, rescuing when required and when the first rescue is required, take advantage of yet another great teaching opportunity. Whistle everyone down to you. As you perform the rescue, talk the students through the other factors you are considering whilst you're rescuing, factors other than the rescue itself, e.g., observation of location within the race, observation of other group members, search for slack water, management of any tows required, etc. I teach people to tow and do flat water rescues on day one of any course, even if it's 'intro sea kayak'. Having people familiar with capsizing and towing, seeing it as a fundamental part of sea kayaking is important for them and for me (see Rescuing Others below).

By the end of your rough water handling session, people will have enough skill and confidence to turn around and play, the next time you go through an overfall.

RESCUING OTHERS

This is a particularly useful session to run at the start of any 2 day or 5 day course. Rescue skills save lives. Paddling skill will prevent rescues from being needed, but these take time to develop. So as a coach and guide I have thanked my lucky stars I've covered basic rescue techniques and towing early, as time after time I have needed client help in the swift management of a situation, even if all they know is how to be rescued on the sea.

Ideal Teaching Location

Session 1 - in warm water or in a pool (if possible). If a pool is not available, calm sheltered water.

Session 2 - revision in calm water, followed by rougher water as appropriate, e.g. a small tidal race or flow or increased sea state (only ever use onshore wind conditions for rescue work – testing conditions, low consequences).

Skills You Need To Coach And Practise

To learn a variety of rescues and tows (physical skills) and manage an incident (cognitive skills) involving a selection of appropriate rescue and towing techniques are the key points for this session.

Session Progressions

▶ Session 1 - Rescues

In the pool revisit or teach safe capsize drills, eskimo rescues. The paddle presentation eskimo rescue is particularly useful on the sea, also look at turning an upturned kayak from another kayak and finally revisit or teach a deep water rescue and casualty re-entry.

Providing your students with a basic model from which to adapt other techniques for use with different crafts is very useful. The X rescue is recognised as a good basic model and within sea kayaking has been modified to the TX for use with sea kayaks that have bulkheads. (If a boat has no bulkheads a full X rescue will be necessary.) With respect to re-entering the kayak with assistance, a side-on re-entry is easy to execute and is less prone to causing injury to the person in choppy water compared to coming up between the two kayaks.

Experiential learning is not the most appropriate teaching method for this session. A lot of information needs to be put across in a very short space of time. 'IDEAS', with a very big 'A' is perfect. Learning all the different rescues is very engaging and can be a lot of fun with the opportunities for mini-races and games in a warm pool. Furthermore, operating in buddy pairs, even 3's is a necessity for the rescues to work and also facilitates plenty of opportunity for lots of collaborative teaching and all its benefits.

▶ Session 2 - Revision Plus Towing

Once the techniques have been mastered in a nice warm environment head outside. It would be wise in

---

 KEY POINT - TESTING CONDITIONS / LOW CONSEQUENCES

Your choice of tidal race is paramount, not just to your students' learning but also their safety and thus your group control. Remember you are looking for:

Testing Conditions/Low Consequences

Consider these two scenarios:

• Consider the direction the tidal stream flows – does it go along shore or out to sea? If your group is at the level where they can quickly rescue their buddies then (b) is fine (given the weather conditions are favourable too), otherwise consider using (a).

• Also consider the wind strength and direction – will it flatten the waves or increase them?

• Consider whether it is springs or neaps – how big do your clients need the waves to be?

You may not get a choice and can only use what there is in certain weather and tidal conditions.

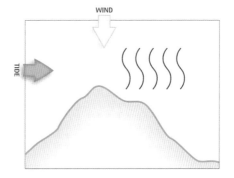

a) Testing Conditions/Low Consequences

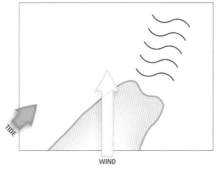

b) Testing Conditions/High Consequences!

Photo 18 Anchored tow. To prevent him being blown onto the rocks the rescuer is towed off as he performs the rescue.

Have a variety of lines available for use and encourage people to try different systems. Introduce them to waist, boat and contact towing systems and facilitate a variety of simple scenarios that allow for their use. Discuss issues in feedback sessions after the tow.

Begin to make the scenarios involve more people. More people means more management and so the group begin to learn about incident management, communication, etc.

Finally reintroduce the earlier rescue session. Allow the group to try each rescue in turn, allow them only one or two goes. They must not get so cold that their concentration goes before you have had the chance to finish your session. If rescue attempts continue to fail suggest they wait until the very end before trying again and/or practise later in the pool. Once they have tried all the rescues learned earlier, set them a new scenario involving a multiple rescue and tow to finish off the day.

The analysis of this final scenario may be best left until everyone is back in the warm again.

cold-water areas to do other drier sessions, a strokes session for example, followed by the towing session. Leave yourself an hour at the end to try each rescue learned in the pool.

The towing session lends itself to some careful use of guided discovery. There are many different methods of towing. Ultimately, your sea kayakers need to affect an emergency tow over a short distance, a close quarter contact tow and a long distance tow. Key coaching points must include emphasising the need for releasable systems, how and when to release, an ability to tow a buddy and be towed safely, the value of rafted tows and anchored tows and the advantages and disadvantages of the various towing techniques.

▶ Session 3 – Practice In Rough Conditions

The next session involves moving to rougher conditions, a sea state of Force 2-3 (onshore) would be ample for this session. A consolidation session practising these skills for real occurs by default on any rough water handling day. Throughout the rest of the course rescue opportunities between buddies will arise naturally and build perfectly on the foundations you have laid.

Before venturing into rougher water and looking more at the application of the various rescues and tows through the incident management of various scenarios you will be setting, take time to have a brief theory session on Risk Assessment (see Risk Assessment and Incident Management skills section below.)

Photo 19 Rafted tow. The person being towed is supported by another and the pair of them are towed.

INCIDENT MANAGEMENT SESSION

On the sea begin with simple scenarios requiring simple rescues and tows and progress on to ever-harder ones. (The following progression is based on incident management sessions run by Aled Williams of Rock Pool Kayaks). Students will begin in buddy pairs and progress through a series of typical incidents, which progressively get harder and require more group members to affect a rescue. Set each scene and ask the group to consider each of the questions below before rescuing the casualty (the casualty should wait in their kayak until everyone is ready to begin). Once each group has a plan ask the casualty to hop in, which signals the start of the rescue.

Questions that should be asked as each scenario unfolds:

'Can I rescue in situ without damage to myself?

Typical incidents might include: Capsizes in deep water, where there are no rocks, no overfalls or tidal races.

• Yes – should warrant an X rescue (or assisted X rescue).

• No – and the students need to ask a new question.

'Do I need to relocate?'

Typical incident might include: Rocks e.g. a narrow cleft, no swell, no or light offshore winds.

• Yes – A contact tow or bow/stern carry or tow to a 'safe' area then X rescue (or assisted X rescue)

• Yes – But I can't manage it by myself!

'Do I need help to relocate?'

Typical example incident includes: Overfalls, tidal races, rocks and/or onshore winds.

• Yes – An anchored bow or stern contact tow/carry, then an X rescue (or assisted X rescue)

• Yes – but could still hurt myself getting into position to rescue!

INCIDENT MANAGEMENT SESSION – CONTINUED

'Do I need help getting into new location?'

Typical examples include: Hideous shelving rocks, onshore winds and swell. Set this one up with a lot of care. If you are remotely unsure that you can pull back the rescue if all begins to go wrong, just discuss this scenario. (I'm often the casualty for this one, so that if it comes to it I can re-enter my kayak and get myself out.)

• Yes – attach a tow line before you go in, then use towed bow or stern contact tow followed by an X rescue.

• Yes – but still too big and scary!

'SHOULD I BE HERE?

At the end of each scenario discuss the effectiveness and risk management of the rescue. If necessary, repeat it. Each new scenario should be exercised with different members of the group taking on different roles, rescuer, casualty, communicator and leader's eyes, tower(s), others.

ROLLING AND SELF–RESCUE

It is not often that a sea kayaker will need to roll, however the ability to roll or at least perform a self-rescue would be the difference between life and death if a situation required such measures.

There are many good texts on learning to roll, especially in some of the playboat books, and on performing self-rescues in a sea kayak. Become familiar with a variety of different rolls and self-rescues. Not every student will be able to perform the same type of roll or rescue and certain conditions, injuries or events may preclude a person from rolling altogether and necessitate another form of self-rescue. When coaching a rolling and self-rescue session, suggest everyone wears a dry suit. This is not always possible, but very useful from a training point of view. If they are only in wet suits or the temperature is not conducive, limit the amount of getting wet everyone has to do and take advantage of any local swimming pools. If dry suit or warm seas are available then this session is a lot of fun.

Working on the whole-part-whole and the silent demo principles, begin the session by demonstrating all the self-rescues you want them to try such as emptying their kayaks and climbing in over the stern, paddle float rescue, re-entry and paddle float roll, half roll or full roll. This shows the flow and timing of each technique and provides everyone with an overview of the self-rescues available to them as sea kayakers. Later, more demos will be needed in order to coach each individual rescue.

Photo 21a *Emptying the kayak*
Photo 21b *Crawling up the back deck*
Photo 21c *Getting into the cockpit. A good sense of balance and a fairly stable kayak is required for this particular technique to succeed. There are others.*

Next, buddy up your students and ask the students to take it in turns jumping in and out of their kayaks, have them empty their kayaks, scrabble up over the backs to start with. Their buddies may assist by gently steadying the kayaks – set the challenge of aiming for no help from the buddy.

Stop the fun and gather everyone around to observe a second demonstration of the next self-rescue, if necessary. Firstly silent, then again focusing people's attention on key points that will help them succeed, e.g. maintaining a low centre of gravity, keeping the kayak flat. Stress not every method suits everyone's body type and that they might find variations on the same theme work better for them.

Send them away again to practise further and experiment with what works best for them.

Work your way through each of the self-rescues in this way, including the rolling. When getting them to practise rolling have them work in buddy pairs, a rolling buddy and a rescuing buddy.

▶ Eskimo Rescues

Briefly revisit Eskimo rescues if necessary, they will need to do a lot of these during the next session. Ultimately have the rescuing buddy position themselves in such a way that they Eskimo rescue their friend on the side they anticipated them rolling up on.

Even if the roll fails, an Eskimo rescue on this side reinforces the correct messages to the brain about the rolling sequence. Taking students to an area with some tidal flow next helps them to consolidate the timing of the roll and helps them feel for that all-important water pressure on the blade.

Demonstrate the roll focusing the group's attention on your front blade and your head.

Photo 22 *Hopping out, keeping one's head dry*

Photo 23 *Eskimo rescue*

✅ Do a second demo, this time demonstrating the job of the rescuing buddy during the practise. You will need a volunteer roller (ask them to try a roll, fail, bang on their kayak and await Eskimo rescue from you). Encourage everyone to look at you, the rescuer, and not the roller. Specifically highlight your position in relation to the roller.

▶ Rolling

You need to train them to the stage where they are aware of water pressure on the blade. Feeling that water pressure signifies the moment to pull/brace on the pressure and initiate their hip flick. It is the 'command word' or rather sensation (i.e., intrinsic feedback through one's kinaesphere) that triggers the roll.

Making your students aware of that pressure to pull against, coupled with keeping their head down on the way up will benefit their roll no end. Some sort of mantra, (I use 'This side over to the other side' as a mantra for 'C to C' rolls) or the deliberate focusing of one's mind on feeling for that pressure spot to trigger the roll by the body (self 2) also helps to block out any anxiety rising in the mind (self 1) from being upside down. This is another example of using the principles of the inner game.

At the beginning of your session your students may have known they couldn't roll too well - they were consciously incompetent. The above progression moves the students from being consciously incompetent to consciously competent to varying degrees, but the final aim is to make them unconsciously competent - responding with reflex-like reactions to being upside down.

Reflex reactions do not come from the brain, but the spine; the information required would take far too long if it had to come from the brain. We need to make our sea kayaker's roll a reflex and as such we need to get them into water where capsize opportunities are plentiful. The surf zone, overfalls and tide races that form big waves are perfect for such practice, creating depth to their understanding and permanently writing the muscle memory for the reflexes.

Much of the sea we paddle on does not involve fast flowing tidal streams and so ultimately we must train our sea kayakers to roll without the assistance of water flow. Their final progression therefore must be to practise their rolling in a variety of non-tidal conditions, for example, in short chop, in clapotis, in long swell, in rough seas generated by the wind only. However remember whichever location you choose, ensure testing conditions but low consequences; risk assess every venue you choose.

24

Photo 24 Long boat surfing, a great way to sort out your rolling reactions.

▶ COACHING COGNITIVE SKILLS

Coaching cognitive skills requires you to bring to a conscious level all those seamanship decisions made by you at an unconscious level every time you go out on the sea. Look at the following list of cognitive skills needed by your sea kayakers. Reflect for a moment on what you think about when considering these items whilst you are out paddling.

Consider:

- ◎ Group awareness
- ◎ Wind and water awareness
- ◎ Planning skills
- ◎ Navigation skills
- ◎ Leadership skills
- ◎ Risk assessing skills and incident management

Raising awareness in your students of how and when you are applying these cognitive skills to your paddling, leading and coaching, can be very tricky. The balance between talk and activity is very fine and there is a tendency to talk far too much and not allow enough time for the students to experience conditions in which the awareness can be developed.

Nevertheless, cognitive skills do require quiet time off the water to assimilate theory with practise. As such all the above require an introductory classroom session, followed by a practical, and then another classroom or dry land review session, consolidated with more practical work in a variety of conditions (see flow chart at start of the chapter for other conditions).

Ultimately if your students are still unsure of what to look for or be aware of after your training sessions, encourage them to look for change or be aware of changes in conditions, people, etc.

GROUP AWARENESS

Making your students work, almost all of the time, in buddies on the sea encourages awareness of one another more than any other teaching method. Furthermore, experience and positive reviewing of the consequences of any poor group awareness occurring during the day is invaluable. The rescue work and especially the incident management sessions begin to encourage awareness of a much larger body of people as well as awareness of how the weather and water are affecting the rescue. Reinforcing any good group awareness behaviour after scenarios are dealt with also forms part of the acquisition of this skill. The section on Leadership Skills – (CLAP) is as important for friends paddling as peers, as it is for those training to lead, guide or coach.

WIND AND WATER AWARENESS

Being able to react to the wind and water takes physical skill, but being able to read the water ahead or wind above and anticipate what the effect will be doing around the corner, is a cognitive skill primarily learned from experiencing the sea physically. However, cognitively being able to understand why the water does what it does, helps them to know when it is necessary for them to avoid conditions beyond their capabilities.

Many texts have excellent sections describing the effects of wind and water. Study these and choose those that will help you to explain in the classroom:

- How moving water is affected by rocks, the seabed and other topographical features.
- How the tide works.
- How the weather affects the sea state.
- How the wind is affected by topography.

Ideal Teaching Locale

Classroom for planning, followed by complicated piece of tidal or wind affected water.

Skills You Need To Identify, Coach And Practise

Finding out what sea conditions are expected (from your tide table, weather forecast, tidal diamonds, atlases, etc); anticipating the effect of these conditions on the stretch of coast to be paddled (using maps and charts to see what topographical features are in the area).

Session Progressions

A wind and water awareness session works well once your students have seen water features and experienced them first hand in the close quarter manoeuvring session.

Begin by nurturing the group's awareness of the effects of wind and water by introducing it into their planning session (i.e. as part of their risk assessment of what to expect on the water for the day - see Planning and Risk Assessing sessions below). From their own tidal timing matrix and from weather and swell forecasts they will be able to draw a picture of what the sea will be doing at any time during the day.

As the day unfolds, and providing there have been no delays affecting your student's timing, they will be able to see the anticipated water and wind features just as they expected from their planning. As always review the day's events in the warmth of a minibus or classroom. Other trips your students make whilst with you should be planned by them, and include an assessment of how the wind and tide will affect the sea that day. Do make your own plans, so should things not work out as they expect, you have your notes to work out why. If the reasons why are not noticeable immediately, don't bluff, but work it out later, even at home and give the students the answer the next day.

Practical coaching of wind and water awareness can occur in many of the sessions above. However, a journey forming part of the planning skills sessions is best.

Working out tactics for:

🌀 Going against wind and tide using eddies, staying under cliffs.

🌀 Going against the tide around headlands.

🌀 Going across tidal streams or wind funnelled areas.

🌀 Going with a following or beam sea.

All these and others can be anticipated, planned for, and then experienced on the trip.

PLANNING SKILLS

There are many sea kayaking and yachting texts on passage planning that will supply you with lots of excellent teaching tools, pictures, diagrams and ideas for use when teaching your students to plan their day. The Royal Yachting Association also has many texts on and tools for specifically teaching navigation. Any good chandlery will have a selection of publications for you to buy. If you don't understand any of the terms used here, refer to those publications.

Identify the elements you use in your own journey planning and deliver only those that are necessary for your client's present needs. Ensure you pitch your planning sessions at an appropriate level. There are 2 distinct levels: Introductory planning for linear trips and more advanced planning involving tidal open crossings. At any level the 'What if' factor(s) should always be part of the plan. Most people will need to plan and do several trips before moving up to the next level of planning.

▶ Introduction To Planning Linear (Coastal) Trips

Ideal Teaching Locale

The classroom for the planning, the water to implement the plan.

Skills You Need To Identify, Coach And Practise

You need to be able to:

• Read charts, OS maps, pilots, tide tables, weather forecasts.

• Use a compass, plotter, dividers, sliding rule (not essential), other available navigation tools.

• Make risk assessments, predict conditions.

• *Create flexibility within the plan.*

Session Progressions

Firstly, spend time introducing the students to the various pilots, charts, forecasts and tide tables they need to become familiar with. Demonstrate how the information is gained and interpreted from each, and set your students exercises to find relevant pieces of information.

Sourcing information from:

- Maps and Charts
- Tide Tables
- Pilots
- Tidal Atlases
- Almanacs
- Weather and Swell Forecasts

Reading charts and maps:

- Symbols
- Features
- Latitude and Longitude (Charts)
- Grid references (Maps)

Making estimations of:

- Direction
- Distance
- Time
- Tide, Weather, Swell and Topographical effects

Secondly, have your students brainstorm what information they consider important in making their plans. Encourage them collectively to come up with a proforma of questions to use when planning. This will invariably be a guided discovery session by you as there are key pieces of information that they would not necessarily consider necessary. The way I have my students plan is the same as that outlined at the beginning of the chapter. I can't stress enough that it is only one way of planning, especially my tidal timing matrix. There are lots of ways of passage planning and lots of kayaking and yachting publications that give good step-by-step templates, so find one that you like, but above all one that is simple for you to teach to your students.

Photo 25 The necessary items for the planning exercise

Thirdly, work through a simple linear route with your students. Ensure you have enough copies of the relevant information for each student. Everyone should have a coloured copy of the section of the chart and the OS map required together with a pencil, ruler and eraser.

Next some homework. Ask each student to plan, on their own, tomorrow's linear trip. This 'homework' will allow them time and space to revise all that you have taught in the classroom. This time spent alone to think and work through the theory is very important, especially for those not used to maths or more cognitive work.

Hour	Hour	HW	Tidal Diamond D		Tidal Diamond E		Way Points	Notes
from	to	+/-	Direction	Rate	Direction	Rate	Tick off features	
0919	1019	-5						
1019	1119	-4						
1119	1219	-3						
1219	1319	-2						
1319	1419	-1						
1419	1519	HW						
1519	1619	+1						
1619	1719	+2						
1719	1819	+3						

Fig. 6 Tidal Timing Matrix

In the morning, as a class, review their plans and ensure that the students are all saying the same thing and if not, correct where necessary. Have them pop their plans into a waterproof case ready for use later. Throughout the journey refer back to the student plans and work through any anomalies with them should they occur.

Finally, encourage your students to plan all the paddles for the remaining days of their course. Continue to do your own plans so anomalies can be ironed out and so you are still prepared for what the day's sea is likely to bring.

▶ Planning Open Crossings

Ideal Teaching Locale

The classroom for the planning, tidal section of open water, involving a crossing of sorts to implement the plan.

Skills You Need To Identify, Coach And Practise

As above plus understanding the use of tidal diamonds or tidal atlas to construct vector diagram.

Session Progressions

This theory session should not be done before your students have physically experienced the effect of the tide.

Firstly, review how the tide affects their progress when paddling with the tide, against it and whilst crossing it. Refer them back to their earlier practical session on water awareness. Remind your students how they used transits to cross a particular piece of tidal flow or current.

Through questioning technique, draw from them the following information:

🖐 How did they know what ferry glide angle to set off on? (Answer - transit)

🖐 Did they have to change that angle at all as they crossed the tidal flow in order to maintain the transit? (Answer - yes)

🖐 What made them have to change their angle? (Answer - The current changing rate and direction as we crossed from one side to the other.)

Next ask:

🖐 How would they know what ferry glide angle to use as they set off to reach the other side, with no transits to help, i.e. it is too foggy or the other side is too far away to see transits. (Answer - a vector diagram).

Again many publications give excellent step-by-step accounts of creating a vector diagram; choose one that is clear and concise and that you consider you can teach your students effectively.

For me it is important that the method I use can be built into what I have already taught them. For example my tidal timing matrix is expanded thus to include tidal diamond information that I need to draw on my vector diagram.

As with coaching linear trip planning, go through a worked example together and then provide homework once more for the following day's trip.

One very important factor to note when teaching planning for crossings is that vector diagrams are hard to do unless your crossing point happens to coincide with tidal information given on a chart or tidal atlas. You can use information from a pilot book and estimate the flow using the 'Rule of Thirds' though the resulting information is less accurate than that provided by a tidal diamond. In fact vector diagrams are more often than not actually not necessary.

For example, crossing with an equal amount of time either side of High or Low Water will enable you to

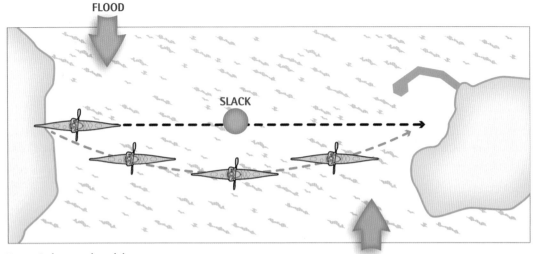

FLOOD

SLACK

EBB

Fig. 7 Balancing the tidal streams

cross directly from A to B, if the tidal stream is evenly balanced either side of High or Low Water (Fig. 8).

A crossing that begins a long way uptide, requiring a gentle ferry glide out until at 90° with the desired island for example, followed by literally 'drifting' onto the island, works very well and makes for an exceptionally comfortable paddle (Fig. 9).

Next day, head out and do the trip you set for homework. Make sure the weather and conditions are appropriate before you give them the planning to do, otherwise the potential benefit is lost, if plans cannot be practically tested. As and when anomalies arise work through them, using your own plans.

Do vary their practice in planning crossings. Vector diagrams are not always practical or possible and more often than not 'crossing equi-time either side of HW

or LW' or 'drifting onto an island' will be far more appropriate, so do ensure that other trips during a course employ other such strategies.

Finally, the first open crossing day should be a dedicated planning and deck-top navigation day and should not involve leadership or incident management. A dedicated leadership day, however, should definitely involve planning and navigation as part of that day, where any planning or navigation anomalies are dealt with by the students themselves. Such a session should form the final teaching progression/the culmination for this planning module.

▶ Deck Top Navigation Skills

Many of your sea kayakers' navigation skills will be used when planning their trips. Nevertheless simple deck top navigation skills will also be required whilst

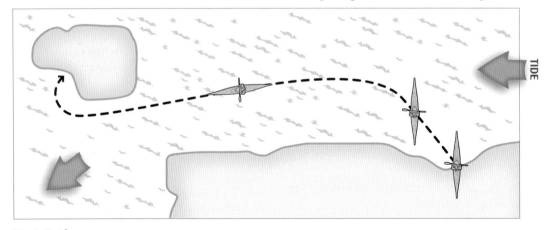

TIDE

Fig. 8 Drifting onto your target

paddling. A day deck top navigation session on the water should follow an introductory planning session. The two could be designed to form a complete day dedicated to planning and navigation.

Ideal Teaching Locale

Initial session in the classroom, with a follow-up practical session involving some tidal movement or wind funnelled area and a very short crossing of the tide or wind.

Skills You Need To Identify, Coach And Practise

Simple deck-top navigation skills as listed below.

Session Progressions

Begin in the classroom following the introductory planning session outlined above. Take the plans with you on the sea and ensure that every student has a copy of the chart and OS map, a chinagraph pencil on elastic, a compass on some string (to prevent loss, but more importantly to provide a measuring tool on the water), a watch.

Your practical session should include:

 Isolating the various navigation strategies

    a. Timing

    b. Hand-railing the coastline

    c. Simple fixes

    d. Transits

    e. Following a bearing

    f. Using a transit and bearing fix

    g. Resections

    h. Maintaining awareness of position during an incident.

Demonstrating and practising these skills in isolation.

Applying the learned navigational skills to a variety of situations. (Do this during other sessions, e.g. wind and water awareness journey, rough water handling and incident management days.)

Many of your students may already have a range of land or yachting navigational skills so try to build on what they already know, shaping that knowledge and adapting it for use in a sea kayak. Keep it simple and follow a logical progression.

The example session below looks at a few of the navigation skills above, but all can be taught in a similar manner.

Firstly, on the beach prior to getting on, split the group into smaller groups of 3. Buddy groups will encourage further collaborative teaching, freeing you up to give extra tuition as needed and your students more independence. The first exercise revises the fundamentals: Position given by lat and long and grid references, timing, hand-railing and simple fixes. This will set the base line from which references can be built upon later and allows you to see what skills your students do have compared to what skills they still need to learn.

Look at the section of map overleaf, circled are some typical exercises for students to do during a deck top navigation session:

 Exercise 1 (A) - 'What's my location?'

Before getting on the water, ask each student to give you the grid reference of their current location on their OS maps. Then ask them to give you the lat and long of the same position on their charts. Next ask them to take it in turns to give one another the lat and long of a feature the other must identify.

Exercise 2 (A to B) - How fast do I paddle?

For this exercise the students would ideally set themselves a distance of 1nm and time how long it will take to paddle. The area available to them above, which is unaffected by the tide, is quite small and your students would have to choose a distance over a fraction of a nm and multiply it up in order to work out how fast they had paddled.

Exercise 3 (B-C) - Find the feature on the map.

Once the average speed has been worked out, ask one of the buddies to pick a point (giving lat and long rather than pointing to it) for their buddies to paddle to. The two buddies should work out how to get there, its distance and suggest how long it will take. The two should paddle to the point whilst the first paddles behind. Once on arrival at the point the first buddy should feedback to the other the level of their success. Each buddy should take it in turns to pick a point.

Exercise 4 (C-D) - Transits

Explain what a transit is and demonstrate the use of one to the group by identifying a transit that everyone sets off for 'en masse'. Next have the students take it in turns to guess the transit their buddy leader is using.

Exercise 5 (D-E) - Following a bearing (with or against the flow only)

Take a break and land. Introduce the compass; explain what it is used for, describe what features it has, and explain how it works. Have each student try and take a bearing from the chart (or map). Help anyone who is having difficulties or needs a little extra tuition, regroup the students if necessary so more able can assist less able, etc. Ask the buddies to work out a simple circuit between them to 3 points up and/or down tide of them. Once they have worked out the 3 bearings required they can set off. If you make the 3rd point a set point on the chart (e.g. Point E) all the teams will arrive back at the same point ready for the last exercise. Check no one is working on points across the tidal flow.

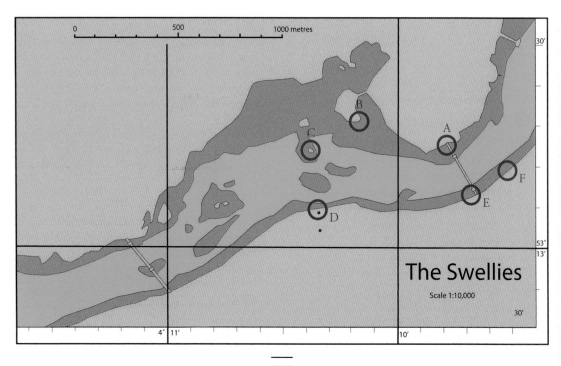 Exercise 6 (A to F) - Use a compass bearing (across the flow)

Back at Point A have the buddy teams take a bearing that goes directly across the tidal flow. Ask what they anticipate will happen. Insist they must paddle on the bearing at all times and not switch to transits, and that they must stay together. Set off. Once on the far side, invariably with the buddy groups strung out, bring those furthest downstream and highest upstream to those in the centre. Ask them to locate this position they were in and mark it and the time, on their charts for use later.

Exercise 7 - Lastly have them cross to another point across the flow using any method they wish,

e.g. straight across on a guessed ferry glide, straight across on a transit, up the eddy and across, drifting down, etc. Exercise 6 and 7 form the ground-work for methods of planning open crossings, but there is no need to mention that at this stage.

After a day dedicated to planning and deck top navigation skills, build on this by planning a day trip, doing it and en-route reinforce the lessons learned from the previous navigation session, by asking simple questions such as: 'Can you give me the lat and long for where are you now?' 'What is that building on the cliff?' etc.

▶ **Poor Visibility Or Night Navigation Skills**

Getting back late off a trip and paddling into the twilight hours is not uncommon. Teaching your students to paddle safely and look after one another at night could be very useful to them in the future.

Ideal Teaching Locale

The classroom initially, then a section of coastline that has some interesting features to find. If windy at all choose an onshore venue. If very rough conditions persist use a sheltered harbour or estuary. Beware of other users in such venues and ensure you have a white light available and a VHF. Inform the coastguard you are in the harbour on a night navigation exercise if appropriate.

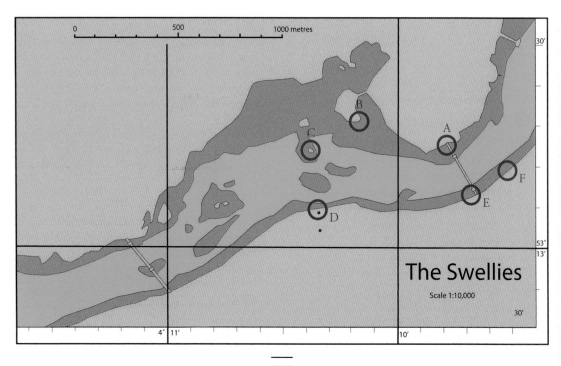

The Swellies

Scale 1:10,000

Skills You Need To Identify, Coach And Practise

Desktop navigation at night, group management and leadership considerations at night. Ensure everyone has a light stick attached to their body rather than kayak, just in case they capsize and become parted from their kayak.

Session Progressions

Introduce the session inside.

Before setting out ensure everyone has a map, large-scale 1:25,000 OS maps are the best for this exercise. During the day you would have had your students using the coastline as a handrail, checking off features as they went. The process is the same now, except they need to really concentrate. Distance will be covered far quicker than they expect and water lapping over the rocks will make things sound far closer than they really are. Give your students time to study their route and mark on the map key features they hope to see.

Look at the section of map below, circled are some typical points for students to find during a night navigation exercise:

A. The mouth of the stream.

B. The gap between the island and mainland.

C. The small island in the bay.

D. The island of rock off the larger island.

E. This harder inlet can be verified by lining oneself up with the 2 sailing markers on the land and West Mouse in transit.

F. This small inlet.

On route ask individuals or buddy pairs to find specific locations. These can be features along the coastline which students can handrail to or features that require a bit of transit work or compass relocation work to get a fix on their position, using a resection.

During this exercise it's best if students are given a point to find just before it's their turn to navigate, otherwise they spend too much time looking at their maps and don't concentrate on following the current leader and consequently get left behind.

Spend your time near to the navigator/leader ready to help them as required, yet remain vigilant of everyone else. It is easy to get stragglers engrossed in work-

Photo 26 Night navigation

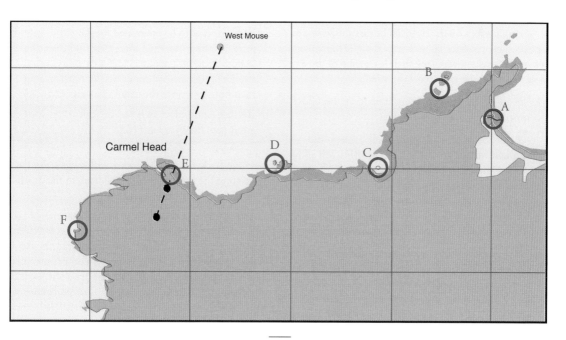

ing something out on their deck. Keep count of light sticks and make sure everyone is there at all times. Giving everyone a number to call out, (you as leader begin as number one) may help in your management and should be encouraged when coaching trainee leaders to manage groups at night.

LEADERSHIP SKILLS

All of the above cognitive and physical skills are required if your student is to become an effective leader on the sea, but it is important that you address leadership skills within its own session at some stage. A day journeying through a variety of conditions requiring good planning and navigation and the opportunity for tactical use of wind and water as well as incidences to occur naturally, really works well for covering many leadership issues.

As with incident management it is dangerous to teach in such a way that students believe there is only one solution for type 'A' incident and another for type 'B', without realising in fact that one should be using a combination of the same techniques adapted to fit the new scenario facing them. To help in this matter and to help them remember in the future, give your students a generic incident management framework (see next session below) to follow and suggest rescues and towing skills to adapt as necessary. We need to provide a similar framework for leaders to follow and provide them with the rescue, navigation and planning skills they need to know in order to adapt to the conditions of the day and to the individuals on each trip.

The mnemonic CLAP often used in leadership coaching sessions on the river can be easily used on the sea too and provides us with an excellent framework on which students can hang their leadership of the day and you can hang your coaching strategy.

🖐 Begin in the classroom looking at the CLAP mnemonic:

🖐 Divide your class into small groups and go through the above written exercise. This will allow your students to brainstorm their ideas, drawing from their own experiences and knowledge. This discussion time amongst the group will affect their learning far more positively than if you just told them or worse, went out with no framework at all.

🖐 Make the session even more effective by using their solutions once you are on the water. On the water, work through as many of the above as you can, taking advantage of any other opportunities that arise. However, do leave time at the end to

CLAP – THE ART OF GOOD LEADERSHIP

Communication

- Voice, whistle, hand(s), paddle, eyes.
- There should only be a few signals and all must be clear, simple and discussed before leaving the shore.

Line of Sight

- Ideally everyone, but definitely through using other group members, if headlands, rocks, etc are in the way.
- Line of sight ensures line of communication.

Avoidance is Better than Cure

- Appropriate group control.
- The teaching of group awareness.
- Buddy system.
- Leader's awareness of water ahead, weather all around and group's psychological/emotional state on the water - teaching this in others can only help.
- Teaching those capable to assist in rescues, do rescues themselves and to tow will pay dividends should things go wrong.

Position of Most Effectiveness/Usefulness

- Position yourself to enable the most effective communication.
- Position yourself to manage/prevent any likely incident. Best to be positioned for the most likely incident rather than the most disastrous, bearing in mind that most major incidents occur following a series of unmanaged minor incidents. Managing minor ones prevents the major one occurring.
- You are most effective if you are safe, then your group and finally the casualty.

come back to the classroom and review the day relating the principles of CLAP back to the practical session they have just had.

After you have spent time with them encourage them to go on trips with peers or others with less experience than themselves. Consolidation is the next level of progression and that can only come from trips in which they have to make all the decisions, do all the planning, manage any rescues. This injection of 'sharp end' kinaesthetic input is what they need now.

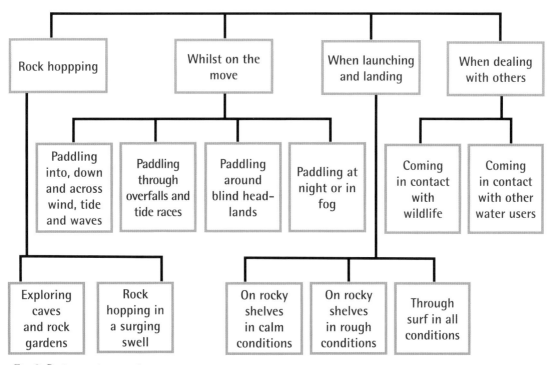

Using the principles of CLAP

How can I communicate, maintain line of sight, anticipate problems and position myself with most effectiveness in the following situations?

- Rock hoppping
- Whilst on the move
- When launching and landing
- When dealing with others

- Paddling into, down and across wind, tide and waves
- Paddling through overfalls and tide races
- Paddling around blind head-lands
- Paddling at night or in fog
- Coming in contact with wildlife
- Coming in contact with other water users

- Exploring caves and rock gardens
- Rock hopping in a surging swell
- On rocky shelves in calm conditions
- On rocky shelves in rough conditions
- Through surf in all conditions

Fig. 9 Brainstorming exercise

It will provide them with valuable intrinsic feedback from their good and bad days, allowing them to build upon the solid foundations you have laid.

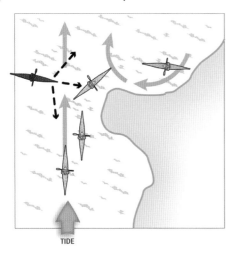

TIDE

Fig. 10 By drifting sideways the leader is able to see all the paddlers and would be able to paddle to anywhere they are needed if someone got into difficulties.

▶Risk Assessing And Incident Management

Risk assessment does form a big part of your planning and incident management sessions, but the skill of risk assessing and the techniques involved are so important I like to teach them as a sub-session on their own.

Ideal Teaching Locale

First session in the classroom, subsequent risk assessing on the water in a variety of conditions and situations including the handling of kayaks to and from the water.

Skills You Need To Identify, Coach And Practise

To make an assessment of the hazards and identify the risks involved. Prepare strategies to avoid and manage the risks.

Session Progressions

Initial classroom introductory session, subsequent sessions for part of planning, incident management and leadership days.

As previously said, frameworks to hang the session on work really well for you when structuring your sessions and for your students to have a proforma to follow and a means of remembering both the theoretical and practical input given.

Encourage your students to build the flow chart and mnemonics into their planning preparation, leadership considerations and incident management scenarios. Laminated versions for your students to refer to whilst being buffeted by the sea would be very helpful to them. Operating at this level requires one to think a lot about many things all at once and so any crib sheets or diagrams, mnemonics, plans they have will help them stay fully *aware* of the now very big picture. Feel free to copy the following flow chart to help you with this session.

WHAT ARE THE RISKS?

▶ Definition

Risk Assessment is all about recognition and avoidance of hazards and deciding whether the hazard constitutes an acceptable risk or unacceptable risk.

▶ Making An Assessment Of Risk

Look at the possible hazards that face you, consider the consequences of messing up if you have to paddle through any of these hazards. Then considering your group's abilities, the weather, the time of year, the amount you've paddled already, how you feel yourself about going in to rescue, estimate the likelihood of messing up.

If the consequences and the likelihood of messing up are high then your risk assessment is to avoid the

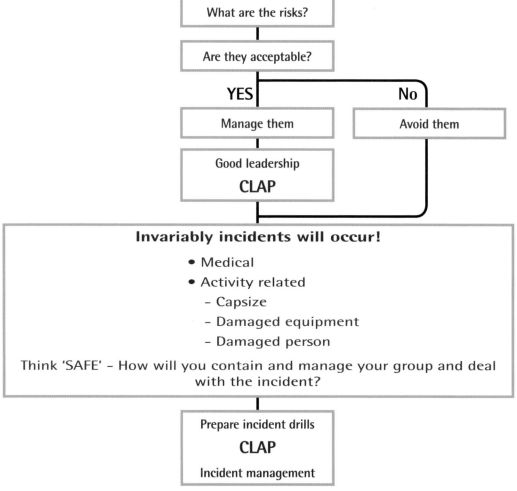

Fig. 11 Risk assessment and management flowchart

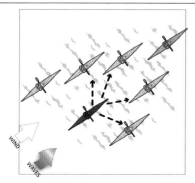

Fig. 12 By being at the centre/rear of the group the leader can see everyone and is in a position to reach anyone who gets into difficulties.

hazard. If the consequences are high, but the likelihood low then consider going ahead. If the consequences are low, and the likelihood high, it is probably an excellent teaching opportunity… go for it.

Remember, tomorrow's assessment of the same site, same group, different state of the tide could be any other issue and requires a new risk assessment.

▶ Manage Them (The Risks)

CLAP – The art of good leadership

See Leadership notes for more detail but in summary when managing an acceptable risk do so with the following in mind, ready for any incident that may occur as a result of taking the risk.

- ◎ Communication
- ◎ Line of Sight
- ◎ Avoidance better than Cure
- ◎ Position of most effectiveness/maximum usefulness

▶ Avoid Them (The Risks)

Not all risks are avoidable. In fact you may have to make a choice between 2 risks. Weighing up the greater and going with the lesser after considering all the options is the only solution. Managing it as best as you can, following your incident management drills (i.e. SAFE) is the best way to deal with an incident or hazard.

▶ Invariably Incidents Will Occur

Ensure your students know that invariably incidents will occur, through no fault of their own. As such they need to manage them as above and have ready some incident management drills based around the mnemonic SAFE.

SAFE - The art of successful incident management

🕐 **S**top
- Take a deep breath

🕐 **A**ssess the Situation
- What further risks are there:
  - To me
  - To the rest of the group
  - To the casualty

🕐 **F**ormulate a plan
- Which rescue is applicable in this situation
- Do I need to fix damages on land or at sea

🕐 **E**xecute & Evaluate the plan
- See the rescues and towing session for suggested scenarios

As before, ensure there is plenty of time at the end of the day to review the incidents. Any scenarios listed but not covered should be given as homework or discussed. On the sea incidents will invariably happen… make sure your sea kayakers have enough skill and know enough about the sea environment to avoid most problems, but enough skill and knowledge to deal with them, without you!

▶ ENVIRONMENTAL AWARENESS

Being aware of the environmental factors that affect the sea, such as weather and topography, has already been covered. However, the sea environment contains a lot more than just salt water and weather and your sea kayakers will want to know about the many varied marine wildlife they encounter on their journeys. Learn what you can and carry with you laminated details of the wildlife less common to your area.

As a sea kayak coach you look to the sea for your living as do many other humans and wildlife. Knowing as much as possible about other nautical users and other creatures, and being aware of times and areas that require special consideration are very important. As the coach/guide, you are a role model and watched continuously by your students. Much of your environmental awareness coaching will be seen by your students through your attitude and actions, so demonstrating a personal responsibility for the environment is essential if your livelihood is to continue.

CONCLUSION

Training others to become sea kayakers is a wonderful job. The rich diversity of both physical and cognitive skills a sea kayak coach has to teach their clients, in order to enable them to paddle safely and efficiently in an ever-changing environment, is vast. Sea kayak coaches have an incredible classroom to work in and just the most fantastic array of natural teaching opportunities that they share with so many other extraordinary living things. I can't for one moment imagine ever tiring of coaching people to sea kayak. I hope this chapter helps you to understand a little more about what a sea kayak coach coaches, and inspires you and helps you to train others to paddle on the sea.

FURTHER READING

Sea Kayak Navigation, Ferrero F, 1999, Pesda Press, 0-9531956-1-9
How to Read a Nautical Chart, Calder N,2003, ME USA, McGraw-Hill, 0-07137615-1
Inshore Navigation, Cunliffe T, 1987, Arundel, Fernhurst Books, 0-90675431-3
RYA Yachtmaster Theory Booklet, Haire P, Hampshire, Royal Yachting Association Publications
Learn to Navigate, Mosenthal B, 1995, London, Adlard Coles Nautical,0-71366870-9
Reeds Skipper's Handbook, Pearson M, 1993,Bradford-on-Avon, Thomas Reed Publications, 0-90128192-1
Sea Kayaking, Foster N, 1991, Brighton, Fernhurst Books, 0-906754-60-7
Sea Canoeing, Hutchinson D, 1976, London, A & C Black Ltd, 0-7136-5602-6
Sea Kayaking, Dowd J, 1988, Vancouver, Douglas& McIntyre Ltd, 0-88894-598-1
Kayak Rolling, Collins L, 2004, Pesda Press, 0-9531956-8-6

DVDS

This is the Sea, by Justine Curgenven
This is the Sea II, by Justine Curgenven
Over and Out, by Gordon Brown
Sea Kayak Rescues, by Olly Sanders and Leo Hoare
The Kayak Roll, by Performance Video and Instruction Inc.

WEBSITES

There are several excellent websites on the tide and weather and provide excellent explanations and pictures for use in your teaching. The RNLI and Met Office also have excellent educational website, and e-safety DVDs available.

TRYS MORRIS

Originally a river paddler, Trys was soon converted to the sea when she began university in North Wales, studying sports science. The vast array of wildlife and the unique tidal waters and weather of the Welsh coast provided a new and exciting playground for her to explore, learn about and develop skills in.

Trys is a Level 5 Coach Sea, Level 4 Inland and now divides her work time between freelance coaching and running an activity booking agency and coffee shop, Café Active. She formerly taught at Plas y Brenin and Plas Menai and still works the sea kayak symposium circuits in the UK, USA and Norway. She has done several expeditions, her most notable being an 8 month journey from the UK to Greece and more recently as one of three females to be the first to circumnavigate Tasmania.

16 SURFING

Coaching surfing can be as frustrating as it is exciting and rewarding. The environment is such that trying to organise structured practise can be a nightmare. However when you find that perfect spot, or wait for the tide to change, and a clean shouldering wave is produced, all the doubts and disbeliefs are dispelled. That environment can also challenge your observation and feedback skills, calling on you to draw on more imagination skills than knowledge (thanks Einstein). But the thrill of watching someone emerge from a first run with a beaming, 'I'm hooked' smile makes it all worthwhile.

INTRODUCTION

In this chapter we will look at the coaching of surfing. We will try and keep terms generic to kayak/ski collectively known as craft or boat and primarily deal with coaching of manoeuvres on green waves. The soup or broken wave has its place as a coaching zone, however the range of skills that can be performed there are transferable from the freestyle chapter.

▶ THE ENVIRONMENT

The coach must have a good understanding of the environment he is working in both from a coaching and a safety perspective.

COACHING ZONES

The areas we have to consider can be divided into the following:

- Outside, flat water environment, e.g. to practise rolling.

- Green wave surfing.

- Inside of break, soup e.g. to practise edge control.

- Use of reforming waves for surfing.

- Beach - drawing pictures, mental rehearsal, sand dunes for modelling waves.

It is the quality of wave the coach should look for not the quantity. During the session the swell may decrease or increase in size and possibly character (e.g. dumping at

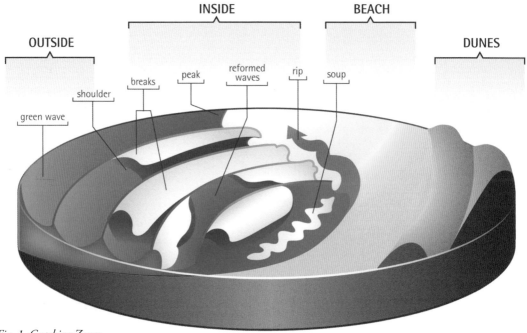

INSIDE

BEACH

OUTSIDE

DUNES

green wave

shoulder

breaks

peak

reformed waves

rip

soup

Fig. 1 Coaching Zones

low water) and this can have a catastrophic effect on the student's performance if not taken into consideration.

Surf is a chaotic environment and that chaos easily transfers to the coach. Take your time, ensure your aims are achievable given the environment, students and time available. If it all goes belly up don't be afraid to bin the session and start again or even move sites.

▶ Session Aims

When considering the choice of site the aims of the session must go hand in hand. If you have decided that addressing your student's needs will be best met by setting them a goal of trying to accomplish this on 3 waves left 3 waves right, you will need to choose a site that gives right and left shouldering waves and good observation opportunities.

If your choice of site is limited you may have to work the other way around. Decide what the environment will allow and address those aspects of your student's performance that are best tackled on that break.

SAFETY CONSIDERATIONS

Remember, "the ultimate safety of the learner is the coach's responsibility".

Get into the habit of carrying out risk assessments of the sites used. Do it with your students to allow them to learn the process. Factors to consider include weather, onshore/offshore wind, tides, obstacles, rips, undertows and other water users. Dynamic risk assessments include what changes as the tide comes in and goes out, and the wind changes in direction/strength.

Look after yourself. Dress appropriately, you may find yourself standing on a windswept beach or in the water for some time. Are you also dressed appropriately to effect a rescue?

Are the students equipped appropriately. Air bags and end grabs?

Emergency kit (should be close to hand).

Rescue kit, own boat, tow line, throw line and knife, swim fins, torpedo buoy.

(Certain rescue methods and equipment will be favoured by some and not others. Practise so that you are not drawn into attempting a rescue where you are ineffective and endanger yourself.)

First aid kit, simple repair kit, shelter, flask, spare clothes, means of recall or attracting attention, for example: paddle, whistle, air horn, flares, mobile phone, VHF.

Session safety. Use paddle out, surf in zones. Ensure your students know surf etiquette, collision avoidance procedure (emergency capsize) and promote good relations on and off the water.

Photo 1 Beach whiteboard

🌀 Mark out the beach to enable the surfers to gauge where they are and the surfing zone. Explain the use of transits to help them to maintain their position, (the change in view of a near and far fixed object, as the paddler drifts).

🌀 Warm up and cool down exercises. See Chapter 2.

▶ Group Management

Group management in a surf environment is essential for a safe and effective coaching session. You and your students must be clear on what signals are to be used, how long you want individual sessions to last, (should they have a watch on?) and what to do in the event of an incident or a total recall.

▶ COACHING CONSIDERATIONS

In the following sections we will examine some of the key coaching behaviours and how they are affected when working in the surf environment.

DISCIPLINE AND PACE

As a coach you will need to be quite firm with your students to avoid them getting carried away. Ensure they concentrate on the task at hand; if you say only take 3 waves make sure they do.

▶ Avoiding Burn-Out

The surf environment is also very tiring. Often the coach will need to enforce frequent breaks and comfort stops to allow students to take on fluids and snacks to rehydrate and raise blood glucose levels and possibly get warm. There is also a tendency to over-coach, allow your students time to surf.

⊙ KEY POINTS

- An appropriate sequence for a paddlesport warm-up would begin with a pulse raiser and then light mobilising exercises before the lifting of any boats. Once on the beach/water a secondary boat specific pulse raiser and mobilising exercises can be carried out. All flexibility exercises should be carried out at the end of the session.

- Warm-ups are now frequently used as part of a training session for paddlers. The most appropriate are those that closely match the demands of the discipline and can be carried out in-boat. Cool-downs are less frequently carried out at the end of a session but can have a very positive impact upon recovery from training

- Flexibility exercises for paddlesport should focus on the shoulder, trunk rotation, flexion and extension, lateral flexion and extension, and hip flexion.

Photo 2 Supervising a session.

OBSERVATION

If you cannot observe you cannot give feedback based on observation.

▶ Position

Where you observe from will be decided by a combination of what aspect of your student's performance you are trying to observe and safety considerations.

🌀 The beach allows a full picture to be seen. On some beaches headlands can be used to get a side view.

🌀 In or on the water either paddle/swim out and sit in a useful position to observe; a boogie board may provide some support.

▶ Safety Considerations

Outside, beyond the line of breaking waves, the ultimate risk is being carried further out to sea by offshore winds. In this instance you may consider keeping paddlers within the break line or positioning yourself at the point of most usefulness, i.e. out back.

Inside the break line with minimal offshore wind any swimmers will be washed ashore. Remember to instruct paddlers to grab the seaward end of the boat. Rips and undertows can affect this and a risk assessment would prescribe where activity took place or appropriate instruction was given to paddlers. Within this zone effective rescuing is usually best carried out from the beach side.

▶ Use Of Video

This is covered in greater depth in Chapter 11. Given the restraints in observation in surf and the low prices of video equipment the video is a very useful tool.

◉ Try and use it to highlight specific points, remember it is giving feedback so don't overload!

◉ If you can afford it buy one with a flip out screen, thus allowing you to view performances on the beach, cave, kisu or minibus.

◉ Keep your batteries charged.

◉ Use a tripod.

Pre-recorded video and DVD's can be used to good effect for giving students demonstrations and models to understand surfing techniques and manoeuvres. They can also be used to check their understanding by questioning. Often closed questions gain more information than very open questions, e.g. "At the top of the wave where is the surfer looking?"

FEEDBACK

Research tells us that feedback should be given long enough after the performance to allow both the student and coach to internalise the performance and short enough to give maximum potency. When a surfer is sometimes 50m from the coach this can be positive or negative depending on your point of view. Positive as you can only give small bites of visual feedback and not overload the student. Negative in that unless you have a lengthy repertoire of signals some of the ability to reinforce or change the performance are lost.

▶ Reviewing Skills

You may need to compensate for a lack of technical feedback by making the most of your reviewing skills.

Photo 3a Visual feedback signal - "Arms out"
Photo 3b "Shoulder going this way"

Use the beach as a white board to draw pictures to give feedback. Build a small wave and use a model of a boat on the wave to describe movements.

▶ Intrinsic Feedback

Structure exercises so as to allow the student to tune in to their intrinsic feedback. Coach the student to feel!

This will be the most effective tool you can use as a coach and will require you working with your student to develop their kinaesthetic awareness. Remember your smart rules for goal setting.

✔ INTRINSIC FEEDBACK

• *exercise:* An important tool is that of using extremities. An exercise to help the paddler find the most effective position in which to hold the paddle is to:

1. Paddle with their hands gripping the shaft very close to the blades.

2. Paddle with their hands touching each other in the middle of the shaft.

3. Paddle with their hands in the most comfortable position between these two points.

The concept of scoring these positions can also be added e.g. 0 for least effective and 6 for most effective.

Photo 4 Wave model

 WALKING THE WAVE

• *exercise:* Build/draw a wave or use a sand dune and get the student to run the wave preferably with their paddle as if they were on the real wave.

Often by the student closing their eyes they can concentrate greater on the movement of the body.

Remember when drawing/walking the wave, ensure the wave is drawn in the same manner as the waves washing up the beach.

QUESTIONING

With the use of immediate feedback so limited by the environment, effective questioning has some very important roles.

The coach needs to receive the specific answers to aid their analysis, e.g. "On that last wave were you attempting to make the section or go for a top turn?"

Questioning can also be used to help the student review a performance and visualize what changes they wish to make on the next run.

IMAGERY AND MENTAL REHEARSAL

Given the communication problems in the surf environment these are very useful and powerful tools. See the PETTLEP model in Chapter 3.

Photo 5 Walking the wave

COLOURS

"When I coached Martine from our squad she had a problem of throwing her trim violently forward to bottom turn and upright when at the top of the wave. I used colours in a similar way here. She is a very visual activist. We labelled the upright position Green and the forward Red. I suggested that there should be room for Amber. She used a foamy on the beach to climb and drop on a Karrimat wave, identifying the appropriate colours as she surfed the wave.

Prior to this exercise Martine was not always able to feed back to me what had happened out on the wave. She went out for 5 waves and came back in. Her trim of the boat was still jerky but she said con-fidently "I can get Green and Red, but not Amber!". She had created both a new awareness and a language of colour. As well as now having a common language, Martine could easily work off the water to improve her performance. She worked with the foamy to analyse her performance, could overlay colour to the video footage I had taken, and easily pre-practised using visualisation.

She went back out and put Amber into her runs. Her movements were smooth, and the kayak carved without shedding speed."

Ian Sherrington - Level 5 Surf Coach

► CORE KNOWLEDGE

As coaches we need to identify which factor (technical, tactical, physiological or psychological) is the rate-limiter at any stage in our student's development. For example, when paddling out, does the student have knowledge of the techniques involved such as forward paddling, what strategy to use (e.g. position, waiting, enough power), or are they scared about being back looped.

Within surfing all four factors are of equal importance; it is very hard to isolate them individually. The following are some examples of the core knowledge that your students must possess.

TACTICAL

► Wave Selection

Here the coach has to actively encourage their students to watch and paddle a wide selection of waves, size, direction, shapes, speed and character (fat sluggish waves or steep fast waves). The effect of the wind onshore/offshore, how it holds up the wave. Look at tidal height and beach morphology.

► Wave Awareness

The student should be aware of the shoulder. Will it break? Which way… left or right? Probably not if there is a head of another wave just in front of it. Will it close out? That is does the wave break along its whole length therefore not really allowing a long run for the paddler.

► Position On The Wave

Where the paddler is on the wave will affect their speed and what manoeuvres they can achieve. For maximum potential speed the paddler needs to be higher on the wave or on the steepest/most critical part of the wave known as the shoulder or pocket.

The coach has to put the student in positions where they are able to feel the differences, i.e. structure exercises where the student 'explores the wave.'

► Choreographed Runs

In the early stages of surfing, the paddler may only be concerned with catching a wave. A pro-active approach would be to diagonal run along the wave. A reactive approach is one that would occur if, on seeing the wave break, the paddler either exits the wave by turning off it, or if too steep, running before it.

AWARENESS ON THE WAVE

- *exercise:* Allow the student to catch a wave and to surf out in front of it. Question them to gauge whether they were aware of the drop in speed and change in noise? Now get them to do the same but turn before the boat loses speed. Get them to surf away from the pocket until they slow down.

KEY POINTS

- **Attention style** - Broad or narrow external or internal (see Chapter 3). Where is your student concentrating… on the front of the boat, or looking both ways to check where the shoulder is? Coach your student to have a broader external view.

- **Bilateral transfer** - Where possible, always get paddlers to practise both sides.

Choreography is another form of goal setting. The student should be encouraged to put together a run made up of a number of manoeuvres.

Here we can take an example from competition judging, which looks at:

The take-off including wave selection.

The run, making the best use of the wave.

Exiting the wave.

"It is the ability to read and predict the wave that separates the average from the good surfer, rather than flashy manoeuvres."
(Keeble and Andreisson)

KEY POINT

- The key themes for a coach to take away is that we should encourage individual customisation of strokes and skills, allow students to practise their techniques in a variety of environments, and foster decision-making in their application.

► Speed

Without optimising speed it is impossible to master many of the surf manoeuvres. The achievement of speed is governed by position on the wave

Photos 6a-d Wave selection

and affected by some of the following technical and physiological points.

TOP TIP

- If the paddler is continuously slowing the boat with the paddle (providing conditions allow), get them to take off and then throw their paddle away and surf without it.

TECHNICAL

It is worth talking here briefly about some key aspects of hull design, a huge subject.

Photo 7 *A variety of surf craft*

▶ Waterline Length

When a kayak is in displacement mode, that is when paddling out and taking off, the longer the waterline length the greater speed achieved.

However, when planing/surfing only the mid to back third/tail of the boat is in the water so a flat, wide hull profile will increase speed. General river playboats with a flat mid-section and kicked up tail will be slower.

▶ Rails

For grippy fast turns the kayak will require rails, that is the angular shape at the gunwale. The nearer to 90° the angle, the greater the grip.

The rails of the craft will not only affect its grip on the wave face, to a certain extent they will also affect the arc of a turn, particularly the bottom turn. Once planing, only half to one third of the rear of the craft is in contact with the water, therefore it is important that the rails here are sharp to effect positive water release and therefore ultimate speed. As the rail shape moves forward it will progressively become 'tucked' under, too soft at the bow to avoid them catching during slow or stalled turns.

PHYSIOLOGICAL

Dynamic seating position and dynamic balance should be maximised to enable body, blade and boat control.

The paddler must have good contact with the craft so that when they move the craft moves. Care should be taken to pad out the craft to allow this. Surf wax can be used on the seat of a ski.

▶ Range Of Body Movement

Mobility is the key, especially upper body, front to back trim and rotation. The answer here is to make the student aware of the extremities of trim and rotation so that they can work within or aspire to those extremes. (Using the scoring method mentioned earlier will help).

Photo 8 *Coaching edge control and body movement. The use of the inflatable rubber ring allows this to be done on the beach and even indoors!*

The nature of the seating position on a ski allows greater use of the lower body especially by tensioning the body by pulling on the toes.

▶ Edge Control And Core Stability

Developing edge control and core stability is vital for surfing and effective craft control. The student must be coached to use edging in much the same way as a dimmer switch rather than just off and on. The paddler must be able to effectively control edge to climb and drop on the wave and to allow for the vagaries of the wave.

TOP TIP

- It is important to coach below-decks paddling using the processes of relaxing and tensing alternate legs, so that the rails are engaged. The analogy of skiing and locking and unlocking edge is a good one.

Photo 9 Sand simulator

▶ Power

Generally surfing requires short bursts of anaerobic power (development of this is covered in Chapter 2).

Paddling out may require more power and breath but both very much rely on technique. The student must be made aware of correct forward paddling technique (see Chapter 14).

▶ Paddle Size And Length

The paddle is made up of two main components: the blade and the shaft. The relationship between the two is very important, depending on the size and age of the paddler and the use the paddle is put to. Surfing, which requires a short burst of power, may use a big blade and short shaft. However, young or smaller surf paddlers may use a smaller blade and longer shaft.

PSYCHOLOGICAL

See also Chapter 3.

There are many factors that may affect a paddler's performance. The coach should be aware of these and have strategies and session progressions to cope with each. Here are a few:

- Past paddling history, recent bad experiences.
- Who you surf with, peer pressure, motivation.
- Intimidation from other water users.
- Size and nature of wave.
- Nature of break, reef breaks with nasty rocks.
- Cognitive (mental) excitement can impede physical performance, which can lead to some manic runs until the paddler settles in. This is especially true if they have not been able to surf for a while.

Relaxation Techniques

Yoga offers the best training for relaxation techniques. The two I have found useful are to practise tensing and relaxing muscle groups and the concept of breathing deeply using the diaphragm in a circle, not just in and out. Another approach is to listen to music.

Inner Game

Inner game strategies allow self-2 to do its job, i.e. to control fluid movement (see Chapters 1 and 2).

▶ BASIC SKILLS

Remember when reinforcing or correcting a performance to firstly coach from a body perspective, this will invariably lead to a correction in the blade or boat.

When coaching specific skills or manoeuvres it is vital that the coach isolates that skill or manoeuvres in order that the paddler only concentrates on that skill or manoeuvre, for example:

✓ Take-offs

Ask the student to try 3 without surfing the wave then come in for review and correction.

✓ Bottom turns

Ask the student to take off, go to the bottom of the wave, turn then exit the wave. Do this 3 times left, 3 times right, then come in.

THE BONGO SLIDE

This is about preventing the boat from capsizing once it has been broached by a breaking wave. In its most basic form this can be described as:

- 1. Edge into the waves to prevent them tipping you in.
- 2. Use a low support stroke to assist this.

It can be argued that this position is a secure position for a beginner, but what about the other water users who get bounced over as the kayak makes its way to the beach?

By over-developing this secure position the coach may be hindering the paddler's development and the safety of other water users.

By coaching a few more techniques we can ensure that, even when broached, the paddler has a degree of control over their craft by being able to have some forwards and backwards movement as opposed to just sideways.

1. Edge into the waves.

2. Use a low support stroke to assist this.

3. Trim forwards (to go backwards), trim backwards (to go forwards).

4. Continue to paddle forwards or reverse to change position.

5. Progress to changing edge and using sweep strokes to turn (unlocking and locking the edge).

Photo 10 Trimming in the soup

▶ Getting Ahead

With the ever-decreasing length of craft the severity of broaching, turning parallel to the wave, will be reduced. In modern craft, after the drop is taken it can be more effective to point the craft at the beach and lean back? With low volume back decks the craft is spat out in front of the wave.

PADDLE OUT

To get off the beach put your hands either side of the boat, or one hand one side and a vertical paddle on the other, and push down and slide the boat forwards.

Paddling out through the surf is more about strategy than brute force.

Photo 11 Paddle out

The coach should give their students experience of watching the waves, and asking them where is the path through?

Time the waves - how long between the sets?

Set courses that make the paddler change direction and speed and wait.

Coach dynamic forward paddling, vertical paddle shaft close to boat, good trunk rotation, and forward trim. Head down, high style during punch through to avoid paddle shaft in face.

The concept of continuous paddling to provide momentum and using the blade to anchor the boat as they go through the wave.

Sometimes, if the wave is too steep it may be better to turn and run.

If paddlers have trouble understanding these skills the coach could set up a follow the leader exercise.

▶ Use Of Rips

Rips provide a very useful, often dry conveyor belt to the outside, often allowing the paddler to save energy even if it means paddling further back to it after each run.

▶ Angle Of Attack And Edge

Attacking the waves at up to 45° or on edge minimises the likelihood of being back looped.

▶ Bunny Hops

As the paddler paddles up the wave they lift their feet/knees and thrust forwards with their hips whilst pulling on the paddle, causing the boat to hop over the wave.

▶ Rolling Under Waves

It is possible for the paddler to perfect timing to roll under the waves by capsizing towards the beach. The wave will assist with the roll.

TAKE-OFF

Prior to take-off the paddler should give some thought to the type of wave. Has it got a peak? Will it close out? Is it a double wave? Which direction will the shoulder go?

The paddler should position themselves on the steep peak of the wave to allow for minimal paddling:

Dynamic forwards paddling (practise exercise of max speed in the minimum number of strokes).

Trim forwards.

Photo 12 Take off

🛶 Depending on the wave initially take off at a 45° angle to prevent the boat nose-diving.

🛶 As timing and the ability to read the waves improve the paddler can progress to taking off straight down the wave and then doing a bottom turn.

🛶 Once surfing, look around you. (Where is the shoulder and where are the other surfers?)

DIAGONAL RUN
'SURFING DOWN THE LINE'

The coach should get the paddler to take off and gain as much distance along the wave parallel to the beach as possible before the wave breaks, the use of beach markers may help. Emphasise that increased speed equals greater distance. To improve:

🛶 Position the boat in the top third of the wave.

🛶 Trim forward.

🛶 Keep the paddle in front of you, with a sufficient gap between the shaft and the body, forward paddle if necessary. On steep waves the paddle may need to be held to the side.

🛶 Use edge to maintain height.

Photo 13 Diagonal run

▶ The Role Of The Stern Rudder

For the purposes of this chapter a stern rudder is a rudder stroke performed behind the hip. Depending on its purpose the stroke is varied or blended by either:

🛶 1. Placing the stroke further back or deeper.

🛶 2. Changing the angle of the blade.

🛶 3. Varying the distance from the back of the kayak.

The variety of the stroke has led it to be called a Low Brace Stern Rudder. We should already know that it is a dynamic stroke that is performed whilst the craft is travelling forward. Conversely the very act of using the stroke slows the craft down, it also tends to make the paddler lean back.

It is a useful stroke to have in the repertoire because it is essential in steering a kayak without edges and also sets up a good lower body position. However it can easily become a bad habit and takes skill to effectively use. It may be far better to coach the use of edges and forward sweeps to steer (especially at slow speeds).

Photo 14 Encourage the paddler to lean forward with the paddle and surf without using it.

CLIMB AND DROP

At 90° to the wave (facing the shore). Experiment with body trim. Lean forward to go down, back to slow down and therefore climb back up the wave.

▶ Whilst Tracking Along The Wave

The coach should set an exercise that makes the student go to the bottom and right to the top of the wave using edging, relaxing one leg whilst tensioning the other to edge up and down the wave to gain awareness, trim forwards to maintain speed.

▶ Optimum Trim

It is important that the paddler develops these techniques until they have developed 'optimum trim'.

Photo 15a *Heading for the beach*

Photo 15b *Punching out*

At this point the craft is in harmony with the wave, maximum speed is combined with effective trim to put the craft in perfect balance. No paddle strokes are needed, the craft held there by tensioning various muscle groups.

This position is the key to all other surf manoeuvres and it is vital that the paddler can replicate and return to this 'optimum' position with the least amount of effort. Only once the student has 'got this down' in long term memory should you move on to more advanced techniques.

EXITING THE WAVE

Used to get off the wave either because the wave is about to break or another surfer is in the way. There are two methods:

1. Flatten out and head for the beach.

2. Gain some speed and punch back out through the wave.

A power draw blade combination will help pull the boat through the wave if it breaks.

WIPE-OUTS

Following the inevitable wipe-out the paddler should adopt the crash position i.e. tuck in and put the paddle to the side. If the paddle gets hard to hold take one hand off the paddle.

The benefit of a ski is that the paddler can jump off prior to the wave and hold the foot straps.

▶ Rolling

Rolling is covered in depth in Chapter 15. The key points in surfing are to use a number of environment strategies:

Use the wave to roll up on, that is roll up on the same side as the incoming wave.

Hesitate so that you roll up between sets.

In shallow water use the bottom.

On a ski, taking one leg off the ski can assist the roll.

CHANGING DIRECTION

▶ Bottom Turn

This is a turn at the bottom of the wave, the speed that is gained from the drop down the wave enables

Photo 16 *Bottom turn* (see also Fig. 2)

the surfer to lean outside of the boat, engaging the rails, allowing an effective turn without loss of speed. When coaching the main emphasis is on getting the paddler to lean outside of the boat whilst maintaining forward trim to enhance speed, and engage the inside edge. The head should be looking to the top of the wave (future water). It is the head that is the pivot point paddle in the low brace stern rudder position.

The bottom turn is a complex manoeuvre and can be varied through:

 1. Position on the wave. There will be a 'sweet spot' to turn to give maximum speed however this may have to be sacrificed in order to make the section or to set up for a manoeuvre.

 2. Blade position. Initially the blade can be used to provide support but blade entry should be minimum to prevent loss of speed. To prevent spin-out master the use of edge. In more rounded boats pull in on the drive face of the blade, so that as you squeeze in with the back hand and lock the elbow, the boat shoots forward like a squeezed bar of soap.

TOP TIP

Many paddlers have trouble grasping the body extension required for the bottom turn . A physical guidance land drill will help (see Photo 8).

▶ Cut Back

Whilst mastering going along the wave the paddler may deliberately venture too far from the shoulder and will need to turn or cut back towards it (see Fig. 2).

Look where you want to go and twist the body.

Unlock the edge and steer using front sweep or stern rudder dependent on speed.

Maintain forwards trim.

Having returned to the shoulder the paddler can use the broken water to turn back to the green wave (known as a bouncer). When surfing back towards the shoulder, lift the nose and hit the broken part of the wave, to initiate the turn (towards the beach) and turn as above.

▶ Top Turn

A top turn follows a good bottom turn and the speed that this has induced and is performed in the

Photo 17 Cut back

upper part of the wave. It can also be used to stall the boat to regain the shoulder.

On the way back up the wave flatten the edge.

Look down the wave and twist the body.

Down wave stern rudder pushes away.

Trim forwards.

▶ ADVANCED SKILLS

Before attempting these the surfer must have mastered the concepts of speed and position on the wave and core manoeuvres outlined previously.

The nature of the moves are governed by the paddler. It is dependant on their speed, what the wave will allow and what they are trying to achieve, e.g. a stall, skid, pivot or carve.

RE-ENTRY, SLASH TOP TURN – OFF THE LIP

(See Title Photo).

This is where the paddler uses the breaking lip of the wave to turn back towards the beach similar to a top turn. The planning of the turn should take place prior to and will affect the nature of the bottom turn.

Pick a spot to attempt the re-entry.

Bottom turn accordingly.

Flatten the boat in relation to the wave face.

Once the feet have cleared the top of the wave look back down the wave and rotate the body.

Down wave stern rudder pries away (and acts as a pivot) whilst the hips push in the opposite direction.

Lean back and flatten the boat to land.

AERIAL

The ultimate top turn manoeuvre and extension of the re-entry (see Fig. 2).

- Requires speed and a steep vertical attack and the appropriate wave.

- At the top of the wave the beach-side blade powers and stays in the wave.

- Thrust forward with the hips.

- When the boat feels weightless, look back down the wave, twist the body, push away with and pivot around the blade.

- To land flatten the boat and lean back to keep the nose from diving or catching an edge.

To give optimum feedback as the coach, position yourself behind the wave and gauge the amount of boat that clears the top of the wave.

REGAIN, FLOATER

A regain is when the paddler regains another shoulder, this is when a section of wave breaks in front of their path. They can either surf around the section back on to the shoulder or, providing they have enough speed, float over the section ensuring they thrust the nose over the top of the white water.

- Create speed by using a bottom turn.

- Flatten the boat.

PADDLE OUT TAKE OFF

This allows the paddler to catch the wave in the pocket, whilst paddling towards the break. It requires a wave with a distinct shoulder, good timing and maximum speed (see Fig. 2).

- Paddle towards the shoulder, paddling throughout.

- As the nose of the craft is about to hit the white/broken water, lean back and flatten the hull.

- Twist the upper body down the wave (towards the beach) and then lean forward.

- Pry the back of the craft around using the white water and gravity to push/pull the nose down the wave.

- Keep the craft flat or even lift the down wave rail slightly as the turn progresses to avoid the rail from catching and tripping up the nose.

THE LINE UP

One thing I teach (borrowed from Jock Young) is to do with how we set ourselves up for the take-off. I teach a "Charc" as in the squirt boating term meaning Charging Arc. I feel that this can improve success and safety at the take-off. A Charc should provide the following:

- Vision
- Position
- And therefore, Precision

The idea being that if we paddle a slowly accelerating arc towards the take-off we can keep the wave's progression in view. We can tighten up or open out the arc and all the time the craft is gaining momentum. Using this method surfers will catch more waves in the place they want. Also the progressive acceleration means that boats are up and planing early and can then start steering early, i.e. less chance of being closed or pearled.

At a peak you can perform this as an inside or outside charc. One coming from deep, providing good vision for a bold take-off. The other works from a position of safety when we are concerned not to get caught too deep.

Ian Sherrington

Photo 18 Two different fin set-ups

USE OF FINS

Fins are used to prevent the craft's tendency to spin out or slide on the wave, i.e. they provide grip and directional stability in the turns. Providing they are set up correctly fins provide lift and thrust which therefore maximises the speed potential of the craft. The use of fins is best learnt through experience. Here are some guidelines:

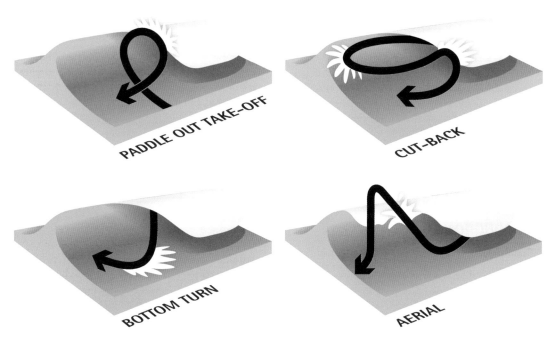

Fig. 2 Manouevres

Choose a site that will limit damage to fins whilst getting on or off the water.

Hone your edging skills first to understand the limitations of the craft.

Assuming a tri-fin set up, experiment first with one centre fin, then 2 side fins and finally all 3. Usually the third fin is positioned behind the side 2.

Remember that there is a trade off between increasing the number and size of fins and the increase in drag.

Generally, positioning fins further forward increases turning ability. Positioning them further back increases speed whilst making the craft stiffer.

"Within the parameters of normal use and assuming the fins are correctly foiled, the shape of skis is of little importance. On the other hand the area (or size) of the fins and the mounting position is of great importance. The fin shape, size and configuration can be varied to suit the rider and is a personal one. Most tri-fin sets use fins of even shape and size but sometimes a larger centre fin will be used when more drive in turns is required." **Roger Shackleton**.

The result is edge to edge surfing and full top and bottom turns.

TOP TIPS

• Practise with a purpose. All too often it is easy to get carried away in the surf environment and neglect what you are trying to practise.

• Allow time to reflect and evaluate your surfing.

• Get someone to observe you, even better video your surfing.

• Be self critical with relation to Body Boat Blade Brain.

• As a coach continuously update your coaching knowledge, e.g. transfer your paddling/observations between different craft.

• As paddlers we need to identify which factor (technical, tactical, physiological or psychological) is the rate-limiter at any stage in our development, e.g. knowledge of how to do a top turn, when to do a top turn, lack of upper body mobility or fear of wiping out.

• Examine your training programme to ensure that it has specificity and variety.

• Are your goals intrinsic process goals?

▶ SESSION PLANS

The following are suggested session plans for a variety of beginner/novice surfer groups. They will of course have to be tweaked to suit the conditions and the individual needs of your students, so remember to question and observe extensively to allow you to receive maximum information prior to session. There is no timescale specified for these sessions; it is dependent on the student, site, coach, weather, etc. Each session assumes appropriate risk assessment and warm-ups are covered.

With thanks to **Howard Jeffs** for his contribution.

INTRODUCTION TO SURF

An introduction to surf session for 2-3 star paddlers.

✔ Bongo slide, secure position, support and edge.

✔ Explore trim.

✔ Catch a wave.

✔ Concept of speed and position.

✔ Diagonal run using edge and downwave low brace stern rudder.

✔ Wave awareness and exiting the wave.

✔ Turning.

BEGINNER

Ensure a safe progression by firstly using the shore and soup zone.

✔ Edging on beach, maybe dry roll.

✔ Paddle parallel to soup practising edging and low brace.

✔ Take off at varying angles and move across the beach, play with edges, maintain forward paddling.

✔ Explore relaxing the edge to allow the kayak to turn whilst still preventing being tipped in.

✔ A common fault will be paddlers leaning back. Coach forwards trim.

✔ Coach turning. Head looking for future water, plant paddle, twist upper body, unlock edge. (Land drill useful).

▶ Progression

✔ Turns, zigzag across the wave, emphasis on moving along the waves. (Set up beach markers to help gauge distance covered.)

✔ If available use a small green wave, talk briefly about paddling out, wave selection and take-off.

The downwave stern rudder should only be used where the paddler is having difficulty preventing the kayak broaching. Explain that it is a short term fix due to it acting as a brake.

✔ TOP TIPS

• To help gauge both trim and edge it is beneficial to give a measurement or score. If student and conditions allow get the student to take one hand off the paddle and control the boat with their lower body.

• Another common fault is where the paddler holds the paddle shaft too close to their body. Get them to hold it a beach ball distance away from their chest.

PLAYBOATER, NO SURFING EXPERIENCE

Typically catches the biggest wave, heads straight for the beach, gets nailed, rolls up performs three 360's and the beginnings of a blunt, surfs all the way to the beach. Ask yourself do they want to change? They do not have to, however they might like to know what it is all about.

✔ Introduce the concept of the shoulder, watch the waves, the need to move along the wave.

✔ Catch 3 waves with a definite shoulder. Look where you want to go, ride the wave and get off before it breaks.

✔ Trim the boat to allow for better speed.

✔ Control the edges to allow you to climb and drop, explore the top and bottom of the wave.

✔ Use manoeuvres to maintain speed and maintain proximity to shoulder.

✔ Steer from the front of the boat, keep the paddle in front of you.

3 STAR PADDLER, CAN BOARD SURF

Typically will head for the green wave and a forming shoulder. Finds the boat slow and cannot manoeuvre it accurately.

✔ Reinforce transferable skills of edge and trim, and using the whole body to turn the kayak.

- Separate edge and trim into two different units.

- Concentrate on trim first to get the speed up.

- Focus on staying in the pocket and/or the upper portion of the wave, to maintain speed.

- Progress onto moving away from the pocket by forward trim, backwards trim to move back into the pocket.

- Finish exercise by good wave selection, positioning and venturing out onto the wall using forward trim and exaggerated edge control.

INTRO TO SKI

Introducing students to wave skis can be a very rewarding experience, especially if they are new to the sport and have never paddled before!

Unlike the kayak, the initial impression of entrapment under the deck is alleviated, however if you wish to have a productive and safe initial session then there are a few points to consider.

▶ Dry Land Drill

- Consider the fins, if they are fitted. Avoid damage by sinking them in the sand before getting into the boat, or do not use them.

- Get the paddler to sit on the ski. Adjust any footrest, straps and lap straps until you can fit a minimum of two fists underneath the paddler's knees and the deck. The seat should be grippy, use either a seat pad or surf wax.

- Ensure the foot straps are sufficiently tight enough to prevent the feet from sliding through them.

- Get the paddler to assemble the lap strap system (anything other than a 'fail safe' system is unacceptable!) and release a number of times. Try again with their eyes shut. Tip the ski on its side so there is now load on the system and repeat the above.

- Review the paddler's 'on water' clothing to ensure that nothing can catch or become trapped in the release mechanism.

- Show how to fit and remove ankle or paddle leashes. Some paddlers attach their paddle to the ski with a telephone cord type leash, others use their leash around their ankle to keep the ski with them if they bail out. (If they are not the coiled telephone cord type but the long surfboard style, then explain about looping the excess leash through the lap strap belt to avoid a large loop forming by the side of the ski and inevitably entangling the paddle! Also explain that this loop of excess leash should be stored on the opposite side of the lap strap release system.)

- Show the various options of carrying the ski to the water's edge.

▶ Flat Water Session

A flat-water (lagoon, lake, out back on a calm day) session is very useful to introduce the paddler to paddling a ski and later on learning to roll the ski. If this cannot be done use a sheltered section of the beach.

- A ski is notoriously tippy until it is moving. By keeping one or both legs either in the water or alongside the ski will assist balance until momentum is gained. This is a useful technique to provide balance even as an expert paddler. If the ski is still too tippy check it is the correct size for their height and weight, if not change it.

- In the beginning it may also assist balance to adopt a lower paddling style and slowly bring the shaft more vertical as momentum increases.

- Forward trim essential to keep the weight forward. If it doesn't hurt they are not far enough forward.

- Get them to paddle a short circuit until they can get both feet into the foot straps, without capsizing!

- Introducing the lap strap. Here coach must instil confidence and ultimate trust with their student, similar to an intro rolling session.

- Get the paddler to put their hands by the side of the ski and grip the rails. Tell them to remain in this position and you will pull them back upright after they have capsized.

- Get the student to capsize in their own time and pull them back up immediately! At this point you can usually judge how water confident they naturally are and how much more practice they need to gain personal confidence.

- Once you the coach are confident in their performance, revisit the lap strap as a surface exercise with their eyes shut. This time move into slightly deeper water, let the student capsize and release the belt. Reconfirm beforehand that if they have any problems, you are by their side, put their hands back on the rails and you will pull them back up.

- Let them practise until they can complete the task with confidence with you not close by.

NO SURF

Generally if there is enough wave to push the boat along you can coach surfing. In fact the student will really have to work hard to get the optimum speed out of their craft. Strategies will have to be sought for keeping speed throughout the turns e.g. forwards paddling, lots of forwards trim.

This may be the ideal time for the student to try a different craft such as a ski or a surfboard.

However, there will always be that occasion when everything conspires against the coach to give a flat day. Don't despair, here are a few options:

🖐 Practise forwards paddling technique, recreate the variation required for taking off on the wave, and strategies required for paddling out.

🖐 Choreograph imaginary runs, firstly on land and then on the water, use buoys to help.

🖐 Rolling, practise hesitation, and position awareness.

🖐 Rescues, being involved with the surf environment. The students should familiarise themselves with a range of techniques to rescue themselves and others. By practising first on flat water aids the progression through to bigger surf.

🖐 Practise swimming in full kit pushing the boat, carrying the paddle.

🖐 Practise shepherding a swimmer, giving encouragement.

🖐 Practise carrying a swimmer on the craft.

🖐 Practise using other lifesaving devices e.g. a torpedo buoy.

🖐 Practise rescuing and treating an unconscious swimmer.

🖐 If you still have time watch surfing videos. Get the students to practise their observation skills.

▶ Theory

Finally there is a huge chunk of theory that needs to be imparted as practically as possible:

🖐 Safety.

🖐 Craft type and design.

🖐 Equipment.

🖐 Weather and wave forecasting, beach morphology.

🖐 Tides and rips.

🖐 Etiquette, why not re-enact some examples on a beach wave?

These are just some ideas to be getting on with. Use your imagination, be prepared to learn from others and always be open to new ideas.

FURTHER READING

BCU Canoe and Kayak Handbook (Surf Chapter), BCU, Pesda Press, 0-9531956-5-1
Kayak Surfing, Bill Mattos, Pesda Press, 0-9547061-0-2
All about Wave Skis, Shackleton R, 1985, Surfside Press

NIGEL ROBINSON

'Nige' Robinson has paddled, surfed and coached throughout Europe, North America and Papua New Guinea. As well as a Level 5 Surf Coach he is a Level 5 Sea Coach and was formerly Coaching Development Officer for the Welsh Canoeing Association.

He now runs courses from his home in Pembrokeshire where he was born and brought up either close to or on the sea. That passion for the sea continues to grow whether kayaking, surfing or sailing.

17 WHITE WATER

The job of a white water coach has many elements, all interrelated and complex. The best analogy I can find is that of a juggler.

INTRODUCTION

As with everything on white water it's a question of understanding the components and how they relate to each other. The two main components are:

- Safety - And how the coach manages it.
- Fundamentals - Body, Boat, Blade, Background and Brain.

▶ SAFETY

One of the more frequent comments about coaching goes something like this…

'Steve Redgrave's coach can't row faster than Steve Redgrave'.

It is offered to justify why a coach need not be able to paddle. Well the statement is essentially correct, however Steve Redgrave's coach doesn't need to travel on white water to do his job. As a recreational white water coach you do!

To fulfil your role as a coach you must ensure the session is safe. That means being able to paddle if you are to supervise your students.

Safety, when you're a recreational white water coach is about:

- Your own skill.
- Your ability to make judgement calls about locations, activities and realistic goals for your paddlers.

The reality is that coaching is both a physical and mental activity for the white water coach. We know as coaches that if we are having to focus our efforts on performing physical skills it is very difficult to think about other things. You should not need to focus your attention on yourself when coaching. Your attention should only be on your students and coaching them.

This all means that you must be able to paddle!

KEY POINT

- Demonstration as a teaching tool and/or a method of feedback is a valuable tool. You have to be able to paddle to use this tool!

MASLOW'S HIERARCHY OF NEEDS

White water, especially for novices, can be a very scary place. The need to feel and be safe is one of the basic instincts (it's the foundation of Maslow's Hierarchy of Needs).

Not a lot of people know this but Maslow was a white water coach! He developed a theory identifying that fundamental elements of security, respect and self-worth need to be addressed if our students are to develop. Although primarily a motivational theory it is very applicable to white water coaching, especially when it comes to safety, security and learning.

If we interpret Maslow for the coach, he suggests that for people to be motivated (learn), they have to be physically secure (warm), fed and watered and their basic needs addressed. Once these are covered, the immediate physical safety needs to be addressed (the student should feel at no physical risk). He then states that psychological security needs to be covered (a positive, respectful learning environment without fear of ridicule). For learning to be possible Maslow also suggests that the learning environment needs to be one that recognises achievement and responds to it in an individualised way.

▶ Qualities Of The White Water Coach

In a nutshell the white water coach has to be friendly, caring and compassionate.

Empathise with your students, try learning something new yourself just to make sure you know how it feels.

You must be safe. You will need to be considerate, modest, patient, understanding, honest and able to do this in your boat from an eddy or from the bank if the conditions permit.

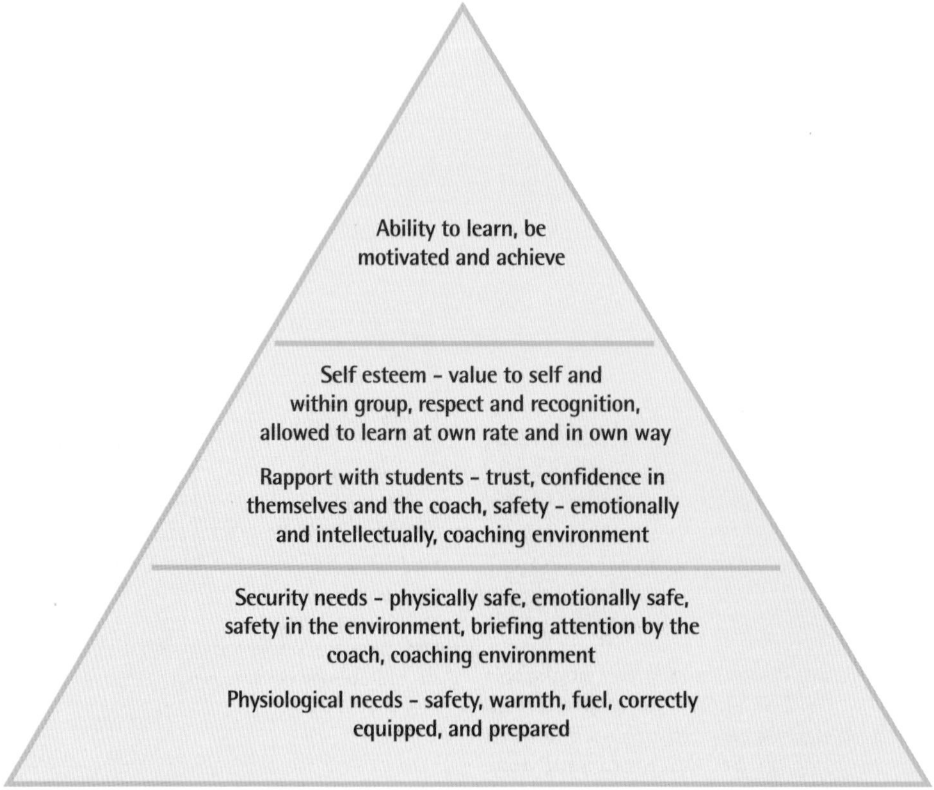

Ability to learn, be motivated and achieve

Self esteem – value to self and within group, respect and recognition, allowed to learn at own rate and in own way

Rapport with students – trust, confidence in themselves and the coach, safety – emotionally and intellectually, coaching environment

Security needs – physically safe, emotionally safe, safety in the environment, briefing attention by the coach, coaching environment

Physiological needs – safety, warmth, fuel, correctly equipped, and prepared

Fig. 1 Maslow, the White Water Coach!

Qualities of the white water coach:

- Friendly
- Caring
- Compassionate
- Considerate
- Modest
- Patient
- Understanding
- Honest

Photo 1 *An enjoyable experience*

You need to enjoy your boating, you don't have to be a zealot but you do need to be able to paddle and enjoy it! The passion and enthusiasm you have will inspire people to take part. You need to be, and appear to be confident.

The safety of your clients is about your judgement. The responsibility lies with you to ensure the immediate safety (what you do on the water), the long term safety (injury prevention, appropriate skill development for the future) and the overall well-being of your student (the rate of development and the nature of the coaching environment).

The safety of your clients is paramount. However maintaining your student safety is not simply a case of supervising them so closely that an accident can't happen.

► THE NUTS AND BOLTS OF SUPERVISION

Your supervision skills should be a natural process. (You should be able to paddle to ensure the CLAP principles are maintained on the grade of water you are coaching on. You will not be a bank-based coach).

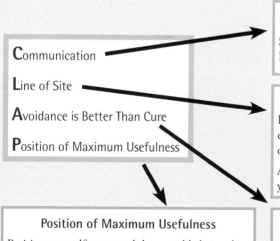

Communication

Signals - Left, Right, Come on down, Stop, Paddle harder, Help

Line of Sight

Ideally every paddler should have two attainable eddies between themselves and the river going out of sight.

Always endeavour to have your fellow paddlers in your line of sight.

Communication
Line of Site
Avoidance is Better Than Cure
Position of Maximum Usefulness

Position of Maximum Usefulness

Position yourself to control the most likely incident and manage it, rather than the most disastrous. This revolves around the idea that most incidents occur following a series of unmanaged minor incidents rather than a single catastrophe. Control the minor incidents to prevent the major.

Avoidance is Better Than Cure

a) Mutual support

b) Clean rope

c) Self, team, casualty

d) TRTRG (Talk, Reach, Throw, Row, Go)

Fig. 2 CLAP - the principles of white water safety

MAINTAINING A SAFE COACHING ENVIRONMENT

In particular your skills should extend to applying the 'A' (Avoidance is better than cure) very well because both safety and coaching will hinge on your judgement to maintain a safe coaching environment. Often the recreational coach manages risk rather than removes it. A great deal of this is about selecting a venue that the student finds challenging enough to develop, but not so intimidating as to prevent learning (it's an arousal level and a Maslow thing). Your students will not learn if they are too preoccupied with their own safety and security, but do need to be challenged in order to gauge their achievements. This is a hard level to find. The physical demands of white water may suggest quite a high level of arousal yet the cognitive processes of learning to paddle on white water may suggest a lower arousal level.

Photo 2 A safe coaching environment

▶ Striking A Balance

A balance has to be struck that creates a safe environment in which to work but is not so secure that it fails to challenge the paddlers. This can only be based on experience and is definitely not an excuse to compromise safety.

Consider safety when coaching as a balance: students' ability versus risk posed by the environment. The balance will change as your students improve, as the skills being coached develop, as the session progresses and the students become increasingly tired. There is a point at the start of a session when student ability and environment will be furthest apart and the coach will be more directly involved with practical safety issues. As the ability of the paddler develops the

gap closes, the coach has to ensure a gap remains suitable between ability and goal to ensure progress can be gauged by both parties. This can be achieved in one of three ways: changing the technique, changing the environment, changing both, all of which are appropriate and effective.

Broadly speaking:

⭕ Changing the technique creates a range of options that the paddler may select from when paddling.

Photo 3a Low brace turn breakout

Photo 3b Bow rudder turn breakout

⭕ Changing the environment can be used to create a robust individual technique, i.e one may be used in a greater range of situations or with greater reliability in the continually changing environment of white water.

⭕ Changing both allows you to explore the application of different techniques in different applications.

The skill of the white water coach lies in maintaining the arousal level at the appropriate point for each student in relation to the type of activity. If you want to develop physical components of white water skill you may want a higher arousal level. When refining

Photo 4a Spangle (Speed and Angle) breakout
Photo 4b Spangle breakout in different eddy

Photo 5a Bow rudder breakout into tight eddy
Photo 5b Spangle breakout into deep eddy

skills and when you want a variety in performance you will be working with a lower level, and when developing judgement/cognitive skills you will be even lower. As you move within this 'coaching zone' (an imaginary box defined by an upper limit 'scared' and a lower limit 'bored'), your practical supervision will change and a new balance has to be considered, that of observation versus supervision.

▶ Observation VS Supervision

When environment and performance are close, you need to consider the point at which the paddler or the group can take greater responsibility for their own safety.

Photo 6 Coaching from the bank, boat and equipment to hand.

The coach in the first photograph has elected to coach from the bank. His student's ability is high and he can handle the difficulty of the water easily, he has a reliable roll and the site has a large slow moving pool at the bottom. The rest of the group are of similar standard and can help in the unlikely event of a swim. The coach can watch the complex actions of the move, use a video and focus on the coaching rather than safety, the student is comparing, contrasting and thinking.

Photo 7 Coach in boat

The same coach and student are at a different venue. This time the site does not have a safe run-out and is busy. The coach has elected to coach from the boat and will move around to get the best possible supervision and observation. He will physically move around the eddy to ensure both roles are maintained, to physically time his feedback, maintain line of sight for supervision and observation.

▶ CHOICE OF VENUE

The choice of venue can lie with the coach or the student if they have sufficient experience. The environment for effective learning will be different for each individual and the student's perception of the security of the coaching venue will have a dramatic effect on the effectiveness of your coaching. The venue should challenge the paddler but not intimidate them. It should have scope for moves to be practised on both sides, have an area that allows for feedback to be provided and allow you to observe the paddler effectively.

Same coach, same student, different skill, different venue... different approach.

Consideration must be given to:

Feature - Does the venue have the kind of water/bank you need to teach the skills you have identified. Is it appropriate? An easier venue could be better than a hard venue. Is it consistent? How long will you work here? Will it be tiring for the students?

River downstream - What is downstream? Is it safe? Do you need to brief your students about it? What will you do if you need to deal with a swim, can you see or will you need to move?

Other river users - How busy is it? Tours and events tend to be very busy and are not the best place to coach or be coached.

Other paddlers and etiquette - The attitude of some paddlers would lead you to believe they must have learnt to paddle by the laying on of hands method. Unfortunately the 'wannabes' may not be patient or considerate to your students. A quiet word to explain or physically helping your student by appropriate boat positioning can help.

Other coaches - Talk to the other coaches using the site. This will make sure you don't get in each other's way. Don't move slalom gates if they're in use. Likewise don't encourage your group to queue jump. Keep an eye out upstream for downriver traffic. Perhaps you could use a different venue?

VENUE AND PRACTICE

We aspire to create a performance that is skilful, robust enough to be performed in a variety of places and that has solid foundations. To achieve this a white water coach should endeavour to use a variety of different venues and should be wary of overusing a single site as this leads to the development of 'narrow based' skill. Initially, as the foundation moves are learnt, it many be necessary to work a single site to generate a solid foundation of technique BUT at the earliest opportunity the venue should be changed to generate a robust basic model for the students' performance.

"Variety is the spice of practice"

The skill for the coach is in judging the impact of the venue on your student. This enables you to ensure the environment/task is pitched at the optimum level for the student and skills you are coaching. The impact of the environment cannot be overstressed because its effect can be catastrophic. I would consider the venue in terms of four elements:

Positive - The consequences of mistakes are not significant and the results achievable. The objective is to achieve, not avoid!

Understandable - The venue is clearly defined with the kind of features needed being easily recognisable by the students.

Realistic - At a level of activity that has a relation to the ability of the student.

Enjoyable - Not physically exhausting or boring.

PURE

Whether you're getting it right or wrong there are indicators the coach can pick up on:

Listen to your group - There should be conversation within your group. If you can't hear it they could be intimidated by the site. If the conversation is about what you've asked them to do it should be positive, you will need to keep a careful eye on performance. Try to encourage conversation by asking people to consider setting their own goals or using a reciprocal approach that has people working in pairs or threes, so they can watch and coach each other under your guidance.

Watch for changes in performance - If the performance level drops the site could be too difficult (expect it to fall initially as they get used to the site). If there is no improvement the site could be too much. You may not need to change the venue, you may get away with de-tuning the exercise initially. The intensity of the environment has the potential to occupy many aspects of the students' learning capacity; reducing the complexity of the exercise can sometimes help. A rule of thumb: capsize and roll or swim more than once and the exercise could be too hard, consider changing.

Watch for changes in behaviour - If the person who has been 'go for it' now becomes quiet and waits till last, the exercise or environment could be too hard. The quiet person now starts to ask loads of questions when they haven't in the past, consider changing the exercise for them. Are they asking if you think they'll be OK? This is because they have doubts!

Look at your students - Have they physically drawn back from you, are they pale, do they look scared or concerned. Possibly this is because they are, so don't ignore it.

▶ OBSERVATION STRATEGIES FOR THE WW COACH

Observation is the key skill for the coach. It doesn't matter how well timed, structured or delivered your feedback is if it's wrong! The quality of your observation and your understanding of what you are looking at is a foundation skill.

'Look and Listen'

The practicalities of observation must be considered. Often the best place to observe a performance is not the best place to ensure your student's safety. For the environment to be suitable for learning to take place there should not be a real risk to your students, so if you are working in an appropriate environment the bias can be towards the observation. Nevertheless, you should never neglect the safety issues of your role.

The act of observation will change a student's performance; formal observation will have the greatest impact, informal will have least. As a coach you will need to consider: what you actually see, what you don't see, and what you can't see.

What you actually see - With what you do see, look for several repetitions of similar actions, look for a root cause to a common problem before dealing with individual specific problems, i.e. look for common causes.

What you don't see - This is particularly important with informal observation strategies. It is easy for the paddler to do only what they feel comfortable doing, not what they don't feel good at doing (and it could be this that you want to coach). Sometimes the venue may not allow you to see some things. You may need to ask to see what you've missed, change a venue or move your observational position.

What you can't see - You will not be able to see the work going on with the legs within the boat or the amount of work the paddler feels they're actually doing. The only way to address this is to create a way in which the paddler can provide you with quantifiable answers to your questions.

Observation is like any skill… with practice its use will become refined and improve. The more we observe the more experiences we can draw on when we observe in the future.

We can classify our observation approaches into three broad categories: Analytical, Deductive and Holistic. A white water coach will use all three methods of observation, often at the same time (see Chapter 1).

▶ FOUNDATION SKILLS

Getting to grips with white water assumes a level of competency in foundation boat handling skills by the student. Without solid foundations none of the fancy stuff works. Flat water foundation skills are the basis for white water skills and white water foundation skills are the basis for freestyle skills. If you can't ferry glide you can't get to the wave to pull the moves, and if you can't ferry or break out you can't get back into the eddy. Not fashionable or 'new school' but true!

You could easily argue that the job of a white water coach starts on flat water. Some of the things we learn on the pond in preparation for white water aren't actually what we do on white water.

It is the weaknesses of the component parts that lead to the rapid onset of exhaustion in the novice paddler. The emphasis on foundation skills should be equal to the importance of understanding the impact of environment on their performance.

It's a Gestalt thing.

'The whole is greater than the value of the component parts.'

REVISITING FLAT WATER SKILLS

Accordingly the good white water coach should not be afraid to revisit some skills on flat water. It is primarily a presentation problem for the coach because many people want to be on 'the white stuff'. Hence the use of the term 'foundation' rather than 'basic'. More importantly, the coach will need to approach these skills with the same enthusiasm and in the same, student-centred manner. For these sessions to work the coach will need to consider the context of the skills being taught and placing them in context for the paddlers.

At a foundation skill level the coach will want to focus on balance, speed and direction. This will require the coach to consider an active posture for the paddler, i.e. one that has stability at a core level (strength from physical position) allowing muscles to remain relaxed and flexible, giving greater boat/blade control and better intrinsic feedback.

In a preparation for a white water pond-based session the coach will want to consider:

◎ How to balance the boat, being able to control the amount of edge a boat has, both when stationary and when moving. (These aren't support strokes… that's about being off balance!)

◎ To do the 'when moving' of the above, the coach will need to make sure the paddlers can propel the boat forwards and backwards, accelerate and maintain speed… all with the boat on edge.

◎ Finally, once proficient with the above foundation skills, the student will need to be able to steer the boat with the boat on edge and moving forwards.

Foundation skills first, specifics later.

▶ Consider The Context Of The Final Skill

This means the coach can often avoid strokes which are best taught wholly in context, i.e. bow rudder, because when breaking in and out the blade angle is set relative to the current, and the low brace turn where the angle of boat sets the angle of the blade to the water when breaking in (not by feathering the blade as we do on flat water).

Photo 8 The bow rudder in context.

The sweep, knee, brace combination is only suited to flat water and has subtle differences that do not work well when breaking in or out. Flat water is a good place to develop the skills to achieve balance, by edging through dynamic balance to leaning and to develop confidence in the legwork, bottom position and body movements to

EXERCISES – FLAT WATER PREPARATION FOR WHITE WATER

• *Paddling the Plughole:*

Aims: - Increase boat awareness.
- Increase boat control.
- Linking , modifying and blending strokes.

Place a buoy in a clear area of water. Paddle the boat in ever-decreasing circles in towards the buoy. Once at the buoy paddle out in ever-increasing circles without losing speed or control.

Set the boat into a skid, control the skid with a long power stroke. Gradually shorten the power stroke from the stern and allow the circles to tighten. When the skid is at its tightest start linking a bow draw to the front. For even tighter turns add a stern push away, creating a 'C' stroke. At its tightest keep the blade in the water in a continual movement.

Keep the boat moving.

To move out, add a little more emphasis to the forward power part of the stroke until the slice can be removed. Then lessen the correction at the stern; the radius of the turn will increase. To increase the radius further, lessen the bow draw until only the bow sweep remains. Gradually lengthen the sweep and bring it closer to the boat until it is a full-length power stroke and bring the boat onto a straight course with an effective stern sweep.

• *'Syncro' paddling:*

Aims: - To have fun.
- Encourage variety in strokes, length, shape, etc.
- To encourage thought about stroke choice.

Delegate a 'Team Leader'; this person is the main co-ordinator for this exercise and should be confident. Identify a short course that has three distinct 'legs'. A simple game of 'follow the leader' starts the ball rolling. Specify to the leader that they should include a certain variety of movements, 360° spins with sweeps, quick stops, four strokes in reverse, etc. The group should follow on straight behind each other. Once you've completed the exercise, pick a new leader and specify a new content to the route, more spins, sideways, etc. Rather than following 'line astern', attempt the whole course in a 'Delta' formation, leader at the front. Finally, identify another leader, redesign the course and its content and perform the whole course in' Diamond' formation.

Other variations include:

• *'Follow the Leader':* On a rocky shoreline or rapid.

• *'Custer's Last Stand':* With the leader in the centre, have the group circle and on the leader's command change direction, spin, draw in or out.

• *'North, South. East, West':* In a defined area specify a North side, South side, East side and West side. The team leader shouts out the point of the compass and the whole group have to move to that side. The boat should always be facing the same direction so forwards, backwards strokes and draw strokes can be used.

Photo 9 The brace often turns into a reverse sweep thus killing all the forward speed - not good!

achieve that. However, the tendency is for paddlers to create a turn on the flat with no edge and a brace that actually becomes a reverse sweep. On white water this kills all the speed and doesn't allow the boat to cross into or out of eddies. This is often why people miss eddies!

A true understanding of the boat handling skills is essential to understand the context of the technique if it is to become skilfully applied. It's the only way the coach can truly understand the end result and the goal-setting process.

► RECREATIONAL BOATERS ARE PEOPLE TOO!

The ability to surf a wave and move around it is essential. Learning how the boat reacts on all the different parts of a wave will develop a great understanding of positioning, and positioning is key to achieving the more advanced freestyle moves such as blunts, flip turns, donkey flips and a host of other tricks that are still being invented.

Ask yourself what motivates you to paddle white water? The answers will be as varied and as individual as you are. Our individual motivations may be varied but we can be sure that if people don't feel safe, enjoy the activity and enjoy the learning, their motivations and goals cannot be met. It's a Maslow thing.

It is probably unfashionable to say that some people have a natural aptitude for white water paddling, in the same way that some people have a natural aptitude for playing a musical instrument. This does not preclude people but it does mean that the coach needs to anticipate the kind of problems they are likely to encounter.

Some people will struggle with the continually changing and active environment. Others may enjoy the apparently unpredictable water but struggle with the subtle changes in technique required to control the boat. They may find it difficult to handle the concepts and principles of boat control and want specific techniques which are not the best overall answer. For some the actual speed can be too much.

FINDING OUT ABOUT YOUR PADDLERS

As the coach you will be building on something. Your observations will help, but coaching and learning are personal skills; it is people we teach after all! Take some time to find out a little bit about the people you are teaching. Name, age, what they do? What other sports they do? When did they last paddle... and what? How was it? Did they like it? What do they want from you? What do they feel they need to work on? When they've been learning new things in the past what worked best? What doesn't work? Listen to the answers, not just their content but also how they are presented.

DEVELOPING CONFIDENCE

Developing confidence can mean a great deal of things. Confidence is the key to white water. Simply doing lots of it will develop confidence. However, people will come to you because they want to develop that confidence more rapidly and without having it knocked back. This puts you in a privileged position and is one you should accept carefully. People will want to learn to be confident and you can coach that in the same way you coach any skill. People can lack confidence because they are new to the sport, have had an experience that knocks them back before skills are developed sufficiently, or because they haven't had their confidence topped up recently. This can be intrinsically via their own experience (i.e. they haven't been paddling recently or they haven't seen an improvement in their own performance recently) or extrinsically (they haven't been told they are doing well recently or they haven't seen themselves doing well recently).

Sometimes little things can knock fragile confidence. Two words have a big influence, *but* and *should*. The word *but* negates anything positive you've said before the *but*, and *should* implies there is a correct way to do something and therefore an incorrect, i.e. wrong way. Try to take *but* and *should* out of your coaching vocabulary.

Photo 10 *No such words as 'but' and 'should' in Loel Collins' Dictionary.*

What we do know is that the more predictable an environment becomes the less anxiety a paddler feels and the greater opportunity they have to pre-empt actions. This reduces fear and on the whole improves performance. This is why confidence comes from experience. We know judgement is based on experience and judgement for paddlers is having the experience to pick the right skills to paddle the rapid. We know that experiences have to be varied and positive but that this has to be gauged against negative experiences that are to some degree less successful. The role of the coach is to ensure those experiences are appropriate and safe. It's another one of those play-offs but here the balance is one of independence or dependence. As coaches we aspire for our students to be independent of us. Coach dependency can be a real problem but so can independence that comes too soon.

▶ Implications

When coaching the ability to read and understand white water, we need to take a very supportive and student-centred approach, one in which the students have ownership of the process and the information they are discovering. You know what you want them to find out and you ensure it's a safe environment, with you guiding the process. This is not and must not be exploratory because the safety issues will make it guided in nature, you must know what you want to achieve. Exploratory used poorly can be little more than an excuse to let the worst happen under the out-dated guise of 'character building'. Simply throwing someone into a stopper and then picking up the pieces isn't coaching. It's massaging your ego and destroying your students, and is not what we do!

▶ UNDERSTANDING WHITE WATER

The clue is in the name! White Water Coach. The biggest single step!

Many people, when they first sit on moving water literally cannot make out the different parts of the river. To many novices the banks are dry, the river is wet and the water is flowing downstream, and that is the limit of their understanding. As a consequence, choice of venue becomes vitally important, not simply to ensure an appropriate teaching/ learning physiological environment, but in terms of the easy identification of features and the physical details of the site.

'Eddy, chute, eddy, just ain't enough!'

For instance at a basic site the coach will want to explain:

- The location of eddies.
- The location and direction of eddy lines.
- The location and direction of chutes.

- The direction the water moves within the chutes and within the banks.
- The waves and what they mean.
- The direction the water is moving in each of these features.

The coach will need to develop strategies to enable him to do this, both from the bank and from the boat.

COPING WITH RIVER MOVEMENT

Many paddlers initially struggle with the speed of a moving river. This stems from the need to appreciate the fact that, even if the paddlers do nothing, the river is still moving. Developing confidence and understanding of the speed of the water can be approached very effectively by drawing analogies with the paddlers' other experiences. Skiing, mountain biking, driving, all work and are often a good place to start. People who lack these previous experiences or who have struggled with this aspect of their other sports may need a more methodical approach. Illustrating the speed with a demonstration and even experiencing the movement by having people float past a point are useful strategies. Having people paddle up current and down current can be used to start to develop a feel and appreciation of the forces involved. Any warm-up should allow the student to experience the site in order to reduce the impact of the environment on the paddler.

▶ Video Game

An analogy of a video game works well for people who are increasingly using the TV. Encouraging the paddler to sit in their boat and imagine this action as it passes them by puts the movement into a context many people will understand.

▶ Dancing On The Bank

Walking or dancing on the bank works well. People can throw a log in the water and walk opposite the log on the bank. The same approach can be used for complex sequences. These are aspects of visualisation and physical rehearsal. Two aspects must be considered, firstly the paddler must have some experience in order to visualise effectively (even in this rudimentary way) and the emphasis must be on position rather than stroke sequences (particularly with inexperienced paddlers).

▶ Variations

The limitless variations of the white water environment will force the coach to teach in terms of the con-

EXERCISES ON WAVES

• *Off at a Tangent*

Aims: - Illustrate the effect of waves on a boat.

    - Develop understanding of moving water.

    - Illustrates the principle of gravity (water always runs downhill).

    - Use of a wave to move a boat.

Find a small diagonal breaking wave, ideally crossing the current at 45°. Identify an obvious marker immediately below the wave to act as a reference point to gauge the results.

Run a comparative session that encourages the paddlers to hit the wave in different ways to examine the results (Fig. 3).

• *Zigzags*

Aims: - Illustrate the use of waves to cross current.

    - Develop reading water skills.

    - Develops timing of strokes.

    - Develops use of head and body in rotation.

On a series of standing waves, from the eddy on one side get the paddlers to 'ferry glide' across the wave into the opposite eddy. The key principle is to move onto the wave at its lowest point (in the trough).

Once achieving the initial cross with no paddle strokes on the wave, encourage the use of a stern rudder on the upstream side. Plenty of upstream edge. Get the paddler to surf back to the opposite eddy in that position. As they cross the eddy line get the paddler to raise the front hand and look back on to the wave. 'Visualise sliding your bottom away from the paddle'.

Once achieved, aim to paddle back onto the second wave and then repeat onto the third and then the fourth.

Aim to get the turn closer to the wave each time by reducing the strokes needed to get back on to the wave and starting the sequence on the eddy line and even before whilst still on the wave. The final result is that the surfer can surf and change direction on a single wave.

• *Waltzing:*

Aims: - Water awareness.

    - Timing strokes.

    - Accuracy.

    - Forwards and reverse work.

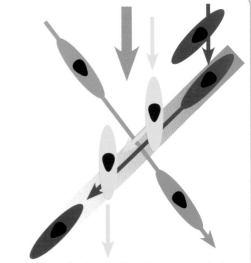

Fig. 3 Plan of a diagonal breaking wave with the path of different approaches.

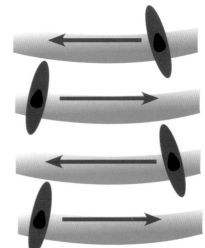

Fig. 4 Zigzags

On a rapid with clearly defined eddy lines, pick a sequence of eddies. The exercise is to 'tickle' the top third of each eddy with one end of the boat. As the boat crosses into the eddy the paddler uses a gentle opposing sweep to help spin the boat and keep it in the current. The boat re-enters the current facing the opposite direction. The paddler then has to put the downstream end of the boat into the next eddy and be spun round to face the original direction again.

This exercise can be combined with ferries and also only done with single strokes between eddies. Even eyes shut works in some places.

EXERCISES ON WAVES – CONTINUED

• *Mogul Turns*

Aims: - Illustrates the appropriate place to turn in waves.

- Develops timing of strokes.

- Develops water reading skills.

- Illustrates the 'free end principle'.

On a series of standing waves, create an exercise in which people float from the top through the waves. Allow people to do this a couple of times, eyes shut, eyes open, facing upstream, facing downstream and across the current.

Once the paddlers have become confident at that site, run a comparative exercise in which the paddlers are encouraged to try to turn the boat on the top of the waves and then in the troughs.

The paddlers may need several runs but the points should be illustrated that easier turns happen when the boat is on the crest of the waves whilst the ends are free, as opposed to being in the trough of the waves when the bow and stern are trapped by the wave upstream and downstream.

Once demonstrated try to turn 360° in 3 waves, then in 2, then on 1.

Try turning the boat to face one bank then the other. Turn on one wave above an eddy to create the ideal angle of attack.

• *Choreography*

Aims: - To combine previous exercises.

- To put exercises into realistic practice.

Design runs down a rapid that meet the following criteria:

1. Changes in direction.

2. Changes in speed.

3. Changes in height.

4. Fluency.

5. Use of the whole rapid.

6. Variety of movements.

Allow the paddlers to choreograph their runs, discuss what meets the criteria best and how they will achieve it. Use visualisation to enhance the run, then walk down the bank performing the run, and finally perform the run.

cepts and principles for effective paddling rather than set piece moves. The initial building blocks must be in place and these must be introduced within the context of the principles that underpin good white water technique. As the environment changes the principles will remain the same even though the exact technique may differ. It is important to reference the techniques back to the principles you wish to illustrate. Part of this process will be for the coach to accept variation in performances, and will require the coach to consider the performance in terms of how the form presented could be applied in other environments and gauged relative to the principles rather than technique. This positive and supportive approach actively encourages a variety in performance, all of which we want to achieve as a coach.

A vital skill for any paddler and any student is the ability to read water from the boat. The impact of continually getting out of the boat to examine the site or the rapid is significant, and the value of being able to spot a clean and predictable line on moving water will make exercises work and illustrate techniques as being applicable. A few simple points from the coach may allow you to move more fluently between venues, run

simple single drops and improve the paddlers' ability to anticipate what will happen to them. Simply verbalising your thought process about line selection is a good place to start, and simple concise points that are clearly visible can be highlighted.

The coach, using his line to demonstrate the effect of the water, is a particularly good tool and works well. However, the key to learning to understand moving water is for the student to experience its effects.

Horizon lines mean a change in gradient and the steeper the rapid the closer you will have to get to the top of the rapid to inspect it. Mist below the horizon line is a bank inspection. Bits of splash and spray with no sequential standing waves need to be avoided.

Water within a wave will always move to the downstream end. Therefore the water will have that effect on you. Given a safe environment, an exercise that has the paddlers hitting diagonal waves at different angles will clearly illustrate the points. Setting sequences that specifically use the troughs of standing waves or even just the faintest hint of a trough can achieve some smashing results and if combined by reducing the number of strokes used to complete a move will rapidly confirm that using the water is best.

▶ Looking At Features

Rather than looking for individual features look for sets of features. Standing waves should come in lines and the direction of the line is the direction the current is moving. An isolated standing wave is best avoided. A horizon line followed by an area of flat water is often a stopper; if that water is aerated the point at which the white area is furthest downstream is often the line. If there is no bubble line to make the point, get out and look. If the water is unaerated, get out and look. If in doubt, get out and look.

Look at how the water moves. Anything that is not constantly formed is doubtful, so get out and look.

▶ PLANNING A SESSION ON WHITE WATER

Increasingly the physical fitness of paddlers will limit the duration and content of the coaching sessions. The pace of each session, the structure of the whole day, and the nature of sessions in the long term will need to be considered. Paddlers will be unable to learn effectively if they are tired, indeed it often contributes to the 'grooving in' of poor technique and should be avoided.

THE PACE OF THE SESSION

White water paddling can be very exhausting but is particularly tiring if you are being coached. The enthusiasm of the coach can often lead to repeated cycles of practice that rapidly become tiring. With many people a good warm-up will be tiring and the coach must ensure that the warm-up is considered as part of the session. The coach should guard against over-tiring the paddler by structuring the practices so that the site allows for rests and enables the paddler to take 'time out'. Overusing a site does not allow for the variety required in effective practice when skills are being refined, and also adds to the onset of boredom which will lead to tiredness and demotivation. The coach should keep a careful eye for unexplained drops in performance, people sitting out. Listen to people when they say they feel tired and watch for negative body language. A useful strategy is to deliberately change the exercises at a given site so it is not repeated more than 3 times and after 3 different exercises move to a different site. Having said that, one single go is not enough so the coach will need to strike

the happy mid-ground. A single session of around 90 minutes would be productive maximum.

Once they begin to get tired, the ability of your paddlers will diminish throughout the day. A simple structure can be applied as a guide. A two-session day can be used with paddlers who are taking on strenuous sessions or are unfit. A 90min session with a good rest with water and food, followed by a 60min teaching session can work. A three-session structure can work with fitter paddlers, 90min (teaching), break (water and food), 60min (coaching of skills from session 1) rest (water) followed by a 45min supervised paddle with minimal input (only when requested from paddler).

▶ COACHING ON THE MOVE

Increasingly, white water coaching as a discipline has two sides, the 'park 'n play' and the 'play the river'. Much of the specifics mentioned in this chapter will apply equally to both aspects of the coach's role, however it is worth considering coaching within the context of a river journey. For many people who learn to paddle on white water, it is not the paddle waggling and gymnastics of freestyle that attract them, it is the travelling that they aspire to. An important role for the white water coach is that of coaching within the journey and that does raise some issues for the coach that are best considered within a guiding/coaching framework.

In the long term the coach will want to address the actual fitness of the paddler and will need to structure the sessions to develop the fitness required (see Chapter 2).

This is no 'big thing'; the context of coaching within the journey can be different to that of a site-based session in something as simple as the fact that your paddlers will predominantly be facing downstream rather than upstream. This literally changes the paddler's view of the river and their ability to interpret the water can be lost.

The trip will take longer if you are going to coach en route. The river should be predominantly within the ability of the group but you should not discount a river that has sections at the limit of your group or above. Ideally these sections should be short and positioned along the trip as the 'highlights' of the trip or act as punctuations between sections. Sometimes the things we take for granted are the kind of things people want; these are not so much coaching points, more practical points or top tips. For instance, ensuring the clothes are in the car at the bottom of the river and making sure someone has the car keys for that car.

Photo 11 Rapid seen from high on the bank

Photo 12 Same rapid seen from boat level

So our job as the coach can also be to consider the practicalities of doing a trip, its planning, and its problems. Practical hard skills like navigation, map work, accident procedures, river strategies, setting up a shuttle, getting a weather forecast, understanding it, access and egress and living from a boat all fall within our remit as coaches. Safety, rescue and river etiquette are of particular importance.

Choice of river can make a big difference. Consider the weather for the day. Trying to coach on a river that is exposed and being hit by a gale is almost impossible so pick a section of river that could be sheltered. The access and egress points should be considered; a long hard carry out at the end of the day will undo all your good work. Likewise the hardest rapid at the end of the day can mean ending the trip on a low point if someone swims, so pick a section where the hardest point is not right at the end and if you have time make sure you finish the river on a high note. The trick is to know the river or have good guidebook and map info at hand so you can plan ahead.

The pace of the day will need to be watched. It is very easy to coach eddy to eddy; this overloads your paddlers and takes most of the day to cover 2km on a 5km trip, leaving you to rush the rest. Here you need periods of coaching on the fly, set exercises to work on and even simply free paddle, with paddlers working to individually identified goals. The trick is to vary the pace and content of the sessions for the individual. This does mean for the coach that you will be working intensively throughout the day because as one person needs some 'down time' the next will possibly need your attention.

The great thing with coaching on journeys is that the environment will vary as you travel downstream. It is really easy to miss things that would be good to coach and likewise easy to spend too much time at one point when the better spot is just round the bend. The trick is to use everything once, good things twice and excellent things three times but then move on. Some things you can only use once and the coach will need to plan and brief some things very well prior to the actual exercise. Some rivers by their character are continuous and the coach will end up working via sequences and circuits. Other rivers may be more pool-drop in nature and the coach could run a series of linked individual sessions.

LEADING AS A COACHING STRATEGY

A good river for coaching will have both. The trick here is for the coach to know the river well but also for the coach to have lots of different exercises that he can use on the river. Coaching your way down the river maintains control as effectively as any formal leadership style. The coach will want to consider the value of different guiding and leadership strategies from the coaching perspective.

For instance, basic eddy hopping is a great way of developing the skills for breaking in and out and river reading. The difference is that the coach will select eddies on the basis of coaching rather than leadership (i.e. CLAP). See Chapter 15 Sea Kayaking for some very transferable ideas on the teaching of leadership.

The eddy-hopping type exercises prove to be very useful for the coach because they enable a variety of different river skills to be covered and specific issues to be addressed. For example:

Eddy-hopping sequences can be followed that use water features, the troughs of waves, diagonals, etc.

A paddler has difficulty understanding the need to have an angle of attack into eddies, so the coach can set an eddy-hopping sequence that uses alternate sides, has wide crosses or returns to the mid-point of the current.

A paddler has difficulty identifying eddies. The paddler can actually lead but the coach joins them in each eddy to discuss/examine possible strategies before the paddler moves off to the next area. Simply verbalising the process you employ can be very effective as long as you know what you're doing!

Using an eddy-hopping system that relies on coordinated signals ensures the paddlers start to pick eddies that have line of sight with each other.

To refine coping strategies how about playing a game where each person has to catch the next possible eddy to the one chosen by the previous paddler.

The options are actually endless and these are not definitive. They all maintain supervision by coaching rather than 'leading' and they all make progress downstream. They all stem from common practice for river runners.

FURTHER READING

White Water Safety and Rescue - 2nd Edition, Ferrero F, Pesda Press, 2006, 0-9547061-5-3
Kayak Rolling, Collins L, Pesda Press, 2004, 0-9531956-8-6

LOEL COLLINS

Loel Collins was formerly the Director of the National White Water Centre, Canolfan Tryweryn and is now the head of the canoeing department at Plas y Brenin, the National Mountain Centre. Loel is one of the UK's leading coaches.

His passion lies in coaching white water skills and exploring and travelling in both kayak and canoe. He has paddled and taken part in first descents in many parts of the world including Papua New Guinea, Pakistan and Iran.

18 CANOE SLALOM RACING

3... 2... 1... Go! Ten strokes to the first drop – jump right, land left and drive hard at left pole on gate one – aim to flick off big wave en route to gate two – wetter than intended but still OK – high into gate two upstream and squeeze out tight – good start – track hard across river – shoulder under right pole on three – roll off diagonal – dry bows and a touch of upstream edge on the lift into upstream four – sweep fix and away – arms feel strong – fight to hold a straight line for tricky offsets five and six – just OK... late on the jump into seven and lose touch with entry pole – half a sec gone but fast exit helps retrieve – stuff high into upstream eight on single stroke – sneak out tight and we're back on track – pull hard away – first crunch move – tight offset nine to eleven needs a hard pivot at nine just to make the full spin at ten – 'tight as', but great exit through eleven – halfway... fast and clean so far!

This is canoe slalom racing 2006 style...

The Olympic discipline of Canoe Slalom has to be one of the most spectacular and exciting canoeing disciplines for paddlers and spectators alike. Racers must negotiate a time trial course of up to 25 gates as quickly as possible with penalty seconds added if they hit or miss a gate. Depending on the level of competition, races are decided on either a single run, the aggregate of two runs or the best of two runs and can be held on any kind of water from the flat right up to grade 3+.

▶ So What Makes Slalom Different?

It's a time trial event that races over a different course every time. Each new race is a new challenge of river characteristics, river levels and gate placements that racers have to pit their wits against and 'do battle with'. Good course design will be a test of the physical, the technical, the mental and the tactical, as well as being just cool to paddle.

▶ Why Cool?

In the most basic sense, slalom takes all its moves from a white water river play environment, linking selections of them together into measurable tests graded for whatever ability levels are involved. It also has endless choices and variables.

It offers a great way to develop boat, blade and physical skills as well as watermanship, whatever your paddlesport discipline. It demands 'on the spot' decisions and reactions to all manner of unexpected situations, requiring a determined focus and an instinctive 'flair' for athletic ability, at times using the water, at others combating and defying it.

Who Can Race And In What?

Canoe Slalom UK has a national ranking system split into divisions for all abilities.

> **There are 4 individual classes, 2 for kayak and 2 for canoe to choose from:**
>
> • Men's Kayak (MK1)
>
> • Women's Kayak (WK1)
>
> • Men's Canoe Singles (C1)
>
> • Men's Canoe Doubles (C2)
>
> • All 4 cater for junior right through to veteran competition.

In addition to the above classes there is Slalom Team Racing where three boats race together over the same course, timed from first starting to last finishing. It is possibly the most visually impressive, spectacular and FUN class of them all.

▶ GB Slalom Medals

Over the past thirty years Great Britain has developed a winning history in Canoe Slalom, consistently placing its paddlers in the world top ten since the early 1970's, and this against all the odds considering the lack of consistent and accessible white water on offer. GB paddlers have developed reputations for being technically excellent and physically well prepared. The major world opposition comes from the Alpine countries: France, Germany and Italy, also the recently emerging Eastern block countries of the Czech Republic, Slovakia, Slovenia, Poland, and the USA, Canada and the Australians.

▶ Artificial Or Natural?

Increasingly since the 1980's artificial slalom courses have taken over from natural river sites. An Olympic sport 5 times since 1972, three of these five courses have been run on man-made channels with pumps recirculating the water. Advantages here are that they can be built near large centres of population with the design of the river features absolutely controlled. With multi-user features coming as standard this has made a big impact

on 'access' with rafting, freestyle and recreational users benefiting as well as world class slalom racing.

▶ Rule Changes And Links To Freestyle

Over 1989 - 2004 the running time for international canoe slalom dropped by 50% from an average 200secs to somewhere in the region of 85-95secs. Improvements and adjustments both in the rules and in boat design have resulted in a much more attractive event for paddlers and spectators alike. More of each race is on white water and at many venues spectators can see most of the race from start to finish without moving.

Over this same period a typical slalom boat has changed shape dramatically with the biggest change coming in 2005 with a cut in the minimum length of 0.5m. The full impact of this has still to be felt but already technique and the possibilities for new moves are changing slalom forever and interestingly bringing slalom moves more into line with freestyle techniques.

▶ GENERIC DEVELOPMENT IN SLALOM

LONG TERM PADDLER DEVELOPMENT (LTPD)

Slalom is committed to the best principles of LTPD which is crucial to the development of a balanced and successful slalom athlete, in it for the 'long haul' whether it be for elite performance or 'canoeing for life'. The development of a robust white water skill base does not happen overnight and can only be achieved through a well structured, varied and wide ranging programme commitment over a period of years.

The importance of the FUNdamental movement skills and their transfer into basic paddling during the Paddlesport Start and Development stages is key to the development of a young slalomist and provides the bedrock to developing moving water skill, white water confidence and gate technique that underpin later success in slalom. The key 'slalom window' here is predominantly in the age range 9-15 years. If variety of canoeing 'movement experience' is missed out on in these years, the ceiling of potential will have been lowered and is virtually impossible to make up at a later stage.

We are not talking slalom competition here. Experience indicates that a range of experiences involving WW touring, play, games, polo, surf, canoe as well as kayak, in addition to short course mini-slaloms and the new X Stream Challenge opportunities can all provide essential and relevant multi-discipline input and make for a natu-

ral LTPD progression, an 'in house benefit' for canoeing that not many sports can match.

As we move on into this chapter to focus on the specific slalom development of the 'Training to Train' & 'Training to Perform' stages - namely Technique and Skill Development, Physical Development, Planning & Mental Skills Development, Tactical and Racing Skill Development - it is important to be aware of the generic template of the recommended training progressions as they apply from the FUNdamentals stage to the onset of puberty by the end of the Start and Development stages. Areas not covered here will almost certainly lead to remedial work or compromises at a later stage.

 See Chapters 1 and 10 and BCU LTPD document.

▶ GOAL SETTING AND EFFECTIVE PLANNING

Success in slalom cannot be achieved without good goal setting and planning skills. The following points underline how they underpin the whole slalom coaching process and are key factors in developing performance for both coaches and paddlers.

- They allow the paddler to take responsibility.

- They promote a philosophy of 'athlete driven... coach steered' and will define a coach-athlete relationship.

- They underpin any evaluation and planning process.

- They support the reviewing, replanning and restating process.

- Whilst being essentially individualised they can also have a powerful 'team effect', tapping into group support systems not normally associated with either slalom or paddlesport.

Goal setting and planning - see also Chapter 1, pp. 19, 35-36; and Chapter 3, pp. 3-5.

Goal setting can also have a positive impact on mental skill development by:

- Boosting confidence

- Enhancing motivation

- Reducing anxiety

- Focusing attention better

- Promoting a positive attitude and self image.

See also Chapter 3 'Planning & Mental Skill Development'.

MAIN GOAL TYPES WITH SLALOM EXAMPLES

▶ Outcome/End Goals

End goals are the 'end result' or the dream.

Examples of these might be to win, to medal or to make national team selection. They can be motivating and inspiring and are essential and necessary over the long term. Everyone should have them – coach and paddler.

The downside with end goals is that they are not always in the athlete's control and can therefore be demotivating and create anxiety when not achieved or are perceived to be unrealistic.

▶ Performance Goals

Performance Goals are measurable benchmarks linked clearly to outcome goals and process goals.

Examples of these might be beating previous personal best times on a time trial / set course or posting a set number of clean runs over an identified period. In essence they are easily measurable, personal benchmarks within a paddler's control.

▶ Process Goals

Process Goals are task-related, focussing directly on the 'individual how' and they should relate directly to the 4 core elements: Technical, Physical, Mental and Tactical requirements of reaching Performance goals.

Achieving process goals should always be 'Within the paddler's control'.

Examples might be:

- Developing specific stroke sequences or key blade understanding.

- Developing a robust race day routine that you own.

- Improving balance/stability on a particular lift in the weights room.

- Improving the number of competitive first attempts.

GETTING THE BEST OUT OF YOUR GOALS

- Revisit goals regularly.
- Constantly seek to link outcome goals to performance and process goals.
- Face up to replanning where necessary.
- Restate for motivation and encouragement.
- Seek a group 'buy in' for a powerful dynamic and motivating effect.
- Allow the athlete to take responsibility.
- Maintain a constant focus on what 'performing well means for the paddler'

▶ FUNCTIONAL STABILITY AND FLEXIBILITY FOR SLALOM

Acknowledging this key area of slalom development – BCU World Class Slalom has followed up the programme of research instigated by Sprint Racing and Joanne Elphinston (see Racing Chapter). Outlined below are the key areas relevant to slalom and short boat WW paddling in general.

To follow up this section properly it is essential for coaches to attend a L1 Functional Stability workshop and obtain a copy of the CD resource "Functional Stability for the Paddling Athlete" (info for both on the BCU website).

The general thrust here is to develop a more functional approach to conditioning, in turn enabling a more holistic approach to a paddler's overall strength, power and flexibility development.

Slalom coaches are in the business of preparing paddlers to carry out a high skill, whole body activity with complex linked movements occurring from hands through to feet. A common misapprehension, amongst short boat paddlers in particular, is that what goes on under the spraydeck is 'not that important'. Nothing could be further from the truth.

Functional stability for paddlesport is important for two reasons:

 Performance optimization – best results for least effort.

 Reduction of injury risk – body structures working in their optimal range and position.

KEY AREAS

It is often impossible for athletes to develop beyond certain points technically - in training and in competition - without a sound level of functional stability in the following two key areas:

- **Shoulder** - If the paddler cannot lock the blade at the catch and hang onto that blade without the shoulder area stability breaking up, they will not be able to improve their skills and maximise good technique and performance when racing in any discipline.

- **Trunk** - If the trunk area is weak and unstable, then the power generated by the body will not be transmitted into either effective forward movement of the boat or the dynamic rotational manoeuvres required in slalom and the other short boat disciplines.

Functional stability can also influence speed, power, strength, flexibility and technique and should form an integral part of a slalomist's preparation from the very earliest stages. Paddlers with poor functional stability will borrow muscles whose prime role is in movement to prop up their stability. These 'movement muscle groups' will fatigue early because they are also heavily involved in stabilising the body rather than just in moving the boat.

▶ ACHIEVING CORRECT POSTURE FOR PADDLING KAYAK

By Tim Deykin - Lead Physiotherapist, BCU World Class

This section will focus on the key areas of posture that go into paddling a kayak efficiently. The origins of this work are in slalom boats but there are wider implications for all kayak paddlers especially those of closed cockpit boats where the fittings dictate a tight body position with the knees low and spread apart.

KEY AREAS

The kayak paddling position should show:

- A mild curve in upper back (not hump).
- A shallow hollow in lower back.
- The pelvis in neutral or anterior tilt (forwards).
- An overall impression of sitting tall and upright but with gentle lean forwards coming from hips (not from back).

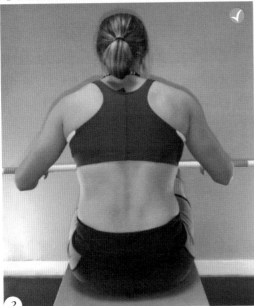

Photos 1 and 2 Correct kayak posture

To achieve this position (form) you need to be able to anteriorly tilt pelvis.

This can be limited by three parameters:

1. Tight shortened muscles.
2. Weak lengthened muscles.
3. Poor equipment selection (ergonomics).

The predominant reason in over 90% of cases is parameter 1: Tight, shortened or stiff hamstrings (posterior thigh muscles).

Next but equally as important is 2: Weak core stability exacerbated by:

Weak lower back muscles.

Weak postural abdominal muscles.

Weak gluteal muscles (buttock).

For closed-deck kayaks short, tight or stiff adductor muscles (inner thighs) or stiff hips may also pose a restriction in anterior pelvic tilt (i.e. with feet together and knees out to side).

Finally 3: Poor equipment selection, in particular:

Seat fittings.

Foot rest for toes only and not heel.

Back support or back strap to support anterior tilt of pelvis.

Deck or cockpit is too low for amount of flexibility in hamstrings, adductors and hips.

COMMON FAULT STAGE ONE

Due to any one or combination of the above, the pelvis cannot be maintained in an anteriorly (forwards) tilted or even neutral (vertical) position for forward paddling. Posterior tilt of pelvis sets lower back into a forward curve rather than a shallow hollow, and the upper back continues with an increase of its curve into a marked hump.

The natural position of the head and neck on top of the upper back in this position would be looking down into your lap, so to look forwards in the direction you're going, you have to lift up your head, creating an angle between the back of the head and upper back. (Equivalent of sitting upright in a chair and looking right up at the ceiling!) The effect is of the head and chin poking forwards.

As the upper back is no longer upright but curved forwards, the shoulder blades which follow the line of the upper back are also angled forwards, so the paddler tends to hunch up the shoulders to effect the stroke. This has the resemblance of the arm action of climbing up a ladder.

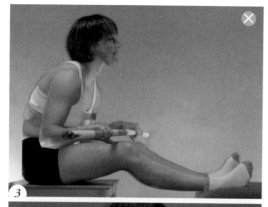

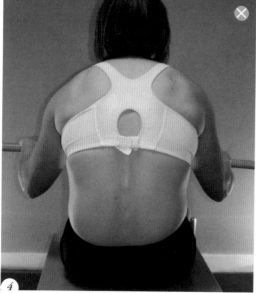

Photos 3 and 4 Stage one fault

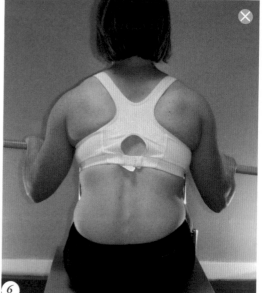

Photos 5 and 6 Stage two fault

COMMON FAULT STAGE TWO

It is suspected that this arises as a result of a failed attempt to correct the Stage One fault, when the paddler tries to sit up straight and not slump.

The muscles of the hamstrings are very large, and can be considered as a very stiff set of springs, pulling on their attachment to the sitting bones which in turn pulls the pelvis into a backwards tilt. The lower back muscles in comparison (and the core stability muscles also) are much smaller and thinner in size, and can be considered comparatively as weaker springs. As in the Stage 1 fault they cannot maintain the shallow hollow in the lower back against the strong pull of the hamstrings.

However, your upper back muscles tend to be functionally stronger than your lower back muscles,

and can pull harder into extension, so much so that the mild hump disappears and it becomes a shallow hollow instead! Don't forget that this is happening whilst the lower back has changed its hollow to a curve! So consequently the lower back is pulled back into its pelvic tilt whilst the upper back compensates and hollows out.

It gives the overall appearance of being upright, but the two curves of the back have been reversed, limiting optimal function of the back into rotation, and changing the quality of the platform upon which the shoulder blades work, so limiting the effectiveness of the transmission of force from paddle to trunk to boat.

This tends to be more common in females and hyper-mobile adolescents, whilst the upper back is still flexible enough to be able to reverse its curve.

WHY ARE THE HAMSTRINGS SO SHORT AND TIGHT?

Several factors can contribute to short hamstrings:

1. Postural factors
2. Underlying nerve sensitivity
3. Genetic

▶ Postural Factors

This is the predominant cause of shortened hamstrings, and happens very simply as a result of poor posture when standing, and subsequently whilst walking.

The hamstrings are used inappropriately to do postural holding instead of the gluteal (buttock) muscles and they become weak. They are key to the control of pelvic tilt, and are very important in making the connection between boat and opposite shoulder/arm.

The gluteal (buttock) muscles are essentially postural holding muscles, to help you stand your trunk and pelvis on top of your hips. If you feel them whilst standing up and they feel mushy, then they are most likely not working. But this would make you fall over, (and you obviously don't), so you must be using something else in instead.

Now feel your hamstring muscles whilst standing, and notice how tight they feel compared to your gluteal muscles. Your body recruits your hamstrings which are really designed to be mover (walking/running) muscles and to work powerfully. However they are now working with a sustained contraction leading to an increased 'resting tension' and ultimately shortening.

▶ Sensitised Sciatic Nerve

Normal healthy nerves can be twisted and stretched momentarily, without damage or producing any nasty symptoms. Nerves have to bend and stretch where they cross around the outside of a joint like the elbow.

The nerve becomes sensitised by chemicals (inflammatory agents released from unhealthy or injured tissues) which make the nerve unable to tolerate stretching anymore. In large quantities these chemicals also cause pain and swelling. In fact even before it gets much of a stretch, it asks the brain to help by getting surrounding muscles to remain short and resist any forces to stretch them. So the hamstring automatically stays tight and the harder you try to stretch it, the harder it will fight back so as not to allow the underlying nerve to be stretched.

▶ Genetic Factors

You may simply be predisposed to having short hamstrings, as an inherited trait from your parents.

HOW TO STRETCH THE HAMSTRING MUSCLES AND THE SCIATIC NERVE

Now that you have evaluated the posture and determined that the hamstrings are limiting good posture and form, it is likely that you will need to give advice on how to elongate them. In order for you to stretch the hamstrings you must isolate them, and avoid stretching adjacent parts of the body instead. As such, the normal bend and reach your toes is not a useful exercise, as it encourages upper and lower back stretching more than hamstring stretching, rather like when you sit in a kayak and try to lean forward just by bending your back.

1. Set-up and Pre-load
2. Muscle Stretch
3. Nerve Stretch

▶ Set-Up And Pre-Load

Arrange chairs, stool or other suitable weight-bearing surface as in Photo 8, so that you can sit on only one of the sit-on bones in your buttock and the other buttock is over the side of the chair. Put the leg of the side you are sitting on (on-chair side), out in front of you with the heel on a surface of similar height, knee locked-out straight and toes pointing away. Then position the thigh of the other leg (off-chair side) pointing down to the floor with the knee, which is bent, and with toes on the floor.

▶ Muscle Stretch

As you sit up tall, tighten the thigh of the leg that is up and feel the stretch in the back of your thigh. At the same time, use the foot of the leg which is down to assist in pulling the thigh backwards and behind you. Bending at the ankle increases the intensity of the stretch on your hamstrings (the muscle stretch).

▶ Sciatic Stretch

To put some stretch on the sciatic nerve all you need to do is pull your toes of the straight leg up towards your shin. The stretching sensation will rise to another level, but will ease immediately you point your toes down again. Keep sitting tall, without slumping, and attempt to hold stretches for longer periods of time. Start at 15 seconds and gradually increase to a minute or more!

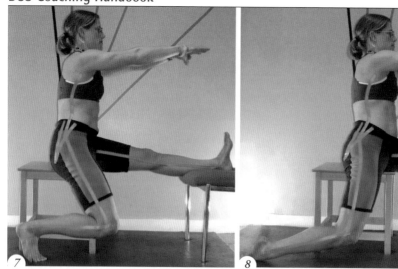

Photo 7 *Starting position to stretch hamstring muscle.*   Photo 8 *Loading stretch hamstring muscle.*

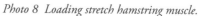

Photo 9 *Adding tension on the sciatic nerve.*

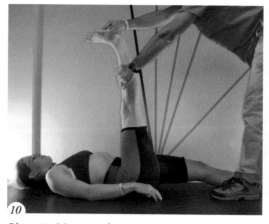

Photo 10 *Measuring hamstring and sciatic nerve stretch.*

You can measure your progress by estimating the angle at the hip with the knee locked out straight. Marking some lines at 10° intervals on a wall with tape will help you estimate the angle of leg raise. Assistance is needed to lift up the leg as in Photo 10.

OBSERVATION OF PELVIS, LOWER AND UPPER BACK

It goes without saying that it is unrealistic to try to see what is happening through a thermal, a cagoule, and a buoyancy aid. We need to expose the back to view from the rear and from the side to see how it is working. This brings with it its own problems in relation to Child Protection and Privacy especially with young girls, boys and females etc.

It is *only* an *observation*, and therefore there must be no physical contact whether accidental or with intent to make contact. If you are at all unsure, then *STOP* immediately, and explain that you are not comfortable in continuing the observation.

If you would like a professional to assist you with the observation, then it would be best to seek the expertise of a Chartered and State Registered Physiotherapist or Graduate BSc Sports Rehabilitator. You can find an accredited list on the internet under CSP or BASRaT.

You will need to ascertain permission and informed consent. This should be in the form of signed consent by those over 18 years of age. For those under 18 years, informed consent will be needed by parents or guardian. It should be arranged for a convenient time when parents or guardian are able to attend, and it would be advisable to record their presence at the meeting. For those over 18 years, they too should be given the opportunity for them to bring parents or a close friend. You must make clear the reasons for wanting to make these observations, and explain the reasons before you start. It would be sensible to document these clearly. Only do the observations of what you have said you are going to do, and do not deviate from the planned actions.

The place of the observation should be clearly defined, private, warm and with adequate lighting.

▶ THE CORE ELEMENTS OF CANOE SLALOM

Canoe Slalom is a highly technical sport which also demands high levels of strength, explosive power, endurance and mental toughness.

◎ 1. Technique And Skill Development

Effective technique - Development of strokes, boat line, pacing, edging, trim, in a dynamic yet controlled and repeatable way.

Watermanship - understanding of the shape, feel and possibilities of a white water environment. Developing and maintaining a high white water confidence.

◎ 2. Physical Development - Strength, Power, Speed And Endurance

Physical ability to develop & deliver skilful slalom performance in training and competition environments.

◎ 3. Planning And Mental Skills Development

Psychological abilities – Visualization, Concentration, Mental toughness. Maximising strengths and minimising the effects of individual weaknesses.

Goal-setting, preparation, planning and review.

◎ 4. Tactical And Racing Skill Development

Decision making - Which technique? Where? Tactical awareness in different formats.

Reactive ability – Applying successful plan B's and C's to unexpected situations.

Best practice in the key areas of nutrition, health, rest/recovery and the more general areas of lifestyle support such as family, school/college and work are also essential in preparing athletes for a successful long-term career in slalom.

The following sections will look at each of the key core elements for canoe slalom in more detail.

▶ TECHNIQUE AND SKILL DEVELOPMENT IN CANOE SLALOM

Canoe Slalom is an open skill sport where a wide variety of techniques are brought to bear in a skilful way on a constantly changing white water environment. A successful slalomist must be technically, physically, tactically and mentally prepared to respond to whatever the river and the course design demands.

This choice of 'how fast' versus 'how clean' remains a compelling one for any level of slalomist.

COACH'S TIP

- An individual's physical build (predominantly height and length of levers) will define that individual's paddling technique and be a key determinant in the focus of physical preparation. The wide variety of solutions available in slalom make it possible for a wide range of body types and paddling styles to be catered for. Within the basic defined developmental framework for slalom, as outlined in this chapter, a coach must always be ready to develop strengths and limit weaknesses by individualizing both the approach and the preparation.

The Technical Demands of Slalom can be broken down into developing understanding of:

- Water shape, strength and direction.
- Course design/character/demands.
- Stroke sequence/key stroke around slalom gates.
- Boat position/angle/trim/lean.
- Body position and function.
- Impact of boat speed.
- Rhythm/tempo.

Traditionally the introduction of the basic slalom techniques of forward paddling, turning and steering, basic flat water gate sequences, take place on flat water – both with and without gates. This allows the key basic principles to be felt and understood, and remains an important part of day-to-day slalom training at all levels.

From the start there should be an early focus on the stop/start element inherent in slalom. This looks at the effectiveness of 8 -10 stroke accelerations and force production from single stroke whilst retaining good technique. Careful, regular coach observation and use of video is important here with work done both with and without gates.

FORWARD PADDLING IN A SLALOM BOAT

◎ See also the new Slalom Technique DVD available through the BCU website and Chapter 20 under 'Racing Stroke'.

What Is The Importance Of An Effective Forward Stroke In Slalom?

◎ Up to 80% of any course is broken down into forward strokes.

◎ Most of these strokes are re-acceleration strokes to move the boat forward again after completing technical slalom gate moves.

◎ Good forward paddling technique can deliver more power for less energy, especially when fatigue sets in near the end of a competition run.

Below are some key considerations for the slalom kayak and canoe stroke.

The Forward Stroke In Kayak
▶ Boat

◎ Flat boat whenever possible with rock-solid edges.

◎ A well adjusted footrest - tight but allowing some movement to prevent cramping.

◎ Knees out wide with strong grip upwards and inwards.

◎ Loose hamstrings are vital to facilitate good boat grip and a relaxed effective paddling action (see also section on Functional Stability).

◎ Have a close-fitting backrest, flexible enough to allow layout over the stern when necessary.

▶ Body

◎ Visible torso rotation, with power derived from major back muscles before arms.

◎ Core stability central to maintaining good posture in boat with forward lean from cocking the pelvis and not by bending the mid and upper back.

◎ Top arm – fairly straight, some bend to allow efficient mechanics.

▶ Blade

◎ Paddles – stiff shaft for 15+ years. Younger juniors need a more flexible shaft.

◎ Paddle length and grip - no less than a third of total paddle length between hands.

◎ Blade size – very individual, important to assess/measure, through visible fatigue and feedback over full course efforts and longer, (reassess regularly with juniors).

◎ Neck of blade to travel through water (visually assess).

◎ Clean entry of blade, driving downwards at the catch.

◎ Vertical stroke to side of boat - optimal pull of blade through water.

◎ Exit of stroke at latest by hip.

Key Elements – Forward Stroke For Slalom Canoe
▶ Catch

◎ Fully submerged blade.

◎ Blade vertical and as close as possible to boat.

◎ Back straight.

◎ Torso rotation, with lower arm fully extended.

◎ Bent top arm (pushing down).

◎ Form the 'A' shape with boat, paddle and body.

▶ Pull

◎ Vertical paddle.

◎ Pulling with back and arms.

◎ Winding in the torso twist.

◎ Rigid set lower back.

◎ Back then arms apply force to the paddle, gripping through the water, thrusting all the power from the paddle through the knees into the boat, trying to push the boat past the paddle.

- There should be a strong focus on visible size of impulse –fast and powerful – allowing the blade to apply real 'grip' to the water.

- Exit of stroke at latest by hip.

▶ Boat

- Keep the boat even, with as little rocking as possible.

▶ Back Posture

- Back should remain solid and straight throughout the stroke.

- The forward lean coming from the hips and not from the mid or upper back.

- Posture the same as when lifting a heavy weight or squatting weights in gym.

Onside And Offside Issues For Canoe

▶ Onside

- For more advanced paddlers the boat can be steered back onto the onside stroke by putting a little offside edge on at the end of the stroke, thus reducing the need for cross-bow strokes.

- 'J' stroke should be a fluid component of stroke, left as late as possible to effect maximum pull along stroke.

▶ Offside

- Strong trunk rotation essential with good top arm flexibility.

- Well-developed core stability needed to facilitate this cross-bow rotation.

DEVELOPING THE BASIC SLALOM STROKES AND TECHNIQUE MODELS

Revised and updated in 2005 these models cover the basic boat lines, stroke patterns and key blades for the main upstream and downstream moves in slalom. Starting with basic strokes and drills, moving onto basic flat water gates and progressing onto white water gates, they underpin all the basic technique moves of canoe slalom and represent a common agreed start point for skill development in slalom.

Slalom Technique DVD & Website

All the above strokes, models and progressions (Basic strokes, flat water gates and WW gates) are now available on DVD via the BCU website. Using new rules 'short' slalom boats and covering Kayak, C1 and C2 - top GB and international paddlers demonstrate all the key techniques and moves involved in slalom. Coaching bullet points and sequence descriptions plus a comprehensive glossary and notes section make this a 'must have' coaching and paddling resource for 2006.

Technique models are also available in diagrammatic form in the *Slalom Coaching Manual* via BCU supplies.

Also check out the website:

www.slalomtechnique.co.uk

where most of the DVD content is available to view online via flash viewer and still shots with bullet points. Essential viewing for coaches Level 1-4.

Visit www.bcu.org.uk for more information.

CONTROLLING ROTATION

Slalom boats by definition are designed to turn quickly and easily. White water river environments and slalom course designers combine to test not only turning skills but also the skill of negotiating a course on moving water without over-rotating.

The developing slalom paddler very soon learns that it is this understanding and feel of the creation and control of rotation that is one of the key skills to racing 'fast and clean' in slalom.

The term commonly used in slalom is 'keeping the bows downstream' and is very similar to the skiing term 'keeping your shoulders facing down the hill'.

BASIC STROKES AND BEHAVIOURS

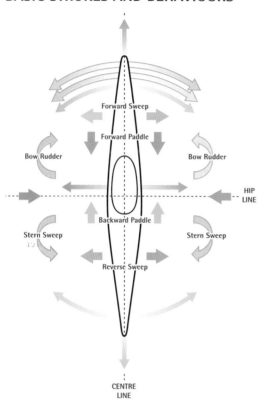

Fig. 1 Basic Strokes and Behaviours

It is fundamental to understand and feel that what slalomists do is either:

- Pull the boat past the Blade.
- Pull the boat towards the Blade.
- Push the boat away from the Blade.

These are key to acceleration/deceleration, and creating and controlling rotation in slalom.

What about strokes where neither boat nor paddle appear to move? These are holding strokes and their role is:

- To decelerate.
- To control rotation.
- To counteract water flow.

Different types of strokes turn the boat in the same directions. Who or what decides? This is the challenge of slalom!

THE KEY BLADE PRINCIPLE

Because a slalom boat is hardly ever going in a straight line, the principle of 'Key Blade' is crucial. For virtually every position on a slalom course (or river for that matter) the dominant blade will provide the most effective control. Watch C1 paddlers; if they are 'on track' with the boat running well then they will be on the key blade whether it's onside or offside. Every coach's toolbox should contain the question, 'If you could only have one blade in that position…which would it be?' Eventually as paddlers get more skilful they will be able to answer correctly before their first attempt.

> ### COACH'S TIP
>
> • Every aspiring kayak paddler in any discipline or class should paddle a C1 to better understand the key blade principle (and to improve white water confidence). With two blades to choose from and the frequent encouragements to 'keep paddling' it's all too easy for kayak paddlers to be on the wrong blade at the wrong time.
>
> When developing the basic slalom models or working out any slalom sequence, matching or planning every stroke is not as important as recognizing the key blade and 'feeling' when to either move off it or repeat it. Incorporate single blade work into your tech sessions on a regular basis – only when paddlers feel it will they believe.

FLAT WATER VERSUS MOVING WATER TRAINING

As soon as possible all basic techniques (forward paddling and gate work) should be introduced into moving water situations so that the ability to apply them in a changing environment starts to develop. This is especially so for the development of edging, leaning and trimming skills and the understanding of how to create and control rotation.

SOME USEFUL TECHNIQUE PROGRESSIONS

The basic technique models should be developed with juniors to allow further progressions as seniors. From very early on the coach/paddler relationship should aim to develop a toolbox of skills, allowing paddlers to choose the appropriate technique - with/without the coach - developing ultimately paddler responsibility for decision making.

Focus on a sound understanding of the three key stroke areas of Power, Turning and Linking/Slicing stroke.

Develop an understanding of the interplay of boat line, pacing and key blade.

Develop basic skills on flat or easy moving water to groom technique.

From early on practise choosing, holding and retrieving the 'racing line' on a course, with choices/decisions being reviewed and evaluated by how fast and how clean (times and penalties).

Gate work – start with single gate moves then slowly building complexity of sequence.

Experience the feel of 'holding the line, using the inside poles, pivoting around poles to allow swift exits, torso moves where the body movement is radical but does not adversely affect the run or the trim of the boat.

Focus on keeping body lean within the balance of the boat, the boat remaining balanced without losing the edge or requiring blade support.

Try to paddle (and feel) wider lines first then tighten up to notice/believe any difference.

Practise the ability to have a plan A / plan B option of equal commitment and be able to deliver in a race setting without any visible difference.

Groom techniques through short sequences and build these skills into longer runs (halves and fulls in training) and then into race situations (simulated and real).

A key role of the slalom coach is to facilitate choice/understanding/feeling of most effective options on a sequence with the emphasis on efficiency, maintenance of boat speed and reducing the number of strokes.

Never lose focus of single stroke power and efficiency with regular assessments over 8-10 strokes maximum.

See testing protocols in Physical prep section.

PRACTICE STRATEGIES FOR YOUR COACHING 'TOOLBOX'

Methods for structuring technique work or practice are normally grouped into three pairs of areas (see also Chapter 1 p. 31):

Massed Practice – where the rest interval between practices is short or non-existent (less than 1:1).

Distributed Practice – where rest is more frequent or longer (over 1:1).

These two methods focus on the recovery interval as the key variable. See Physical Preparation section for more info on the interplay of the training variables.

Blocked Practice– execution of one technique repeatedly (maybe up to 50 times) with a small amount of variation say in direction or pace.

Random Practice – the deliberate mixing of a variety of techniques throughout a session.

These two methods are both task focused – the first overloading just one move or technique with a little variation – the second focusing on as mixed a variety/combination of techniques/skilful applications as possible.

Constant Practice – where the same move or specific technique is repeated in the same uniform way a high number of times.

Variable Practice – where the execution of a technique is deliberately varied throughout the practice session.

These two focus on the execution of the task. The first looking for as exact a grooving/repetition of the technique as possible – the second providing varied and challenging environments for the skilful application of a technique.

Applying the correct practice method is crucial in targeting / isolating particular techniques without them getting too boring and repetitive.

WATERMANSHIP AND WHITE WATER CONFIDENCE

As indicated in the earlier section on LTPD, it is important to underline here the vital development for slalomists (particularly in the J12 - J16 age range) that must take place away from slalom gates on just about any type of moving/white water in pretty well any kind of appropriate boat. There are no short cuts here and failure to put in these 'white water minutes' will severely limit any future development in slalom. white water touring, freestyle, white water racing and surfing offer these key opportunities to a balanced slalom development as well as bringing real variety and enjoyment.

TECHNIQUE DEVELOPMENT VERSUS SKILL DEVELOPMENT

Slalom is a highly technical discipline and it is important to understand the distinction between techniques and skills. The two are often used interchangeably and can at times cause confusion.

Techniques - the specific strokes and patterns of movement that are canoe slalom.

Skills - the effective application of those techniques in a slalom environment.

- To improve techniques 'develop the action'.

- To improve skill (i.e. to become more skilful) we need to develop the ability to perceive a need and apply the correct technique.

Slalom competition by definition tests both techniques and their skilful application. However a common pitfall in training for slalom is to persistently practise slalom, which by its very nature links and combines all varieties of move to 'test out' the racer.

In training, coaches should ensure:- Adequate time is spent on individual technique themes so that sufficient mastery takes place before it is exposed to a typical slalom race environment. A key aspect of this for coaches is ensuring that the correct practice strategy is applied.

▶ Contextual Interference (CI)

This is similar to random or variable practice and is a term used to describe ways in which a coach might vary or interfere with the 'task' to better promote learning, feel or awareness.

Slalom examples of this might be:

- Paddling sections of courses with eyes closed, (improves kinesthetic awareness).

- Restricting the use of either blade (helps better understand the key blade).

- Use a different class of boat (C1 instead of K1).

- Denying use of a particular stroke on a sequence (key blade awareness and breaking of comfort zones).

- Controlling the number of strokes used on a sequence (developing either stroke efficiency, quickness of transfer, acceleration and pacing skills).

- Not allowing any visual preparation of a course at all (overload instinctive reactions and plan B's).

- Deliberate last-minute changes of plan to test a paddler's race-day routine, (mental skills overload).

- Overloading of race facilitation or simulation strategies, personalized commentary, loud music, etc. (mental skills overload).

COACH'S TIPS

- Combining practice strategies can also be useful – so for instance distributed and constant can be used in a 'carry back' situation where the aim of the session is to repeat a hard technical white water move a number of times but with a carry back recovery to work ratio 4:1.

- Achieving balance in the 'practice mix' with clear links to the session/programme aims is vital to successful slalom coaching (see Chapter 1, pages 31-32).

- Use goal setting to be clear whether the aim is to learn/consolidate a technique or to become more skilful at applying it in a slalom context. This is a vital consideration when planning and periodising technique training.

- Remember... to develop the specific actions consider - massed, distributed, blocked, constant practice strategies.

- To develop the perception/skilful application consider - random, variable, contextural interference strategies.

AS A SLALOM COACH – WHAT DO YOU DO NOW?

Whilst slalom coaches might touch on all of these at some stage – especially if they have a wide range in paddler age and ability - random and variable practice strategies are probably the most common. With slalom being such an open skill (i.e. the conditions, requirements, environments are never ever exactly the same) and slalom gates difficult to re-set in the same position – they are liable to get over-used. Consider trying some of the following:

🛶 Varying approach and exit lines to the same gate or 'task'.

🛶 Using different types of eddies to focus on the same upstream technique.

🛶 Courses that have combinations of different moves - as in a race.

🛶 Progressive courses where paddlers repeating a move immediately is not possible, (see sample sessions section).

🛶 Deliberately setting particular moves at the end of a course (or session) to provide a physical overload and adaptation.

IDEAS FOR TECHNIQUE/SKILL DEVELOPMENT SESSIONS

🛶 1. Coaching is usually a lonely business – how much do you know about how other coaches do run their tech sessions? Preferences for what works/doesn't work are closely guarded secrets – the 'black art' of slalom if you like. Go out of your way to observe (not assist) other coaches and vice versa. Insist on a debrief/feedback opportunity. Be as descriptive as possible in your feedback, rather than evaluative and critical. The process is guaranteed worthwhile.

🛶 2. Course design and choice of white water environment – how planned and systematic are you? Ask yourself how many times do you return to the exact same move or skill on your next tech session/or block of sessions? Have we got the balance right between practice strategies? How often do you use the gate positions already set?

🛶 3. Devise your own test courses or sites where you can reset the same or very similar character of moves. Only in this way can you set about evaluating training progress in slalom.

Photo 11 Devise your own test courses or sites

🛶 4. Numbers of course and reps – when as a group did you last revisit these and ask yourselves why you use the numbers/multiples you do?

🛶 5. How often do you play around with the rest intervals on technique sessions? (Massed vs distributed).

🛶 6. How does your session structure differ when coaching new techniques in comparison to remedying/changing old ones?

🛶 7. Be imaginative on your race simulation/contextural interference sessions.

🛶 8. Check out what methods are used in similar technically-based sports such as skiing, sailing, cycling, etc.

🛶 9. Periodisation: A lot of time can be spent planning a training year for physical development. How much time do you spend on planning technique development over the year? How many times do you revisit/review the tried and tested formulas of your normal speed tech, speed league, quarters, halves and fulls? Are there alternatives/new ideas/adaptations of these to consider? See also sample sessions in the following section.

As ever with all best coaching practice, goal-setting should be at the heart of good technique and skill development, with the specific needs of the paddler calling all the shots.

► PHYSICAL DEVELOPMENT FOR CANOE SLALOM

This section concerns the physical preparation necessary to develop and deliver skilful slalom performance in training and competition environments.

THE IMPORTANCE OF WARM-UPS AND WARM-DOWNS IN SLALOM

See also Chapter 2 p. 76 and Appendix A.

Warm-ups and warm-downs are crucial in the delivery of consistent performance whether in racing, training or testing. As we have seen, a time trial event such as slalom requires 2-3 repeated efforts throughout a day (each needing the paddler to be 100% ready on GO!) with a fair amount of inactivity in between. Every individual will be different and require different types of warm-up and warm-down both in content, timing and duration and the 'start of day warm up in particular will need to be different to any subsequent warm ups in the day. In training the intensity and type of the session will be a determinant factor in the make-up of each warm-up and warm-down.

Neglecting warm-ups and warm-downs in slalom can result in:

• Failure to produce best form in a race.

• Poor quality training for the early part of each training session.

• Delayed recovery and underperformance in any subsequent performance, or session.

• Overall increased injury risk.

Essential elements for warm ups should be:

Warming up body - increase body temperature and blood flow.

Preparing muscles for the appropriate level of use in session.

Coordination warm-up - speed of movement and range of movement.

Technique preparation.

Sharpening mental focus on session or race.

Essential elements for warm-downs should be:

Essential physically and mentally.

Aids dispersion of chemicals in body (especially upper body.)

Lowers body temperature in a controlled way.

Allows arousal to drop and regain mental calmness.

Opportunity to recall and reinforce good technique.

Allows focus on fluids and food replenishment.

► CANOE SLALOM TRAINING TYPES

Two types of training develop the physical side of canoe slalom:

  • Water-based training - with or without slalom gates on either flat water or white water.

  • Land-based training - predominantly strength/power development and conditioning; flexibility and functional stability development, or general aerobic development.

This section will focus on these two training types, examining the key physical elements involved and in particular the significant amount of crossover involved between the various training types.

THE INTERPLAY OF THE KEY TRAINING TYPES INVOLVED IN SLALOM

The Training Types table over the page is designed to illustrate and simplify the complex relationships between training sessions, water types, power demand and metabolic stimulus (energy training systems) in canoe slalom. The aim of this table is to help the coach and athlete understand the typical demands and possible stimuli arising from carrying out training of the types described. The variable nature of white water means that this chart should only be used as a guide.

► What Are Training Stimuli And Why Are They Important?

Training Stimuli is the term used to describe the training demands imposed by any training session.

TRAINING TYPES Barney Wainwright, BCU World Class, 2004.

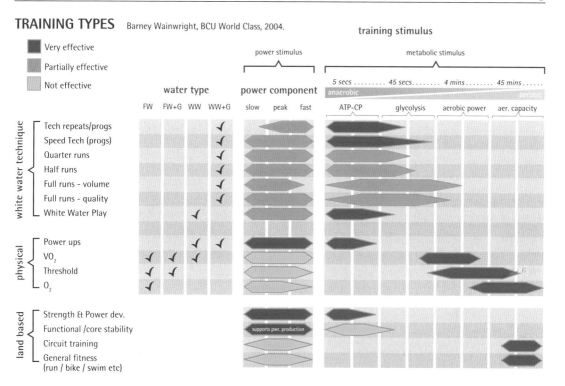

Table 1 Training Types

Simply speaking they are the demands put on the paddler to elicit a training response or adaptation.

Key variables to provide these demands are:

- Length of effort in time and distance.
- Number of repetitions and sets.
- Intensity of effort.
- Frequency of effort (recovery).
- Technical demand of the gates (tight or open).
- Physical demand of the gates and water (slow/peak/fast power; anaerobic; O2).
- Tactical/strategical/mental demand (race simulation or training volume).

These stimuli are the building blocks of any slalom training session and define the aim of that session (see also Chapter 2).

▶ The Challenge In Defining The Training Stimulus

Slalom training types allow much variation in the actual stimulus. For example a particular 'Tech Progs' training session may consist of gate combinations that create a stimulus more towards the fast power component than the slow power component.

Or on a more physically demanding 'Tech Progs' course the rest interval between sections may be short, moving the metabolic stimulus more towards aerobic power and away from an anaerobic stimulus.

Due to the nature of the sport and the water environment it is often found that two athletes carrying out the same training session can actually receive very different stimuli for adaptation. For this reason the training should be carefully planned for each individual where possible and observed or monitored in order that any differences in planned stimulus against actual stimulus can be evaluated then adjusted in the future training plan.

The chart should ideally be used to obtain an improved understanding of the potential stimulus that the different modes and types of training currently used in Canoe Slalom have upon the athlete. Careful consideration should be given when planning training cycles or individual training sessions, and also during the training session itself to make sure that the correct stimulus is provided as part of the short and long-term development of the athlete in question.

As the athlete adapts and develops, modification to the chart on an individual basis will be required. More demanding and specific training sessions will be required to further develop physical abilities alongside techniques and skills that have become enhanced.

Achieving the correct balance of all the different components is both the skill and art of canoe slalom coaching, but the careful planning and recording of training sessions and athletes' progressions will certainly help in understanding as much of this complex process as possible.

▶ The Importance Of 'Power'

This applies both in slalom performance and in any short burst paddling activity such as canoe polo, freestyle or white water play.

Slalom has more recently been described as a power sport, or more specifically a sport where the mechanical power that can be produced has a large influence upon the performance. We must be careful not to be confused by the different meanings that power can convey in relation to slalom or any form of canoesport.

Power can refer to the ability of the metabolic system to provide rates of energy production. The amount of energy which the body can provide at certain rates over durations of time is often referred to as power and can be measured via physiological assessments as anaerobic power or aerobic power (see Chapter 2 Physiology).

Power is also used to refer to the type of mechanical work that the body can generate. For canoesport this specifically refers to the speed and magnitude of force that can be produced in a single paddle stroke or a series of paddle strokes. The result of this is the power. As we have already seen in slalom there is a spectrum of mechanical power requirements that is determined by the white water, the moves, the strokes and the speed at which the paddler wants to travel.

Very simply, mechanical power is a product of the speed at which the blade is being moved and the amount of force being applied to the blade during this stroke. At times, for example when paddling upstream or crossing the flow, on an individual stroke the speed of the pull will be high, but the actual load on the blade will be relatively low. In other circumstances (for example - a holding bow rudder or the first 4-5 strokes re-accelerating downstream after breaking in) the speed of the pull will be quite slow but the load on the blade will be high. The power produced may be exactly the same in each of these circumstances, but it was created by two different loads and speeds on the paddle. You can soon see that in Slalom there are many situations on white water where the combinations of these two factors that influence power are very different.

The faster you want to travel over a particular section or course, the more mechanical power must be produced. However, the additional power may not be spread evenly over the duration of this section as some stroke may require more power than others.

These different types of power on the spectrum can also be thought of as being slow power at one end and fast power at the other end. This refers to the speed of the pull or to application of the force (see Table 1 Canoe Slalom Training Types).

▶ Using The Slalom Training Types Table
(N.b. Use The Table From The Left-Hand Column.)

Column 1 lists the main training types and the main sessions in each. Note, under white water technique 'progs' is short for progressives. Also flat water gates have been included in the physical section although it is recognised that in the early stages of development this will contain a high technical component.

Column 2 lists the four main water training types in with ticks to indicate where the session outlined in column 1 would normally take place: flat water, flat water gates, white water and white water gates.

Columns 3 & 4 show a 'training stimulus continuum' for assessing slalom sessions. The third column shows the power component split into three levels. By using a colour coded system (red = very effective; orange = partially effective; yellow = not effective) shows how effective a particular session is in developing slow, peak and fast power.

The centre and right of the continuum covers the metabolic stimulus (energy training systems) This is time-based from 0 seconds to 45 minutes and shows the relationship of anaerobic and aerobic work to the key energy systems of ATP-CP/glycolysis/aerobic power/aerobic capacity. Again using the colour coded system the table shows how effective a particular session is in developing a particular energy system for slalom.

SAMPLE SESSIONS FOR SLALOM

Sessions To Develop Fitness

▶ Power Ups

⚙ 12sec max course on WW with 1 or two upstream gates (left/right for balance).

⚙ 2-4 courses with 2-4 repetitions on each.

⚙ At least 2min rest between efforts.

⚙ Maximal intensity.

Notes: The key to this session is to adjust pace for the move then to re-accelerate.

This should not be used as a learning technique – the power must be delivered in the optimal direction. It can be used to consolidate or 'groove' good technique.

Penalties count! Finish session when fatigued or when technique breaks down.

▶ VO₂ Sessions

⚙ Perform a 5min loop on flat water at max effort - Rest for 5 min - Repeat 3-5 times.

⚙ Perform a 4 min loop at max effort - Rest for 4min - Repeat 3-5 times.

⚙ Perform a 3min loop at max effort - Rest 3-4 min - Repeat 4-5.

▶ Threshold Sessions

⚙ 6 - 8 flat water loops - Approx. 6min loop - 60sec rest between loops.

⚙ 10 x flat water loops - 9min loop - 60sec rest between loops.

⚙ 30 - 40min constant flat water paddle - Taking first 5 mins to steadily work up to threshold HR.

⚙ 6 - 8 x flat gate loops (easy open course) - 6min loop - 60sec rest between loops.

⚙ 6 – 8 x white water 5min loops (very open course, 2 ups max) - 60sec rest.

⚙ 4 x white water loops (open course, 2 upstreams max) - 9min loop - 60sec rest between loops.

▶ O₂ sessions

⚙ Recovery O₂: 45 - 60min, very light pace - HR 140-150 bts/min.

⚙ Steady State O₂: 40 - 60min - HR 150-155 bts/min.

⚙ Extensive O₂: 40-50min HR 160-165.

Sessions To Develop Technique

These are the names and details of the most commonly used gate training sessions in canoe slalom. The multitude of terms and names given to sessions can be confusing so an attempt has been made here to reduce some of the 'jargon' and start the process of agreeing a common terminology.

▶ Tech Repeats

These are short courses usually between 10 and 25sec in length – normally with a specific technical theme. They are used for learning or consolidating techniques. Coach and paddler will agree a set number of reps (repetitions) that are repeated before changing to another course. Recovery is normally long – up to 10 times longer than work. Depending on the river conditions paddlers will either paddle back to the start (circulate) or get out of the boat and walk back to the start (walk-backs).

▶ Tech Progressives (Progs)

These are similar to tech repeats but with 2 or more courses paddled consecutively before walking or paddling back to the start. These are also used for learning and consolidating techniques but put more pressure on the paddler by not repeating moves straightaway.

The following group of sessions are all based on a normal full length slalom course (18-25 gates with a running time somewhere between 85 – 105 secs for the fastest MK1.

▶ Speed Techs/Progressives (Progs)

This is a full course split into fifths or sixths (course lengths varying between 10-20sec) so that it provides a complete mixture of course types and challenges. Some open, some tight, some rough and some flatter. Often done in the build-up to races it challenges the paddler to paddle fast and clean. It can be very competitive if done in a group and penalties should always be recorded. Coaches often add the 5 or 6 course totals together to give an aggregate score for each run.

▶ Quarter Or Half Runs

As the name implies these are full runs split into quarters (25-30sec approx) or halves (50-60sec approx). They can be paddled progressively or as repeats depending on the aim of the session. Progressively means far more pressure technically and physically; repeats less demanding technically and more speed based.

Half runs whether repeat or progressive put serious pressure on the anaerobic system.

▶ Full Runs – Quality

These are simulated race day practice and can be based on any of the formats outlined in the Tactical and Racing Skill Development Section. Single run, 2 run aggregated or 2 run with best run counting. Rest between runs should be 30 to 90min depending on time available and there should be a full competition warm-up and course preparation routine. As well as the technical, the physical and the mental this session tests the tactical challenge of putting a competitive run down 'on the board' in the allotted number of attempts.

▶ Full Runs – Volume

These are full runs (rest in the 8-15 minute range) repeated anywhere from 3-8 times. These put particular pressure on the technical and the physical plus the mental challenge of sustaining full run consistency when fatigued. They are a key indicator of a paddler's ability to be competitive in slalom.

▶ WW Play

This is an informal session with or without gates where the emphasis is on play, experimentation and confidence building. Often pushing the boundaries, it can be in slalom boats or play boats, kayak or canoe. Emphasis should be on the 'relatively' unplanned and on having FUN. Generally there should be long recoveries between efforts.

▶ MEASURING PERFORMANCE

There are many reasons why one might choose to test or assess the athlete:

• To see changes in aspects of physical ability over a period of time to assess the effectiveness of the training undertaken during this period.

• To be able to make comparisons between athletes to help understand the differences in performance between them.

• To help identify physical areas of strength or weakness.

• To try to identify whether an athletes changes in performance are due to physical or technical reasons.

The test that is used is determined by the information that is required. Where possible the tests should be as specific as possible to the event while still allowing you to isolate the aspects of performance that you are interested in. They must also be sensitive enough so that real changes in physical ability can be observed. Tests can either be water-based or land-based (see also Chapter 2).

Outlined below are two effective and simple slalom specific boat-based tests that most people with access to a stretch of flat water should be able to carry out (and easily re-test). They are ideal for a typical flat water club site. These can be timed electronically with beams to 100ths of a second or hand timed to 10ths of a second.

THE 20–100 TEST

Rationale This test was designed to stress the body in a similar way to that which is experienced in a slalom race. It consists of repeated high intensity efforts with some recovery as well as a series of boat accelerations from stationary. It is an excellent indicator of ability to perform in a slalom environment and may also be of interest to similar short boat 'burst activities' such as canoe polo and freestyle.

Protocol To carry out the test you will require 3 buoys or posts. They should be used to mark out a 20m distance and then a further 30m beyond this to create a 50m straight section.

The protocol for the test is shown below:

Protocol For 20-100 Test

Effort distance	Rest Interval
20m	2 minutes
20m	5 minutes
20m	10 seconds
20m	10 seconds
20m	10 seconds
20m	10 seconds
20m	10 seconds
100m (to 50m buoy and back)	5 minutes
20m	10 seconds
20m	10 seconds
20m	10 seconds
20m	10 seconds
20m	10 seconds
20m	finish

Table 2 Protocol for 20-100 Test

The three 20m sprints at the start of the test are opportunities to record a fastest 20m time, and as such there is sufficient rest between them for a full recovery. The third opportunity is then part of the next section of six 20m repeated sprints. Each of these has a quick turn, with the sprint going back in the other direction.

The 100m effort starts after a 5min rest and is an all-out effort without any pacing, turning around the buoy at 50m. Another set of six 20m sprints then follows after the 100m has finished with a 10sec rest.

TIMING PROTOCOL FOR THE COACH

For each sprint there is a verbal start command 3-2-1 go! (paddler's hips sitting stationary level with the post or buoy with the finish as the paddlers hips cross the finish post or buoy) This can be quite difficult with only 10sec between efforts and needs practice. It is in the best interests of the paddler to be as consistent as possible when lining up at the start.

The time for each 20m effort should be recorded as well as for the 100m effort.

Below are some times from the Great Britain National Slalom Teams that can be used for comparison purposes. The total test time is the sum of the first six 20m sprints, the 100m effort and the second set of six 20m sprints. It excludes the first two 20m sprints even if one of these is the fastest 20m sprint of the test. Check your paddlers out against these times, keep a record, do some training then re-test. If the times improve then see if your paddling performance improves as well.

Protocol For 20-100 Test

Class/Age	Fastest 20m	Fastest 100m	Fastest total
Senior MK1	5.8secs	33.3secs	114.9secs
Junior MK1	6.3secs	34.5secs	119.8secs
Senior WK1	6.5secs	37.6secs	129.0secs
Junior WK1	7.4secs	42.1secs	141.5secs
Senior C1	7.0secs	40.2secs	135.0secs
Junior C1	7.5secs	44.0secs	142.0secs
Senior C2	6.1secs	36.0secs	119.9secs

Table 3 GB squad times for comparison purposes

For further information on training the physical in slalom contact: The National Development Coach (moving water) c/o BCU HQ, Tel: 0115 982216 E mail – alan.edge@bcu.org.uk.

▶ PLANNING AND MENTAL SKILLS DEVELOPMENT

This section focuses on the key areas of preparation, profiling, planning and review, goal-setting, developing better concentration and attention skills, developing mental rehearsal and imagery skills, developing the ability to deal with high pressure situations by 'stepping back' and dealing with race day nerves.

PREPARATION, PROFILING, PLANNING AND REVIEW

See first Chapter 1 pp. 16-20.

The starting point in any planning and preparation process has to consider: What are the essential elements in your discipline's profile? What are the strengths and areas of improvement of your performer's profile? What are the time frames for action?

The main areas involved will be :

- Physical
- Technical
- Attitudinal
- Psychological
- Lifestyle

At its simplest planning is a series of inter-related goal setting exercises with the following key points to be observed.

The coach must act as a collection point of all the information needed to profile and plan effectively. This can involve:

○ Creating an athlete development pathway identifying where they as an athlete want to end up (long term/outcome goal) and where they've come from.

○ Agreeing exactly where they are at that point in time (not always easy).

○ What they want from their paddling (often different from what they think they want).

○ Agreeing what is realistic yet challenging by referring to any Paddler Development Model (PDM - see section below).

○ Agreeing how and when to review, evaluate and re-plan or restate.

This process creates a profile of all the issues that could impact on performance and feeds them forward into the long-term plan for the athlete's paddling career. A PDM is essential in this process as a proven pathway of performance, based on what has produced successful medal winning performance in the past.

MENTAL SKILLS DEVELOPMENT

Here we are considering maximising strengths and minimising the effects of individual weaknesses, goal setting, attention and concentration, mental toughness, mental rehearsal and visualization, stepping back, dealing with race day nerves (see also chapter 3).

As mentioned earlier, goal setting can also have a positive impact on mental skill development by: boosting confidence, enhancing motivation, reducing anxiety, focusing attention better and promoting a positive attitude and self image.

▶ Concentration And Attention

Despite recognizing its importance as a key slalom skill, development of concentration is often left to chance.

The key to concentration is awareness. If a paddler can be completely aware of what he or she is doing or aiming for there is much less chance of 'losing concentration'.

The aim is to control distractions which represent wrong focus at the wrong time. This is especially so if it is known what they need to be aware of at any particular time.

Attention is the act of directing awareness, and can be usefully labelled either internal, narrow external or broad external.

Internal attention is when we predominantly notice our bodies, feelings, or thoughts. It can help to monitor effort or pacing by allowing awareness of fatigue or acid build-up. Our thoughts and inner dialogue can help or hinder depending on what sort of messages we give ourselves, and feelings can be a useful indicator of how we are dealing with the demands of an upcoming race.

Narrow external attention is like a spotlight that illuminates a small area very brightly to the exclusion of all else. Studying a particular move from the bank, or targeting in on the bottom of a pole when approaching a break-out are times when we use this type of attention.

Broad external attention occurs when we are taking in the 'big picture' and need to be aware of overall considerations. When you first arrive at a new race-site it is likely you will be in this mode, taking in as much information from as many sources as possible. This is of course useful, but care must be taken as it's sometimes easy to get swamped by too much information, just as it is possible to miss important detail.

Stress and anxiety tend to change our ability to use these different attentional styles. Under stress (however caused) we often narrow down, as though we are wearing blinkers. Also, we can become too concerned with our inner feelings and get sidetracked by fears of illness or feel weak and unprepared because of 'churning guts'.

Some ideas to incorporate into your training:

✓ Learn to be aware of where you direct your attention. On flat water sessions deliberately switch your attention around; e.g. for 10 strokes notice your breathing (internal), for 10 strokes the bow of your boat (narrow external), for 10 strokes look as far ahead as you can (broad external). Notice how this affects you, and whether you tend to get stuck in a particular style, or whether you lapse in your efforts to maintain a style.

Become aware of the important cues you use when paddling on gates. What specific part of the gate do you look at when approaching an upstream? Where do you look on the exit? At the start of a full-length run, is your attention focused internally or externally? Is this consistent ?

Monitor your inner conversations. What sort of messages do you give yourself? Are you 'present' or 'off on a daydream'. Notice this at different times of the day, not just when training. Are you thinking about training over lunch, then... wondering what's for tea half way through a session?

▶ Mental Toughness In Slalom

It's vital in slalom to develop the ability to paddle towards the next gate as if it were the first gate off the start, in other words to remain at all times in the 'here and now'.

This is achieved with a combination of super-effective concentration - having the right attention on the right things at the right time - and well planned process goals that maintain a narrow focus, keeping the next cue or trigger much stronger than anything else. In this way, with practice, it will not be possible to recall events or penalties from a run until after the finish. Nothing is stronger than what is next.

It's also very effective in developing a 'never quit' mentality, a golden rule of any time trial.

▶ Mental Rehearsal And Imagery

These are fundamental skills of racing slalom successfully. Some key principles are:

○ Physically relax first.

○ Use all your senses: vision, sounds, feelings, taste and smell.

○ The image may be outside looking in, or inside looking out. There are no rights or wrongs, so discover which is best for you or which method works best when.

○ Always try to think through or 'see' the actions at the right speed. A watch can be used to check accuracy but recognise that it is a skill to be learned

and developed so don't expect to be too close to start with.

○ Sometimes it is appropriate to slow down the action - to identify a crux move or new technique.

○ Always focus on what you want to do. Try to "re-edit" errors once only and then focus on the positive 'getting it right' image.

○ If necessary, break a complex course down into sections first, but try to finish with a complete 'full run' image.

○ You have to believe in the image, so what you are rehearsing needs to be within, not beyond, current abilities.

○ Short regular practice is best. On and off the water right from the start of learning to paddle.

▶ Stepping Back

There are times when we each get 'caught up' in what it is we are doing, sometimes this is helpful if it means we are concentrating and focusing effectively on the job, but sometimes it means we are lost in anger, worry, or just daydreaming. One way of dealing with this is to practice 'stepping back' or to use the jargon misidentifying from how we are feeling or behaving and consider what options we have.

Japanese samurai warriors used this as part of their lifelong training for battle; when scared or fearful they were instructed to think, "There is a warrior who is scared, what should he do now?", rather than "I am scared!". This allows a clearer understanding of what is happening, and allows you to control the feeling rather than allowing the feeling to control you.

To give an example: During a training session you set yourself the goal of paddling 100% clean. The session starts well, but in the second course you start to have trouble with a move and hit a pole. There is no way to recover and the goal of 100% clean is lost; worse, you're having increasing trouble getting the move, you get more and more upset and your paddling gets worse. A vicious cycle erupts; the original mistake leads to anger or disrupted concentration, which leads to more errors, which leads to worse anger.

Stop, take a moment just to settle and relax. Take a few deep breaths and get centred to recover your composure. In your imagination pretend you are an impartial observer and ask, "What is happening here?" Don't be judgmental at this point, with an answer like "That idiot just ruined his session" - that is not what's needed now.

🕊 Describe the situation to yourself as clearly and calmly as you can, e.g. 'The paddler in the yellow boat hit the left hand pole of the gate with his paddle as he left the gate. He stopped paddling and started to beat the front of his boat with his fist".

🕊 Then ask yourself how is the person feeling or responding, e.g. "He is angry and upset because it was important for him to have a perfect session". Then, still acting as though you were watching this scene as an observer, ask yourself what options does the paddler have e.g. "He can get off and finish the session now or he can repeat the move having learned from the previous run and continue".

🕊 Don't get caught up with 'Why?' questions. They are more likely to drag you back into self-blame or analysis which is less useful in terms of creating a change in your attitude.

🕊 Once your attitude has changed you'll be in a better position to look at the reasons for any mistake.

🕊 Stepping back gives you the option to break out of a vicious cycle. The vicious cycle need not be caused by anger. It may be worry, distracting thoughts, fatigue; anything that disrupts your attention. Its easy to practice stepping back because you can do it anytime and anywhere, driving your car, watching T.V , eating. The more practiced you are the easier it will become at times when you are really worked up, such as important races or the weeks up to selection.

To summarise the stages in Stepping Back:

1 Recognise that something about your mood, attitude or performance is inappropriate or unpleasant:

2 STOP! Take a few breaths and centre yourself.

3 Use your imagination to view the situation as an educated but neutral observer.

4 Ask 'What is happening here?'

5 Ask 'How is that person feeling ?'

6 Ask 'What options does he have to move on from here ?'

7 Don't ask 'why?' - it doesn't lead to new options as easily.

BUILDING BLOCKS FOR SUCCESS

Pay attention to detail - before and on race day. There are several areas that they will have dealt with well before the big race arrives. This might include:

◎ Don't be fazed by race day - no matter what's at stake.

◎ Be fiercely competitive and determined to always give the max in training and racing.

◎ Have realistic goals that maintain a focus on what's most important. Don't create unnecessary stress.

◎ Know how to maintain concentration on and off the water, and how to refocus when necessary.

◎ Develop the ability to look at moves on a course and work out what will be the best way to tackle them. Use visualization and imagery on the moves and relate back to practice and training. Make sure you've been there before (or very close).

◎ Know/practise how to get useful information from coaches, splits and video analysis that is available. Control it, to be right for you.

◎ Maintain an outer calm and confidence when performing - even when you aren't.

Get on with other paddlers so that they aren't distracted by team hassles.

◎ Manage your time and lifestyle so they are in top condition to race.

▶ Race Day Butterflies - What Are They And How Can We Manage Them?

A natural physical response to an important situation – especially in a day long time trial environment such as slalom – where there is a lot of time to kill or fill. The gap in your mind between the present and a (catastrophic?) future. Excitement and energy.

Every competitor gets the nerves - some regularly, some once in a while. They needn't prevent you from enjoying racing and performing at your best. Here are some strategies to deal with them:

🕊 Re-frame – put a positive personal spin on them by acknowledgment and acceptance - e.g. welcoming them as a sign you're ready to race.

🕊 Learn how to quickly calm yourself through centreing. Use of a central breathing pattern from your stomach to regain/take control. This can also be used with a strong positive personal image/memory.

🌀 Concentrate fiercely on the 'here and now' - your breathing, your movements, your immediate activity.

🌀 A well prepared and individualized race day routine is essential here.

🌀 Have clear process goals that are within your control and focus on the important things you need to do.

🌀 Prepare for race day in your mind - use imagery to imagine yourself dealing with the race the way you want to, feeling strong and confident.

Finally, remember the difference between amateurs and professionals - amateurs can perform well when they're feeling great, professionals can perform well no matter how they feel.

▶ TACTICAL AND RACING SKILL DEVELOPMENT

In this section we will cover tactical challenges of a time trial race demands of the different slalom formats, getting the best out of demonstration (demo) runs, having an effective race week/race day plan, using a stopwatch in training and on race days, the role of the coach on race day, mental skills on race day, use of video on race day and taking and evaluating split times.

THE TACTICAL CHALLENGES OF A TIME TRIAL

Slalom is a time trial event that races over a different course every time with races decided on either a single run, the aggregate of two runs or the best of two runs. The demands of time trials are quite different to any other race format - especially when aggregate runs are involved. Below are just a few 'golden rules' for coaches and paddlers to consider:

🌀 In a time trial it's not possible to see how the other competitor is doing compared to you. It is vital that a paddler races their own run and retains a focus only on what they are doing and not what others may or may not have done. (Even if they have watched an opponent before their run it is risky to make assumptions over the outcomes of an aggregate format.)

🌀 Never ever quit on a time trial. Someone could always do worse than you. Be tough and paddle towards that next gate like it's gate one. From the very start this rule should be applied in all technique training. Never quit; complete the move; finish the course whatever – these are key slalom mantras.

🌀 Time trial racing means long race days with a lot of boats doing the same thing. It is not easy to be competitive racing on your own and completely unsupported. Time trials challenge the competitors to organise how they will plan their day and who will help:

• to gather feedback, (watching, videoing or timing).

• to rest, relax encourage and support them.

• just to 'be there for them' in an 'expected' and normal way.

🌀 Mental pressures and expectations in time trials, whilst more indirect and less 'in your face', are nevertheless just as intense. In a two run time trial a simple way of putting pressure onto other competitors is to put a competitive run down on the first run. It might not be the fastest or the winner but it serves the purpose of putting the onus and the pressure to produce onto opponents for the second and final run. Route decisions, risk v time to be gained, quality of feedback gathered, confidence in and knowledge of a paddler's ability are the key paddler/coach challenges here.

Demands Of The Different Slalom Racing Formats

Coaches and paddlers must be alert to the different challenges of the slalom race formats especially in the UK where there are several to deal with. Outlined below are the main race formats and some tips on preparing for them.

▶ ICF Championship Race Format

This is used for all major championships and is prevalent in most countries other than the UK. Day 1 is a two run aggregate qualification race with between 20-40 boats per class, advancing to a 1 run semi-final in the morning of Day 2 and then the top 10 boats in each class going forward to a final run on the same course. Semi-finalists are scored on just one run and finalists on 2 runs aggregated. Up to 6 course changes are made by the course designers for the semi and final runs.

• Taking maximum feedback from the demo runs on both the qualification and semi/final days. For early boats off these can be the only chance to assess the course - see the section below on using demo runs well.

• Being solidly consistent in qualification to avoid the big 'blowout mistake'. In training there's no avoiding volume full run skills here, where hours of white water gates grooving skills over full race run length at just under maximum pace will develop the consistency needed to 'feel in control' of qualification.

• Going fast enough in qualification to avoid too early a start number in the semi-final. If you start early then later starters can watch you on the new course.

• Taking qualification seriously enough to maximize familiarity with the sections of the course that remain the same for both days. A lot of the course stays the same so in effect you have 2 practice runs before the semi and final runs. Expectations should be high on these sections.

• Being prepared for the sudden death qualification of 40 to 10 in the semis. This requires much preparation in training with considerable emphasis on bankside preparation, 'getting it right first time' and risk-taking whilst retaining control. Lots of 1 run races, changing the course slightly every run and running some courses 'blind' (i.e. with no visual prep) will all build up the necessary skills and confidence to handle the 'semi-final guillotine'.

• Being controlled enough on the final (4th) run of the event to place a competitive final aggregate result. This final run brings the technical pressure of paddling some familiar sections fast and clear for the 4th time, of repeating the new 3rd run moves as well as dealing with the physical demands of the 4th run in two days. With these pressures top notch runs in the final aren't always needed to win the medals.

▶ Single Run Race Format

Used only in the UK for senior selection purposes and equating closely to the demands of the ICF Championship Semi-final, this format places maximum pressure on 'getting it right first time' with no second chance. It is also a key part of training and preparation for the ICF Championship format.

▶ Super Final Format

Used only in the UK for some domestic races and in 2005/2006 for Junior selection. This format has three runs in a day, first two are qualification with up to 50% qualifying through to a 'winner takes all' 3rd run on a course with up to six changes. This format allows a classic 1 day race (see below) to be run for UK ranking purposes alongside a qualification format race.

▶ Classic Format

A conventional two run race day with both runs aggregated. This is still the most common format in the UK and has been in use since 1997.

▶ Div 1 Format

A three run race day with practice run, followed by two race runs, best of the two runs to count. This is very much how slalom has been for the past 30+ years. With varying types of practice conditions at the lower divisions it is the standard format for all UK Slalom Divisions 1-4.

GETTING THE BEST OUT OF DEMONSTRATION RUNS

At all races without official practice (in the UK – Premier and above) the organizers must provide boats normally from each class to demonstrate the course in sections. This has two purposes: i) To allow the course designers/jury to approve the course. ii) To allow competitors (especially the early start numbers) a view of the course being paddled. Coach and paddler must have a clearly planned approach as to how information is to be gathered. Here are a few options to consider:

Make sure you have walked the course before demos so that you already have a clear idea of the areas of particular interest, (particularly important if the paddler has an early start number).

Decide early which bank will be best to watch from. Which view of the key moves is best?

If there is access to a video camera try to get someone else (coach/parent/support) to video the sections of most interest. It's important that the paddler (and coach if possible) gets the chance to watch demos 'live' without being tied to a camera position.

Careful note needs to be taken of the quality of paddler doing the demos. Are they giving appropriate information on the key moves. The coach might need to 'translate' the demo performance into what is realistic and what isn't. Some moves can be made to seem hard or easy. Be vigilant, coach and paddler should be crystal clear about current race capabilities.

Have a stopwatch ready to measure any options of the route that the paddlers might demonstrate. Beware of 'big penalties' distorting the split time (see section on taking split times below).

Coach and paddler need a clear rendezvous soon after demo runs to look at the video and discuss issues arising from the demos that will affect the race plan.

HAVING AN EFFECTIVE RACE WEEK / RACE DAY ROUTINE

By definition slalom race days are long with lots of time to fill between extremely active, high stress competitive race moments. Without a well-planned, tried and tested, personalized and flexible race routine, performance 'on the day' will be compromised. Devising a winning routine starts in training and at less important races –sometimes taking several years to refine. It should cover the 4-5 days prior to the race, race day and the journey home and should consider most of the following:

All meals during this period – especially the evening meal prior to race day. Most paddlers will be 'on the road' – what are the plans to avoid 'junk'?

All training during this 'taper' period (see physical preparation section).

Transport to and from the race.

Accommodation at the race.

Who will be travelling with and there for the paddler at the race.

Race day warm-ups and warm-downs - where, when and how?

Who will carry the boat to the start/from the finish?

Race run times - how early in the list? Impact on breakfast and warm-up? Effect on demos?

How is it intended to watch demo runs and with who?

When to walk the course - and with who?

When will the race plan be fixed (everything that you have decided to do from start to finish of the course – key strokes and boat positions, pacing, plan B's etc.) Minor adjustments can still be made after this but the major decisions will have been taken.

When to look at video and splits - and who with.

Where to spend 'down time' before and between runs – and who with.

Does the plan accommodate all possible weather conditions?

Why such a detailed plan? Well, part of it is because all possibilities need considering if you're serious about performing well, such as being able to answer "What if?" with "So what if?". However there is also a subtler reason that is connected with retaining control in stressful situations. A strong, personal race day routine that a paddler has confidence in can reduce stress and race-day nerves, prevent distractions and help keep a firm focus on the key race day goals.

▶ Race Day Goals

Goal setting comes into its own on race day. In the week before a race, coach and paddler should revisit and restate the goals for the race, revising and updating them if necessary. This is one of the key mental and tactical skills at a paddler's disposal for coping with all the varied pressures of race day. Get the process and performance goals for a race right and there is every chance of staying in control and producing a personal best performance. (See also section on goal setting at the start of this chapter).

▶ Use Of Video On Race Day

Video is a key player on race day, but who operates it and how is not straightforward. No matter how experienced a coach is, watching any performance through the camera lessens the quality of 'first hand feedback' that can be given. Action seen 'through the lens' can be severely limited and paddlers will know straight away when a coach's live recall is flimsy and vague. Nothing should compromise what can be seen live especially at key pre-run times like the demo runs.

So whenever possible get someone else to work the camera for you. Be prepared and make sure whoever is asked to help has used the camera several times before and been given feedback and advice on the footage they have taken.

Clearly this needs advance planning as your operator will need to be familiar with the camera and the kind of shots you want. If you have no support, try to set up a video share arrangement with another paddler or parent where you agree to video each other and share the footage. (This can also work well with splits).

Golden Rule: Video is a key part of a coach's race day 'toolbox' and time should be spent in training sessions practising (coach and operators) with the camera - in record and playback mode - so that operating it becomes second nature.

▶ Video Of Demo Runs And Early Boats

Gathering information prior to the first attempt is paramount in any time trial situation, especially where it is a two run aggregate format and 'everything counts'. Here are some top tips to follow:

🕐 Always try to video demo runs but here it is even more essential to offload the camera onto someone else. Plan ahead for this, maybe buddying up with another coach if necessary (see above section).

🕐 Video only key moves/problem areas and especially those with choices or options.

🕐 Time will be short for both videoing and review. Be strict about what needs to be 'seen' and what just needs to be 'split' or observed.

🕐 Review and (if necessary) take split times through the camera right there on the bank after demos. Practise doing this in training.

🕐 Always consider the standard (high or low) of the subject. Are comparisons valid/ useful? Are they worth watching? (See also demos section).

🕐 The coach should always be prepared to look at a video alone without showing it to the paddler – in this way it can be sifted, edited and interpreted.

🕐 Use the footage as a reminder, confirmer of decisions already made. If other options that might confuse have been videoed, the correct decision might be not to show them.

▶ Race Day Simulation In Training

All the areas covered in this section should be practised and simulated in training. Only then will the 'What ifs' stand a better chance of becoming 'So what ifs'. Simulation is a developing and proving ground for race week and race day routines: warm-ups/warm-downs, use of demo runs, walking the course and for-mulating a race plan, use of video during training and competition, testing pacing and route choosing decisions, taking and using splits, putting race day mental skills under pressure, and much more. It is a fun part of training and can present an enjoyable change from the other maybe more boring or painful types of training.

▶ Using A Stopwatch In Training And On Race Days

Using a stopwatch is part and parcel of training and racing slalom. Coach and paddler both need to own one and be 110% familiar with using it. Most 'Casio style' wrist watches have a lap split facility that will do the job for paddlers. Coaches will need a more conventional stopwatch that offers some memory functions as well. Beware overuse but be 110% familiar with it and have a clipboard and at least 2 pencils (and a pencil sharpener) tucked away in your coaching rucksack.

Why do we need a stopwatch?

• As a measure for hard feedback on where time has been gained or lost, to augment other types of feedback such as video, verbal, kinaesthetic etc.

• As a comparison used alongside a penalty count on choices of route.

• As a motivator - Beat this time! You were faster than him!

• As a record to be recorded and re-tested at a later date to determine progress.

• Used alongside video a stopwatch can provide invaluable augmented feedback.

• As a monitor of pace - Useful when training specific energy systems or developing a paddler's self-pacing ability.

When must we be careful of using a stopwatch?

• In the early stages of development where 'racing it' too fast too soon can lead to poor technique.

• When some paddlers in the group might suffer from competitive or unfair comparisons.

• Too much or too frequent 'on the line' racing can demotivate.

• Too much use of the stopwatch can have the same effect as using a camera - the coach does not see or remember the 'live event' clearly enough! Times will be recorded that cannot be interpreted effectively. You have been warned!

▶ What Are Split Times?

These are clearly identified section times on a course that isolate specific moves so that comparisons (of either route or paddler) can be made to assess time lost, time gained or consistency of repetition. They are most useful on demos and 1st runs but in a Championship Format race over 2 days, 2nd run splits can give vital information on the sections of the course that remain unchanged; 2nd run splits are also important as a record for review after the race, often showing interesting trends and patterns over a series of races.

Here are some guidelines on setting them up:

◉ Have a clearly marked out clipboard that shows routes and times in adjacent columns. Circle the fastest on each route for ease of reading.

◉ Always have clear start and finish points in 'neutral positions' (that isolate the move in question) and that can be accurately seen by the splitter.

◉ Use the body or the helmet as the 'trigger' for the start and finish of the watch.

◉ Never use 100ths on handheld splits. 10ths are quite adequate for split purposes. (NB - decide in advance whether to round up/down or ignore the 100th).

◉ Remember the shorter the split the more susceptible it may be to error.

◉ The longer the split the more mixed/combined moves it will contain.

◉ In interpreting split times beware the 'big penalty' that renders the split worthless. A good rule of thumb is use only clear runs unless the penalty is very slight or careless.

◉ Look for trends in consistency v speed when comparing routes and making recommendations for the next attempt.

▶ Role Of The Coach On Race Day

Clearly much of this 'Race Day' section will involve the coach in a central, supporting and advisory role from start to finish. However as a paddler develops and as the coach/paddler relationship strengthens an important decision has to be mutually agreed. Will the paddler over time develop greater dependency on the coach or greater autonomy from the coach.

In my opinion, taking the long view on this, the only realistic choice is that the ultimate goal of the coach should be redundancy. It may not happen overnight but the end game of any coach should surely be to have prepared as independent a paddler as possible, one who does not need a particular coach there all the time and has the skills and confidence to seek out and use whichever coaches or support services may be available in any racing or training situation.

There are clearly stages of progression towards this but, right from the start in training as well as racing, the coach should start to empower and encourage ownership of all training and race day skills. In fact there is much evidence to suggest that long-term coaching goals such as these are some of the major factors in optimum skill retention and transferability, outcomes vital in producing successful Canoe Slalom performance.

To encapsulate this philosophy a phrase favoured by the BCU World Class Slalom Coaches is to define the Coach/Paddler relationship as being…

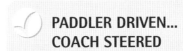

PADDLER DRIVEN...
COACH STEERED

ACKNOWLEDGEMENTS

Thanks are due to Tim Deykin - the Lead Physio-therapist, BCU World Class for his section on Achieving Correct Posture for Paddling Kayak.

Thanks are also due to Barney Wainright, Richard Lee and John Males for their contributions to the writing of this chapter.

ALAN EDGE

A National Coach since 1982, Alan started to work full-time with the British Canoe Union in 1985. He coached Britain's canoe slalomists to their first-ever Olympic medal in 1992 and in the period 1983 - 2000, National Teams under his guidance won nine World titles, 11 World Cup titles and six European titles.

Alan competed as an elite athlete throughout the 1970's, competing at 3 World Championships and becoming World Team Champion at the 1979 Worlds in Jonquiere, Canada.

He coached 3 times World Cup Champion Paul Ratcliffe to Olympic Silver in Sydney and was involved between 1997-2000 in the production and implementation of the Canoe Slalom World Class Performance Programme. In the period 1992-2000 Alan's coaching knowledge and expertise also made a significant contribution to the British Olympic Association's Coaches Advisory Group.

In his current position as National Development Coach, Alan has been responsible for overseeing the implementation of the World Class Development Programmes for Canoe Slalom and is currently involved with the development of the United Kingdom Coaching Certificate across all disciplines within the BCU.

Alan is married and based in Nottingham, spending most of his non-canoeing time keeping up with his young family and trying to master golf and the mandolin!

19 FREESTYLE

When I first started coaching freestyle, or playboating as it was then, people were finding the basic moves really hard to master and this led to frustration and a much slower learning curve. I soon realised that a lot of the freestyle moves required the paddler to break some fundamental rules that they were taught at a much earlier stage in their paddling life. Freestyle developments constantly challenge both the limits of paddling, and the people coaching this very dynamic and ever-evolving discipline of our sport.

▶ Do You Have To Be A Great Freestyle Paddler To Be A Great Freestyle Coach?

This question pops up all over the place partly because a lot of retired freestyle paddlers get into coaching and they're the ones we hear about in the paddling press. It does help if you can do the moves, especially for demonstration purposes, but the answer is no. You just need a great understanding of freestyle and an ability to observe and analyse the moves and be able to break them down into individual techniques that make up a move. A top tip for this is to visit good freestyle locations and spend time watching. Using a video is a great way to look closely at technique because you can slow motion and pause the action.

▶ What's So Different About Coaching Freestyle?

In most if not all aspects of paddlesport the aim of the game is to keep the craft upright, to get through stoppers and use waves merely to move around the river. In the sport of freestyle it's about the boat being upside down, in the air, on its edge whilst rotating and deliberately staying in a hole or pour-over. This is why the freestyle coach needs to think outside the box of normal thought to discover what is possible. It challenges and develops the individual's spatial awareness and alters their kinaesphere. As coaches we have to be able to help develop these areas with our students and some of the techniques needed are outside the paddlesport coach's normal repertoire of coaching skills.

▶ EQUIPMENT AND SAFETY

Getting the right kit for your students plays a huge part in their learning. A boat or paddle that is either too large or too small will certainly slow their progress or even lead to injury. The softwear they use is also important as they need to be able to move, so getting a specific freestyle buoyancy aid will give more freedom and look the part.

Photo 1 A well equipped freestyle paddler.

FOR THE COACH

Obviously, normal boating and safety kit is needed if you are going to be on the water. If bank-based, consider having a safety boater on the water; this could be the rest of the group if they are competent. As a minimum the coach should be wearing a buoyancy aid, have a throw bag, and a first aid kit should be at hand. Finding yourself on the edge of a weir with your student going round in the hole with no way of helping will be difficult to justify. Other useful kit is a video camera, small whiteboard and a model canoe/kayak as visual coaching aids.

LOCATION, LOCATION, LOCATION

Get this wrong and you will have a disaster! A huge amount of freestyle happens on weirs and these are very often the most dangerous places that you can paddle. Therefore it is essential that you have local knowledge and are aware of any changes that different water levels may bring. Choosing a location that is user-friendly and safe will have the knock-on effect of your students feeling comfortable and able to learn. Most of the fundamental work can be done on very easy sections of river such as eddy lines, small surf waves and even flat pools… you don't need a world class play feature to teach the fundamentals.

▶ THE EARLY YEARS

The sooner you get your paddlers spinning around, balancing the boat and even standing up in it and generally experimenting, the better. Even if it's their first time in a boat you can give them some great skills that can be developed for the future. Just give them loads of time to see how the boats move and understand how they affect its movement.

Think outside of canoesport as well. Other sports such as gymnastics, dance, diving and martial arts all have areas that link well to freestyle because they all require a high level of spatial awareness and body control.

BREAKING THE WHITE WATER RULES

❌ Rule 1. "Always edge into the turn when turning into or out of the current."

❌ Rule 2. "Never edge the boat upstream when side-surfing a stopper."

❌ Rule 3. "Don't let the bow or stern get sucked under."

When coaching white water skills we often use phrases like these to make sure our students don't keep falling in. Fair enough, but what happens after they have been paddling by these rules for a couple of years and then want to progress into freestyle? It makes even the most fundamental move, the tailsquirt, a really hard concept to grasp because you need to edge upstream. If we start paddlers out with the concepts above as rules they will stay as rules. If we change our language to reflect the fact that in most situations you edge into the turn but some more advanced skills mean edging away from the turn or upstream, your students will be more open to try things that before they would have been told never to do.

Photo 2 Warming up.

▶ WARMING UP

Freestyle is a very dynamic sport using a huge range of movement and muscle groups. It is essential that your students are ready for this type of activity. Try to warm up in a way that will reflect the movements that your students will be performing; this doesn't mean stretching, just getting the body warm, the blood flowing and the limbs mobile.

THE BRAIN

You will be expecting your students to try new things and coordinate their bodies in some new and unusual ways. By including some coordination exercises into the warm-up you will both warm the body and the brain, and then they will be both mentally and physically ready to learn and perform.

▶ As A Bonus

If you think about how to structure the warm-up and take time to observe your students' warm-up session, you can find out loads about them such as physical ability, coordination, flexibility, their ability to acquire new skills and even their preferred learning style in terms of VAK (visual, audio and kinaesthetic).

▶ FOUNDATION SKILLS

There are certain elements we should address before moving on to specific moves. These are balance, posture and edge.

BALANCE

This is an essential part of becoming a freestyle paddler. In other words the ability to balance your chosen craft both with static and dynamic balance and in a variety of body positions. Every time the body changes position the balance point will change, so it's important to practise balancing the boat with a variety of body positions.

POSTURE

This is how you sit or kneel in the boat. Poor posture can lead to poor technique or worse still injury. Posture is a personal thing depending on the physical make-up of the individual, for example whether a person has the flexibility to sit forward in the boat.

The seat position in the boat is also a factor to consider as most boats come with the seat fitted in the most convenient position for the fitters in the factory. Get your students to sit in the boat on the water and

look to see if it's balanced correctly for the paddler's size and shape. It should be balanced equally at each end; if it's not set up right then the paddler will struggle to perform through no fault of their own. A boat that is bow heavy will bury very easily. A stern heavy boat will feel very twitchy and the edges will catch, making it very unforgiving.

Photo 3 Posture

 TOP TIP

Using a Swiss ball is a great way to develop better balance, posture and core stability. Get some good advice on how to use one and give it a go.

Photo 4 Using a Swiss ball.

EDGE

Edge control is one of the most important elements of freestyle paddling. From being able to stay upright in a hole to initiating the front end of a cartwheel, most if not all moves are based around a change of edge or holding an edge and rotating around it. To achieve good edge control the posture must be good and so must the outfitting of the boat so as to prevent

PROGRESSIONS

• *exercise one:* Get students wobbling the boat from side to side then try it leaning back then forwards and see which technique gives more control over the edge (this will help them to understand good posture and the best position for edge control).

• *exercise two:* Facing and edging towards the partner.

• *exercise three:* Edging towards partner with body and head facing away.

• *exercise four:* Edging and leaning forwards and backwards.

• *exercise five:* On the move, paddling in a circle, try edging both to the inside of the turn and then the outside, (this gets the paddler used to the water pressure on the edge of the boat on the outside of the turn).

5c

5a

5d

5b

5e

Remember everything must be practised on both sides!

the paddler sliding around inside. Take time to help outfit your students' boats to ensure a good fit.

Take time to get them to understand the ways in which edge can be achieved, such as a knee lift or hip drop/buttock push. Have them consider how body rotation causes the boat to edge and how each different technique affects the boat and which technique or combination of techniques is used for each different move. For example a back stab uses a very dynamic hip and knee lift combined with body rotation, whereas a cartwheel uses more of a buttock push, progressing to knee lift, then into body rotation edge to create edge.

The ability to change edge is just as important. So make sure your students practise on both sides and have the ability to change from one edge to the other without a thought.

► USING THE POOL

Even though freestyle is a white water sport a huge amount of learning can happen in the pool, from rolling to flat water loops, stalls and cartwheels.

ROLLING

Whilst learning freestyle your students will soon be capsizing in a huge variety of positions and situations. Take time in the pool to develop a bombproof roll that works from a whole range of positions, from front and back loops and falling in whilst pirouetting. All will help when they are in the hole and getting power-flipped time and time again. The ability to roll quickly is essential so as to maintain position in the feature.

SPATIAL AWARENESS

As mentioned earlier this is fundamental for freestyle and the pool can be a great place to develop these skills by playing some games such as:

1. Pair up. One partner is to tuck up into a ball and the other picks a target for the partner to point at after they have been tumbled around in the water. This will help them to know where they are whilst spinning. This can then be repeated in the boat as well by rolling up and pointing to the target.

2. Modelling other moves. For example a semi-straight legged somersault (piked) is similar to the front loop.

► Introducing Balance And Rotation Moves

Fill the boat with water and get your students to try balancing the boat, first on the front end then the back. As the coach you help them by holding the position for them until they have found the balance point, this can be done both in the middle of the pool or using the edge for a bow stall. Then go on to do the same with the boat empty.

Photo 6 Bow stall

For the rotation fill the boat with water and get them to try pirouetting the boat around, firstly by using the paddle and secondly by only using body rotation.

Photo 7a Rotation with the paddle
Photo 7b Rotation without the paddle

► Vertical Moves

As a coach you can help your paddlers with their cartwheels by spotting them much like a gymnastics coach would. Be careful as there are boats and paddles being thrown around very close to you.

Photo 8 Loops

You can even coach loops in the pool by giving your paddler enough angle and down force that they can get the feel and the timing needed.

▶ WAVE SURFING

The ability to surf a wave and move around it is essential. Learning how the boat reacts on all the different parts of a wave will develop a great understanding of positioning, and positioning is key to achieving the more advanced freestyle moves such as blunts, flip turns, donkey flips and a host of other tricks that are still being invented.

ZONING AND POSITIONING

Stage 1 - Start by getting them to be able to split the wave into zones and identify the differences across the wave. This will help them to understand the shape of the wave and which zone can be used.

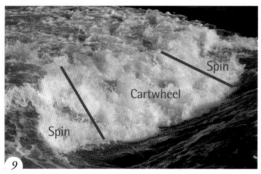

Photo 9 Split the wave into zones.

Stage 2 - Get them to move around each zone and then hold position in each zone. They will soon learn which zone of the wave they can stay in and which zones mean they have to keep moving, which parts give them speed and which zones give them time to rest or set up for a move.

Stage 3 - Encourage them to use their body to position the boat, using trim to gain or lose speed and edge control to move across the wave.

Photo 10 Using the body.

HOLE SURFING

Choose carefully. The right hole can be great fun, the wrong hole can be a very frightening experience.

Photo 11a Good hole!
Photo 11b Bad hole!

As with the wave, the hole can be split into zones. They can look for steep sections, release points, sticky sections and radials.

Before any moves can be learnt it's essential that they are comfortable in the hole and can exit the hole whenever they wish. Once this has been achieved it's time to start to move around the hole, with your students finding their way around the zones. They need to learn what each zone can be used for, such as the corners for spins or setting up cartwheels and loops, and using the sticky zones for regaining the hole.

Photo 12 Getting comfortable in the hole.

▶ GETTING VERTICAL

This is the one thing that every freestyle paddler wants and needs, the boat on end. Almost all the current moves are based around the boat being on end. Without the previous parts this just will not happen, so make sure they have good balance and edge control.

Find a good feature for performing enders and pop outs and you can work a whole host of vertical moves from pirouettes to cartwheels. This could be a small ledge drop, a pour-over or just a feature where the water comes off a corner creating a drop. It ideally needs to be deep and have good eddy service.

By getting them to be able to control the boat on end they can progress to pirouettes and then to cartwheels.

TOP TIP

• When trying transferring flat water cartwheels to a hole, practise on the flat as if you were in a hole. Pick a target on the bank to aim the bow and stern at, and spot the point with your head. Make sure that every end falls in line with the target and this should stop the boat walking around.

EXERCISES FOR CARTWHEELS

• *exercise one:* Get your paddler to think about using their legs when turning on the spot, a scissor action with the legs and paddle.

• *exercise two:* Lifting the bow with combo of edge, body and paddle.

• *exercise three:* Pushing the bow down with the same combo.

• *exercise four:* Combine 2 and 3 to get the boat spinning around without using the paddle.

13b

This exercise is good for encouraging paddlers to use the body more than the blade when cartwheeling. If this technique is then converted to a vertical axis it will lead to a smoother style.

With all the above exercises make sure they are not just throwing their weight backwards and forwards but are using the legs and hips in conjunction with the paddle.

13c

13a

13d

► LOOKING AT SHAPE AND MOVEMENT

All freestyle moves involve the boat moving through from 0° to 180° to 360° on one axis or another. The way in which it moves is important as it can give away clues to how the paddler is performing it, its efficiency and whether or not it's actually performed correctly.

SOME COMMON PROBLEMS WITH THE FOUNDATION MOVES:

► Tail Squirts

⊙ The paddler keeps falling in when crossing the eddy line. This is commonly due to one of two problems:

• Either the angle out of the eddy being too aggressive, which can usually be cured by letting the boat turn further downstream before the initiation reverse sweep.

• Or because the paddler is not comfortable in dropping the upstream edge whilst rotating the body the opposite way.

► Cartwheeling

⊙ When cartwheeling ask yourself if the boat's ends travel through a circular motion? If they are, the paddler is using well-timed rotation between ends and will be able to retain the feature and have more control.

⊙ Are the boat's ends forming an elliptical movement? If they are the paddler is using a forwards and backwards weight throw to force the ends around. This will lead to the paddler flushing from the hole and losing control and will make it hard to link to other moves. The technique described earlier can help solve this.

⊙ Does the boat flatten out on the second end? This could be because the body is rotating too early for the next end. Get them to wait until the stern of the boat reaches 12 o'clock.

► Spinning

⊙ The paddler initiates the spin with the paddle after they have looked back upstream. This can lead to an inefficient sweep and the amount of spin created will be reduced.

⊙ The boat is badly positioned on the wave or in the hole. This will make the spin either impossible or a lot harder than need be. Can be solved by using the zoning described earlier.

⊙ When flat spinning, look at the path the boat travels through, and ask yourself is the boat spinning on the spot or does it travel across the wave or hole? If it travels then the most common problem is that the paddler is edging the boat too much, leading to the boat starting to carve. This is common if paddlers lean back whilst applying the forward sweep in the final 180° part of the move. If the boat does not travel then good technique is being applied and the boat is flat spinning.

CLEAN MOVES

These are moves that only use the paddle for part of the move, for example with a cartwheel. If you only use the blade for the first end and body rotation for the second end that would be a clean cartwheel. If you went to the third end it would be a super clean cartwheel. These type of tricks involve an enormous amount of control over the boat and body. The ability to spin the boat without using the paddle is essential. You can work towards this by giving them a C1 paddle as it forces them to use the body and not the blade for the stern end.

► OFF WATER EXERCISES

There are many things that can affect your student's learning. It could be the environment being too exciting, the paddler having to concentrate on staying upright or it could be that there is too much to think about, with the feature, the boat, the paddle, and capsizing all getting in the way of learning. By removing some of these factors we can coach the basic technique then put the environment back.

DRY WAVES

Using a dry ski slope or sand dune is a great way to help your paddlers to get the feel of speed under the hull. It can be used for coaching basic straight surfing, flat spins or carving turns. The paddler can try many new things without the fear of wiping out and taking a beating or the fight to get on the wave. They can practise the technique time and time again and gain a good understanding of the move.

► Safety

Be careful with using dry ski slopes as a crash can be nasty. Paddlers should be wearing gloves and helmet and the coach should do a test run to check how high up the slope you need to take them. It's not normally as high as you would expect or like.

CANES

Tie two garden canes together at each end. Your student can then step between the two canes and hey presto they have the outline of a boat that sits on the hips and moves when they do! This is a great way of helping your students understand movement and where the boat, body and blade is during each move, whether it's surfing a wave, spinning on the corner of a hole or learning the sequence of a cartwheel in the car park next to the river. It works really well for getting the timing between edge changes, rotation and paddle switch.

MAPPING THE FEATURE

To help your students understand the different zones and where to position themselves on a particular feature, you can get them to draw the feature on paper or in the sand or dirt. A throw line works really well as they can get very detailed with it and there is no trace after you have finished. They can then walk through the different zones and model the moves on dry land. Add in the canes idea and the world's your oyster.

MAKING IT WORK EVERYWHERE

To help your students be able to repeat their performance in other features they must fully understand how the moves work and how each wave, hole and eddy line can be used. They need to be able to identify features and recognise which moves can be performed in each feature before going in to paddle it.

Photo 14 Canes

▶ COACHING MORE ADVANCED MOVES

Lots of coaches say: "I wouldn't know where to start with coaching the new moves". In truth the new moves are mostly adaptations of the easier moves or a few moves linked together, for example:

Pheonix monkey = Pirouette into front loop.

Tricky whoo = 2 split wheels together but using one blade throughout the move.

Take a look at any move and break it down, bit by bit and see what other moves are hidden within it. If you can use a video camera to do this it will be easier to slow the action down.

Freestyle is a fast-developing discipline of canoesport. As a coach you will need to stay in tune with all the developments, both in the moves and boat design, as new boats mean new thinking as to what is possible. This may mean going to freestyle events or purchasing good videos. Even better, go out and play. Freestyle moves are complex and a good demo goes a long way.

PETE CATTERALL

Pete Catterall is a Level 5 Inland Coach and works full time at Plas y Brenin, the UK National Mountain Centre. He is also the head coach for the GB Freestyle Team and helped them to medal successes at both the 2004 European and 2005 World Championships. As well as coaching, Pete has paddled extensively in Europe, India, Africa and South America and has accomplished three multi-day first descents in the previously unexplored region of Arunachel Pradesh in north-east India.

20 RACING

*P*reparation for competition paddling is a long-term process. As a governing body we are committed to the guidelines of our Long Term Paddler Development framework, and this gives coaches a sound basis to look at this process, with particular emphasis on the best preparation at each physiological age grouping.

INTRODUCTION

This section outlines some of the key issues relating to this long-term preparation process.

It is not a definitive guide as the issues are vast, but both the BCU and Sports Coach UK and other agencies can provide more in-depth training for coaches in this and other related fields.

Racing paddling is a power, endurance and skill activity. Preparation for a racing athlete includes a range of elements that build these capacities.

1. Endurance

2. Strength and Power

3. Speed

4. Functional Stability

5. Technique and Skill Development

6. Psychological Skills

7. Racing Skills

Good nutrition, health, rest, supportive families and educational establishments, supportive programmes for promising athletes all play their additional but vital part in preparing successful athletes for racing.

All these elements will be relevant to the development of each paddler throughout their career from beginner to Olympic Champion.

Some elements will take priority at certain phases of development as shown in the Long Term Paddler Development framework.

As examples, endurance and cardiovascular development will be particularly central to development in the phase up to mid-teenage, the Train to Train phase.

Strength and power development will be central in different ways to the stage from puberty in girls and from 12-18 months after puberty for boys.

Table 1 shows an outline of the training progressions as they apply in the junior stages, following on from the onset of puberty and the end of the Start and Development stage.

► BUILDING ENDURANCE AND SPEED ENDURANCE

The physiological key to going fast in the boat is speed endurance, the ability to maintain a high speed for a relatively long period, i.e. 500m or 1000m and to be able to tolerate high levels of lactic acid. This can be a period of between 1.40 to 6 minutes according to the level of paddler.

To improve this we need to concentrate on *Aerobic and Anaerobic Power* development. We can develop these through both our water and land-based training depending on the time of year and the developmental stage of the athlete.

Before looking at training methods, it helps to have a basic understanding of how we produce energy and the different energy systems, so read Chapter 2 before you continue if you haven't already.

In our sport we are dealing with paddlers who may have aspirations to compete at distances between 200m and 36km and their individual training needs will differ, however there is a great deal more crossover than may first appear in terms of the physical requirements needed for both sprint and marathon racing.

For instance while it is true that a 36km marathon would rely primarily on a well developed aerobic (oxygen) system, the ability to tolerate lactic acid build up following the start, during a burn or at the finish is just as important in gaining a good end result. Likewise a 500m race requires good lactate tolerance following the start but also the speed endurance, which comes from the ability to work at the upper end of the aerobic system.

To develop these attributes we need to follow some basic principles when setting our programmes.

The key elements of all training programmes are:

- Frequency - how often we need to do the session
- Intensity - how hard the session should be done
- Volume - varies depending on athlete
- Duration - how long is the session
- Sets - how many
- Reps - how many
- Rest - how much

TRAINING ZONES

The Training Zones Table gives a guide as to how we put these elements into practice. We need to follow these principles otherwise, while we may be aiming for one outcome from our sessions, the final outcome may be completely different.

If the aim of the session was to develop sub-race pace a good session would be 6 x 1000m starting every 8min, maintaining a stroke rate of 95 per min. Increase the number of efforts to 8 x 1000m, reduce the rest and reduce the stroke rate and the session soon changes to a mix of threshold and core aerobic pace.

We also need to take into account ability and developmental stage of our athletes. Again taking the above session as an example, while an elite athlete may be able to complete the session properly, a younger, less experienced paddler may only be able to complete 4 x 1000m at sub-race pace.

(See Table 3- Training Zones).

AEROBIC POWER

How do we develop Aerobic Power?

◎ It is training at threshold level and particularly sub-race pace which will help increase aerobic power. We therefore need to make sure that we programme this type of work during the year whether it is land based or water based.

◎ We also need to take into account the developmental stage of the athlete and the windows of opportunity laid out in the Long Term Paddler Development Model (LTPD).

◎ While aerobic development is crucial throughout the athlete's career, there is a window of opportunity during the Train to Train phase (male 12-15 female 11-14) that is the optimum time to develop first aerobic capacity and then aerobic power.

Table 3 'Training Zones', shows how we can fit in the different types and elements of training into programmes during the paddler's different stages of development.

Some examples of threshold and sub-race pace paddling sessions are shown on Table 3 Training Zones. To get the same effect from running or swimming, the paddling sessions can be adapted based on time and intensity. For example to get a similar benefit from a threshold paddling session of 6 x 1000m (4.30 pace or 80% RP) with 4min rests, a paddler might run 6 x 1200m with 4min rests or swim 6 x 300m with 4

	Train to Train				Train to Perform	
	Year 1	**Year 2**	**Year 3**	**Year 4**	**Year 1**	**Year 2**
Typical developmental age	boys 12-13 girls 11-12	boys 13-14 girls 12-13	boys 14-15 girls 13-14	boys 15-16 girls 14-15	boys 16-17 girls 15-16	boys 17-18 girls 16-17
Windows of opportunity Key times for development	Skill Aerobic capacity Strength development girls	Peak Speed Window Analactic aerobic capacity Strength development Hypertrophy g+b	PSW boys contd. Aerobic power Strength Development Hypertrophy g+b Girls +power	Aerobic power Strength development Hypertrophy g+b + power	Anaerobic power Strength development Max strength + power	Anaerobic power Strength development Max strength + power
Maintenance General development areas	Functional Stability	Skill Functional Stability	Skill Functional Stability	Skill Functional Stability	Skill Functional Stability General aerobic	Skill Functional Stability General aerobic
Skill	Different environments Wide range of skill developments Stability and feel Specialising on skill beginning	Increasingly discipline specific Stability and feel Still widening skill base Group and crew skills	Discipline specific Higher intensity Pace changes Group and crew skills	Discipline specific Higher intensity Increasingly race focussed Pace changes Crew skills	Discipline specific Racing performance focus Powerful paddling Boat feel in racing	Discipline specific Racing performance focus Powerful paddling Boat feel in racing
Volume Actual training time	4 –6 hours + other sports + non-activity coach time	6-8 hours + other sports	8-10 hours + other sports	10-12 hours	Up to 15 hours	Up to 20 hours
Sessions	3-4	4-5	5-7	8-9	8-11	8-11
Periodisation	Single	Single	Single	Single	Double or triple	Double or triple
Strength and Conditioning Land-based sessions Olympic lifting	2 per week often joint Girls general strength and begin structural hypertrophy Boys general conditioning Olympic lifting included	2 per week often joint Structural hypertrophy Coordinated strength Olympic lifting included	3 per week Structural hypertrophy Muscular endurance Coordinated strength Olympic lifting included	3 per week Structural hypertrophy into strength and power Muscular endurance Coordinated strength Olympic lifting included	3-4 per week Some structural hypertrophy Max strength and power Muscular endurance Coordinated strength Olympic lifting	3-4 per week Some structural hypertrophy Max strength and power Muscular endurance Coordinated strength Olympic lifting
Running Length and type a/c to season	2 per week + CAP joint sessions	2 per week + CAP joint sessions	2/3 per week	2/3 per week	2 per week min.	2 per week min.

Table 1 'Training To Train' and 'Train To Perform' training progressions.

min rests. Likewise in the gym, weight training sessions need to be adapted to meet the requirements for the different types of training. This of course is highly individual and will be determined by their abilities at running or swimming and here we may need to adapt programmes to suit the individual.

TESTING AND MONITORING

To get a clear picture of the intensity athletes need to work at we should test and monitor them individually. Table 3 Training Zones gives a guide to test distance to be performed at % of 1000m race pace, however heart rate and lactate levels are highly individual. Using a paddler's 1000m race time as a baseline we can then monitor heart rate and stroke rate on the test distances and in turn we can ascertain the level at which paddlers should work during sessions. Finding individual lactate levels is difficult in club situations, as it requires taking and testing blood samples.

▶ Comfortable Pace And 3 Point Test

While not highly scientific the comfortable pace and 3 point test can give us a more individual guide to the level at which an athlete needs to work. To do this we need to be able to monitor workload and heart rate.

Below is an example of the test carried out on a treadmill using gradient to increase workload, but on a paddling machine this could be done by stroke rate.

The procedure for the test is:

1. Find the athlete's comfortable pace (this is done by observing and talking to the athlete); they should be working but still able to hold a conversation. We then keep the athlete at this level for 4 min. (In the example this was at a workload of 8.3, Minutes 10-13, Workload 1).

2. The athlete then reduces to a very easy workload until the HR drops below the level it was at 4min into the test (in this case 3 mins, Minutes 14-16).

3. The workload is then increased to 15% above comfortable pace for 4min and heart rate is monitored each min. (Minutes 17-20, Workload 2).

4. The athlete again reduces to a very easy workload until the HR drops below the level recorded at 4min into the test (minutes 21-22).

5. The workload is then increased a further 15% for another 4min, once again HR is monitored. (Minutes 23-26, Workload 3).

Once the test is complete we can plot the data on the graph (see Fig. 1 overleaf).

HOW DO WE DEVELOP ANAEROBIC POWER?

Training at race pace and peak race will increase our lactate tolerance and increase anaerobic power.

Once again programmes need to fit the individual requirements of the athlete.

There are windows of opportunity in the Train to Train phase and continued development in the Train to Perform phase.

The important thing to remember is that Race Pace Training is *not* race practice. It is training the athlete to paddle at the pace they require to reach their end goal.

For example:

If we are aiming for 500m at 1.43, then we are looking for 200m at 40sec speed.

Time*	Work	HR	Time	Work	HR	Time	Work	HR
1	3.0	87	11	8.3	178	21	2.1	135
2	3.5	90	12	8.3	179	22	2.1	125
3	4.5	114	13	8.3	181	23	10.9	200
4	5.5	129	14	2.1	173	24	10.9	200
5	6.0	144	15	2.1	128	25	10.9	203
6	6.5	149	16	2.1	128	26	10.9	206
7	7.0	152	17	9.5	182	27		
8	7.5	162	18	9.5	192	28		
9	8.0	169	19	9.5	194	29		
10	8.3	176	20	9.5	195	30		

Table 2 Example of results from a Comfortable Pace and 3 Point Test.
  * Time in one minute periods.

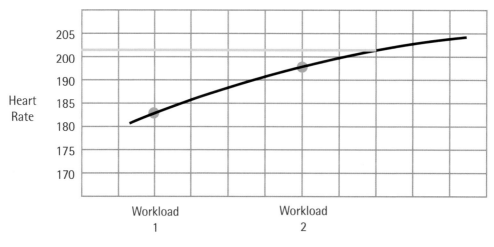

Workload 1 = Aerobic Threshold

A = Anaerobic Threshold (mid-point between Workload 2 and 3)

Workload 3 = Max HR

Fig. 1 Graph from a Comfortable Pace and 3 Point Test used to find athlete's Anaerobic Threshold.

To train for this:

1. Work to achieve 200m in 40sec.

2. Then work to do this with a more controlled powerful stroke.

3. Over a period of a few months extend the distance at which race pace can be maintained, i.e. 200m – 300m – 400m.

Peak Race Pace training is the top pace you will reach in a race. It is important to train at this level, as it is difficult for the muscles to give up their energy, as there is a bottleneck effect. Training at Peak Race Pace makes this bottleneck less restrictive.

For a guide to training levels and sessions refer to Table 3 Training Zones.

CANOE RACING TRAINING ZONES

▶ Background

The creation of the training zones for Canoe Racing has come about due to the demand that we all use the same terminology for describing what training we are prescribing or carrying out. In the past there have been many different terms used to describe the same type of training. None of the terms were particularly wrong, it's just that they were different. Many of the terms originated from those used in other sports, athletics or swimming for example, and may not have been completely transferable to canoeing. What we have tried to do here is to create a specific terminology which is as distinctive to canoeing as possible, but which also describes the type of training that needs to be carried out.

Once the same terminology is used and everyone is carrying out the training correctly, it is easier for squad programmes to be set with a continuum from young athletes to senior athletes. Progressions of training types, volumes and intensities can be set and followed more easily. Annual evaluations of an individual's or a squad's training can be accomplished with more accuracy than before, allowing more effective changes to take place.

▶ The Zones

We have tried to make the zones both practical and physiologically correct as much as possible. This is by no means comprehensive, and you could argue that some training intensities or types are missing, but included here are the ones that everyone involved felt covered the main requirements and needs of the flatwater paddler.

As can be seen the training speeds, heart rates and lactic acid levels will be different for each person, unless they have very similar competition results and physiological make-up, and so should be set individu-

Abbr.	Pace Name	Specific Physiological and Technical Aims of Training	Speed (% of 1,000m race pace)	Stroke Rate (% of 1,000m race pace)	Heart Rate (To be set individually)	Test Distance	Speed (To be set individually)	Perceived Levels of Exertion
CAP	Core Aerobic Pace	GENERAL ENDURANCE General improvements to aerobic system. Improving fat metabolism. Technique foundation.	60%	60+/-5		10km	1-2	Moderately comfortable. Intermittent conversation.
THR	Threshold Pace	SPEC. AEROBIC CONDITIONING Higher intensity aerobic improvements. Start of some aerobic work and lactate tolerance. Acceleration off the blade.	80%	75+/-5		5km	3-4	Slightly uncomfortable. Breathing heavily. More concentration.
SRP	Sub Race Pace	AEROBIC POWER Improving maximum ability to consume oxygen. Increasing lactate tolerance as anaerobic metabolism increases. Consolidation of near race pace technique.	90%	95+/-5		2000m	6-8	Hard, breathing very heavily but under control.
RP	Race Pace	RACE ENDURANCE Race practice, increasing ability to sustain high work rate. Maximum oxygen consumption and high lactic acid levels. Improving race technique.	100%	110+/-5	Max	750m	10+	Painful, breathing extremely hard. Lactic acid accumulation.
PRP	Peak Race Pace	PEAK RACE PACE Improving ability to sustain maximum speed. Improving anaerobic system and lactate tolerance. Keeping strong technique.	110%	130+/-5	N/A	200m	8+	Very hard, local muscular pain. High levels of lactic acid.
MP	Max. Pace	MAXIMUM SPEED Max. speed and power development. Improving anaerobic abilities - lactic and ATP-PC. Increasing maximum stroke rate.	112%	130-140 Max	N/A	100m	6	Fast and powerful, but physiologically comfortable.

Left margin labels: AEROBIC METABOLISM — ENERGY SYSTEM INTEGRATION — ANAEROBIC METABOLISM

NOTES

Resistance Work - Additional resistance work may be added to the kayak during any of these sessions, by either adding weight to the kayak, or putting bungees or balls on the outside of the kayak.

Technique - Separate technique sessions have not been identified. A technique emphasis, or goal, should be placed on every session. The aims of technique development may determine the type of session which can be prescribed, or the aims of the physiological development may determine the technique emphasis during a particular session. The priority of technique development versus physiological progression will change throughout the year.

Table 3 Training Zones

ally, based on 1000m times, on-water lactic acid profiling or ideally both.

The most important aspect of using these or any other training zones is their periodisation through the year, and ensuring that the mix of training is correct to allow consistent advances in physiological abilities and technique, and therefore performance. This is where the coach's role lies: programming training for individuals and groups but allowing for differences in capabilities and rates of progression. More assistance in this area can be gained from talking to other coaches who have had many years experience of going through this process.

▶ Technique

The development of effective and efficient paddling technique is essential for success at high levels of competition. Its development can take place within these training zones, and each prescribed session should have a technique emphasis. This emphasis may range from development of fundamental aspects of technique at lower intensities to purely maintaining some of these aspects at higher training intensities. Due to this approach a separate 'technique training' zone has not been identified.

▶ FUNCTIONAL STABILITY

Before moving on to Resistance Training we should look at the concept of balanced training as developed in canoesport.

We are teaching paddlers to carry out a high skill, all-body activity. It is often impossible for athletes to develop beyond certain points technically and in performance in competition, without a sound level of functional stability.

If the paddler cannot lock the blade at the catch and hang onto that blade without the shoulder area stability breaking up, they will not be able to improve their skills and maximise good technique and performance in racing.

If the trunk area is weak and unstable, then the power generated by the body will not be transmitted into the forward movement of the boat in racing, or manoeuvres in moving water competition.

The BCU has instigated a programme of research and training to address this vital area, working with Joanne Elphinston, a leading physiotherapist and specialist in this field.

This programme has dovetailed with an English Institute of Sport promotion of a wider examination of functional strength training, looking at a holistic approach to the paddler's development, strength, power and the application of the power to produce a high level of skill and performance.

WHAT IS STABILITY?

Stability will be defined as the ability of the body to withstand, support and generate forces with optimal efficiency and minimal musculoskeletal stress.

▶Efficiency

This is the best result for the least effort.

This minimises muscular/skeletal stress where structures are working in their optimal range and position.

As Racing Coaches, we are therefore interested in stabilising mechanisms for two reasons:

• Performance optimisation

• Reduction in injury risk

Stability can influence all the major areas of performance by our paddlers.

Speed

Power

Strength

Flexibility

Endurance

Paddlers with poor functional stability will borrow muscles whose prime role is in movement to prop up their stability.

Their movement muscle groups will fatigue early because they are also heavily involved in stabilising the body rather than just in moving the boat.

Their secondary stabilisers, controlling their movement, will quickly be ineffective.

To be successful with their paddlers, coaches need to be able to recognise the biomechanical elements of paddling.

They then need to be able to recognise the muscle groups and their role in the paddling movement, and their role in stabilising the body for that movement and controlling the movement.

A series of simple assessments has been devised where coaches can discover fundamental and then more detailed areas where their paddlers do not have adequate functional strength.

These assessments identify problems that may affect technical paddling skill, under-performance in training and competition and areas prone to injury.

Armed with the identification of areas to work on, the coach can then institute a general and specific programme of regular exercises using little equipment other than fitness balls, medicine balls, broomsticks and a mat.

This can soon become a general programme of high quality physical preparation for the sport, starting at the age of 8, rather than a remedial activity for paddlers who have been injured or who are identified with performance restricting problems.

Workshops and a CD/DVD resource, "Functional Stability for the Paddling Athlete" support a regular BCU programme of workshops for coaches.

▶ RESISTANCE TRAINING

The outline here of a Strength Training programme for athletes preparing for competition paddling is necessarily brief compared with the extent of the material involved in becoming an expert in this field.

It is the recommendation of the BCU and racing disciplines that coaches who are involved in preparing young and adult paddlers will need to be trained and qualified specifically in this area.

To this end the BCU runs British Weight Lifting Association Leader, Instructor and Tutor courses on a regular basis, as well as in-house workshops and resources on the discipline-specific aspects of strength and power training.

BWLA workshops are also available around the country, though these are targeted more at Olympic lifting coaches.

The advantages to be gained from working alongside Olympic lifters is considerable. We can gain from some of their attributes in terms of speed, control and power.

Further joint resources from BCU/EIS are also available, illustrating good practice in programmes for flexibility, sport-specific strength and power.

There is a BCU programme of Functional Stability workshops and paper and CD/DVD resources available to back this up.

Contact either of the National Development Coaches at BCU Head Office for details of workshops or resource availability.

RESISTANCE TRAINING FOR PADDLERS – THE RATIONALE AND THE PROCESS

"The direct correlation between strength and speed and performance is a proven fact"

Csaba Szanto Hungary and ICF

▶ The Target

Coaches in racing clubs are looking to develop paddlers who can move their boat, be it kayak or canoe, single or crew boat, faster over distances ranging from 200m to 26 mile marathons and beyond. All our training is aimed at that long-term goal.

▶ The Process

It is clearly accepted by physiologists that people cannot 'play' themselves into good shape for their sport, whatever sport it is.

Paddlers cannot paddle their way into best shape for being elite kayak and canoe paddlers.

It is necessary to do specialised training to develop certain qualities required in the sport, as well as working on the skills necessary, if they are to develop to a high level and avoid injury.

In canoe and kayak racing there are a variety of ways of approaching this process of development and the balance will vary at different times of the year and with different age groups. Ongoing reference to the earlier Train to Train and Train to Compete training progressions is necessary here.

○ *Strength* is identified as a crucial area for moving the boat faster.

○ *Endurance* is a crucial area as all racing competition is over a distance that is heavily endurance oriented.

○ *Coordination* is essential as paddling is a highly technical skill.

○ *Functional Stability* and *Functional Strength*. The general thrust here is to develop a more functional approach to conditioning, in turn enabling a more holistic approach to a paddler's overall strength, power and flexibility development. This enables the paddler's body to use the strength and power gained more effectively in moving the boat.

The muscle that paddlers develop must therefore be muscle with the necessary qualities of endurance, speed and coordination if paddlers are to be successful. Muscle bulk alone does not make paddlers go faster or have better technique.

To this end, the essence of strength development can be split into two areas:

- Building more muscle - structural hypertrophy.

- Refining the qualities of that muscle to make it useful for propelling boats quickly, in terms of endurance, speed, power and pure strength and coordination - functional hypertrophy.

As in most sports, the need is however largely for power.

 Strength is merely the ability to move a load.

 Power is the ability to move a load quickly.

ALL-ROUND ATHLETES

Coaches of younger paddlers are looking to create all round athletes in the 9 -13 age range, Start and Development and early Train to Train phases for boys.

Paddling in canoe or kayak is an all-body exercise, so paddlers need strength, power and coordination in their upper body, in the trunk and in the legs and lower body. This strength and body stability is the core of the body's ability to move the boat quickly and with good technique.

Most of these qualities will of course be applicable for use in all sports. Therefore the whole body should be trained.

Gaining a balanced whole body strength at this age is crucial to the future development of the athlete and their general health.

From 8-12 (notional age for girls) and 9-13 (for boys), the Start and Development phase is the age when the young athlete is prepared for the rigours that future, more intensive training on land, and boat training and competition will put on the body.

This process is much simpler than that for post-puberty paddlers, for most improvements in strength are based around improved neural connections to the muscles. Existing muscle is made more efficient, with better coordination and speed.

Moving to the Train to Train phase, after puberty, from 12 for girls and around 13+ for boys, is the prime age for developing more muscle

through hypertrophy training, and developing functional strength and stability.

From 15/18 years and onwards into senior level is the time to continue to build up more muscle, sport-specific strength and power and maintain functional stability.

▶ Where Are Junior Paddlers To Gain Strength?

Strength can be gained:

- In the gym - all muscle groups.

- On the water - most muscle groups.

- On land - running/swimming - some muscle groups.

In a paddler there is a demand for highly coordinated muscle with good speed, speed endurance and endurance qualities.

Each sprint race will require the paddler to repeat a load exercise 200 times for 500m, perhaps 400 times for a 1000m and many times more in a marathon.

The load in working a modern wing paddle can be up to 35kg with an elite adult, or even 40kg with a bungee. It may be 20kg in a junior or female paddler.

This load can be easily exceeded in the gym with weights exercises, with consequent gains in strength from the overload, so it is desirable to use periodised resistance training to build up more strength and power as fast and efficiently as possible.

It is usually seen that increases in strength and power are gained most effectively in the gym.

MAKING THE MUSCLE!

The periodisation of good training will devote a considerable proportion of time available from October to January to building muscle and strength. Especially in paddlers who have passed puberty, this will be heavily centred on building more muscle as body hormones will be supporting this process. For girls this is immediately post puberty, but of course is more pronounced with boys from 12-18 months after puberty onset.

Coaches will need to be aware of this process of hormonal change in their athletes and react to it in well prepared paddlers, by increasing strength training accordingly.

There will never again be such a receptive time to build muscle!

Coaches are advised to keep a close record of individual height on a weekly basis so they can recognise the onset of puberty in their athletes, and adjust their programmes accordingly.

There is evidence that younger athletes also produce some small increases in muscle before puberty, though most improvements here are neuro-muscular.

▶ Training The Muscle For Power!

From January onwards, both in the gym and on the water, that muscle will need specific training to increase its endurance and speed qualities and create power.

If this is neglected the paddler will be 'stronger' but this will not translate into power and paddling speed. In an extreme case of bad periodisation the paddler may just have acquired muscle bulk and the ability to move more weight slowly, and be slower on the water than before – something that has given strength training an anecdotal bad reputation in the past.

▶ Maintenance Of Strength

With the paddler well prepared for racing, using the new muscle acquired over the winter, the racing season will need to have time set aside to maintain that strength and power.

As the load on the paddler in the boat will always be less than that possible in the gym, the paddler will tend to gradually lose strength during the racing season unless gym strength maintenance training is carried out twice weekly at least.

This cyclical pattern over a period of years will see the paddler increasing the amount of muscle but translating this into boat speed on the water.

PROGRESSION AND REGULARITY OF TRAINING

As in all training, progression is of vital importance for improvement.

In strength and resistance training, stressing the muscles will cause change as long as that process of stress is progressive and is repeated often enough.

To ensure that the muscle reacts to the stress by changing, these muscles must be re-stressed at the level worked at, within 72 hours approximately, if there is to be improvement.

After 3 days there is full recovery.

After 4 – 5 days the effect is lost.

The implication is that the stressing of the muscle, i.e. the resistance training sessions, must take place ideally 3 times a week or more.

If only two sessions are completed each week, then only in younger juniors below puberty will this be a tolerable situation.

Two sessions or less for older juniors and seniors, and the effect will certainly be one of strength maintenance not strength improvement.

The muscle stress that prompts change and more muscle to develop or become more effective will also be dependent on the stress remaining at a high enough level. In the 3 sessions per week therefore, the load or number of reps must always be aimed at pushing the athlete to demand change from his/her muscles.

Junior elite athletes will be able to tolerate a maximum of 4 strength development sessions per week.

Potential elite level athletes will manage 5 sessions within a balanced programme.

All athletes at any age should move from one level of training to another in stages.

A 16 or a 21 year old will be badly advised if he moves from 1 - 5 sessions a week without a series of stages in between.

Moving from 1 - 3 sessions, 2 - 4 sessions, 3 - 5 sessions is recommended as being appropriate.

The coach is crucial in monitoring this process and encouraging the athletes to push themselves to new higher levels in a safe environment where progression is controlled, well recorded and informed.

Two extremes will need to be dealt with:

• Very competitive groups of often male athletes may push themselves to increase loads too often and by too much. This will need to be restrained to allow the body to adapt and prevent injury.

• Some athletes will be content to keep loads at the same level because it is easier or less 'painful'. They will need to be motivated to go for bigger loads and more intensity if they are to develop strength.

MATCHING THE TRAINING TO DEMANDS OF PADDLING

It is vital to make execution of exercises match what we are trying to encourage in the paddler.

This implies:

◉ Executing exercises with emphasis on powerful movement. A 12 reps sessions should run at 1 second per rep. Slow exercising encourages slow reacting muscles and has little or no place in our preparation of athletes.

◉ Extension of arms etc. should reflect the movements needed in paddling technique.

◉ Good technique, e.g. both arms working symmetrically and in a controlled way in Bench Press encourages the coordination requirements of paddling.

◉ Isolation of parts of the body, e.g. locking body on a pull down machine encourages the necessary upper/lower body contrary movement skills.

◉ Any sloppy technique in the gym will replicate in sloppy paddling on the water.

▶ Programme Duration

🌗 **Start and Development (Pre-puberty level) 8 to 12/13**

For these athletes the strength development programme may take place throughout the winter with periodisation looking for maintenance only in the racing season.

🌗 **Train to Train (post puberty, puberty) 12/13 to 15/16**

Hypertrophy and strength development demands programmes of a minimum of 6 weeks, perhaps up to 8 weeks before a change of emphasis is required. This usually implies one hypertrophy phase per winter, followed by work to build maximum strength, speed and endurance. It is possible to run 2 cycles in one year but this is usually precluded by competition demands.

🌗 **Train to Perform - 15/16 to 18-20**

Once again the basis of one structural hypertrophy phase followed by maximum power and endurance strength phases that are tailored to the competition programme is the effective layout. Maintenance throughout the racing season is essential. Coaches will need to be more specific in planning individual programmes that reflect the strength development needs of individual athletes at this stage.

▶ PSYCHOLOGICAL SKILLS

Confidence, inner calm and my strength and belief in myself all come from working hard to prepare for performance. I think areas such as pre-race visualisation are the key to secure this confidence. It ties everything together. I think it is a very important area to master as a junior.

Ian Wynne (GB and Olympic Bronze medallist in K1)

Most coaches acknowledge that mental skills are an important aspect of top performance and need to be developed along with technique, strength and fitness. A guide has been prepared by sport psychologists who work with sprint and marathon athletes, from junior to World Champion ability. It contains some basic reference material and ideas for how you can incorporate essential mental skill development into regular training sessions. It is not a comprehensive guide – there are plenty of these already. What they have tried to do is distil the essentials and make them very sport-specific.

The skills are presented under a number of topic headings, but in fact they are all interrelated. Developing more effective goals, for example, is an essential aspect of a successful race routine which in turn helps improve concentration and builds confidence. Whilst the material is pitched at juniors, the content is applicable to competitors at all ability levels.

The full manual was written by Sarah Cecil, Tony Gleadell, Jonathan Males and Ian Raspin. It has one version for the athlete and one for the coach.

The contents cover Self Confidence, Goal Setting, Concentration, Imagery, Relaxation and Emotional Control, Race Routines, Team Building.

The BCU offers training workshops to support coaches to understand their paddlers' needs and support them in learning these vital skills.

Resources and details of courses can be obtained from National Development Coaches at the BCU.

Chapter 3 Psychology summarises the issues raised in the full manual and below I have included the more racing specific issue of team building.

RACE ROUTINES

Race routines improve the consistency of performance by removing variation. A good routine focuses attention on the right factors and enables learning by making it easier to identify the impact of any changes. Routines should incorporate all the relevant physical, technical and mental elements of a race performance. By having a clear plan, the paddler is less stressed, more relaxed, and can feel more confident that everyone is in place for a good performance.

A good routine should be simple and adaptable to all races. There needs to be some flexibility and the ability to deal with unexpected events. It's important to be clear about the real priorities in a routine, so that if a routine is disrupted, the disruption itself doesn't cause additional stress. Over time the routine should allow the paddler to become increasingly autonomous and less reliant on you, support staff or parents.

An effective race routine starts at least a day before the race and needs to pay attention to diet, sleep and travel arrangements. On the day of the race the routine should allow time for boat preparation and physical and psychological warm-up.

The routine should include a specific race plan for the events. The race plan is formulated in consultation with the coach and includes technical, physical and psychological components.

After a competition, spend some time to review your performance and your race routine. Discuss with your paddlers what worked well and what they might want to change. Remember, there are two types of error - errors in decision and errors in execution. The same applies to race routines – a paddler may have chosen to have done the right thing but executed it poorly, or chose to do the wrong thing but executed it well.

TEAM BUILDING

Although canoeing is largely an individual sport (except crew boats) team relationships off the water can have an impact on paddler's self-confidence and performance.

Any team has 'norms', which are unwritten rules of behaviour that are just as significant as any formally agreed rules. It's important that team mates have shared expectations about acceptable behaviour within a team, relating to, for example, punctuality, bad mouthing others, leaving training areas tidy and managing a bad training session. This becomes particularly important during team trips when paddlers are sharing accommodation and eating together, when lack of agreement on room etiquette can be a major source of unnecessary stress.

Achieving high quality training can often demand mutual support between the training group and/or the coach.

Smoothing the way – the key is listening effectively and being sensitive to others' feelings.

As a coach you are an important role model for the way people communicate within a squad. It's particularly important for you to set the right tone regarding humour. Banter and 'taking the piss' is inevitable in any group of energetic, fit, and ambitious athletes, particularly young men. Where the humour is predominately good natured it leads to greater team spirit and can defuse tension. Some humour, especially sarcasm, is instead used as a way of establishing and maintaining a 'hierarchy' in the group and can lead to resentment and a loss of confidence amongst those who are the targets of such 'humour'. Pay attention to the banter in the team and be very clear about what's acceptable and what's not.

One essential skill that you can demonstrate and encourage is Effective Listening, which involves:

- Restating and summarising to show that you have understood what the other person has said.

- Using appropriate 'non verbal' signs such as nodding, looking at the person who's speaking, and the occasional 'uh huh'.

- Openness to new ideas/ways of doing things.

- Making the time to really understand others' point of view rather than assuming you know what they mean.

CONTRIBUTORS

Thanks are specifically due to:
Barney Wainwright (BCU World Class Sports Science)
Steve Train (Fladbury Paddle Club and BCU World Class Coach)
Narelle Sibte (formerly of English Institute of Sport)
Joanne Elphinston (Elphinston Performance)
Graham Campbell (BCU)
Sarah Cecil (St. Mary's Twickenham)
Ian Raspin (BCU World Class Coach)
Tony Gleadell,
Jonathan Males
Many other BCU and BCU World Class staff

RESOURCES

Resources and workshops available for the Racing Coach from the BCU National Development Coach for Slalom, Polo and Freestyle, and the BCU National Development Coach for Flat-water and Wild Water Racing. (These resources are sometimes only available at an approved workshop).

Functional Stability for the Paddling Athlete CD	*BCU/Joanne Elphinston*
Strength and Resistance Training booklet	*BCU*
British Weight Lifting Association Training Manual	*BWLA*
Strength and Conditioning CD	*BCU/EIS*
Teaching Technique in Kayak booklet	*BCU*
Racing Canoe Paddling booklet	*BCU*
Circuit Training for Racing booklet	*BCU/Imre Kemecsey*
Warm-up and Recovery booklet	*BCU*
Medicine Ball Training booklet	*BCU*
Video use and Dartfish software	*BCU*
Library of training sessions and analysis CD	*BCU*
Programme Setting Software CD	*BCU/Chris Jones*
Psychological Skills	*BCU*
Mental Training	*Imre Kemecsey*
LTPD the BCU pathway	*BCU*

GRAHAM CAMPBELL

Graham is a L4 coach, specialising on the placid water and Racing side. He worked as a volunteer coach for nearly 20 years and for 4 years as National Development Coach for flat water. While coaching international juniors and seniors, he developed his interest in teaching technique and worked with top international coaches to search for the most effective way of introducing these high level skills.

He has recently retired to France, but is still involved in coach development.

21 HIGH PERFORMANCE COACHING

To Get A Sip

There are no shortcuts for winners
No free rides
The winner does not look for handouts or freebies
He or she knows that the only worthwhile things to achieve in life
Are things that we earn through sweat and hard work
Things we had to fight for
Things we had to hit limits to get or to achieve
These are things worthwhile achieving
They are the true champagne of life
Go and get yourself a sip

Ralph Kruger, Swiss National Ice Hockey Coach

INTRODUCTION

High Performance Coaching is the term increasingly used to describe the expert coaching and support of performers and athletes who aspire to perform at the highest levels of sport, whether it is winning medals consistently at International Championship level, taking on the most extreme river or sea expedition challenges or setting the record time for the Devizes to Westminster. It is a term frequently associated with coaching at Levels 4-5.

For this chapter, input from a group of expert paddlesport coaches, working with or having worked with elite performers, has been drawn on and summarized in an attempt to crystallise the essence of what being a High Performance Coach means. The aim has been to discover, for the reference of future coaches, what is accepted as World's Best Practice, with a view to identifying the key factors, attributes and behaviours that distinguish a High Performance Coach. The words 'high performance' and 'elite' should not distract the reader. They are part of the language of coaching and we can all consider them in relation to where we may see ourselves, either within the performance continuum or the coaching spectrum. They are terms often associated with coaching at Levels 4 and 5.

The collective thoughts of the group of expert coaches were focused via a series of questions and are presented here in two key areas:

◉ **Defining and understanding High Performance Coaching.**

◉ **Key skills, processes and tools that High Performance Coaches use in their coaching.**

Wherever possible there has been an attempt to keep to the generic 'how' of coaching so that the points made are relevant to canoe coaches whatever the discipline, competition or recreation-based and hopefully also to sports coaches from outside of canoeing.

Prior to progressing it is worth commenting that for many readers, whether paddler or coach at development or elite level, some of the observations and comments here may seem obvious and already second nature. If so then please reflect on the fact that we may not have been able to fully highlight the degree of 'competency refinement' recognisable at a high performance level.

Hopefully the reader will be able, depending on their own current coaching level, to reflect on their own current degree of understanding of the coaching process and coaching delivery, and consider areas where this can be refined and 'individualised' to move forward. In reading this as the concluding chapter of the book you will be able to consider how the preceding chapters will enable you to consider your own development action plan.

▶ DEFINING HIGH PERFORMANCE COACHING

KEY ASPECTS OF HIGH PERFORMANCE COACHING

High Performance Coaching is all about having a thorough appreciation of the technical, physical and psychological attributes required to deliver improved performance. Coaches working at this level would hold a fascination in challenging and advancing these areas.

Key areas that should be associated with coaching performance at this level and in achieving continuing advancements are:

◑ **High Performance Athletes** - With the appropriate age range, potential and possessing the necessary qualities, drive and commitment to perform at the highest level.

◑ **Cutting Edge Skills and Techniques** - Always with success in its sights and keeping ahead of the rest by reinventing itself and being innovative. Using measurable performance points, indicators and programmes that monitor, evaluate, adapt and then move forward.

◑ **World class training venues** - Both water and land-based in the UK or abroad to aid their development.

◑ **A Big Picture Approach** - An integrated vision with a sense of purpose and a clear vision of the end game, always thinking holistically, embracing all lifestyle aspects of an athlete's development.

◑ **Self-belief** - There should be a confidence and self-belief to drive a project forward and a passion to succeed.

◑ **An implicit high level of understanding** - Particularly regarding the demands of the sport, with all coaches kept updated and abreast of world best practice. This would include continuous professional development and a strong desire from both staff and athletes to develop and update knowledge.

◑ **A consistency of message, attitudes and provision** - Success will not come from 'jumping around' from idea to idea, but from consistent progress along a journey with a singular message to the athlete. This is an essential part of developing inclusive, robust and productive relationships between coaches and athletes to aid success.

◑ **Close supportive links with all partner organizations** - Good communication fostered with the BCU, other sports, Sports Institutes, Sports Councils and Media.

WHAT ARE THE KEY QUALITIES OF A HIGH PERFORMANCE COACH?

The High Performance Coach would be someone with a comprehensive understanding of the sport, with an up-to-date knowledge in sports science and the use of technology to augment rather than to lead their coaching. They should be a good analytical thinker with a breadth of experience and the ability to problem solve.

They would have a clear sense of purpose and vision, and be capable of pushing the boundaries and perceived ceilings of excellence. They would be a confident coach with an unshakeable belief both in self and in the performers, demanding the highest levels of performance.

They would be a coach who is enthusiastic, passionate and committed but also resilient, determined and mentally very tough, who can stay grounded at all times, a coach who can be a positive role model to both athletes and peers.

> **The High Performance Coach can be categorised into two types:**
>
> • A coach of elite athletes.
>
> • An expert coach of elite athletes.

Both of these can be characterised on a development continuum. Expert coaches, however, while seeing the same world as others, can view it differently and transform athlete performance as a result. By definition each sport has very few of these expert coaches at any one time.

ESSENTIAL EXPERIENCES, ATTITUDES, SKILLS AND PRINCIPLES

What are the essential experiences, attitudes, skills and principles in the development of a High Performance Coach?

▶ Essential Experiences

It is important not only to have had grass roots coaching experience with responsibility for all areas of a paddler's development but also to have worked closely with a number of paddlers from beginner right through to expert. Implicit here is longevity in the sport. The coach should show evidence of development and experience outside paddlesport either in another sport or in a relevant work place, especially involving process-oriented environments with access to a sharing knowledge network that stimulates and challenges the status quo. A coach should have had experience (not necessarily as a performer) of a high performance arena with all the accompanying high stress, pressures and expectations, including handling both success and failure in coaching.

The coach should also have worked as an apprentice to or been mentored by other experienced HP coaches either in paddlesport or in other sports covering a wide spectrum of different coaching environments.

He should have had experience of observing how the High Performance end of paddlesport operates across a range of disciplines and activities along with having a good working knowledge of the BCU and its volunteer support systems.

A coach should have embraced a culture of continuous professional development (CPD) with a commitment to attending workshops, training courses, seminars and conferences on a regular basis. In particular those covering the analysis of performance, technical aspects of intervention strategies and observational training and the overall impact sports science can have on paddlesport performance.

▶ Essential Attitudes

A coach should take a holistic approach, be it with a person or issue. He should be vicarious in looking anywhere for opportunities to advance, never being satisfied with the status quo, always looking for ways to maintain momentum in improvement.

A coach would need to be committed 100% plus to the project with an expected reciprocity from the athlete and they should be ambitious, although not always apparently so on the surface. He views competition and challenge as an experience that essentially enriches the individual – whether athlete or coach.

Coaches should be honest with themselves and in dealings with others, promoting a culture of openness, with an ability to admit mistakes and move on.

▶ Essential Skills

A coach should be a great communicator with superb people management skills, completely at ease in creating and managing a coaching environment, with good time management, planning and organising skills. In short he should be a planning perfectionist with an ability to review, assess and use information quickly and profitably.

A coach should have an extremely high technical knowledge base and excellent observational techniques, possessing an unerring ability to pinpoint the 'key elements' of a sport and relentlessly revise and update them. He should be familiar with all aspects of differentiation.

▶ Essential Principles

This is a coach who looks to apply the basic principles of trust, fairness, respect, honesty and integrity throughout their coaching career, supporting fair play and the rules of the game. They put 'Person' first and 'Person as an athlete' second, with winning not the 'be all and end all', understanding that fallibility is a normal human state and that promoting activities that help raise self-esteem is the key to an athlete or coach flourishing. They would have an ongoing 'fascination for the process' of coaching and a continuing commitment to performance self-improvement.

HOW DOES COACHING AT A HIGH PERFORMANCE LEVEL DIFFER?

How does coaching at a high performance or elite level differ from coaching at development level?

▶ The Nature Of The Process

The High Performance environment is much less forgiving, meaning results are harder to get and the increase in performance levels of athletes much smaller. This can lead to frustration and the need for this to be managed by athlete and coach. At elite level you have to look so much harder for potential areas of improvement, which can be tiny, and sometimes not there. It is more about changing behaviour and technique that may already be ingrained.

Developmental coaching is often about educating the athlete in many aspects of the sport. When working at this stage, athletes often have a clean slate and progress can be quicker. Development athletes have a lower skill level and may require more feedback, and at times may actually need to be physically shown by the coach or a better athlete in the boat what to do. Their attention time span is usually shorter as they are less accustomed to long periods of intensive training, making session content a key decision.

KEY POINTS

- **Recognition of success** - for both athlete and coach – It's easier for the outside world to see a World/Olympic Champion than to see when a young athlete has started to master a new skill. There are implications for good goal setting in both cases.

- **Taking into account sacrifices** - The athlete is likely to be making huge sacrifices and therefore the coach needs to take this into account. Expectations of everyone involved are far greater and therefore require good management, again with sound evaluation, planning and goal setting.

▶ Coaching Style

The relationship between athletes/performers and their coach can and will vary at different levels; at a development level there may be more of a 'leading' style but at High Performance level it is more of a partnership. For the development paddler/coach the commitment levels, the greater need for encouragement and a recognition that the physical, technical and tactical challenge is at a different level dictates the style and pace of delivery.

The High Performance Coach can afford to be harder on an athlete who is performing at an elite level as they should be totally focused on improving performance. As an athlete's balance of the physical and neural challenges changes, as they become more feeling and expert and their technical side becomes more autonomous, the physical and tactical considerations come more to the fore.

▶ Challenging The 'Norm'

At elite level ideas and principles are always being challenged - it is performance driven. There is a national responsibility to drive the process forward, onwards and upwards. There are rich seams of within-sport experiences to draw upon, especially so in a small sport like slalom. A High Performance Coach needs to know what the opposition is doing worldwide, needs to train with them and talk to them, and then confidently share, measure, evaluate what they see… then reject or take on board.

HANDING THEM ON

Should a coach move with his/her athletes as they develop *or* at key stages 'hand them on' to more experienced coaches?

▶ Coaches Handing Athletes On

This depends upon the skills of the individual coach, options and resources available and the coaching culture of the nation involved. It raises the importance of every country having an agreed coaching philosophy.

In many cases coaches work with athletes of a standard that they are most effective (and comfortable?) with. If the primary objective is to develop the athlete then 'not handing on' runs the risk of not providing the best support for the athlete. All athletes approaching transition need to be looked at individually by all coaches in the equation. Several factors are crucial - coach availability, coach location, athlete location, location of training partners and regular quality water (white water in the case of slalom) and not least the opinion of the athlete.

In an ideal world it would be great for the coach to move through with younger athletes. Unfortunately not all kids make it and move through at the same speed of progression. This would also leave you with a high number of coaches at senior level with perhaps no coaches coming back into programmes at junior levels - a difficult balancing act.

Well-managed transitions are the best way to go. Athletes can choose personal coaches but NGBs must offer pathways of formal coaching. Very few elite juniors progress to elite seniors and I would be concerned if an athlete had only one coach throughout their career. In some sports this 1:1 relationship is limiting, risky and can in some cases be catastrophic. In a more established, better resourced nation, logistics tend to make this more difficult. So it would probably be better to 'hand on'. However this requires careful planning with coaches and athletes to try to minimise the disturbance during the transition periods.

There should always be *the opportunity for an athlete to retain a coach in a mentor capacity,* which can be beneficial for both parties. Clearly defined roles and responsibilities are the key here.

▶ Moving Through With Athletes

With a new/developing nation, or one with small resources, it may be better to progress with the athletes and absorb younger athletes into what in effect becomes a mixed group. There can be real training opportunities here for fast tracking especially with Juniors and the minor classes (e.g. in slalom C1/C2/WK1). The gains for athletes and coaches can be tangible although there can be issues in the race season when athletes will be racing at different events over the same weekend.

If the objective is to develop the coach then every attempt should be made to stay involved with the athlete in at least some capacity. Coach and athlete should be allowed to progress whilst they are achieving the desired growth, development and technical outcomes. A good system is one that can be flexible enough to accommodate individual coach and athlete needs.

PERFORMANCE BACKGROUND?

Should a High Performance Coach have performed at a high level themselves?

There are two points of view outlined below. The fact is that both backgrounds have advantages and dis-

advantages. *The key issue for me is the demeanour, care and style of the coach rather than the level of competition they may have competed in.*

▶ High Level Paddling Experience Essential

Yes, wherever possible. In a technical sport they require in-depth knowledge to succeed, which generally comes from performing themselves. Very few successful coaches in slalom have not had a background in international performance. Without this you nearly always have to work a squad system to get athletes to draw from each other. On 1:1 coaching the development may be limited by the knowledge of the coach, which is likely to be less effective if there's no background of international experience.

Aspects of paddlesport such as slalom are very technical, unlike sprint racing or swimming where knowledge of training and motivational aspects may be more important. Nowadays elite athletes might not accept a coach if they had not been a successful athlete themselves. There are exceptions, such as Mike Druce in the Aussie C1 class and Kev McHugh with the GB C1/C2 classes as an example from slalom.

Having a coach without an elite paddling background becomes more difficult if there is no appropriate elite 'technical bench mark' within the group. One solution here is for the group either to travel or invite better paddlers in to train.

▶ Elite Level Paddling Experience Is Not Essential

This view is based on the belief that any systematic observer can coach and can apply principles to bring about behavioural change. Access to, and not necessarily involvement in high performance sport can transform a coach's understanding and approach.

It is not essential to compete at a high level in the sport in which you coach and I have concerns about any sport that demands this as an entry requirement. A skilled performer does not necessarily make an effective coach. However as previously mentioned a HPC should have a clear 'big picture' of high performance development and how to achieve it and an understanding of the demands of the sport. This can be achieved through competition, or equally well through effective observation of the sport over a period of time. It can be easier if the coach has competed at a high level, as the coach will then have an inside view of the demands an athlete is under. However, this can also cause problems, for example, if a coach was previously an extremely successful athlete, they may not be able to relate to, or understand the problems or stages of development a less successful athlete is undergoing.

Having not competed can lead to a more open and questioning viewpoint but if the coach hasn't competed at a high level it can sometimes be harder for them to gain respect from the athletes. The solution is not a quick one and they need to immerse themselves in the sport and gain a real understanding of the elite end of performance.

It also needs the coach to take a slightly different approach when dealing with the athletes (for example approaching them from a position of strength in an area where they may be expert – say psychology or physiology). Another good technique is to throw the challenge back to the paddlers by asking 'how can you best use me?' In most cases *the best coaches operating like this also have the back-up of some top technical coaches/or very experienced athletes.* In fact many groups feel a mix of both types of coaches works best

ATHLETE DRIVEN – COACH STEERED

That coaching should be 'athlete centred' is pretty well taken as read but is that enough? How much and how early should an athlete be encouraged to be independent and the process become Athlete Driven – Coach Steered?

The aim should be always to encourage independent decision-making, promote a positive self-image and develop self-confidence. The sub text should always be to coach the athlete to become non-dependant and the coach to become redundant.

From the very start discuss programme and co-ownership in the project, and present them with choices to encourage self-belief. Encourage independence in thinking, planning, and decision-making at events. Encourage paddlers to take responsibility in groups for leading sessions, designing courses, organising feedback, running video sessions, giving the whole process a '2 way feel'. Don't be there for every race. Encourage self-sufficiency and dealing with the 'What ifs'.

At the end of the day the coaching of elite athletes should become (gradually) a more and more invisible occupation. The coach drops more into the background, steering, advising and just being there. Empower them wherever possible as long as the choices they make in your care are safe and ethical. This should happen naturally in any good coaching relationship. Self-direction and operation is important and ultimately makes for stronger athletes and coaches.

There will always be those athletes who can only ever be partially autonomous. All athletes require some direction at times. There will be individual differences and character traits that will define how they like to be coached and how fast, if at all, they progress towards operating autonomously. Managing this is a key art of coaching.

KEY SKILLS, PROCESSES AND TOOLS

▶ Managing The Process Of An Athlete-Driven – Coach-Steered Approach

When an athlete is developing they have gaps in their understanding and often do not know what it is they need to know. A coach can help ensure this knowledge is imparted at the right time in their development. However the motivation should always come from the athlete. The athlete needs to be intrinsically motivated whenever possible, such as creating a motivating and positive environment when things are tough.

⊙ How to develop? - Ensure athlete realises that drive and enthusiasm are the fuel to succeed, but without the right map and direction, the tank will soon be empty with little to show for it.

⊙ How to manage? - A thorough and intense trusting relationship between the athlete and coach. The coaching should continually educate and empower the athlete to take responsibility for his/her own destiny.

This underpins how coaching for high performance develops. Organise the basics for them but give them ownership and point out to them their responsibilities on the programme. There should be absolute clarity on their roles and responsibilities, on the coach's role and also of the expectations on them. Constantly monitor training to make sure they are adhering to agreements. Always be willing to help but it must come from the athlete as a request, not an expectation… Critical here is how successful coaching is measured.

Young athletes should not be coached prescriptively. A coach's role is to induct people into the sport and hope they will make it the sport of their choice. The key is an approach that works with small groups and creates a guided discovery environment. Although some athletes appear to always need more driving and support than others, any coach with enough sensitivity and awareness to pick up individual differences and needs can address this.

Coaches should also work more in 'development age' groups rather than 'chronological age' groups. It is within every coach's remit to promote multi-class, multi-age learning opportunities. Careful mixing of groups vertically on a regular basis will create learning opportunities that cannot be achieved amongst peers or with bigger groups. Young people are outstanding observational learners and we should continually be seeking to enrich their worlds with lots of different stimuli.

These issues reflect the personal responsibility of the athlete. To assist in this, involve the athlete in planning and review processes, so that they understand where they are, where they want to get to and how they plan to get there. This way they take ownership of the process, instead of being told what to do, where and when. Hopefully they are then more likely to put more into the whole process, and so get more out of it.

On the programme side there are far more occasions when this has to be coach-led and more prescriptive. The coach's role here should be:

- To keep an overview of how the athlete fits into the 'programme'.
- To help define boundaries (agree acceptable behaviour or operate within 'the rules' for instance).
- To look at the relevant support services available.
- To constantly 'feed in' new ideas.
- To think strategically on how to help the goal-setting process.
- To organise the feedback data, and overall facilitate the athlete to revisit, review and plan ahead.

It's often easy for one side or the other to dominate thinking and oversimplify this whole 'coaching process' by trying to 'pigeonhole it' into just one box.

Canoeing is not a natural occurrence and as such needs quite specialist technical direction. The coach's job is to refine and develop the qualities that the athlete has rather than rebuild something that he or she would like. The amount of input depends on the individual make-up and progress of the athlete. That said, 'coach input with athlete drive' is a great combination and is slightly different to the initial statement above.

SUPPORTING HIGH PERFORMANCE COACHING

What are the most important tools and coaching processes for supporting High Performance Coaching?

Coaches And Athletes

The coaches... their knowledge, their attitudes and their professionalism, and of course the athletes.

The quality of observational and critical feedback analysis is paramount. All coaches should have a broad knowledge of all the key support mechanisms or there can be no effective use of the information received. The coach needs access to information that can be understood and easily delivered to the athlete. As each athlete is different the coach needs plenty of options on where to gain the necessary information and on the appropriate ways to deliver it.

It is also important not to lose sight of the athlete in this support process. Without their desire and commitment to be the best at what they do nothing works.

▶ Funding – National And Regional

The key sources of support that allow coaches and athletes to commit both financially and lifestyle-wise to the programme.

▶ Support Services

High Performance Coaching has to make the most of the services provided by sports science and medicine.

The challenges that sport science/medicine support services present to High Performance Coaching:

- Not enough time, money or staff to fully utilise efficiently and effectively. Also a CPD challenge to coaches as often they will feel less knowledgeable and possibly intimidated by the science experts.
- Co-ordination - Being able to fully integrate the support for the athlete into the big picture..
- Successfully integrating them into the package, so that they feed into one another, rather than operating as distinct 'packages', e.g force measurement data will inform strength and conditioning, tieing into physiotherapy and video analysis, and maybe psychology. The whole is more than the sum of its parts. Sports sciences and medicine can challenge the coach's and athlete's thinking, as well as the conventions of the sport. This can lead to tensions and arguments when trying to 'move forward' unless the thinking behind them is clearly explained and managed.
- Getting sports science and medicine to understand the language and intricacies of the sport is essential. Their challenge is to adapt testing to fit the sport and not the other way around.

• The more people that are brought into the coaching process, the more chance of conflicting, or mixed messages, leading to confusion or a crisis of confidence in the athlete. There is a massive responsibility/pressure on the coach to keep working with the service providers (sports scientists etc) and understand what they are doing. Plus there is an equal responsibility on the service providers to get a real understanding of the sport, the athletes and coaches before 'jumping in' with advice. Equally when advice is given it should be either given through the coach, or a real effort made to make sure any advice is consistent with the coach's message. If there is an area where the coach and service provider disagree, then it has to be managed effectively before the athlete is approached.

• Sport scientists very often believe they know more than the coach and can sometimes undermine the coaching process in place.

• The key issue is how sports science can support coach knowledge rather than the sport being driven by the requirements/opinions of the sports scientists who sometimes have little real knowledge of the sport's or athlete's requirements.

• Funding priorities and choices – deciding where will the biggest gains be made? All the 'ologies' can be expensive to access. Knowing whether they are really adding value and getting the hard evidence to back it up is not easy. There is so little published or ongoing research on canoeing that there isn't much evidence around of what has worked before.

SUMMARY

Throughout this coaching handbook the focus has been on the journey towards best practice in coaching delivery. It provides for the first time a unique centralised training resource for coaches in all the BCU disciplines, whether recreational or competition based. There is without doubt plenty in it for every paddlesport coach.

The key aim of this High Performance chapter has been to open up an awareness of what is required at the highest levels of coaching. It has focused on some of the key skills, experiences and processes that a coach might need to acquire, develop and support in order to move their coaching delivery onto a high performance level whether it be coaching at the emerging United Kingdom Coaching Certificate Levels 4 & 5 or coaching to the LTPD levels of Training to Perform and Training to Excel.

Clearly there is much of interest here to coaches in the competition disciplines but if a clear focus is kept on the search for ways of improving paddlesport performance then I feel there can be tangible benefits and crossover to many recreational coaches as well.

ACKNOWLEDGEMENTS

I'd like to thank Bill Endicott, Hugh Mantle, Keith Lyons, Dave Crosbee, Reg Hatch, Shaun Pierce and Ian Raspin for their contributions to this chapter.

ALAN EDGE

In his current position as National Development Coach, Alan has been responsible for overseeing the implementation of the World Class Development Programmes for Canoe Slalom and is currently involved with the development of the United Kingdom Coaching Certificate across all disciplines within the BCU.

Alan is married and based in Nottingham, spending most of his non-canoeing time keeping up with his young family and trying to master golf and the mandolin!

For more details of his career and achievements see Chapter 18 Canoe Slalom Racing.

GENERAL WARM UP REGIMES IN CANOE SLALOM

Exercise Type	Range of warm-up activities	Intensity of warm-up	Duration
Base aerobic	• Paddling. • Some dynamic and static stretches in the boat.	• Low intensity. • Slowly raise heart rate up to training range.	5min
Threshold	• Paddling. • Some dynamic and static stretches in the boat.	• High intensity. • Slowly raise heart rate up to training heart rate range and hold for at least 2min.	10-12min
VO_2 peak intervals	• Ideally a land based pre-water warm.up e.g. jogging. • Paddling. • Some dynamic and static stretches in the boat.	• Moderate intensity. • Slowly raise heart rate up to training heart rate range and hold it within the range for at least 2min.	15min, including 3-4min land based warm-up
Half runs, full runs, speed, technique and lactate tolerance	• Ideally a land based pre-water warm-up e.g. jogging, step ups, star-jumps, jogging on spot. • Some land based stretches. • Paddling. • Increased static and dynamic stretches in the boat - stroke specific.	• On land pre-water moderate intensity. • Very high intensity. • Slowly raise heart rate to same range as for VO_2 peak intervals, and hold for at least 2min. • After a 1min recovery start 4 to 5 progressive build up sprints lasting no more than 20 seconds. The final sprint should finish at max pace.	20-25min, including land-based warm-up
Races and race practice	• Ideally a land based pre-water warm-up e.g. jogging, step ups, star-jumps, jogging on spot. • Some land based stretches. • Paddling. • Incr. static & dynamic stretches in boat – stroke specific. • Pre-race mental rehearsal techniques during this period. • Attention should also be made to final hydration strategy. • Pre-second run warm-up can be reduced in volume, but not intensity or diversity, as long as you have been active during the period between runs, and not cooled down.	• On land pre-water moderate intensity. • Very high intensity. • Slowly raise heart rate to same range as for VO_2 peak intervals, and hold for at least two minutes. • After a 1min recovery start 4 to 5 progressive build up sprints lasting no more than 20 sec. The final sprint should finish at maximum pace. • Avoid periods of inactivity over 1 min in duration.	25-30min, including land-based warm-up Pre-second run warm up, 15-20min

GENERAL WARM DOWNS FOR CANOE SLALOM

Exercise Type	Lactic acid level post exercise	Range of warm down activities	Duration and intensity	Additional recovery strategies
Base aerobic	2-3 mmol/l	• Paddling. • Preferably some water based and land-based stretching.	• 5 -10 min paddling below training heart rate range. • Heart rate should drop to approximately 120 to 130 b/min. • 10min of stretching.	Ingest snack and fluids within 20min of the finish of the session.
Threshold	3-5 mmol/l	• Paddling. • Preferably some water-based and land-based stretching.	• At least 10min of paddling below heart rate training range. • Heart rate should be stepped down from training range to approximately 120 to 130 b/min over the 10min period. • 10 min of stretching.	Ingest snack and fluids as soon as possible after the finish of the session.
VO₂ peak intervals, speed, technique, half runs	5-7 mmol/l	• Paddling. • Preferably some water-based and land-based stretching.	• 15 minutes of paddling below heart rate training range. • Heart rate should be stepped down from training range to approximately 120-130 b/min over the 15min period. • 10min of stretching.	Fluids should be taken in during the session. Ingest snack as soon as possible after the finish of the session.
Full runs, lactate tolerance, races, race practice	7-12 mmol/l	• Extensive paddling, or support this with jogging, step ups, star-jumps if paddling is not possible. • Water-based and land-based stretching.	• 20-25min of paddling below heart rate training range. • Heart rate should be stepped down from training range to approximately 120-130 b/min over the warm-down period. • 10 -15 minutes of stretching.	Fluids should be taken in during the session or between runs. Ingest snacks as soon as possible after the session, or first run.

EXAMPLE JUNIOR SLALOM K1W WINTER TRAINING PROGRAMME OVERVIEW

21 week training programme (Nov - Apr) for 17 year-old junior women's K1 preparing for junior selection events at the end of March/start of April.

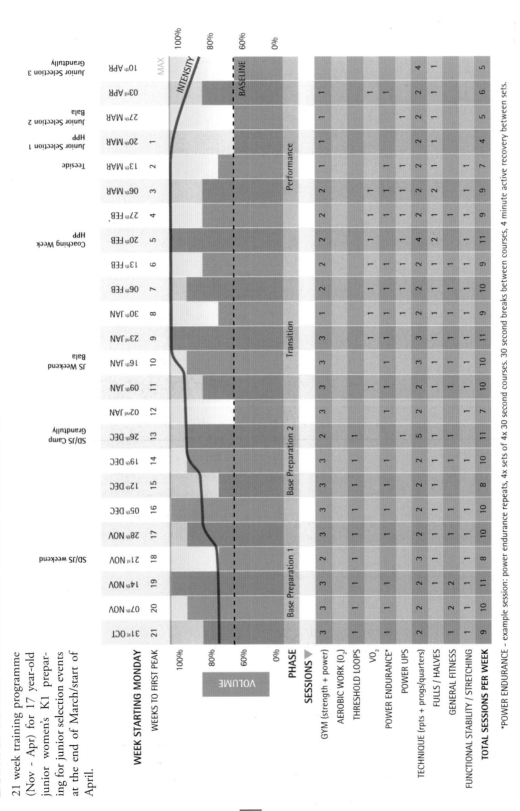

*POWER ENDURANCE - example session: power endurance repeats, 4x sets of 4x 30 second courses, 30 second breaks between courses, 4 minute active recovery between sets.